CHECKLISTS

THE McGRAW-HILL COLLEGE HANDBOOK

McGRAW-HILL, INC.

New York   St. Louis   San Francisco   Auckland   Bogotá
Caracas   Lisbon   London   Madrid   Mexico City   Milan
Montreal   New Delhi   San Juan
Singapore   Sydney   Tokyo
Toronto

THE
McGRAW-HILL
COLLEGE
HANDBOOK

FOURTH EDITION

Richard Marius
Harvard University

Harvey S. Wiener
Adelphi University

THE McGRAW-HILL COLLEGE HANDBOOK

This book was developed by STEVEN PENSINGER, INC.

Copyright © 1994, 1991, 1988, 1985 by McGraw-Hill, Inc. All rights reserved. Printed in the United States of America. Except as permitted under the United States Copyright Act of 1976, no part of this publication may be reproduced or distributed in any form or by any means, or stored in a data base or retrieval system, without the prior written permission of the publisher.

This book is printed on acid-free paper.

Acknowledgments appear on pages 696–698, and on this page by reference.

11 12 13 14 15 DOC/DOC 0 9 8 7 6 5 4 3 2 1

ISBN 0-07-040481-X

This book was set in New Baskerville by Ruttle, Shaw & Wetherill, Inc.
The editors were Steve Pensinger, Jeannine Ciliotta, and David A. Damstra;
the designer was Jo Jones;
the production supervisor was Kathryn Porzio.
The cover was designed by Joseph Gillians.
R. R. Donnelley & Sons Company was printer and binder.

Library of Congress Cataloging-in-Publication Data

Marius, Richard.
    The McGraw-Hill college handbook / Richard Marius, Harvey S. Wiener. — 4th ed.
        p.   cm.
    Includes index.
    ISBN 0-07-040481-X
    1. English language—Grammar—Handbooks, manuals, etc.   2. English language—Rhetoric—Handbooks, manuals, etc.   I. Wiener, Harvey S. II. Title.
    PE1112.M33   1994
    808'.042—dc20   93-29714

INTERNATIONAL EDITION

Copyright 1994. Exclusive rights by McGraw-Hill, Inc. for manufacture and export. This book cannot be re-exported from the country to which it is consigned by McGraw-Hill. The International Edition is not available in North America.

When ordering this title, use ISBN 0-07-113482-4.

ABOUT THE AUTHORS

Richard Marius has been the Director of Expository Writing at Harvard since 1978, in charge of a course that all Harvard students must take. His program includes a large writing center and interdisciplinary work in writing across the undergraduate curriculum. He teaches a popular advanced writing course, and in 1990 the student government at Harvard gave him the Levenson Award for outstanding teaching by a member of the senior faculty. In 1993 he was awarded the Harvard Foundation Medal for furthering good race relations in the Harvard community.

He was born on a farm in Tennessee and worked on a small county newspaper for five years while he finished high school and then took a degree in journalism at the University of Tennessee, Knoxville. Later he took the M.A. and the Ph.D. at Yale. He is the author of two biographies, *Luther* in 1974 and *Thomas More* in 1984. *Thomas More* was a finalist in the nonfiction category for the National Book Award. He has published three novels, *The Coming of Rain* in 1969, *Bound for the Promised Land* in 1976, and *After the War* in 1993. He writes a regular book review column for *Harvard Magazine*, and his articles have appeared in publications as diverse as *Esquire* and the medieval journal *Traditio.*

He has published many articles about the teaching of writing, and he has written or coauthored three writing textbooks. Since 1986 he has directed a two-week Governor's Academy for Writing each July for Tennessee teachers from kindergarten through twelfth grade to help them teach writing more effectively. By 1994 over 1500 teachers had attended the Academy, and Tennessee's governor has made him a Tennessee Colonel for his efforts in their behalf. In 1992 then Governor Bill Clinton of Arkansas made him an Arkansas Traveler for his work with schools and teachers in that state.

Harvey S. Wiener is Vice Provost for Academic Affairs at Adelphi University. He is the author of many books on reading and writing for college students and their teachers, including *The Writing Room* (Oxford, 1981). His book for parents, *Any Child Can Write,* was a Book-of-the-Month-Club alternate. A revised edition appeared in 1990. He has written two other books for parents, *Talk with Your Child* (1988) and *Any Child Can Read Better* (1990). He has written for network television and was trained in the Columbia Broadcasting System's daytime television Writer Development Project. He was founding president of the Council of Writing Program Administrators (CWPA) and chaired the Teaching of Writing Division of the Modern Language Association (1987).

Born in Brooklyn, he has worked in education for more than thirty years. He has taught writing and literature at every level from elementary school to graduate school. A Phi Beta Kappa graduate from Brooklyn College, he holds a Ph.D. in Renaissance literature from Fordham University. He has won grants from the National Endowment for the Humanities, the Fund for Improvement of Postsecondary Education, the Exxon Education Foundation, and the Ford Foundation.

CONTENTS
IN BRIEF

CONTENTS

BOOK THREE
SPECIAL WRITING TASKS   403

PREFACE

The fourth edition of the *McGraw-Hill Handbook* is a sign of the solid place it has gained in the teaching of English composition in colleges and universities in the United States. We are proud of its acceptance by the women and men who teach this most demanding of disciplines and the steady dialogue in person, by mail, and increasingly by E-mail that we have had with teachers who use the book in the classroom. We have incorporated a great many suggestions from these conversations in this edition.

We are also gratified by the recognition of our efforts to present a handbook that does not condescend to students or to teachers. Like all living languages, English changes as the people who use it change. Our language is not a dead butterfly in a glass case; rather, English flutters brightly in the sun of human experience and at times does things that no one quite understands. Why does "ain't" have such a bad reputation? Why do words like "shrewd" dramatically change meaning from one century to another? Where do new words come from? Unlike some handbooks, ours admits the puzzles when we find them. We believe that good writing is a matter of principles rather than rules, and we try to be honest when we find the principles fuzzy.

English does have some rules, but we make a distinction between those that can be broken now and then and those that cannot. We do not scream in agony at the sight of a split infinitive, but we do think tacking a plural verb onto a singular subject confuses readers. We think some sentences can end with a preposition, but we don't think good writers can use double negatives. We try to hold to principles, to state them clearly, and to illustrate them by the work of good contemporary authors.

We are proud that our handbook has been widely recognized as treating women and minorities with respect, and gratified by Professor Deborah Kennedy's special commendation of *The McGraw-Hill College Handbook* for its attention to gender and inclusive language in her article "Inclusive Language" in the spring 1992 issue of *Women and Language* (p. 46). We have presumed throughout that women and minorities should be treated with the same dignity and respect accorded to white males, and we have examined every line of the fourth edition to make sure that we maintain our own high standards.

Our handbook offers no easy route to glory: *The McGraw-Hill College Handbook* assumes that students must write regularly and revise continually if they are to become good writers.

We have practiced our own philosophy in preparing the fourth edition. In the previous three editions, we worked hard at providing clear explanations of both the process and the product of writing. How do writers write? What can they do to make their work clear, logical, and (we hope the word is not out of date) elegant? We considered these issues always with students in mind, always with the desire to convey the results of our study in a way that was friendly without being condescending, clear without being shallow, and accurate without being pedantic. The testimony of the hundreds of teachers and thousands of students who have used this book throughout the United States and Canada has been that we succeeded.

Once again in this edition, we focus as much on process as we do on product. Too often handbooks concentrate on showing students correct written products without telling them how to produce one. In our writing process chapters we have given a realistic account of how writers write. We have provided drafts of a typical first-year student's paper and showed the changes on the way to a final draft. Students who follow our trail through this process will arrive at a piece of work that will make them proud of their effort and their accomplishment.

Note that we have not forgotten product in our interest in process. To provide process without giving some idea of a goal is a bit like constructing an elaborate rocket to be fired off into space without a target. We try to help students write essays that will be coherent expositions of their own thoughts about evidence, however the evidence is defined. We show students how to revise and how to think about their writing so that they become their own best critics.

We expect this book to be used in composition classes for first-year students and in other courses in writing offered by English departments. We value literature, and we draw many examples from it. But we also think that students should write well in courses across the entire curriculum. We assume throughout that students can be helped by our book in whatever courses they take. In a new chapter and throughout the text, we provide examples from writing about history, psychology, economics, physics, biology, business, engineering, sports, and other fields to illustrate our conviction that good writing is necessary to any discipline.

Above all, we want students to learn to write by writing. If we taught kids to play baseball in the way that we have traditionally tried to teach them to write, baseball would not be our national sport. Just imagine saying, "Now in first grade, we are going to study the *Baseball Rulebook.* We are going to study that rulebook every year for twelve years. And if you memorize the rulebook, we may let you finally play a game." We teach baseball by letting kids play, by telling them a step at a time that three strikes make an out, three outs make a half inning, a caught fly ball is an out, and so on. We should teach writing the same way. Let writers write; help them with the conventions as they go along. We all learn to write by discovering that we all have something to say if we try hard enough. We want to help students make that great discovery.

In This Edition

We worked hard to shorten the third edition and keep it comprehensive. In this fourth edition we have done some further tightening, eliminated some examples and added others, and reworked the entire text to make it even more readable. We have added many more Checklists. We have revised and rewritten exercises, and added some in a continuing effort to make the book serviceable to the first-year student. We have added an ESL appendix for students who want more help with some of the more difficult problems of idiomatic usage. We have also worked on the design, to make it more attractive and functional.

We have returned to our earlier practice of providing two research papers, one in literature and one in science, to buttress the interdisciplinary character of the book. Once again we show both the APA and the MLA reference styles, with examples and in detail.

Reviewers and users of the three previous editions of *The McGraw-Hill College Handbook* have continually commented warmly on its stylistic excellence. We have worked hard in this revision to hold to the standard we have set for ourselves. We have been told that we have written a handbook that can be read with pleasure and used with profit. We think we have written a handbook for these times, and yet a book that respects and uses the strengths of tradition.

Supplements

We have provided a package of aids that teachers will find helpful throughout the course, and supplements that students will find useful in enhancing their work.

For teachers, the aids consist of:

An **Instructor's Manual** that contains teaching tips, answers to exercises, and additional testing materials for the classroom teacher; and the McGraw-Hill **Computerized Diagnostic Tests.** For these we thank Santi Buscemi of Middlesex County College.

For students, the supplements include:

The **McGraw-Hill Workbook,** which includes exercises that may be assigned by the teacher, prepared by Mark Connelly of Milwaukee Area Technical College, for which an **Answer Key** is available. The **McGraw-Hill On-Line Handbook** is a computer disk that can be stored in memory and accessed to answer questions about grammar and usage. The **McGraw-Hill Practice Program** is an interactive software tutorial with exercises. **Writer's Tools** is a HyperCard stack with two sets of tools to help with writing.

Acknowledgments

We are grateful to the many people who have helped us with this book in all four of its editions. Teaching English composition is probably the most difficult job in any university—and often the least rewarded. Perhaps the very difficulty of our profession makes its members feel so strongly the mutual obligations and respect that bind us all together. We have been the beneficiaries of helpful opinions from many teachers in the field who have reviewed this book in its various stages, and we could not have done our work without their searching commentaries, their occasional sharp criticism, and their generous and steadfast encouragement.

Because so much of the structure and personality of the three previous editions persists in this revision, we want once again to thank and acknowledge all those who helped with their reviews of this and the many drafts of the previous editions: Jay Balderson, Western Illinois University; Raymond Brebach, Drexel University; Richard H. Bulloch, Northeastern University; Santi Buscemi, Middlesex County College; David Chapman, Texas Tech University; John Chard, Gloucester County College; Joseph J. Comprone, Michigan Technological University; Virgil Cook, Virginia Polytechnic Institute; Harry H. Crosby, Boston University; Janet Eber, County College of Morris; Robert M. Esch, University of Texas at El Paso; Peter Farley, Adelphi University; James A. Freeman, University of Massachusetts at Amherst; Dennis R. Gabriel, Cuyahoga Community College; Pablo Gonzales, Los Medanos College; Frank Hubbard, Marquette University; Maurice Hunt, Baylor University; Lee A. Jacobus, University of Connecticut, Storrs; Ben Jennings, Virginia Highlands Community College; Larry Kelly, Widener University; Russ Larson, Eastern Michigan University; Peter D. Lindblom, Miami-Dade Community College; Joe Lostracco, Austin Community College; William MacPherson, Essex County College; Sheila J. McDonald, C. W. Post Center, LIU; Donald A. McQuade, University of California, Berkeley; Robert Meeker, Bloomsburg University; Doris Miller, U.S. Air Force Academy; Pat Murray, DePaul University; Sharon Niederman, Metropolitan State, Denver; Rosemary O'Donoghue, Western New England College; Jack B. Oruch, University of Kansas, Lawrence; Margaret Panos, Southeastern Massachusetts University; Compton Rees, University of Connecticut; Karen Reid, Midwestern State University; Kathleen W. Ritch, Santa Fe Community College, Gainesville; Annette T. Rottenberg, University of Massachusetts at Amherst; Donald C. Stewart, Kansas State University, Manhattan; John Stratton, University of Arkanas, Little Rock; Margaret A. Strom, Eastern Maine Technical Institute; Sebastian J. Vasta, Camden Community College; Bryant Wyatt, Virginia State University.

John C. Bean, Seattle University; Kathleen Bell, Old Dominion University; Mark Coleman, Potsdam College; Larry Corse, Clayton State College; Joe Glaser, Western Kentucky University; Rosalie Hewitt, Northern Illinois University; Pat C. Hoy II, New York University; Beverly Huttinger, Broward Community College; Larry P. Kent, William Rainey Harper College; Patricia Maida, University of DC; David A. Martin, University of Wisconsin, Milwaukee; Joseph McLaren, Mercy College; Albert H. Nicolai, Jr., Middlesex County College; Della H. Paul, Valencia Community College; Dorothy U. Seyler, Northern Virginia Community College; Donnetta Heitschmidt Suchon, Daytona Beach Community College; Carroll L. Wilson, Somerset County College; and members of the English faculty at the United States Military Academy, West Point.

We want to say again how much we have enjoyed working on this book. We have had the pleasure of thinking through our long experience as deeply engaged teachers of writing and the greater satisfaction of thinking through our glorious English language in its rich and lively American version. We have worked far into the night more times than we can possibly count in producing the four editions of this book. We have never been content to study other textbooks and to rephrase their advice; we have gone directly to the English prose that we both love to see how it works and to express our finding in the spirit of discovery and excitement that stands behind all true scholarship.

We have picked up many debts through the years. Dozens of people at McGraw-Hill have helped, sometimes giving us excellent technical advice, sometimes making evenings ring with laughter over the dinner table after long, long hours of difficult work.

For this edition we are especially grateful to C. Steven Pensinger, who cheerfully and energetically took this project under his general editorial wing for the third edition and remains steadfastly with us in this one. Jeannine Ciliotta has served as the developmental editor for the last two editions, spending hours with us on the telephone, working out an infinity of details. Developmental editors should have a special place in heaven, reserved for those patient and responsible shepherds who keep their sheep from running off in twelve different directions at once. David Damstra has been steadily on the mark in seeing that the text we wrote is the one that gets bound and printed. His friendly voice, booming through the telephone, has kept us on schedule during the long production of this book.

Both our families have put up with our silences at our computers while we labor to prune back old prose and to write something fresh and new. Our wives receive our loving gratitude not only for their support, but for the enthusiasm they have always managed to muster when we felt compelled to read to them something we had written that we thought deserved to be memorized by schoolchildren. They managed to like our words, and after a great many years, they seem to like us, too.

Perhaps most remarkable, we have worked closely with each other now for fifteen years through four editions with a mutual respect and affection that endure.

Richard Marius
Harvey S. Wiener

TO THE STUDENT

The best way to use this book is to keep it handy as a reference. Pick it up every day and browse through it at random. When your teacher assigns a section, read it carefully and do the exercises to fix its principles in your mind. By all means read Chapters 1 through 3 before you begin to write your first paper.

The index and the contents will help you locate information that deals with your special problems and interests. For easy reference, the correction symbols appear inside both front and back covers. The checklists, which you can use to review or as handy summaries of important points, are listed inside the front cover. Topics covered in the ESL appendix are listed inside the back cover. The appendix itself, which offers additional help (guidelines, examples) with special problems in English, is keyed into the text by a tree logo and a table number in the margin at the appropriate point.

The ability to write well can give you both pleasure and power. You owe it to yourself to discover the joy of writing, the excitement of expressing your ideas, your feelings, your thoughts, your discoveries, your opinions about everything from daily events to the demands of a promising future. As you learn to write well, you will also discover that people are more likely to respect and accept your opinions because you express them in writing that engages and persuades your readers.

Some textbooks seem to promise that they can make writing easy. They are wrong. Good writing always takes hard work, and all writers are sometimes discouraged. Effective writers go back to work after their discouragement and try again. We hope that *The McGraw-Hill College Handbook* can make writing less difficult and can give you guidance and pleasure along the way.

Richard Marius
Harvey S. Wiener

THE
McGRAW-HILL
COLLEGE
HANDBOOK

PART ONE
WRITING ESSAYS AND PARAGRAPHS

PART TWO
WRITING CLEAR AND EFFECTIVE
SENTENCES

PART THREE
USING WORDS EFFECTIVELY

THE
WRITING
PROCESS

ONE

WRITING ESSAYS AND PARAGRAPHS

1

PLANNING
A PAPER

In your composition course—and all the way through college—you will be writing papers. The first two chapters of this handbook describe the steps you take from choosing a subject to completing the final copy. These steps are the **writing process.** It begins when you start thinking about a topic, continues through your first efforts at shaping it, passes through several revisions, and concludes with the final copy you turn in to your instructor. The writing process may include taking notes, making lists, sketching outlines, and experimenting with sample sentences and paragraphs. It involves writing drafts of the whole paper and changing them dramatically as you develop a clearer sense of what you want to say.

Writers develop their topics in many ways, so don't think of the writing process as a sequence of activities that are the same for everyone or that, even for the same writer, are the same for every writing project. Nor do the activities always proceed in the same sequence. Some take place almost simultaneously. But from the time they consider writing something until they produce the final copy, most writers take similar steps. Sometimes you can skip one step or another, but most often you will do them all, and you might even have to do one several times. Few writers can dash off a sensible essay; most have to work long and hard. It will help you to think ahead of time about the different activities involved in the writing process so that you can organize yourself to work efficiently and well (see Checklist 1.1). The first step in preparation is called **prewriting.**

1a
Using Prewriting Techniques

Prewriting includes a number of steps that prepare you to begin your essay. They help you think about your topic and define it. Here are some steps to help you work out ideas for writing.

Thinking: Let Ideas Float

Good writing begins with clear thinking, but most of our thinking begins in a muddle. Many different ideas crowd into our heads, some of them useful, some useless, some contradictory. Some are so vague that we don't know at first whether they're useful or not. Thinking about your subject is a process of sorting out good ideas from bad ones, the relevant from the irrelevant, the shallow from the creative.

Remember, too, that all your thinking does not go on at your desk. You may get good ideas when you are walking, riding a bike, taking a shower, or talking with friends. Keep your writing task on your mind. Think about it whenever you can. Bring it up in conversations. Ask yourself how you can use material you learn in other courses to enrich a paper you write in composition.

✔ CHECKLIST 1.1: PREWRITING STEPS

- Practice prewriting: thinking, listing, reading, talking, questioning, freewriting, clustering.
- Limit the topic.
- Plan your approach.
- Consider your audience.
- Choose supporting evidence.
- Draft a thesis statement.
- Organize your ideas.
- Create a rough outline.
- Review the rough outline.

Listing: Jot Down Ideas

Sometimes the best way to think about your subject is to jot down some ideas in a notebook—disconnected sentences that may provoke other ideas. Moving a hand across a page seems to move the brain. One idea generates another. The more you write, the more inspiration you get. Carry the list around with you. Let it grow over several days as your thoughts develop and become more specific—one or two sentences or phrases scribbled in the morning, another few dashed off as you return from class, perhaps something jotted down in class itself. Ideas come at unexpected times. Keep a notebook ready to catch them.

Here's a sample prewriting list. It develops an example we'll follow throughout Part One. The composition instructor has assigned her students to write "a personal reaction to something you have read recently."

John Williams, a student in her class, thinks he'll write about Stephen King's novel *The Shining*, which he read over the summer. He jots down some ideas.

Stephen King and horror

Why do people like Stephen King?

He writes horror stories – but so do lots of people.

but all my friends read Stephen King, so do I – why?

He writes about familiar things but gives them a twist – families, fathers and sons.

That's the real horror of <u>The Shining</u> – a father turns against his son.

happens in real life, children are abused.

Danny Torrance loves his father, and I think the father loves him.

the horror comes from something familiar turning ugly, murderous.

science fiction never did grab me; it's unreal, but Stephen King writes about things we know – or think we know.

like a big house, a hotel, up in the mountains of Colorado, a family goes up there to be caretakers for the winter.

house is <u>haunted</u>.

hotel has been used by criminals, owned by the mob and all sorts of criminal types.

The evil hangs in the building, and it infects Jack Torrance, Danny's father, and Jack tries to kill his family.

Danny is rescued by a black man who has the same mysterious power Danny has – to communicate as though by radio from mind to mind over miles and miles.

We all want a loyal friend like that, somebody who rescues us when the time comes.

What does it all mean?

King writes with lots of suspense, but that's not the only reason people read him.

more to The Shining than just a suspense story.

This list records many fragmentary ideas about Stephen King's *The Shining* and how one student set about writing about it. John has an idea but does not yet have a topic. He knows only that he has been strongly affected by the book, and he wants to write something about it. He goes on thinking about the book and making notes. He comes to recognize that what fascinates him about *The Shining* is King's talent for portraying horror. Then John makes another list.

Subject: Stephen King's Secret of Horror

the feeling of feeling threatened.

For a child the world is mysterious and sometimes frightening.

Parents are bigger than we are.

Most of the time they love us.

We love them, too.

But sometimes they get mad at us.

We know they can hurt us.

Some parents do hurt children.

Stephen King takes this natural love/fear relationship and turns it into a great story.

Jack Torrance, a man down on his luck, becomes caretaker to an old hotel in Colorado during the winter when the hotel is closed.

He takes his wife and son back there with him.

The boy Danny has a strange power.

The hotel has been owned by criminals.

As the months pass, the ghosts in the hotel take over Jack Torrance's soul.

He tries to kill his son, but the son is rescued by a black man named Dick Hallorann who also has the power, the shining, that allows him to communicate with Danny.

Many things in the world can hurt us, things very near and dear to us.

The Shining teaches us to keep on doing what we can, even when everything turns against us, even parents and friends.

That conclusion seems weak.

How do I think about horror and make it worthwhile?

Why do we read horror stories?

With the second list, John has explored ideas of horror in *The Shining*. He has defined a topic. Successive revisions of the list will eliminate some points, expand others, and add some that are not now on it. Writing a list of ideas prepares you to write the paper itself.

You can use the same process in planning a paper based on a written text instead of a personal experience or personal reaction. If your assignment is to analyze a short story, an essay, or some other text, read it through quickly. Then read it again and jot down ideas about it. Make connections. Let your mind rove freely. As you jot down your thoughts, your mind will generate other ideas, and you can write them down too.

Save *everything*: all your lists, your scribbled notes, your practice sentences. You may want to come back to them as you develop your topic. Only when your assignment has been completed and graded should you consider throwing anything away.

Reading: Learn About Your Topic

Good writing flows from knowledge. You must know something about a topic to write about it well. A paper that merely asserts uninformed opinions will rarely interest anybody—not even the person who writes it. We read to learn, and mere opinion is not interesting unless the person with the opinion is a widely recognized authority or famous. Otherwise we want to know the facts that made the writer form the opinions he or she has. Only then can we decide whether the opinions are worthwhile. Facts come from study: lots of study.

Of course, many interesting papers do not depend on research. Writing about a personal experience or a personal reaction may not require you to work in the library. But seeing how others have written about similar experiences or reactions may help you focus your ideas, and most topics will be much better if you do some general reading about them. Often reference books and magazine articles will suggest ideas you have not thought of. Several hours of browsing in the library and taking notes give many writers just the materials they need to develop a topic with confidence. You may also wish to interview people who know about your subject.

For example, if you decide to write about a novel by Stephen King, you will find abundant materials in the library: articles about King, interviews with him, reviews of his books, biographical blurbs. Your reference librarian will assist you in finding these articles, and they may help you shape your ideas. Be sure to keep track of your sources so you can give credit to these articles if you use them in any way.

Reading about and around your topic broadens your understanding and will give you facts you can draw on later.

Talking: Listen to What You and Others Have to Say

Talk to everyone you can about the topic. Talking about a subject is not just a good way to know what you are thinking and express it better; talking can actually be a process of discovery. Sometimes ideas and connections come out in conversation that you didn't know were there.

Talking is also a good way to uncover areas where you don't have enough information and to narrow your topic to something manageable. Your instructor may divide your composition class into small groups so that you can talk to others about the topic you're considering and hear about their topics.

Talk about your topic with your roommates, with friends over lunch, with the friends you jog with or with some of the people you work with. "I'm writing a paper on Stephen King's novel *The Shining*. Have you read it? I think he really understands some of the fears children have. What do you think?"

Of course the purpose of discussing your topic with others isn't simply to hear yourself talk. Listen to what your friends and colleagues have to say. Their questions will let you know where you haven't explained your ideas clearly, and their opinions will suggest new angles, fresh approaches, and reasonable cautions that can help you shape your topic.

Questioning: Ask the Journalist's Questions

To stimulate ideas, writers frequently ask themselves questions about a subject. One good way to organize questions is to think of the five *W*s of journalism. In writing a news story, reporters are taught to ask, and answer, *who, what, where, when,* and *why.*

To use the journalist's questions, identify your subject at the top of the page. Then, with ample space for your answers, write *who, what, where, when,* and *why.* Here are John's questions.

Subject: Stephen King's Secret of Horror

<u>Who</u> are the main characters?

<u>Who</u> exactly is the father, Jack Torrance?

<u>Who</u> exactly is Danny?

<u>Who</u> are the most important minor characters?

<u>What</u> happened in the hotel when Danny and his father and mother went there?

<u>What</u> are the supernatural elements in the story?

<u>What</u> happened to Jack Torrance?

<u>What</u> had Danny's father done before the story opens that lets us know he's a dangerous man?

<u>Where</u> does the story take place?

<u>Where</u> is Dick Hallorann when he gets Danny's call for help?

<u>Where</u> does the end of the story take place?

<u>When</u> does the story take place?

<u>When</u> did the criminal things in the hotel happen?

<u>When</u> does Danny recognize he had the power of "the shining"?

<u>Why</u> does the story scare us so much?

<u>Why</u> does Stephen King write about children so much?

Why does the evil in the hotel take possession of Danny's father?

Why does Danny say at the last that the man trying to kill him is not really his father?

If you ask as many versions as possible of the five Ws, you begin to see how much you have to write about. You will not want to answer all the questions you ask. Not all of them will contribute to your essay as you develop your thesis. But as you ask questions, you will open mental doorways that will help you think of things to write.

Freewriting: Write Nonstop for Ten Minutes

Some writers discover that they can overcome writer's block if they make themselves sit down at a table—or a computer—and write without stopping for ten or fifteen minutes. If you suffer anxiety when you get ready to write a paper, try this technique, which is called **freewriting.**

Sit down and write anything that comes into your head about your subject. Write without trying to control the direction or the organization of your prose. Don't worry about spelling, grammar, or punctuation. Just write. Here is John Williams's freewriting:

```
King. Stephen King. I don't know what to write. What am I going to
write about? Well, when I read Stephen King's stories, I feel a thrill of
terror down my spine, and somehow I love it, but I don't think it's just an
excuse to take an emotional bath. My English teachers don't always think
that King is a serius writer, not like Hemingway or Falkner or Morison or
Austin or all those people we read in the litrature textbooks and the
anthologies. I like Stephen King, and my friends like him, and we read him
when we don't read anything else sometimes, and ever once in a while I find
out that one of my English teachers in schools reads Stephen King on the
sly and likes him, too. Now why do we like to be scared out of our wits? And
why does he scare us so much? When you think about it, there have been a lot
of good writers who scared the wits out of the people at the time--Edger
Allen Poe for one and even Nathaniel Hawthorn for another with his story
about the man who had a garden of poisoned plants, and when the daughter
raised in that garden tried to kiss somebody or get out of the garden, she
was likely to die. And maybe there have been a lot more writers who tried
to scare us and couldn't pull it off, which is what happens in a bad
```

mystery or a bad horror story or some of the horror flicks that get so stupid that you laugh where you are supposed to scream. I think King scares us because he talks about the things that make little children afraid, and he remembers that when we grow up, we are still little children inside, and we still have our fears only now they are translated into a lot of fears that surround us in life that are a lot more real than the fears we had as kids. I'm afraid of failing this course or of not graduating from college or of not getting a job or of not being able to afford my car payment. Maybe all these things will turn out all right, but I don't know that now, and I'm scared. It's almost a happy thought to remember when I was afraid of the dark or thought that there might be a monster under my bed at night or in the closet or somewhere out there in the dark trying to get in the window. I've grown up, and I don't think much about those fears in my childhood anymore, but when I read Stephen King, they all come back, and I remember them, and it's almost like saying, Hey, you got through all those fears and made it to being an adult more or less, and so you are going to get over all these fears, too, and they are going to go the same way that those old fears of yours did. Still, Stephen King remembers that we don't get rid of all our fears, and we shouldn't because there are a lot of things in life to be afraid of even when we grow up, and he says I think that we ought to remember what it is to be afraid when we are children because life is scarry. But if we keep on and face our fears and make friends and try to be loyal to them, we will get through most of the things that scare us.

These sentences are a long way from being a finished essay. But ideas are beginning to flow. The writer is beginning to get thoughts in order.

Clustering: Draw a Subject Tree

As your ideas begin to take shape, begin **clustering** them—tying related ideas together. As you put ideas together you begin to expand them, to complicate them and make them more interesting, and to see connections that help you organize your paper.

You might cluster thoughts by listing or even outlining, but if it helps you to visualize connections, try drawing a subject tree like the one shown here for John Williams's ideas for a paper on Stephen King. The subject tree allows you to jot down ideas in a rough organization, with your general subject as the trunk from which more specific ideas branch out. As you

can see, a subject tree produces a number of ideas that can be developed
into a paper. Drawing a tree helps you identify possible topics in relation
to a general subject. The subject tree breaks knowledge down into manageable chunks, and you can then put those chunks together. Many writers
find that drawing a subject tree is a good way to tie related ideas together.

1a

plan

Subject Tree

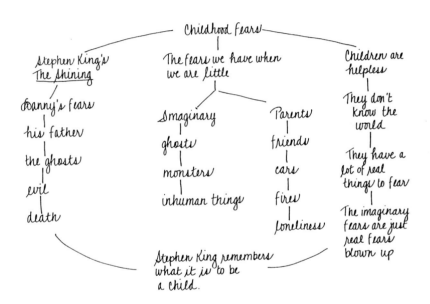

■ **Exercise 1.1**   Use some of the prewriting techniques explained
on the previous pages to explore three of these general subjects.

1. a book or article you have read recently
2. AIDS and morality
3. violence in the movies
4. gun control
5. attitudes toward the homeless
6. advertising of alcohol and tobacco
7. the work ethic during a recession
8. gender roles for children
9. feminism and multiculturalism

10. the pressures on college and professional athletes
11. sexual harassment on campus or in the workplace
12. free speech vs. politically correct speech
13. the responsibilities of citizenship in a democracy
14. religion and politics

1b
Limiting the Subject

The subjects of some papers you write in college will be assigned. In other cases you may be free to select your own subject. Sometimes you will know immediately what you want to write about. But more often writers find their topics by a slow, uneven process. Perhaps you may want to write about feminism and multiculturalism—how to reconcile a feminist viewpoint with an appreciation of the many different cultures that coexist in the United States and throughout the world. Hundreds of books and articles related to this general topic have appeared in the last five years alone. Where do you begin? You can't treat the topic in its entirety, and generalizations by themselves aren't interesting or convincing. Pick a specific place or time or incident, and start there.

The Persian Gulf War, for example, focused a great deal of attention on the Muslim view of women in their place in society. An interview with a thoughtful woman in a National Guard unit called to service during the war could focus the problem—an independent American woman in Saudi Arabia, where women are not allowed to drive cars—and be the basis of an excellent paper. Further reading might help you address more broadly the conflict between a feminist perspective and traditional societies. You might not be able to solve the problem, but you could explore the implications of the tension between respect for self and respect for others.

Limiting your subject not only makes it manageable; it sharpens your focus and makes it interesting as well. Checklist 1.2 suggests a series of steps that will help you trim and focus your subject. Even topics in the ''still less broad'' column my be further narrowed. Only you can decide how much to limit your subject. Your decision will depend, in part, on the sheer physical demands of the task: How many pages do you have to write? How long will that take you? How much time do you have? Also consider the limits the subject itself may impose: How much has been written about the subject already? What do I have to do to say that is new or different or mine alone? Can I learn enough about the subject to write about it well before my deadline?

✔ **CHECKLIST 1.2: LIMITING A TOPIC**

■ Too broad	gender roles for children	The Shining
	children depicted in movies	horror in The Shining
■ Still too broad	bravery on the part of little girls and boys in the movies	horror in The Shining comes from the familiar turned ugly
■ Less broad	Dorothy in The Wizard of Oz vs. Kevin McCallister in Home Alone. How are they alike? How are they	the natural love/fear between parent and child is universal and is the basis of
■ Still less broad	different? Have gender roles for children changed in the past half century?	the horror in The Shining

As you limit your subject, you bring it more and more under control. Your mind will start generating ideas about it. As your focus becomes more specific, it will also get more penetrating. Record ideas as they come to you, and add them to your prewriting materials.

■ **Exercise 1.2** Using Checklist 1.2 as a model, limit, in a series of steps, two of the subjects you selected in Exercise 1.1.

1c
Planning Your Approach

How will you present your topic to your reader? Writers use four long-established **modes** of writing and speaking: description, narration, exposition, and argument.

- *Description* tells how something looks or sounds or tastes or feels or smells.
- *Narration* tells a story, usually in chronological sequence.
- *Exposition* explains.
- *Argument* usually maintains a point of view against some opposition.

Most writing involves combinations of these modes. You rarely find a description that does not involve narration, a narration that does not have some description in it, or an exposition or argument that does not include the other two. Many essays use all four modes. It helps to know the modes so you can plan how you'll approach your subject.

Much college writing is expository because college papers usually explain texts, statistics, events, or observations. The line between an expository paper and an argumentative paper may be thin. You may explain your interpretation of a short story, for example, to prove that someone else's interpretation is incorrect. Then your exposition becomes an argument.

Checklist 1.3 shows how John Williams might plan his approach to his subject along four distinct lines. You can see how easy it is to move from one mode to another. You can also see that the final purpose of your paper will lead you to emphasize one of these modes above the others. A news story for your college paper may tell of the dean's decision to close the library on Friday night without telling how the dean looks when she makes the announcement and without arguing that the decision is right or wrong. But it may explain why the dean has made her decision, and it may tell the story of student reactions. If you write an editorial arguing that the library should remain open on Fridays, you may not use description or narrative at all, but you will probably use some exposition to set up your argument.

✔ **CHECKLIST 1.3: APPROACHING THE TOPIC**

Mode	Purpose
■ Description	To describe what I imagine the Overlook Hotel looks like—not Stephen King's word-for-word description, but the picture in my mind that he has created.
■ Narration	To tell the story of what happened to the Torrance family during that winter.
■ Exposition	To explain how an isolated house that looks like a dream-come-true turns into a nightmare.
■ Argument	To argue that Stephen King understands that the worst fears for children and adults are those threats that no one can understand.

■ **Exercise 1.3**   Using Checklist 1.3 as a model, select one of the topics you used in Exercise 1.2 and jot down some thoughts about how you would approach it using each of the four models. If you would find it helpful, devote a short paragraph to each of these questions:

> **What do I want to describe?**
> **What stories do I want to tell?**
> **What do I need to explain?**
> **What do I want to argue?**

1d
Considering the Audience

Who will read your writing? Don't think of your audience as only the teacher who will grade your paper. Write to interest others—your friends, other members of the class, relatives, other people you know. Try to write a paper for people you admire.

For some writing assignments, the audience is "built in." If you are preparing a résumé, for example, and writing a letter of application, your audience is a potential employer in your field. Keep that reader in mind as you write. You will want to sound polite, convincing, self-confident without being boastful. If, on the other hand, your assignment is to review a school play or a local production for submission to the school or local newspaper, you will want to sound knowledgeable and enthusiastic without being bubbly or discerning without being snobby.

For all types of assignment, you will need to consider the **discourse community**—people who share certain interests, knowledge, and expectations and who also share some customary ways of communicating with each other. Each of us belongs to several discourse communities. Baseball fans make up a discourse community. They talk and write about the game in familiar ways, and they understand each other, even if people outside the community don't know what the fans are talking about. Consider this sentence:

> Mickey Mantle switch-hit for the Yankees for eighteen seasons, compiling a .298 lifetime batting average and a phenomenal slugging average of .557.
>
> —DICK CURRY

Every baseball fan would understand this sentence, but for someone outside the fans' discourse community, the sentence is gibberish. Now consider this statement from the discourse community that includes biologists:

Endocytosis of liposomes occurs in a limited class of cells; those that are phagocytic, or able to ingest foreign particles. When phagocytic cells take up liposomes, the cells move the spheres into subcellular organelles known as lysomes, where the liposomal membranes are thought to be degraded.

—MARC J. OSTRO

To a biologist, these sentences are clear; to people outside the discourse community of biology, they are gibberish—just like the baseball fan's language to the nonfan. Historians, specialists in literature, economics, philosophers, astronomers, model-railroad enthusiasts, pilots, engineers, surgeons, lovers of fishing, and thousands of other groups have their own discourse communities. In each of these communities, certain expectations about language control the way members communicate with each other. Think about your audience when you write. What do you have to explain to your readers? What do they know? You don't have to define *switch-hitter* to a baseball fan; you don't have to define *liposomes* to a biologist. But you should probably define both terms to someone outside those discourse communities.

In a college composition class, you usually assume that your audience includes the other members of the class and the instructor. What do they know about your subject? How much do you have to tell them? If you are working on a paper about *Hamlet* and everybody in the class has read the play or seen it, you waste time and space by summarizing the plot. But if you write about a novel or short story you know others have not read, a short plot summary might be in order. It might help to keep the journalist's questions in mind. When you introduce a new character, identify the person: "Margaret Fuller, the nineteenth-century New England writer"; "Richard Wright, author of *Native Son* and other books." As your essay unfolds, keep your readers informed about *who* is acting, *what* is happening, *where* the action is going on, *when*, and, if possible, *why*.

Think of your readers as good people whom you deeply respect, and you will get just that kind of reader for your work.

In some ways, you create your audience as you write. If you write sensibly, interestingly, clearly, and with occasional flashes of wit, you will win the audience that does most of the reading in America. If you try to be cute or show off or fill your pages with slang and private jokes, you aren't taking your readers seriously, and they won't take what you have to say seriously either—including your opinions. If you write with passionate emotion and uncompromising anger, your audience will be a small group of people whose passions rule the way they look at the world. If you write in a dull, plodding effort to fill pages and to avoid taking risks, you probably will not get any audience at all—except your instructor, who is paid to read your writing no matter how dull it is.

■ **Exercise 1.4**   Explain in a brief paragraph how each audience listed below might influence the content, style, and language of John Williams's essay on Stephen King.

1. people your age who share a liking for Stephen King
2. people your age who do not share your opinion
3. a class of eighth graders
4. older people who dismiss horror stories as having no intellectual content at all
5. older people who argue that violence depicted in fiction and in the movies generates violence in real life

1e
Choosing Supporting Evidence

Generalizations are boring. Assertions are convincing. When you make them, you must give evidence to back them up. You may have strong opinions, but unless you're a well-known authority no one will accept them just because they're yours. And even if you are an authority, you won't get away for very long with telling people what they ought to think without giving them the reasons why.

Explain yourself. Provide evidence. If your instructor writes "Be specific" in the margin of a paper, she is probably asking you to give some details to support the generalization you have made. If you say "Using a computer has made writing easier for me," you have not explained anything. But if you say this, you are using details to support your generalization:

```
My computer has made writing easier for me because it has reduced the
physical strain of writing. I can insert and delete without having to type
the whole essay over again. I can move sentences and paragraphs around in
my work so that it all fits together better. I can revise on the screen,
and I can correct my errors. The computer also has a spell checker so that
I can avoid misspellings. And the automatic formatting means that I do not
have to be careful about margins; the computer does all that for me, and my
work comes out looking clean and neat and authoritative. I can also keep
copies of all the versions of my work.
```

If you say, "The comic strip 'Calvin and Hobbes' is interesting," you have not persuaded anybody to read it. But if you explain how the strip shows a little boy's imagination working with a stuffed animal that comes to life when no one else is present, you may interest your reader enough to open the newspaper to the comics and read the strip.

Kinds of Evidence

There are several kinds of evidence you can use to support your generalizations and assertions:

- ▪ *Personal observation and experience:* These include details that appeal to the senses—actions, colors, sights, sounds, smells, tastes—and stories from your own life. These help readers bring their memories to you and give credibility to your beliefs.
- ▪ *Authorities:* These include quotations, paraphrases, summaries, and descriptions from books, magazines, radio, television, films, or interviews. They support your arguments by presenting the opinions of experts.
- ▪ *Statistics and cases:* These include information not easily challenged. They lend weight to your assertions.

These kinds of evidence do not exclude one another. A paper that uses statistics or quotes authorities may also use images to call forth concrete sensory responses. A recent newspaper article explaining that the U.S. debt was approaching $1 trillion included these graphic details: $1 trillion is enough dollar bills to give one to every ant in the United States or, placed end to end, to reach the star Alpha Centuri, more than five light-years from earth. By converting numbers into something we can see or imagine, we make the meaning of the numbers more vivid.

When you consider your subject and your audience, think about the evidence that will best suit your purpose. Ask yourself how you will gather the evidence you need. For most papers, questions like those in Checklist 1.4 will be helpful.

✔ CHECKLIST 1.4: FINDING EVIDENCE

- ▪ What experiences in my own life will help me make this topic interesting?
- ▪ What have I read recently—or what can I read before I write—that will help me develop or support my topic?
- ▪ What have I heard on the radio or seen on television or in the movies that will help me develop or support my topic?
- ▪ What have I learned in recent conversations with friends, parents, relatives, teachers, and others that will help me develop or support my topic?

■ What reference materials are likely to include the facts I need?

■ What do people in my audience know about my topic? What will interest them? What will bore them? What may even surprise them?

■ **Exercise 1.5**   Go back to the topic you used in Exercise 1.3. Write a paragraph describing your intended audience and suggesting some types and sources of evidence you might use.

1f
Writing a Thesis Statement

Define your main idea, or **thesis**—the essential thing you want to say about your subject—before you sit down to write your paper. You do not have to put a thesis statement in every paper. It would be awkward to write, "The thesis of this paper is that the threat that Jack Torrance is to his son is much like the threat that many parents are to their children." But you should be able to write out a thesis statement that summarizes the point you want to make in your paper.

As you write and revise, you may change your mind about your thesis. Writers often start a paper and discover that their original thesis is not exactly what they want to say. Listen to the proddings of your mind, and when they become insistent, change your thesis. Revision and refinement are essential to the writing process.

All the same, you will save yourself much time, and you will write much more to the point, if you formulate a main idea before you begin your first draft. You may change it slightly or transform it into something altogether different later on. But you may very well keep the same main idea from first draft to final copy. Having a thesis focuses the mind and helps you control the sentences and paragraphs that make up your composition.

Once you have narrowed the focus of your topic, construct a **thesis statement**—one sentence or more that tells your readers what they will be reading. The thesis statement also establishes the tone of the essay and tells readers why they should read your work. It lets them know what to expect and helps them decide whether to read on. It may show your position on the subject as well. The following limited topics at the left led writers to produce the thesis statements at the right.

Limited topic	Possible thesis statement
Surprise endings in fiction	The good surprise ending, as in William Faulkner's short story, "A Rose for Emily," makes us feel that we should have expected it, for in subtle ways the writer prepares us for it throughout the story.
The morals of lyrics in video and rock music—reality and fantasy	The lyrics in rock music, including the music that we see on videos, are often filled with references to sex that may seem vulgar and obscene, but they also often express a longing for enduring love and loyalty in a world where young people know that most love affairs and half the marriages do not last very long.
Special effects in movies and what they do to our feelings about reality	Special effects in movies do such a good job of making us believe the unbelievable for a couple of hours that our whole conception of reality has changed, so that we expect special effects in everything—including the classroom.
The fears of childhood in Stephen King's *The Shining*	Stephen King's novel *The Shining* is a modern parable of the fears of childhood and the fantasies that children manufacture to get over those fears—which are often real.

■ **Exercise 1.6** Return again to the topic you used in Exercise 1.3. Write a broad phrase that covers the subject, then write a thesis statement.

1g
Organizing Ideas

With your thesis statement before you as your controlling idea, begin organizing your supporting ideas. As you write your thesis statement, you will probably think of more ideas related to your topic and ways to expand ideas you have already recorded. Don't hesitate to add these new ideas to your prewriting notes. At this time, review all those notes. Select the ideas that are relevant, and cluster them. Think of how to fit your thoughts into a coherent essay. What do you have to put first so that readers can understand what comes later on? Which ideas belong together? If you cluster ideas before you write, you improve the chances of producing a clear essay that moves confidently from point to point from beginning to end.

You can do this clustering in many ways—by cutting and pasting, by drawing lines and arrows from one point to a related one, or by identifying ideas that belong together with a letter or a symbol in the margin. Some writers look at the lists or jottings produced in prewriting and recopy them into groups of connected thoughts. Some writers draw another subject tree. This time, however, the ideas need to be put in some sequence or hierarchy. If you do this cutting and pasting on a computer, make a backup copy before you start. You may change your mind and want to return to your first arrangement.

Arranging Information

Different topics and different purposes call for different kinds of organization. You can present your ideas in several different ways. Here are some common principles of organization:

- A *chronological arrangement* relates events as they happened in time. The first event is the first one you treat in your essay, and the last event comes at the end of your paper. Accounts of personal experiences and overviews of historical events are often arranged chronologically.

- A *spatial arrangement* presents ideas in the order of their physical relationship to one another. Choose a logical starting point and move through space systematically. A description of a painting in a university museum or in a local art gallery might begin with the central focus and then move outward to the edges of the canvas, up, down, right, and left.

- A *deductive arrangement* moves from the general to the specific. An essay examining surprise endings in fiction might begin with the generalization that such endings are best when they sneak up on us and go on to cite examples of stories in which, on reflection, we find that the endings were inevitable but we were kept from being able to predict them by the skill of their authors (see also 35c).

- An *inductive arrangement* moves from the specific to the general. John Williams's essay on childhood fears in *The Shining* might begin by citing examples of Danny's fears, move to similar examples from John's own childhood, and conclude that King has written a modern fable of childhood fears and fantasies (see also 35b).

- An arrangement by *order of importance* assigns a hierarchy to ideas. An argument for term limits for members of Congress might present five reasons, moving from the trivial to the profound. Most deductive and inductive essays also present ideas in descending or ascending order of importance, respectively. An essay on the morals of rock music might begin by quoting some lyrics and acknowledging that many are raw and sexual and imply a lack of commitment, then quote other lyrics to show a fear of loneliness and a desire for love that lasts longer than a night, and finally conclude that the lyrics of rock music express the desire for love that many young people do not see in their parents. To make a cumulative argument like this, you must decide which ideas are more important than others and choose the order that fits your subject and your thesis.

Creating a Rough Outline

When you arrange your ideas, when you put them in sequence, you have created a rough outline. This outline is an informal list, a private convenience for you. It does not need to follow a prescribed form but should be detailed enough to help you see the shape and direction of your paper. It will also help you decide what you have to say and how to say it. It will raise helpful questions about limitations. Checklist 1.5 shows the elements that should be included in your outline.

From prewriting notes, John Williams prepared this rough outline:

Thesis statement: Stephen King's The Shining illustrates the frightening

fantasies many children have in a world where they are helpless and the

fantasies that help them get through their fears.

Introduction: Start with my fears at sleeping alone in the upstairs back

bedroom of our house when I was a little child and my fantasies of having

Spider Man as a big brother to protect me.

1. Summarize briefly Stephen King's novel The Shining. How pleasant the

   prospect of a winter with a mother and father in an old hotel in

   Colorado, all alone, all they could eat, a great old house to roam

   through.

2. How King's child character Danny has fantasies about an imaginary

   friend Tony, but how he also has psychic powers, and in the end a sort of

   big brother character comes to rescue him from the evil that has

   overwhelmed the hotel.

3. The story makes most people remember childhood fantasies--

   helplessness before a world that children do not know very well and

   cannot control, a world that seems mysterious. Fantasies of having a

friend who will help even against your parents when they become
threatening.

4. In a lot of ways, Stephen King's novel is like the comic strip "Calvin
   and Hobbes," where the mean little kid Calvin has a stuffed tiger named
   Hobbes who becomes a real tiger when nobody else is around. The tiger is
   the older friend who takes care of a little boy.

5. When we grow up, we still live in a world that can be a scary place. But
   we don't have imaginary friends to take care of us. We make up other
   things to imagine--organizations, sports, fame, whatever. And we
   expect these things to take care of us.

6. Life may not be a mystery of the sort that Stephen King gives us in The
   Shining, but it is a mystery of its own kind, and a lot of times we feel
   helpless when we face parts of it. I wish I had a big brother or sister
   right now to give me advice about this paper.

Conclusion: Stephen King is a serious writer who uses a different kind of
story to say serious things.

✔ CHECKLIST 1.5: MAKING A ROUGH OUTLINE

A rough outline should include

- thesis statement
- introduction or opening
- ideas or main points, in numbered sequence
- conclusion

You might prefer to write up a fully developed, formal outline (discussed in 34b). But a rough outline, a list of points you want to cover, is usually enough. As you write the first draft of your paper, you may change your rough outline around and include some new ideas. But even if you don't follow your original plan exactly, the outline is a first stab at unity and coherence. A paper has *unity* if all the ideas support the thesis. A paper has *coherence* if each thought flows logically into the next, allowing readers to see the connections.

Reviewing the Rough Outline

Reviewing his rough outline, John recognized that he was not going to be able to tell a simple story in chronological order. He had several points to make within the framework of an essay that takes Stephen King's novel *The Shining* very seriously, and somehow he must wrap these points around his thesis—that King is writing about life in such a way that most of us can recognize our own fears and fantasies in his work.

John can see several difficulties. He does not want to be preachy, and he does not want to make anyone think that the main reason we read a novel is to take lessons from it. He has read *The Shining* and enjoyed it, and he sees some serious ideas in it. Approaching those ideas will take some hard thinking about organization and tone.

You will find reviewing your rough outline similarly profitable. It will save you time later on. Sometimes you may write several drafts of the rough outline—just as you may write several drafts of the paper itself. Each outline and each draft allows you not only to think more about your sentences and your style, your audience and your evidence, but also to think more about the subject and to reconsider your earlier ideas about it. As you work through drafts, your mind becomes a lens that takes a sharper and sharper focus on what it is seeing so that finally you are clear about what you are writing and where you want your paper to go.

■ **Exercise 1.7**   Make a rough outline for an essay on the subject you selected for Exercise 1.6. Repeat the thesis statement, then write a series of statements that support your thesis. Exchange outlines with someone in your class. When you have read each other's outlines, discuss them using Checklist 1.6 to guide your comments.

✔ **CHECKLIST 1.6: GETTING READY TO WRITE**

- Is the thesis clear enough and limited enough to make for a good paper?
- Does every entry in the outline relate to or support the thesis statement?
- Is the introduction interesting enough to make you want to read on?
- Is the conclusion satisfying, and does it follow logically from the points that have been made?

WRITING AND REVISING A PAPER

This chapter will take you through the steps involved in producing successive drafts of a paper and the final copy. Follow the steps carefully. John Williams's essay on *The Shining* is again used as an example to help you understand what you are doing in drafting your own composition.

2a
Preparing the First Draft

With the benefits of your prewriting and your rough (or formal) outline at hand, you can start writing. Don't try to make your first draft perfect. Don't worry about errors of facts, questionable spellings, or awkward constructions. Write your first draft as fast as you can. Concentrate on producing a flow of ideas. Once you have written a draft, you can correct your errors, smooth out the rough places, and shape the whole into a pleasing design.

Don't worry about a title now. If you think of one, fine. If not, come up with your title later on. Don't even labor over your opening at this point. Just get started. A good way to start your essay may occur to you as you write. Here is the first draft of John Williams's essay. The comments in the margins were written in peer review by another student in the class.

When I was a little boy, I slept in an upstairs room with
my older brother Fred. Our house was on the edge of the town
where we lived, beyond our house were fields woods, and at   *and*
night it was quiet as the grave. Fred was ten years older than
                                        ^
I was. He worked six hours a day in the local Burger-King and

went to night school at the community college near our house. My parents made me go to bed before he came home.

So I went to bed with the lights out. Alone in a room upstairs that seemed huge. I listened to the house creak and pop like old wooden houses do in the night when it gets cool, and I was afraid. There's this scene in the comic strip "Calvin and Hobbes" where Calvin imagines the monsters coming out from under his bed, and I can understand it because I could imagine gangstters under my bed hiding from the police and having guns, and when I turned the light out, I thought they would come out and kill me. Our house was a hundred years old. I don't know how many people owned it before we bought it. Especially I thought about the guy who built the house, you know, the person who owned it first a hundred years ago and thought that since he had designed it and built it or had it built, it was his forever. You know what the three bears said about Goldilocks. "Whose been sleeping in my bed?" And I thought of ghosts really mad at me and saying, "Who's been sleeping in my room."

So I used to lie up there and turn up another fantasy, that Spider Man was my friend, maybe even my older brother, and he was standing guard over me in the dark and that when gangsters came out from under the bed or out of the closet, Spider Man would wrap them all up in his web stuff that he carries around with him all the time, and they would be absolutely helpless, and the police would haul them off to jail, and I would definitely be a hero.

I thought of all that in reading <u>The Shining</u> by Stephen King. It's a story about a father named Jack, a mother named Wendy, and a boy named Danny. Jack is a writer, a former drunk, out of a job. At some point in the past he has abused Danny. Probably when he was drunk, and he has lost his teaching job because he has a terrible temper. Anyway, he gets a job looking after a big old hotel in Colorado through the winter when the place would be snowed in and just needs somebody there to take care of it. The whole family would be cut off from the rest of the world when the first big snow comes.

[margin annotations, handwritten:]
sentence fragment?

Is there just one scene? Do you need this? spelling?

I like all this. But I'm not sure what you are writing about? When are you going to get to the point?

Now I see what you are doing. Why not put the Stephen King part first so we will have your thesis right away?

sentence fragment?

In one way, the story looks like the American dream, a family with everything they want, bound together for months when they have to depend on each other. They have to eat all their meals together and talk to each other, and you'd think it'd be just great.

This is good.

But the old hotel is filled with ghosts of the evil deeds that have gone on there in the past when it was owned by criminals and used for all sorts of evil purposes, including murder. Danny has a kind of power called the "shining", and he can see things other people can't. He sees the ghosts. And then jack begins to see them, too. All the evil ghosts living in the house, haunting it, and they try to possess both Danny and Jack. In the end Jack goes crazy--or else he is possessed by the ghosts. But Danny resists because he is innocent, and Jack comes after him and tries to kill him.

Comma should go inside quotation marks.

Danny uses the shining to send a call for help through space to a friend. A cook he has met at the beginning of the book named Dick Hallorann who also has the shining. Hallorann throws down everything to come across the country to rescue Danny and saves Wendy, but Jack dies, and the hotel burns up.

sentence fragment?

Stephen King has taken these childhood fantasies and made a really good story about them. Only in his book these fantasies are real, and the house truely is haunted. Danny has his own superhero, Dick Hallorann, to help him, a kind of big brother the way I made Spider Man my big brother when I was a child and afraid. But of course we know the book is <u>not</u> real. It is a story, a novel. We know Stephen King has made it all up.

spelling?

But we also know he is making it all up from something we know--fantasies. We meet ourselves and our fears in <u>The Shining</u>. And yes, most of us when we are children both love our parents and fear them at the same time. Stephen King has picked up that idea, too. What happens to us if the people who are supposed to protect us, suddenly start trying to kill us. In real life, children really do suffer abuse from their parents sometimes. Sometimes parents even kill them.

I would put the Stephen King part first, and I would expand this part.

Stephen King is dealing with all these ideas. It is a very powerful story, and Stephen King is a serious novelist.

Your conclusion seems to fall off. I would expand it.

You probably noticed lots of errors in this first draft: many ideas are rambling and unclear, and some sentences are shaky. Remember that John concentrated on recording his thoughts and did not worry about being correct. He got his ideas down on paper and can fix his errors later.

■ **Exercise 2.1**   Revise John's paper. You may not have read *The Shining*, but by now you know enough about it to follow John's argument. Correct any errors you see, smoothing out sentences, eliminating unnecessary words and phrases, and perhaps adding thoughts of your own.

2b
Revising the Draft

After you complete the first draft of a paper, take a long break. Put some time and distance between you and your essay, and clear your mind. Your mind has a powerful ability to work when you don't realize it's working. When you're incubating an idea, your mind is working whether you realize it or not.

You will also find it helpful to do what John has done with his first draft. He has given it to someone else for **peer review,** a reading for comments and suggestions for revision by friends or classmates. John, likewise, has read and commented on the first draft of the person who read his paper. Your instructor may divide your class into writing groups for this purpose. If you aren't in a class-assigned writing group, consider starting one with a few friends. You'll find their serious attention to your writing extremely helpful.

In your writing group, ask for comments and corrections of the kind your instructor would make. Keep your criticism constructive and to the point. Don't simply ask, "What do you think of my paper?" Your reader will almost always say, "I like it." Ask, rather, "What do you think I'm trying to say?" As your reader tells you what he or she reads in your text, you may discover that you have not made your purposes clear. Once you and a friendly reader have agreed that the most important issue is what you want to say, you can talk about the paper in such a way that you learn from the discussion. Talking is an excellent way to think. Checklist 2.1 will help guide peer comments and discussion.

✔ **CHECKLIST 2.1: PEER REVIEW GUIDELINES**

- Put comments as they occur to you in the margins.
- List three things you really like about the essay—what are its strengths?
- List three things in the essay that need improvement—say what's wrong *and* suggest how the problem might be fixed.

When you return to your draft, reread it carefully several times. Study the comments made by others during peer review. Be prepared to change the content, the words, the sentence structure, the organization, and even the thesis of your essay. After talking your paper over with your writing group, you may have decided to go off in an entirely different direction. As you revise, you'll cut some things out and add others. You'll change some words, and substitute more precise language for generalities and clichés. You may want to shift sentences from one place to another or shorten or combine them. If you have a title already, look at it carefully to be sure it fits your topic and the readers you want for your essay. At this point, work on your opening and introduction to make sure they, too, engage your readers and point them in the right direction.

Revised drafts can get messy. Whenever your draft gets too messy to read easily, prepare a new draft. If you use a computer, you can mark up your printed copy, make the changes in your computer file, and print out a new copy—which you may mark up again. Most writers need to write at least two drafts of anything they compose. Professional writers and good student writers nearly always do more. In revising, be as clear as you can. Be sure every sentence makes a clear statement. Some sentences, hastily written in a first draft, will require radical surgery. Try to anticipate the clarifications your readers will need and clarify before they have to ask. Finally, check your draft for errors in spelling, punctuation, and grammar. Make sure each sentence ends with a period or a question mark. (Don't overuse the exclamation point! It can become tedious!) Look for troublesome forms of verbs, vague pronoun references, misplaced modification, or any other kind of error that may distract a reader from what you have to say. Checklist 2.2 outlines things to consider as you revise. When you have produced a readable draft, show it again to a friend or your writing group. Now read your draft aloud to yourself. As you hear what you've written, awkward sentence structures and even errors in grammar will jump out at you, and often improvements simply flow.

✔ **CHECKLIST 2.2: REVISING DRAFTS**

Revising ideas

- Is the thesis clear? (1f)
- Does the paper speak consistently to an audience? (1d)
- Are there enough details, enough facts, to support your major points? (1e)
- Does the paper show unity? Does it stay on track? Do all the ideas relate clearly to each other? (1g)
- Is the paper coherent? Are the internal transitions from point to point clear? (1g)
- Is the language of the paper precise? (3c, 9c, Chapter 13) Should any general words be made more specific?

Revising organization and structure

- Do the opening and the introduction capture and hold the reader's interest?
- Does the conclusion complete the ideas established and supported in the paper? (3d)
- Do the first and the last paragraphs in the paper somehow reflect one another? Are some words or ideas mentioned in the introduction mentioned again in the conclusion?
- Does the title engage the reader's attention?

Revising sentences and words

- Are periods and other end marks used to set off sentences?
- Have run-on sentences been separated by end marks or combined with connecting words and suitable punctuation? (Chapter 13)
- Have sentence fragments been connected to other sentences by adding subjects, verbs, or both? (14a)
- Are parallel ideas expressed in parallel forms? (Chapter 6)
- Have needless shifts in tone or point of view been corrected? (Chapter 20)
- Do modifiers stand near enough to the words they describe to avoid ambiguity?
- Do subordinate sections relate correctly to main clauses? (6b)
- Does each sentence state its information clearly?
- Is there variety in sentence structure?
- When read aloud, does every sentence sound right?

Verbs and other words

- Do subjects and verbs agree? (Chapter 15)
- Are verb tenses correctly formed and consistent? (16a–b)
- Have unnecessary shifts in tense, mood, voice, number, or emphasis been corrected? (Chapter 20)
- Are the pronoun references clear? (Chapter 17)
- Have all unnecessary words been eliminated?

Punctuation and mechanics

- Are punctuation marks used correctly to make meaning clear?
- Are apostrophes placed to show possession or contraction? (Chapter 24)
- Are quotation marks used in pairs to set off someone's exact words? (25a)
- Do italics, numbers, and symbols follow conventional uses? (Chapters 29, 30)
- Do capital letters follow the conventions of American English? (Chapter 28) Is the title correctly capitalized and punctuated?
- Have troublesome words been checked in a dictionary or with your computer's spell checker for accurate spelling? (Chapter 27)

John reconsidered his first draft (pages 27–29) carefully. His peer reviewers helped him find errors in grammar and spelling and some confused diction. But he realized that correcting these errors was not the major task he faced. He had to reshape the thoughts in his first draft into a coherent essay. That took some careful revising.

He also had to think about his audience. Who would read this paper? How could he make the paper appeal to people who did not know him and who did not think that horror stories were worth writing about or reading? What was his thesis?

He went back to his rough outline and studied it, then went back even further to his freewriting. This retracing of his steps showed him how far he had come and gave him confidence to continue. It also gave him a better sense of what he wanted to say and how he needed to shape his essay. The comments made by a fellow student during a peer review helped focus John's attention on some essential issues.

John worked through his first draft carefully, willing to make drastic revisions. Here's his readable revision. This is the second draft, which his instructor said she would read and comment on. The comments in the margin are hers.

**2b
dev**

Stephen King in <u>The Shining</u> has written a novel about childhood fears that may seem fantastic but that have a reality in the modern world that we all know, either personally or by reading the newspapers and seeing the television news. This is not a novel to be dismissed as a horror story filled with cheap thrills. This is a novel to make us think about life as it is in the world.

Opening sentence includes essential information but is awkward, wordy

A lot about the novel seems fantastic. Because it deals with the supernatural. Jack Torrance is a bad-tempered writer, not very successful, who has lost his teaching job because he got into trouble. Now he gets a chance to be the guardian of an old resort hotel in the mountains of Colorado, the Overlook, for a winter when the place is shut in by snow.

*sentence fragment
Rewrite this sentence to make it smoother*

Torrance takes with him his wife Wendy and his little son Danny. Earlier, during a drunken rage, he broke Danny's arm. But that was a while ago. Now the three of them are going to be alone in the hotel all winter long.

In some ways it looks like the American dream—a big house, all the food they can eat, lots of room and lots of time to do whatever they want, time to be together and enjoy each other, and time for Jack to finish writing a play he is working on. But the American dream exists in fiction to be torn apart.

Danny has a supernatural gift, a kind of second sight, that allows him to read minds. When he and his parents arrive at the Overlook as the hotel is getting ready to close down for the winter. He meets a black cook named Dick Hallorann who also has this gift. Hallorann is on his way to Florida to spend the winter, but he will become essential to the story.

transition

fragment

Part of the story is, of course, that the hotel is haunted, it has been owned by criminals, and it has been the scene of every kind of evil from sexual orgies to murders. As the snows come, and Wendy, Danny, and Jack are shut away from the world, the ghosts try to posess both Danny and Jack. Jack, with his weak character, falls victim to them, but Danny in his inocence does not. In one of the most scarriest scenes in the book, Jack is tracking Danny through the hotel to kill him.

Ok, I see—do you want to give this away at this point in your essay?

*spelling
tense shift
spelling spelling*

Danny, however, sends a mental message to Dick Hallorann, begging for help. And Hallorann comes all the way across country, rents a snowmobile, gets to the Overlook just in time to save Danny. The hotel burns. Jack dies. Wendy and Danny escape.

I recognize a lot of my own childhood fantasies here. I suppose other readers do the same. When I was a little boy I had to go to bed in an upstairs room of our big house all alone. I used to imagine monsters under the bed or murderers in the closet waiting until I turned out the light before they did something terrible to me.

spelling

It was scarry, but I fought the fear by pretending that Spider Man was my big brother and that he was there in the room with me and that he would protect me from anything. I would whisper, "Goodnight Spider Man," and I would go to sleep, leaving him to protect me.

Dick Hallorann is to Danny like Spider Man was to me or like Hobbes is to Calvin--a big brother who will do anything for Danny, who loves him, protects him, and talks to him. Stephen King has taken our fantasies and made them work for him and for us in the novel.

Children live amid lots of fears. When we are very small, we even fear our parents. They are a lot bigger than we are. They know a lot more than we do. Sometimes they get mad at us. And we know they can hurt us. Yet they love us, and we love them.

sense?

Most children, I hope, grow up to realize that the love is much more important than the fear, and when we are grown, we think back on the good things our parents have done for us rather than linger over the bad. A lot of the bad turns out to be fantasy, we imagined some evil there when our parents were trying to do us good.

But wait a minute! It isn't all fantasy. Some parents abuse their children and even kill them. And in countries at war, children may be killed by bombs and guns. Even in many of our big cities, innocent children get caught in the crossfire of gang wars and are shot down dead just because they happened to be in the wrong place at the wrong time.

Where is this detail going?

2b

dev

You can even say that some of these children are killed by ghosts from the past. A father may abuse his children because he was abused by his own father when he was a child. That's what seemed to happen to Jack Torrance in the novel. He carries the ghost of memory in his head and in his impulses.

good conclusion – makes connections

So when you think about Stephen King's The Shining, and when you read it and feel scared, you may be reading a parable about human life and history. That's why I think Stephen King is so powerful. And that's why I think he can be so scarry. He thinks up stories that, when we think about them, go right down to the heart of the way human beings are. It looks like fantasy when we read it, but it holds onto us because we know deep inside that he is writing about truth.

spelling; avoid repeating word think.

This is a nice essay on Stephen King that makes me take him seriously as a novelist. You have done a good job relating the book to life. I think you may spend a little too much time on plot summary. See if you can reduce this section.

I've marked some sentences that you might rewrite to make more clear, and I've marked some places where you repeat words unnecessarily. You make several comma faults in this paper. This is an error that you can easily correct. See 14a in the McGraw-Hill Handbook.

■ **Exercise 2.2**   Study the second draft of John's paper and 2e. Compare your revision of his first draft (Exercise 2.1). List three ways his second draft is better than yours. List three ways yours is better.

■ **Exercise 2.3**   Divide your class into small groups and compare John's second draft with his first draft. Where has he revised sentences? Where has he changed paragraphs around? Where has he expanded information? What has he cut out? Why do you think he made each of the changes he made? Do you approve of all the changes? Why?

2c
Proofreading

Both before and after you prepare your final copy, comb your essay for mechanical mistakes and correct them. This step is called **proofreading.** Proofreading requires careful examination of each line of text. Proofread your first draft before you rewrite it into your second draft, proofread the second draft, and proofread the final copy before you submit it. Hold a ruler or a blank sheet of paper beneath the line you are studying. Examine each sentence for missing words and punctuation. Check each word for missing or incorrect letters. Proofreading a paper by reading backward from the last sentence to the first is another good technique. It makes you see each letter and each word and each punctuation mark independently of the context. Some writers touch the point of a pencil to each syllable to help them read more slowly. Again, it is always a good idea to read your work slowly aloud to yourself.

2d
Preparing the Final Copy

Remember that your instructor must grade many papers, and remain alert and careful through them all. Messy papers make life hard for the busy instructor—just as a poorly printed article, filled with typographical errors, makes life hard for any reader. Sometimes you will find a mistake in a paper just as you are ready to hand it in. Always correct the mistake, but do so as neatly as you can. If you proofread carefully before you are ready to hand in your finished draft, you can avoid messing up your paper with lots of handwritten corrections, especially if you write with a computer. See Checklist 2.3 for some general guidelines.

✔ CHECKLIST 2.3: STANDARD ESSAY PRESENTATION

Format

- Use one side of each page.
- Number pages consecutively, starting with page 1 of your paper. Unless your instructor or the usual style requires it, do not count the cover page. Outlines may be paginated with roman numerals or as part of the 1-2-3 sequence; ask your instructor.
- Use arabic numbers in the upper right-hand corner or centered at the top of each page. Be consistent in whatever form of pagination you use.

- Leave margins of $1\frac{1}{4}$ or $1\frac{1}{2}$ inches at the top, sides, and bottom of each page. On typewriters, a left margin at 10 and a right margin set at 70 are usually acceptable. On word processors, turn justification off for a "ragged right" margin and better word spacing.

Title

- Center the title on the first page, $1\frac{1}{2}$ inches below the top margin, or on the first line for handwritten copies.

- Leave one line of space below the title.

- Capitalize the first letter of all major words (nouns, pronouns, verbs, adjectives, adverbs) in the title, including the first and last words, no matter what part of speech they are, e.g.:

    Choosing the Right Running Shoes

- Capitalize the first letter of prepositions of five or more letters, e.g.:

    Going Against the Current: Life on a Houseboat

- Do not place a period at the end of the title or underline the title or enclose it in quotation marks. (The title of a book, an article, or a poem that appears within your title does need correct punctuation. See 28c and 33a.)

- If you use a cover page, repeat the title at the top of the first text page of your essay.

Cover page

- The cover page usually includes your name, your course name and number, the submission date, and the instructor's name. But your instructor may have different requirements.

Typed and word-processed papers

- Use $8\frac{1}{2} \times 11$ unlined white bond paper, not onionskin and not paper treated to allow corrections with pencil erasers, which smudges easily and often becomes unreadable. If you use a computer printer with tractor-fed continuous-form paper, tear off the perforated strip on each side of the paper and separate each page.

- Use *only* black ribbon; if the type looks faded, change the ribbon. Instructors have a hard time reading an almost illegible paper typed with an exhausted ribbon. Be kind to your instructor.

- Double-space between lines; indent paragraphs five spaces.

- After periods, question marks, exclamation points, and colons, use two spaces; after commas and semicolons, use one space.

- Do not use a space before or after a hyphen. To type a dash, use two consecutive hyphens (--) without any spacing between the dash and the words on each side.

    Dashes--as in this example--set off thoughts for emphasis.

- If you use a typewriter, make corrections with a typewriter eraser, a correcting tape on the typewriter, or a correction fluid. Do not strike over incorrect letters. For errors discovered after you have removed your pages from your typewriter or printer, make corrections in pen with blue or black ink, or do the pages over.

- If you use a computer, be sure you have not left in words you intended to delete or deleted words you meant to leave in.

- If you use a typewriter, be sure the type is clean and the letters clear.

- If you use a computer and a dot matrix printer, try to use a printer or typeface that has true descenders. That is, the tails on the letters *g, j, p, g,* and *y* should come down below the baseline for the rest of the type. (See Appendix B.)

Handwritten papers

- Use $8\frac{1}{2} \times 11$ paper with lines spaced about $\frac{3}{8}$ inch apart. For a clear layout, skip every other line.

- Use blue or black ink; write on one side only.

- Indent the first line of every paragraph about one inch.

- Make occasional corrections with an ink eraser or correction fluid, or draw a neat line through words you want to delete. Write in the new words above the deletions, using skipped lines and marginal space for additions. If there are more than a few corrections, write the page over again.

- Make your handwriting readable. Like it or not, willingly or not, your instructor will be profoundly influenced by your handwriting. Don't let good thoughts be condemned for bad script. Use a firm, clear period at the end of each sentence, and leave space before the next sentence. Dot *i*s and *t*s directly above the letter. Avoid loops and curlicues, especially when you make capital letters. Make sure readers can distinguish between the *r* and the *n*, the *v* and the *u*, the *u* and the *n*, the *o* and the *a*, the *l* and the *t*, and the *e* and the *i*. Be careful to round off the *h* so it does not look like an *l* followed by an *i*. Be sure to make the letters *m* and *n* so that they do not look like the letter *u* standing alone or combined with another letter.

■ **Exercise 2.4**   Write an essay describing a personal experience or a personal reaction to something you have read recently. As you go through all the steps involved in writing, save the materials listed below. Put them in a large envelope and submit them to your instructor with the final copy.

1. prewriting notes
2. a limited topic for the paper
3. a description of the audience for your paper
4. a list of your supporting evidence

5. a thesis statement
6. an outline, if your instructor requires it (See 36b)
7. a first draft
8. a second draft and any subsequent drafts
9. a final copy

2e
Making Further Revisions and Corrections

When your instructor returns your paper, read it carefully. Study the summary remarks that describe the strengths and weaknesses of your work. Examine the marginal notations, and be prepared to make revisions on the basis of the commentary you find there. You can learn to prevent errors next time around by correcting your mistakes and by responding to suggestions about style, organization, and content.

Revision toward perfection is the essence of the writing process. Some instructors build stages for revision into their course structures. They may, for example, make it a practice to read and comment on second drafts of student essays, grading only the third and final copy. Other instructors require students to revise essays after they've been graded and to submit them a second time. The point is that you learn from doing—from actually revising—rather than simply reading the instructor's comments. Even if your instructor does not require revisions, revise and correct your papers on your own. You'll be amazed at what you learn in the process, and you probably won't make the same mistakes again. See Checklist 2.4 for guidance.

✔ CHECKLIST 2.4: CORRECTING EVALUATED PAPERS

- Follow your instructor's guidelines for revisions. Some instructors read drafts and make comments *before* the paper goes into final form. Others encourage full rewriting based on comments written on final drafts. Be sure to correct errors before you do complete revisions of graded papers.

- Learn the symbol and comment system your instructor uses.

- Make all corrections in pencil or a different color ink so that you and your instructor can see what you have done.

- As you make corrections, draw a line through the marginal symbol to help yourself keep track of what you have finished.

- Write short corrections clearly, directly above the error noted by your instructor.

- Rewrite any weak sentences in the margin (if there is room) or on the reverse side of the page. If you rewrite on the reverse side of the page, put an arrow in the margin to signal your instructor to turn the page over to see your revision.

- Keep a record of your mistakes. All writers tend to fall into patterns of error. If you keep a record of your errors, you can discover your own patterns and so be on the lookout for the errors you are most likely to make.

Your instructor may evaluate your paper with comments, questions, and marking symbols. An alphabetical list of common correction symbols keyed to this handbook appears on the inside front cover. If you see ∥ in the margin of your paper, for example, the list on the inside cover tells you that ∥ is a shorthand notation for faulty parallelism and that Chapter 6 explains the problem and how to correct it. If your instructor uses chapter and section numbers to indicate corrections needed, check the inside back covers of this handbook for a quick guide. If you don't understand a comment or a symbol, make an appointment to discuss the paper with your instructor. Or you may want to visit your campus writing center and go over your paper with a tutor.

■ **Exercise 2.5**   Following the instructor's comments on John Williams's second draft of his essay on *The Shining* (pp. 34–36), make revisions and corrections. Rewrite sentences or entire paragraphs.

■ **Exercise 2.6**   Revise and correct the composition you prepared for Exercise 2.4 according to your instructor's comments.

3

WRITING STRONG PARAGRAPHS

Paragraphs are the building blocks of essays, and it's fair to say that an essay's structure is only as strong as its paragraphs. This chapter examines the structure within paragraphs and focuses on opening and closing paragraphs in particular.

3a
Understanding Paragraphs

Paragraphs help writers organize their work in steps, and they help readers follow the writer's thought through a text.

Paragraphs also relieve the eye. Few sights are as forbidding as a long block of printed text with no indentations. The indentation assures us that a text is manageable, that it can be broken down into parts which the mind can absorb one at a time. Without the white space of the indentations, a text looks like some monstrous thing we must swallow whole.

Paragraphs do not stand alone. They are not essays in themselves, although some textbooks pretend they are. Once in a while you may write a single paragraph—a caption for a photograph, for example, or a brief memo in an office. Otherwise paragraphs are part of the flow of a larger text. They have meaning only as they are joined to the whole.

How long should a paragraph be? There are no absolute rules. The decision is partially visual. Newspaper editors favor short paragraphs, sometimes only one or two sentences long. Newspaper readers often skim rather than study, and newspaper columns are thin; a long paragraph might run down an entire page. Magazines and books have longer paragraphs, largely because type columns are wider. As you read the paragraphs in this book, you'll see much variety in length. In your college writing, it is usually good to have at least one or two indentations on an $8\frac{1}{2} \times 11$ inch sheet of paper.

A new paragraph usually signals a slight change in emphasis in the paper, a step from one subtopic to another within the body of the text. This paragraph, the one you are reading right now, deals with the purpose of paragraphs in general. The previous paragraph considered how paragraphs look. When we, as authors, sensed our topic changing from the appearance of paragraphs to their purpose, we made a new paragraph by indenting.

The first sentence in a paragraph shows the direction of the sentences that follow it. The writer decides to change emphasis, indents, and then writes a sentence that indicates the shift. The next sentence must develop in some way the thought announced by the first sentence. Here is an example in a story from *Sports Illustrated* about the 1992 winter Olympics.

American women finished higher than American men in every sport in which both fielded teams, except cross-country and biathlon, in which the two sexes were equally inept, neither one cracking the top 10. In every other discipline, on snow and on ice, in traditional sports and in first-time Olympic sports, the dynamic and surprising U.S. women outdid their brethren. Composing just 34% of the U.S. team—55 of 161 athletes—the ladies wearing stars and stripes took home 82% of the medals.

—E. M. Swift

The first sentence in this paragraph announces that American women did far better than American men in the winter games. The following sentences build on the first, adding details that support the generalization.

Always be sure in your paragraphs that every sentence has a clear relation to the first sentence. When you change the emphasis slightly, indent and start a new paragraph. Here is the next paragraph from the article in *Sports Illustrated*.

This imbalance is a new phenomenon. Taken as a whole, in the previous two Winter Olymics, the American medals have been split—eight for men, eight for women. So why, in 1992, is there suddenly a gulf? What has enabled American women to succeed in Winter Olympic sports at a rate U.S. men can't match?

—E. M. Swift

E. M. Swift, the writer of this report for *Sports Illustrated,* changed emphasis from the first paragraph to the next. The first sentence of the second paragraph announces, "This imbalance is a new phenomenon." Every other sentence in this paragraph relates directly to the first sentence, proving first that the imbalance is new and then asking for an explanation.

Smith's paragraphs thus move through the article in blocks of factual information carefully organized to amplify the first sentence in each paragraph.

3b
Building Unified Paragraphs

Now that we have seen the importance of the first sentence in the structure of the paragraph, we can talk about the *controlling idea* of the paragraph. We expect a paragraph to have some single purpose, some point that all the sentences of the paragraph work together to make. A paragraph achieves unity if it supports a controlling idea.

Giving Each Paragraph a Controlling Idea

To speak of the controlling idea of the paragraph is another way of saying that every sentence in the paragraph must be related to a topic introduced by the first sentence. Sometimes the controlling idea is expressed as a generalization, usually in the first sentence. Both paragraphs from *Sports Illustrated* quoted above illustrate this kind of generalization. The generalization in the first paragraph is this: American women finished higher than American men in almost every sport in which both fielded teams. The generalization in the second paragraph is this: This imbalance is new. Every sentence in each paragraph supports the generalization made in its first sentence.

Traditionally, textbooks have called such a general sentence the **topic sentence.** Nearly always, the generalization that makes a topic sentence comes first in the paragraph. But sometimes the generalization will occur later on. In the paragraph below, the generalization comes in the second sentence.

The steam locomotive evokes nostalgia among many people. **The nostalgia is better than the experience of the steam locomotive ever was.** The steam locomotive was a dirty, dangerous, and generally disagreeable companion to American life for well over a century. It spread filthy, black smoke over large areas of every city it served, and it usually left a thick film of oily grime on the face of every passenger in the cars behind it. It started fires along the sides of the tracks in woods and fields. It was so heavy that it pounded rails until they broke, and when it crashed and turned over—as it frequently did—it poured flames, steam, and boiling water onto the fireman and the engineer in the cab. It had so many moving parts under high stress that it often broke down, stranding passengers for hours. And it was absurdly in-efficient and costly to operate.

—Dick Curry

Notice that although the second sentence is the generalization that unites all the facts in the paragraph, the first sentence does a necessary job of introduction. The first sentence announces the subject, and the rest of the paragraph develops its controlling idea by building on some thought expressed in the first sentence.

Many paragraphs do not contain a generalization, a sentence that can be called a *topic sentence* in the old meaning of that term. A paragraph that describes something or that tells a little story will seldom have a general sentence. Here's a paragraph from an article about chili peppers.

In her kitchen, where a *ristra*—a bouquet of deep-red peppers—hangs, Zamora serves me some green chiles she has just pulled from the freezer and cut up. The mesquite imparts a wonderful smoky flavor. For Christmas, she tells me, the feast at her house will feed 50 people, and will include homemade tortillas, tamales, and *carne adovada*, a dish with garlic, pork, and red chiles that cooks all night in the oven. "I don't know what it is," she says, "If I don't eat chiles on a regular basis, I get weird." She's not the only one. Zubin Mehta, former music director of the New York Philharmonic, who now lives in Los Angeles, grows hot peppers in his garden. He carries them in a jeweled silver case so that when he goes to a restaurant he can supply the chef with his favorite ingredient.

—Jim Robbins

This paragraph does not have a generalization, but we know from the setting established in the first sentence that the subject is chili peppers. Sentence by sentence, the writer details the love some people have for this blindingly hot spice.

Some paragraphs begin with a broad statement that is then limited by a second sentence. The rest of the paragraph builds on the second sentence. Some writers call this a "funnel" paragraph. In the following example, the paragraph begins with a general statement, but the rest of the paragraph is built on the second sentence.

Much modern technology for the home focuses on the kitchen, seeking to combine energy efficiency with convenience. The micro-wave oven does both, but does it cook food as well as the gas or electric models? Yes, if you are baking potatoes or cooking bacon or warming up a TV dinner or thawing out a package of frozen spinach.

Microwaves are great for cooking fish. But if you want to brown a steak or boil an egg or bake a pie, your microwave will not do the job.

Many paragraphs begin with a statement that the rest of the paragraph contradicts. This is the way the Rev. Martin Luther King, Jr., began the following paragraph on the actions of police in Birmingham who arrested black Americans for protesting racial segregation in 1963.

> It is true that they [the Birmingham police] have been rather disciplined in their public handling of the demonstrators. In this they have been rather publicly "nonviolent." But for what purpose? To preserve the evil system of segregation. Over the last few years I have consistently preached that nonviolence demands that the means we use must be as pure as the ends we seek. So I have tried to make it clear that it is wrong to use immoral means to attain moral ends. But now I must affirm that it is just as wrong, or even more so, to use moral means to preserve immoral ends. Maybe Mr. Connor and his policemen have been rather publicly nonviolent as Chief Prichett was in Albany, Georgia, but they have used the moral means of nonviolence to maintain the immoral end of flagrant racial injustice. T. S. Eliot has said that there is no greater treason than to do the right thing for the wrong reason.
>
> —MARTIN LUTHER KING, JR.

Some paragraphs introduce the topic with a direct quotation that intrigues the reader about the information to come. In this example, the controlling idea comes in the second sentence.

> "I thought it would be a quick in-and-out job," John Hohmann told me as we stood on the rim of a basalt cliff and looked at the ancient ruins below. In the summer of 1990, the 37-year-old archaeologist had come to east-central Arizona to investigate this prehistoric village. Known to white settlers for more than a century as Casa Malpais (Spanish for "house of the Badlands"), it had been surveyed by previous archaeologists but never excavated.
>
> —DAVID ROBERTS

Some paragraphs introduce the topic by posing a question at the outset. The rest of the paragraph offers some kind of response. The response may be the writer's answer, or it may suggest or report an answer that someone else has given, or it may be a comment on why the question has been asked. In the following paragraph, an economic writer for *Time* ponders the effect of a slowdown in the Japanese economy.

But will the stall in Japan spell trouble for the fragile American economy? Last year American companies shipped $48.1 billion worth of goods to Japan, making it the second largest U.S. export market. A recession in Japan could hurt the recovery by slowing demand for American products. In addition, Japanese business could try to bolster sagging domestic profits by aggressively selling more products overseas, an action that would surely worsen trade tensions. Finally, since Japan helps finance the U.S. budget deficit, some fear that a significant curtailment of Japanese investments in the U.S. could drive interest rates higher.

—*Time*

As these examples demonstrate, not all paragraphs are structured in the same way. Moreover, the position of a paragraph in an essay may make special demands. The paragraphs that open and close essays have a relationship to the essay as a whole that alters their form. The opening paragraph of an essay must present not only its own controlling idea but the controlling idea of the essay as well. Or an opening paragraph may set the scene, with its final sentence summing up the scene and explaining its importance. Or that explanation may not come until the second paragraph. Scene-setting first paragraphs often open articles in popular magazines because they make readers want to know what will happen next. Although the first sentence in such a paragraph is not, strictly speaking, a topic sentence, it sets the direction for what comes next. The following opening paragraph is another example of a funnel paragraph.

The bands are marching, the tailgates swinging open for the ritual of picnics and parties. The beverages are heady, the boosterism infectious, the old school colors vivid and bright. This is college football, as the television slogan goes, a great way to spend an autumn afternoon.

—*Newsweek*

Often an introductory paragraph simply tells a story. The first sentence begins with a striking detail, and the following sentences build on it. A later paragraph introduces the topic illustrated by the opening story. The role of the first sentence in such an opening paragraph is to catch the interest of readers and to make them keep on reading.

Some five hundred years ago, just about the time of Columbus's voyages to the New World, a massive springtime mud slide, set off possibly by a small earthquake, swept out of a canyon during the night, burying a large part of the village of Ozette in the territory of the

Makah Indians on the northern Pacific coast of present-day Washington State's Olympic Peninsula. In a few frightful minutes, humans and their buildings, canoes, utensils, and other possessions were covered under many feet of silt and sand.

For centuries they lay hidden in silence. Then, beginning in the 1960s and continuing for eleven years, archaeologists excavated this remarkable miniature New World Pompeii, revealing—in a completeness almost unparalleled in American archaeology—the details of Native American life as it existed in this part of the continent about 1492. Because of subsurface drainage, the silt and clay deposits above the village had remained moist throughout the years, preserving in excellent condition the lower walls of the structures and a stunning variety of the contents of the houses. Although animal tissue, hair, and feathers had not survived as well, objects made of wood and other vegetable fibers were found in almost the exact condition they were in at the time when the spirits turned against the people.

—Richard D. Daugherty

The standard topic sentence is most valuable when you write paragraphs about ideas, when you explain something, or when you make an argument. Such paragraphs help an essay develop its thesis step by step. Topic sentences define these steps clearly and help both writer and reader know where they are going. In narratives and descriptions, you may write paragraphs that do not have a topic sentence. But in all paragraphs, the first sentence should introduce words or ideas that are developed in the following sentences. Follow your first sentence in a paragraph with a second sentence that expands on some thought or idea. Follow that sentence with a further development of thoughts you have expanded on in the second sentence—and so on until the end of the paragraph.

■ **Exercise 3.1**　Write a couple of pages about something you have recently witnessed—an episode on the street, an athletic contest, a program you saw on television, some trouble you had with a car. Don't labor over your writing. Get your ideas on paper quickly.

Now study your writing and see how the first sentence in each paragraph introduces the subject you explore in the rest of the paragraph. You will usually discover that when you tell a story of something you have seen or experienced quickly, the paragraphs develop naturally from the first sentence.

Now write a couple of pages on something you have been thinking about lately—a political campaign, the ideas expressed in a difficult course, some problem you have seen reported on television or in the newspapers. Examine your paragraphs to see if they develop naturally from the first sentence in each one. How many of your paragraphs include a standard topic sentence, a generalization that summarizes the rest of the paragraph?

■ **Exercise 3.2** Develop each of the following sentences into a topic sentence, and write a paragraph about it.

1. Some people say that football is popular because it is a violent game.
2. Owning an automobile creates personal independence but damages community life.
3. Attending college while one has young children at home is an ordeal.
4. The long hours I spend on my job make it hard for me to study sometimes.
5. The person who comes back to school after years in the so-called real world brings a lot of experience that is helpful in learning.

■ **Exercise 3.3** State the topic of each of the following paragraphs in your own words. Then say whether the writer states that topic in a topic sentence. That is, does the writer's first sentence merely provide the first thought in a series of thoughts about a general topic? Or does the writer summarize the paragraph in a general sentence? Explain how some words in the first sentence of each paragraph are developed in succeeding sentences.

The Africans who were to become Americans came from a region of West Africa that fanned from its westernmost tip, around the Senegal River, south and east, along the Bight of Benin, and south again below the Congo River to include a region we now call Angola. Hardly a people living within this vast region, stretching inland for two to three hundred miles, was unrepresented in the creation of the Afro-American people. Bambara, Fulani, Mandinka, and Wolof from the Senegambia, the collection of peoples from Dahomey called Whydahs, the Ashanti, Coromantees, Fanti, Ga, Hausa, Ibo, Yoruba, Angola—they all came, like migrants from Europe and later from Asia, to mix their seed and substance in the making of the American.

It was a treacherous and awful journey from whatever point they started, down the coast, through the unimaginably inhuman Atlantic crossing, into American slavery. Nor was that journey vast and torturous merely in physical distance and bodily pain. Those who were forced to make it traversed worlds of mind and spirit, leaving what they were and becoming the forebears of a people yet to be. Each man, woman, and child made that internal journey alone; but collectively, their odyssey is one of the great epics of modern times.

Some who started out did not make it. Disease, frailty, brutality, and suicide took a heavy toll. But those whose way was stopped short for whatever reason will not hold us long, for ours is the story of those who have endured, whether due to strength or chance or will to survive or abject surrender. These were the people who would become Afro-Americans.

NATHAN IRVIN HUGGINS

Making All Sentences in a Paragraph Support the Main Idea

Every paragraph needs a logical structure based on a main point. The succession of sentences and the flow of ideas help create that structure. Any sentence that distracts readers from the main idea violates the architecture of the paragraph. In the following paragraph, several sentences wander away from the main idea.

After strenuous exercise, the body enters a dangerous period that cooling off can help prevent. When you are swimming or running, a large blood supply from the heart brings your arms and legs the oxygen required for muscle activity. The human heart works like a pump. When the right upper chamber of the heart (the *auricle*) fills with blood, blood rushes down into the right lower chamber (the *ventricle*). When this chamber fills, the strong muscles in its wall pump tired blood into an artery that speeds the blood to the lungs. As you exercise, the muscles squeeze, and blood going back to the heart gets an added push as long as you move your limbs. But if you stop suddenly, all this extra blood stays there; your arm and leg muscles are no longer helping your heart pump the blood around. Blood that remains in the arms and legs is blood kept away from vital organs like the brain. But if you *cool off,* that is, slow down your activity gradually, you'll help bring your pulse rate and your body temperature down slowly, helping your muscles rid themselves of metabolic waste, and, most important, you'll keep the blood flowing normally through your body.

—DICK CURRY

The controlling idea of this paragraph may be stated like this: If you stop doing vigorous exercise suddenly, you can cause a strain on the heart and other body organs. But a gradual cooling off after vigorous activity prevents this strain.

Now look at sentences three and four. These details about how the heart operates are interesting, but they distract from the controlling idea of the paragraph. These sentences have no place here, although they might work well in another part of the paper. The paragraph is clearer and reads more smoothly with the distracting sentences removed.

In revising your essays and paragraphs, check each sentence in a paragraph carefully against its main idea, and remove sentences that do not support that idea.

■ **Exercise 3.4**   The following paragraphs contain sentences that distract from the controlling idea. Locate those sentences, and rewrite the paragraph without them.

> School textbooks can make some children feel excluded from American life. Only a few years ago first graders learned to read out of books about Dick and Jane and their dog Spot. Children in the first grade are very impressionable. We know that television commercials can create materialism in them and that all sorts of subtle influences shape their view of the world. Dick and Jane were white. They lived in a nice single-family house in a suburb with sidewalks and friendly policemen and postmen, and their dog Spot never bit anybody. The textbooks were on slick paper and had cloth bindings. Daddy wore a suit to work and carried a briefcase. Mother stayed home and kept house and cooked a lot. Mother and Daddy never got a divorce, and Dick and Jane never played with any black or Hispanic children because such children were not to be found in the suburb— or in the textbooks. No father in the neighborhood was unemployed, and nobody ever went without a meal, and there were no homeless people anywhere. Even Spot looked well fed. Children whose parents were divorced, or children who were not white and middle-class, or children who lived in housing projects where there was violence and other kinds of crime could hardly find anything familiar in Dick and Jane.
>
> —DICK CURRY

■ **Exercise 3.5**   Write out the controlling idea for each of the following paragraphs. Explain how each sentence in each paragraph supports that controlling idea.

Lunch-Hour Courage

In grade school, she and I were in the same class—even though she was two years my senior—called "E.S.L.," short for English as a Second Language, where a hodgepodge of non-English-speaking children sat in varying degrees of shameful ignorance. It was a strange class made up of youngsters from extremes of culture and maturity, from an 8-year-old girl just arrived from China to a 15-year-old Cuban boy with dyslexia who had been left back four times.

Our teacher tried, in vain, to bring some sanity to the impossible task that she had been charged with, and here, in this atmosphere of chaotic uncertainty tinged with the shame of not belonging, Sukhee, a proud sixth-grader, and I, her diffident younger sister, first learned our ABC's.

Our classroom, although chaotic, was a haven of sorts from the outside throughout most of the day, but lunch period robbed us of this shield, and we were subject to all the belittling remarks and stares of other children. In actuality, these were nothing—a snicker or two, a mimicry of our accents—but they bothered my timid mind sufficiently to make the lunch hour the most dreaded one of my day.

At these times, Sukhee seemed to me an incredible pillar of strength. She would adopt none of the cowed stance that I couldn't help from adopting, and would look back, if anyone mimicked her appearance or accent, with as much blaze in her eyes as the other person dared to match. Others were never able to insult her because she never let herself become degraded in her own eyes.

On one occasion when she spoke rather loudly in Korean in the cafeteria, I, worried of the foreign inflections of our language becoming the butt of their joke, begged her to speak quietly as to be inaudible. I will never forget her reply as she answered me with a quiet puzzlement in her eyes. "Would you then have me speak in a language that neither I nor you understand? Until I become proficient enough in English to speak comfortably, the only language I know is my own, and I will not have your fear of some bully stop me from making use of my voice as loudly as I like."

It has been some six years since our E.S.L. experience, and Sukhee and I have managed to learn enough English to communicate without discomfort. We have also grown; we have changed. Sukhee, however, remains the one person of my acquaintance who possesses true integrity of character. She has an intimate sense of the woman that she is. She does not compromise her person for easy conveniences, nor does she make apologies for her being. She doesn't need to because she has pride springing from a hard-gained knowledge of what she can and cannot do.

Her self-respect, real and as essential a part of her as her eyes or brain, frees her from petty preoccupations concerning self and allows her to contemplate the scheme of things beyond her own individual will or desire. For this I think humans are said to be above animals and for this I will always envy and admire her unreservedly.

—YOUNGJU RYU

3c
Building Coherent Paragraphs

In coherent paragraphs, thoughts follow one after the other, with connections easy for readers to see and understand. Readers don't like to feel that something has been left out, that a new term has been introduced without adequate preparation, or that a person is mentioned as though they should know who it is when in fact the writer has not mentioned the person before.

Coherence is achieved through the arrangement of information. In revising your essays and paragraphs, look carefully at the first sentence in each paragraph to see what ideas in it you will develop in the next sentence and so on through all the sentences in the paragraph.

Linking Sentences and Ideas

Several techniques can help you achieve coherence. Repeating important words or phrases is one, and using parallel structures is another. Transitional words and expressions such as *therefore, since, moreover, for example,* and *in the first place* (see below and 13e) are an excellent way to bridge sentences and even paragraphs. Combine these techniques to write paragraphs that hold together around a central topic.

Repetition

In the following paragraphs, boldface print highlights repetition that creates coherence. Study the paragraphs carefully to see how ideas are developed, how words tie previous information to new information being introduced, and how various thoughts are explained. You can draw circles around the words in boldface and connect the circles to see how the patterns of repetition hold the essay together. But notice that each repeated word or phrase appears in a sentence in which new information is being introduced.

When Thurgood **Marshall** stepped down from the Supreme Court, it marked the passing of a **generation** of **black civil-rights lawyers** who, in the words of one observer, "linked the passion of Frederick Douglass demanding **black freedom** and of William Du Bois demanding **black equality** to the undelivered promises of the **Constitution** of the United States." **Marshall** was perhaps the most visible member of that **generation,** but it's key figure—a **lawyer** who in many ways pioneered the idea of using the **Constitution** to promote **racial justice**—was a man named Charles Hamilton Houston, who is today largely unknown.

The grandson of slaves, Houston was born in Washington, D.C., in 1895, attended **segregated** schools there, and then went off to Amherst College, in Massachusetts, from which he graduated, magna cum laude and Phi Beta Kappa, in 1915. After serving as a lieutenant in the Army during the First World War, Houston attended Harvard Law School, became the first black member of the law review, and earned his LL.B. in 1922 and a doctorate in 1923. Over the next dozen years, first as a teacher at Howard University Law School and later as its dean, he became one of America's preeminent legal educators, and he transformed an unaccredited night program into an accredited full-time institution with a national reputation for training **black civil-rights lawyers.** "A **lawyer's** either a **social** engineer or a parasite on society," he used to tell his Howard students.

No armchair academic, Houston was himself a brilliant **trial lawyer** and **social engineer.** When he started practice, in 1924, federal and state laws imposed **racial segregation** throughout American life. Eleven years later, he became special counsel to the Nationl Association for the Advancement of Colored People, and in that post he devised the long-range legal strategy that ultimately led the Supreme Court, in **Brown** v. Board of Education, to declare such laws contrary to the **Constitution. Thurgood Marshall,** one of Houston's star pupils, briefed and argued the **Brown** decision, and credited Houston with being "the **engineer** of all of it."

—*New Yorker*

Observe the careful development of these paragraphs by examining the patterns of repetition that the words and phrases in boldface show. The tribute opens with a reference to Thurgood Marshall's retirement from the Supreme Court. The paragraph gradually narrows, funnel fashion, to the main subject, Charles Hamilton Houston. In this paragraph and those that follow, repetitions of words and ideas, such as *generation, black, civil rights lawyer, constitution,* and *engineer,* provide coherence. These repetitions keep us tracking the thought of the writer. The conclusion, with its reference back to Marshall, neatly ties the entire tribute together.

Every sentence after the first sentence in a coherent essay looks both backward and forward. The writer brings up a word or a related idea he or she has used before, repeats it, and adds to it. This pattern of repetition and addition is essential to any good piece of writing.

Sometimes the repetition of a single word or phrase is so insistent that it sounds like a drumbeat. This deliberate repetition can be effective in an occasional paragraph. Be sure, if you use such a form, that you include some new information along with the repetition. The information should develop some thought important to your essay.

> We do not choose to be born. We do not choose our parents. We do not choose our historical epoch, or the country of our birth, or the immediate circumstances of our upbringing. We do not, most of the time, choose to die; nor do we choose the time or condition of death. But within all this realm of choicelessness, we do choose how we shall live, courageously or in cowardice, honorably or dishonorably, with purpose or in drift.
>
> —Joseph Epstein

Parallel structure

Repeating the forms of clauses, phrases, or sentences can also tie thought units together in paragraphs. In the paragraph below, parallelism (discussed in Chapter 6) dramatically links criticisms of Britain's King Charles I (1600–1649), the only English king to be judged a criminal by his people and executed by beheading.

> We charge him with having broken his coronation oath; and we are told that he kept his wedding vow! We accuse him of having given up his people to the merciless inflictions of the most hot-headed and hard-hearted of prelates; and the defense is, that he took his little son on his knee and kissed him! We censure him for having violated the articles of Petition of Right, after having, for good and valuable consideration, promised to observe them; and we are informed that he was accustomed to hear prayers at six o'clock in the morning! It is to such considerations as these, together with his Van Dyck dress, his handsome face, and his peaked beard, that he owes, we verily believe, most of his popularity with the present generation.
>
> —Thomas Babington MacCaulay

Transitional expressions

Transitional expressions are words or phrases that tell a reader something like this: "I now lead you carefully from the point that I have just made to another that I want to make. Stay with me." The most obvious transitional expressions are words such as *moreover, furthermore, nevertheless, however, but, or,* and *and.* These expressions, in boldface in the paragraph below, look back to the thought just expressed and announce that readers will now move to a related but slightly different point.

> Asian students may have trouble with English because most Asian languages lack the articles *the* and *a.* Verb tenses may **also** create difficulties, **for** in Asian languages the past and the present tenses are often expressed not by verbs but by adverbs. **For example,** to form the future tense, Chinese speakers may say, "Tomorrow I go to Beijing." **Or** to make the past tense they say, "Last week, I go to Shanghai." **However,** difficulties in the use of English articles may be overcome with practice.

Transitional expressions are useful, but don't overdo them. Most well-constructed paragraphs hold together without obvious transitional words and phrases. Punctuation often links ideas, as in this example. (The dash is discussed in 26a.)

> Many things we take for granted today would have seemed like magic to people even twenty years ago—the desk-top computer, for example.

Two sentences in succession may sometimes imply cause and effect.

> My parents quarreled incessantly. They were divorced when I was seven.

To make your writing efficient, you may end up deleting unnecessary transitional expressions as you revise. The rule comes down to this: don't use traditional expressions unless you *must* use them to be clear. A steady repetition of *moreover, furthermore, nevertheless, but,* and so on can easily bore your readers.

■ **Exercise 3.6** Rewrite the following paragraph, putting in transitional devices where they are needed and taking them out when they are not necessary. Be prepared to explain why you have removed a transitional device, why you have put one in, or why you have left one in the original paragraph.

> Writing is difficult for almost everybody, even professional writers. Specifically, writing requires hours of concentrated work. Further-

more, writers must usually withdraw from others while they write. In addition, writing exposes many writers to a constant sense of failure because they do not think they are doing well. For example, Thomas Hardy became disillusioned with his fiction. He therefore stopped and turned to poetry after he had produced some of the greatest novels in the English language. In the same way, Virginia Woolf fell into such despair about her work that she eventually committed suicide. Accordingly, we can see that both teachers and students are perhaps pursuing a false hope if they think writing can be made easy. In other words, a writing course may make your writing better. But it may not make it easier.

Linking One Paragraph to the Next

In an essay, the transitions between paragraphs are as important as coherence within paragraphs. Transitional expressions can help readers follow the direction of your thought as you move from one paragraph to the next. But coherence is complex, and merely patching over gaps between ideas with transitional expressions won't help you achieve it.

TRANSITIONAL EXPRESSIONS

To show relations in space

above, adjacent to, against, alongside, around, at a distance from, at the, below, beside, beyond, encircling, far off, forward, from the, in front of, in the rear, inside, near the back, near the end, nearby, next to, on, over, surrounding, there, through the, to the left, to the right, up front

To show relations in time

afterward, at last, before, earlier, first, former, formerly, further, furthermore, immediately, in the first place, in the interval, in the meantime, in the next place, in the last, later on, latter, meanwhile, next, now, often, once, previously, second, simultaneously, sometime later, subsequently, suddenly, then, therefore, third, today, tomorrow, until now, when, years ago, yesterday

To show something added to what has come before

again, also, and, and then, besides, further, furthermore, in addition, last, likewise, moreover, next, nor, too

To give examples or to intensify points

after all, as an example, certainly, for example, for instance, indeed, in fact, in truth, it is true, of course, specifically, that is

To show similarities

alike, in the same way, like, likewise, resembling, similarly

To show contrasts

after all, although, but, conversely, differ(s) from, difference, different, dissimilar, even though, granted, however, in contrast, in spite of, nevertheless, notwithstanding, on the contrary, on the other hand, otherwise, still, though, unlike, while this may be true, yet

To indicate cause and effect

accordingly, as a result, because, consequently, hence, since, then, therefore, thus

To conclude or summarize

finally, in brief, in conclusion, in other words, in short, in summary, that is, to summarize

---

The opening sentence of a paragraph in the body of an essay usually looks back to information in the previous paragraph and forward to information about to be disclosed. Boldface print in the excerpts below shows how that first sentence in a paragraph looks both backward and forward.

> When Africans first got to New York, or New Amsterdam as the Dutch called it, they lived in the farthest downtown portion of the city, near what is now called The Bowery. Later, they shifted, and were shifted, as their numbers grew, to the section known as Greenwich Village. The Civil War Draft Riots in 1863 accounted for the next move by New York's growing Negro population.
> **After this violence** (a few million dollars' worth of property was destroyed, and a Negro orphanage was burned to the ground) a great many Negroes moved across the river into Brooklyn.
>
> —LEROI JONES

> Among those who now take a dim view of marijuana are Dr. Sidney Cohen, a drug expert at the University of California at Los Angeles, who once described marijuana as "a trivial weed," and Dr. Robert I. DuPont, former director of the National Institute on Drug Abuse, who had lobbied for marijuana's legalization.
> **According to these and other experts,** it is no longer possible to say that marijuana is an innocuous drug with few if any health effects aside from intoxication.
>
> —JANE E. BRODY

Sometimes the sentence that looks both backward and forward is the last sentence in a paragraph.

Why is marking up a book indispensable to reading it? First, it keeps you awake. (And I don't mean merely conscious; I mean wide awake.) In the second place, reading, if it is active, is thinking, and thinking tends to express itself in words, spoken or written. The marked book is usually the thought-through book. Finally, writing helps you remember the thoughts you had, or the thoughts the author expressed. Let me develop these three points.

If reading is to accomplish anything more than passing time, it must be active. . . .

—MORTIMER J. ADLER

Sometimes you may want to write a bridge paragraph, one that calls attention to your sense that you are carrying your readers from one part of your essay to another that is somewhat different.

I have, I hope, cleared the ground for a dispassionate comparison of certain aspects of Shakespeare's technique in the Henry VI plays with his technique in the "romance" histories. Now, perhaps, some general remarks about the structure of the trilogy will be helpful.

—PAUL DEAN

■ **Exercise 3.7**   Discuss the various devices used to build coherence within and between paragraphs in the following selection from an essay in *Sports Illustrated* on the revelation by the media that former tennis star Arthur Ashe had the AIDS virus.

Discuss these questions: What theme joins all these paragraphs? What words carry the theme from one paragraph to the next? How do the last sentences in each paragraph look forward to the next paragraph? How do the first sentences in each paragraph look back to the last paragraph?

The first telephone call came to my office in early September. Another call came two months later, just days after Magic Johnson had stood at a podium in Los Angeles and delivered the shocking news that he was infected with the AIDS virus. Both callers were credible members of the tennis community, and both had the same message: "You know about Arthur Ashe. He's got AIDS." Maybe I should have reacted to this disturbing information strictly as a journalist. After all, I'll wave the First Amendment flag until my arm falls off. And I'll defend until my last breath the public's right to know practically everything about anyone who falls into the category of "public figure."

But now my journalistic instincts were overcome by compassion and concern. I had been well acquainted with Ashe personally and professionally for more than a decade. Long before that, I had admired his athletic skill—and more important, his dignity. My admiration for him had grown even stronger in recent years as I watched him fight racism, apartheid, and inequities in college athletics, and as he shared with me some of the insights and convictions that made him a respected champion of human rights throughout the world.

So that's why I said nothing. Not to the managing editor of this magazine. Not to my friends. Not even to Arthur. I could have picked up the telephone and asked him. But I didn't. I could have broached the subject during one of the many conversations we had since I received the first tip about him. But I didn't. In November, soon after Magic's announcement, Arthur and I spoke on the phone about AIDS and the backlash that Magic would surely face because of his promiscuous life-style. The questions were on the tip of my tongue. Were my sources right? And, if so, did Arthur feel any compulsion to join Magic as a spokesman in the fight against AIDS? But I didn't ask. I couldn't.

Last month Ashe was my guest at the United Negro College Fund's annual dinner in New York. Magic was one of the honorees. At one point the discussion at our table turned to Johnson's efforts to promote AIDS education and awareness, but by then I had just about put the calls about Arthur out of my mind. I had decided that if he wanted me to know about his condition, he would tell me. Otherwise, it wasn't my business. I had placed his privacy ahead of any desire to break the story in SI—and it wasn't a tough decision.

—Roy S. Johnson

Arranging Paragraph Ideas According to a Coherent Plan

How you organize information in any one paragraph is similar to how you arrange information to support the point you want to make in the paper as a whole (3d).

Chronological arrangement

Perhaps the most familiar way to present information in a paragraph is chronologically—telling events in the order in which they happened, one after another. We tell most stories chronologically.

The sun rose slowly out of the hazy sea as we hiked through the great olive grove at the foot of Mount Iouktos on the Greek island of Crete. By seven o'clock, we had started our slow climb up the mountain, following a trail that twisted back and forth as it snaked its way towards the summit. We left the olive trees behind quickly and entered a rocky world where a few poplars cast an occasional weak shade. By ten o'clock, the sun had burned the haze off the sea, and its heat bore down on us. We became thirsty, but we had brought no water. By eleven, our clothes were soaked with sweat, and the heat made everything shimmer so that the tumbled rocks seemed to dance crazily amid heat waves. By now we could see for miles down the island, and to the west the huge bulk of Mount Ida rose into the hot blue sky. By noon, nearly crazy with heat, thirst, and fatigue, we got to the top. A little whitewashed chapel with a tile roof stood there, and beside it was a cistern with a bucket attached to a long rope. We dropped the bucket down into the darkness of the cistern and heard a great, reassuring splash. Quickly we pulled the bucket to the top and drank greedily. Then we sat in the shade of the church and looked out over one of the most beautiful landscapes I had ever seen.

—DICK CURRY

Spatial arrangement

You might also decide to present information spatially, by locating yourself and your readers somewhere in a scene and then moving through space— from back to front, from top to bottom, from left to right, or in some other logical way. In describing landscapes, paintings, buildings, streets, and all geographical areas, you can move through space, taking your readers with you.

Practice writing paragraphs such as the one below by standing in front of the scene you are to describe and mentally blocking it off in sections. If you carry a notebook, jot down some things you see in each section of your imaginary frame.

I walked out on the bridge and looked down at the lock. The canal flowed into the lock through a sprung wooden gate just under the bridge. It ran between two narrowly confining walls for about a hundred feet. Then, with a sudden boil and bubble, it broke against another gate, spilled through, and resumed its sluggish course. The walls of the lock were faced with big blocks of rust-red sandstone. Some of the stones were so huge that they could have been hoisted into place only with a block and tackle. It was beautiful stone, and it had been beautifully finished and fitted. Time had merely softened it. Here and there along the courses I could even make out the remains of a mason's mark. One device was quite distinct—a double-headed arrow. Another appeared to be two overlapping equilateral triangles. I went on across the bridge to the house. The windows were shuttered and boarded up, and the door was locked. No matter. It was enough just to stand and look at it. It was a lovely house, as beautifully made as the lock, and as firmly designed for function. It gave me a pang to think that there had once been a time when even a lock tender could have so handsome a house. A phoebe called from a sweet-gum tree in the dooryard. Far away, somewhere down by the river, a mourning dove gave an answering sigh. I looked at my watch. It was ten minutes after ten. I started up the towpath.

—BERTON ROUECHÉ

Chronological and spatial arrangements often work together, as you can see in both previous paragraphs.

Deductive arrangement

Paragraphs may also be arranged for a balance of generalization and specific details. In a deductive arrangement, the generalization comes first, and the details that support it follow.

We tell stories in order to affirm our being and our place in the scheme of things. When the Kiowas entered upon the Great Plains they had to tell new stories of themselves, stories that would enable them to appropriate an unknown and intimidating landscape to their experience. They were peculiarly vulnerable in that landscape, and they told a story of dissension, finally of a schism in the tribe, brought about by a quarrel between two great chiefs. They encountered awesome forces and features in nature, and they explained them in story too. And so they told the story of Man-Ka-Ih, the storm spirit, which speaks the Kiowa language and does the Kiowas no harm, and they told of the tree that bore the seven sisters into the sky, where they became the stars of the Big Dipper. In so doing they not only accounted for the great monolith that is Devils Tower, Wyoming (in Kiowa, Tsoai, "rock tree"), but related themselves to the stars in the process. When they came upon the Plains they were befriended by the Crows, who gave them the sun-dance fetish Tai-Me, which was from that time on their most powerful medicine, and they told a story of the coming of Tai-Me in their hour of need. Language was their element. Words, spoken words, were the manifestations of their deepest belief, of their deepest feelings, of their deepest life. When Europeans first came to America, having had writing for hundreds of years and lately the printed press, they could not conceive of the spoken word as sacred, could not understand the American Indian's profound belief in the efficacy of language.

—N. SCOTT MOMADAY

Inductive arrangement

An inductive arrangement builds through pieces of information to support a generalization that comes at the end of a paragraph. The writer presents details one after another and draws a conclusion from them. In the following paragraph, historian Nell Irvin Painter tells how the late nineteenth-century United States conquest of Hawaii, the Philippines, and Puerto Rico, with their populations of nonwhite natives, made some white Americans think of depriving black Americans of the vote.

> The white supremacist solution to the "Negro problem" was the repeal of the Fifteenth Amendment to the U.S. Constitution, which gave blacks the vote after the Civil War. White supremacists had wanted to reverse the amendment for years, but northern Republicans had objected. By 1900 the notion no longer seemed so farfetched to the northerners. The realities of empire enlightened northern Republicans who had previously championed universal manhood suffrage for the South. "The mind of the country North and South, especially since the acquisition of Hawaii, Puerto Rico and the Philippines," noted the new mayor of Wilmington, North Carolina, "is in a more favorable condition to consider such a proposition than ever before." The Fifteenth Amendment stood, but in name only. Before the twentieth century had advanced very far, all the sizable nonwhite populations under American control enjoyed only limited civil rights, whether as noncitizen Native Americans or Chinese, subjects in the islands, or disenfranchised black citizens in the South.
>
> —NELL IRVIN PAINTER

Arrangement by order of importance

You may also decide to arrange the elements by order of importance, starting with the least significant or least dramatic information and building to a climax with the most significant or most dramatic.

> Shakespeare came to London at a fortunate time. If he had been born twenty years earlier, he would have arrived in London when underpaid hacks were turning out childish dramas about brown-paper dragons. If he had been born twenty years later, he would have arrived when drama had begun to lose its hold on ordinary people and was succumbing to a kind of self-conscious cleverness. But his arrival in London coincided with a great wave of excitement and achievement in the theatre, and he rode with it to its crest. William Shakespeare brought great gifts to London, but the city was waiting with gifts of its

own to offer him. The root of his genius was Shakespeare's own, but it was London that supplied him with the favoring weather.

—MARCHETTE CHUTE

■ **Exercise 3.8**   Explain the arrangement of the following paragraphs—whether the main idea comes first and then is supported by details or whether the details come first and the main idea comes last. Decide whether the paragraph primarily tells a story or argues a point.

Last week, as President Bush was preparing a major televised appearance to mark the unmet deadline for congressional passage of his economic program, a recently published collection of President Franklin D. Roosevelt's radio addresses known as "fireside chats" arrived in the mail from the University of Oklahoma Press, and we began reading. The historians Russell D. Buhite and David W. Levy, who edited the book, point out in their introduction that the Great Depression was a domestic crisis like no other, and they don't suggest that the fireside chats might offer any guidance for the nineteen-nineties. Yet it is hard to read them and not think that among Roosevelt's ideas there is at least one that a great many Americans would be ready to see revived in the near future: the notion of a Presidential address as a way of actually talking to people about something.

—*New Yorker*

The preacher preached a wonderful rhythmical sermon, all moans and shouts and lonely cries and dire pictures of hell, and then he sang a song about the ninety and nine safe in the fold, but one little lamb was left out in the cold. Then he said, "Won't you come? Won't you come to Jesus? Young lambs, won't you come?" And he held out his arms to all us young sinners there on the mourners' bench. And the little girls cried. And some of them jumped up and went to Jesus right away. But most of us just sat there.

—LANGSTON HUGHES

Once in a long while, four times so far for me, my mother brings out the metal tube that holds her medical diploma. On the tube are gold circles crossed with seven red lines each—"joy" ideographs in abstract. There are also little flowers that look like gears for a gold machine. According to the scraps of labels with Chinese and American addresses, stamps, and postmarks, the family airmailed the can from Hong Kong in 1950. It got crushed in the middle, and whoever tried to peel the labels off stopped because the red and gold paint came off too, leaving silver scratches that rust. Somebody tried to pry the end off before discovering that the tube pulls apart. When I open it, the smell of China flies out, a thousand-year-old bat flying heavy-headed out of the Chinese caverns where bats are as white as dust, a smell that comes from long ago, far back in the brain. Crates from Canton, Hong Kong, Singapore, and Taiwan have that smell too, only stronger because they are more recently come from the Chinese.

—Maxine Hong Kingston

Linking Ideas with Pronouns

By replacing nouns, **pronouns** help achieve coherence, joining one part of a paragraph to another. Pronouns with clear antecedents refer readers to a previously identified noun and help the writer connect ideas in a paragraph without having to mention the nouns again and again.

When you use pronouns, pay attention to the antecedents. Be sure they are clear. When used well, pronouns fix attention on ideas that hold a paragraph together. Look how confusing this paragraph is because of the pronouns:

Crowds came to look at the rare books and manuscripts in the exhibit to mark the fiftieth anniversary of the college library. They were from all over the world, representing many different languages and races and customs. The president and the dean circulated among them with great satisfaction, because with so many different people interested in them, and crowding around them and exclaiming over them, they were sure to collect more money to help the librarians do their job better in the future.

Are the books and manuscripts from all over the world, or is it the crowds that come from many different languages, races, and customs? Are the president and the dean circulating among the books and manuscripts or among the crowds? Are so many people interested in the president and the dean or in the books and manuscripts? Are the librarians going to help do their own jobs better in the future or will they help the president and the dean do *their* jobs better?

To eliminate these confusions, the entire paragraph has to be revised:

Crowds poured into the library to see the exhibit of rare books and manuscripts, an exhibit celebrating the library's fiftieth anniversary. The exhibits represented languages, races, and cultures from all over the world. The president and the dean circulated among the crowds, pleased with the excitement visible everywhere and knowing that it would now be easier to solicit donations that would help the work of the librarians.

Using Supporting Details

Coherence is also achieved through a balance of generalization and detail. Paragraphs that contain details only are flat. Paragraphs that contain nothing but general statements are weak. Strong paragraphs display a balance of the general and the specific. This subordination of some ideas to others also helps tie the paragraph together.

Read the following paragraph carefully. What's wrong with it?

> The parking problem here at school is really terrible. Everybody complains about it. It sometimes takes hours and hours to find a space. Students are late to class because they can't park their cars. Why can't the administration do something about it? With all the money the university is spending on football, you would think they could put a little into student parking. It's really hard on commuter students who have to come from jobs to classes with little time to spare. The situation is a disgrace.

Now compare that paragraph, which consists of nothing but assertions, with the one below, which includes substantiating details. Notice, too, the way the details build in intensity and the concluding sentence of this paragraph anticipates the next.

> On Friday of last week I drove to school from my night job at a hotel and arrived at 9:45 for a ten o'clock class. A parking sticker that cost me $250 for the year tells me that I have the right to park in any student parking lot. But on Friday I drove around parking lot A, and parking lot B, and parking lot C without finding a space. Finally, in desperation, I drove up to parking lot M a mile away from my class. There I found plenty of parking, but by the time I raced to the Mahan Building, where my accounting class was in progress, it was 10:20, and Professor Lewis stopped his lecture as I came in and said, "Well, we are certainly happy that Mr. Jenkins has decided to join us this morning. I hope you didn't disturb your sleep just to be with us this morning, Mr. Jenkins." I felt my face turn hot, and I knew I was blushing from anger and embarrassment. What can we do about parking? I have ten suggestions to make to the administration.

As the effects of these two paragraphs demonstrate, generalizations are always more powerful if buttressed with specific examples. Readers want to know why you think what you think. Giving them details and evidence makes them see the steps that led to your conclusions and makes your paragraphs convincing and coherent.

Of course not every point you make in a paragraph can or should be supported by specific details. In a long essay, a paragraph may present several generalizations or abstractions without supporting data. But effective writing uses details of the kinds elaborated below. Without them, readers would remain vague about what the writer is trying to say, and if they do understand, they may not be convinced.

Sensory details

Sensory details help readers bring their own memories to your prose. When you write, use nouns that tell us of sights, smells, sounds, tastes, and feelings. Don't overdo it, but try for some sensory effects. The writer of the following paragraph could have said something prosaic like this: "After 1821, traffic along the Santa Fe Trail became heavy." Instead, he chose to make the scene more vivid:

> They sailed the Great Plains like naval flotillas, four columns abreast, each column counting as many as 25 high-wheeled wagons, stowed with trade goods and canopied by billowing canvas, pulled by plodding 12-ox teams, churning long wakes of dust on winds that rippled the prairie grasses. They were headed for Santa Fe.
>
> —ROWE FINDLEY

✔ CHECKLIST 3.1: FINDING AUTHORITIES TO QUOTE IN A PAPER

- Who has studied this topic and written about it?
- Who has been an eyewitness to some of the events I am writing about?
- Who has been affected by the subject of my paper?
- Is there any scientific evidence that I can quote in support of my position?
- Is there any statistical evidence on this topic?
- Has an important person made a statement about this topic?
- Do I have any experience that will help persuade my audience?

Statistics and cases

Statistics and cases are the language of facts and figures. You can often use them effectively to support a topic (see Checklist 3.1). *Statistics* are numerical data; *cases* are specific instances involving people and events.

Statistics give authority to your statements. Notice how the numbers in the first paragraph below help the writer make his point that although many American Indian children leave the reservation to attend public schools, some tribes feel a strong need to preserve their traditional schools on their reservations.

In 1969 there were 178,476 Indian students, ages five to eighteen, enrolled in public, Federal, private and mission schools. Approximately 12,000 children of this age group were not in school. Of the total in school, 119,000 were in public schools, 36,263 in boarding schools operated by the Bureau of Indian Affairs, 16,100 in Bureau day schools, 108 in Bureau hospital schools, and 4,089 in dormitories maintained by the Bureau for children attending public schools. The Bureau operated 77 boarding schools, 144 day schools, 2 hospital schools, and 18 dormitories. The number of Indian children being educated in public schools has steadily increased, aided by the financial assistance provided local school districts under the Johnson-O'Malley Act of 1934 (which provided financial support, in cooperation with the Department of Health, Education, and Welfare, to aid federally affected areas). The closer relationship between state school systems and the Indian system has been welcomed by many Indian groups. Sixty-one tribes have established compulsory education regulations that conform with those of the states where they live.

On the other hand, some more traditional Indian groups have rebelled at efforts to close down reservation schools. The attempt of the Bureau of Indian Affairs to close down, on July 1, 1968, a small grade-school at Tama, Iowa, created an instant reaction. Forty-five Mesquakie Indian children were attending school there on the reservation purchased by their ancestors, a separate body of the Sac tribe which, with the Fox, had a hundred years earlier been pushed out of Iowa into Kansas. The Mesquakie Indians, who had not been consulted about the closing of the school, promptly sought judicial relief. They got it in September 1968, in the Federal District Court at Cedar Rapids, when United States District Court Judge Edward J. McManus ordered the school reopened in the fall. The Mesquakie were able to call upon a number of influential white friends in their attempt to retain their Indian school. The validity of integration into a white school system that is often both distant from and cold toward Indian values can be questioned, as the Mesquakie questioned it.

—WILCOMB F. WASHBURN

■ **Exercise 3.9** Here are several opening sentences. Choose one, and finish the paragraph, using supporting details to make your writing vivid.

1. When I came to this country, my first attempts to speak English became adventures.
2. Why don't we judge human nature by the many people who do good things rather than by the few who do bad things?
3. The comic strip "Calvin and Hobbes" tells us of a little boy and his imagination.
4. Students can use computers for many purposes.

3d
Using Appropriate Paragraph Forms

The purpose of a paragraph also affects its structure. Telling a story almost always means a chronological arrangement, for example, while analyzing cause and effect may shape a paragraph into two parts. Likewise, a paragraph that serves to open or conclude an essay must be structured to meet the special demands of placement.

Shaping Paragraphs to Function

The purpose of a paragraph—sometimes the same as its controlling idea—often imposes a certain structure on it. The following examples of paragraph forms are offered for your study and imitation: narration, process analysis, comparison and contrast, classification, cause-and-effect analysis, and definition. In the next few weeks, as you read to complete course assignments or simply for pleasure, stop and look at the paragraphs before you. Try to figure out what they're doing and how they work. Do they tell a story, explain something, analyze an event, describe a place or a person? As you construct your own essays, use the examples here to help build the kinds of paragraphs you need to develop your topic.

Narration

Use narrative paragraphs to tell a story. Such paragraphs usually proceed in chronological order.

> Banyan Street was the route Lucille Miller took home from the twenty-four-hour Mayfair Market on the night of October 7, 1964, a night when the moon was dark and the wind was blowing and she was out of milk, and Banyan Street was where, at about 12:20 A.M., her 1964 Volkswagen came to a sudden stop, caught fire, and began to burn. For an hour and fifteen minutes, Lucille Miller ran up and down Banyan Street calling for help, but no cars passed and no help

came. At three o'clock that morning, when the fire had been put out and the California Highway Patrol officers were completing their report, Lucille Miller was still sobbing and incoherent, for her husband had been asleep in the Volkswagen. "What will I tell the children, when there's nothing left, nothing left in the casket," she cried to the friend who called to comfort her. "How can I tell them there's nothing left?"

—JOAN DIDION

Process analysis

Use process analysis in paragraphs to explain how to do something or how to make something. These paragraphs also generally proceed by chronology. Here is a paragraph on how to check the inflation on your bike tires if you don't have an air pressure gauge with you.

There's a great *curb-edge test* you can do to make sure your tires are inflated just right. Rest the wheel on the edge of a curb or stair, so the bike sticks out into the street or path, perpendicular to the curb or stair edge. Get the wheel so you can push down on it at about a 45 degree angle from above the bike. Push hard on the handlebars or seat, depending on which wheel you're testing. The curb should flare the tire a bit but shouldn't push right through the tire and clunk against the rim. You want the tire to have a little give when you ride over chuckholes and rocks, in other words, but you don't want it so soft that you bottom out. If you are a hot-shot who wants tires so hard that they don't have any give, you'll have to stick to riding on clean-swept Velodrome tracks, or watch very carefully for little sharp objects on the road. Or you'll have to get used to that sudden riding-on-the-rim feeling that follows the blowout of an overblown tire.

—TOM CUTHBERTSON

Comparison and contrast

Organize paragraphs by comparison and a contrast if you want to highlight similarities or differences or both.

You may make comparisons between conditions existing at two or more times or between people, places, or things existing at the same time. But be sure that your comparisons are sensible and teach something. You can compare any two things with each other—a computer train with a short story, for example. Both have a beginning, a middle, and an end. Both are designed to carry people along. But meaningless and trivial comparisons like these annoy most readers. Annoyed readers usually stop reading.

The following paragraph compares a 1992 Buick with a 1952 model.

The 1952 *Buick* measured an inch shorter and two inches wider than the 1992 model. Inside, the old car has five inches less shoulder room in front, seven-plus inches in back. Yet we found the old car's seating much more comfortable, even with three abreast. Not even modern ergonomics can compete with the old-fashioned extravagance of a high roof, high bench seats, and flat floor. The back seat felt like a limousine's, with wide-open spaces to stretch one's legs.

—*Consumer Reports*

Classification

Use classification to divide a large group into several smaller parts so that readers can see different elements in a group that, at first glance, may seem to be without variation. Like comparison, classification helps to organize complicated information. Here is a paragraph that classifies maple syrups.

When syrups are graded, it's primarily according to color and flavor, with Grade A assigned to the more delicately flavored syrups. Grade A syrup usually comes in one of three colors: light amber (called Fancy in Vermont), medium amber, or dark amber. The darker the color, the stronger the caramelized sugar taste. Stronger-tasting than dark amber, and darker still, is Grade B syrup, used mostly in cooking.

—*Consumer Reports*

Causal analysis

Organize paragraphs around an explanation of cause and effect when you want to explain why something happened or to report on the results of a happening. Here are two paragraphs that give the cause and effect of the plague that ravaged Europe in the late Middle Ages. Note that the analysis of cause and effect is given partly in the form of a narrative—an *analytical* narrative that explains as it tells a story.

In October 1347, a fleet of Genoese merchant ships from the Orient arrived at the harbor of Messina in northeast Sicily. All aboard the ships were dead or dying of a ghastly disease. The harbor masters tried to quarantine the fleet, but the source of the pestilence was borne by rats, not men, and these were quick to scurry ashore. Within six months, half of the population of the region around Messina had fled their homes or succumbed to the disease, Four years later, between one-quarter and one-half of the population of Europe was dead.

The Black Death, or plague, that devastated Europe in the 14th century was caused by bacteria that live in the digestive tract of fleas, and in particular the fleas of rats. But at that time, the disease seemed arbitrary and capricious, and to strike from nowhere. One commentator wrote: "Father abandoned child, wife husband, one brother another, for the plague seemed to strike through breath and sight." The pestilence was widely held to be a scourge sent by God to chasten a sinful people.

—CHET RAYMO

Definition

Use paragraphs to define objects, concepts, ideas, terms, political movements, and anything else that may be important to your essay. A useful definition first identifies something as a member of a class of similar things; then it states how it differs from everything else in its class. Simple, concrete objects may be identified in a single sentence.

A feast is a meal that is rich and abundant and that usually includes many guests.

Here a feast is first classified as a meal. What distinguishes it from a picnic, a breakfast, a lunch, a dinner, or a snack is that it is rich and abundant and usually includes many guests.

Always define the essential terms in any essay you write. Definitions of abstract terms may require an entire paragraph or several paragraphs. A defining paragraph usually comes near the beginning of an essay so readers will be sure to understand the term as the writer uses it throughout.

We have a roster of diseases which medicine calls "idiopathic," meaning that we do not know what causes them. The list is much shorter than it used to be; a century ago, common infections like typhus fever and tuberculous meningitis were classed as idiopathic illnesses. Originally, when it first came into the language of medicine, the term had a different, highly theoretical meaning. It was assumed that most human diseases were intrinsic, due to inbuilt failures of one sort or another, things gone wrong with various internal humors. The word "idiopathic" was intended to mean, literally, a disease having its own origin, a primary disease without any external cause. The list of such disorders has become progressively shorter as medical science has advanced, especially within this century, and the meaning of the term has lost its doctrinal flavor; we use "idiopathic" now to indicate simply that the cause of a particular disease is unknown. Very likely, before we are finished with medical science, and with luck, we will have found that all varieties of disease are the result of one or another sort of meddling, and there will be no more idiopathic illness.

—LEWIS THOMAS

■ **Exercise 3.10**   Here is an excerpt from an essay on *JFK,* a film directed by Oliver Stone purporting to prove that President John F. Kennedy's assassination in 1963 was the result of an elaborate conspiracy that included agencies of the United States government. Discuss the various paragraph forms the author uses to make his point—narration, process analysis, comparison and contrast, classification, causal analysis, and definition.

There is no single way to do history on film. The traditional division into the dramatic work and the documentary is increasingly irrelevant as recent films (*JFK* included) often blur the distinction between the two. My own research has suggested that history on film comes in a number of different forms. *JFK,* despite the many documentary elements it contains, belongs to what is certainly the most popular type of film, the Hollywood—or mainstream—drama. This sort of film is marked, as cinema scholars have shown, by a number of characteristics, the chief being its desire to make us believe that what we see in the theater is true. To this end, the mainstream film utilizes a specific film language, a self-effacing, seamless language of shot, editing, and sound designed to make the screen seem no more than a window onto unmediated "reality."

Along with "realism," four other elements are crucial to understanding the mainstream historical film:

Hollywood history is delivered in a story with beginning, middle, end—a story with a moral message and one usually embodied in a progressive view of history.

The story is closed, completed, and, ultimately, simple. Alternative versions of the past are not shown. . . .

History is a story of individuals—usually, heroic individuals who do unusual things for the good of others, if not all humankind (ultimately, the audience).

Historical issues are personalized, emotionalized, and dramatized—for film appeals to our feelings as a way of adding to our knowledge or affecting our beliefs.

Such elements go a long way towards explaining the shape of *JFK.* The story is not that of President Kennedy but of Jim Garrison, the heroic, embattled, incorruptible investigator who wishes to make sense of Kennedy's assassination and its apparent cover-up, not just for himself but for his country and its traditions—that is, for the audience, for us. More than almost any other historical film, this one swamps us with information. Some of it, in the black-and-white flashbacks that illustrate the stages of the investigation, is tentative or contradictory. (So much is thrown at us that, on a single viewing, the viewer has difficulty absorbing all the details of events discussed and shown.) Yet, even if contradictions do exist, the main line of the story is closed and completed, and the moral message is clear: the assassination was the result of a conspiracy that involved agencies and officials of the U.S. government, the aim of the assassination was to get rid of a president who wished to curb the military and end the Cold War, and the "fascist" groups responsible for the assassination and subsequent cover-up are a clear and continuing threat to what little is left of American democracy.

—ROBERT A. ROSENSTONE

■ **Exercise 3.11**　Write a short paragraph on two of the following topics, and discuss with the class the technique of development you have used in each.

1. the difference between intelligence and education
2. different types of eaters
3. how to repair a bruised ego
4. different types of roommates
5. movies you hate

■ **Exercise 3.12**　For each paragraph form, select one topic and write a practice paragraph.

1. *Narration:* (*a*) what you and some friends did on a Saturday night recently, (*b*) a visit to a doctor, (*c*) your decision to buy a new or used different car
2. *Process analysis:* (*a*) cooking a simple recipe, (*b*) how to study for an exam, (*c*) learning a foreign language, (*d*) adjusting to a new town when you move
3. *Comparison and contrast:* (*a*) a novel and a film based on the novel, (*b*) two movies featuring the same actor or actress, (*c*) the writing courses you had in high school and this writing course, (*d*) downhill skiing and cross-country skiing, (*e*) writing with a pencil and writing on a computer
4. *Classification:* (*a*) supermarket shoppers, (*b*) clothing styles for different activities, (*c*) television programs, (*d*) trees in your neighborhood

5. *Causal analysis:* (*a*) effects of nuclear war, (*b*) why some people write well and others do not, (*c*) why some people like to read and some do not, (*d*) why people smoke cigarettes

6. *Definition:* (*a*) racism, (*b*) an examination, (*c*) a triathlon, (*d*) argument, (*e*) religion, (*f*) jazz, (*g*) rock music, (*h*) heavy metal music, (*i*) folk music.

Constructing Opening and Closing Paragraphs

Opening and closing paragraphs are extremely important to your essay. Your opening paragraph makes readers decide to keep reading or to lay your work aside. Your closing paragraph wraps up your essay and gives your readers some final thought to remember.

Your opening paragraph should announce the general topic of your essay and be interesting enough to make people read on. The opening paragraph usually implies a promise you make to readers to do something in your essay. Your concluding paragraph should end with the promise kept. Often the concluding paragraph repeats the thoughts and words of the opening paragraph to give readers the sense of having come around to the goal the first paragraph set for them.

A few audiences may expect your opening paragraphs to outline everything you intend to do in your essay. Descriptions of scientific experiments almost always start with such an outline, called an *abstract* in the scientific discourse community. But if you are writing about some personal topic or about something you wish to explain or report, your first paragraphs usually give only an inviting glimpse of what lies in store for the reader.

Note how the opening paragraphs that follow introduce a subject and set the tone.

> Nearly 70 percent of Americans are worried about the quality of their drinking water, according to a recent survey. Much of their concern centers on how water looks, tastes, or smells. Unfortunately water that is hazardous to your health usually looks, tastes, and smells just fine.
>
> —*Consumer Reports*

> Juliette Sauget set out for Paris at the age of seventeen in the company of an elder, married sister who resided there. Born in 1886 into an impoverished woodcutter's family, Juliette left home as a gesture of solidarity with another sister, whom her father had struck in anger. In Paris, her married sister advised her to work as a domestic servant, because Juliette needed lodgings as well as a job. In her first position, she complained one night at supper that the seventeen-year-

old son of the family had come to her room with the intention of having sexual relations with her. The family laughed in reply, so she felt she had to leave. This incident marked the beginning of a series of jobs: first in Paris, then in Amiens—the capital of her home province, where other of her siblings resided—then back in Paris. Eventually, she developed a social life at the public, outdoor dances in Paris. At age twenty-four, she became pregnant.

—RACHEL G. FUCHS AND LESLIE PAGE MOCH

Television has all but swallowed American politics and sport. Now it is closing in on the nation's moral dilemmas. Debates of the toughest questions (abortion, the death penalty, for example) look like wrestling or professional football. When Robert Harris was executed in California last week, the event had a strange gaudy quality, somehow commercial and electronic. Perhaps one day prisoners will go to the gas chamber with product-endorsement logos on their prison pajamas.

—LANCE MORROW

Introductory paragraphs which summarize the paper that follows are standard format for scientific writing. They assume a previous interest by specialists, who can quickly see if the topic of the paper fits their specialty.

In this paper I shall consider several educational issues growing out of A. R. Jensen's paper, "How Much Can We Boost IQ and Scholastic Achievement?" (Jensen, 1969). The first deals with the question of how education should adjust to the incontestable fact that approximately half the children in our schools are and always will be below average in IQ. Following this, I take up some of the more moot points of the "Jensen controversy"—what does heritability tell us about teachability? What are the prospects for reducing the spread of individual differences in intelligence? And what are the educational implications of possible hereditary differences in intelligence associated with social class and race?—ending with some implications that these issues have for educational research.

—CARL BEREITER

Most professional writers never end an article or an essay with a summary. A good concluding paragraph completes the paper logically and clearly, perhaps drawing a conclusion that expresses some meaning to be found in the information presented in the essay. The following paragraphs, from two of the essays whose opening paragraphs appear above, express the general meaning of the essays they conclude.

Single pregnant migrants were integral to the process of urbanization and geographic mobility. Pregnancy motivated some migrations and was the result of others. These women's experience enriches our understanding of migration, urbanization and life in the metropolis. Likewise, the complex patterns analyzed here echo in other cities and in other times.

—RACHEL G. FUCHS AND LESLIE PAGE MOCH

The answer is all of the above. Emphasis on the entertainment. People pay millions to watch terminators and terminations. They have a taste for it. The distinction between actual death and special effects get blurry in this culture. It thins to vanishing. Reality and unreality become ugly, interchangeable kicks. Perhaps if Harris had been spared, he might, like Audie Murphy, have been hired to play himself in the docudrama.

—LANCE MORROW

■ **Exercise 3.13**   Look at all the articles in a popular magazine that you enjoy reading, and carefully compare the first and last paragraphs of each article. What relation do you see between the two paragraphs even before you read the article? Describe to others the connections between each first and last paragraph that you study.

■ **Exercise 3.14**   Take one of your own essays and compare the first and last paragraphs. What similarities do you note between them?

3e
Revising Paragraphs

As you revise the rough draft of your essay, focus on each individual paragraph. Make sure each one is unified, coherent, and well developed (see Checklist 3.2).

Because the controlling idea of your paragraph should guide any changes you make, start by rereading your paragraph carefully to determine the controling idea you want to express. You may want to add elements, eliminate elements, or subordinate one element to another. A paragraph such as the one that follows requires revision.

✔ **CHECKLIST 3.2:** REVISING PARAGRAPHS

■ Is the paragraph an appropriate length? Does a new paragraph begin where there is a change in emphasis?

■ Does the paragraph have a controlling idea? Does each sentence in the paragraph support the controlling idea?

■ Does the paragraph demonstrate coherence? Does each sentence flow into the next, expanding a thought or idea already introduced?

■ Does the paragraph use repetition to advantage? Does it display parallel structure? Are transitional expressions appropriate?

■ Does the paragraph look back to the one before it and forward to the one after it?

■ Are the ideas in the paragraph arranged to suit the purpose?

■ Are supporting details used effectively?

■ Are generalizations and specifics balanced?

■ Does the opening paragraph interest the reader and announce the topic?

■ Does the concluding paragraph pick up on words and ideas announced in the opening paragraph and demonstrate to the reader that the essay has done what it promised?

Wood-burning stoves are helping many Americans beat the cost of fossil fuels and save money. Wood is still plentiful in the United States. Many states set off parts of their state forests where residents can cut designated trees at no charge. Some wood stoves give off emissions that may cause cancer, and people in big cities find wood more expensive than other sources of heat. But the technology of wood stoves has improved so that they can be very safe as well as efficient. The federal government now has standards that wood stove manufacturers must meet. Unfortunately, wood stoves are sometimes bulky and ugly and take up too much space in small rooms. Sometimes they make rooms too hot. Many homeowners who have gone to wood stoves for heat report savings of hundreds of dollars each year over the former price of heating their houses with oil. And many of them enjoy the exercise of cutting wood.

Here the paragraph has been revised:

Wood-burning stoves are helping many Americns beat the high costs of fossil fuels. In recent years, the prices of oil and gas have come down, but these are limited fuels, and the prices are bound to rise again. So the availability of cheap fuel is still worth considering—

and wood is cheap in some parts of the United States. A cord of wood, a stack measuring 4 × 4 × 8 feet, costs just over a hundred dollars in a typical heating season. Many states like Massachusetts and Montana set off parts of their state forests where residents can cut designated trees at no charge. On a warm summer morning, one may see dozens of families sawing trees and loading vans or pickup trucks with logs for use as a winter fuel. Not only can wood be obtained cheaply, but also the technology of wood stoves has improved; the new models are far more efficient than the old ones. Now a family can heat a house with a wood stove with a minimum of waste or expense. A good airtight wood stove heats a room far more efficiently than does a conventional fireplace or a Franklin stove. Many homeowners who have turned to wood stoves for heat report savings of hundreds of dollars each year over the price of heating their houses with oil.

■ **Exercise 3.15**   Revise the following paragraph for unity, coherence, and development.

The blizzard began early on the morning of February 6. The snow began falling before dawn. The flakes were small and hard. The snow itself was very thick. By nine o'clock, six inches of white covered the streets. Commuting traffic was reduced to a crawl. None of this affected me, since the schools were closed, and I stayed home, warm and cozy by the fire. I read the morning newspaper, which had arrived before the snow was very deep, and I kept refilling the coffee mug that sat beside me on a glass-topped table. By ten-thirty, the streets were impassable, and motorists were abandoning their cars. By noon, the offices in the city that had opened despite the storm were closing and sending workers home. At three o'clock, the mayor declared a state of emergency and asked schools, churches, and synagogues to give shelter to people stranded by the storm. Seeing all those people gathered together in houses of worship gave you a nice feeling about human nature, which some writers have claimed is evil. By six o'clock, the city was locked in the enchantment of a profound silence. Two feet of snow lay in the streets, and more was falling.

TWO

WRITING CLEAR
AND EFFECTIVE
SENTENCES

BASIC SENTENCE GRAMMAR

To write well and to understand how you can revise your writing to make it better, you must know how to use the elements of the English sentence—elements traditionally called grammar. **Grammar** is two things:

1. A collection of forms that make sense in sentences
2. The language we use to talk about such forms

4a
Recognizing Basic Sentence Forms

The first definition of grammar is much more important than the second. We use grammar all the time as a set of forms that make sense. Most of us use grammar well enough to make people understand what we mean. We use English grammar and the forms of the English sentence almost instinctively. We learned them when we learned to talk, and we use them every day all our lives.

The word *forms* is essential to understanding grammar. We react to sentences as forms, familiar patterns that we recognize because they are so common. We have heard them since we first heard language, and we have used them since we first began using words in sentences. We cannot change them on whim because everyone else who uses English knows them and uses them by habit.

We probably started by giving something a name that got results. "Milk!" we shouted, and somebody gave us milk. A little later we said, "Give me milk." Still later we said, "Will you please give me some milk?" or "I prefer milk, please."

As we grow older, we learn to work many kinds of thoughts into the basic sentence forms. If you hear somebody say, "I picked up the telephone," you know what the speaker means. But if somebody says, "Picked

I the telephone up," you run the statement through your mind again. What is this person saying? The form is not right. People don't say, "Drove I the car this morning to work" or "Stood bravely he the last until."

The sense of sentence form is so strong in us that we can frequently understand a sentence even when we don't know what every word means. If somebody says, "Give me the phlumpis on the table," we hear the form or pattern, recognize it as a request or a command, and look on the table to see what the "phlumpis" is. The form tells us to do something with something called a "phlumpis," and we do it. The sentence form is grammar in action.

**4a
gram**

In English, there are only a few basic sentence forms, although as you will see, you can make some changes in the basic form of any sentence.

The most common sentence form tells us that someone or something does something to something or someone else.

The man next door kills ants by spraying them with window cleaner.

This is a simple pattern. The man next door does something to the ants. It may seem odd to kill them with window cleaner. Even so, the sentence tells you he does it, and you can imagine him pumping away with a little spray bottle aimed at the ants. Using this common pattern, you can substitute nonsense words and still have an idea of what the sentence means.

The aardcam next door grinks ants by cooming them with dab.

You know that something called an "aardcam" is the actor in the sentence. You know that "grinks" expresses the main act and that "cooming" expresses a helping act to the main act. "Dab" is some kind of tool, some instrument, something used in the action. You know that something is doing something to the ants because you recognize a basic pattern of the English sentence.

Another sentence form tells us that something acts but nothing receives the action.

The telephone is ringing.

The thermometer exploded.

The lilacs bloomed.

Another sentence form describes a state or condition of being. The actor in the sentence exists in a certain way. The sentence expresses no action; it is simply a statement that something *is* (or was or will be), or that it exists with a certain quality.

The telephone is black.

The man was old and feeble but still witty and interesting.

Another sentence form tells us that something is acted upon. In such a sentence the recipient of the action is the most important thing in the sentence.

Amy Huang was honored by the Rotary Club today.

The striking airline workers were ordered back to work.

These basic forms help sentences make sense. That is what the word **sentence** means—a group of words that make sense. They make sense because they communicate through patterns that we recognize and expect. We can easily understand the sense of the following statements.

It rained last night.

The dust on the book made me sneeze.

Junior soccer leagues are becoming popular in suburban communities.

The Toronto Blue Jays won the 1992 World Series.

She fixed five flat tires in an hour.

Some word groups look like sentences at first glance. They begin with a capital letter and end with a period. But we cannot make sense of them because they don't follow a familiar pattern that communicates.

Shafts of light into the valley.

Driving through the rain.

The most frequently abused drugs.

None of these groups of words has a recognizable sentence form. In each case, we must add words to make a pattern that communicates a sensible statement.

The rising sun threw shafts of light into the valley.

Driving through the rain, Bill shuddered at the cold.

The most frequently abused drugs are alcohol and tobacco.

As all these examples prove, you do not have to know or use grammatical terms to recognize sentence patterns. But if you do know the terms, you can talk more precisely about grammar and you can understand better what your instructor says to you in class and in comments on your papers. The rest of this chapter reviews basic grammatical terms.

4b
Reviewing Basic Sentence Structure

The part of the sentence that names what the sentence is about is called the **subject.** The part of the sentence that makes a statement or asks a question about the subject is called the **predicate.** The boundaries of the sentence are clearly marked off by a capital letter at the beginning and a period, a question mark, or an exclamation point at the end. Within these boundaries, every sentence contains at least one subject and one predicate that fit together to make a statement, ask a question, or give a command.

4b
gram

Here are some examples of basic English sentences.

Desert winds blow fiercely.

The sun is rising over the Caribbean.

Your computer blew up yesterday.

The Soviet Union no longer exists.

Sarah repairs automobiles.

Is Carlos allergic to cigarette smoke?

Does Aida own her own business?

[You] Bring me the report.

[You] Pass the spaghetti.

The Subject

The subject and the words that describe it are often called the **complete subject.** Within the complete subject, the word (or words) that serve as the focus of the sentence may be called the **simple subject.**

ESL 1*

In the following examples, the complete subjects are in italics and the simple subjects are in boldface.

*The quick brown **fox*** jumps over the lazy dog.

Shing-Wen Lee won the game with a triple in the ninth.

*The huge black **clouds** in the west* predicted a violent storm.

*Each ESL appendix box is referenced at the appropriate point in the text by a marginal icon (the tree) and the box number.

A **compound subject** consists of two or more subjects joined by a connecting word such as *and* or *but* (discussed in 4c).

*Original **thinking** and bold **design** have distinguished her architectural career.*

The Predicate

The predicate asserts something about the subject. The predicate, together with all the words that help it make a statement about the subject, is often called the **complete predicate.** Within the complete predicate, the word (or words) that reports or states conditions, with all describing words removed, is called the **simple predicate** or the **verb.** A verb expresses action or a state of being.

In the following sentences, the complete predicates are in italics and the simple predicates (the *verbs*) are in boldface.

The quick brown fox *jumps over the lazy dog.*

Shing-Wen Lee *won the game with a triple in the ninth.*

The huge black clouds in the west *predicted a violent storm.*

Original thinking and bold design *have distinguished her architectural career.*

Like subjects, predicates may also be compound. In a **compound predicate,** two or more verbs are joined by a connecting word.

The huge black clouds in the west *predicted a violent storm and ended our picnic.*

Sometimes one verb combines with another to form a verb of more than one word, called a **verb phrase.** The verb phrases are in boldface in the sentences that follow.

Gold **was discovered** in California in 1848.

He **might have seen** that film before.

Original thinking and bold design **have distinguished** her architectural career and **have made** her rich.

The oldest building on campus **would have been demolished** if she **had** not **made** a generous donation to save it.

Another way to locate verbs is to memorize the verbs that serve as **auxiliaries**—that is, helpers to other verbs. These auxiliaries are always verbs and never anything else. The most common helping verbs are *am,* *is, are, was, were, shall, will, could, would, have, has, had, do, does, did, be, been, might, can, may,* and *must.* (Verbs are discussed further in Chapters 15 and 16.)

Recognizing Subjects and Predicates

One way to find the subject and the predicate components is to look at what the sentence says and to ask two questions about its meaning.

4b
gram

1. Who or what is the sentence about? *(subject)*
2. What statement is the sentence making about the subject? *(predicate)*

Perhaps the best way to find basic sentence components is to first look for the verb (the *simple predicate*). Remember that verbs express action or state of being.

> Churchill **spoke** to England.
>
> The hippopotamus **was** beautiful.

It is even easier to find verbs if you remember that they change their form in accordance with the way they are used in a sentence. Because verbs change their forms to show time, or *tense* (discussed in 4c), you can locate verbs easily by forcing such a change in a sentence. If you use a word like *yesterday, today,* or *tomorrow* at the start of a sentence whose verb you are trying to identify, the only word that changes will be the verb.

> I eat green vegetables.
>
> *Yesterday,* I **ate** green vegetables.

> Mr. Smith goes to Washington.
>
> *Tomorrow,* Mr. Smith **will go** to Washington.

✔ CHECKLIST 4.1: TESTING FOR VERBS

- Change a sentence by using *yesterday, today,* and *tomorrow* at the beginning. The word that changes is a verb.

  > He played shortstop.
  > Tomorrow he **will play** shortstop.
  > Today he **plays** shortstop.

- Learn the most familiar helping verbs: *am, is, are, was, were, shall, will, could, would, have, has, do, does, did, be, been, might, can, may, must*

■ Use *I, he, she, it, you, we,* or *they* before the word you think is a verb.

If you make sense with this combination, the word you are testing is a verb.

Word	Test	Verb?
try	I try she tries	yes
olive	I olive (?) they olive (?)	no
laugh	they laugh	yes
laughing	I laughing they laughing	no

Once you find the verb, you can find the subject easily. Just put the verb in a question asking who or what does the action of a verb. Say the word *who* or *what;* then say the verb. The answer to your question will be the subject of the sentence. Generally, subjects of verbs are **nouns** or **pronouns,** words that name persons, places, things, ideas, or objects (discussed in 4c). But other words may sometimes be subjects.

We **have been working** all night. (*Who* has been working all night? **We.**)

Trout fishing **is** a popular sport in northern New England. (*What* is a popular sport in northern New England? **Trout fishing.**)

Lee **invaded** the North twice during the Civil War. (*Who* invaded the North twice during the Civil War? **Lee.**)

■ **Exercise 4.1**   Draw a vertical line dividing the complete subject and the complete predicate in each sentence below. Then draw one line under the simple subject and two lines under the simple predicate, as in the following example.

My writing <u>assignments</u> in school/<u>have always caused</u> me much difficulty.

1. After many years, Ottawa finally has accepted a land of self-rule for Canada's Eskimos.
2. Twenty percent of the country will be carved out from the Northwest Territory.
3. More than 17,500 Eskimos will live in Nunauut, which means *our land* in Inuktituk, the Eskimos' language.

4. The vast region unfamiliar to most Canadians begins at the six-tieth degree of latitude and stretches more than fifteen hundred miles to Alert, the last settlement before the North Pole.
5. Human traces have been identified more than four thousand years back.
6. Norsemen explored the region during the eleventh century A.D.
7. Maritime explorers, missionaries, and adventurers followed.
8. Ottawa, Canada's capital city, was required to assume responsibility for Eskimos by a 1939 court order.
9. Eskimos, or Inuit, no longer hunt seals, whales, and polar bears as nomads.
10. Government centers with typical problems of urban life now form the core of many Eskimo communities.

4b

gram

■ **Exercise 4.2**   Write five original sentences. Draw a slash between the complete subject and the complete predicate. Then draw one line under the simple subject and two lines under the simple predicate.

Other Predicate Parts

In addition to verbs, complete predicates may also include sentence elements that modify, or help describe other elements.

Direct objects

The **direct object** tells who or what receives the action done by the subject and expressed by the verb. Not every sentence has a direct object, but many verbs require one to complete their meaning. Such verbs are called transitive verbs, from the Latin *trans,* meaning "across." A **transitive verb** carries action from the subject across to the direct object. In the examples below, direct objects are in boldface.

Catholic missionaries established the **school.**

Snopes burned **barns** all over the country.

Louis Gosset, Jr., lost thirty-five **pounds** for his role in *Diggstown.*

I have read that **story.**

We heard the distant **voice.**

In these examples, the verbs are transitive. They report actions done by the subject to the direct object.

A verb that does not carry action to a direct object is an intransitive verb. An **intransitive verb** reports action done by a subject, but it is not action done to anything. The following verbs are intransitive.

The ship **sank** within three hours after the collision.

Our dog **vanished** in the summer.

She **jogs** to keep fit.

✔ **CHECKLIST 4.2:** TESTING FOR DIRECT OBJECTS

In looking for direct objects in sentences, ask the question *what* or *whom* after the verb. The answer will be the direct object.

- The children crossed the street.
  The children crossed *what?* the street. *Street* is the direct object.
- The Jets beat the Colts again.
  The Jets beat *whom?* the Colts. *Colts* is the direct object.

Direct objects, like subjects, are generally nouns or pronouns (discussed in 5c) or are word groups that act like nouns or pronouns.

Indirect objects

ESL 9

Sometimes, in addition to a direct object, a predicate also includes a noun or pronoun specifying to whom or for whom the action is done. This is the **indirect object.** It appears after the verb and before the direct object. Indirect objects occur fairly infrequently and are usually used with verbs such as *give, ask, tell, sing,* and *write.*

The tenants gave the **manager** their complaints.

Tell the **teacher** your idea.

Jack asked **George** an embarrassing question.

✔ **CHECKLIST 4.3:** TESTING FOR INDIRECT OBJECTS

If you ask the question *to whom* (or *for whom*) or *to what* (or *for what*), the answer will be the indirect object.

- He sang me a song.
  He sang to whom (or for whom)? me. *Me* is an indirect object.

■ My father gave the television set a furious kick.
  My father gave to what? the television set. *The television set* is an indirect object.

■ Bettina told the children a story from West Africa.
  Bettina told to whom? the children. *Children* is an indirect object.

■ **Exercise 4.3**   In each sentence below, write *DO* over the direct object of the verb and *IO* over the indirect object.

**4b
gram**

1. Poverty-stricken laborers often suffer malnourishment from birth.
2. In Brazil's Northeast a poor diet of manioc flour, rice, and beans has given many workers minimal chances for normal lives.
3. Malnourishment produces retarded mental development, and some Brazilian laborers have brain capacities that are 40 percent less than average.
4. Diets drastically low in protein give adults far less than average heights as recorded by the World Health Organization.
5. Pediatric experts have told the Ministry of Health the grim news that more than 40 percent of the children in Northeast Brazil are born malnourished.

Complements

Complements complete descriptions of subjects and objects.

A **subject complement** is located on the other side of the verb from the subject and adds information about the subject. The verb that joins a subject and its complement is called a linking verb. A **linking verb** joins a subject to some further description of itself not included in the subject.

The most common linking verbs are the "to be" verbs—*is, are, was,* and *were.* But many other verbs also link a subject to a descriptive word. Observe the subject complements after the linking verbs in the following sentences.

My father is **a welder.**

America looked **good** to me after my long absence.

The poodle smelled **fresh** after his bath.

An **object complement** comes immediately after a direct object and helps complete the description of the direct object by the verb.

She called me **a bonehead.**

She said I drove her **crazy.**

My aunt dyed her hair **blue.**

I liked my eggs **scrambled.**

Like subject complements, object complements add to the description of the object. Complements may be nouns, pronouns, or adjectives (discussed in 4c).

4b gram

■ **Exercise 4.4**   Complete the following sentences in any appropriate manner, and indicate whether you have supplied a subject complement or an object complement by writing *SC* or *OC* after each sentence.

1. The university was _____.
2. The breeze felt _____.
3. He got the answers _____.
4. I was often _____.
5. My professors were _____.
6. I shut the door _____.
7. The patient grew _____.
8. You look _____.
9. I'll give you _____.
10. He took his coffee _____.

✔ **CHECKLIST 4.4:** TYPICAL SENTENCE PATTERNS

You have already seen how important sentence patterns are in English. Here are the most typical sentence patterns.

Pattern 1   **subject + verb**

We	laughed.
The flowers	bloomed.
The house	was destroyed.

Pattern 2   **subject + verb + direct object**

Ann	used	the jackhammer.
Dickens	wrote	*David Copperfield.*
She	told	the story.

Pattern 3   **subject + verb + subject complement**

Our house	was	large and cold.
He	looked	good.
The crowd	became	noisy.
The contract	seemed	fair.

Pattern 4   **subject + verb + direct object + object complement**

They   called   Lindbergh   a fool.

He   named   his son   John.

Pattern 5   **subject + verb + indirect object + direct object**

Lee   gave   Longstreet   the orders.

Smoke   gives   me   a headache.

The basic patterns can be rearranged in a variety of ways.

4c
gram

subject complement + verb + subject

Fair   lie   the fields of England.

direct object + subject + verb

These bones   he   removed.

4c
Reviewing the Eight Parts of Speech

Sentence elements consist primarily of a subject and predicate. Each is made up of one or more words that themselves can be classified as **parts of speech.** The eight parts of speech are verbs, nouns, pronouns, adjectives, adverbs, conjunctions, prepositions, and interjections. We classify words as one or another part of speech according to the role they play in a sentence.

Verbs

Verbs report action, condition, or state of being. Verbs are the controlling words in predicates, but verbs themselves are controlled by subjects.

Number and person

The **number** of the subject determines the number of its verb. If a subject is only one thing, we say that it is *singular.* If it is more than one, we say that it is *plural: dog* is singular; the plural form is *dogs.* Verbs reflect these differences in subjects by taking a singular or a plural form.

In the **first-person singular,** I speak of myself. In the **first-person plural,** we speak or write of ourselves. In the **second-person singular and plural** (the forms are the same), you are addressed. In the **third-person singular,** someone speaks or writes about somebody or something who is not being addressed. In the **third-person plural,** someone speaks or writes about more than one person or about more than one object.

Verbs also show whether the action of the sentence is taking place now, took place in the past, or will take place in the future. Study the following examples.

	Singular	Plural
First person	I read.	We read.
Second person	You read.	You read.
Third person	She reads.	They read.
First person	I loosen.	We loosen.
Second person	You loosen.	You loosen.
Third person	It loosens.	They loosen.
First person	I build.	We build.
Second person	You build.	You build.
Third person	He builds.	They build.

All these verbs are in the present tense. Notice that the only change that takes place is in the third person singular; a final -*s* is added to the common form of the verb. Most—but not all—verbs will add this -*s* in the third person singular.

Verbs must agree with the person of the subject. In the present tense (explained in more detail below), an -*s* is usually added to the verb in the third-person singular. Other tenses are shown by a change in the helping verb.

I **run.**	He **runs.**	They **run.**
I **am running.**	He **is running.**	They **are running.**

Helping verbs and verb phrases

ESL 4

Helping (or **auxiliary**) **verbs** help a single verb express a meaning that it could not express by itself. A **verb phrase** is the helping verb plus the main verb. The final word in a verb phrase, the **main verb,** carries the primary meaning of the verb phrase. Sometimes more than one helping verb accompanies the main verb. In the following sentences, the verb phrases are in boldface; HV appears over each helping verb, and MV appears over each main verb.

HV   MV   HV MV

The plane **will have left** before we **can get** to the airport.

    HV   MV   HV   MV

He **had been walking** for hours before he **was found.**

   HV MV

He **is biking** to Vermont from Boston.

    HV   MV

They **will arrive** in time for the game.

                  HV   MV

Contrary to his opinion, he **does** not **have** any imagination.

     HV   HV   MV

Cy Young **has** always **been considered** one of the best pitchers in baseball history.

4c
gram

Notice that sometimes words not part of the verb phrase come between the helping verb and the main verb.

Here are some typical helping verbs.

be	do	can
being	did	shall
been	does	will
is	has	might
am	have	could
are	had	would
was	must	should
were	may	

Sometimes particles are added to verbs. **Particles** are short words that never change their form no matter how the main verb changes. They sometimes look like other parts of speech, but they always go with the verb to add a meaning that the verb does not have by itself.

Harry made **up** with Gloria.

He made **off** with my pen.

She filled **out** her application.

Tenses

English has three simple **tenses** (or times): present, past, and future.

> **Present:** She **works** every day.
>
> **Past:** She **worked** yesterday.
>
> **Future:** She **will work** tomorrow.

4c
gram

The simple past tense of most verbs is formed by adding a final *-ed* to the common form of the present, or a simple *-d* if the common form of the present ends in *-e.*

> **Present:** I **save** a little money every month.
> The dogs in our neighborhood **bark** at night.
>
> **Past:** I **saved** a thousand dollars last year.
> The dog next door **barked** all night long.

But many verbs in English are irregular. **Irregular verbs** form the simple past tense by changing a part of the verb other than the ending.

> **Present:** We **grow** tomatoes every year on our kitchen window shelf.
> I **run** four miles every day.
> I **go** to the grocery store every Saturday morning.
>
> **Past:** We **grew** corn back in Iowa.
> Coe **ran** the mile in three minutes and forty-six seconds in August 1981.
> I **went** to the grocery store last Saturday.

The future tense of verbs is always formed by the addition of **shall** or **will** to the common form of the present.

> **Present:** I often **read** in bed.
>
> **Future:** I **shall read** you a story before bedtime.
> She **will read** you the ending tomorrow morning.

Chapters 15 and 16 provide a detailed discussion of verbs.

■ **Exercise 4.5** Underline the verb phrases in the following sentences. Include particles as part of the verb phrase. Write HV over the helping verbs and MV over the main verbs.

1. Firebombs had forced the closing of the London subway system for almost four hours.

2. Has she rebuilt the Jeep engine?

3. The Cleveland Indians have not won a World Series since Harry Truman's administration.

4. She ought to be here any minute.

5. We send out for pizza every Saturday night.

6. Our friend Miguel Borinquen has spent Thanksgiving with us for years.

4c gram

7. They should never have used up all the bok choy in the stir-fry.

8. He was regularly falling off the water skis.

9. People are moving to California every day.

10. They made out their route to northern Burma.

Nouns

Nouns are the names we use for people, places, animals, things, ideas, actions, states of existence, colors, and so forth. In sentences, nouns serve as subjects, objects, and complements. (Nouns may also be appositives; see the entry for *appositive* in the Glossary.)

ESL 10

Common nouns name ordinary things. Common nouns include the following words and thousands more.

ability	democracy	justice	rope
baseball	desks	library	showcases
beauty	geometry	man	smell
car	glory	music	students
cattle	glove	philosophy	synagogue
color	horses	profession	tension
defeat	house	proficiency	woman

Proper nouns are the names given to persons, places, and things to set them off from others in a group. Proper nouns always are capitalized. Proper nouns include the following—and thousands more.

Amtrak	Germany	New York
Donald A. Stone	Greek Orthodox	Omaha
Frenchman	Helen	State Department
General Dynamics	Ms. Howard	

**4c
gram**

Compound nouns consist of two or more words that function as a unit. They include such common nouns as *heartache, mother-in-law, father-in-law, great-grandmother,* and *world view.* Compound nouns also may be proper nouns—*International Business Machines, Federal Bureau of Investigation, Suez Canal,* and *Belmont, Tennessee.*

How do you recognize nouns? Sometimes nouns reveal themselves by their endings. Words that end in *-ty, -tion, -sion, -or, -ism, -ist, -ment, -ness, -ship, -ture, -ance,* and *-ence* are usually nouns.

But be careful. Some words with these endings may also be verbs, such as *mention.*

Jackson made **mention** of you in his letter. (noun)

I hope you will **mention** my request to him. (verb)

Articles

ESL 12

Often nouns appear accompanied by **articles,** which limit or specify their function (see below). Articles are *a, an,* and *the.* One of the best ways to test whether a word in a sentence is a noun is to see if you can put an article in front of the word and still make sense of your sentence.

Number

Nouns can be singular or plural. You usually form the plural by adding the *-s* or *-es.* You form irregular plurals by other endings or by internal changes. (Regular and irregular plural forms are discussed in Chapter 27.)

Singular	Plural
nest	nests
dog	dogs
humanist	humanists
bush	bushes
church	churches
child	children
woman	women

Possessive form

Some nouns show ownership or a special relation to another noun in the sentence. The possessive form of nouns is formed by adding -'s or a simple apostrophe ('). Possessives can be either singular or plural.

Singular	Possessive	Plural	Possessive
girl	girl's notebook	guests	guests' invitations
insect	insect's sting	neighbors	neighbors' car

4c gram

These qualities of plurality and possession can help you identify nouns in sentences. If you can make a word plural or make it show possession, it is a noun.

✔ CHECKLIST 4.5: TESTING FOR NOUNS

■ Use *a, an,* or *the* before the word.

Word	Test	Noun?
razor	a razor, the razor	yes
book	the book	yes
raining	a raining, the raining	no
laughingly	a laughingly, the laughingly	no

■ Make the word plural.

Word	Test	Noun?
egg	eggs	yes
soon	soons	no

■ Make the word show possession.

Word	Test	Noun?
child	the child's blanket	yes
criticize	the criticize's thing	no

■ **Exercise 4.6** Write a short paragraph about something you did yesterday. Underline all the nouns.

Pronouns

Like nouns, pronouns serve as subjects, objects, and complements in sentences. A **pronoun** is a word used in place of a noun. As pronouns stand in for nouns, you must always make clear to readers what nouns the pronouns stand for. A pronoun that lacks a clear antecedent causes great confusion. (Pronouns are discussed more fully in Chapter 17.)

There are many kinds of pronouns, and we use them for different purposes.

Personal pronouns refer to one or more persons: *I, you, he, she, it, we, they.*

Indefinite pronouns make statements about a member of a group when we are unable to name which one we mean: *all, any, anyone, each, everybody, everyone, few, nobody, one, someone.*

Reflexive pronouns refer to the noun or pronoun that is the subject of the sentence; they always end in *-self: myself, himself, herself, yourself, ourselves.*

> She allowed **herself** no rest.
>
> He loved **himself** more than he loved anyone else.

Intensive pronouns have the same form as reflexive pronouns; they add special emphasis to nouns and other pronouns.

> I **myself** have often made that mistake.
>
> President Harding **himself** played poker and drank whiskey in the White House during Prohibition.

Demonstrative pronouns point out nouns or other pronouns that come after them: *this, that, these, those.*

> **That** is the book I want.
>
> Are **those** the books you bought?

Relative pronouns join word groups containing a subject and verb to nouns or pronouns that the word groups describe: *who, whom, that, which.*

> Dravot in Kipling's story was the man **who** would be king.
>
> The tools **that** I lost in the lake cost me a fortune to replace.

ESL 1

4c

gram

The doctor **whom** you recommended has been suspended for malpractice.

Possessive pronouns show possession or special relations: *my, his, her, your, our, their, its.* Unlike possessive nouns, possessive pronouns have no apostrophes.

She was **my** aunt.

Their cat sets off **my** allergies.

The fault was **ours,** and the worst mistake was **mine.**

Interrogative pronouns introduce questions: *who, which, what.*

What courses are you taking?

Who kept score?

Which of the glasses is mine?

Like nouns, pronouns can be singular or plural, depending on the noun they replace.

4c gram

KINDS OF PRONOUNS

Personal pronouns	Indefinite pronouns		Reflexive pronouns	Intensive pronouns
I	all	no one	myself	myself
you	any	one	yourself	yourself
she	anybody	ones	herself	herself
he	anyone	somebody	himself	himself
it	anything	someone	itself	itself
we	each	whichever	oneself	oneself
they	everybody	whoever	ourselves	ourselves
me	everyone	whomever	yourselves	yourselves
her	few		themselves	themselves
him	many			
them	nobody			

Demonstrative pronouns	Relative pronouns	Possessive pronouns	Interrogative pronouns
this	that	my	what
that	which	mine	who
these	what	your	which
those	who	yours	
	whom	her	
	whoever	hers	
	whomever	his	
	whose	its	
		our	
		ours	
		their	
		theirs	

4c gram

■ **Exercise 4.7** Fill in the blanks with any pronouns that make sense. See how many different pronouns you can use in each blank.

1. _____ always wanted to put a small motor on _____ hang glider.
2. _____ house is on the street next to _____ school.
3. _____ who can square dance is welcome to _____ party.
4. The president _____ said he would be at the party.
5. _____ is in charge of _____ goat?
6. _____ must we do to pay _____ mechanic?
7. _____ of the parts must be replaced?
8. The snake was _____, but I kept quiet when _____ was found on the couch of the adjoining apartment.
9. "The most important principle in dancing," _____ told _____, "is to think of the music and not _____ feet."
10. When _____ drove the car through _____ kitchen window, the impact ruined _____ cake _____ happened to be in the oven at the time.

Adjectives, Articles, Adverbs

Adjectives and adverbs describe other words more fully or more definitely. Adjectives and adverbs modify other words; that is, they change, expand, limit, or otherwise help describe the words to which they relate.

Adjectives

Adjectives modify nouns and pronouns. That is, they help describe nouns and pronouns in a sentence by answering questions such as *which one, what kind, how many, what size, what color, what condition, whose.* Adjectives appear in boldface in the sentences below.

> The **pale** sun shone through the **gloomy** clouds.
>
> **Six** camels trudged across a **vast white** desert.
>
> **Harry's little blue** Volkswagen died **one icy winter** morning.

Adjectives come immediately before or immediately after the words they modify, although they usually come before.

> The **tired, thirsty,** and **impatient** horse threw its rider and went back to the barn.
>
> The horse, **tired, thirsty,** and **impatient,** threw its rider and went back to the barn.

**4c
gram**

ESL 13

Subject complements

An adjective modifying the subject of a sentence sometimes appears on the opposite side of a linking verb from the subject.

> The horse looked **tired, thirsty,** and **impatient.**
>
> My friend was **ill,** and I was **worried.**

In these examples, the adjectives are subject complements.

✔ **CHECKLIST 4.6:** TESTING FOR ADJECTIVES

Ask questions such as:

- Which one? **That** man was the murderer.
- What kind? The **dead** leaves clung to the old tree.
- How many? The train had **six** cars.
- What size? The **tall** building is Holyoke Center.
- What color? The **brown** grass showed that we needed rain.
- What condition? **Sick** people often have no energy.
- Whose? **My** coat is the one with the hole in the sleeve.

Articles

An **article** is a word used with a noun to limit or specify its application. The articles *a, an,* and *the* function as adjectives. The articles *a* and *an* are indefinite and singular; they call attention to any one of several things.

> He sent me **a** card.
>
> Richard III cried, "**A** horse, **a** horse, my kingdom for **a** horse!"

4c
gram

The article *a* appears before words that begin with a consonant sound; *an* appears before words that begin with a vowel sound.

> a dish, a rose, a year, an apple, an entreaty, a European, an hour, a historian, an ideal, an enemy, a friend, an umbrella, a union, an understanding

ESL 12

The word *Europe* begins with the vowels *eu,* which in this case are sounded as *yu.* So we speak of "*a* Europe at peace" or "*a* European in America." A few English words that begin with the consonant *h* have a vowel sound and are preceded by *an.*

> an hour, an honest man, an honor, an honorable schoolboy

The article *the* is used with both singular and plural nouns. It always means "this and not any other." Often the difference between using *a* or *an* and using *the* depends on the writer's idea of how specific the following noun is.

Definite: He came down off **the** mountain and found **the** road. (No other mountain and no other road will do.)

Indefinite: He came down off **a** mountain and found **a** road. (The writer does not know or care what mountain the man descended or what road he found. Maybe the man himself didn't know.)

Degree

In comparisons, adjectives show degree or intensity by the addition of an *-er* or *-est* ending or by the use of *more* or *most* or *less* or *least.* In the **positive**

degree, no comparison is intended. The **comparative degree** singles out one object in a set of two. The **superlative degree** singles out one object among three or more.

Adjective: large

Positive degree: She owned a **large** hat.

Comparative degree: Her hat was **larger** than mine.

Superlative degree: She owned the **largest** hat in the theater.

4c gram

Adjective: sophisticated

Positive degree: Joan's analysis of *Moby Dick* was **sophisticated.**

Comparative degree: Joan's analysis of *Moby Dick* was **more sophisticated** than Emily's.

Superlative degree: Joan's analysis of *Moby Dick* was the **most sophisticated** in her class.

Adverbs

Adverbs modify words or sentence elements that cannot be modified by adjectives. Since adjectives can modify only nouns and pronouns, adverbs are left to modify everything else. They usually modify verbs, adjectives, and other adverbs, but they sometimes modify prepositions, phrases, clauses, and even whole sentences. (Adverbs are discussed more fully in 19c.)

Adverbs answer several questions, such as *how, how often, to what degree (how much), where,* and *when.*

Wearily he drifted **away.**

She did **not** speak **much today.**

Adverbs may modify by affirmation or negation. *Not* is always an adverb.

He **surely** will call home before he leaves.

They shall **not** pass.

We **never** will see anyone like her again.

Many adverbs end in *-ly,* and you can make adverbs of most adjectives simply by adding *-ly* to the adjective form.

Adjective	Adverb
large	largely
crude	crudely
beautiful	beautifully

4c
gram

✔ CHECKLIST 4.7: TESTING FOR ADVERBS

Ask questions such as:

■ How? He **cheerfully** gave up the money.

■ How often? **Sometimes** I wonder what she means.

■ To what degree? I **intensely** dislike having to look for a parking place.

■ Where? Odysseus, following the defeat of Troy, turned **homeward.**

■ When? **Yesterday** I took my last exam.

ESL 14

A great many adverbs do not end in *-ly*.

> often, sometimes, then, when, anywhere, anyplace, somewhere, somehow, somewhat, yesterday, Sunday, before, behind, ahead, seldom

And many adjectives end in *-ly*.

> costly, stately, lowly, homely, measly, manly, womanly

Conjunctive adverbs

Some adverbs can serve to connect ideas between clauses. These are **conjunctive adverbs,** such words and phrases as *accordingly, consequently, hence, however, indeed, meanwhile, moreover, nevertheless, on the other hand,* and *therefore* (see 13e).

> Descartes said, "I think; **therefore** I am."

> He opposed her before she won the primary election; **however,** he supported her afterward in her campaign.

Swimming is an excellent exercise for the heart and for the muscles; **on the other hand,** swimming does not control weight as well as jogging and biking do.

Unlike *coordinating conjunctions* (discussed below) or *transitional expressions* (discussed in 3c), conjunctive adverbs cannot bind clauses together. If you use one of the conjunctive adverbs between clauses, you also must use a semicolon or a period. This rule makes it easy to tell a conjunctive adverb from a coordinating conjunction. Conjunctive adverbs may shift positions within a clause.

4c gram

> **Coordinating conjunction:** Swimming is an excellent exercise for the heart and for the muscles, **but** swimming does not control weight as well as jogging and biking do.
>
> **Conjunctive adverb:** Swimming is an excellent exercise for the heart and for the muscles; **on the other hand,** swimming does not control weight as well as jogging and biking do.

The best test for an adverb is to find what it modifies and then to ask yourself the appropriate adverb questions. If a modifier does not help describe a noun, a pronoun, or some other noun substitute, it has to be an adverb. If it does modify a noun, a pronoun, or some other noun substitute, it cannot be an adverb.

Degree

Adverbs, like adjectives, show degrees by the addition of an *-er* or *-est* ending or by the use of *more* or *most* or *less* or *least.* Whether modifying an adjective or another adverb, the words *more, most, less,* and *least* are themselves adverbs.

> **Adverb:** *fast*
> **Positive degree:** Olga ran **fast.**
> **Comparative degree:** Olga ran **faster** than Jack.
> **Superlative degree:** Olga ran **fastest** of all her playmates.

> **Adverb:** *sadly*
> **Positive degree:** My visitors said goodbye **sadly.**
> **Comparative degree:** They spoke **more sadly** than I did.
> **Superlative degree:** I spoke **most sadly** when they told me that they had decided not to leave.

POSITIVE, COMPARATIVE, AND SUPERLATIVE DEGREES

Positive (one object is)	Comparative (of two objects, one is)	Superlative (of three objects, one is)
Adjective:		
swift	*swifter*	*swiftest*
She was **swift**.	She was **swifter** than Tom.	She was the **swiftest** runner in the fifth grade.
Adverb:		
swiftly	*more swiftly*	*most swiftly*
She ran **swiftly**.	She ran **more swiftly** than she ever had.	Among all the fifth graders, she ran **most swiftly**.

4c gram

■ **Exercise 4.8**   In the following sentences, underline the adverbs and draw a circle around the adjectives.

1. Later he drifted silently across the warm, moonlit street.
2. Clearly solar heat offers many advantages, but both the equipment and its installation have high costs.
3. Japanese planes roared swiftly over the motionless battleships at Pearl Harbor early on Sunday, December 7, 1941.
4. Many state education departments now enthusiastically support the use of hand-held calculators on various mathematics and science tests in elementary and secondary school classrooms.
5. I learned to appreciate Hebrew by hearing our cantor sing during the Friday-night Sabbath services, but I never understood exactly what the songs meant because I did not know the language well enough.

Conjunctions

Conjunctions join elements within a sentence. These elements may be words, or they may be groups of words like clauses or phrases (see 4d, 4e).

Coordinating conjunctions (or, simply, **coordinators**) join elements of equal weight or function. The common coordinating conjunctions are *and, but, or, for,* and *nor*. Some writers now include *yet* and *so*.

She was tired **and** happy.

The town was small **but** pretty.

They must be tired, **for** they have climbed all day long.

You may take the green **or** the red.

He would not leave the table, **nor** would he stop insulting his host.

Correlative conjunctions are conjunctions used in pairs. They also connect sentence elements of equal value. The familiar correlatives are *both . . . and, either . . . or, neither . . . nor,* and *not only . . . but also.*

Neither the doctor **nor** the the police believed his story.

The year 1927 was **not only** the year Lindbergh flew solo nonstop across the Atlantic **but also** the year Babe Ruth hit sixty home runs.

**4c
gram**

Subordinating conjunctions (or **subordinators**) join dependent or subordinate sections of a sentence to independent sections or to other dependent sections (see 4e). The common subordinating conjunctions are *after, although, as, because, if, rather than, since, that, unless, until, when, whenever, where, wherever,* and *while.*

The stylus will not track records **if** there is not enough weight on it.

Although the desert may look barren and dead, a vigorous life goes on there.

He always wore a hat **when** he went out in the sun.

Stories about divorce are common on television and in the movies **because** so many Americans have been divorced.

The use of conjunctions to improve your writing is discussed in Chapter 6.

Prepositions

Prepositions are short words that work with nouns or pronouns as modifiers, often specifying place or time. The noun or pronoun is the **object** of the preposition. In the following sentence the prepositions are in boldface and their objects are in italics.

ESL 15

Suburban yards now provide homes **for** *wildlife* that once lived only **in** the *country.*

The preposition, its noun, and any modifiers attached to the noun make up a **prepositional phrase.** Prepositional phrases act as adjectives and adverbs. The main function of prepositions is to allow the nouns or pronouns that follow them to modify other words in the sentence. Here are common prepositions.

about	below	from	to
above	beneath	in	toward
across	beside	including	under
after	between	inside	underneath
against	beyond	into	until
along	by	like	up
amid	despite	near	upon
among	down	of	via
as	during	on	with
at	except	over	within
before	excluding	since	without
behind	following	through	

4c gram

Some prepositions consist of more than one word.

according to	except for	instead of
along with	in addition to	on account of
apart from	in case of	up to
as to	in front of	with respect to
because of	in place of	with reference to
by means of	in regard to	
by way of	in spite of	

Prepositions usually come before their objects. But sometimes, especially in questions, they do not. Grammarians debate whether prepositions should end a sentence. Most writers favoring an informal style will now and then use a preposition to end a sentence.

> Which college do you go **to?**
>
> Which lake does she live **by?**

For more formal choices, you could restate these questions.

> **To** which college do you go?
>
> **By** which lake does she live?

Many words used as prepositions serve as other parts of speech as well. They often serve as adverbs or as subordinating conjunctions.

He arrived **after** midnight. (*preposition*)

Jill came tumbling **after.** (*adverb*)

After Jack broke his crown, Jill fell down, too. (*subordinating conjunction*)

Interjections

Interjections are forceful expressions, usually written with an exclamation point, though mild ones may be set off with commas.

They are not used often in formal writing except in quotations of dialogue.

4c

gram

Hooray!	Ouch!
Oh, no!	Wow!

"Wow!" Davis said. "Are you telling me that there's a former presidential adviser who hasn't written a book?"

How Words Act as Different Parts of Speech

A word that acts as one part of speech in a sentence may act as other parts of speech in other sentences or in other parts of the same sentence. The way the word is used will determine what part of speech it is.

The **light** glowed at the end of the pier. (*noun*)
As you **light** the candle, say a prayer. (*verb*)
The **light** drizzle foretold heavy rain. (*adjective*)

The cobra glided **outside.** (*adverb*)
The child played on the **outside.** (*noun*)
The mongoose waited **outside** the house. (*preposition*)
The famous **outside** linebacker was terrified by this scene. (*adjective*)

When will he come home? (*adverb*)
He will come **when** he is ready. (*conjunction*)
They decided the where and **when** immediately. (*noun*)

■ **Exercise 4.9**   Fill in the blanks in the following sentences with any words that make sense. The word in parentheses at the end of each sentence tells you the part of speech that will go in the blank. But don't worry about that. Look at the names of the parts of speech, and use your intuition to fill in the blanks. The exercise will prove that you have a feeling for the parts of speech even if you don't readily come up with the names. You will build confidence as you study the other sentences.

1. The dinosaurs _____ extinct millions of years ago. (verb)
2. Emma bought _____ a hamburger for lunch. (pronoun or noun)
3. The _____ swerved and hit the guardrail. (noun)
4. The leaves on the maple tree in the yard _____ red. (verb)
5. "_____!" he cried. "That hurt." (interjection)
6. The English troops retreated _____ from Lexington. (adverb)
7. Collecting hand-painted tin soldiers was _____ hobby. (pronoun)
8. I had to buy textbooks _____ supplies on the first day of the semester. (conjunction)
9. Alcohol is one of the _____ dangerous common drugs. (adverb)
10. Our arrival was delayed _____ we had a flat tire. (conjunction)
11. She welded the _____ to the bicycle. (noun)
12. Come _____ my house for the party. (preposition)
13. It rained all _____ the game. (preposition)
14. France _____ California produce some of the finest wines on earth. (conjunction)
15. Radios _____ from cars in cities by the thousands every year. (verb)
16. The _____ problem was how to buy a motorcycle without going into debt. (adjective)
17. The _____ bicycle is much more complicated than its ancestors. (adjective)
18. We painted the bedposts _____. (adjective)
19. The trip turned into a _____. (noun)
20. The New York Mets began playing baseball _____ 1962. (preposition)

■ **Exercise 4.10**   Write original sentences in which you use each word below according to the directions. Use a dictionary when you need help. Dictionary entries identify the various ways words are used and may give examples that will help you create sentences of your own.

1. Use *leap* as a noun, a verb, and an adjective.
2. Use *beyond* as an adverb, a preposition, and a noun.
3. Use *after* as an adverb, a preposition, and a conjunction.
4. Use *rain* as a noun, a verb, and an adjective.
5. Use *lapse* as a noun and a verb.

4c gram

4d
Identifying Phrases and Clauses

A **phrase** is a group of related words without a subject and a predicate.

> They **were watching** the game.
>
> The child ran **into the lake.**
>
> **Grinning happily,** she made a three-point shot.
>
> **To succeed in writing,** you must be willing to revise again and again.
>
> **Diving for treasure** is sometimes dangerous.

**4d/e
gram**

A **clause** is a group of grammatically related words containing both a subject and a predicate. An **independent clause** can usually stand by itself as a complete sentence. A **dependent,** or **subordinate, clause** often cannot stand by itself because it is introduced by a subordinating conjunction or a relative pronoun and therefore the clause alone does not make sense. In the sentences below, the independent clauses are in boldface, the dependent clauses in italics.

> **She ran in the marathon** *because she wanted to test herself.*
>
> **She said** *that she felt exhausted after fifteen miles.*
>
> **They took** *what they could find.*
>
> *When we had done everything possible,* **we left the wounded to the enemy.**

See also 4f.

4e
Reviewing Types of Phrases and Their Uses

English sentences contain three basic types of phrases: prepositional phrases, verb phrases, and absolute phrases.

Prepositional Phrases

Prepositional phrases always begin with a preposition and always end with a noun or pronoun that serves as the object of the preposition. The noun or pronoun in the phrase can then help to describe something else in the sentence. A prepositional phrase generally serves as an adjective or an adverb in the sentence in which it occurs.

ESL 2

Adjective prepositional phrase: The tree **in the yard** is an oak.

Adverb prepositional phrase: He arrived **before breakfast.**

To identify an adjective prepositional phrase or an adverb prepositional phrase, use the same tests you used for simple adjectives and adverbs (see 4c). In the sentence below, the adjective prepositional phrase (in italics) answers the question *which book;* the adverb prepositional phrase (in boldface) answers the question *why.*

4e gram

Ditmars's book *about North American snakes* sold well **because of its outstanding photographs.**

Verb Phrases

ESL 4

Verb phrases are combinations of verbs including a main verb and one or more auxiliary verbs (see 4b, 4c). But verb phrases, or **verbals,** also include words formed from verbs that do not function as verbs in sentences. Verbals can stand alone as parts of speech, or they can be part of words attached to them to make a verb phrase. There are three kinds of verbals: infinitives, participials, and gerunds.

Infinitives and infinitive phrases

The infinitive of any verb except the verb *to be* is formed when the infinitive marker *to* is placed before the common form of the verb in the first-person present tense.

Verb	Infinitive
go	to go
make	to make

Infinitives and infinitive phrases function as nouns, adjectives, and adverbs. Here, too, the tests for adjectives and adverbs come in handy. In the sentences below, examine the various ways the infinitive phrase *to finish his novel* can function.

To finish his novel was his greatest ambition. (noun, the subject of the sentence)

He made many efforts **to finish his novel.** (adjective modifying the noun *efforts*)

He rushed **to finish his novel.** (adverb modifying the verb *rushed*)

Participles and participial phrases

Participles are made from verbs. **Present participles** suggest some continuing action. **Past participles** suggest completed action. The present participle of verbs is formed when *-ing* is added to the common present form of the verb. (The present participle *being* is formed from the infinitive *to be*.) The past participle is usually made by the addition of *-ed* to the common present form of the verb, but past participles are frequently irregular. That is, some past participles are formed not by an added *-ed*, but by an added *-en* or by a change in the root of the verb.

ESL 16

4e gram

> I have **biked** five hundred miles in two weeks.
>
> I have **driven** five hundred miles in a morning.
>
> I have **fought** to change speed limits on two-lane roads.

Because they do represent action, participles can be used in a wide variety of ways. In the sentences above, the participle is part of a verb phrase. But participles also can act as adjectives. In the sentences below, the participial phrases modify the subjects.

> **Creeping through heavy traffic,** the messenger on the bike yelled angrily at pedestrians.
>
> **Insulted by the joke,** the team stormed out of the banquet.

Gerunds and gerund phrases

A **gerund** is the present participle used as a noun. A **gerund phrase** includes any words and phrases attached to the gerund so that the whole serves as a noun.

> **Walking** is one of life's great pleasures. (subject)
>
> **Walking swiftly an hour a day** will keep you fit. (subject)
>
> She praised his **typing.** (object)
>
> He worked hard at **typing the paper.** (object)

Absolute Phrases

An **absolute phrase** consists of a noun or pronoun attached to a participle without a helping verb. It modifies the whole sentence in which it appears. Remember: the inclusion of a helping verb would make the participle part of a verb phrase.

> **Her body falling nearly a hundred miles an hour,** she pulled the rip cord, and the parachute opened with a heavy jerk.

Falling nearly a hundred miles an hour, she pulled the rip cord, and the parachute opened with a heavy jerk.

The storm came suddenly, **the clouds boiling across the sky.**

4f
gram

■ **Exercise 4.11**   Write sentences using the following phrases.

1. was dreaming (verb phrase)
2. beside the river (prepositional phrase)
3. the train having arrived (absolute phrase)
4. to use a computer (infinitive phrase)
5. sleeping in the woods (participial phrase)

■ **Exercise 4.12**   Identify the phrases in **boldface** in the following sentences. Tell what kind of phrase each one is and how it is used in the sentence.

1. The sheriff strode into the bar, **his hands hovering over his pistols.**
2. "Where is that cat?" he shouted, **his eyes darting around the room.**
3. **Whispered softly and urgently,** the question rippled down the bar.
4. **Opening the door softly,** the cat slinked into the room.
5. **Over the barroom** a great hush fell as the sheriff and the cat stared at each other.
6. The sheriff wiped his eyes **to see better.**
7. "Time's up for you, cat," the sheriff shouted **in the great, expectant silence.**
8. **Licking his fur indifferently and sitting down,** the cat seemed to nod behind the sheriff.
9. **Frightened and dismayed,** the sheriff looked behind him.
10. A thousand cats were softly padding **through the open door.**

4f
Recognizing Clauses

Clauses have subjects and predicates and may be independent or dependent. Sometimes we call independent clauses *main clauses* and dependent clauses *subordinate clauses.*

An **independent clause** usually can stand on its own as a complete sentence. A **dependent clause** cannot. It serves another clause as an adjective, an adverb, or a noun. In the sentences below, the independent clause is in boldface, the dependent clause in italics.

He swam across the lake *after the sun set.*

He claimed *that he swam across the lake after the sun set.*

An easy test for dependent clauses is to see if they are introduced by a subordinating word or group of words (see 4c and 6b). The subordinator tells you that the clause to follow is to serve another clause. In the following sentence, the subordinate clause (in boldface) serves as an adverb answering the question *why.*

I am going to bed **because I am tired.**

Here are some subordinating conjunctions: *after, although, as, because, before, if, once, since, that, though, till, unless, until, when, whenever, where, wherever, while, as if, as soon as, as though, even after, even if, even though, even when, for as much as, in order that, in that, rather than, so that, sooner than*

Some subordinators are relative pronouns: *what, which, who, whom, whose, that.* The subordinators *that* and *which* are sometimes left out of sentences before dependent clauses. In the following sentences, the dependent clauses are in boldface, and the subordinator has been omitted.

Many poor people in Latin America believe **they can gain dignity only by revolution.**

She said **she would enroll in evening school and work during the day.**

We thought **Miami might win the Orange Bowl this year.**

English sentences contain three basic types of clauses: noun clauses, adjective clauses, and adverb clauses.

4f
gram

ESL 17

Noun Clauses

A **noun clause** is a clause that acts as a subject, object, or complement.

Subject: **That English is a flexible language** is both glory and pain.

Object: He told me **that English is a flexible language.**

Complement: His response was **that no response was necessary.**

ESL 18

ESL 19

4f gram

Adjective Clauses

An **adjective** (or **adjectival**) **clause** modifies a noun or pronoun. A relative pronoun is used to connect it to the word it modifies.

> The contestant **whom he most wanted to beat** was his father. (adjective clause modifies the noun *contestant;* relative pronoun *whom*, which stands for its antecedent *contestant*, serves as the direct object of the infinitive *to beat*)

> The computer **that I wanted** cost too much money. (adjective clause modifies the noun *computer;* relative pronoun *that* serves as the direct object of *wanted*)

> The journey of Odysseus, **which can be traced today on a map of Greece and the Aegean Sea,** made an age of giants and miracles seem close to the ancient Greeks. (adjective clause modifies *journey;* relative pronoun *which* serves as the subject of *can be traced*)

Adverb Clauses

An **adverb** (or **adverbial**) **clause** serves as an adverb, frequently (but not always) modifying the verb in another clause. Adverb clauses are often introduced by the subordinators *after, when, before, because, although, if, though, whenever, where,* and *wherever*, as well as by many others.

> **After we had talked for an hour,** he began to look at his watch. (adverb clause modifies the verb *began*)

> He reacted as swiftly **as he could**. (adverb clause modifies the adverb *swiftly*)

> The desert was more yellow **than he remembered**. (adverb clause modifies the adjective *yellow*)

■ **Exercise 4.13**   Identify the clauses in each of the following sentences. Draw one line under any dependent clause and two lines under the independent clause.

> *Example:*
> When he was a pilot on the Mississippi River in his youth, Samuel Clemens learned the lore of the people along its banks.

> 1. Before she set out on the Appalachian Trail, she had to buy a good backpack.
> 2. A retrospective of Georges Seurat's life was presented to the American public on the centenary of the artist's death.

3. Although Hollywood remains the film capital, New York City's Upper East Side and Greenwich Village have provided memorable settings for several important movies.
4. When knighthood was in flower, life was bloody and short.
5. Women now do many things that society prevented them from doing not long ago.
6. In college football, the running game is more important than it is in professional football.
7. A joyous feature of modern American music is New Orleans polyphony, which is the blare and howl of a marching band's horns along with vibrant drum rhythms.
8. The state of Texas has decided that high school athletes must pass all their academic work if they are to play sports.
9. George Armstrong Custer and the Seventh Cavalry perished because they attacked a village where thousands of Indians were ready to fight.
10. Medical evidence has been building up for years to prove that cigarette smoking causes lung cancer and heart disease.

**4g
gram**

■ **Exercise 4.14**   Write sentences using the following dependent clauses. Tell whether you make each an adjective, an adverb, or a noun.

1. because we awoke late
2. when she spotted the fox
3. as soon as she could
4. after she had won the state lottery
5. although he erased the answers
6. where the dinosaur bones were found
7. whenever he stirred the sauce
8. before the fire started
9. though the night had long since fallen
10. if she would fix the muffler on her car

4g
Identifying Types of Sentences

We can classify sentences by numbers of clauses and how the clauses are joined. The basic sentence types in English are simple, compound, complex, or compound-complex. We also classify sentences by purpose: declarative, interrogative, imperative, and exclamatory.

Simple Sentences

A **simple sentence** contains only one clause, and that clause is independent, able to stand alone grammatically. A simple sentence may have several phrases. It may have a compound subject or a compound verb. It may even have both a compound subject and a compound verb. But it can have only one *clause*—one subject and one verb that combine to make a clear statement. The following are simple sentences. Some are quite complicated, but they are *all* simple sentences, each with one independent clause.

4g

gram

> Large land reptiles have been unable to evolve in the presence of large land mammals.

> The bloodhound is the oldest known breed of dog.

> He staked out a plot of high ground in the mountains, cut down the trees, and built his own house with a fine view of the valley below.

> Historians, novelists, short-story writers, and playwrights write about characters, design plots, and usually seek the dramatic resolution of a problem.

> Singing, brawling, shouting, laughing, crying, and clapping every moment, the fans turned out every night hungry for a pennant.

Compound Sentences

A **compound sentence** contains two or more independent clauses, usually joined by a comma and a coordinating conjunction such as *and, but, nor, or, for, yet,* or *so.* A compound sentence does not contain a dependent clause. Sometimes the independent clauses are joined by a semicolon, a dash, or a colon.

> The sun blasted the earth, and the plants withered and died.

> He asked directions at the end of every street—but he never listened to them.

A compound sentence also may consist of a series of independent clauses joined by commas or semicolons, usually but not always with a conjunction before the last clause.

> They searched the want ads, she visited real estate agents, he drove through neighborhoods looking for for-sale signs, and they finally located a house big enough for them and their pet rattlesnakes.

The trees on the ridge behind our house change in September: the oaks start to redden; the maples pass from green to orange; the pines grow more dark.

Complex Sentences

A **complex sentence** contains one independent clause and one or more dependent clauses. In the following sentences, the dependent clause is in boldface type.

4g gram

> He consulted the dictionary **because he did not know how to pronounce the word.**

> She asked people **if they approved of what the speaker said.**

> **Although football players are reputed to be the most powerful athletes in team sports,** the winners of the World Series beat the winners of the Super Bowl in a celebrity tug-of-war on network television one year.

Compound-Complex Sentences

A **compound-complex sentence** contains two or more independent clauses and at least one dependent clause. In the following sentences, boldface type indicates dependent clauses.

> She discovered a new world in international finance, but she worked so hard investing other people's money **that she had no time to invest any of her own.**

> **Although Carrie Nation was an extremist in the temperance movement,** her belief **that God had called her to break up saloons with her hatchet** was widely applauded in her time.

> **After Abraham Lincoln was killed,** the government could not determine **how many conspirators there were,** and **since John Wilkes Booth, the assassin, was himself soon killed,** he could not clarify the mystery, **which remains to this day.**

Classification by Purpose

We also classify sentences by the kind of information they convey—by whether they are statements, questions, commands, or exclamations. End punctuation helps identify the purpose of the sentence.

Sentence type	Meaning	Example	End punctuation
Declarative	Makes a statement	He stopped watching *Gilligan's Island* reruns.	Period
Interrogative	Asks a question	Did he stop watching *Gilligan's Island* reruns?	Question mark
Imperative	Gives a command, makes a request	Please stop watching *Gilligan's Island* reruns.	Period
Exclamatory	Expresses strong emotion	I'll smash the TV if you don't stop watching *Gilligan's Island* reruns!	Exclamation point

4g gram

■ **Exercise 4.15** Classify the following sentences as simple, compound, complex, or compound-complex.

1. The winter of 1542 was marked by tempestuous weather throughout the British Isles: in the north, on the borders of Scotland and England, there were heavy snowfalls in December and frost so savage that by January the ships were frozen into the harbor at Newcastle.

—ANTONIA FRASER

2. Prints, with woodblocks as the oldest form, began life humbly, not as works of art but as substitutes for drawings or paintings when multiples of a single image were needed, probably as long ago as the fifth century A.D. in China.

—JOHN CANADAY

3. Using her own surreal version of the stream of consciousness monologue, Tatyana Tolstaya depicts the missed connections and lost opportunities that define her characters' lives with uncommon compassion and humor.

—MICHIKO KAKUTANI

4. True to his species, the white-tailed buck moved in ghostlike silence over a deep carpet of leaves lying faded, dry and crisp as cornflakes on the Ozark ridge.

—MICHAEL PEARCE

5. Until recently the main preoccupation of Cuban dissidents was monitoring human rights violations.

—ANNA HUSARSKA

6. Although America has some fine native cherries, some of the very best wild cherries to be found came originally from seedlings of cultivated varieties, and the birds have been the chief agents of scattering the seeds.

—EUELL GIBBONS

7. The notion of the painter as a sort of boon companion to the hangman is carried on by Leonardo, who was fond of attending executions, perhaps to study the muscular contortions of the hanged.

—MARY MCCARTHY

8. When he had eaten seven bananas, Mr. Biswas was sick, whereupon Soanie, silently crying, carried him to the back verandah.

—V. S. NAIPAUL

9. The people who developed the English language were more interested in making distinctions between boats than they were in the differences between colors and feelings, not to speak of tastes and smells.

—WALTER KAUFMANN

10. Inside the tough-talking, hard-jogging man of 40 who is identified largely by his work, there is a boy trying not to cry, "Time is running out."

—GAIL SHEEHY

■ **Exercise 4.16** Combine the following groups of sentences into compound, complex, or compound-complex sentences. You will often have to add conjunctions or relative pronouns. Sometimes you will want to delete some words. See how many combinations you can work out from each group.

1. A pitcher can throw a baseball faster than ninety miles an hour. Batters may be severely injured if they are hit. Every batter must wear a helmet at the plate.

2. Singapore banned the sale, production or import of chewing gum. The ban started early in the New Year. It is another in a series of restrictive measures for the island. These measures have given Singapore the reputation of an overly regulated, highly antiseptic community.

3. Orson Welles terrified the United States with his radio presentation of *War of the Worlds* in 1938. Hitler was pushing Europe into war. News bulletins regularly interrupted broadcasts. Welles made the program sound like a news broadcast. He made people think that Earth was being invaded from Mars.

4. The Mississippi Delta has some of the richest farmland in the world. It grows more cotton than any comparable area on earth. It was not thickly settled until after the Civil War. Mosquitoes gave people in the Delta yellow fever.

5. Almost a million accountants now work in the United States. The profession is still growing. Positions will increase by 30 percent over the next ten years. These figures have been reported by the Bureau of Labor Statistics.

4g
gram

SENTENCE LOGIC

Every sentence should make a clear statement that readers can understand. Often sentences answer some or all of the journalist's questions, the questions we want answered when we read a report of an event: *who, what, when, where, why,* and sometimes *how.*

Short, simple sentences like these offer little difficulty.

The world came to life at dawn.

The Soviet Union crumbled in 1991.

The snow fell softly all night long.

Even when your sentences are long and complicated, you can simplify your thinking by asking which of the six questions they answer. In writing, you need to strive for clarity and logic. To write clear and logical sentences and paragraphs you can use five strategies that most writers know: (1) Prune irrelevant details that can derail your readers. (2) Give proper emphasis to the most important parts of your sentence. (3) Clearly establish cause-and-effect relations. (4) Limit your generalizations. (5) Use concrete terms when you define a word.

5a
Pruning Irrelevant Details

Unnecessary information may confuse your readers by blurring the central thought of your sentence. Everything in a sentence must support the central statement. If ideas are not related to the central statement, prune them.

In a first draft, you may include irrelevant details as you try to put down everything you know about a topic. When you revise, cut out these details so that everything in each of your sentences will contribute to the major statement you wish to make.

Draft: *The Adventures of Huckleberry Finn,* by Mark Twain, who lectured widely in the United States and Great Britain, received only one review when it was published in 1884.

Revised: *The Adventures of Huckleberry Finn,* by Mark Twain, received only one review when it was published in 1884.

Often you can revise a sentence so that all the details in your first draft can be made to support the major purpose of the sentence.

5a

logic

Revised: Although Mark Twain lectured widely in the United States and Great Britain and was well known to the public, *The Adventures of Huckleberry Finn* received only one review when it was published in 1884.

But you should never cram too many ideas in a sentence. As a general rule, aim at stating one central idea in every sentence. When you have several important ideas to communicate, put them in separate sentences.

Draft: World War I began on July 28, 1914, when the Austrians, whose army was huge but badly commanded and badly supplied and was also made up of many rival nationalities, attacked the city of Belgrade, in what was then called Serbia, though recently part of the nation of Yugoslavia, a country once again in turmoil after the Soviet Union loosened its grip on Communist Europe and rival nationalities began fighting.

This sentence contains too much information. What is its purpose? Is it to tell us when the war began? Or is it to tell us why the Austrian army was much weaker than it appeared? Or is it to tell us where Belgrade is? Or is it to describe rival nationalities in the Balkans?

Revised: World War I began on July 28, 1914, when the Austrians attacked the city of Belgrade, in what was then called Serbia. The Austrian army was huge, badly commanded, and badly supplied, but the Serbians were no match for it by themselves, and so they had to call on the Russians for help. The Austrians thereupon called upon the Germans for help against the Russians. The German war plan called for defeating the French before turning against Russia, thereby avoiding war on two fronts. The Germans attacked France through Belgium, compelling Britain to come to the aid of its Belgian ally. Suddenly all Europe was in conflict.

■ **Exercise 5.1**   Rewrite the following sentences to clarify the main statement in each of them. You may choose to revise to make two sentences with related thoughts if you want to express two distinct statements. You may want to leave out some of the information given in the sentences so that the statements you preserve will be clear.

1. My mother, who always hated to wash windows or clean house but preferred to work in her flower garden, worked on newspapers for twenty years in places as diverse as Beaumont, Texas, and Montgomery, Alabama.

2. Notoriously hard to spell and difficult grammatically, the English language has spread all over the world largely because of the power and influence of the United States and the British Empire and Commonwealth.

3. Scurvy, a disease once common among sailors who spent many weeks at sea, can be prevented by eating citrus fruits, which grow in warm climates and can be preserved at sea because of their thick skins.

4. If Lincoln had not sent ships to supply the federal garrison at Fort Sumter in Charleston Harbor, the British might have recognized the Confederacy as an independent nation so that they might ensure a steady supply of southern cotton to British textile mills, which by 1861 were using steam engines.

5. Terrorism is one of the frightening symbols of modern society because it is violent, bloody, and merciless and often completely anonymous, since the terrorists sometimes do not know and do not care who their victims are, but they know that a bomb exploding in an airport or a bullet tearing through the body of a police officer will get publicity, which they think will make them look important in the eyes of the world, and they think that if they are important, they may be able to get their way.

5b
logic

5b
Deciding on Proper Emphasis

The most emphatic places in a sentence are the beginning and the end. Most sentences begin with the subject. The person, place, or thing that the sentence is going to be about comes first, so that readers will have it in their minds for the rest of the sentence.

In your first draft, you may be concerned only to get ideas on paper. When you revise, think about what element in each sentence you want to stress. Then make sure to arrange your sentence to provide the intended emphasis. Eliminate statements that don't contribute to that emphasis. For more information on emphasis, see Chapters 6 and 7.

> **Draft:**   When you are looking for a good book, try *Moby-Dick*, which you will find to be a great one.
>
> **Revised:**   *Moby-Dick* is one of the greatest books in American literature.

5c

logic

5c
Expressing Cause and Effect

Simply by being close to one another, elements within a sentence may imply a causal relation. If you do intend to suggest cause and effect, make sure the link is clear. Be logical when you attribute an effect to a cause, and avoid statements that imply causality you do not intend.

In your first draft, you may put elements together in a sentence. When you revise, ask yourself if they belong together and, if they do, if the link between them is apparent or requires expansion.

> **Confusing:**   In 1950 the most popular song in America was "Tennessee Waltz," and the United States went to war in Korea.

Was the popularity of "Tennessee Waltz" the cause of the Korean War? The thought needs filling out to clarify the writer's point: that two contradictory things were happening at the same time.

> **Revised:**   In 1950, when the most popular song in America was the slow, dreamy "Tennessee Waltz," the United States went to war in Korea, and a peaceful dream ended for thousands of young men.

Confusion may also result from joining a dependent clause to an independent clause in such a way that a cause-and-effect relation seems to be implied.

> **Confusing:**   When he saw the movie *Casablanca*, my friend Bert had a heart attack.

Did the movie *Casablanca* cause Bert to have a heart attack? Probably not. But a rapid reader might think that it did. Again, a solution is to expand the thought so that readers will not think you are implying cause and effect.

Revised: While he was watching the movie *Casablanca* last week, my friend Bert had a heart attack. He seemed to be in perfect health, and he was enjoying himself, but suddenly he was doubled over with a near-fatal seizure.

Some conjunctive adverbs and coordinating conjunctions establish negative relations. Words such as *but, although,* and *however* alert the reader to a contrast or qualification. Use them only when you intend such a contrast. Again, you may have to fill out the negative link you are implying. Confusion results if you use one of these words to join two statements that are unrelated to each other.

Confusing: **Although** I like to read, television is exciting.

Revised: **Although** I like to read, it is easier for me to watch an exciting television show in the evening when I am too tired to concentrate on the printed page.

■ **Exercise 5.2** Rewrite the following sentences to eliminate faulty patterns of cause and effect. Add information when it is necessary to clarify sentence logic.

1. Personal computers were unknown thirty-five years ago, and Elvis Presley was in his prime.
2. Anabolic steroids have been shown to produce a host of illnesses including cancer while they are helping build huge, muscular bodies for weight lifters and football players, and athletes often use them.
3. Because the thief was finally captured, some politicians do not believe in light sentences for chronic criminals.
4. If you see a Woody Allen movie, he captures the humor and suffering of middle-class urban men and women today.
5. When you go to college, many teachers love to write and talk to students about research and writing.

5d
Limiting Generalizations

Statements that assert too much on too little evidence have little credibility. They reveal that the writer has not studied the material enough to be aware of the exceptions serious observers know about. Be especially careful of sentences that assert *all, always,* and *never.*

In your first draft, you may want to do little more than express your opinion or main point. When you revise, examine your generalizations to make sure that they are valid, and limit them if they are not.

5d logic

Misleading: Students nowadays lack dedication and seriousness, and they seldom read anything but the sports pages and the comics.

Revised: Some students I have known lack dedication and seriousness, and they seldom read anything but the sports pages and the comics.

Misleading: There never has been another play as good as *Macbeth.*

Revised: *Macbeth* is an excellent play because Macbeth's flaws are the flaws of all of us.

Misleading: Everyone is agreed that Faulkner's story "A Rose for Emily" is not one of his better works because it is too melodramatic.

Revised: Some critics believe that Faulkner's story "A Rose for Emily" is not one of his better works because, they say, it is too melodramatic.

■ **Exercise 5.3** Rewrite the following sentences to qualify sweeping generalizations. Don't hesitate to change words if the changes improve the sentences.

1. On the expressway the other day, the driver of one car shot another driver who dented his fender. This kind of thing happens because people in big cities are stressed beyond limits and prone to violence.

2. My cousin Charles was furious because he could not get anybody to speak English when he asked directions in Paris no matter how much he shouted at them. His experience proves that the French all hate the Americans except when France needs American help in time of war.

3. Members of the crime syndicate are always photographed smoking cigars, and the cigar has long been regarded as a symbol of success by everyone who thinks about such things.

4. The photographs of the ship *Titanic* lying on the bottom of the Atlantic Ocean since it sank in 1912 prove that travel by ship was much more dangerous than travel by airplane is today.

5. Colstrop's necktie was found at the scene of the murder along with his wristwatch, his notebook, and a pair of his trousers. So he was the killer, and the courts will convict him.

✔ **CHECKLIST 5.1: MAKING SENTENCES MAKE SENSE**

As you revise your sentences, consider internal sentence logic. Ask yourself these questions.

- Is all the information related to the central statement?
- Does the sentence emphasize the central statement by appropriate arrangement of elements?
- Does the presentation of information clarify the relation between cause and effect?
- Are generalizations reasonable and supported?
- Are intended definitions clear and not reliant on cognates?

**5e
logic**

5e
Defining Terms

Defining a word by repeating it or by using one of its cognates is not helpful. **Cognates** are words that come from the same root. *Grammar* and *grammatical* are cognates. So are *describe* and *description, narrate* and *narration, compute* and *computer,* and *nostalgic* and *nostalgia.*

In your first draft, in order to get your point across, you may use words that you yourself understand. When you revise, however, think about your words from your reader's point of view, and define or explain those that need explaining.

> **Poor:**   A grammar book teaches you grammar.
>
> **Revised:**   A grammar book explains the system of rules about word endings and word order that allows a language to communicate.

> **Poor:**   A community is a group with communal interests.
>
> **Revised:**   A community is a group that shares similar ceremonies, goals, habits, and patterns of work.

In defining, avoid using the words *is when.*

> **Awkward:**   Fascism is when a military dictator rules with the help of secret police and won't allow freedom of the press or assembly.
>
> **Revised:**   Fascism is a political system ruled by a military dictator with the help of secret police and characterized by terror and strict censorship of the press to limit popular assemblies and suppress freedom of speech.

■ **Exercise 5.4** Rewrite the following sentences to give proper definitions. Use a dictionary when necessary (see 12b).

1. An accident is when you have something happen accidentally that is unexpected and usually harmful, although accidents can be lucky, too.
2. A traffic jam is when traffic is jammed up on the streets.
3. A computer is a machine used for computing.
4. A quarterback is a back on a football team.
5. A poet is a man or a woman who writes poetry.

5e
logic

COORDINATION, SUBORDINATION, PARALLELISM

To develop sentences effectively, distinguish between main ideas and subordinate ideas and bind related thoughts together with parallel construction. Your readers should be able to follow your train of ideas from the beginning of a sentence through to the end. Improper coordination or subordination can interrupt the flow and make your readers struggle to understand the main points you are trying to make. A lack of parallelism disrupts the relation between the parts of a sentence and weakens its force.

6a
Expressing Equal Ideas: Coordination

Establish equal emphasis between parts of a sentence by using coordinating conjunctions or suitable punctuation or both.

Coordinating Words, Phrases, or Clauses

The conjunction *and* always calls for equal emphasis on the elements that it joins.

> The bear **and** her cubs ate the food in camp.
>
> The bear **and** her cubs ate the food in camp **and** destroyed our tent.
>
> At the end of our climb we were hot **and** tired.
>
> He drank only coffee, tea, **and** milk for a week.

A comma can sometimes replace the *and* in a series.

He zigzagged, fell, rolled, ran into my waiting hand.

—E. B. WHITE

Wistfully, admiringly, the old voice added, "It's snug in here, upon my word!"

—KATHERINE MANSFIELD

6a
coord

The conjunction *or* also joins equal sentence elements.

He could go by bus **or** by train.

They knew that they must work out their differences over money **or** get a divorce.

Coordinating Clauses

Coordination can establish clear relations among equal thoughts or ideas by joining clauses or short consecutive sentences.

They hesitate, and they regret, and sometimes they petition; but they do nothing in earnest and with effect.

—HENRY DAVID THOREAU

When you use *and, but, or, for, nor, yet,* or *so* to connect independent clauses and thus coordinate related statements of equal importance, use a comma.

To act is to be committed, and to be committed is to be in danger.

—JAMES BALDWIN

I buried my head under the quilts, but my aunt heard me.

—LANGSTON HUGHES

You can also use a semicolon to connect related statements that are equally important.

We walked, and he talked; the musical irresistible voice seemed to set the pace of our march.

—EMLYN WILLIAMS

Sometimes both a semicolon and a coordinating conjunction introduce an independent clause (discussed in 23a).

The hands of the man who sawed the wood left red marks on the billets; and the forehead of the woman who nursed the baby was stained with the stain of the old rag she wound around her head again.

—CHARLES DICKENS

■ **Exercise 6.1**   Rewrite the following sentences to provide proper coordination. You may want to write more than a sentence for some of the examples.

1. He loved to shave in the morning because he liked the softness of shaving cream, the clean feel of the razor on his cheek, the smell of his after-shave, and he enjoyed taking a shower, too.
2. We drove to Baltimore last month, and to Wilmington the month before that, and next month we hope to drive to Providence.
3. Police officers in old movies often seem hard, cynical, and yet they are honest.
4. Truck drivers in this country complained bitterly about unreasonable speed limits, the high price of diesel fuel, and many of them refused to slow down.
5. Our friends would eat out on Saturday night, go to a movie, visit with each other, or they would do something else to have a relaxing good time.

6b
subord

6b
Expressing Unequal Ideas: Subordination

In some sentences, one idea depends on another. For example, one condition or event may cause another; one event may come before another; one observation may explain another. **Subordination** establishes the dependence of one idea on another by shifting emphasis away from supporting elements so that major statements emerge clearly.

Clauses, phrases, and single words can all be subordinate units in a sentence. The subordinate element usually enlarges on some element in the main part of the sentence. As you write and revise, keep clearly in mind the main thoughts you want to communicate. Then subordinate other elements to those main thoughts.

Subordination Within Sentences

In the following paragraph, readers would have trouble finding the statements that carry the writer's major line of thought. Each sentence in this paragraph is clear, but together the sentences create confusion because they do not show proper subordination.

**6b
subord**

Draft: Columbus discovered the New World in 1492. He made his voyage in three tiny ships. No educated person at that time believed that the world was flat. Columbus was well educated. The Greeks had taught that the world was round. They had taught that two thousand years before Columbus. On a round world, a sailor might head west to lands others had found by sailing east. Columbus wanted to find a new route to China and to other lands in Asia. Others had reached those lands. They had sailed around the southern tip of Africa to get there. Columbus thought the world was much smaller than it is. He thought he could get to Asia in about a month. Suppose America had not been in the way. He would have had a voyage of three or four months. He did not find the East Indies or China or Japan. America was in the way. It is a good thing America was in the way. Columbus might have sailed his three ships into an enormous ocean. His sailors might have starved to death. The ocean would have been far larger than anything Columbus could have imagined.

Revised: With tiny ships, Christpher Columbus discovered the New World in 1492, although he never understood just what he had done. Neither he nor any other educated person in his time believed that the world was flat. From the time of the ancient Greeks, two thousand years earlier, educated people had believed that the world was round, and that a ship might reach Asia by sailing west, around the tip of Africa. Because Columbus thought the world was much smaller than it is, he expected to find the East Indies, China, or Japan. Instead he found America. Had this continent not been in the way, he might have sailed his crews to starvation in an enormous ocean far larger than any sea he had imagined.

ESL 17

Subordinating conjunctions, often called **subordinators** (see p. 109), help to build subordinate clauses. Some examples are *after, because, since,* and *when.* Commas may also set off subordinate sections from a part they modify, especially when a subordinated element opens the sentence (discussed in 22b).

Where the road forks, you will find the graveyard.

Unless you object, I will plug my ears at the rock concert.

Because great horned owls are so big, they can sometimes kill and eat cats.

Until you remove the engine head, you cannot see the pistons.

He taught me **how to throw a curve.**

Although she looked tiny, she was a superb police officer.

The position of a subordinator in relation to the clause it introduces affects the meaning of a sentence.

6b
coord

She did not eat **because she was angry.**
She was angry **because she did not eat.**

When the police arrived, the burglars ran away.
When the burglars ran away, the police arrived.

After he had completed a fifty-yard pass, we cheered him.
After we cheered him, he completed a fifty-yard pass.

Relative pronouns—*who, whom, that, which, what, whoever, whomever, whose*—also signal subordinate elements in a sentence (discussed on p. 100).

The plane rose into the sky **that had turned fierce and gray.**

Uncle Kwong, **whom no one liked anyway,** refused our invitation.

Notice how the use of subordinators speeds up the pace of the following sentences.

Without subordinators: My cousin does my taxes every year. He is an accountant. He helps me with many suggestions. These suggestions allow me to take several deductions. These deductions reduce my tax bill considerably.

With subordinators: Because my cousin is an accountant, he does my taxes every year, suggesting several deductions that reduce my tax bill considerably.

Embedding

As you've already observed, short sentences are easy to understand, but several of them in a row may be monotonous even if they are clear and correct. Look at this example.

She was sad. She did not look back. She mounted the seawall. She was bowed by her burden of failure, sorrow, and self-contempt.

Now consider this example. With the same ideas and words several sentences have been reduced to modifiers. This technique is called **embedding.**

> Sadly, without looking back, she mounted the seawall, bowed by her burden of failure, sorrow, and self-contempt.
>
> —CONSTANCE HOLME

Embedding compresses a great deal of information into a few words by establishing subordination. Consider these additional examples.

> We can turn poetry toward biology. We can suggest a closer relationship between them. This creation of a relationship would follow a long line of similar suggestions. Other disciplines have made these suggestions.
>
> To turn poetry toward biology and to suggest a closer relationship between them is only to follow in a long line of similar suggestions made by other disciplines.
>
> —ELIZABETH SEWELL

> The White Star liner *Titanic* was the largest ship the world had ever known. The *Titanic* sailed from Southampton on her maiden voyage to New York on April 10, 1912.
>
> The White Star liner *Titanic,* largest ship the world had ever known, sailed from Southampton on her maiden voyage to New York on April 10, 1912.
>
> —HANSON W. BALDWIN

> She was falling asleep. Her head was bowed over the child. She was still aware of a strange, wakeful happiness.
>
> Even as she was falling asleep, head bowed over the child, she was still aware of a strange, wakeful happiness.
>
> —KATHERINE ANNE PORTER

Using this technique, you can embed several enriching thoughts within one base sentence and transform a whole group of ideas into a statement in which unstressed elements modify main ideas precisely. By using coordination along with subordination, you can expand your options for embedding and transforming sentences. Look at these examples.

The fissions generate heat, and in a power reactor this heat produces steam, which drives electric turbines.

—JEREMY BERNSTEIN

Equality with whites will not solve the problems of either whites or Negroes if it means equality in a world society stricken by poverty and in a universe doomed to extinction by war.

—MARTIN LUTHER KING, JR.

6b subord

■ **Exercise 6.2** Using the subordination techniques illustrated in 6b, revise the following sets of sentences. Make any necessary changes to create logical, correct sentences. You may want to see how many different combinations you can make of each example.

1. Bilingual education is expanding in many schools. It is designed for children. The native language of these children is not English. It may be Spanish. It may be Chinese. It may be Vietnamese. It may be Korean. It may be some other language.

2. This auditorium was huge. The acoustics were terrible. The tenor nearly screamed at us. But no one could hear him beyond the ninth row. The soprano looked as if she was trying. But her voice sounded like a whisper in the balcony. The singers walked off the stage. They had played only two-thirds of the first act. The baritone was in tears.

3. *JFK* was released in 1991. It was directed by Oliver Stone. Stone's film reopened the controversy over President John Fitzgerald Kennedy's death. The conspiracy theory is alive again. Many people fault Stone for giving the American public a false view of history.

4. A uniform can symbolize a worker's status. Status means power. People see authority in some uniforms. A person in a police uniform shows by dress that he or she has authority to make people stop. A person in a nurse's uniform shows by dress that he or she can dispense medications. Sometimes uniforms are not prescribed. But people try to wear clothing that makes them look as if they belong. Male college professors used to wear tweed jackets. Their tweed jackets were a kind of uniform.

5. I read the same want ads over and over. I was looking for a job for the summer. The recession clearly had affected the job market. Few jobs were available for college students. I would have done anything reasonable. I would have worked nights or days. All I found was a job shining shoes. This was at the airport thirty miles away. I quit after two days.

Avoiding Too Many Subordinate Structures

Too much subordination may distract readers and confuse your main statement. Be sure not to overload your sentences.

Overloaded: He was a stamp collector of considerable zeal who bought stamps at the post office on the day they were issued and fixed them with loving care in large books which had leather bindings, treasuring them not merely for themselves but for the enormous profit that he hoped to gain from them in the passage of years when they had increased in value.

Revised: A stamp collector of considerable zeal, he bought stamps at the post office on the day they were issued and fixed them carefully in large, leather-bound books. He prized them not only for themselves but for the enormous profit he hoped to gain from them when, after many years, they had increased in value.

Overloaded: Jackson Bingle, leader of the rock group called the Howlers, who had been known for his ability to scream over the sound of drums, a primal shriek that had amazed critics and delighted audiences while dismaying parents, learned during his annual physical, administered by T. J. Summers, head of Whooping Crane Hospital, that he had lost seven-eighths of his hearing, so he told reporters this morning.

Revised: Jackson Bingle told reporters this morning that he had lost seven-eighths of his hearing. Bingle, leader of the rock group called the Howlers, had been known for his ability to scream over the sound of the drums. His was a primal shriek that had amazed critics and delighted audiences. It also dismayed parents. Bingle said he learned of his hearing loss during his annual physical administered by Dr. T. J. Summers, head physician of Whooping Crane Hospital.

■ **Exercise 6.3**   Revise the following sentences to eliminate excessive subordination. You will have to write at least two sentences for each one that appears below.

1. Big city mayors, who are supported by public funds, should weigh carefully using taxpayers' money for personal needs, such as home furnishings and decorations, especially when municipal budget shortfalls have caused extensive job layoffs, angering city workers and the general public.

2. The new sun creams, which contain various sun-blocking chemicals, help protect against skin cancer, long a hazard to people who spend too much time in the sun, and against aging, which seems

to be at least partly a consequence of the ultraviolet rays of the sun, and they have also been shown to retard the graying of hair.

3. Literacy should mean not only the ability to read and write, which is an essential skill in our culture, but also the ability, which is very much appreciated by academics, businesspeople, and professionals, to talk about many topics with intelligence—which may be another way of saying that true literacy embraces curiosity and the love of learning.

6c
Writing Balanced Constructions: Parallelism

Some sentences repeat the same form for balance or emphasis. This repetition of form is **parallelism.** The elements in a parallel construction are equal or nearly equal in grammatical structures and importance. Parallel constructions may help you make lists, join similar ideas, or build emphasis. The coordinating conjunctions *and, but, or, nor,* and *yet* always join parallel structures.

The simple parallel structure is the series with two or more elements in it.

> She loved to read **magazines** and **newspapers.**

> She loved to read **books, magazines,** and **newspapers.**

> At Gettysburg in 1863, Abraham Lincoln said that the Civil War was being fought to make sure that government **of the people, by the people,** and **for the people** might not perish from the earth.

> He **did the dishes, ran the vacuum, put out the garbage,** and **swept the walk.**

> He **runs marathons** and **she runs sprints,** but **they train** together.

> Many performers live **to hear** the roar of the crowd, **to feel** the love of their fans, and **to enjoy** the attention of reporters.

Making Comparisons and Contrasts

Parallelism helps make comparisons and contrasts more emphatic.

> **Weak:**   She preferred **to buy** a house rather than **renting** one.

> **Parallel:**   She preferred **to buy** a house rather than **to rent** one.

> **Better:**   She preferred **buying** a house to **renting** one.

Weak: The new library was larger than the old one, more beautiful than any other building on campus, and **it cost too much money.**

Parallel: The new library was **larger** than the old one, **more beautiful** than any other building on campus, and more **expensive** to build than anyone had imagined.

6c parallel

Coordinating Elements

Some word pairs help coordinate elements in parallel forms. Examples are *both . . . and, either . . . or, neither . . . nor, not only . . . but also,* and *whether . . . or.* Such pairs, often called **correlatives,** always indicate a choice or a balance between equal elements. If you use these pairs to join unequal elements, you disrupt the relation between those elements and lose the grammatical sense of the sentence.

Faulty: Most soldiers in the Civil War were **neither heroic nor were they cowardly.**

Parallel: Most soldiers in the Civil War were **neither heroic nor cowardly.**

Faulty: The parking lot for commuters was **both small and it was crowded.**

Parallel: The parking lot for commuters was **both small and crowded.**

When you use a single coordinating element, such as *and* or *or,* be sure that you join equal elements.

Faulty: His favorite pastimes were reading, walking, **and he liked to skate on frozen ponds in winter.**

In this sentence, the words *reading* and *walking* prepare us to find a similar word after *and*—a gerund, such as *skating* or *thinking.* Instead we find not another gerund but an independent clause, and we feel that something has been left out. You can amend the sentence in this way.

Parallel: His favorite pastimes were reading, walking, **and skating.**

Confusion can arise with a breakdown in parallelism when *or* joins unequal elements.

Faulty: They could see a movie, a play, **or** talk all night.

Something is missing in such a sentence; the breakdown in parallelism makes it seem that they could "see talk" all night. The writer must mean this instead.

Parallel: They could see a movie or a play, **or** they could talk all night.

Making Lists and Outlines

In lists and outlines the meaning is clear only when the items are parallel.

Faulty:

Americans now rely on the automobile because:
1. cities are sprawling; public transport poor
2. habit
3. the cheapness of gasoline for so long
4. parking lots provided for employees and students by businesses and schools.

Parallel:

Americans now rely on the automobile because:
1. cities are sprawling and public transport is poor
2. they have formed the habit of driving cars everywhere
3. gasoline was cheap for a long time
4. businesses and schools provide parking lots for employees and students, encouraging them to drive.

Repeating Words

Repetition helps achieve parallelism and adds a certain rhythm or emphasis to your sentences. You do not always have to make that choice, but from time to time, repetition will strengthen your style.

Note that the sentences *without* repeated elements in the following examples are correct and parallel. They are simply not as strong.

They thought it was better **to** agree than quarrel.

Parallel: They thought it was better **to** agree than **to** quarrel.

They searched for the lost keys **in** the house, yard, and street.

Parallel: They searched for the lost keys **in** the house, **in** the yard, and **in** the street.

For the handicapped, getting an education is often **a** tribulation, necessity, and victory.

Parallel: For the handicapped, getting an education is often **a** tribulation, **a** necessity, and **a** victory.

I decided to leave when I realized **that** I had offended him, he was angry, and my apology would do no good.

Parallel: I decided to leave when I realized **that** I had offended him, **that** he was angry, and **that** my apology would do no good.

■ **Exercise 6.4** Rewrite the following sentences to create parallel forms.

1. Harrison Ford was a hot-rod driver in *American Graffiti,* a rocketship pilot in *Star Wars,* and he played Indiana Jones, the archaeologist in *Raiders of the Lost Ark,* and was an injured lawyer in *Regarding Henry.*
2. Orson Welles starred on radio, he directed and appeared in movies, and toward the end of his life advertised wine on television.
3. We biked around the reservoir, over the hills, enjoyed the country roads, and we ended at the ice cream store.
4. In the summer I like to visit Lake Louise, race along the shoreline by bike, or enjoy fishing from my uncle's rickety boat.
5. Many people in America are unhappy because of jobs not leading anywhere, with their families, and they don't like where they live either.

■ **Exercise 6.5** Revise the following sentences to repeat introductory words before parallel forms to make the parallelism more striking.

1. The new ultralight aircraft can land on a sandbar, back lot, or open field.
2. She enjoyed buying antique cars, refinishing them, and to drive a shining vehicle down Main Street every Sunday afternoon.
3. They piled their books on the sofa, tables, and beds.
4. She made three promises—that she would try the machine out, write up a report about it, and tell her friends if she liked it.
5. The railroad tracks passed through a tunnel and then over a river and highway.

Parallel Clauses

To make clauses parallel, introduce them in the same way. If you begin a clause with *and which, and that, and who,* or *and whom,* be sure that it follows a clause that begins with *which, that, who,* or *whom.*

> The peach tree, **with** its sugary fruit and **which** was not known in the Middle Ages, seems to have developed from the almond.
>
> **Parallel:** The peach tree, **which** has a sugary fruit and **which** was not known in the Middle Ages, seems to have developed from the almond.

6c
parallel

> Walt Whitman, **influenced by Emerson** and **whom multitudes loved,** was the first great American poet to praise cities in his verse.
>
> **Parallel:** Walt Whitman, **whom Emerson influenced** and **whom multitudes loved,** was the first great American poet to praise cities in his verse.
>
> Walt Whitman, **whom Emerson influenced and multitudes loved,** was the first great American poet to praise cities in his verse.

✔ CHECKLIST 6.1: ARRANGING SENTENCE ELEMENTS TO CLARIFY MEANING

As you revise your sentences, consider the relation of sentence structure to meaning. Ask yourself these questions.

- Are ideas of equal importance presented with coordination?
- Are ideas of equal importance presented through parallel structures?
- Are ideas of unequal importance presented through subordination?

■ **Exercise 6.6** Revise the following sentences to make good parallel constructions.

1. The movie *Gone with the Wind,* filmed in Technicolor and which cost millions of dollars to make, was the first talking movie about the Civil War to be a success at the box office.
2. Television, the great rival to the movies and which movie people hated at first, was not allowed to show the Academy Awards until 1952.
3. Many Japanese Americans, treated badly in this country during the war and who were sent to internment camps, shared their thoughts and feelings at the recent Pearl Harbor memorial services.

4. She hoped to win her first marathon, the one she entered at Boston and which led over a hilly course.
5. He brought home a new computer, very compact, expanded memory, expensive, and which he could not afford.

EMPHASIS
AND VARIETY

Two ways to gain and keep readers' attention are to provide proper emphasis and to supply variety. When you arrange information carefully in a sentence, you can emphasize important ideas and put less emphasis on less important ideas. When sentences vary in pattern and length, your ideas will engage your readers' attention more readily and the monotonous repetition of the same forms will not distract your readers.

7a
Using Periodic Sentences

A **periodic sentence** has a strong word or phrase at the end, just before the period. The complete meaning is apparent only when you come to the end and have read the last few words.

> If asked to name the central quality in Faulkner's work, one is likely to give the quick answer "Imagination."
>
> —MALCOLM COWLEY

Sometimes a periodic sentence ends with a striking thought rather than with a striking word.

> The original Hopalong Cassidy was created by Clarence E. Mulford, a Brooklyn marriage-license clerk who at the time had never even seen the West.
>
> —JAMES HORWITZ

When you have several facts to convey in a sentence, it is nearly always a good idea to put the more important ones toward the end to give a sense of building toward a climax. The most important fact in the following sentence is the part played by John Muir in establishing Yosemite National Park, not the fact of his wearing a beard:

> **Wrong emphasis:**   John Muir, the naturalist who was more responsible than any other single person for establishing Yosemite National Park, took long, solitary walks and let his beard grow long and tangled.

> **Revised:**   John Muir, a naturalist who took long, solitary walks and let his beard grow long and tangled, was more responsible than any other person for establishing Yosemite National Park.

**7b
emph**

7b
Avoiding Weak Endings

A weak ending lets readers down because it leaves them with a sense of unfinished business or a sense that they've been taken in—that the writer has no real goal in mind.

> **Weak:**   Young people in 1946 and 1947 turned from the horrors of World War II to a love affair with the jukebox, however.

> **Better:**   Young people in 1946 and 1947, however, turned from the horrors of World War II to a love affair with the jukebox.

> **Weak:**   The huge demonstrations in Washington against the Vietnamese war in the 1960s may not have been supported by a majority of the American people, nevertheless.

> **Better:**   Nevertheless, the huge demonstrations in Washington against the Vietnamese war in the 1960s may not have been supported by a majority of the American people.

■ **Exercise 7.1**   Rewrite the sentences below to make periodic sentences. If necessary, delete some words and phrases or invent others that capture the central idea.

1. Adlai Stevenson, laboring against the awesome power of Dwight Eisenhower's smile, lost the presidential elections of 1952 and 1956, as everyone knows.
2. Fiction writers do not often talk very well to interviewers about how they write, so Malcolm Cowley says.
3. The inspector found the body in the kitchen. When she had arrived on the scene, the house was locked and silent. She had the officers break down the door.

7c
Using Free Modifiers and Absolutes

In a **cumulative sentence,** several free modifiers or absolutes are appended to the predicate, thus giving new layers of meaning to the basic assertion of the clause.

A **free modifier** is a participle or participial phrase that occurs at the end of a clause and modifies the subject. The free modifiers in the following sentences are in boldface type.

> The motorcycle spun out of control, **leaving the highway, plunging down the ravine, crashing through a fence, coming to rest at last on its side.**

> The ocean beat against the shore in long swells, **roaring above the sound of the wind, threatening the tiny houses, slamming against the great rocks on the beach.**

An **absolute** (discussed on p. 115) consists of a noun and a participle. At the end of the clause it modifies, an absolute adds meaning to the whole. The absolutes in the following sentences are in boldface.

> He crossed the finish line in record time, **his lungs nearly bursting with his effort.**

> The barn burned, **the flames rising two hundred feet into the night sky.**

A cumulative sentence may use absolutes or free modifiers or both. A noncumulative sentence completes its thought with a subject complement, a direct object, or an adverb with an adverbial phrase. The sentence below concludes its thought with an adverbial phrase.

> The house stood silently **on the hill.**

But the sentence can be revised so that it completes its thought with absolutes and free modifiers.

> The house stood silently on the hill, baking in the hot sunshine, its broken windows gaping open to the ragged fields, its roof collapsing, its rotting doors hanging open, its glory departed.

Study the following cumulative sentences, and see how elements added to the end of the predicate help them accumulate force.

He emptied them thoroughly, **unhurried, his face completely cold, masklike almost.**

—WILLIAM FAULKNER

Another characteristic was that once a Veragua had caught and gored a man or a horse he would not leave him but would attack again and again, **seeming to want to destroy his victim entirely.**

—ERNEST HEMINGWAY

■ **Exercise 7.2** Combine the following sentences to make cumulative sentences.

Example:
He sat at the typewriter. His teacup was at his left. The wind was blowing outside. The clock was ticking over the fireplace.

He sat at the typewriter, his teacup at his left, the clock ticking over the fireplace, the wind blowing outside.

1. She studied the map of the block. She was thinking of the fine old buildings that would have to be torn down. She was thinking of her own creation that would take their place. Her ideas were rushing in her head like a flood.
2. He got down from the train and looked around. He saw the courthouse. He saw the city square. It was vacant at this hour of the morning.
3. She saw him. He was working in the field. He was holding a long black hoe. His father gave it to him many years ago.

■ **Exercise 7.3** Look around the room where you are sitting and write three cumulative sentences that describe some of the things you see.

7d
Using the Active Voice

In general, use the active rather than the passive voice. The subject of a sentence in the active voice performs the action of the verb; the subject of a sentence in the passive voice is acted upon. (The active and passive voices of verbs are discussed on p. 257.) Look at the difference:

Weak: His decision not to run for reelection to the presidency in 1968 was announced on television on March 31 of that year by Lyndon Johnson.

Revised: On March 31, 1968, President Lyndon Johnson announced on television that he would not run for reelection in the fall.

As a rule, use the passive voice only when the actor or agent in the sentence is much less important to your statement than the recipient of the action.

Estes Kefauver **was elected** to the Senate in 1948.

She **was taken** to the hospital last night.

Passive voice constructions have a way of creeping into our writing, and it pays to look at your revisions with an eye to using the active voice. A good rule of thumb is that whenever you use the passive voice, explain to yourself why you chose it over the active voice.

7e
Emphasizing with Repetition

Add emphasis by repeating key words or phrases in consecutive clauses or sentences.

Let every nation know, whether it wishes us well or ill, that we shall pay *any* price, bear *any* burden, meet *any* hardship, support *any* friend, oppose *any* foe to assure the survival and the success of liberty.

—JOHN F. KENNEDY

7f
Varying Sentence Length

Give special emphasis to ideas by writing a very short sentence to follow several long ones.

The real objection to capital punishment doesn't lie against the actual extermination of the condemned, but against our brutal American habit of putting it off so long. After all, every one of us must die soon or late, and a murderer, it must be assumed, is one who makes that sad fact the cornerstone of his metaphysic. But it is one thing to die, and quite another thing to lie for long months and even years under the shadow of death. *No sane man would choose such a finish.*

—H. L. MENCKEN

7g
variety

■ **Exercise 7.4**   Rewrite the following sentences to emphasize the elements you think are most important or most dramatic. You may change or delete words and phrases as long as you keep the central idea. Try to find several ways of dealing with each sentence.

1. The college library was locked up by the head librarian, G. W. Cranshaw, who said he got tired of seeing all those careless and sweaty students handling the books.
2. How strongly we believe in something, especially when it is something we think we ought to believe and maybe don't but won't admit it, and somebody comes and asks us if we believe it, is not measured well by statistics.
3. Now swimmers can buy little floats with bright colors on the top and clamps on the bottom under the water, and they can swim out to sea and take off their bathing suits and clamp them with the clamps and go skinny dipping if they want to.

7g
Varying Sentence Type

Sentence variety is the spice of lively writing, and you should strive to write sentences varied enough to hold your readers' attention throughout your paper.

   Vary the patterns and the lengths of sentences to keep readers alert and involved. If you repeat any sentence pattern too often, you will bore your readers. It is a good idea to learn and practice variations in the basic writing pattern. The basic pattern in modern English writing is *subject + predicate* (discussed on pp. 85-92). In this example, the subject is in bold and the predicate is in regular type.

   My father and my stepmother left on the noon plane to Atlanta.

The most common variation on this pattern is to begin with some kind of adverbial opener.

By the late afternoon, they will be at home.

Because they live so far away, we see them only once or twice a year.

Tomorrow they will telephone.

Another variation is to begin with a participle or a participial phrase that serves as an adjective.

Smiling, he walked confidently into the room.

Stunned by the stock market crash, many brokers committed suicide.

Sentences also can open with an infinitive phrase or a coordinating conjunction.

> **To protect my mother,** I'd made up stories of a secret marriage that for some strange reason never got known.
>
> —SHERWOOD ANDERSON

> **But,** say you, it is a question of interest, and if you make it your interest, you have the right to enslave another. Very well. *And* if he can make it his interest, he has the right to enslave you.
>
> —ABRAHAM LINCOLN

In the first passage below, the sentences all begin with the subject; they are all about the same length; and they are all short. They are clear and understandable, but notice the improvement in the second passage, where the combined and embedded elements create a pleasing variety in both length and sentence structure.

He dived quickly into the sea. He peered through his mask. The watery world turned darker. A school of fish went by. The distant light glittered on their bodies. He stopped swimming. He waited. He thought the fish might be chased by a shark. He satisfied himself that there was no shark. He continued down. He heard only one sound. That was his breathing apparatus. It made a bubbling noise in operation.

He dived quickly into the sea, peering through his mask at a watery world that turned darker as he went down. A school of fish went by, the distant light glittering on their bodies, and he stopped swimming and waited a moment to see if the fish might be chased by a shark. Satisfying himself that there was no shark, he continued down. The only sound he heard was the bubbling noise of his breathing apparatus.

The improved version combines thoughts, reduces the number of sentences, and cuts down the repetition of the pronoun *he*. The sentence patterns now are more varied and interesting.

7h
Using Rhetorical Questions

Asking a question will require your reader to participate more actively. Questions that require no answer or for which the answer is demonstrably obvious are called **rhetorical questions.**

> Is not marriage an open question, when it is alleged, from the beginning of the world, that such as are in the institution wish to get out; and such as are out wish to get in?
>
> —RALPH WALDO EMERSON

Rhetorical questions that allow the writer to supply the answer can sometimes be effective transitional devices.

> The movie is called *Rock 'n Roll High School,* and for anyone not into punk, it has only one conceivable point of interest: Can Van Patten act as well as he hits a tennis ball? The answer is no, which is not to say that he isn't a promising young actor. It's just that as a tennis player he is a good deal more than fine.
>
> —*Sports Illustrated*

But avoid beginning an essay with broad rhetorical questions that might better be phrased as sharp thesis statements. ''Why should we study *Huckleberry Finn?*'' ''How did the Peace Corps begin?'' ''Was Rodney King guilty as charged?'' Such openings may lead readers to suspect that the writer did not take the trouble to think of something better. Save your rhetorical questions for an occasional paragraph that comes in the body of a paper after you introduce your subject in some other way.

7i
Using Exclamations

Occasionally an exclamation helps vary a series of declarative sentences, but use this sentence type only on rare occasions and for special effects.

Clearly, even if there were a limit on the length of sentences to twenty words, it would not be possible to characterize any individual knowledge of English by claiming that he carried around a list of all its sentences in his head! But there is in fact no limit to the length of a sentence. A sentence twenty-one words in length can be made longer by adding another modifier or a subordinate of some kind—and so on.

—HELEN S. CAIRNS AND CHARLES E. CAIRNS

7i

variety

✔ **CHECKLIST 7.1: STRENGTHENING SENTENCE EMPHASIS AND VARIETY**

As you revise your sentences, consider reworking sentence patterns for proper emphasis and pleasing variety.

Emphasis

Analyze one sentence at a time. For appropriate emphasis, consider these options.

- Promote rhythm or cadence through deliberate repetition.
- Strengthen the sentence ending by making the sentence periodic.
- Strengthen the sentence ending by making the sentence cumulative.
- Strengthen the sentence action by making the voice active.

Variety

Analyze one paragraph at a time. If the sentences are monotonous, consider these options.

- Vary sentence length.
- Vary sentence openings with adverbs.
- Vary sentence openings with participles or participial phrases.
- Vary sentence openings with infinitive phrases.
- Vary sentence openings with coordinating conjunctions.
- Invert subject and verb.
- Use a rhetorical question.
- Use an exclamation.

7j
Inverting Subject and Verb

For variety, you can put the verb before the subject. This is another device to use only rarely:

> Beyond is another country.
>
> —ROBERT M. PIRSIG

7j

variety

> From high above in the swirl of raging wind and snow came a frightening, wonderful, mysterious sound.
>
> —MARK HELPRIN

■ **Exercise 7.5**   Revise the following set of simple sentences to form two coherent paragraphs made up of sentences that are varied in style and in length. You may change or add words but not facts. Look for places where you can subordinate one idea to another, both to reduce the number of words and to create a pleasing style. Experiment. Try the techniques of sentence revision described in Chapters 5–7. Compare your version with the work of others in your class.

1. Bluegrass music was popular in the rural south before World War II.
2. It features hand-held instruments.
3. These include the banjo, the guitar, the fiddle, the mandolin, and sometimes the dulcimer and the bass fiddle.
4. Bluegrass songs are in the tradition of the mountain ballad and the Protestant hymn.
5. It began as the music of poor southern American mountaineers.
6. Bluegrass songs are about love affairs gone wrong.
7. Sometimes they speak about the fear of hell.
8. Sometimes they describe conversion experiences.
9. Sometimes they express the yearning of the soul for heaven.
10. Bluegrass bands never use electrified instruments.

THREE

USING WORDS
EFFECTIVELY

CHAPTER

8

CHOOSING TONE AND DICTION

The language you choose conveys more than the meaning of individual words. It says something about you—the writer—as well as something about what you think of your audience. Careful writers control their language so that their writing conveys what they mean on all levels. In revising drafts of paragraphs and sentences, be sure to pay attention to tone and diction. **Tone** is the style and manner of your expression—formal or informal, highly technical or broadly appealing. **Diction** is the specific word choice that achieves clarity, accuracy, and effectiveness.

In writing and revising, your goal should be to use language appropriate to your subject. Choose the tone and diction that fit your topic. Select words that state your meaning exactly. Avoid a style that is too informal or chatty, but don't be stiff and pompous. A breezy, informal tone is not appropriate for a paper on cancer treatments, nor is a sober tone appropriate for an essay on hang gliding. Don't write about the World Series or the Super Bowl as if they were as important as war or disease.

The best way to gain a sense of language is to read as much as you can. Whether you are preparing to write about literature or natural science or history, take some time to read what writers in the field have written. Try to use their tone and diction as models for your own style.

8a
Checking Diction

When you revise, examine your word choice to be sure it is appropriate for your subject and purpose. Slang, dialect, jargon, and foreign terms have a place in communication, but they may create barriers and wrong impressions.

Using Slang

Slang words are emotional but inexact; they are also only briefly in use. Use slang only when it is appropriate to the subject and tone of your essay. Consider the following pairs of sentences.

Inappropriate: In *Heart of Darkness,* we hear a lot about a dude named Kurtz, but we don't see the guy much.

Revised: In *Heart of Darkness,* Marlow, the narrator, talks almost continually about Kurtz, but we see Kurtz himself only at the end.

Inappropriate: When Thomas More saw how Henry VIII was going, he might have run off to France to save his hide, but he stayed on and got his head chopped off for his trouble.

Revised: When he saw the direction of Henry's mind, Thomas More might have fled to France to save himself, but he stayed on until he was imprisoned and put to death.

**8a
diction**

Some slang terms are always entering the mainstream of the language, and many American journalists adopt a breezy, informal tone. But even these journalists do not fill their prose with slang. Instead, they use slang to fit a special mood that they are trying to convey.

But Boston is also a city that historically has pricked the social conscience of many well-heeled undergraduates.

—Howard Husock

Minutes before the camera's ruby light flashed on, cable TV's garrulous impresario was already well into his inaugural address before a gathering of Atlanta VIPs.

—*Time*

Even when an informal tone is appropriate, be cautious. Slang can spoil good writing and make careful readers scorn your work. Never try to be cute when you write.

You must use slang, however, if it is part of a direct quotation. There the prose is not yours but that of your source, and you must quote that source exactly if you are using quotation marks.

"He whopped me good," Turner said of the tackle that made him fumble.

Using Dialect

Some inexperienced writers use dialect to show the ethnic or regional origins of people, but dialect is very difficult to do correctly. Inexperienced writers frequently get it wrong and may appear to be making fun of the people they are writing about.

> **Dialect:** "Ah'm a-goin' raght over thar," she said, "an if'n you'd go along, hit'ud be a big hep, and Ah'd be much obleeged."

> **Revised:** "I'm going right over there," she said with a strong Appalachian accent, "and if you'd go along, it'd be a big help, and I'd be much obliged."

Avoiding Jargon and Technical Terms

**8a
diction**

Jargon is the language of specialists. It includes unfamiliar words, new compounds, and ordinary English words used in ways that are unfamiliar to most people. For example, people who use computers speak of "booting a disk," making "hard copies," and "accessing the program."

Jargon has a place when specialists talk to each other, but if you want to be sure your readers understand you, avoid jargon. It not only makes simple thoughts seem complicated, but it puts people off, making them feel like outsiders. Experienced readers rarely take jargon seriously. Consider this paragraph written by an academic author.

> **Jargon:** Romantic love is characterized by a preoccupation with a deliberately restricted set of perceived characteristics in the love object which are viewed as a means to some ideal ends. In the process of selecting the set of perceived characteristics and the process of determining the ideal ends, there is also a systematic failure to assess the accuracy of the perceived characteristics and the feasibility of achieving the ideal ends given the selected set of means and other pre-existing ends.

The paragraph means something like the following.

> **Revised:** People in love see only what they want to see in the beloved. They want to believe in an ideal, so they do not question the accuracy of what they see or ask themselves if the ideal they imagine can be attained.

Here is another example. Notice how pompous the unrevised writing sounds.

Pretentious: Baxter felt a pang of existential anxiety when he contemplated his English exam.

Revised: Baxter worried about his English exam when he thought about it.

Jargon and technical terms from one field are always inappropriate in another.

Jargon: The interface of the Honors Committee and the dean's office impacted student access to rare books.

Revised: Relations between the Honors Committee and the dean's office affected student access to rare books.

When you think you may be using unnecessary jargon, ask yourself what you are really trying to say. Put that meaning in the simplest sentence you can write. Don't use words most people do not understand unless they are necessary to say exactly what you want to say.

**8a
diction**

Avoiding Obsolete and Foreign Terms

Obsolete or archaic words and expressions can confuse your reader or misstate your meaning; they may also distract your reader from your subject into wondering about you.

Archaic: It was clear ere she left that the problems had not been resolved.

Revised: It was clear before she left that the problems had not been resolved.

Use foreign words only when they are necessary. It is pretentious to use foreign expressions when English will do.

Pretentious: Her collection of exotic clamshells was her only *raison d'être.*

Better: Her collection of exotic clamshells was her only reason for living.

Pretentious: Sarah's *Weltanschauung* extended no further than her daily whims.

Better: Sarah's view of the world extended no further than her daily whims.

■ **Exercise 8.1**   Rewrite the following sentences to change language that might be inappropriate in a formal paper. Try to keep the meaning of each sentence intact.

1. When the ump called nine consecutive strikes on three batters, Manager Sparky Anderson got his back up.
2. When the Germans were presented with the Treaty of Versailles in 1919, they really got sore.
3. Maybe the concert of the Boston Symphony Orchestra will be so wicked that the audience will fork over megabucks to go with the flow.
4. Ross Perot was a shrewd old geezer who made a pile of money and decided to go for broke in 1992 by running for President.

■ **Exercise 8.2**   Rewrite the following sentences to eliminate foreign words or stilted expressions. You may need to look up words in your desk dictionary. Don't try to translate the foreign words literally; try to put their meaning into fresh, idiomatic English.

1. The freshmen thought that the *summum bonum* of college life was to own a convertible.
2. Max said that if his roommate kept on smoking cigars in bed at night, it would be a *casus belli.*
3. A common multidimensional learning problem for students of the typewriter and the violin is the dexterity factor, for in both cases erroneous application of the fingers has the end result of a negative production response.
4. A sophomore is a kind of *tertium quid* between freshman and upper-class students.

8b
diction

8b
Using Idioms Correctly

Idioms are habitual ways of saying things, and they usually cannot be translated from one language to another. Sometimes they cannot be transferred from one region to another within a country. If you say in French to a Frenchman, "I'm going to eat a hot dog with mustard," he will hide his pet poodle. If you ask a mountain southerner in the United States for a poke, he will hand you a paper bag; if you ask a New Yorker, he may hit you in the mouth.

Idioms involve more than regional speech. They are customary forms of expression that are not always logical. Often they involve selection of the right preposition. We are not angry *against,* but angry *with;* we do not go *with* the car but *in* the car or, simply, *by* car. The same point can be made about the phrase *different than.* We say "Fred is *different from* his older brother," not "Fred is *different than* his older brother."

Some verbs may take particles (see p. 95) to clarify their meaning. Particles look like prepositions, but they are really a part of the verb form, and they can make a big difference.

Harry made **up** with Gloria.

Harry made **off** with Gloria.

Harry made **out** with Gloria.

Selecting the right particle involves knowing idiomatic English. Sometimes particles aren't needed, and they should be eliminated when they don't add or detract meaning.

8b diction

Draft: We will meet **up** with him in Denver.

Revised: We will meet him in Denver.

Idiom is difficult because it is a reflection of customary speech patterns, and custom often refuses to obey logical rules. Inexperienced writers often have trouble with idioms when they use unfamiliar words or expressions and do not know how to put them together the way experienced writers use them.

■ **Exercise 8.3**   Rewrite the following sentences to correct mistakes in idiom.

1. We celebrate Labor Day at the first Monday after the first Sunday in September.
2. Lyndon Johnson became president on November 1963.
3. My mother introduced me with her friend.
4. Previous to the meeting, we agreed to talk only an hour before adjourning.
5. Newton's general principle states that all bodies have a force of gravity proportionate with their mass.
6. Jazz music has been traditionally centered around the experience of black musicians playing in small groups.
7. He deaned the faculty for ten years and then returned to teaching because he wanted to make something of himself.
8. The sun arose that morning at six o'clock.

9. Shiela's dress needs ironed.
10. Where's it at?
11. Computers promise to us much more efficiency than typewriters could ever give.
12. Tom used a strip of masking tape to get the fur of cat off the seat.

✔ **CHECKLIST 8.1: CHECKING TONE AND DICTION**

As you revise paragraphs and sentences, think about tone and diction—the tone you want your writing to set and the impression you want it to convey. Examine your choice of words. Ask yourself these questions.

- Is the tone appropriate for the subject?
- Is the tone appropriate for the audience?
- Are slang words, dialect, jargon, obsolete and foreign terms, if they appear at all, used deliberately and with full awareness of their meaning and the impression they convey?
- Are idioms correct?
- Are connotations correct?

8c
Undertanding Denotations and Connotations

Words have both primary meanings, called **denotations,** and secondary meanings, called **connotations.** Connotations allow some **synonyms—** words with the same meaning—to work in some contexts and not in others. You can say that your friend Murdock *evaded* the requirement that everyone learn how to swim before graduation, or you can say that he *flouted* it, or you can say that he *escaped* it. Each way we know that Murdock did not learn how to swim and that he did not obey the rule. But if he *evaded* the rule, he slipped away from it slyly. If he *flouted* the requirement, he may have announced publicly and arrogantly that he did not intend to observe the requirement. If he *escaped* the requirement, something may have happened to make the college forget to enforce the rule for him.

Here are some words with similar denotations but different connotations.

requested, demanded
ignored, neglected
unsympathetic, intolerant
confused, dazed

Beginning writers often have trouble with connotations. The best remedies are to note how experienced writers use different words and to study the dictionary for various connotations. Beware of using a thesaurus, as it lists synonyms only. If you're not sure of a synonym's connotation, consult a dictionary.

■ **Exercise 8.4**   Write sentences that use the following words correctly. You may use several of the words in one sentence if you can do so gracefully.

1. ambitious, greedy
2. successful, enterprising
3. proud, arrogant, haughty
4. hit, smash, collide
5. drink, guzzle, sip
6. eat, gobble, pick at

**8c
diction**

USING IMAGERY AND FIGURATIVE LANGUAGE

Lively writing creates word pictures for the reader. With concrete nouns and verbs that appeal to the senses, you can change an abstract idea into something vivid and specific. If you write, "The trees were affected by the bad weather," you do not give your readers much to picture in their minds. But if you write, "The small pines shook in the wind," the concrete nouns and the verb create an image.

Figurative language helps you build images. A **figure** states or implies a comparison between your subject and something else. If you write, "The small pines shook in the wind," you are being literal. If you write, "The small pines trembled with fear like children scolded by the wind," you are being figurative. The figure compares the trees to frightened children and the wind to a person scolding them. The English language is rich in figures because they help express ideas clearly and succinctly.

9a
Using Concrete Nouns and Verbs

Nouns and verbs that are specific rather than general create an image and have an impact. Generic, unspecified nouns (*tree*, instead of *pine*) and verbs (*were affected*, instead of *shook*) merely report that something happened, but not what. Examine this paragraph.

Often the positions people take on energy are an index to how they stand on other issues. Conservatives, liberals, and radicals tend to congregate in causes, and if you tell me where you think we ought to get our energy, I can probably tell you what you think about what we ought to eat and how we ought to spend our time. But nearly everybody on every side of every current issue agrees that we should use solar energy.

This paragraph contains no errors in grammar, and it is fairly clear. But its prose style does not engage our attention, and when we finish reading it, we have a hard time remembering it.

Now study this version (italics added).

> Every source of energy seems to have become a political issue. Tell me whether you think the path to a happy future lies with *solar heating* or with *nuclear furnaces,* tell me how you feel about *oil shale* and *coal* and *corn-fed gasohol,* and I'll tell you where you stand on *welfare reform, environmental policy, vegetarianism, busing, back-packing,* and *abortion.* But there is one kind of energy that attracts a diverse following: *photovoltaics,* the art of converting *sunlight* into *electricity.*
>
> —TRACY KIDDER

9b imag/fig

Notice how the italicized words—all concrete nouns—create a strong impression.

■ **Exercise 9.1**   Read the following paragraph and pick out the concrete details.

> In the smallest of these huts lived old Berl, a man in his eighties, and his wife, who was called Berlcha (wife of Berl). Old Berl was one of the Jews who had been driven from their villages in Russia and had settled in Poland. In Lentshin, they mocked the mistakes he made while praying aloud. He spoke with a sharp "r." He was short, broad-shouldered, and he had a small white beard, and summer and winter he wore a sheepskin hat, a padded cotton jacket, and stout boots. He walked slowly, shuffling his feet. He had a half acre of field, a cow, a goat, and chickens.
>
> —ISAAC BASHEVIS SINGER

9b
Using Metaphors and Similes

Comparisons can make your prose more vivid, but be sure they are appropriate to your subject, your tone, and your audience.

A **simile** is a comparison that uses the word *like* or *as.*

My love is **like** a red, red rose.

—ROBERT BURNS

Tom Birch is as brisk **as** a bee in conversation.

—SAMUEL JOHNSON

Mortality weighs heavily upon me **like** an unwilling sleep.

—JOHN KEATS

A **metaphor,** or implied comparison, speaks of things or of actions as if they were something other than what they are. Because of its compression, a metaphor may have stronger force than a simile.

The dice are the gods of the backgammon wars.

—E. J. KAHN, JR.

Marcel Duchamp once referred to dealers as ''lice on the backs of artists''—useful and necessary lice, he added, but lice all the same.

—*New Yorker*

At least half of all writers, major or minor, have suffered from writing blocks—from inner resistance to dragging oneself, hour after hour, to the bar of self-judgment, and forcing oneself, before it, to confront that most intimidating of objects to any writer: the blank page waiting to be filled.

—WALTER JACKSON BATE

■ **Exercise 9.2**   Complete the simile that will describe each of the following actions or objects. Try to avoid any similes that you have heard before. Add as many words as you need.

   1. My mother was as angry as _____.
   2. The biscuits were as light and fluffy as _____.
   3. The coin gleamed in his hand like _____.
   4. My flower garden was as wild as _____.
   5. Our football team was as inept as a group of _____.

■ **Exercise 9.3**   Write a descriptive paragraph on two of the following subjects, using a simile and a metaphor in each.

   1. the first time you voted in a national election
   2. a child learning that her parents will be divorced

3. the announcement that your father has won a beauty contest
4. deciding to buy a new car
5. recognizing that a friend is an alcoholic

✔ **CHECKLIST 9.1: BUILDING WORD PICTURES**

As you revise, look for ways to make your language strong and lively. Reflect on how you express yourself. Can you make your expressions more memorable? Can you recast them to build word pictures? Ask yourself these questions.

■ Are there generic, unspecified nouns that can be replaced with concrete nouns?

■ Can static verbs or passive voice constructions be replaced with strong, action-oriented verbs?

■ Can a simile be introduced?

■ Can an action or impression be recast as a metaphor?

■ Are cliché's making the prose seem tired (and the reader, too)?

**9c
imag/fig**

**9c
Avoiding Clichés**

A **cliché** is an overworked expression. The moment we read the first word or two of a cliché, we know how it will end. If someone says, "She was as mad as a _____," we expect the sentence to be completed by the words *wet hen* or *hornet*. If someone says, "My biscuits were as light as _____," we expect the sentence to be completed by *a feather*. If someone says, "His prose is as heavy as _____," we expect the sentence to end with *lead*.

We have heard these expressions so often that our minds are dead to them even when we understand what they mean, and they no longer create vivid pictures in our imaginations. The table on the next page lists some common clichés to avoid. You can probably think of others.

Usually it's best to rephrase a cliché as simply as you can in plain language.

Cliché: When John turned his papers in three weeks late, he had to *face the music.*

Better: When John turned his papers in three weeks late, he had to take the consequences.

Cliché: Harvey *kept his nose to the grindstone.*

Better: Harvey gave close and unceasing attention to his work.

■ **Exercise 9.4**   Rewrite the following sentences to eliminate the clichés. Be adventurous. Try to think up some similes or metaphors that convey the meaning of a cliché without repeating its tired words.

1. Although he had worked like a dog all week long, the conductor seemed as cool as a cucumber and as fresh as a daisy when he mounted the podium and raised his baton to his orchestra.
2. The letter announcing the prize came to her like a bolt from the blue, making her friends green with envy, while she herself felt worth her weight in gold.
3. Bollinger believed that he had a right to be president of the university, since he had paid his dues as a lower functionary for years, sometimes feeling in the depths of despair over the way people treated him like a dog, believing often that he was doomed to disappointment in life, but determined to put his shoulder to the wheel.

**9c
imag/fig**

COMMON CLICHÉS

abreast of the times	bustling cities	every dog has his day
acid test	calm, cool, and collected	face the music
add insult to injury	cold, hard facts	fair sex
agony of suspense	come to grips with	few and far between
beat a hasty retreat	cool as a cucumber	fire-engine red
better half	crazy as a loon	flat as a pancake
beyond the shadow of a doubt	dead as a doornail	gild the lily
blind as a bat	deaf as a post	green with envy
blue as the sky	deep, dark secret	heave a sigh of relief
bolt from the blue	depths of despair	heavy as lead
bottom line	diabolical skill	hit the nail on the head
brave as a lion	distaff side	in this day and age
brown as a nut	doomed to disappointment	ladder of success
brutal murder	drunk as a lord	

last but not least

little lady

live from hand to mouth

livid with rage

nose to the grind-stone

nutty as a fruitcake

110 percent

the other side of the coin

paint the town red

pale as a ghost

pass the buck

pick and choose

poor but honest

poor but proud

pretty as a picture

primrose path

proud possessor

quick as a flash

quiet as a church-mouse

reigns supreme

right as rain

rise and shine

rise to the occasion

sadder but wiser

sharp as a tack

shoulder to the wheel

sink or swim

smart as a whip

sneaking suspicion

sober as a judge

straight and narrow

tempest in a teapot

tired but happy

tried and true

ugly as sin

undercurrent of ex-citement

untimely death

walk the line

wax eloquent

white as a ghost

white as a sheet

worth its weight in gold

**9c
imag/fig**

CHAPTER 10

MAKING EVERY WORD COUNT

One key to good writing is making sure you have all the words you need to make your meaning clear—and no more. Extra words are something to avoid.

10a
Including Necessary Words

Include all the words that are necessary to make sentences clear and complete.

Completing Verbs

Many verb forms include several words. Helping verbs and particles are needed to make tense or meaning clear. Be sure to include all necessary verb parts.

> He **is writing** about the beehives.
>
> I **have seen** what he **has done.**
>
> She **has taken** a minute to rest.
>
> The plum pudding **was scorched** around the edges.
>
> Josie and Phil **felt** like **dressing up.**

Do not leave out part of a compound verb when the tense of one part of the verb varies from the tense of the other part.

> **Incomplete:** Caldwell **has** long and always **will be** sympathetic to those who think jogging is boring.

Revised: Caldwell **has** long **been** and always **will be** sympathetic to those who think jogging is boring.

Using the Subordinator *That*

In **indirect discourse**—statements rephrasing the statements of others without directly quoting—the subordinator *that* introduces the subordinate clause. Sometimes it is necessary.

> He sent the message **that** canoes were unable to navigate the Platte River.

But sometimes it is not. Omit *that* only if the subordinate clause is so simple that its meaning is instantly clear.

> Loretta Lynn sang songs women love.

**10a
clar**

■ **Exercise 10.1**   Check the following sentences for missing words. Add words where they are needed. If a sentence is clear and grammatical as it stands, put a check by the number.

1. He told the staff men and women deserve equal pensions.
2. He taken the car to a junkyard and found many people in business suits now go to junkyards to get parts for old cars they want to keep running a few more years.
3. I been here now for thirty years and never seen so little rain.
4. Air travel getting so expensive only the rich and people on business able to afford it now.
5. She told her daughter driving across the country and staying in motels were much more expensive than flying.
6. I will have been sick for two weeks on Monday and tomorrow see a doctor.

Using Articles, Prepositions, and Pronouns

Include the articles, prepositions, and pronouns that are necessary for idiomatic expressions.

ESL 12

> All **the** people in the room had quit smoking.
>
> A dog that bites should be kept on **a** leash.
>
> He gave me **the** books he liked best.

This kind **of** dog is noted for its affection.

He did not like taking **from** or giving **to** the fund.

You do not have to repeat a preposition before every word in a series, but if you do repeat it before any of those words, you must repeat it before all the words.

> **Draft:**   He loved her for her intelligence, her beauty, and **for** her money.

> **Revised:**   He loved her **for** her intelligence, **for** her beauty, and **for** her money

Making Comparisons Clear

Include a possessive form when you are comparing possessions or attributes.

> **Wordy:**   Plato's philosophy is easier to read than **that of** Aristotle.
> **Revised:**   Plato's philosophy is easier to read than **Aristotle's.**

Use *other* and *else* to show that people or things belong to a group with which they are being compared.

> *Gone with the Wind* won more awards than any **other** film in Hollywood history.

> Professor Koonig wrote more books than anyone **else** in the department.

Use the word *as* twice when you use it to compare people or things.

> His temper was **as** mild **as** milk.

Avoid the vague comparison implied in the word *that* used as a weak synonym for *very*.

> **Weak:**   Professor Koonig was not **that** dull.
> **Revised:**   Professor Koonig was not **very** dull.

When you are tempted to use *that* as a vague comparative, think of something concrete and lively, and use the comparative form *as . . . as* instead of *that*. Or use *so . . . that* and a clause.

Professor Koonig was not **as** dull **as** some cows I have known.

Professor Koonig was **so** dull **that** he could make flowers wither.

Be sure your comparisons are always complete. If you have just said, "Professor Koonig is dull," you can say immediately afterward, "Professor Donovan is more interesting." But you cannot say in isolation, "Professor Donovan is more interesting." You need to name who or what forms the rest of the comparison. You may say, "Professor Donovan is more interesting than Professor Koonig."

■ **Exercise 10.2**   Add words as they are needed in the following sentences. If a sentence is correct as it stands, put a check by the number.

1. She was happy as I have ever seen anyone when she graduated from West Point.
2. He took the car in to have the transmission replaced, the body painted, and seats covered.
3. This type grass seed does not do that well in shade.
4. The car I drove to the beach was worse than any car I have ever driven.
5. Pete Rose was not that fast, but he always played hard as a boy even when he was forty years old.

**10b
clar**

10b
Avoiding Wordiness

If you eliminate words that do not contribute to your meaning, you make every word count. Avoiding wordiness does not mean that you must write in short, choppy sentences or that you must reduce your prose to its bare bones. It does mean that every word should be necessary to your thought, because words that add nothing will obscure your meaning and bore your readers.

Eliminating Unnecessary Words

The following paragraph, a response to an assignment requiring an explanation of **expository writing,** is a good first draft, but it is entirely too wordy. The writer put down thoughts as fast as they came to mind, without pausing to edit. Then she revised the draft to eliminate wordiness and to make her points more effectively.

Draft: Briefly, expository writing is the kind of writing that develops an idea. It is not quite the same as narration, which tells a story, though you and I both know that narratives may contain many ideas. But that is not their main purpose. If I tell you that last night I was eating in a restaurant and found a pearl in my oyster, that is narration. And expository writing is not the kind of writing that describes something, though descriptions may include several of the most important ideas that a writer considers significant. If I describe how the campus looks under a deep, thick white snow and describe the way people wade through the snow and leave tracks on its pure and immaculate surface, then that is description. But if I go to the theater and see a play and come home and write down an interpretation of it, then I am doing expository writing even if part of the exposition is to describe the action of the play itself. And if I go on and talk about the aforesaid snow that I have talked about falling on the campus and if I tell the story about how the history department got out in it and started aggressively and energetically throwing snowballs at the dean, and if I then go on and try to explain why historians on this campus are at this point in time and always have been bellicose, then I am combining description, narration, and expository writing. But the main thing I want you to be conscious of is how you should classify the kinds of writing that are likely to go on in a single piece of writing and you've simply got to remember that it is not an example of expository writing unless it is writing about expounding an idea.

10b
clar

Revised: Expository writing develops ideas; narration tells stories; descriptions tell how things look. If I tell you that last night in a restaurant I found a pearl in an oyster, I am narrating. If I write of a deep snow on campus and how people wade through it and leave tracks, I am describing. But if I interpret a play, I am writing exposition, even if part of my essay describes the action of the play itself. And if I describe snow, and tell how the history department threw snowballs at the dean, and try to explain why historians at this university are bellicose, I am combining description, narration, and exposition. Remember that all three kinds of writing may appear in a single piece, but only expository writing interprets an idea.

The writer has recast the entire paragraph as well as several of its sentences. She has found ways to shorten sentences. She has presented her definitions at the beginning, as quickly as possible, and she has combined sentences to save words. (Helpful discussions are found in Chapters 5 and 6.)

Eliminating Redundant Constructions

As you revise for wordiness, look out for redundant words and phrases, the unnecessary repetitions that slip easily into first drafts. Conscious, deliberate repetition can help you emphasize ideas (see p. 151); meaningless repetition only makes for flabby sentences. Avoid redundant constructions.

The candidate repeated the answer again.

He expressed a number of clever expressions much to the audience's delight.

Her dress was blue in color.

■ **Exercise 10.3** Edit the following paragraphs to make them more concise.

I am going to tell you how much fun and profit there is in it for you to build your own house. If you have the time and a little energy and common sense, then you can build your very own house, save a ton of money, and have lots and lots of fun as you build your house. When it's all done and your house is standing there, built by you and maybe some members of your family, you will be proud of it, really proud. And think of all the fun you've had!

Most of us, including probably you and me, usually think there is some kind of strange, secret mystery to the occult art of carpentry, but building things with wood is not a mystery at all. It takes lots and lots of care and lots and lots of hard work, but just about anybody can do it. You can do it too. The enjoyment you'll experience as well as all the money you'll save will make you enjoy this experience.

10b

clar

■ **Exercise 10.4** Underline the redundancies in the following examples.

1. at three A.M. in the morning
2. in modern times in the twentieth century today
3. return to the old neighborhood again
4. in my opinion, I think
5. the autobiography of her life
6. resultant effect of the report
7. quite tiny in size
8. the surrounding environment
9. unemployed workers now out of work
10. rectangular in shape

Eliminating Fillers and "Waiting Words"

When we speak, we often use phrases that serve as "waiting words"—they let us keep talking while we think of something more to say. These waiting words often creep into writing, where they take up valuable room without doing any work. Common waiting words include *like, you know, sort of, kind of, what I mean is, so to speak, in other words,* and *in the final analysis.*

Other common phrases are cumbersome, roundabout, habitual ways of saying something when we need only a word or two. And some of them are junk—words we can get rid of altogether without losing any real meaning.

Study the checklist and the recommended substitutions.

✔ CHECKLIST 10.1: ELIMINATING FILLERS

10b clar

When you see	Substitute
■ at the present time ■ in the present circumstances ■ at this point in time ■ at this moment ■ in this day and age	now, today, nowadays
■ at that point in time ■ in those days ■ in that period	then
■ in many cases	often
■ in some cases	sometimes
■ in exceptional cases	rarely
■ in most cases	usually
■ consider as, consider as being	consider
■ prior to	before
■ subsequent to	after
■ despite the fact that ■ regardless of the fact that	although
■ due to the fact that ■ for the purpose of ■ by virtue of the fact that ■ the reason is because	because
■ in a position to, in order to	can
■ in the area of	near, in
■ in the event that ■ in the event of ■ in case of	if (*with a verb*): If fire breaks out . . .

■ in terms of	*Usually recast sentence to elimi-nate:*
The new curriculum was de-signed in terms of student needs and faculty ability.	The new curriculum considers both student needs and fac-ulty ability.
	The new curriculum was de-signed to match faculty abil-ity with student needs.
■ in the final analysis	finally, *or drop entirely*
■ in no uncertain terms	firmly, clearly, *or eliminate*
■ in the nature of	like
■ refer back	refer

10b

clar

■ **Exercise 10.5**   Edit the following sentences to eliminate redun-dancies and fillers.

1. He is of a complex character.
2. She is of a generous nature.
3. The car was of a green color.
4. The weather conditions are bad.
5. Traffic conditions are congested.
6. Ted's leg injury was a serious crisis for the soccer team.
7. LaToya gave the officer her personal opinion.
8. Wesley looked at the referee in a suspicious manner.
9. Through repeated practice Elise was able to master the free throw.
10. The old post office was razed to the ground to make way for the new shopping mall.

■ **Exercise 10.6**   Edit the following paragraph to eliminate unnec-essary words and phrases. You may find some words and phrases that are not in the checklist. Think hard about each sentence to see if you can eliminate padding and wordiness.

   Due to the fact that at this point in time we have an energy crisis of a severe nature, we need to devote ourselves to a good rethinking of the academic calendar. At the present time, schools in the area of the United States begin in September and end in May or June. The reason is because schools once upon a time used to begin right after the harvest in societies of an agricultural character. But by virtue of the fact that buildings must be heated in the wintertime, schools in the cold regions of the earth are now paying out millions of dollars for fuel bills—money that might do much more good if it were put into faculty salaries, student scholarships, the library fund, the athletic program, or things of these kinds and of that nature. A solution to the problem may be of a simple nature: make the academic calendar according to the weather conditions prevailing in the different areas where the schools happen to be located.

Avoiding Word Inflation

Do not inflate simple thoughts with overblown language (see p. 175).

10b
clar

Inflated: Owning a gun for protection could be a consequence of several other factors. It could be the logical extension of a general home defense orientation. One mode of behavior for individuals who are vulnerable to crime is to increase their personal security, which leads them to a general home defense orientation and the acquisition of a gun.

Better: Some people buy guns to defend their homes, especially when they feel threatened by crime.

Inflated: Lucinda Childs's early development as a choreographer in the 1960s paralleled the rise of minimalist art. And while her work is extremely complex in its patterning and ordering, this complexity is grounded in the permutations of simplicity expressed in a few steps and their repetition.

Better: Lucinda Childs' early choreography in the 1960s developed alongside the work of the minimalist painters. Although she creates complex patterns and sequences, she uses only a few simple steps repeated with slight changes.

✔ CHECKLIST 10.2: MAKING EVERY WORD COUNT

As you revise, check to see that all necessary words are in place. Examine each sentence. Ask yourself these questions.

- For multiple verbs, are all verb parts present?
- Is the subordinator *that* used when necessary?
- Is use of articles, prepositions, and pronouns idiomatic?
- Are comparisons complete?

Then look for words you can trim.

- Can any words be eliminated without sacrificing meaning?
- Have all redundancies been eliminated?
- Have fillers been eliminated or replaced?
- Has word inflation been successfully avoided?

■ **Exercise 10.7**   Edit the following sentences to make them more concise and clear. You may want to make two sentences where the writers have written one. Use the dictionary when you must.

1. A total site signage program is being studied, and if the study analysis dictates to relocate the stop sign, it will be done as a part of the total signage program and not as a result of your suggestion.
2. Dissatisfaction over the lack of responsiveness and accountability of decision makers is itself a primary source of the recent precipitous decline in confidence and trust that citizens hold for the national government.
3. We had no primary intention at that point in time to micromanage the news from the Persian Gulf war, but we did want to implement directives to keep people from knowing more than was good for them.

**10b
clar**

11

AVOIDING BIAS

Words can wound. No moral writer should ever wish to wound anyone by using words that injure others. Our language reflects the sad tendency of some human beings to identify groups as "the other," as people who are different and who are therefore to be scorned, mocked, humiliated, and even despised. Avoid **biased writing**—writing that continues stereotypes or that demeans, ignores, or patronizes people on the basis of gender, race, religion, country of origin, physical abilities or disabilities, sexual preference, or any other human condition. As this chapter makes clear, avoiding bias is a lot more complicated than simply not using derogatory words and slurs.

11a
Avoiding Sexism in Writing

Men and women should be treated as individuals, not primarily as members of opposite sexes. Neither sex should be stereotyped or arbitrarily assigned to a leading or secondary role.

Even those who are committed to the principle of equality have to guard against bias in writing. Our language is full of concepts, conventions, labels, and clichés that can slip into writing, perpetuating stereotypes and inequality even when we honestly do not mean to do so. Make sure your written expressions match your principles and intentions.

Avoiding Sexist Labels and Clichés

Many labels and clichés imply that women are not as able or as mature as men. Consider the meaning of words and phrases such as *lady, the weaker sex, the fair sex, the little woman, girl, gal, broad, dame, my better half, working mother, housewife, poetess,* and *coed.*

All these terms imply that women have only one proper role in society. *Ladylike,* for example, is often intended as a compliment but may in fact disparage women. A "ladylike" woman is polite and cooperative. She does not assert herself as successful men are expected to assert themselves, and she is not taken quite so seriously as men are. Behavior that in men is admired as *assertive* is often criticized in women as *abrasive* or *aggressive.*

Here are some clichés and labels to watch out for.

Women as appendages

Traditional titles such as *Mrs.* and *Miss,* identifying women either by their relationship to husbands or as without husbands, are an example of the way in which the conventions of the English language perpetuate inequality. Do not refer to women as *Mrs.* or *Miss* unless you are also referring to men as *Mr.,* and be certain when you use *Mrs.* or *Miss* that it is the woman's preference. If you are uncertain, use *Ms.,* a title introduced in the early 1970s to parallel *Mr.,* which identifies an individual by sex but does not specify marital status. If a woman has another title, such as *Dr., Rev., Prof.,* or *Lt.,* use it in the same contexts in which you would use such titles for a man.

**11a
bias**

> **Biased:** Albert Einstein and Mrs. Mead
> Einstein and Mrs. Mead
>
> **Revised:** Dr. Einstein and Dr. Mead
> *or*
> Albert Einstein and Margaret Mead
> Einstein and Mead

Here is another example.

> **Biased:** Jane Austen, Mrs. Gaskell, and George Eliot described life in the provinces; Dickens described life in the city.
>
> **Revised:** Austen, Gaskell, and Eliot described life in the provinces; Dickens described life in the city.

Another way to revise the sentence would be to use first names for all authors—Jane Austen, Elizabeth Gaskell, George Eliot, and Charles Dickens. This solution prevents any confusion between George Eliot and T. S. Eliot.

Avoid unnecessary reference to or emphasis on a woman's marital status. Refer to a woman by the name she prefers, whether that name is her birth name or her name by marriage. Do not describe women as if they were appendages to men.

Biased: Elizabeth Wallingford, wife of car salesman John T. Wallingford, has been appointed chief justice of the State Supreme Court by Governor Emily Katz.

Revised: Elizabeth Wallingford, dean of the Law School at Sourmash State University, has been appointed chief justice of the State Supreme Court by Governor Emily Katz.

Also avoid identifying women by reference to their children if the children have nothing to do with the subject you are discussing.

Biased: Molly Burdine, mother of six, will represent Sourmash State University at the national meeting of the American Association of University Professors in Washington.

Revised: Molly Burdine, professor of government, will represent Sourmash State University at the national meeting of the American Association of University Professors in Washington.

11a

bias

Women described in terms of appearance

Don't write as if the most important quality a woman has is her appearance.

Biased: Major is a remarkably talented automobile mechanic, and his wife Estelle is pretty enough to have been a Miss America when she was young.

Revised: Major is a remarkably talented automobile mechanic, often employed by his wife, Estelle, who designed some of the cars he works on.

Women described as unusual in the workplace

Don't describe women's jobs as though special attention must be called to the fact that a woman holds such a position. Such language indicates that a writer is surprised a woman has accomplished such things and implies that most women are incapable of such feats. Don't refer to some jobs as if only women can hold them.

Biased: Judge Wallingford has been a poetess as well as a lady lawyer and judge.

Revised: Judge Wallingford is a much-published poet, and she has managed to keep writing poetry while she has worked first as a lawyer and then as a judge.

Biased: Emily Katz decided early in life that she would be a career woman.

Revised: Governor Emily Katz decided early in her life to go into politics.

Biased: I thought the waitress was very pretty, so I left her a big tip.

Revised: The server did a very good job. She refused to give my friend Clarence another drink when she saw he was having too much, and I gave her a large tip as a mark of my gratitude.

Biased: We advertised for a new secretary because we thought we needed another girl in the office.

Revised: We advertised for a new staff assistant because we had too much work for the staff on hand.

Biased: Although Monique was a woman, she refused to be satisfied with being a receptionist in the hospital.

Revised: Monique worked as a receptionist at Mt. Auburn Hospital one summer while she was in college. There she became so interested in the sick and their problems that she went on to medical school and became a psychiatrist and now counsels the terminally ill and their families at the same hospital where she once had a summer job.

11a bias

Women described as not equal with men

Don't refer to women as inferiors who should be protected from situations that might be acceptable to men. Don't describe them as weak, hysterical, or helpless, nor their concerns as trivial, humorous, or unimportant.

Biased: It was not the sort of story that should have been told with ladies present.

Revised: It was the sort of story that could only have been told by a man who had been deluded since he was six years old by the idea that using vulgar words for natural functions made him seem grown-up.

Biased: After much negotiation Queen Isabella, with a woman's intuition, gave Columbus his chance.

Revised: After much negotiation, Queen Isabella decided to support the venture Columbus proposed.

Don't write as if men were the only people who counted in certain situations or as if women are or were invisible. When you use the word *man*, be sure you are referring to an adult male and no one else. Avoid the use of *man* and *mankind* to stand for all members of the human race.

Biased: Man has spread all over the world from his origins, probably in Africa.

Revised: Human beings have spread all over the world from their origins, probably in Africa.

Biased: We needed people to man the telephones during the fund drive.

Revised: We needed people to answer the telephones during the fund drive.

Biased: Politicians try to guess what the man in the street thinks about the issues.

Revised: Politicians try to guess what typical citizens think about the issues.

11b
bias

Biased: The pioneers moved west, taking with them their women and their children.

Revised: The pioneers moved west, men, women, and children enduring the hardships of the long journey.

Avoiding Bias Against Men

Most of the recommendations and examples given so far in this chapter relate to bias against women. It is equally important to avoid stereotyping men, especially in the context of home and family life. Do not assume that men are dependent on women for advice on what to wear or eat. Nor should men be characterized as inept in household maintenance or child care. Avoid using expressions such as *henpecked husband* and *boys' night out.*

Biased: Ryan was a house husband, taking care of Beth when she wasn't in preschool.

Revised: Ryan took care of Beth when she wasn't in preschool.

11b
Recasting to Avoid Sexism

Writing bias-free prose requires careful thinking. Here are some specific techniques to help you recognize and check bias. A careful and accurate choice of words often provides a ready solution.

Parallel Language

Use parallel language for men and women.

Biased: men and ladies
man and wife

Revised: men and women *or* gentlemen and ladies
husband and wife *or* man and woman

Genderless Nouns and Verbs

Many English words assume that the doers are men. Examples are given below. Replace gender-specific words with genderless words whenever you can.

> *not* policeman *but* police officer
>
> *not* stewardess *but* flight attendant
>
> *not* cameraman *but* photographer
>
> *not* businessman *or* businesswoman *but* businessperson, business executive, store owner, manager, proprietor, merchant
>
> *not* clergyman *but* minister, priest, rabbi *or* member of the clergy
>
> *not* forefathers *but* ancestors
>
> *not* spokesman *but* spokesperson
>
> *not* chairman *but* chair *or* presider
>
> *not* congressman *or* congresswoman *but* representative *or* member of Congress
>
> *not* man-made *but* artificial, synthetic, manufactured, constructed, *or* of human origin

**11b
bias**

If there is not a simple substitute for a gender-specific word, revise the expression in another way.

Biased: There are only six crews available to **man** the trucks.

Revised: There are only six crews available to **operate** the trucks.

Biased: The sob sister's account was less than truthful.

Revised: The account in the newspaper was so sentimental that it wasn't truthful.

Avoiding Masculine Pronouns and Nouns

Whenever possible avoid using the pronouns *he, him, his,* and *himself* as indefinite pronouns. One satisfactory way to avoid masculine pronouns is to use the plural forms.

> **Biased:**   Every student who wrote his name on the class list had to pay a copying fee in advance and to pledge himself to attend every session.

> **Revised:**   Students who wrote their names on the class list had to pay a copying fee in advance and to pledge themselves to attend every session.

Often you can avoid the maculine pronouns by revising the sentence to eliminate the pronouns altogether.

11b

bias

> **Another revision:**   Every student who signed up for the class had to pay a copying fee in advance and pledge to attend every session.

In many instances you can say *he or she, his or her, her or him.* We seem to accept such constructions readily nowadays.

> If anyone finds a rock in the soup, **he or she** should be careful not to break a tooth.

> Anyone who reads Shakespeare eventually finds **his or her** life reflected in some of the characters.

> Once the winner of the lottery is known, we will send **him or her** to Ptomaine Ptolemy's Turkey Tavern for a free meal.

Avoid cumbersome constructions such as *his/her* and *s/he.* As yet these constructions are not acceptable English. Also try to avoid cumbersome repetitions.

> **Awkward:**   Each student in the psychology class was to pick up a different book according to his or her interests, to read the book overnight and to do without his or her normal sleep, to write a short summary of what he or she had read, and then to see if he or she dreamed about the book the following night.

Such sentences must be entirely rewritten.

Revised: Every student was to choose a book, read it overnight, do without sleep, write a short summary of the book the next morning, and then see if he or she dreamed about the book the following night.

Some writers alternate *he* and *she, him,* and *her,* using one gender in one paragraph and another in the next. This alternating may be effective, especially when combined with plural forms and with sentences requiring no personal pronouns referring back to indefinite pronouns. But switching back and forth can also be distracting.

Many speakers and some writers use a plural pronoun to refer to an impersonal singular antecedent: "The person who left *their* suitcase on the bus can call for it at the office." But writers and editors often consider such usage nonstandard. You can revise the sentence to avoid the pronoun: "The person who left a suitcase on the bus can call for it at the office."

Using the neuter impersonal pronoun *one* can help you avoid the masculine pronouns.

> The American creed holds that if one works hard, one will succeed in life.

But again, probably the best way to handle such a problem is to rewrite the sentence.

> The American creed holds that those who are willing to work hard will succeed in life.

In the past, some writers have used the feminine personal pronoun *she* for references to ships and countries. This usage is no longer recommended. Use the pronoun *it* for such references. Keep in mind that *it* is not genderless; it's gender is neuter.

11b
bias

■ **Exercise 11.1** Rewrite the following sentences to eliminate biased writing.

1. A sports writer must try to be fair to his own favorite teams and to their opponents.
2. When the dishwasher breaks down, we grit our teeth and call the repairman, knowing that he will charge us too much money and that we may have to call him again soon.

3. Any country musician worth his guitar knows that true bluegrass music does not use drums. He would also refuse to use an electric guitar.

4. Working women often have to come home from the office or the shop and fix supper for their families and do the laundry.

5. Deborah Townsend, the chairman of the city council, used her cellular telephone to summon policemen after the councilmen got into a fight over where to have their annual picnic.

6. An old wives' tale holds that if you see a black cat run across a graveyard at night, you can listen very carefully and hear the dead talking with their wives and children.

7. Although she was the mother of three children, Professor Helen Burns of the Sourmash University's History Department wrote three books on Egyptian religion in two years and led a tour of faculty members and their wives to the Nile Valley.

8. The ladies worked in the kitchen to prepare the meal while the men sat around the television set watching football.

11b
bias

■ **Exercise 11.2**   All of the following words and expressions display bias. Suggest at least one alternative for each. If a word or phrase should probably be avoided altogether, put a check beside it. If a word or phrase cannot be avoided, explain why.

1. manpower	19. manhole
2. seamstress	20. Jewess
3. manslaughter	21. yes-man
4. lady doctor	22. divorcee
5. tomboy	23. workmanship
6. early man	24. journeyman
7. widower	25. suffragette
8. actress	26. freshman
9. landlord	27. one-upmanship
10. housewife	28. bachelor's degree
11. busboy	29. sissy
12. middleman	30. longshoreman
13. fellow worker	31. majorette
14. career girl	32. fish wife
15. cleaning lady	33. handyman
16. ombudsman	34. workman's compensation
17. heroine	35. gal Friday
18. right-hand man	

11c
Avoiding Other Kinds of Bias

Women are not the only people to be humiliated by stereotypes. Ethnic and religious groups, the handicapped, gays and lesbians, and some occupations are often degraded by the way some people talk and write about them. Analyze your prose to avoid biased assumptions and implications.

Avoiding Assumptions About Groups

All stereotyping is unfair. Making generalizations about people ignores individual differences and potentials. Ascribing qualities to people based on their religious, racial, or ethnic backgrounds reveals the writer's limitations while also doing an injustice to the groups described.

Ethnic and religious groups

**11c
bias**

When writing on topics in history and the social sciences, inexperienced writers need to take special care not to use their own cultures as the standard for comparison. The term *culturally deprived,* for example, implies that one group has culture and another does not. The American Psychological Association recommends this test: substitute your own group for the group you are discussing, and if you are offended by the resulting statement, revise your comments to eliminate bias.

Study the examples of bias below to detect unwarranted assumptions about people and language that can insult and humiliate.

The Bonfiglio family seems to have become wealthy without help from the Mafia.

The assumption is surprise that a wealthy Italian family is not connected to a criminal organization.

Blacks may not make a lot of money, but they know how to have fun.

The assumption is that all blacks are poor and somehow care more about having fun than working.

I offered him the apples for five dollars a bushel, but he tried to jew me down to three dollars.

Using *jew* as a verb implies that Jews are always seeking bargains and that the rest of us are not.

> Some of my best friends are Jews, but you have to watch them in a business deal.

This sentence is a crude way of excusing oneself for prejudice but then affirming the prejudice just the same.

> Greeks and Chinese don't know how to do anything but open restaurants.

This sentence ignores all the contributions of Greek and Chinese people to culture, politics, business, and good order in American history.

> Although the Browns are Catholic, there are only three children in the family.

This sentence implies that Catholics have lots and lots of children because of their religion.

11c
bias

> I was surprised to learn that although she is a Baptist, she has a Ph.D. in nuclear physics from Cal Tech.

This sentence implies that Baptists are usually ignorant.

Other groups

No group should be the victim of careless generalizations or stereotyping. Study the examples below to detect unwarranted assumptions about people on the basis of their abilities, disabilities, occupations, or sexual orientations.

> Although Conrad is confined to a wheelchair, he is a good receptionist.
>
> Football players are not known for their great intelligence; be sure you give him an easy question.
>
> Gays and lesbians in the military services would be dangerous companions in combat. The rest of us would be trying to save our lives, but all they would think about under fire would be sex.

Several terms in the past have been used to refer to individuals with disabilities, and groups representing their interests have at times promoted one or another. *Special education* is now widely used to describe programs for students with physical, mental, or emotional disabilities. Federal regulations implementing the Americans with Disabilities Act (1991) point out that the term *handicapped,* used in earlier federal legislation, is today objected to by individuals with disabilities and organizations representing them. The regulations recommend the term *disability,* recognizing that "the terminology applied to individuals with disabilities is a very significant and sensitive issue. As with racial and ethnic terms, the choice of words to describe a person with a disability is overlaid with stereotypes, patronizing attitudes, and other emotional connotations."

References to Black and Other Americans

Language has been cruel to American blacks. They have been the victim of a great many terrible words. And in some respects they have been the victim of efforts not to discriminate against them. The word *Negro,* capitalized, was the polite word of choice for two centuries. It was derived from the Latin word for *black,* and in the 1960s the Rev. Martin Luther King, Jr., used it regularly, as did the celebrated black writer from Tennessee, Alex Haley, author of *Roots.*

Black leaders such as Malcolm X objected to *Negro* because it seemed to put black Americans into a special and inferior category. The word *Negroid* had a vaguely pejorative sense; "Negroid" features were not considered attractive. The slogan "black is beautiful" challenged the Hollywood notion that the only beautiful people were blond white women. Blacks also resented *Negro* because it allowed many prejudiced people to imagine they were not prejudiced because they used it instead of an ugly word. Many whites could use the word and still refuse to admit black people to the country club or the fraternity or even the public schools. To many, *Negro* became a symbol of hypocrisy.

In the 1970s, *black* became the word of choice, a neutral description parallel to *white.* Almost overnight the word *Negro* dropped out of use. Careful writers never use it now unless they are quoting from speeches and documents from the past.

A few years ago the black leader Jesse Jackson suggested yet another change. Instead of *black,* he advocated the term *African-American.* Despite polls that show that about 70 percent of black Americans don't like the term and prefer to be called *blacks,* it is used more and more frequently. If the term is generally adopted, it runs counter to the general trend of language to shorten and simplify frequently used terms.

No one can ever predict how language will be used in the future. For now, hardly anyone considers *black* a prejudiced word. Attentive writers will consider carefully the changing connotations of words and will always strive to use words that are both common and untainted with bias. Obviously pejorative names used for any ethnic group are to be avoided at all costs.

**11c
bias**

In recent years the terms *people of color* or *colored people* seem to be coming back into general use. These terms were considered derogatory in the early years of the civil rights movement, though the leaders of the National Association for the Advancement of Colored People, founded in 1910, never felt compelled to change the organization's name. Of course the term *people of color* also includes Asians and American Indians.

The term *Native Americans* has been increasingly used for the peoples who occupied the American continents at the time of Columbus. Because Columbus and others assumed he had sailed to India, he called these people *Indians,* and all European languages quickly adopted the name. But it was clearly off the mark, and in recent years many people have objected to it.

Still, American Indians resolutely call themselves *Indians* and *American Indians.* The American Indian Movement has been one of the most active civil rights groups among the various tribes without feeling any compulsion to change its name. Currently it seems that both terms—*Native American* and *American Indian*—are acceptable. Unacceptable are terms that assume American Indians are more savage and bloodthirsty than the general run of human beings or that label them by a supposed skin color. "Redskin" is the most common of these terms, and attentive writers will not use it. "Wild Indian" is another such term. Terms like "Indian giver" for those who give a gift and then demand it back are equally unfair and should be avoided.

11c

bias

Writers and others should not assume that all Indian tribes were alike, that they all wore Sioux war bonnets, or that they all hunted buffalo or that they said "How" when they greeted each other. If anything, Indians in the Americas were far more diverse than Western Europeans have been for centuries, and the various tribes maintain many differences. Nor should Indian cultures be depicted as frozen in time, forever like those whites described at the time of contact. Like all human cultures, Indian cultures develop and adapt.

The term *Hispanic* has been used to designate anyone from Latin America, but it is coming under increasing attack by many who find it overgeneral. A Mexican is not identical to someone from Argentina; a Panamanian has a different culture from that of a Cuban or a Bolivian. It would seem wise to identify such people by their country of origin instead of by some assumed general identity in the word *Hispanic.* (The same cautions apply to words such as *Latino, Anglo,* and *Chicano,* all of which may carry pejorative meanings.) For many of the same reasons, persons from Asia often object to the label *Oriental,* a word that also embodies a European perspective on the world. Again, it would seem wise and fair to identify a person by country of origin instead of by some assumed general identity.

The best rule is always good faith and sympathy. Imagine how it would feel to be insulted for some quality over which you have no control. Imagine how it would feel to be assumed ignorant or incapable because of some physical attribute you possess, when you know yourself to be educated and able.

■ **Exercise 11.3** Look up the etymology of the following words in a dictionary. If you don't know what *etymology* means or how to use a dictionary, consult Chapter 12. When you have learned the word origins, decide whether or how you will use these words. Discuss them with your classmates.

1. paddy wagon	11. Mongoloid
2. gyp	12. Eskimo
3. Indian giver	13. jerry-built
4. Near East	14. flesh (color)
5. German measles	15. maiden name
6. Mohammedan	16. gringo
7. dumb	17. sinister
8. nonwhite	18. Caucasian
9. Scotch	19. hunk
10. mulatto	20. Dutch treat

**11c
bias**

✔ **CHECKLIST 11.1: AVOIDING BIAS**

Habits of thinking and conventions of speech sometimes work against your honest and unbiased intentions. As you revise, look carefully at your prose to make sure it is saying what you want it to say. Ask yourself these questions.

■ Are titles, clichés, or labels presenting a limited view of women?

■ Are women referred to as appendages of men—as daughters or wives or mothers, instead of as individuals in their own right?

■ Are women described in terms of their appearance when appearance isn't relevant?

■ Are women's accomplishments, particularly in the workplace, treated as curious or exceptional?

■ Are assumptions made about the roles and abilities of either sex?

■ Are gender-specific words used when they refer to individuals of both sexes?

■ Do pronouns assume that individuals are of a particular sex when, in truth, they are not?

- Are assumptions or implications made about ethnic or religious groups?
- Are certain qualities ascribed to individuals or groups on the basis of background or physical features?
- Are the terms selected for reference to any group pejorative or not the term that most members of the group prefer?
- Are any word choices or underlying assumptions potentially hurtful?

If the answer to any of these questions is "yes," rethink your intentions and revise your prose.

11c
bias

USING A
DICTIONARY
AND THESAURUS

A good dictionary is an essential tool for every writer. You should consult your dictionary every time you have the slightest doubt about the spelling, meaning, proper use, pronunciation, or syllabication of a word.

12a
Choosing Useful Dictionaries

The most useful dictionaries for college writers are desk dictionaries—books of a convenient size to keep on the desk, handy to consult as the need arises. Words and usages that do not appear in the standard desk dictionaries may be found in an unabridged dictionary or in an appropriate specialized dictionary. Any good library has many excellent dictionaries in its reference room.

Selecting Desk Dictionaries

A standard desk dictionary contains 140,000 to 180,000 entries. It may include drawings as well. Illustrations are useful because they can show something that otherwise cannot be defined easily in words.

Many dictionaries are called "Webster's." The name means only that they follow the general methodology of Noah Webster's two-volume *American Dictionary of the English Language,* published in 1828.

The following desk dictionaries are all useful to college students:

■ *Random House Webster's College Dictionary.* McGraw-Hill Edition. New York: Random House, 1991. With 180,000 entries, this is one of the largest desk dictionaries. When it was published, it created a great deal of controversy because it includes many new coinages related to feminist and multicultural issues. It also offers "usage notes" that give advice on the connotations of words. Here, for example, is a note on the word *lady:*

> Uses that are commonly disliked include LADY in compounds or phrases referring to occupation or position (*cleaning lady; forelady; saleslady*) and as a modifier (*lady artist; lady doctor*). Increasingly, sex-neutral terms replace LADY (*cleaner; supervisor; salesperson* or *salesclerk*). When it is relevant to specify the sex of the performer or practitioner, *woman* rather than LADY is used, the parallel term being *man: Men doctors outnumber women doctors on the hospital staff by three to one.*

This dictionary lists definitions in order of common usage, beginning with the most commonly used meaning of the word and proceeding through less common meanings.

12a dict

■ *Webster's New World Dictionary.* Third College Edition. Cleveland, Ohio: New-World Dictionaries, 1988. The prefatory materials in this dictionary do not tell us how many entries it includes, but it is large and readable. Like the *Random House Webster's College Dictionary,* the biographical and geographical entries are in the main body of the work and not confined appendixes at the rear. The editors of the dictionary especially pride themselves in their listings of Americanisms—those many words that have one meaning or connotation in American English and another or none in the British isles.

■ *Webster's Ninth New Collegiate Dictionary.* Springfield, Mass.: Merriam-Webster, 1983. This dictionary is based on *Webster's Third New International Dictionary,* generally regarded as the standard one-volume unabridged dictionary in English. Biographical and geographical entries appear in appendixes. The dictionary has about 160,000 entries, many from the sciences. It lists the meanings of words in the order in which they came into use. Exemplary sentences from works of well-known writers illustrate usage, and an occasional usage note offers guidance in the different connotations of synonyms.

Consulting Unabridged Dictionaries

In theory, an unabridged dictionary should include every word in the language. In practice, such inclusiveness is impossible. Yet a couple of unabridged dictionaries come close to the ideal, and college writers should learn about them and continue to use them long after college.

■ *Webster's Third New International Dictionary of the English Language.* Springfield, Mass.: G. & C. Merriam, 1961 and later enlarged editions. This enormous unabridged dictionary occupies a prominent place in the reference room of any respectable library. When it first appeared, purists greeted it with howls of outrage, and a few people burned it in protest. Because it is descriptive rather than prescriptive, many people thought that it symbolized the decay of the English language. It takes a relaxed attitude about usage; if a large number of people define a word in a certain way, the dictionary includes the definition in its list of definitions. The dictionary includes *ain't* and other words not regarded as standard English, and in the editions after 1967, profane and obscene words are also included. Although the *Third* is now generally recognized by publishers as the authoritative dictionary for American English, many also concede that it can lead inexperienced writers astray because it does not warn them that certain usages are unacceptably casual, confusing, or avoided by careful writers.

■ *The American Heritage Dictionary of the English Language.* Third Edition. Boston: Houghton Mifflin, 1992. The long-awaited third edition of the *American Heritage Dictionary* is much larger than the second edition and in size now occupies a place somewhat between the standard desk dictionary and the so-called unabridged dictionaries that usually have a special stand in the reference rooms of libraries. It is renowned for its panel of writers and editors who, during the preparation of each edition, vote on the usage of controversial words. Their votes are included in usage notes, but the dictionary's editors are not reluctant to dispute their own panel, as they do in the usage note to *hopefully* used as an adverb meaning "It is hoped." A great majority of the usage panel voted against this usage, but, say the editors, "It is not easy to explain why critics dislike this use of *hopefully*." This dictionary is great fun and carries enormous prestige. But it is heavy enough to need a handle if you carry it from room to room.

12a dict

■ *The Oxford English Dictionary.* Second Edition. Prepared by J. A. Simson and E. S. C. Weiner. 20 volumes. Oxford: Clarendon Press, 1989. This is the premier dictionary of the English language, the indispensable tool for any serious scholar of English literature. The project conceived in Britain in 1857 and was published in parts (the first covered *A* to *ant*) between 1884 and 1921. It was ultimately ten volumes. Supplements immediately followed, and the second edition is twenty volumes. The *OED*, as it is known, lists every word the editors have been able to find in English manuscripts and books, provides variant spellings (American spellings are variants), and identifies the most common spellings in each century. It provides definitions of words and illustrates all the definitions by brief quotations. It is now available on compact disk (CD-ROM), allowing for computer searches that speed up the use of the dictionary considerably. A new and much expanded edition is promised shortly. It, too, will appear on compact disk. A two-volume edition of the older *OED* is in print—with type so small that most people must use a magnifying glass to read it.

Using Specialized Dictionaries

Many highly specialized dictionaries may be found in the reference room of any good library—biographical and geographical dictionaries; foreign language dictionaries; medical dictionaries of legal terms; dictionaries of philosophy, sociology, engineering, and other disciplines; dictionaries of slang, word origins, famous quotations, first lines of poems. These dictionaries may help you write an essay or simply enlarge your background knowledge necessary to comprehend and explain various subjects. Browse through them when you are deciding on a topic for an essay. Your reference librarian can help you locate the dictionaries that may be helpful to you in the general field of interest you choose to write upon.

**12b
dict**

12b
Reading Entries in a Standard Desk Dictionary

All dictionaries contain guides to their use. In these guides, usually located in the front of the dictionary, you will find the meanings of the abbreviations used in the entries, and you will also find a list of the special cautions dictionaries use for words that the editors consider *slang, vulgar, informal, nonstandard,* or something else worthy of notation. When you use a dictionary for the first time, study these instructions carefully. They usually contain sample entries that will help you get the most from the time you spend consulting the dictionary.

An entry in the *Random House Webster's College Dictionary* is shown on the facing page.

Spelling, Syllabication, and Pronunciation

Entries in a dictionary are listed in alphabetical order according to standard spelling. In the *Random House Webster's College Dictionary,* the verb *compare* is entered as **com·pare.** The dot divides the word into two syllables. If you divide the word *compare* at the end of a line, the hyphen goes where you find the dot in this example. Phonetic symbols in parentheses show the correct pronunciation; explanations of these symbols appear on the bottom right column of each right-hand page in the dictionary. The second syllable of *compare* receives the greater stress when you pronounce the

Word division — Pronunciation — Part of speech — Past tense and past participle

com·pare (kəm pâr′), v., **-pared, -par·ing.** n. —v.t. **1.** to examine (two or more objects, ideas, people, etc.) in order to note similarities and differences: *to compare two restaurants.* **2.** to consider or describe as similar; liken: *"Shall I compare thee to a summer's day?"* **3.** to form or display the degrees of comparison of (an adjective or adverb). —v.i. **4.** to be worthy of comparison: *Whose plays can compare with Shakespeare's?* **5.** to be in similar standing; be alike: *This recital compares with the one he gave last year.* **6.** to appear in quality, progress, etc., as specified: *Their development compares poorly with that of neighbor nations.* **7.** to make comparisons. —n. **8.** comparison: *a beauty beyond compare.* —**Idiom. 9. compare notes,** to exchange views, ideas, or impressions. [1375–1425; late ME < OF *comperer* < L *comparāre* to place together, match, v. der. of *compar* alike, matching (see COM-, PAR)] —**com·par′or,** n. —**Usage.** The traditional rule states that COMPARE should be followed by *to* when it points out likenesses between unlike persons or things: *She compared his handwriting to knotted string.* It should be followed by *with,* the rule says, when it examines two entities of the same general class for similarities or differences: *She compared his handwriting with mine.* This rule is by no means always followed, even in formal speech and writing. Common practice is to use *to* for likeness between members of different classes: *to compare a language to a living organism.* Between members of the same category, both *to* and *with* are used: *Compare the Chicago of today with* (or *to*) *the Chicago of the 1890s.* After the past participle COMPARED, either *to* or *with* is used regardless of the type of comparison.

— Definitions

Idiom —

— Etymology

Usage —

12b
dict

word correctly. You say "comPARE." In this dictionary, the syllable that receives the primary stress is given an accent mark at the end (′). Down the column from *compare,* you find the word *compartmentalization.* It is pronounced with the heaviest stress on the syllable *za,* but it has a secondary stress on the syllable *men.* The syllable with the heavier stress has the darkest accent mark (′); the syllable with the secondary stress has a lighter accent mark (′).

Plurals of nouns are usually not given special notice if they are formed by the addition of *-s.* Irregular plurals such as *children* for *child* are noted.

Parts of Speech and Various Forms

The abbreviation *v.* immediately after the pronunciation tells you that *compare* is most frequently used as a verb. The *-pared* shows the simple past and the past participle forms. If the past participle differed from the simple past, both forms would be included. (Look at the verb *drink* in your dictionary; you will see the forms *drank* and *drunk.*) The *-paring* gives you the present participle form and shows that you drop the final *e* in *compare* before you add the *-ing.*

The *-n.* indicates that on occasion *compare* can be used as a noun.

The next abbreviation—*v.t.*—stands for *verb transitive,* indicating that the definitions that follow show the verb used in a transitive sense, that is, with a direct object. A little farther down in the entry *v.i.* (verb intransitive) introduces definitions showing the verb used in an intransitive sense, without a direct object. Still later, after the abbreviation *n.* is a definition and an example of *compare* used as a noun, as in the phrase *beyond compare.*

In this entry the word *Idiom* signals a special meaning not necessarily included in the simple definition (see p. 162). To *compare notes* is an idiom meaning *to exchange views, ideas, or impressions. Comparing notes* does not necessarily mean that two people sit down with notes they have made on a subject and compare them. In English, you *compare notes* even when there are no notes, just ideas in your mind that you want to talk about with someone who has similar ideas.

Definitions

As we have seen, the several meanings of the word are arranged according to the parts of speech that the word plays in various contexts. For *compare,* the definitions begin with its meanings as a transitive verb. If appropriate the editors note in italics whether word or a defintion of a word is *non-standard, informal, slang, vulgar, rare, poetic, archaic, regional,* or *foreign.*

Word Origins

At the end of most entries in this dictionary is an **etymology**—a brief history of the word—set off in brackets. There we see the date of the first known use of the word in English together with the earlier words from which it is derived. We see that *compare* came into English between 1375 and 1425 and that it comes from late Middle English, derived from the Old French word *comperer,* which came from the Latin verb *comparāre,* which meant "to place together" or "to match." This word in turn came from the Latin *compar,* meaning simply "alike" or "matching." Just a few lines can reveal a great deal about the history of a word and its related meanings—information that can sometimes be a very great help to a writer seeking a precise meaning for his or her thoughts.

Usage

Finally, a usage note follows some main entries in the *Random House Webster's College Dictionary.* For *compare,* the traditional rule for using *to* or *with* is given, together with examples and some comments on common practice.

Finding Other Information

Other entries and other dictionaries give additional information, including abbreviations, synonyms, and antonyms. Sometimes cross-references send you to words with similar denotations but different connotations. Some dictionaries list alternate spellings, always giving preferred spellings first or placing the full entry under the preferred spelling only.

■ **Exercise 12.1**   Which of the following words can be used as verbs? What cautions does your desk dictionary offer about using them? Indicate with a *T* or an *I* whether a verb is transitive or intransitive. Put *TI* before verbs that can be both.

1. total	**6.** victory	**11.** access	**16.** hype
2. outside	**7.** hipster	**12.** occasion	**17.** keyboard
3. fritter	**8.** interface	**13.** impact	**18.** input
4. issue	**9.** grunt	**14.** envelop	**19.** workout
5. freak	**10.** postulate	**15.** effect	**20.** estimate

■ **Exercise 12.2**   Write out your own short definition for each of the following words, noting the part or parts of speech that you think each word may serve. Then check your definitions with those in a standard desk dictionary. If you don't know a word, try to guess what it means before you look it up.

12b dict

1. effete	**6.** nomenclature
2. jejune	**7.** manufacture
3. jangle	**8.** relationship
4. parameter	**9.** mucus
5. pestilent	**10.** mule

■ **Exercise 12.3**   Look up the etymologies of the following words in your desk dictionary. Do the origins of a word help you understand its modern meaning?

1. gynecologist	**6.** eugenics
2. gymnasium	**7.** democracy
3. geology	**8.** gender
4. infringe	**9.** conceit
5. muck	**10.** otter

■ **Exercise 12.4**   If you haven't done Exercise 11.3, do it now. It is a lesson in using a dictionary as well as in avoiding bias.

■ **Exercise 12.5** Dictionaries differ. Look up the following words in at least two different dictionaries to find variations in spellings and preferred spellings. Compare your answers with your classmates. How do you account for the differences?

1. underway
2. mustache
3. idiosyncrasy
4. indispensable
5. adviser
6. combating
7. theater
8. insure
9. defence
10. glamour
11. traveler
12. catalog
13. archaeology
14. tranquillity
15. sizeable
16. threshold
17. idyll
18. esthetic
19. specter
20. acknowledgment
21. life style
22. decision maker
23. policymaker
24. socio-economic
25. childrearing

12b
dict

The size of a standard desk dictionary limits the information that each entry can include. But either alphabetized with other words or in appendixes you can find the correct spellings of important place names, the official names of countries with their areas and populations, and the names of capital cities. Biographical entries give the birth and death years and enough information about the person to explain his or her importance to society.

Many dictionaries also include lists of abbreviations and symbols, names and locations of colleges and universities, titles and correct forms of address, conversion tables for weights and measures, and even guides to punctuation, capitalization, and the use of italics.

✔ **CHECKLIST 12.1: USING A DICTIONARY**

■ Use the *guide words.* At the top of each dictionary page, *guide words* (usually in boldface) tell you the first word and the last word on the page. Since all entries are in alphabetical order, you can locate the word you are seeking rapidly by looking for guide words that would include your word somewhere between the two of them.

■ Use the *pronunciation key.* The letters and symbols used to indicate pronunciation are explained in a separate section at the front or the back of a dictionary and often summarized at the bottom of each right-hand page of entries. Always pronounce new words carefully aloud to help you remember them and to integrate them in your spoken vocabulary.

■ In checking definitions, pay attention to the *part of speech.* The same word serving as different parts of speech can have different meanings. Thus you can turn on a *light* (noun), but a butterfly that *lights* (verb) on a leaf. You will find both meanings (among many others) in a dictionary, and you will have to choose the meaning appropriate for your use. Parts of speech are often abbreviated (*n.,* noun; *v.,* verb; *adj.,* adjective; *adv.,* adverb). The abbreviations the dictionary uses are usually identified in prefatory material.

■ Always test the meaning you find. To check whether you have selected the correct meaning, substitute the meaning for the word in the sentence you are writing or reading.

■ Try alternate spellings if you cannot find the spelling for the word you are looking up. Don't give up if you can't find a word on a first try. Use alternate phonetic spellings. For example, if you tried to look up a word you thought was spelled *troff,* you wouldn't find it. You should try *trouf, truff,* and *trough.* (*Trough* is correct.) Many spell checkers on word-processing programs for computers will do this searching for you. But *be sure* to check the meaning of the word in a good dictionary. Spell checkers can't tell you if you've used *their* or *there* correctly, only that such a word does exist in English. And they can't always help you find the word you're looking for any more than a dictionary can. The spelling *troff* makes a computer fix on the *tro,* and from this spelling you might get the alternatives *troll, trout, troop,* or *trots*—none the word you are seeking.

**12c
thes**

12c
Using a Thesaurus

A **thesaurus** (the word means "treasury" or "collection" in Latin) is a dictionary of synonyms, sometimes without definitions. Several kinds of thesauruses are available. Many are called "Roget's" after Peter Mark Roget (pronounced Ro·zháy) who in 1852 published the first *Thesaurus of English Words and Phrases.* The guide went through twenty-eight editions before he died in 1869, demonstrating the attraction a handy reference to synonyms may be to writers and speakers and others interested in language. The synonyms are not limited to words but include phrases and expressions.

■ *Roget's II: The New Thesaurus*. Boston: Houghton Mifflin, 1988. In this dictionary of synonyms, each synonym is given a short definition. The word *distinction,* for example, is given four definitions. One is "Readily seen, perceived, or understood." The thesaurus gives as a synonym for this meaning the word *apparent*. On looking up *apparent,* you find the definition, "Readily seen, perceived, or understood," and next to it the synonyms "clear, clear-cut, crystal-clear, distinct, evident, manifest, noticeable, obvious, patent, plain visible." This is an excellent thesaurus to use when you feel a little unsure of the precise meanings of some synonyms.

■ *Roget's International Thesaurus*. Fifth Edition. Edited by Robert L. Chapman. New York: HarperCollins, 1992. This thesaurus holds to Roget's original method, classifying words into various categories that he thought embraced nearly all human concepts. To each general category he assigned a number, and by means of these numbers he made cross-references so that you can readily pass from one category to another in the search of a synonym that will produce just the right meaning. In the fifth edition, words set in boldface are listed in alphabetical order in the index. The user still has to first look up a word in the index in the back of the book, then turn to the number in the front of the book.

This is by far the most popular thesaurus, but it does not define the words it lists. It is therefore most useful for the experienced writer who already knows the definitions of words and merely wants to be reminded of synonyms that may add color, variety, or precision to a piece of prose.

Most writers find a thesaurus a great pleasure to use. But be cautious. Be sure you understand the full meaning of the words you use. Be sure they are not inappropriate for your purposes. And don't use fancy words when simple words will do.

✔ CHECKLIST 12.2: **USING A THESAURUS**

■ Know how the words are arranged. In many thesauruses, the words are arranged in simple alphabetical order. In *Roget's International Thesaurus,* the words are listed in numbered categories. You need to use the index to find the word whose synonyms you seek. In other kinds of thesauruses, the words are listed alphabetically, and you use the thesaurus much as you would a dictionary.

■ Never use an unfamiliar synonym that you pick up from a thesaurus without looking it up in the dictionary first. Otherwise you may write something ridiculous, impolite, or incomprehensible.

■ Test the replacement word carefully in your sentence. Watch particularly for appropriate connotations as well as denotations.

■ Reject high-sounding or multisyllabic words simply for the impression you think they might create. Use a thesaurus to find a more precise word, not a fancier one. Inexperienced writers can be seduced by "fine" or unusual language inconsistent with their writing style and often misleading or ridiculous.

■ **Exercise 12.6**   Find five synonyms for the word *excitement* in a thesaurus. Write a sentence for each of the synonyms, using the words correctly. Use a desk dictionary if you need to check on the connotations of a word.

**12c
thes**

BOOK

TWO

USAGE
RULES
AND
OPTIONS

UNDERSTANDING GRAMMAR AND WRITING CORRECT SENTENCES

13

CORRECTING RUN-ONS AND COMMA SPLICES

Appropriate punctuation and conjunctions can correct two common sentence errors: run-ons and comma splices. A **run-on error** occurs when two independent clauses run together. A **comma splice** occurs when two independent clauses are linked by a comma. You can see both errors in the example below. *A* is a comma splice; *B* is a run-on.

> Fuel emissions at Yosemite National Park can disrupt the delicate ecological balance, [A] authorities have acted firmly against pollution [B] they have banned the automobile in Yosemite Valley.

Independent clauses may be joined or separated correctly in several ways: by using end marks, by using a comma and a coordinating conjunction, by using a semicolon, and by using subordination.

13a
Using End Marks

A period at the end of an independent clause, followed by a capital letter at the beginning of the next word, will give you two correct sentences.

> Fuel emissions at Yosemite National Park can disrupt the delicate ecological balance. Authorities have acted firmly against pollution. They have banned the automobile in Yosemite Valley.

Sometimes you can use a question mark or an exclamation point to separate the clauses.

Run-on: Are liberal arts graduates desirable employees in business many corporations report their strong interest in women and men with humanities backgrounds.

Corrected: Are liberal arts graduates desirable employees in business? Many corporations report their strong interest in women and men with humanities backgrounds.

Comma splice: I made it, I passed the bar exam, I can be a lawyer!

Corrected: I made it! I passed the bar exam! I can be a lawyer!

■ **Exercise 13.1** The items below contain one or more run-on errors or comma splices. Correct them by creating complete sentences separated by appropriate end punctuation and, where necessary, appropriate capitalization.

1. The economy withered in 1991 corporate bankruptcies rose 40 percent over 1990.
2. Despite the rise in fares, short ocean voyages continue to draw vacationers for all over America now "cruises to nowhere" have grown in popularity.
3. Regular cleaning of the Lincoln Memorial in Washington has eroded the marble, the National Park Service will have to repair it.
4. How can noise ordinances protect city dwellers against loud portable radios cradled like babies in the arms of strolling adolescents the police seem reluctant to arrest young offenders, since a loud radio is not a violent crime.
5. When my mother first got a job, I had to make some sudden adjustments, I had to deal with an unexpected feeling of abandonment the first time I came home from grade school to an empty house and realized that Mom was not there to greet me and that everything seemed still and dead.

**13b
run-on**

13b
Using a Comma and a Coordinating Conjunction

A comma alone is not strong enough to mark off one independent clause from another (see p. 113). A coordinating conjunction is also required. **Coordinating conjunctions** join equal elements. The most common coordinators are *and, but, or, for, nor, yet,* and *so.*

Notice how a coordinator is used correctly in the following example.

Fuel emissions at Yosemite National Park can disrupt the delicate ecological balance, **so** authorities have acted firmly against pollution.

The comma and the conjunction *so* coordinate the independent clause in a compound sentence.

Comma splice: Cortez first introduced chocolate to Europe, the Spaniards later added sugar for sweetening.

Corrected: Cortez first introduced chocolate to Europe, and the Spaniards later added sugar for sweetening.

13c
Using a Semicolon

13c

run-on

When the ideas in two independent clauses are closely related, a semicolon stresses the relation. The first word after a semicolon begins with a lowercase letter unless the word is a proper noun. When a conjunctive adverb such as *also, however,* or *therefore* or a transitional expression such as *for example* or *on the contrary* (see 13e) appears between two independent clauses, you can separate them with a semicolon. Remember, however, that the period is a more usual mark of separation than a semicolon. When you use a period, you of course have two sentences; if you use the semicolon, you have one sentence.

Federal authorities in Yosemite National Park have acted firmly against pollution; they have banned the automobile in Yosemite Valley.

By connecting the independent clauses, the semicolon stresses the point that the second clause is a consequence of the first.

Comma splice: A good researcher may not know all the facts however, she should know where to find them.

Corrected: A good researcher may not know all the facts; however, she should know where to find them.

Occasionally a writer will use both a semicolon and a conjunction to mark off independent clauses (see 23a).

Nothing could be more racy, straightforward, and alive than the prose of Shakespeare; but it must be remembered that this was dialogue written to be spoken.

—W. SOMERSET MAUGHAM

When independent clauses are short and closely related in structure and meaning, some writers occasionally join them with a comma to achieve a special effect.

You fly in with the goods, you fly out with the lucky.

—JOHN LE CARRÉ

■ **Exercise 13.2** Correct run-on errors and comma splices in the following sentences. Use either a coordinating conjunction and a comma or a semicolon, but be sure that your corrections yield logical sentences. Mark sentences that require no correction with a check.

1. The snow started falling at five o'clock then the wind began to blow hard from the north.
2. The best way to keep warm in icy weather is to wear layers of clothing moreover wool is much warmer than cotton.
3. In their own countries Soviet scientists are no longer needed for nuclear arms development, however, other countries actively seek their skills.
4. Fewer jobs are open for teachers every year, yet many college students major in education to obtain teaching certificates.
5. The heavy black clouds meant rain, they came on swiftly with thunder and lightning.

**13d
run-on**

13d
Using Subordination

Finally, subordination correctly joins independent clauses into a single sentence. **Subordination** establishes the dependence of one idea upon another through use of a subordinator such as *when* or *because* and a comma at the end of the clause.

Comma splice: Fuel emissions at Yosemite National Park can disrupt the delicate ecological balance of the region, authorities there have acted firmly against automobiles.

Corrected: Because fuel emissions at Yosemite National Park can disrupt the delicate ecological balance of the region, authorities there have acted firmly against automobiles.

Run-on: Authorities have acted firmly against pollution—they have banned the automobile in Yosemite Valley.

Corrected: Authorities who have banned the automobile in Yosemite Valley have acted firmly against pollution.

Also corrected: Acting firmly against pollution, authorities have banned the automobile in Yosemite Valley.

■ **Exercise 13.3**   Use subordination to correct run-on errors and comma splices in the sentences below. Mark correct sentences with a check.

1. Learning to read lips is not easy young children can adapt to this preferred method of teaching language to the deaf more easily than older people can.
2. *Europa Europa,* a brilliant film, was not nominated by Germany for an Academy Award, some people believe that it embarrassed Germans about the treatment of Jews during World War II.
3. Play, which allows a child's free expression, has an important role in early childhood education. However, children must keep some real control over the situation if play is to encourage real learning.
4. The Mediterranean fruit fly larva can leap distances of five inches, it has no legs.
5. The Super Bowl in January has now become an unofficial national holiday, people who hardly follow professional football during the regular season gather at parties before huge color television sets, eating and drinking and enjoying good fellowship and sometimes watching the game.

13d
run-on

■ **Exercise 13.4**   Correct the run-on errors and comma splices in Exercise 13.1, this time by joining complete thoughts either through coordination or subordination (13b and 13d).

13e
Recognizing Sources of Run-ons and Comma Splices

Certain conjunctive adverbs (p. 106), transitional expressions (p. 57), and subject pronouns (p. 100) at the beginning of a sentence can mislead you into producing these errors. Quoting the work of other writers in your text also requires special attention.

Recognizing Conjunctive Adverbs

Conjunctive adverbs connect ideas between clauses. Examples include *accordingly, also, anyway, as a result, besides, consequently, finally, furthermore, hence, however, incidentally, indeed, instead, likewise, meanwhile, moreover, nevertheless, nonetheless, now, otherwise, still, suddenly, then, therefore,* and *thus.* If you use one of the conjunctive adverbs between clauses, you must use a semicolon or a period. Remember that a comma belongs right after a conjunctive adverb.

> **Comma splice:**   The price of gold varies greatly every year, nevertheless, speculators purchase precious metals in large quantities and hope always for a price rise.

> **Corrected:**   The price of gold varies greatly every year; nevertheless, speculators purchase precious metals in large quantities and hope always for a price rise.

> **Run-on sentence:**   Salt air corrodes metal easily—therefore, automobiles in coastal regions require frequent washing even in cold weather.

> **Corrected:**   Salt air corrodes metal easily. Therefore, automobiles in coastal regions require frequent washing even in cold weather.

**13e
run-on**

Recognizing Transitional Expressions

Transitional expressions such as *after all, after a while, as a result, at any rate, at the same time, for example, for instance, in addition, in fact, in other words, in particular, in the first place, on the contrary,* and *on the other hand* also require the use of a semicolon or period. Again, commas belong right after these words.

> **Comma splice:**   Richard Rodgers's music continues to delight audiences everywhere, in fact, revivals of *Oklahoma!, Carousel,* and *The King and I* pack theaters every year.

Corrected: Richard Rodgers's music continues to delight audiences everywhere. In fact, revivals of *Oklahoma!, Carousel,* and *The King and I* pack theaters every year.

Run-on sentence: Americans continue their love affair with the automobile at the same time they are more successful than ever before in restricting its use.

Corrected: Americans continue their love affair with the automobile; at the same time, they are more successful than ever before in restricting its use.

Recognizing Subject Pronouns

The subject pronouns that may lead to comma splices and run-on sentences are *I, you, he, she, it, we, they,* and *who.*

Comma splice: Disneyland is fun for everyone, I think I enjoyed it as much as my ten-year-old niece did.

Corrected: Disneyland is fun for everyone; I think I enjoyed it as much as my ten-year-old niece did.

Run-on sentence: The weather disappointed Vermont vacationers—they wanted snow in January, not warm, sunny skies.

**13e
run-on**

Corrected: The weather disappointed Vermont vacationers because they wanted snow in January, not warm, sunny skies.

Divided Quotations

In divided quotations or in consecutive sentences within a quotation, be sure to punctuate complete sentences correctly.

In a dialogue, commas are not sufficient to set off independent clauses.

Comma splice: "Speak up, amigo," Juanita said, "I can't hear you."

Corrected: "Speak up, amigo," Juanita said. "I can't hear you."

✔ **CHECKLIST 13.1: CORRECTING RUN-ON ERRORS AND COMMA SPLICES**

- Use a period, a question mark, or an exclamation point.
- Use *and, but, or, nor, for, yet,* or *so,* preceded by a comma.

- Use a semicolon to coordinate closely related ideas in consecutive independent clauses.
- Use subordination to relate some ideas that might otherwise be expressed in independent clauses.

■ **Exercise 13.5** Use the words in brackets correctly in the sentences that follow. Correct the punctuation and capitalization where necessary.

1. [they] Federal investigators cleared the Senator _____ found no evidence that he had bribed a Treasury agent.
2. [however] The new regulations restricting study abroad have many loopholes _____, the Chinese government is not enforcing the rules too precisely.
3. [however] He said _____ that the car would never run again.
4. [it] The dulcimer has a soft, sweet tone _____ was long ago replaced by the guitar in bluegrass music.
5. [I] "Not I," she replied with a scowl "_____ never liked him."

✔ **CHECKLIST 13.2: REVISING TO CORRECT SENTENCE ERRORS**

Examine drafts of your papers carefully for run-on errors and comma splices. If you have trouble with these errors, spend extra time trying to locate and correct them. Try these techniques.

**13e
run-on**

- Read your papers aloud slowly. When you read aloud slowly, your ear probably will pick out the independent clauses. They will sound like complete sentences, and you are likely to pause for breath at the end of each one. When your voice clearly stops and drops, look for a period or a semicolon at that point.
- Before you write your final draft, count your sentences. Number your sentences all the way through the draft of your paper. Then see if you have separated them with the right punctuation and capitalization. If the number of sentences seems small in relation to the length of the draft, you may have committed some run-on errors.
- Read your papers backward from the last sentence to the first. When you use this technique, you can consider each sentence as a separate unit of meaning apart from the surrounding sentences. Each sentence appears as a complete statement on its own, and implied connections, such as those made through transitional expressions, adverbs, and pronouns, cannot trap you into making errors. You

must read very carefully, being sure that each group of words you read aloud forms a complete sentence or a complete independent clause.

■ Watch for the words and phrases that often cause run-on errors or comma splices at sentence junctures (see 13e). Subject pronouns, transitional expressions, and conjunctive adverbs frequently appear at sentence junctures. Words and phrases in these groups can trap you into writing run-on errors and comma splices. If you look for those words and phrases when you read over your drafts, you can often locate and correct your mistakes.

■ **Exercise 13.6**   In each item below, underline the sentence element that gave rise to the run-on error or the comma splice. Correct the errors by using any of the methods explained in this chapter.

> 1. Mounting financial problems have forced many colleges to take dramatic steps, for example one college sold its two hundred acre campus and moved to smaller quarters.
>
> 2. A hush fell over the crowd then a small man with an empty sleeve on his coat and a hideously scarred face got out of his seat and hobbled to the platform.
>
> 3. Public transportation is quick and safe on the other hand it does not offer the flexibility and privacy of travel by car.
>
> 4. Sidesaddles allowed women to ride horseback modestly in an age of long, thick skirts, however, such saddles were extremely dangerous because they did not allow women to grip the horse with their legs.
>
> 5. A two-cycle gasoline engine is excellent for lawn mowers and for boats equipped with an outboard motor it is not good for larger machines because its lubrication is uneven at the higher temperatures larger machines generate.

13e
run-on

■ **Exercise 13.7**   Numbers in parentheses at the end of the sentences indicate the number of run-ons and comma splices each sentence contains. Revise any incorrect sentences using any of the methods explained in this chapter.

> 1. Raccoons once won people's hearts as furry creatures with black masks now as rabies is sweeping many metropolitan regions raccoons are feared and hated, they have lost their attractiveness as adorable cuddly animals. (3)

2. In the past police would receive occasional complaints about raccoons, they overturn garbage cans or bite their way through trash bags, however, last year police in some regions received three or four raccoon complaint calls a week. (3)

3. In December police shot and killed four raccoons, one was rabid, in fact raccoons are identified as major carriers of rabies it is a sometimes fatal disease. (4)

4. Many see as essential the need to protect people from rabies nevertheless they are unhappy with the usual way of dealing with the problem—shooting the raccoons. (2)

5. The slaughter may not be necessary apparently only one in six raccoons has rabies, unfortunately people respond to early reports of rabies by trying to destroy every raccoon they encounter, a more humane response might be to innoculate raccoons, there are procedures available to accomplish this goal, the costs are high. (6)

**13e
run-on**

CORRECTING SENTENCE FRAGMENTS

End marks—periods, question marks, and exclamation points—separate grammatical units that are complete sentences. To be complete grammatically, a sentence needs both a subject and a predicate. A grammatically incomplete unit starting with a capital letter and closing with an end mark is called a **sentence fragment.**

In the following sentence fragments, the writer makes an incomplete word group look like a sentence by using a capital letter for the first word and placing a period after the last.

And tried the hot tamales.

Watching the ducks on the lake.

You can easily spot sentence fragments when they appear in isolation. But when a fragment is buried in surrounding sentences, you may have trouble seeing it and correcting it.

We enjoyed our stroll through the park. **Watching the ducks on the lake.** The leaves were changing color.

We visited a new Mexican restaurant downtown. **And tried the hot tamales.** They burned my mouth for a week.

Each of these fragments can be added to the preceding sentence to form one complete sentence.

We enjoyed our stroll through the park, watching ducks on the lake.

We visited a new Mexican restaurant downtown and tried the hot tamales.

■ **Exercise 14.1**   Identify the fragments below. Put a check by any complete sentences you find.

1. Without any funds from the federal government or from foundations.
2. Who ate twelve tacos.
3. Surrounded by rich farmland and dense forests.
4. Driving through the California desert with the temperature at 114 degrees.
5. Johnny Cash sings many songs about prisons and prisoners, their loneliness and their hardships.
6. Since she stopped drinking milk.
7. That woman holds two jobs.
8. Country music wailing with pain and loss.
9. A woman who holds two jobs.
10. Country music wails with pain and loss.

■ **Exercise 14.2**   Identify the complete sentences and the fragment or fragments in each selection below.

**14a
frag**

1. Alcohol can damage heart muscle tissue in a condition called *alcoholic cardiomyopathy.* Which can be fatal. Especially to people who cannot leave alcohol alone.
2. The Federal Communications Commission proposes opening a swath of radio frequencies. Hoping to expand new mobile communications. To reallocate frequencies not used by utilities, railroads and police departments.
3. New studies have revealed important information about dyslexia. A reading problem that affects about 10 percent of children. Not necessarily permanently, the studies show.
4. Human beings develop intellectually in leaps from one stage to another, say some important theorists in psychology. Such as Erik Erikson and Jean Piaget.
5. Working for the government sometimes requires great personal sacrifice, but the rewards of public service are great. By hard work and careful attention to detail, a government worker can do much good for the society at large.

14a

Making Fragments into Complete Sentences

No handbook can give a complete set of rules for converting fragments into sentences, but the following examples show some typical problems and ways to remedy them.

■ Join the fragment to the sentence that comes before it.

Fragment: Television brings current events to life. **Through interviews and dramatic images.**

Corrected: Television brings current events to life through interviews and dramatic images.

Fragment: Jean Rhys's *Good Morning, Midnight* is a novel about Sasha Jansen. **A lonely woman in Paris.** She searches desperately for escape from a dismal past.

Corrected: Jean Rhys's *Good Morning, Midnight* is a novel about Sasha Jansen, a lonely woman in Paris.

■ Add the fragment to the beginning of the sentence that follows or precedes it. Your intended meaning determines whether you connect a fragment to the sentence before or to the sentence after it. Sometimes neither option will produce a sentence that makes sense and pleases stylistically.

Fragment: Watching ducks glide across the lake. Men and women sit everywhere beneath the flowering dogwoods and talk softly in the afternoon sun.

Corrected: Watching ducks glide across the lake, men and women sit everywhere beneath the flowering dogwoods and talk softly in the afternoon sun.

■ Add or remove words to convert a fragment into a complete sentence, or change the wording of the fragment itself.

Fragment: On Sundays in May at the seashore everyone can relax. **Watching the lobster boats come in.**

Corrected: On Sundays in May at the seashore everyone can relax. Children enjoy watching lobster boats come in.

or

On Sundays in May at the seashore everyone can relax. Children watch lobster boats come in.

■ **Exercise 14.3** Return to Exercise 14.1. Correct each fragment by using the techniques explained in 14a. Be sure that your new sentences make sense. Read them aloud.

**14a
frag**

✔ **CHECKLIST 14.1: CORRECTING SENTENCE FRAGMENTS**

Correct sentence fragments according to sentence logic and your own stylistic tastes. Take one of the following steps.

- Connect the fragment to the sentence before or after it.
- Add a new subject, a new verb, or both, and add any other necessary words.
- Remove any words that keep the fragment from being a complete sentence.
- Make a present or past participle into a verb by adding a helping verb such as *am, is, are, was,* or *were* before the participle or by changing the participle into a correct verb form.
- When necessary, add a subject to the fragment to convert it into a complete sentence.
- Change an infinitive to a verb by removing *to* and using the correct form of the verb. Or you can sometimes use *like, likes, want, wants, plan, plans, try, tries, am, is,* or *are* before the infinitive. Sometimes you will have to add a subject to fragments that contain an infinitive.
- Make any necessary changes in the wording of the fragment to convert it into a complete sentence.

14a
frag

■ **Exercise 14.4**   Find the thirteen fragments in the following selection. Correct each one by adding it to an adjacent sentence, by adding words to it, or by removing words from it. Be sure that each sentence has a subject and a predicate.

The yellow ribbons, symbols of support for our armed forces fighting in the Persian Gulf, now torn and pale. Still wrapped around the oak trees near the army air field in Savannah, Georgia. Where crowds once cheered and waved American flags. To welcome home the men and women. Who fought in Operation Desert Storm. Coming back from the war in the Persian Gulf.

As in other places. The war is a faded memory. Something from our past. All over America people talk of other issues. The failing economy. The increase of crime in our cities.

The Gulf War is a war few of us think of any more. As we worry about domestic problems. But the war is not a forgotten dream. For those who fought there. And their families.

14b
Recognizing Words and Phrases That May Cause Fragments

When you begin sentences with present and past participles, infinitives, and certain adverbs and subordinators, you may trap yourself into producing an incomplete sentence. If, when you revise your drafts, you check carefully for words in these groups at the beginnings of your sentences, you may spot unwanted fragments.

Recognizing Incomplete Verb Forms

Some verb forms cannot serve as sentence predicates. They look like verbs, but, as they serve other functions in their sentences, they can be misleading.

Present participles are verb forms ending in *-ing*, such as *singing, running, speaking, trying, shouting, working,* and *flying* (see p. 115, 16a). They are not verbs, but modifiers, and they cannot stand alone in an independent clause.

Fragment: **Running wildly in the hills.** The stallion looked untamed and beautiful and somehow ghostly.

Corrected: Running wildly in the hills, the stallion looked untamed and beautiful and somehow ghostly.

14b
frag

Past participles are verb forms ending in *-ed, t,* or *-n,* such as *dressed, faded, hurt,* and *driven* (see 16a). Like present participles, they function as modifiers and cannot stand alone.

Fragment: The toast popped up. **Burned black as coal.** It looked like a piece of volcanic rock.

Corrected: The toast popped up, burned black as coal.

Infinitives are verb forms introduced by the word *to,* which is called the **infinitive marker** (see p. 114). Infinitives include such forms as *to play, to scream, to study,* and *to eat.* Like participles and participial phrases, they express action vividly and sometimes seem so strong that writers may think them capable of standing alone as sentences.

Fragment: The mayor spoke forcefully. **To convince her audience of the need for tax reform.**

Corrected: The mayor spoke forcefully to convince her audience of the need for tax reform.

Adverbs, subordinators, and connecting words and phrases that often begin fragments include *also, as well as, especially, for example, for instance, just like, mainly,* and *such as.* In speaking we often use fragments along with adverbs and connecting words, but when we write, we must be sure that adverbs and connecting words or phrases lead into complete sentences.

> **Fragment:**   An individual spectrum exists for each element. **For example, hydrogen.** It has a red, a blue-green, and a green line.

> **Corrected:**   An individual spectrum exists for each element. For example, hydrogen has a red, a blue-green, and a green line.

Subordinators that may lead writers into making sentence fragments include conjunctions, such as *as long as, after, although, as, as if, as soon as, because, before, wherever, once, while, how, provided, if, since, so that, though, unless, until, when, where,* and *whether,* and relative pronouns, such as *what, which, who, whoever, whose, whom, whomever, whatever,* and *that* (p. 109).

> **Fragment:**   The University Government Association gives students a voice in making policy. **Because they, too, should influence the university administration in matters of academic, social, and cultural welfare.**

> **Corrected:**   The University Government Association gives students a voice in making policy because they, too, should influence the university administration in matters of academic, social, and cultural welfare.

14b
frag

✔ **CHECKLIST 14.2: CHECKING FOR INCOMPLETE SENTENCES**

To avoid sentence fragments, you must first be able to recognize them.

- Read your sentences aloud, or get a friend to read them aloud to you. Distinguish between the pause that a speaker may make for emphasis and the grammatical pause marked off by a period, a question mark, an exclamation point, a semicolon, or a colon.

- Read your paper from the last sentence to the first, or have a friend read the paper aloud in that way to you. Stop after you read each sentence and ask: Is it complete? Does it make a complete statement or ask a complete question?

- Check for subjects and predicates. Every complete sentence must have at least one subject and one predicate.

- Look at sentences that begin with present and past participles, connective words and phrases, and subordinators.

14c
Using Fragments for Special Effects

Although most formal writing requires complete sentences, sentence fragments can occasionally achieve special effects. Writers of fiction use fragments to record dialogue, since when we speak, we often use incomplete sentences. However, the context always makes the meaning of the fragment clear.

Although they can be effective and acceptable in the hands of skilled writers, fragments are still rare in the expository writing you will do in college. Use them carefully. In writing for your courses, when you write a fragment, you may even want to mark it as such with an asterisk and a note at the bottom of the page. Your teacher will then know that you have made a deliberate choice, not a mistake.

> Jean leaned back, her hands clasped round a knee, looking at the water below them. "I came to a decision last night, Dan." It was unexpected, and he glanced at her. **"Yes?"** She shrugged. **"Nothing momentous.** But I think I'll definitely try for a teacher training course when I get home. **If I can find a place."**
>
> —JOHN FOWLES

> I had a sudden mad impulse to pack my bags and get away from both of them. Maybe it wasn't a question of choosing between them but just of escaping both entirely. **Released in my own custody. Stop this nonsense of running from one man to the next. Stand on my own two feet for once.**
>
> —ERICA JONG

Fragments may also appear in nonfiction, especially when the writer is striving for an informal, conversational effect.

> But such was Autry's impact that even the action-all-the-way Cowboys had to have somebody in their films who could sing a few cowboy songs while the hero stood around listening and tapping his foot. Charles Starrett was good enough not to need any yodeler's slowing up his action. But you couldn't buck the fashion. Anyway, Dick Weston did not exactly stop the show. **And never would if he went on calling himself Dick Weston.** The name was definitely not a bell ringer. **No matter how many times you said it.**
>
> —JAMES HORWITZ

Questions and exclamations often have impact when written as fragments. To call attention to an idea, writers can use fragments effectively.

> **American culture?** Wealth is visible, and so, now, is poverty. Both have become intimidating clichés. **But the rest?**
>
> —Peter Schrag

> Whatever economic sanctions can achieve will be duly tested. A semblance of Western resolve has been temporarily achieved. **At a considerable price.**
>
> —*New York Times*

■ **Exercise 14.5**   In each selection, correct each fragment by adding it to the sentence that comes before or after or by changing it into an independent sentence. Put a check by any selection that is correct as it stands.

1. In 1980, the Supreme Court ruled that scientists could patent bacteria made in laboratories. An important decision that has made profitable genetic engineering possible.
2. In and around Boston, the sixty-eight institutions of higher learning draw both full-time and part-time students, numbering more than 150,000. Of these over 60 percent come from states other than Massachusetts.
3. When I approached him after school for extra help with my algebra. He replied that he had already given me enough time. That I should try to find a tutor. Who could explain things slowly and carefully.
4. A University of Manchester astronomer, who thrilled sky watchers when he reported discovery of a planet around a neutron star. Retracted his announcement.
5. Abigail Adams championed women's rights. Writing about new legislation to her husband John early in the history of the United States. She said, "I desire you would remember the ladies and be more generous and favorable to them than your ancestors." A strong remark, considering the times.

**14c
frag**

■ **Exercise 14.6**   Return to Exercise 14.2. Correct each fragment. Do not change correct sentences.

■ **Exercise 14.7**   Using the following fragments, construct complete sentences. You may add anything you want to make the sentences complete.

1. Slipping across a patch of ice.
2. The coiled snake under my bed.
3. A woman of enormous strength and speed.
4. When I had discovered myself walking in my sleep.
5. When you open the refrigerator door and find the milk spoiled and the bread hard and stale.

■ **Exercise 14.8**   Identify the fragment in the following passages. Then explain why you think each writer used a fragment instead of a complete sentence. If you wanted to avoid the fragment, what would you do?

1. Mr. Fitzgerald and his wife, Kathy Fitzgerald, realized that if their hopes for filming the script were to be realized, they would need more help. Which they got in the form of Tom Shaw, a well known production manager and old friend of John Huston, who left a big-budget Barbra Streisand picture to take charge of *Wise Blood.*

   —LINDA CHARLTON

14c frag

2. And so whenever we go to Detroit we always go to visit this friend of our girlhood. Who knows how we looked before our teeth were straightened. Who knows how we talked before our voice got unBrooklyned. Who knows what we ate before we learned about artichokes. And who, by her presence, puts us in touch with an earlier part of ourself, a part of ourself it's important never to lose.

   —JUDITH VIORST

3. But how many women can name marriage itself as a source of our turbulence? More often than not, we were the ones who most wanted to get married. Besides, if not marriage, what *do* we want? Divorce? That is too fearsome.

   —NANCY FRIDAY

4. Milan is quite an attractive little city. A nice cathedral, *The Last Supper,* a very glamorous train station built by Mussolini, La Scala, and many other enjoyable sights.

   —FRAN LEBOWITZ

MAKING SUBJECT AND VERB AGREE

When a verb is singular, its subject must be singular; when a verb is plural, its subject must be plural. When a subject is in the first, second, or third person, the verb must match it (as we saw on pp. 93–94). This matching in number and person of subjects and verbs is called **agreement.**

In the present tense, the presence of the -*s* suffix at the end of a subject or verb usually indicates a plural subject or a singular verb.

> Our *dog* **sleeps** in the basement.
>
> Our *dogs* **sleep** in the basement.

The suffix -*s* (or -*es*) on a noun subject generally means that the subject is *plural.* The suffix -*s* (or -*es*) on a present-tense verb usually tells you that the verb is *singular.* Singular noun subjects, which usually do not end in -*s,* accompany singular verbs, which usually do end in -*s.*

Agreement: singular noun subject; singular verb, third person, present tense

> An *orchid* **costs** too much.
>
> The *house* **needs** paint.
>
> The *day* **goes** by quickly.

Plural noun subjects, which usually do end in -*s* (or -*es*), accompany plural verbs, which usually do not end in -*s.*

Agreement: plural noun subject; plural verb, third person, present tense

> *Orchids* **cost** too much.
>
> The *houses* **need** paint.
>
> The *days* **go** by quickly.

15a
Making Noun Subjects and Verbs Agree

Using Singular Noun Subjects Ending in -s

The letter -s at the end of a word is not always a suffix denoting the plural form. Some singular nouns end in -s, and they, too, must match singular verb forms.

> *Glass* **breaks.**
>
> *Moss* **grows.**
>
> *Fungus* **spreads.**

Using Plural Noun Subjects Not Ending in -s

Some nouns do not use the suffix -s for the plural form (see pp. 366–367). But no matter what the form is, a plural subject requires a plural verb.

> *Children* **giggle.**
>
> *Men* **guffaw.**
>
> *Alumni* **contribute.**

15b
Making Pronoun Subjects and Verbs Agree

**15a/b
agree**

Using Singular Pronoun Subjects

The third person singular pronouns *he, she,* and *it,* like the nouns they replace, require singular verbs.

> *She* **raises** tomatoes.
>
> *He* **keeps** the cat away.
>
> *It* **eats** all the seedlings.

Using the Pronouns *I* and *You*

Even though the pronoun *I* is singular, it always takes the present tense verb without a singular -s ending.

> **I applaud.**   **I write.**
> **I dream.**   **I cry.**

The pronoun *you* functions as both a singular and a plural, but it always takes a plural verb—that is, a verb without the -*s* suffix.

You **live.**	I **am.**
You **laugh.**	You **are.**
You **love.**	She **is.**

Using Plural Pronoun Subjects

They **applaud.**

We **love** trains.

■ **Exercise 15.1**   In the sentences below, subjects are in italics and verbs are in boldface. If subjects and verbs are singular, make them plural; if they are plural, make them singular. You may need to change other words as well. Follow the example.

Example:
A *field mouse* **takes** cover in the house when the *temperature* **drops.**

Field mice **take** cover in the house when *temperatures* **drop.**

1. The *horses* **gallop** swiftly over the plains.
2. A *city* **provides** many interesting things for people to do.
3. A *flu epidemic* **affects** old people severely.
4. *I* **drive** her to class on Mondays, but on Thursdays *she* **insists** on taking the bus.
5. *Terror* **stalks** some neighborhoods; *people* **face** the possibility of violence every day.

**15c
agree**

15c
Using Plural Verbs with Subjects Joined by *and*

Sometimes a plural subject consists of two singular nouns joined by *and*. These are considered plural subjects and require a plural verb.

Pepper and garlic **flavor** the soup.

Greed and arrogance **disgust** most people.

Queenie and Clarence **work** on cars.

When subjects joined by *and* suggest a single idea, they may take a singular verb, but such uses are rare.

The *tenor and star* of the show **is** out with the flu.

The words *each* and *every* preceding singular subjects that are joined by *and* require a singular verb for the whole subject, even though the subject may sound plural.

In the Nittany Mountains, *each dawn and dusk* **fills** the sky with soft, pink light.

When *every window and every door* **shuts** out drafts, your furnace will burn less oil.

In the rare instances when *each* follows subjects joined by *and*, you may choose either a singular or a plural verb, whichever sounds better to you.

In the Nittany Mountains, dawn and dusk each **fill** (or **fills**) the sky with soft, pink light.

15c agree

AGREEMENT OF SUBJECT AND VERB

Singular subject	Singular verb
I	love
He	loves
The compact disc	was spinning
Our class	laughs
He	sings
The dog	barks
You	are
She	is
Anybody	can
Every one of them	is
Each of us	was
Either Burriss or Ted	is
Neither Dorothy nor John	is
Everyone	is
The friend who	was coming
The committee	is meeting
Mathematics	is

AGREEMENT OF SUBJECT AND VERB (*Continued*)

Plural subject	Plural verb
Dogs, walruses, and seals	bark
They	are barking
He and I	sing
All of them	are
All of us	were
Both Burriss and Ted	are sitting
The three friends who	were coming
The committee members	are meeting

15d
Learning a Special Case: The Verb *To Be*

With the verb *to be*, observe the rules of agreement in both the present and past tense (see p. 248). In the present tense, the various forms of *to be* are irregular and require selective use with subjects.

am: When *I* **am** tired, I cannot think.

is: The *door* **is rattling.**
Martha **is** late again.
He **is serving** tables.
It **is** dawn, and still *she* **is studying.**

are: The *waves* **are racing** to the shore.
They **are gardening;** *we* **are resting.**
When *you* **are finished,** you can go.

In the simple past tense both singular and plural verbs use the same form for all subjects—except for the verb *to be*, which has two past tense forms, *was* (singular) and *were* (plural).

was: The *ball* **was** high.
He **was** merely pink, but *I* **was** lobster-red.

were: As *you* **were reading,** the *children* **were planning** their little surprise.
The *refugees* **were standing** patiently in line.

The rules of agreement also apply to the present perfect tense (see 16a). In the present perfect tense, the helping verb *has* is singular and the helping verb *have* may be either singular or plural.

15d
agree

I **have biked** across the country twice.

He **has** often **complained** about his back.

They **have been** out all night.

TO BE

	Singular	Plural
Present:	I am	we are
	you are	you are
	she is	they are
Past:	I was	we were
	you were	you were
	it was	they were

15e
Watching Out for Intervening Words

Make your verbs and subjects agree when misleading words or phrases come between them.

**15e
agree**

Large *sums* of money **go** to national defense.

One *error* in a column of figures **throws** computations off by thousands.

Words such as *in addition to, as well as, along with, plus, including,* and *together with* do not affect the number of the subject. They usually serve as prepositions introducing the object of a preposition, which can never be the subject of a verb (as we saw on p. 109).

The price, including the tip and taxes, **was** $45.

Although such a sentence may be grammatically correct, it may still be awkward. Revise awkward sentences whether they are grammatically correct or not.

One of my happiest childhood memories **is** of a baseball game between the Philadelphia Athletics and the St. Louis Browns. I can still see the bright colors of the grass and the uniforms, and I can still feel the excitement of the crowd.

The *Marx brothers,* including Groucho, still **make** audiences laugh in *A Night at the Opera,* filmed half a century ago.

The plural subject *Marx brothers* requires a plural verb, **make:** the phrase *including Groucho* does not influence the number of the verb.

15f
Making Subject and Verb Agree: *Or, Either-Or, Neither-Nor*

And connects subjects to make them compound and plural. *Or* has a different effect. It says, literally, take one or the other, not both. Subjects connected by *or* are therefore singular and take singular verbs. So do subjects connected by *either . . . or* and *neither . . . nor.*

> A simple fungus *infection or a rash* between the toes **is** often extremely painful.

> *Either running or swimming* **improves** the heart's performance significantly.

When a subject with *or* or *nor* contains both a singular and a plural part, the verb agrees with the nearest part of the subject.

> *Either fine art or old coins* **make** a good hedge against inflation.
> *Either old coins or fine art* **makes** a good hedge against inflation.

> *Neither Jack Miller nor his friends the Stanleys* **like** beer.
> *Neither the Stanleys nor their friend Jack Miller* **likes** beer.

Combined singular and plural subjects often sound awkward. Consider revising them to make compound subjects that may be expressed easily by a plural verb.

> Old coins and fine art **make** a good hedge against inflation.
> Both the Stanleys and their friend Jack Miller **dislike** beer.

**15f/g
agree**

15g
Keeping Agreement in Special Cases

Making Indefinite Pronouns Agree

Singular indefinite pronouns, such as *anybody, anyone, anything, each, either, everybody, everyone, neither, nobody, no one,* and *one,* require singular verbs.

Use singular verbs with singular indefinite pronouns even when a prepositional phrase with a plural noun comes between the pronoun subject and the verb.

> *Everyone* **is** on strike.
>
> *Nobody* **likes** a losing team.
>
> *Everyone* in all the departments **is** on strike.
>
> *Nobody* among ardent fans **likes** a losing team.

With the more ambiguous indefinite pronouns *all, any, more, most,* and *some,* use singular or plural verbs, depending on whether their meaning is singular or plural in a particular sentence.

> She listens carefully to the children because *some* of them **have** mature ideas.
>
> He made a cake last night; *some* of it **is** still on the table.

The pronoun *none* has been a subject of much debate. Strict grammarians point out that *none* means "no one" and therefore should always take a singular verb. But many writers make the same distinction with *none* that they make with *any.* When *none* refers to a plural noun, some writers use a plural verb. When *none* refers to a singular noun, these writers use a singular verb.

15g

agree

> *None* of my students **are** here yet.
>
> I read his *novel* and discovered that *none* of it **was** any good.
>
> *None* of these ancient peoples **were** horse nomads.

Using Relative Pronouns as Subjects

When the relative pronouns *who, that,* and *which* appear as subjects, use a verb that agrees with the antecedent of the pronoun.

> Readers learn about new products from advertisements *that* sometimes **mislead** by making fantastic claims.
>
> Chow Leung is one of those physicians *who* **work** compulsively.

Be sure you identify the antecedent correctly. In the sentence above, the antecedent is *physicians,* but in the sentences below, it is *one.*

> Chow Leung is the only one of those physicians *who* **works** compulsively.

The Glass Menagerie is one of Tennessee Williams's plays *that* **experiments** with slide photography.

Watching Agreement in Inverted Sentences

When you invert the normal sentence order you have to look carefully for the subject. Don't be tricked by the first noun you see.

Below the waves **lurks** a great white *shark.*

Beside the brook **grow** *tulips* in a profusion of color.

Beginning a Sentence with *There* or *Here*

When a verb follows *there* or *here* at the beginning of a sentence, make sure the subject that follows the verb agrees with it.

Here **lie** the *ruins* of a once-thriving civilization.

There **are** five broken *pencils* on the desk.

There **is** a heavy glass *door* at the end of the corridor.

Making Linking Verbs Agree

Linking verbs must agree with their subjects, not with complements of the subjects.

Scholarship and study **are** her passion.

Her *passion* **is** scholarship and study.

If such sentences sound awkward, revise them to make them smoother.

Her *passions* **are** scholarship and study.

She **loves** scholarship and study.

Making Collective Nouns Agree

Collective nouns stand for or suggest a unit. They are singular in form, even though they have plural meanings. *Army, audience, class, committee, majority, minority, team,* and *group* are examples. When collective nouns stand for a single body acting as a unit, they take singular verbs.

This *class* **meets** too early.

An *army* **needs** good leadership and a good cause.

**15g
agree**

ESL 11

The parking *committee* **issues** permits to students.

The football *team* **travels** to East Lansing tomorrow.

When collective nouns refer to individuals or factions, however, and not to a group acting in concert, they take a plural verb.

The *majority* of the people **were** in favor of reform.

One-third of the team **have** forgotten their jerseys.

Sometimes neither plural nor singular sounds correct.

The graduating *class* **was** already going its separate ways.

The graduating *class* **were** already going their separate ways.

The *couple* **was** arguing with each other.

The *couple* **were** arguing with each other.

These sentences should be revised to make them sound less awkward.

The *members* of the graduating class **were** already going their separate ways.

The *two* **were** arguing with each other.

**15g
agree**

When plural nouns specifying quantities suggest a single unit, they take a singular verb.

Ten minutes **is** not enough time to see the Acropolis.

Two hundred *dollars* **is** not much to pay for a bike these days.

Two-thirds of the pie **was eaten.**

Using Singular Nouns That Look Plural

In contrast to collective nouns, some nouns appear plural in form but are singular in meaning. *Mathematics, politics, athletics, ethics, kudos,* and *pediatrics* are examples. A book or other work that has a plural title is also singular. All these nouns take singular verbs.

Gulliver's Travels **is** both a fantastic narrative and a serious satire on the human condition.

Politics **is** both a science and an art.

Mathematics **is** difficult for many people.

■ **Exercise 15.2** Change the infinitives shown in brackets into the correct forms of the *present tense* verb. Make sure the subjects and verbs agree.

[to be]
1. The two books about health care for the senior citizen _____ not providing enough data.

[to choose]
2. Neither she nor I _____ horror movies.

[to want]
3. Each of the children _____ to do some of the gardening.

[to win]
4. The battery-powered car regularly _____ praise fron environmentalists.

[to require]
5. Economics _____ careful study both for governments and for people planning to buy a new house or car.

[to give]
6. She is the only one of the trustees who _____ any consideration to what faculty members and students want.

[to be]
7. A desk with several drawers _____ all you need.

[to recommend]
8. Our group unanimously _____ an end to parking fees.

[to need]
9. Each man and woman on the boat _____ a life jacket.

[to stand]
10. Beyond the elms _____ a small cabin.

[to be]
11. Connie, as well as both her aunts, _____ looking forward to seeing the movie again.

[to have]
12. Either Theo or his brothers _____ the key.

[to be]
13. Three-quarters of the game _____ over.

[to be]
14. Neither the jewelry nor the silverware _____ missing.

[to be]
15. There _____ considerable politics in-volved in the appointment of Supreme Court justices.

[to be]
16. She wonders which of the students _____ telling the truth.

[to make]
17. An extra fifteen pounds _____ a big dif-ference in how your clothes fit.

[to be]
18. Peanut butter and jelly _____ her favor-ite sandwich.

[to be]
19. "Live and let live" _____ the moral of the story.

[to get]
20. Everybody _____ seasick in gale winds.

15g
agree

✔ **CHECKLIST 15.1: ANALYZING SUBJECTS TO MAKE VERBS AGREE**

When checking sentences to make sure that subject and verb agree, first determine whether the subject is singular or plural. Here are some questions to ask.

- Is the subject singular? Then the verb must be singular.
- Is the subject plural? Then the verb must be plural.
- Is the subject the pronoun *I* or *you?* Then the verb must take the appropriate form, which may look plural but will be correct for these pronouns.
- Is the verb a form of *to be* or another irregular verb? These verbs have many variants, especially in the present tense. You may need to consult a dictionary or a style guide if you don't know the appropriate form.
- Is the subject a compound joined by *and?* Then the verb must be plural, unless the two nouns constitute the same thing (e.g., "first and best"). Analyze the subject carefully.
- Is the subject a compound joined by *or?* Then the verb must be singular, unless both elements or the element nearest the verb is plural.
- Are there intervening words between the subject and verb? Don't let them throw you off.
- Is the subject a singular indefinite pronoun? (Remember that *everybody* and *everyone* are singular.) Then the verb must be singular.
- Is the subject *none?* Then the verb can be singular or plural, depending on *none's* meaning.
- Is the subject a relative pronoun? Then the verb can be singular or plural, depending on whether the pronoun's antecedent is singular or plural.
- Does the sentence begin with *There* or *Here?* Then look for the subject to follow the verb.
- Is the subject a collective noun? Then the verb will likely be singular, unless the noun expresses the idea of individuals or factions operating independently.

15g
agree

USING VERB FORMS CORRECTLY

Verbs can take a variety of forms, depending on how you use them. This chapter teaches you how to make the various verb forms work for you.

16a
Reviewing the Principal Parts of Verbs and Verb Tenses

Tense means "time." Verb tenses show the time of the action described by the verb. To form tenses correctly, you must know the **principal parts** of the verb. The principal parts are the *present* form, the *past* form, and the *past participle.*

The *present* form (the *infinitive* form without the infinitive marker *to*) is listed alphabetically in the dictionary; it is often called the **dictionary form.**

> **Dictionary forms:**   sing, dance, delight, slice
>
> **Infinitive forms:**   to sing, to dance, to delight, to slice

To make the *past* form of most verbs, add the suffix *-d* or *-ed* to the dictionary form.

> I ask**ed,** you play**ed,** he danc**ed,** she slic**ed,** we calculat**ed,** they open**ed**

Recognizing Participles and Helping Verbs

The **past participle** also is usually formed by the addition of *-d* or *-ed* to the dictionary form of the verb. But unlike the past form, the past participle always requires a helping verb to complete the phrase. (The past participle form is sometimes used as a verbal; see p. 115.)

Helping (or **auxiliary**) **verbs** help form tenses. The common helping verbs are *have, has, had, am, is, are, was, were, be, being, been, do, does, did, shall, will, should, would, can, may, might, must,* and *could.* Helpers may also be groups of words such as *have to, ought to, used to, is going to,* and *is about to.*

I **should have predicted** that result.

We **were finished** by noon.

He **had planted** his garden before he left for work.

ESL 16

The important helping verb *do* in its various forms helps other verbs to make emphatic statements, to ask questions, or to make negations.

I **do** work!

Do I work?

I **do** not work.

The **present participle** is formed by the addition of *-ing* to the dictionary form. (Spelling changes that occur when *-ing* is added to some verbs are discussed on pp. 362–363.) Although the present participle is an essential verb form, it is not usually listed among the principal parts. Remember that the **gerund** has the same form as the present participle, but gerunds are always treated as nouns (see p. 115). Here are some present participles.

16a verb

singing, dancing, delighting, slicing

Understanding the Three Simple Tenses

There are three basic tenses in English—present, past, and future.

Simple present

The *simple present* of most verbs is the *dictionary form,* which is also called the **present stem.** To form the third-person singular from the simple present, you usually add *-s* or *-es* to the present stem.

I run	we run	I go	we go
you run	you run	you go	you go
he run**s**	they run	she go**es**	they go

I join	we join
you join	you join
it join**s**	they join

16a
verb

Simple past

To form the simple past of regular verbs, *-d* or *-ed* is added to the present stem. The simple past does not change form.

I escaped	we escaped
you escaped	you escaped
he escaped	they escaped

Sometimes the simple past is irregular. Irregular verbs form the simple past tense not with *-d* or *-ed* but by some other change, often a change in an internal vowel.

I ran	we ran
you ran	you ran
she ran	they ran

Simple future

The simple future is made with the helping verbs *shall* and *will.*

I shall go	we shall go
you will go	you will go
she will go	they will go

Traditional grammar holds that *shall* should be used for the first person, *will* for the second and third persons. In practice, this distinction is often ignored; most people write, "I will be twenty-five years old on my next birthday."

Understanding the Uses of the Simple Present

The *simple present* has several uses. It makes an unemphatic statement about something happening or a condition existing right now.

The earth **revolves** around the sun.

The car **passes** in the street.

It expresses habitual or continuous or characteristic action.

Porters **carry** things.

Dentists **fill** teeth and sometimes **pull** them.

Rocky McKnuckle **fights** with everybody.

The organization of his government always **seems** more important to an incoming president than the organization of his White House.

—THEODORE H. WHITE

It expresses a command indirectly, as a statement of fact.

Periodicals **are** not to be taken out of the room.

It reports the content of literature, documents, movies, musical compositions, works of art, or anything else that supposedly comes alive in the present each time it is experienced by an audience.

Macbeth **is driven** by ambition, and he **is haunted** by ghosts.

The Parthenon in Athens **embodies** grace, beauty, and calm.

Some writers use the present tense to describe historical action on the theory that history happens to us again each time we read about it. This *historical present* is awkward to sustain in English; in general, you should avoid it. A wise rule is to write about the past in the past tense.

Historical present: When Tom Paine **calls** for America's independence, he **is speaking** as an English radical.

Past: When Tom Paine **called** for America's independence, he **was speaking** as an English radical.

16a verb

Understanding the Three Perfect Tenses

In addition to the simple present, past, and future, English verbs have three perfect tenses—the *present perfect,* the *past perfect,* and the *future perfect.* The **perfect** tense expresses an act that will be completed before an act reported by another verb takes place. For that reason, a verb in the *perfect tense* should always be thought of as paired with another verb, either expressed or understood.

Present perfect

In the *present perfect* tense, the action of the verb started in the past. The present perfect is formed by the helping verb *has* or *have* plus the past participle.

I **have worked** hard for this diploma.

The work you began in the past has just ended. This compound sentence is implied: "I have worked hard for this diploma, but now my work is ended."

She **has loved** architecture for many years, and now she *takes* architecture courses in night school.

The interest in architecture began in the past and continues into the present.

Past perfect

The *past perfect* tense reports an action completed before another action took place. The past perfect is also formed with the past participle, but it uses the helping verb *had.*

I **had worked** twenty years before I saved any money.

The act of working twenty years has been completed before the act of saving took place.

They thought they **had considered** all the dangers when they decided on the attack.

The act of considering all the dangers had been completed before the act of deciding took place.

The past perfect, like the present perfect, implies another act that is not stated in the sentence.

He **had told** me that he would quit if I yelled at him. I yelled at him, and he quit.

**16a
verb**

Future perfect

The *future perfect* tense reports an act that will be completed by some specific time in the future. It is formed by the helping verb *shall* or *will* added to *have* or *has* and the past participle.

I **shall have worked** fifty years when I retire.

He **will have lived** with me ten years next March.

Understanding the Progressive Form

The **progressive** form is used with all tenses to show that an action continues during the time that the sentence describes, whether that time is past, present, or future. It is made with the present participle and a helping verb that is a form of *to be.*

ESL 5

Present progressive: I am working.

Past progressive: I was working.

Future progressive: They will be working.

Present perfect progressive: She has been been working.

Past perfect progressive: We had been working.

Future perfect progressive: They will have been working.

Here are some more examples of progressive forms:

I **am working** on a new book.

I **was working** in the kitchen when the house caught fire.

They **will be working** in the garage tomorrow afternoon.

Understanding the Principal Parts of the Most Common Irregular Verbs

Although the principal parts of most verbs are formed quite regularly, many of the most frequently used verbs are **irregular:** their past tense and their past participle are not formed simply by an added *-ed*. The only way to master them is to memorize them.

If you are unsure of the principal parts of a verb, always look in a dictionary. If the verb is regular, a dictionary will list only the present form, and you will know that you should form both the past and the past participle by adding *-d* or *-ed*. If the verb is irregular, a dictionary will give the forms of the principal parts.

The most important irregular verb is *to be,* often used as a helping verb. It is the only English verb that does not use the infinitive as the basic form for the present tense. Study the following forms.

16a verb

TO BE

	Singular	**Plural**
Present:	I am	we are
	you are	you are
	she is	they are
Past:	I was	we were
	you were	you were
	it was	they were
Past perfect:	I had been	we had been
	you had been	you had been
	he had been	they had been

The following is a list of the principal parts of the most common irregular verbs. (Some verbs in this list are not irregular but are included because they confuse many people.) Notice that the past or the past participles of some irregular verbs have more than one form.

COMMON IRREGULAR VERBS

Present stem	Past stem	Past participle
awake	awoke	awoke/awakened
become	became	become
begin	began	begun
blow	blew	blown
break	broke	broken
bring	brought	brought
burst	burst	burst
choose	chose	chosen
cling	clung	clung
come	came	come
dive	dove/dived	dived
do	did	done
draw	drew	drawn
drink	drank	drunk
drive	drove	driven
eat	ate	eaten
fall	fell	fallen
fly	flew	flown
forget	forgot	forgotten/forgot
forgive	forgave	forgiven
freeze	froze	frozen
get	got	gotten/got
give	gave	given
go	went	gone
grow	grew	grown
hang (things)	hung	hung
hang (people)	hanged	hanged
know	knew	known
lay (to put)	laid	laid
lie (to recline)	lay	lain
lose	lost	lost
pay	paid	paid
ride	rode	ridden
ring	rang	rung
rise	rose	risen
say	said	said
see	saw	seen
set	set	set
shake	shook	shaken
shine	shone/shined	shone/shined

16a
verb

COMMON IRREGULAR VERBS (*Continued*)

Present stem	Past stem	Past participle
show	showed	shown
sing	sang	sung
sink	sank	sunk
sit	sat	sat
speak	spoke	spoken
spin	spun	spun
spit	spat/spit	spat/spit
steal	stole	stolen
strive	strove/strived	striven/strived
swear	swore	sworn
swim	swam	swum
swing	swung	swung
take	took	taken
tear	tore	torn
tread	trod	trod/trodden
wake	woke	waked/woke/wakened
wear	wore	worn
weave	wove	woven
wring	wrung	wrung
write	wrote	written

16a

verb

■ **Exercise 16.1**   In the following sentences, supply the correct form of the verb that appears in parentheses at the end of the sentence.

Example:
The book had **been published** before he knew anything about it. (publish)

1. The plane _____ before we can get to the airport. (go)
2. He will _____ the house by the time we get back from our vacation. (clean)
3. He _____ while we were singing in the living room. (cry)
4. They had often _____ together in the same place where the shark attacked. (swim)
5. On the western frontier, horse thieves were sometimes _____ without a trial. (hang)
6. The balloons had _____ before the children arrived for the party. (burst)
7. Macbeth was _____ from a great victory when he met the three witches. (return)
8. She _____ for you at this very moment. (search)

9. Johnson, whom you see over there on the ballfield, has
_____ that bat for an hour and a half. (swing)
10. He _____ to escape from his job whenever he can. (like)

16b
Observing Correct Sequence of Tenses

If you use more than one verb in a sentence, be sure that the time of the verbs flows logically from one to the next. This means that past, present, and future actions must appear in sequences in a logical order.

> While I **am writing,** I **like** to listen to the radio.

In the example above, two actions take place at the same time—the present. Both are reported in verbs using the present tense.

> He **says** that Hamlet **felt** only self-pity.

In this example, the action of *saying* appears in the present; it is a comment on something that happened in the past.

> Dickens **was** already famous when he **made** his first trip to America.

In the example, the two verbs both report past action; both are in the simple past.

> The child **was crossing** the street when I **saw** the car bearing down on her.

In the example, the past progressive is used with the simple past, the action *crossing* continuing to the definite point when I *saw.*

> He **had been** in Vietnam for a year when he **began** to write his book.

In the example above, the past perfect *had been* indicates an action in the past that continued before the action expressed in the simple past tense *began.*

> When I **get up,** he **will have been gone** for hours.

In this example, a future time is indicated by the adverb *when* and the present *get up*. The future perfect *will have been gone* indicates an action that will be completed before the action of getting up takes place.

Ordinarily, a past tense in the first clause of a sentence cannot be followed by the simple present, the present perfect, or a future tense.

> **Incorrect:** Sir Walter Scott **wrote** many novels because he **is** always in debt and **needs** to make money.

> **Revised:** Sir Walter Scott **wrote** many novels because he **was** always in debt and **needed** to make money.

However, you may use the present tense or the future tense in the second clause if it expresses a general truth always in force and follows a first clause containing a verb such as *say, tell, report, agree,* or *promise.*

> They **agreed** that friendships between the sexes **are** not so difficult now.

> He **says** that he **will pay** the bill next month.

> He **says** that he **has paid** the bill already.

> He **says** that he **paid** the bill last month.

For more on the correct sequence of tenses, see 20a.

■ **Exercise 16.2** Fill in each blank with any verb that makes sense. Use the tense given in parentheses.

**16b
verb**

> *Example:*
> After John **had been dancing** for three hours, he realized that the band had stopped playing. (past perfect progressive)

1. He _____ white water rafting five times and plans to go again. (present perfect)
2. Tomorrow _____ the first day of the rest of my life. (future)
3. Ralph _____ in the bank when the robbery took place. (past perfect)
4. Hitchcock always _____ in his own movies. (present)
5. Canada geese _____ continually while they fly. (present)

■ **Exercise 16.3** Fill in each blank with a logical tense of the verb given in parentheses.

1. They were going out the back door when she _____ the bell. (ring)

2. You _____ home by the time you get this letter. (arrive)
3. They _____ for about an hour when the fire broke out in the boat. (sail)
4. Winter _____ by the time you come home from the army. (go)
5. They _____ the split pea soup now. (eat)

16c
Using Mood Accurately

The **mood** of a verb expresses the attitude of the writer. Verbs have several moods—the *indicative,* the *subjunctive,* the *imperative,* and the *conditional.*

Understanding the Indicative Mood

The **indicative** is used for simple statements of fact or for asking questions about the fact. It is by far the most common mood of verbs in English.

> The tide **came** in at six o'clock and **swept** almost to the foundation of our house.

> **Can** he **be** serious?

Understanding the Subjunctive Mood

The **subjunctive** conveys a wish, a desire, or a demand in the first or third person, or it makes a statement contrary to fact.

**16c
verb**

> I wish I **were** a bird.

> Helen wishes she **were** home.

> Would that I **were** home!

> He demanded that his son **use** the money to go to college.

> He asked that she never **forget** him.

> If only I **were** in Paris tonight!

> If I **were** you, I'd read the short story one more time before the test on Tuesday.

The subjunctive form for most verbs differs from the indicative only in the first- and third-person singular. Note that the present subjunctive of the verb *to be* is *were* for the first, second, and third persons, singular and plural.

Were she my daughter, I would not permit her to date a member of a motorcycle gang.

If we **were** born with wings, we could learn to fly.

Even if you **were** to promise that each of you would have the assignment completed, I would not postpone the test.

If they **were** self-confident, they would not have turned down the invitation.

When the subjunctive is used with the verb *to be* to express commands or wishes in the third-person singular or the future tense in the first or third person, the verb form is *be*.

If I **be** proved wrong, I shall eat my hat.

Let there **be** light.

Grammar **be** hanged!

If this **be** treason, make the most of it!

The subjunctive is used in clauses beginning with *that* after verbs that give orders or advice or express wishes or requests.

He wishes that she **were** happier.

She asked that he **draw** up a marriage contract before the wedding.

16c verb

In these examples, a request is embodied in a *that* clause. Since no one can tell whether a request will be honored or not, the verb clause is in the subjunctive.

Should and *had* may also express the subjunctive.

Should he step on a rattlesnake, his boots will protect him.

Should you find yourself unhappy in your new job, don't hesitate to ask to be reinstated here.

Had he taken my advice, he would not have bought stock in a dance hall.

Take care not to confuse the conditional with the past subjunctive. Do not say "I wish we *would have* won the tournament." Say "I wish we *had* won the tournament."

Understanding the Imperative Mood

The **imperative** expresses a command or entreaty in the second-person singular or plural, and the form of the verb is the same as the indicative.

In the imperative sentence, the *subject* of the verb is always *you*, but the *you* is usually understood, not written out.

> **Pass** the bread.
>
> **Drive** me to the airport, please.
>
> **Leave** the room!
>
> **Watch** your step!

Sometimes *you* is included for extra emphasis.

> You **give** me my letter this instant!

■ **Exercise 16.4**   Identify the moods of the verbs in italics in the following sentences. Over each italicized verb, write *I* for indicative, *S* for subjunctive, or *IM* for imperative.

1. If she *was* awake, she must have heard the noise.
2. Soldiers in their last year of service *count* the days until their release.
3. He said that Japan *has* one of the lowest crime rates in the world.
4. If Brian Wilson *were* still *writing* surfing songs, the Beach Boys might not be numbered among rock and roll's great singing groups.
5. *Had* you *been* here, we might not have quarreled.
6. *Don't burn* the toast.
7. If horses *were* smarter, they would never put up with bridles and saddles.
8. You better not *go* in.
9. She demanded that he *eat* the whole banana.
10. If I *had helped* him study, he might have passed the test.

**16c
verb**

Understanding the Conditional Mood

The **conditional** makes statements that depend on one another; one is true on condition of the other's being true. A conditional sentence contains a clause that states the condition and another that states the consequence of the condition. Most conditional statements are introduced with *if.*

ESL 8

> **If** communist governments had been able to produce enough food for their people, they would not have collapsed in 1989.
>
> **If** you will be home tonight, I'll come over.
>
> Even **if** the strike is settled, they will still be angry.

Like the indicative, the conditional requires no changes in ordinary verb forms. The difficulty comes in distinguishing the conditional from the subjunctive. Remember that the subjunctive is used for conditions clearly contrary to fact.

If he **were** here right now, we would be happy.

The example above, in the subjunctive mood, means that he is not here, we know that he is not here, and we are not happy. The following example is conditional.

If he **is** there, we will be happy.

We do not know whether he is there or not. We make a simple statement of fact. If we discover he is there, we will be happy.

If the circumstances are in the past, use the subjunctive for conditions that were clearly not factual and the indicative for conditions that may have been true. The verb *would* or *could* is used as a helping verb for statements that give the supposed consequences of conditions that were not factual.

If he **were** there that night, he **would have had** no excuse.

He was not there; the *if* clause uses the subjunctive, and the clause stating the consequences uses *would*.

**16c
verb**

If he **was** there, he **had** no excuse.

He may have been there; we do not know. If he was indeed there, he had no excuse. The indicative mood is used in both clauses as a simple statement of fact.

The past perfect is used in past conditional statements when the condition states something that was not true.

If Hitler **had stopped** in 1938, World War II **would not have come** as it did.

Avoid using the conditional in both clauses.

Incorrect: If she **would have gone** to Paris, she **would have had** a good time.

Correct: If she **had gone** to Paris, she **would have had** a good time.

Take care not to confuse the conditional with the past subjunctive.

Incorrect: I wish we **would have won** the tournament.

Correct: I wish we **had won** the tournament.

Using the Active and Passive Voice

Learn the difference between the active voice and the passive voice. Use verbs in the active voice in most sentences; use verbs in the passive voice sparingly and only for good reason.

The voice of a transitive verb tells us whether the subject is the actor in the sentence or is acted upon. (A transitive verb carries action from an agent to an object. A transitive verb can take a direct object; an intransitive verb does not take a direct object. See 4b.)

When transitive verbs are in the **active voice,** the subject does the acting. When transitive verbs are in the **passive voice,** the subject is acted upon by an agent that is implied or expressed in a prepositional phrase. (Intransitive verbs cannot be passive. You can say "My brother *brooded* too much," but you cannot say "My brother *was brooded*.") In the passive voice, the transitive verb phrase includes some form of the verb *to be.*

Active: She **mailed** the letter.
John **washed** the dishes.

Passive: The letter **was mailed** by her.
The dishes **were washed** by John.

**16d
verb**

Readers usually want to know the agent of an action; that is, they want to know *who* or *what* does the acting. Since the passive often fails to identify the agent of an action, it may be a means of evading responsibility.

Active: The senator **misplaced** the memo.
The Mustangs lost because Al Tennyson **missed** a tackle on the punt return.

Passive: The memo **was misplaced.**
The Mustangs lost because a tackle **was missed** on the punt return.

Use the passive when the recipient of the action in the sentence is much more important to your statement than the doer of the action.

✔ CHECKLIST 16.1: **AVOIDING COMMON ERRORS IN VERBS**

Verbs present many possibilities for error. Here are a few to watch for.

ESL 6

16d verb

	Faulty	Correct
Irregular verbs		
■ Avoid confusing simple past with past participle.	I **seen** her last night. He **done** it himself.	I **saw** her last night. He **did** it himself. He **had done** it himself.
■ Don't try to make irregular verbs regular.	She **drawed** my picture. We **payed** for everything.	She **drew** my picture. We **paid** for everything.
Transitive and intransitive verbs		
■ Don't confuse *lay* (trans.) with *lie* (intrans.).	I **lay** awake every night. I **lay** my books on the desk when I come in. I **laid** down for an hour.	I **lie** awake every night. I **laid** my books on the desk when I came in. I **lay** down for an hour.
■ Don't confuse *set* (trans.) with *sit* (intrans.).	He pointed to a chair, so I **set** down. She **sat** the vase on the table.	He pointed to a chair, so I **sat** down. She **set** the vase on the table.
Tense		
■ Don't shift tenses illogically.	The car **bounced** over the curb and **comes** crashing through the window. I **asked** him not to do it, but he **does** it anyhow.	The car **bounced** over the curb and **came** crashing through the window. I **asked** him not to do it, but he **did** it anyhow.
Mood		
■ Don't confuse conditional with past subjunctive.	I wish he **would have come** sooner. I would have been here if you **would have told** me you were coming.	I wish he **had come** sooner. I would have been here if you **had told** me you were coming.

My car **was stolen** last night.

Who stole your car is not known. The important thing is that your car was stolen.

After her heart attack, she **was taken** to the hospital in an ambulance.

Who took her to the hospital is unimportant; the important fact is that she was taken.

Scientific researchers generally use the passive voice throughout reports on experiments to keep the focus on the experiment rather than on the experimenters.

When the bacteria **were isolated,** they were treated carefully with nicotine and **were observed** to stop reproducing.

■ **Exercise 16.5**   Rewrite the following sentences to put the passive verbs in the active voice.

1. The paintings on the wall of my kitchen were done by my daughter.
2. At a hundred years of age, Hal Roach was presented with the Smithsonian's highest award for his pioneering film comedies.
3. The movie *Citizen Kane* was made by Orson Welles, was the recipient of many awards, but was not viewed by Welles himself for years afterward.
4. In the 1950s, color was used by filmmakers to compete with television where all the programs were still being shown in black and white.
5. A redistricting plan was revealed yesterday in the state capitol by a joint legislative committee.

**16d
verb**

■ **Exercise 16.6**   The following sentences were all written by professional writers. Analyze each verb to see whether it is in the active or the passive voice. Tell why the passive is used when you do find it.

1. Some birds can be identified by color alone.

—ROGER TORY PETERSON

2. The radio was silenced, and all that could be heard was the echo of the Mayor's voice.

—MARK HELPRIN

3. His purpose on this earth, I was convinced, was to corrupt life. While other kids were plied with fairy tales and ghost stories, he burdened our minds with Tolstoy and Shakespeare and the Bible.

—LINDSAY PATTERSON

4. At this point, a doctor was summoned; a formal pronouncement of death was made; and Big Jim's carcass was dragged, feet first, and for the last time, through the front door of his saloon.

—JOE MCGINNISS

5. Many statesmen feel that weapons are in themselves evil, and that they should be eliminated, as you would crush a snake.

—E. B. WHITE

16e
Using the Infinitive

The **infinitive** is the present tense of a verb with the marker *to*. Grammatically, the infinitive can complete the sense of other verbs, serve as a noun, and form the basis of some phrases.

**16e
verb**

The *present infinitive,* which uses the infinitive marker *to* along with the verb, describes action that takes place at the same time as the action in the verb the infinitive completes.

to go:

He wants **to go.**

He wanted **to go.**

He will want **to go.**

ESL 7

The *present perfect infinitive,* which uses the infinitive marker *to,* the verb *have,* and a past participle, describes action prior to the action of the verb whose sense is completed by the infinitive. The present perfect infinitive often follows verb phrases that include *should* or *would.*

to have seen:

I would like **to have seen** her face when she found the duck in her bathtub.

An **infinitive phrase** includes the infinitive and the words that complete its meaning.

Her attempt **to bicycle through a New York subway tunnel** was frustrated by an express train.

To take such an immense journey required courage and money.

To dance was his whole reason for living.

Her only aim was **to dodge his flying feet.**

He studied **to improve his voice.**

Sometimes the infinitive marker is omitted before the verb, especially after such verbs as *hear, help, let, see,* and *watch.*

She heard him **come** in.

They watched the ship **sail** out to sea.

She made him **treat** her with respect.

In general, avoid split infinitives. A **split infinitive** has one or more words awkwardly placed between the infinitive marker *to* and the verb form. The rule against split infinitives is not absolute: some writers split infinitives and others do not. But the words used to split infinitives can usually go outside the infinitive, or they can be omitted altogether.

Split infinitive: He told me **to** really **try** to do better.

Better: He told me **to try** to do better.

16e
verb

Some writers believe that split infinitives are acceptable.

The government was little altered as Mr. Bush touched down at Andrews Air Force Base at 6:30 P.M. **to** gracefully **assume** the duties but not the powers of the Presidency.

—Time

■ **Exercise 16.7**   Rewrite the following sentences to eliminate split infinitives.

1. Enrique wanted to completely forget his painful romance.
2. They intended to speedily complete the job.
3. The pilot wanted to safely and happily complete the trip.
4. The United States Football League vowed to strictly refuse to sign college football players before they had played in their senior year.

5. Her invitation seemed to really be genuine, but I suspected her intentions.

■ **Exercise 16.8**   Correct the errors in the following sentences. If a sentence is correct as it stands, place a check beside the number.

1. He come home last night and find the dog sick.
2. They take the kickoff and get to work and have a touchdown in five minutes of the first quarter.
3. She worked hard and done a good job.
4. After a long day, it's always good to lay down.
5. He lay his pants over the back of the chair last night and go right to sleep and don't wake up until this morning at ten o'clock.
6. The turtle swum after the goldfish.
7. They hung him by the neck until he were dead.
8. Suzanne Yip drunk three beers and then had passed out on the front steps just as I rung the bell.
9. She shown me the right path but I seen a snake and ran.
10. A blue jay had flew into the storm window and had broke the glass into thousands of pieces.

USING PRONOUNS CORRECTLY

Pronouns take the places of nouns in sentences. If we had to repeat the noun *house* every time we wrote about the ideal *house* in the sentence below, we would have awkward and unwieldy prose.

> The house stood on a shady street, and the house looked large and comfortable, as if the house were perfectly suited for a large family and for two sets of grandparents visiting the house for long periods.

We use pronouns to avoid awkwardness, to simplify style, and to express certain ideas clearly. (See p. 100 on identifying pronouns.)

We could not express some ideas without pronouns. Many sentences require first-person pronouns (*I, we, our,* and *ours*) or second-person pronouns (*you, your,* and *yours*), and no other words can serve in their place.

17a
Coordinating Pronouns and Antecedents

By themselves, pronouns are indefinite words, therefore, most pronouns require an antecedent to give them content and meaning. The **antecedent** is the word the pronoun substitutes for. The antecedent usually appears earlier in the same sentence or in the same passage. In the following example, the antecedent for the pronoun *it* is *snow.*

> The *snow* fell all day long, and by nightfall **it** was three feet deep.

Some pronouns are **indefinite,** taking their meaning not from an antecedent but from the sentences in which they are located.

Anybody who wants to see the concert should get a ticket two months in advance.

Some pronouns are **intensive.** They end in *-self,* and they add emphasis to the noun or pronoun they follow.

John **himself** admitted his error.

The legal battle about who owned the field went on for years while the field **itself** grew like a jungle.

No matter how you may judge my actions, you **yourself** would have done the same thing in my situation.

When these pronouns ending in *-self* are used as direct objects or objects of prepositions, they are **reflexive.**

I hurt **myself.**

Alice went to the game by **herself.**

Making Pronouns Refer Clearly to Antecedents

Pronouns that do not refer clearly to their antecedents or that are widely separated from them may confuse your readers. Often the only way to remedy such confusion is to rewrite the sentence.

**17a
pron**

Confusing: Albert was with Beauregard when **he** got the news that **his** rare books had arrived.

Who got the news? Did the rare books belong to Beauregard, or did they belong to Albert?

Improved: When Albert got the news that **his** rare books had arrived, **he** was with Beauregard.

Now the sentence is clear. The rare books belong to Albert, and he got the news of their arrival while he was with Beauregard.

Generally, personal pronouns refer to the nearest previous noun, but don't count on your readers to understand that or figure it out. Revise the sentence whenever the pronoun antecedent is potentially unclear.

Making Pronouns Agree with Their Antecedents

Pronouns must agree with their antecedents in number and gender.

Singular antecedents require singular pronouns. Plural antecedents require plural pronouns.

The *house* was dark and gloomy, and **it** sat in a grove of tall cedars that made **it** seem darker still.

The *cars* swept by on the highway, all of **them** doing more than fifty-five miles per hour.

Roosevelt and *Churchill* found radio a perfect medium for **their** speaking talents.

Use a singular pronoun when all the parts of a compound antecedent are singular and the parts are joined by *or* or *nor.* Notice how the pronouns in the following examples also agree with their antecedents in **gender,** or sexual reference in grammar.

Either *Ted* or *John* will take **his** car.

Neither *Judy* nor *Linda* will lend you **her** horn.

But if Ted and John own one car in partnership, you should write, "Either Ted or John will take *their* car." And if Judy and Linda own only one horn between them, you should write, "Neither Judy nor Linda will lend you *their* horn."

Sometimes you must revise a sentence because a single pronoun will not do.

Incorrect: Neither *Patricia* nor *John* would let me borrow **his** lawn mower.

Revised: Neither Patricia nor John would let me borrow a lawn mower. Patricia would not lend me her lawn mower, and John would not lend me **his.**

Another revision: Patricia would not lend me **her** lawn mower, nor would John lend me **his.**

**17a
pron**

Referring to Antecedents of Unknown Gender

Books on writing used to recommend the masculine singular pronoun to refer to a noun or pronoun of unknown gender.

Any *teacher* must sometimes despair at the indifference of **his** students.

Everybody can have what **he** wants to eat.

Such language, though grammatically correct, is now viewed as sexist. Writers who are sensitive to the implications of the words they use avoid sexist language. The problem apparent in these sentences is not difficult to fix.

Any teacher must sometimes despair at the indifference of students.

Teachers must sometimes despair at the indifference of their students.

You can all have what you want to eat.

Everybody, order anything you want!

We can all have what we want to eat.

All participants can have what they want to eat.

Chapter 11 explores biased language and describes various remedies for it.

When referring to the whole, collective nouns—*team, family, audience, majority, minority, committee, group, government, flock, herd,* and many others—use single pronouns.

The *team* won **its** victory gratefully.

In elections, the *majority* has **its** way.

The *committee* disbanded when **it** finished **its** business.

However, if the members of the group indicated by a collective noun are being considered as individuals, a plural pronoun is appropriate.

The hard-rock *band* broke up and began fighting among **themselves** when **their** leader was converted to Mozart.

17a

pron

In British English, collective nouns usually take plural pronouns and plural verbs.

The cricket *team* quit playing when **they** discovered that **their** spectators had fallen into a profound sleep.

The *government* have refused to elaborate on **their** earlier brief announcement.

■ **Exercise 17.1** Rewrite the following sentences to correct errors in pronoun antecedents. If you find no error in a sentence, put a check by it. You may rewrite a sentence to keep some pronouns, or you may eliminate the pronouns altogether.

1. The ship sailed under the Golden Gate Bridge as it put out to sea.
2. The painter complained to her model that she was too pale.
3. Everyone on the men's swim team should bring their goggles to tomorrow's practice.

4. It says on the menu that the special is fried eggplant.
5. The traveler bought a melon from the peasant as he stood in the shade on the road below Lamia, the city on the hill.
6. The passengers boarded the buses after they sat idly for several hours.
7. Neither Lewis nor Alfred brought their toothbrush.
8. If anyone wears polyester shirts, they will be much hotter in summer and much colder in winter than with cotton shirts, but they can enjoy them for years.
9. Sara phoned Luz when she was rushing out to take the children to a Cub Scout meeting.
10. Neither Ellen nor Mike rode her bicycle to school that day, although they usually rode in together every morning.

ESL 1

Avoiding Pronouns Without References

Some writers use such pronouns as *this, that, they, it, which,* and *such* to refer not to a specific antecedent, but to the general idea expressed by a whole clause or sentence. Using pronouns in this way is imprecise and often misleading.

> Andy Warhol once made a movie of a man sleeping for a whole night, **which** was a tiresome experience.

Was the movie tiresome to watch? Or was making the movie the tiresome experience?

17a
pron

Revised:

> Andy Warhol once made a tiresome movie of a man sleeping for a whole night.

> Andy Warhol once went through the tiresome experience of making a movie of a man sleeping for a whole night.

Differentiating Between the Expletive *It* and the Pronoun *It*

The pronoun *it* always has an antecedent; the **expletive** *it* serves as a grammatical subject when the real subject is placed after the verb or is understood.

> **Pronoun *It*:**   In rural America when a barn burns, **it** often takes with **it** a year's hard work for a farm family.

Expletive *It:* In rural America, when a barn burns, **it** is difficult for a farm family to recover from the loss.

The expletive *it* serves as the grammatical subject of the independent clause that it begins. The sentence could read, "When a barn burns, to recover from the loss is difficult for a farm family." But such a sentence, although correct grammatically, sounds awkward in comparison with the sentence that uses the expletive *it.*

Try to avoid using the expletive *it* and the pronoun *it* one after the other.

Weak: What will happen to the kite? If **it** is windy, **it** will fly.

Improved: What will happen to the kite? It will fly if the wind blows.

The expletive *it* is correctly used without an antecedent. But other pronouns used without antecedents are both awkward and unclear.

Vague

They say that the heat wave will break tomorrow.

They say Philip dyes his hair.

They say we can expect a higher rate of inflation next year.

They haven't plowed the back roads yet.

**17b
pron**

Who is *they?* Sometimes *they* can be identified. If so, be specific; if not, recast the sentence to avoid vagueness.

Better

The heat wave is supposed to break tomorrow.

Philip's former wife says he dyes his hair.

The front-page article in today's paper says we can expect a higher rate of inflation next year.

The road crew has not plowed the back roads yet.

17b
Addressing Your Readers

In the first example below the writer announces that he will talk with the reader throughout as though in a discussion. The tone is informal and the pronoun *you* appropriate. In the second example, the writer chooses a more formal tone. The pronoun *one* does the service that *you* might perform in a less formal piece.

> The book's no good to you now. Neither is scientific reason. You don't need any scientific experiments to find out what's wrong.
>
> —ROBERT M. PIRSIG

> One notices, as one rarely does when dining in company, the lengthiness and noisiness of one's chewing, the slight awkwardness with which one handles one's cutlery, one's ineptitude with lettuce.
>
> —JOSEPH EPSTEIN

Let the tone and intention of your essay determine whether you will use the pronouns *I, my, me,* and *mine.* Many teachers tell students to avoid using first person singular pronouns to prevent student writers from calling attention to themselves and getting in the way of the subject they should be writing about.

Intrusive

I think Carew is a handsome man, but I don't mean that in the conventional sense. I think that the most arresting features on his face are a tiny turned-up nose and a mouth that in my opinion is a mile wide, and I believe it can exaggerate the mildest emotion. When he smiles, I believe the light can be seen as far away as Newport Beach. When he's downcast, I'd say there's an eclipse of the sun.

Nonintrusive

Carew is a handsome man, but not in the conventional sense. The most arresting features on his face are a tiny turned-up nose and a mile-wide mouth that can exaggerate the mildest emotion. When he smiles, the light can be seen as far away as Newport Beach. When he's downcast, there's an eclipse of the sun.

> —RON FIMRITE

**17b
pron**

The first person singular pronouns are appropriate when you are writing about some personal experience that is the center of your prose.

> From all available evidence no black man had ever set foot in this tiny Swiss village before I came. I was told before arriving that I would probably be a "sight" for the village; I took this to mean that people of my complexion were rarely seen in Switzerland, and also that city people are always something of a "sight" outside of the city. It did

not occur to me—possibly because I am an American—that there could be people anywhere who had never seen a Negro.

—JAMES BALDWIN

First-person singular pronouns are also acceptable when you are weighing two contradictory opinions and want to let readers know which side you are on.

Many scientists believe that all matter in the universe will fall back to a central mass, which will eventually explode again in a ''big bang'' like the one that created the universe. Others believe that the universe will end in the solitary deaths of all those stars scattered at an infinite distance from one another in space. I am inclined to accept the second view.

Avoiding the first person can help you avoid wordiness, but when you believe you must use it, you may do so with a good conscience. No rule of written English or good taste holds that you should always avoid saying *I, me, my,* and *mine.*

17c

17c
pron

Avoiding the Unnecessary Pronoun After a Noun

In the following sentences the pronouns in boldface are redundant and should be omitted.

George Bush **he** liked to fish.

My mother **she** graduated from college when I graduated from high school.

The newspapers **they** admitted that advertising sometimes influences their editorial policy.

■ **Exercise 17.2**   Rewrite the following sentences to eliminate pronoun errors. If a sentence is correct, put a check beside it.

1. He liked to read in the bathtub in the summer and to regulate the water temperature with his toes and to keep the door shut and locked, which was inconvenient for others in the family, since the house had only one bathroom.

2. The movie *Apocalypse Now* was based partly on a novel by Joseph Conrad. It is likely that it suffered because Marlon Brando was so fat in it that it was hard to take him seriously. It looked as if he himself had not taken the movie seriously, and despite the money spent on promoting it, it is clear that it failed to meet expectations about it.

3. As a sequel to *Gone with the Wind* the novel *Scarlet* it was a smash commercial hit but reviewers they attacked it for being dull and inconsequential.

4. The house it was small and cramped for a family of four, and my mother and father, they loved each other, and they made the house seem as big as all creation.

5. The readers of this page will forgive this writer perhaps if he indulges himself in a personal recollection of hearing Hank Williams sing at the Grand Ole Opry in Nashvile.

17d
Recognizing the Proper Cases of Pronouns

Pronouns often change their form according to their use in a sentence. The **case** of a pronoun is a form that shows the pronoun's grammatical relation to other words in the sentence. English has only three cases—the *subjective* (sometimes called the *nominative*), the *possessive* (sometimes called the *genitive*), and the *objective* (sometimes called the *accusative*).

Indefinite pronouns (*anybody, everybody;* see p. 100), the pronoun *it,* and the pronoun *you* change form only for the *possessive* case. We speak of *anybody's* guess, *its* color, and *your* writing. The pronouns *I, we, he, she, they,* and *who* change form in each of the three cases.

**17d
pron**

PERSONS AND CASES OF PRONOUNS

Personal pronouns	Singular	Plural
Subjective		
First person	I	we
Second person	you	you
Third person	he, she, it	they

PERSONS AND CASES OF PRONOUNS *(Continued)*

Personal pronouns	Singular	Plural
Possessive		
First person	my, mine	our, ours
Second person	your, yours	your, yours
Third person	his, her/hers, its	their, theirs
Objective		
First person	me	us
Second person	you	you
Third person	him, her, it	them
Relative pronouns		
Subjective	who	who
Possessive	whose	whose
Objective	whom	whom

Using the Subjective Case

Pronouns that act as subjects or as subject complements are in the *subjective case*.

17d pron

> **He** and **I** read books all summer long.
>
> **She** was the candidate **who** I thought deserved the victory.
>
> It could have been **anyone.**
>
> Mark's best friends were **she** and **I.**
>
> Leave the message for **whoever** comes into the house first.

Notice that the subject of a dependent clause is always in the subjective case, even when the dependent clause serves as the object of another clause. *Who* and *whom, whoever* and *whomever,* are likely to give you the most trouble. When in doubt, find the verb of the dependent clause. Its subject will be *who,* even if *who* in the independent clause is the recipient of the action or the object of a preposition.

Using the Possessive Case

Pronouns that show ownership or a special relation are in the *possessive case*.

> **Their** cat climbed up on **his** roof and ate **our** bird.
>
> **Her** critics were louder than **her** admirers.

My uncle was **my** only relative **whose** tastes were like **mine.**

The decision was **theirs** to make after we had made **ours.**

Notice that personal pronouns in the possessive case have two forms—*my* and *mine,* for example. The first form is an adjective—**my** books. The second form actually means *my ones* and stands alone as a subject complement. *Mine,* in the first-person singular, is the only subject complement that does not end in -*s.*

Those books are **mine.**

The towels are **theirs.**

His is the only pronoun that is the same as both adjective and complement.

These are **his** books.

The books are **his.**

Notice also that, unlike nouns, pronouns in the possessive case do not add -'*s. It's* is not the possessive of *it;* it is a contraction for *it is. Who's* is a contraction for *who is.*

Using the Objective Case

Pronouns that are indirect objects, direct objects, or objects of prepositions are in the *objective case.*

17e

pron

The company gave **her** a contract to design the building.

The team chose **me.**

Just between **you** and **me,** I thought the play was terrible.

They believed **him** to be better qualified.

She asked **him** to call **her** that evening.

She wondered to **whom** she should give the spices.

17e
Using Pronouns Correctly

The checklist below provides useful hints for correct pronoun use in places that sometimes give writers trouble.

✔ CHECKLIST 17.1: **SOME USEFUL PRONOUN RULES**

ESL 1

- The subject of a dependent clause is always in the subjective case, even when the dependent clause serves as the object for another clause.

  Dr. Hiromichi promised the prize to **whoever** made the best grades.

  She was the writer **who** I thought deserved to win the Pulitzer Prize.

  Leave the message for **whoever** comes into the house first.

ESL 3

  The child **who** we believed had fallen from the bridge in fact had jumped to retrieve her ball.

- Objects of prepositions, direct objects, and indirect objects always take the objective case.

  She called **him** and **me** fools.

  It was a secret between **you** and **me.**

  A package arrived for Beverly and **him.**

  The old man pushed Rocco and **her** aside and then hobbled down the stairs.

  She glared at Pei Ching and **me.**

  She gave the driver and **me** quite a lecture on road safety and courtesy.

  Who's kicking **whom?**

17e pron

- When a noun follows a pronoun in an appositive construction, use the case for the pronoun that you would use if the noun were not present. Note that in these examples the presence of the noun does not change the case of the pronoun.

  He gave the test to **us** students.

  Freedom of speech is very important to **us** lawyers.

  We students said that the test was too hard.

  We lawyers must protect freedom of speech.

- *Than* and *as* often serve as conjunctions introducing implied clauses. In these constructions, we understand the idea that follows a pronoun at the end of a sentence. The case of the pronoun depends on how the pronoun is used in the clause we would write if we expressed the thought. (Implied clauses are sometimes called elliptical clauses.)

  Throughout elementary school, Elizabeth was taller than **he.**

  I always thought I was smarter than **she.**

  The Sanchezes are much richer and more miserable than **they.**

- Differences in case can cause differences in meaning. In the first sentence below, *Odetta* likes *Jorge* more than *I* like Jorge. In the second sentence, *Odetta* likes *Jorge* more than *she* likes *me.*

✔ **CHECKLIST 17.1: SOME USEFUL PRONOUN RULES** *(Continued)*

Notice how the difference in case changes the meanings of these two sentences.

Odetta likes *Jorge* more than **I.**

Odetta likes *Jorge* more than **me.**

- Pronouns that are the subjects or the objects of infinitives take the objective case.

They thought **her** to be an excellent choice for department head.

I believe **them** to be tedious and ordinary.

Lincoln decided to consult Johnson and **him.**

The conference leaders wanted to choose Martinez and **her.**

- Use the possessive case before gerunds. Use the subjective or objective case with present participles used as adjectives.

Gerund (an *-ing* verb form used as a noun; see p. 115)

His returning the punt ninety-six yards for a touchdown spoiled the bets made by the gamblers.

Her hanging a light above the painting softened the reds and darkened the blues.

Present participle

They remembered **him** laughing as he said goodbye.

Through the wall they heard **him** sighing with pain.

- Pronouns agree in case with with the nouns or pronouns with which they are paired.

Compound

He and Juan Sebastian del Cano sailed around the world.

She and Carla ran a design studio.

Appositive

The captain chose two crew members, **her** and **me,** to attempt the rescue.

The state honored two women, Carla and **her,** for their contribution to the project.

The last two crew members on board, **he** and I, drew the first watch.

Two teachers in the audience, my mother and I, whistled through our fingers.

**17e
pron**

■ **Exercise 17.3** Circle the correct pronoun within the parentheses in the following sentences.

1. He wrote the book for Nini, for (she, her) of the quick quip.
2. Of all the English kings, Henry VIII was the one (who, whom) I think was most cruel.
3. Between her and (I, me) arguments never occurred.
4. I had no objection to (she, her) walking across the country.
5. The candidates seemed to most Americans, including (I, me), to represent a choice between foolishness and stupidity.
6. They were both scheduled to speak—Brian and (he, him).
7. Jackson is the sculptor (who, whom) I believe to be worthy of the Sting Memorial Award.
8. Clark Gable played the same role again and again for (whoever, whomever) directed him.
9. (Whoever, Whomever) wins the Student Council election is unimportant to you or (I, me).
10. Eisenhower was the president for (who, whom) the college was named.
11. Elizabeth got better grades in algebra than (I, me).
12. (We, Us) students had bought a block of tickets to the hockey game.
13. Henry, Jason, and (I, myself) were selected to review the honors policy.
14. Leroy expected the culprit to be (I, me).
15. Beth watched (she, her) struggle to hold back tears.
16. Professor Wu wasn't as strict with Martha and (I, me) as (we, us) feared.
17. Everyone but Justin and (I, me) made it back to the bus on time.
18. Donald wouldn't think of letting (we, us) women help clear the table.
19. The young boy (who, whom) had stolen the parking place walked swiftly.
20. My father disapproved of (me, my) voting for a Democrat.

17e
pron

ADJECTIVE AND ADVERB MODIFIERS

Adjectives and adverbs are describing words. Because they qualify the meanings of other words, we say that they *modify* other parts of speech.

Adjectives tell us what kind or how many. Adverbs tell us where, when, why, and how. Adjectives modify nouns and pronouns; they do not modify anything else. Adverbs modify verbs (including verb phrases), adjectives, other adverbs, and sometimes whole sentences.

18a
Modifying Nouns and Pronouns with Adjectives

You can identify adjectives by locating words that answer one or more of these questions about nouns or pronouns: Which one? How many? What color? What size? What kind?

The adjectives in the following sentences are in boldface.

The road was **long, hard,** and **twisting.**

She was a **brilliant** architect and a **good** tennis player.

The **red** Buick belonged to my aunt.

The **six large** men were brothers.

Writing is always **difficult.**

You may use adjectives before or after the noun or pronoun they modify.

The building, **ugly** and **tall,** burned down last night.

The **tall, ugly** building burned down last night.

The **old** car, **battered** and **rusty,** finally died.

Present and past participles of verbs often serve as adjectives:

Running hard, the bank robber fired back over his shoulder at the police.

The trip was both **exhausting** and **rewarding.**

The **gathering** night was filled with stars.

Buried alive for days, he survived to tell about the earthquake.

Tired and **discouraged,** she dropped out of the marathon.

A noun can be used as an adjective.

Cigarette smoking harms your lungs.

People who drive six miles for a six-pack do not help the **energy** crisis.

The **Marshall** Plan helped rebuild Europe after World War II.

Adjectives can also serve as nouns. All the words in boldface in the sentence below are normally adjectives, but here they clearly modify a noun that is implicit though not stated: *people* or *persons*. The words therefore assume the function of the implicit noun and become nouns themselves.

**18a
adj/adv**

The **unemployed** are not always the **lazy** and the **inept.**

Using Adjectives After Linking Verbs

A linking verb, usually a form of *to be,* always links a subject with an adjective or a noun that adds to the description of the subject.

Charles was **fast** and **reliable.**

The road became **difficult.**

Avoiding Jargon

Bureaucratic jargon teems with nouns used as adjectives when perfectly good adjectives are available or when the sentence is better recast in standard English. Be careful when you use nouns as adjectives: it's easy to pile them up.

Jargon: An **opposition education** theory holds that children learn Latin best under strict **discipline** conditions.

Revised: An alternative theory of education holds that children learn Latin best when strict discipline is enforced.

In the hands of a seasoned bureaucrat, a multitude of nouns used as adjectives can serve much the same function as the passive voice (see 16d): it can obscure facts that the writer prefers not to make clear.

Pursuant to the environmental protection regulations enforcement policy of the Bureau of Natural Resources, special management area land use permit issuance procedures have been instituted.

We may surmise that the bureau is issuing permits for use of lands designated as "special management areas." But what are "special management areas"? They are ecologically fragile lands that the government had decided to protect against development. In other words, the bureau is inviting firms that want to develop those lands to go ahead and do so now. They need only secure a permit, which the bureau is prepared to issue to them. The bureau's "policy" is to ignore regulations established to protect the environment. The bureaucrat who wrote the statement knows that the developers' lawyers will understand it and that the public will not.

■ **Exercise 18.1**

1. Write a sentence in which the adjective *powerful* appears before a noun subject and the adjectives *frightening* and *fierce* appear as subject complements.
2. Write a sentence in which the adjective *cheerful* is used in a phrase immediately after the noun or pronoun that it modifies.
3. Write a sentence in which the adjective *reckless* is used as a noun.
4. Write a sentence in which the adjective *dreamy* is used to modify the subject.
5. Write a sentence in which the noun *flower* is used as an adjective.

**18b
adj/adv**

**18b
Using Adverbs to Modify Verbs, Adjectives,
and Other Adverbs**

Adverbs modify verbs, adjectives, and other adverbs. They answer the questions When? Where? How? How often? How much? To what degree? Why?

The child ran **quickly** into the house.

The game was **hotly** contested.

The water was **brilliant** blue and **icy** cold.

He spoke **more** slowly at the end than at the beginning.

Yesterday she was in Chicago.

The lamp is right **there.**

He came **painfully** to the door.

She **seldom** comes to visit anymore.

We were **greatly** relieved to receive your letter.

She was **completely** surprised at the results.

Dickens mixed humor and pathos **better** than any other English writer after Shakespeare; **consequently** he is still read by millions.

Most adverbs are formed by the addition of *-ly* to the adjective form, but adverbs may also end in *-wise*, *-where*, or *-ward*. And many adverbs have no special ending. Among them are *anew, soon, never, ever, almost, already, well, very, often, rather, yesterday,* and *tomorrow.*

The surest way to recognize adverbs is by understanding how they work in a sentence.

■ **Exercise 18.2**   Fill in the blanks in the following sentences with adverbs that make sense.

1. She waited _____ at the airport for the team to make its way _____ home.
2. Lincoln was _____ witty, but he was also _____ sad.
3. _____ the sun was shining when I got up, and a great blue heron flew _____ over the waters of the lake.
4. Doctors have _____ accused boxing of being responsible for serious brain injuries among fighters.
5. Gina moved _____ slowly into the room.

ESL 14

18c
adj/adv

18c
Using Adjectives and Adverbs Appropriately

As modifiers, adjectives and adverbs have related but distinct functions. To avoid potential problems, pay attention to these special cases.

Avoiding Adjectives When Adverbs Are Called For

In common speech we sometimes use adjectival forms in an adverbial way; in writing, this colloquial usage should be avoided.

Nonstandard: He hit that one **real good,** Howard.
Both *real* and *good* are adjectives, but they are used here as adverbs, *real* modifying *good* and *good* modifying the verb *hit.*

Revised: He hit that one to the warning track, Howard.

Nonstandard: She **sure** made me work hard for my grade.
The adjective *sure* here tries to do the work of an adverb modifying the verb *made.*

Revised: She certainly made me work hard for my grade.

Using Adverbs and Adjectives with Verbs of Sense

Verbs of sense (*smell, taste, feel,* and so on) can be linking or nonlinking. You must decide whether the modifier after a verb of sense serves the verb (adverb) or the subject (adjective). Study the following examples:

Adverb: The dog smelled **badly.**

Here the sentence means that the dog had lost its sense of smell and could not track anything.

**18c
adj/adv**

Adjective: The dog smelled **bad.**

Here the sentence says that the dog needed a bath.

Adverb: I felt **badly.**

The speaker is saying that her sense of touch was bad, perhaps because her fingers were numb.

Adjective: I felt **bad** because she heard me say that her baby looked like a baboon.

The speaker is saying, "I felt that I was bad because she heard me make such a terrible remark." A similar expression would be this: "I felt *guilty* because she heard me make that remark." You would not say "I felt *guiltily* because I hurt her feelings."

Distinguishing Adjectives and Adverbs Spelled Alike

Some words have the same spelling in adjective and adverb forms. Not every adverb is an adjective with *-ly* tacked to the end of it. In standard English, many adverbs do not require the *-ly*, and some words have the same form whether they are used as adjectives or as adverbs. When you are in doubt, consult your dictionary (see p. 200).

WORDS THAT ARE BOTH ADJECTIVES AND ADVERBS

Adjective	Adverb
fast	fast
hard	hard
only	only
right	right or rightly
straight	straight

■ **Exercise 18.3**   In each of the following sentences, locate the words misused as adjectives and put the proper adverbs in their place or vice versa. You may simplify the sentence by eliminating the misused adjective or adverb.

1. I felt really badly because he took my advice about seeing the film and hated every minute of it.
2. He did terrific on the exam, and I was real unhappy about his success.
3. John sure felt good because he ran so fast in the race.
4. McDonald looked greedy at the fried chicken on his neighbor's plate and decided he would go to Kentucky real fast.
5. She sat still while the poisonous snake twined silent in the arbor just over her head, but she was right scared.

■ **Exercise 18.4**   Fill in the blanks in the sentences below with any adverb that makes sense. Avoid the easy choices of *very, well,* and *badly.*

1. As the rains grew heavier, the houses were _____ damaged by the flood.
2. The procession wound _____ through the narrow streets and across the square, where the police had _____ blocked off traffic.

18c
adj/adv

3. One by one the graduates paraded _____ across the stage, shook hands _____ with the college president, received their diplomas, and stood _____ for a moment while relatives snapped their pictures.
4. Despite their _____ competitive spirit the skaters made friends _____ with other contestants for the pairs final title.
5. Jokes are _____ funny because we do not expect the punch line.

18d
Using the Comparative and Superlative Degrees of Adjectives and Adverbs

Adjectives and adverbs are often used to compare. Usually an *-er* or an *-est* ending on the word or the use of *more* or *most* along with the word indicates the degree, amount or quality.

The simplest form of the adjective or the adverb is the **positive** degree, the form used when no comparison is involved. This is the form you find in the dictionary.

> **Adverb:** The dog ran **quickly** out of the house. (*adverb*)
>
> **Adjective:** The dog was **quick.** (*adjective*)

18d
adj/adv

The **comparative** degree is used when two things are being compared. You can form the comparative degree of many adjectives by adding the suffix *-er,* or by using the adverb *more* or *less* with the positive form. The adverb *more* or *less* is also used to form the comparative of most adverbs.

> **Adverb:** The dog was **quicker** than the rabbit.
>
> **Adverb:** The dog was **more quick** than the rabbit.
>
> **Adjective:** The dog ran **more quickly** than the rabbit.
>
> **Adjective:** The rabbit ran **less quickly** than the dog.

Use the **superlative** degree of both adjectives and adverbs when you compare more than two things. You can form the superlative of an adjective by adding the suffix *-est* to the positive form, or by using the adverb *most* or *least* with the positive form. The adverb *most* or *least* is used to form the superlative degree of an adverb.

Adjective: She was the **happiest** of the three women.

Adjective: George was the **most gloomy** person I ever knew.

Adverb: They sang **most happily** when they had eaten well.

Some adjectives and adverbs are irregular. They change form to show degree.

FORMS OF IRREGULAR ADJECTIVES AND ADVERBS

Positive	Comparative	Superlative
bad	worse	worst
good	better	best
little	less	least
many/much	more	most
far	farther	farthest

Some Rules for Using Degrees

18d
adj/adv

- Do not use the superlative for only two things or units.

  Not: Of the two brothers, John was **quickest.**

  But: Of the two brothers, John was **quicker.**

- Do not use the comparative and superlative degrees with absolute adjectives. **Absolutes** are words that in themselves mean something complete or ideal, such as *unique, infinite, impossible, perfect, round, square, destroyed,* and *demolished.* If something is *unique,* it is the only one of its kind. We cannot say, "Her dresses were *more unique* than his neckties." Either something is unique or it is not. "The answer to your question is *more impossible* than you think," is also wrong. Something is either possible or impossible; it cannot be *more* or *less* impossible.

- Avoid using the superlative when you are not making a comparison.

  Dracula is the **scariest** movie!

  The scariest movie ever filmed? The scariest movie you have ever seen? The scariest movie ever shown in town? In common speech, we frequently use expressions such as *scariest movie* or *silliest thing* when we are not in fact comparing the movie or the thing with anything else. In writing, such expressions lack the vocal emphasis we can give them when we speak. They become merely wordy and imprecise, taking up space without conveying any meaning.

■ Avoid adding an unnecessary adverb to the superlative degree of adjectives.

Not: She was the **very** brightest person in the room.

But: She was the brightest person in the room.

Not: The interstate was the **most** shortest way to Nashville.

But: The interstate was the shortest way to Nashville.

■ Avoid making illogical comparisons with adjectives and adverbs. Illogical comparisons occur when writers leave out some necessary words.

Illogical: The story of the *Titanic* is more interesting than the story of any disaster at sea.

This comparison makes it seem that the story of the *Titanic* is one thing and that the story of any disaster at sea is something different. In fact, the story of the *Titanic* is about a disaster at sea. Is the story of the *Titanic* more interesting than itself?

Illogical: Building houses with brick is harder than lumber.

What is being compared here? Is the *act* of building harder than the *thing* we call lumber? The comparison is illogical because acts are different from things and so cannot be compared with them.

Illogical: Mr. Lincoln's speech was shorter than Mr. Everett.

In this sentence, one might suppose that Mr. Everett was six feet tall but that Mr. Lincoln's speech was only five feet.

18e
Avoiding the Overuse of Adjectives and Adverbs

**18e
adj/adv**

Too many adjectives or adverbs can weaken the force of a statement. Strong writers put an adjective before a noun or pronoun only when the adjective is truly needed. They rarely put more than one adjective before a noun unless they need to create some special effect or unless one of the adjectives is a number or part of a compound noun, such as *high school* or *living room*.

Weak

The **sleek-looking high-speed jet** airplane has radically altered the **slow** and **unsteady** rate at which our **current Western** technology and today's **apparent** culture have spread.

The **clean** and brightly **lit** dining car left a **cold** and **snowy** Moscow well stocked with **large** and **sweet fresh red** apples, **many** oranges, **long green** cucumbers, **delicious chocolate** candy, and **countless** other **well-loved** delicacies.

Improved

The jet has radically altered the rate at which **Western** technology and culture have spread.

—JAMES BURKE

The dining car left Moscow well stocked with **fresh** apples, oranges, cucumbers, **chocolate** candy and **other little** delicacies.

—HEDRICK SMITH

Adverbs should be used in the same careful way. Instead of piling them up, use strong verbs that carry the meaning.

Weak: The train **went very swiftly** along the tracks.

Improved: The train **sped** along the tracks.

■ **Exercise 18.5**   In the following sentences, use any adjectives you choose to fill in the blanks. But whatever adjective you write in must be in the proper degree—positive, comparative, or superlative. Be adventurous. Avoid common adjectives such as *good* and *bad*.

1. On the court Magic Johnson was a _____ dribbler than many other players in the NBA.
2. Alaska is the _____ of all the states.
3. Lassie is a _____ actor than John Travolta.
4. Station wagons are _____.
5. Percy owned the _____ leather vest in his motorcycle gang.
6. Country music recordings now are generally the _____ among a range of musical offerings.
7. Rain is generally _____ than snow or ice.
8. The president of the university is _____ than the faculty.
9. The sea is _____ than the desert.
10. Dick Tracy was _____ than Batman.

■ **Exercise 18.6**   Revise the sentences below to correct inappropriate use of adjectives and/or adverbs.

1. She felt badly that her mother was more prettier than she was.
2. Hopefully, I can find a real good job when I graduate.
3. Her long, thin, red-nailed fingers quickly raced silently over the polished white ivory keyboard.
4. Run to town real quick and find Dr. Clemson.

5. The most happiest days of my life were spent when I was a tiny tough troublemaking child on the large, wide-open ranch owned by my uncle Huey.

■ **Exercise 18.7**   Eliminate as many adjectives as you can in the following paragraph:

The old, bent, wrinkled man stood still and thoughtful on the crowded edge of the crowded, busy, narrow street and looked down to the tall, lighted, brick building which loomed up in the thick, damp, gray mist of the early, chill, autumn, overcast, threatening night. He felt in the deep, warm, dark pocket of his new wool black tweed overcoat for the hard, blue, loaded automatic pistol and checked the tiny metal safety catch on the lethal, heavy, criminal weapon. The important, threatening, dangerous gun was there, ready, waiting, eager to be fired.

18e adj/adv

CHAPTER
19

AVOIDING MISPLACED MODIFIERS

In English, clarity depends on the word order within sentences. We expect most adjectives and adjectival clauses and phrases to stand as close as possible to the words they modify. But other words often separate adverbs and adverbial phrases from the words or phrases they modify. We say, "They began their job yesterday," not "They began yesterday their job." And we also write sentences such as "When she was young, she played softball every Saturday," in which the adverbial clause and the simple adverb are separated from the verb by other words.

We have to know when we can separate modifiers from the words or phrases they modify and when we cannot. And in general we can separate adverbs and adverbial phrases from the words they modify more easily than we can separate adjectives from the words they modify.

Yet even adverbs and adverbial phrases can be misplaced. An adverbial phrase ordinarily modifies the nearest verb. It may be separated from that verb by other words, but English idiom joins adverbs and adverbials to the nearest possible verb. When another verb gets in the way, our writing gets into trouble, as in the following sentences from a humorous squib in The New Yorker.

> Wednesday morning, Lee's oldest son Mike signed a national letter of intent with Indiana University to play football for the Hoosiers in the family kitchen at 3838 Ashland Drive in West Lafayette.

The writer intended to make the adverbial prepositional phrase *in the family kitchen* modify the verb *signed*. But since it is nearer to the infinitive phrase *to play football*, it seems to modify that phrase, giving the impression that Mike is going to be running for touchdowns over the kitchen sink.

During the lecture, Johanson will describe the discovery of a band of the new species of hominids who appeared to have been killed simultaneously by some disaster with color slides.

The writer has intended to make the prepositional phrase *with color slides* modify the verb phrase *will describe.* But it is nearer to and appears to describe the noun *disaster* and seems to be an adjectival phrase.

These errors should remind you to keep the related parts of a sentence as close to each other as you can. Otherwise you may confuse your readers.

19a
Avoiding Dangling Participles

Introductory participles and participial phrases must modify the grammatical subject of the sentence. Participles that do not modify the grammatical subject are called **dangling** or **misplaced participles.** A dangling participle lacks a noun to modify. Study these examples.

Incorrect

Having studied small-engine repair in night school, fixing the lawn mower was easy.

Driving along Route 10, the sun shone in Carmela's face.

Using elaborate charts and graphs, the audience understood the plan.

Running down the street, the fallen lamppost stopped her suddenly.

Having thought for a long time, the idea of a community patrol group emerged.

The work was hard, sweating over hot machinery, bending in cramped spaces, sometimes mashing his fingers, skinning his knees, twisting heavy wrenches, and getting home late and exhausted every night.

19a
dangler

Revised

Having studied small-engine repair at night school, Jane found that fixing the lawn mower was easy.
or
After Jane studied small-engine repair in high school, fixing the lawn mower was easy.

Driving along Route 10, Carmela found the sun shining in her face.
or

As Carmela drove along Route 10, the sun shone in her face.

Using elaborate charts and graphs, the mayor explained the plan to the audience.
or

Because the mayor used elaborate charts and graphs, the audience understood the plan.

Running down the street, she saw the fallen lamppost, which stopped her suddenly.
or

As she ran down the street, the lamppost stopped her suddenly.

Having thought for a long time, the committee finally developed the idea of a community patrol group.
or

After the committee thought for a long time, the idea of a community patrol group emerged.

He worked hard, sweating over hot machinery, bending in cramped spaces, sometimes mashing his fingers, skinning his knees, twisting heavy wrenches, and getting home late and exhausted every night.

Usage Note

**19a
dangler**

Informal usage frequently accepts the following forms, which combine an introductory participle as a modifier of the expletive *it* (see 17a), especially when the participle expresses habitual or general action.

Walking in the country at dawn, it is easy to see many species of birds.

The statement is general, expressing something that might be done by anyone. Many writers and editors would prefer this revision: "Walking in the country at dawn is an easy way to see many species of birds."

When beginning a new exercise program, it is good to have a complete physical examination by a doctor.

The statement is general, and to many writers it seems preferable to an even more informal statement like this one: "When you begin a new exercise program, you should have a complete physical examination by a doctor." But many other writers—perhaps a majority—would revise the sentence to avoid the dangling modifier: "Anyone who begins a new exercise program should have a complete physical examination by a doctor."

■ **Exercise 19.1** Rewrite any of the following sentences that have dangling participles. If a sentence is correct, put a check beside it.

1. Daydreaming about his new job, the doorbell startled him.
2. Working hard through the night, I finished the job by daybreak.
3. Looking up, the long V-shaped flock of geese could be seen by everyone in the valley.
4. Racing through the hall, my nose suddenly detected the acrid smell of smoke.
5. Backed into a corner and hurt, the bell barely saved him.
6. Walking along the street, the city seemed calm.
7. Using a word processor, he was able to revise his paper in a couple of hours and turn in the finished product the next day.
8. Having played hard, the loss was bitter.
9. Taking the child by the hand, the hot dog stand was just a short distance away.
10. Having been aged in an oak barrel for twelve years, he discovered that the wine was exactly to his taste.

19b
Avoiding Misplaced Phrases and Clauses

Place phrases and clauses used as modifiers as near as possible to the words they modify.

**19b
mod**

Prepositional Phrases

Prepositional phrases used as adjectives seldom give trouble. We use them commonly in speech, and these speech habits transfer readily to writing:

The book **on the table** belongs to me.

We lived in a house **near the school.**

Prepositional phrases used as adverbs are harder to place in sentences, and sometimes writers lead readers astray by misplacing adverbial phrases.

He saw the first dive bombers approaching **from the bridge of the battleship.**

The multipurpose knife was introduced to Americans **on television.**

He ran the ten-kilometer race from the shopping mall through the center of town to the finish line by the monument **in his bare feet.**

Revised

From the bridge of the battleship, he saw the first dive bombers approaching.

The multipurpose knife was introduced on television to Americans.

In his bare feet he ran the ten-kilometer race from the shopping mall through the center of town to the finish line by the monument.
or
From the shopping mall through the center of town to the finish line by the monument he ran the ten-kilometer race in his bare feet.

Clauses

A misplaced clause is one that modifies the wrong element of the sentence.

Confusing

Professor Peebles taught the course on the English novel that most students dropped after three weeks.

For five years Dixon worked all day as an accountant to support her family and after supper went to night school to study law, which was hard, but finally she got her degree.

Revised

Professor Peebles taught the course on the English novel, a course that most students dropped after three weeks.

For five years Dixon worked all day as an accountant to support her family and after supper went to night school to study law. It was a hard schedule, but she finally got her degree.

**19b
mod**

■ **Exercise 19.2**   Rewrite the following sentences to correct errors in modification.

1. Marco Polo traveled overland to China with his father and his uncle to visit the Mongol Empire, which was very dangerous.
2. He stood in the middle of the room and shouted at everyone in his pajamas.
3. He apologized to his teacher for his paper over the telephone which was smeared with ink and covered with egg and coffee stains.
4. She wrote the outline of her book on the wall in the kitchen with a black crayon.
5. When she was a little girl, she used to lie awake at night wishing that she had a horse in her bedroom.

19c
Placing Adverbs Correctly

ESL 14

Adverbs can modify what precedes or what follows them. Avoid the confusing adverb or adverbial phrase that seems to modify both the element that comes immediately before it and the element that comes immediately after it, as in these examples.

> To read a good book **completely** satisfies her.
>
> Changing gears **continually** gives mental exercise to people who ride bicycles.
>
> To speak in public **often** makes her uncomfortable.

Revised

> She is completely satisfied when she reads a good book.
> *or*
> She is satisfied when she reads a good book completely.
>
> Continually changing gears gives mental exercise to people who ride bicycles.
> *or*
> Changing gears gives continual mental exercise to people who ride bicycles.
>
> When she speaks in public often, she feels uncomfortable.
> *or*
> Often she feels uncomfortable when she speaks in public.

**19c
mod**

Be cautious when you use adverbs to modify whole sentences. Here are two examples.

> **Unfortunately,** *The Quiz Kids* lost its popularity as an afternoon game show.
>
> **Presumably,** the climber was killed in an avalanche three years ago, although his body was never found.

Some authorities maintain that these adverbs modify the entire sentence; others insist that the adverbs modify only the verbs in the clauses where they appear. In either case, the meanings of these sentences are clear. But other adverbs are much more ambiguous when they modify full sentences.

> **Hopefully** he will change his job before this one gives him an ulcer.

Who is doing the hoping? Is it the person who speaks the sentence or the person who is the subject of the sentence?

Revised: We hope he will change his job before this one gives him an ulcer.

Similar confusions occur when other adverbs modify whole sentences:

Briefly, Tom was the source of the trouble.

Does the writer wish to say briefly that Tom was the source of the trouble? Or was Tom briefly the source of the trouble but he then mended his ways?

Revised: To put it briefly, I think Tom was the source of the trouble.

The following sentence does not mean what it says:

Happily, the mad dog fell dead before it could bite anybody.

The grammar of this sentence indicates that the mad dog fell dead very happily before it could bite anybody. The writer doubtless means that people on the street were happy that the mad dog fell dead before it could bite one of them. Why not write that?

■ **Exercise 19.3**   Rewrite the following sentences to eliminate the confusion caused by the placement of adverbs. If a sentence is correct, place a *C* beside it.

1. The car starting easily made this the best day of my trip.
2. Hopefully, she will be able to buy another red coat like the one she lost on the train.
3. A scholar who studies often goes to sleep over her books.
4. People who love to criticize books sometimes do not write books themselves.
5. Happily the child ran to the father she had never seen before.
6. His mother only could forgive him.

19d
Putting Limiting Modifiers in Logical Places

In speaking we sometimes put modifiers in illogical places, but the sense of what we say is clear from tone of voice, gesture, or general context. In writing, the lack of logic that results from misplacement of modifiers can cause confusion. Limiting modifiers, words such as *merely, completely, fully, perfectly, hardly, nearly, almost, even, just simply, scarcely, only,* must be placed directly before the words or phrases they modify.

Confusing

The **almost** exhausted man finished the marathon.

The restored antique cars paraded proudly through the **completely** admiring town.

Revised

The exhausted man **almost** finished the marathon.

The **completely** restored antique cars paraded proudly through the admiring town.

Confusing

He **only** had one bad habit, but it **just** was enough to keep him in trouble.

They were all **nearly** about to graduate, but they wouldn't **even** send one invitation because all of them decided **almost** that the commencement speaker would insult the intelligence of the audience.

Revised

He had **only** one bad habit, but it was **just enough** to keep him in trouble.

They were **nearly** all about to graduate, but they wouldn't send **even** one invitation because all of them decided that the commencement speaker would insult the intelligence of the audience.

**19d
mod**

■ **Exercise 19.4** Explain the meaning conveyed by the placement of the adverb in each of the following sentences. Make any revisions necessary to clear up the confusion.

1. The lawyer spoke to her *only* client after he quieted down.
2. The lawyer *only* spoke to her client after he quieted down.
3. The lawyer spoke *only* to her client after he quieted down.
4. *Only* the lawyer spoke to her client after he quieted down.
5. The lawyer spoke to her client *only* after he quieted down.

✔ **CHECKLIST 19.1: CHECKING THE PLACEMENT OF MODIFIERS**

English depends on word order for clarity. Adjectives and adverbs are best placed next to the words they modify. When you revise sentences, check adjectives and adverbs. If they are awkwardly placed or possibly confusing, move them. Ask yourself these questions.

- Does an introductory participial phrase modify the subject of the sentence?
- Are prepositional phrases placed next to or near the words that they modify?
- Are clauses placed next to the words that they modify?
- Do limiting adverbs appear directly *before* the words or phrases that they modify?
- Do adverbs appearing in the middle of sentences clearly modify only one sentence element?
- If an adverb modifies an entire sentence, is the meaning unmistakably clear?

**19d
mod**

CHAPTER 20

AVOIDING CONFUSING SHIFTS

To keep your sentences clear and harmonious, you must be consistent in your use of verbs and nouns. Avoid jarring shifts in point of view and sudden outbursts of emotion—what is sometimes called purple prose.

20a
Being Consistent in Verb Tenses

Watch out for shifts from one tense to another within paragraphs or within sentences. Some shifts are acceptable; others are not. When you write about the content of any piece of literature, you usually use the present tense. Be careful not to shift out of the present tense when you have decided to use it for such a purpose. Make sure your tenses are consistent not only within sentences, but from one sentence to another. Be especially careful when you quote a passage that is in the past tense. Do not shift your description of the passage into the past tense if you have been using the present. Here is an example:

> David Copperfield **observes** other people with a fine and sympathetic eye. He **describes** villains such as Mr. Murdstone and improbable heroes such as Mr. Micawber with unforgettable sharpness of detail. But David Copperfield **was** not himself an especially interesting person.

Being Consistent in Narrative

Avoid the temptation to lapse into inconsistent tenses when you are telling a story. Sometimes the events you are relating become so vivid to you as you speak or write that you slip into the present tense. The inconsistency may be acceptable in conversation, but it confuses readers.

> **Inconsistent:**   The wind **was howling** and **blowing** a hundred miles an hour when suddenly there **is** a big crash, and a tree **falls** into Rocky's living room.

> **Consistent:**   The wind **was howling** and **blowing** a hundred miles an hour when suddenly there **was** a big crash, and a tree **fell** into Rocky's living room.

> **Inconsistent:**   Every day the parking lot **fills up** by eight in the morning, and commuting students arriving after that **could not find** parking paces.

> **Consistent:**   The parking lot **fills up** by eight in the morning, and commuting students arriving after that **cannot find** parking places.

Being Consistent in Successive Clauses

Inconsistency may creep into your writing when you combine present perfect and past perfect tenses with present and past tenses of verbs.

> **Inconsistent:**   She **has admired** many strange buildings at the university, but she **thought** that the Science Center **looked** completely out of place.

20a shifts

> **Consistent:**   She **has admired** many strange buildings at the university, but she **thinks** that the Science Center **looks** completely out of place.

In writing successive clauses, you must be sure that you take into account the continuing action of the first clause. The thought expressed in the consistent sentence is like this: *She has admired and still admires many strange buildings at the university, but she thinks now that the Science Center looks completely out of place.* Verbs in successive clauses do not have to be in the same tense, but they should follow each other in tenses that make good grammatical sense.

✔ CHECKLIST 20.1: **SOME RULES FOR SUCCESSIVE TENSES**

■ The present tense may be followed by another present tense:
Dogs **bark** to show that they **are** interested in something, or to show that they **are afraid,** or to announce that someone—perhaps another dog—**is invading** their territory.

- The present tense may be followed by a past tense:

  Michaelson **says** that transistors **made** stereo systems cheaper but **reduced** the fidelity of sound created by vacuum tubes.

- The present can be used with the present perfect.

  Quality control in the American automobile industry **is** a long-standing problem that **has made** millions of Americans **think** that Japanese cars **are** better.

- The present can be used with the future tense:

  We **predict** that word processors **will replace** electric typewriters in most offices by the end of this decade.

✔ **CHECKLIST 20.2:** TIPS FOR TENSE CONSISTENCY

- Do not use the present tense with the past perfect tense unless a suitable tense follows the past perfect.

  Inconsistent: She swears that she **had registered** her car properly.

  Consistent: She swears that she **had registered** her car properly before she **received** a ticket for having an improper license plate.

- If you are not going to follow the past perfect with a clause that contains a verb in the past tense, change the past perfect tense to a more suitable form.

  She **swears** that she **registered** her car properly.

- The simple past can be followed by another simple past:

  College football **was** so violent early in this century that President Theodore Roosevelt **threatened** to abolish it.

- The simple past can be used with the imperfect:

  Everyone **was** eager to know if she **was going** to enter the fifty-mile road race.

- The simple past can be used with the future:

  They **told** me that the tire shipment **will arrive** next week.

- The simple past should not be used with the present perfect, although in informal speech we sometimes do use the two tenses together.

  She **reports** that she **runs** nine miles every morning.

  She **reported** that she **had been running** nine miles every morning.

20a shifts

■ **Exercise 20.1** Examine the verbs in boldface in the sentences below and make any necessary corrections for consistency in verb tense.

1. Researchers who **experiment** with dolphins **had found** that these creatures **are** as sophisticated and devious as humans, especially in courtship.
2. Bottlenose male dolphins **have formed** social units that **recruited** another group of males, which **helped** wage battle on a third group.
3. These actions **were occurring** as the males **look** for fertile females and **could steal** them from competing bands of dolphins.
4. Scientists at the University of Michigan **have observed** male dolphins surrounding females and **determined** that the males' leaping and somersaulting **are** ways to keep females in line.
5. Oceanographic researchers **have reported** their findings to the National Academy of Sciences and **presented** dramatic evidence to support their assertions.

20b
Being Consistent in Mood

**20b
shifts**

The mood of a verb is a distinguishing form that indicates whether or not an assertion is intended as a statement of fact (see pp. 253–257). The indicative mood makes simple statements or asks simple questions. The conditional mood makes statements that would be true if something else were true. The subjunctive mood conveys a wish, desire, or demand, or makes a statement contrary to fact. It is now used rarely in English. (If I *were* in Rome on Easter morning, I would hear thousands of church bells. I am not in Rome on Easter morning, and I may not be there when Easter comes; so I use the subjunctive mood in the clause *if I were*.)

Avoid inconsistent shifts from the indicative to the conditional or from the conditional to the indicative.

Inconsistent

ESL 8

He **will go** to night school and **would take** a course in hotel management.

If he **goes** to night school, he **would take** a course in hotel management.

If he **were** absent, he **will fail** the course.

Consistent

If he **could go** to night school, he **would take** a course in hotel management.

He **would go** to night school, and he **would take** a course in hotel management, if he **could get** out of jail.

He **will go** to night school and **will take** a course in hotel management if he **gets out** of jail.

If he **is** absent, he **will fail** the course.

If he **were** absent, he **would fail** the course.

■ **Exercise 20.2**   Correct the confusing shifts in the following sentences. If a sentence is correct as it stands, put a check by the number.

1. Archeologists have been surveying the earth with satellites, and they found many remnants of a lost city buried in Arabian sands.
2. Mercutio has to die in *Romeo and Juliet,* or else he would have carried the play off from the two young lovers, who are not nearly as interesting as he was.
3. The band hit a sour note, and the drum major gets sore at the tuba section.
4. Children who often are noisy at a concert annoyed their parents.
5. King James I, who died in 1625, had never taken a bath in his adult life, and those who prepared him for burial have to scour his underwear off his body.

**20c
Being Consistent in Voice**

The voice of a transitive verb is either active or passive. In clauses in the active voice, the subject does the acting; in clauses in the passive voice, the subject is acted upon (see p. 257). Inconsistency in voice sometimes arises from a writer's desire for variety in sentence forms. But when the actor remains the same, do not change voice.

Inconsistent

The Impressionist painters **hated** black. Violet, green, blue, pink, and red **were favored** by them.

The bulldozer **clanked** into the woods and **bit** into the ground. The trees and the earth **were ripped up.**

In each pair of sentences above, the writer uses first active voice then passive voice. The shift is jarring.

Consistent

The Impressionist painters **hated** black. They **favored** violet, green, blue, pink, and red.

The bulldozer **clanked** into the woods, **bit** into the ground, and **ripped up** the trees and the earth.

Note that you can go easily from a linking verb of simple description in the active voice to a verb in the passive voice in the next clause, thereby keeping the focus on the subject of greatest interest.

Today the majority of American Indians **are** poor, uneducated, and unhealthy. They **have been isolated** from the rest of the country, deprived of the benefits of the land that **was taken** away from them by force, and **forgotten** by the people who robbed them.

McNabb **rode** his motorcycle through the plate glass window and **was taken** to the hospital as soon as the ambulance could get there.

The best advice about the passive voice is to use it infrequently and only with good reason.

<table>
<tr><td>

20d

shifts

</td><td>

20d

Being Consistent in Person and Number of Nouns and Pronouns

</td></tr>
</table>

In speaking and writing in an informal tone, we often use the pronoun *you* instead of the more formal pronoun *one* (see pp. 268–270). Using *you*—addressing the reader in the second person—is perfectly legitimate. What is not legitimate is shifting between *you* and *one* in the same sentence.

Consistent: If **you** smoke cigarettes, **you** run a high risk of getting lung cancer.

Inconsistent: If **one** smokes cigarettes, **you** run a high risk of getting lung cancer.

Here are some other consistent alternatives:

If **one** smokes cigarettes, **one** runs a high risk of getting lung cancer.
or

Anyone who smokes cigarettes runs a high risk of getting lung cancer.
or
People who smoke cigarettes run a high risk of getting lung cancer.

If you address your reader directly as *you,* you may write in the third person from time to time. But you cannot shift from the third person to the second person or from the second person to the third person in the same sentence.

Consistent: **You** will always find good writing to be hard work. **Good writers** never think that their craft is easy.

Inconsistent: **People** flying across the country nowadays discover that **you** can get many different fares to the same destination.

Make pronouns agree with antecedents, but avoid sexist language (see Chapters 11 and 17).

Awkward: **Anyone** who **rides** a bicycle every day will discover that he or she develops some muscles not developed by jogging.

You can substitute consistent plural forms:

People who ride bicycles every day will discover that **they** develop some muscles not developed by jogging.

**20d
shifts**

Or you can avoid the need for a pronoun:

Anyone who rides a bicycle every day will discover that some muscles that are little used in jogging are being developed.

Anyone who rides a bicycle every day will discover that the exercise develops some muscles that are not developed by jogging.

You can make a much more sweeping revision:

Bike riders do not exercise some of the muscles used in jogging and usually discover that they get sore quickly when they try to run around the neighborhood at night.

Or a simpler one:

Daily bicycle riding develops some muscles not used in jogging.

20e
Being Consistent in Point of View

Maintain a consistent point of view in your writing. **Point of view** is the position from which you present information. Note the example of inconsistency here:

> He sat idly in his seat and looked down at the land pouring beneath the low-flying plane like some immense sea whose waters reached to the sky. The green of the forest enchanted him. Everything was primitive and nearly unspoiled. Here and there a house stood in a solitary clearing that, from above, looked like a raft afloat on the great ocean of green. He saw it for a moment, and then it was whisked away behind him. In the houses, people were sitting down to supper, unfolding napkins, looking expectantly at the head of the table where the father gravely bowed his head to say grace.

The point of view is of someone in an airplane looking down on the land passing underneath. But in the last sentence we shift to a scene that such a traveler cannot see. The writer should revise the last sentence to match the point of view of the rest of the passage.

> **He could imagine that** in the houses people were sitting down to supper, unfolding napkins, looking expectantly at the head of the table where the father gravely bowed his head to say grace.

20e

shifts

■ **Exercise 20.3**   Rewrite the following sentences to eliminate confusing shifts. If a sentence is correct as it stands, put a check beside it.

1. American landscape painters of the nineteenth century viewed the American wilderness as the handiwork of God; signs of God's work were seen by them in lakes, mountains, and prairies.
2. Government paperwork costs forty billion dollars a year, and government accountants are working to trim those costs—and making more paperwork as they do so; you can see the problem.
3. When anyone rides the Green River rapids with your glasses on one can have them knocked off, and you won't see the magnificent rock formations.
4. People who take pictures sometimes find that they get tired carrying a camera, and they often stop taking pictures all at once, the way some people stop smoking.
5. Anyone who writes a long letter of complaint is frustrated when they get a form letter in return.

■ **Exercise 20.4**   Rewrite the following paragraph to correct the confusing shifts.

> In Thomas More's book *Utopia,* which is the name he gave to an island supposedly located off the coast of the New World, the people of his commonwealth wear unbleached wool, eat together in great halls, punish adultery with death when one is convicted twice of the offense, and allow husbands and wives to inspect each other naked before they are married so one will not be deceived by the other. The Utopians have no individuality. They tried as hard as they could to eliminate passion. More had made no mention of any artists among them.

20f
Avoiding Excessive Emotionalism

You may have strong feelings about a subject, and having discussed some of the issues in an essay, you may be tempted to conclude with a highly charged ending so readers will know where you stand. Emotionalism in writing is almost always a mistake. Readers tend to dismiss the opinions of ranters and to laugh at their "purple prose." You may embarrass even those people who agree with you if you present your opinions in an irrational way. Readers want to like the person who has written the prose they read; otherwise they will not enjoy spending time in the writer's company. Few readers like to spend time with an angry or overwrought or sarcastic person.

**20f
shifts**

Consider the excessive emotionalism in this paragraph:

> Lord Crenshaw strode mightily into the room, his bushy eyebrows looking like forests waving in the mightiest of all God's storms, his cold blue eyes flashing like bolts of lightning as he looked around at the assembled guests. Philippa felt her heart go bang in her chest with a wild emotion, wilder than anything she had ever felt before, wild as the incandescent lava that bursts from a volcano and pours down the mountainside, burning up all the reserve and all the hesitation that she might have felt. This was the famous Lord Crenshaw, dauntless leader of Wellington's right at Waterloo, the bold, brave man who flung his great arms skyward and shouted at his troops to hold fast while all around his gallant head the bullets whizzed and whirled, the thunderhead of a hero whose voice sounded like ten thousand organs booming through ten thousand cathedrals. People nodded gravely to him, knowing his reputation for sudden anger, for

the outburst that could lead to the duel at sunrise that had more than once snuffed out the tender flower of a young life before it could grow and flourish and become a mighty tree. As he entered the room, a silence like that of Judgment Day itself fell over everyone, and it seemed that the world held its breath while he walked to the buffet and thundered a command to the trembling waiter here. "Give me a ham sandwich," he said. "And hold the pickles."

■ **Exercise 20.5** Rewrite the passage about Lord Crenshaw.

✔ **CHECKLIST 20.3: ENSURING CONSISTENCY**

Lack of consistency in the use of verbs and pronouns and sudden shifts in point of view can distract your reader from what you are saying to how you are saying it. To help ensure consistency, ask yourself these questions as you revise.

Tense

■ Are tenses consistent, following one another within sentences in correct and logical sequence?

■ Is the mood of each sentence consistent in itself?

■ Does the voice used from one sentence to the next serve to keep the emphasis on the subject you want to emphasize?

20f
shifts

Pronouns

■ Are pronouns consistently formal or informal, with occasional shifts between sentences but no shifts within sentences?

Point of view

■ In narratives, is perspective or point of view consistent?

■ Has "purple prose" been eliminated?

21

SELECTING END MARKS

In English, as in most other languages, the system of **end marks** gives writers a means to separate sentences and signal their purpose. There are three end marks—periods, question marks, and exclamation points.

21a
Using the Period

Use a period after a sentence that makes a statement, that gives a mild command or makes a mild request, or that asks a question indirectly. Commands showing strong emotion require exclamation points, discussed in 21c. Direct questions require question marks, discussed in 21b. The use of ellipses is discussed in 26f.

Making Statements

Simple statements end with a period. Most English sentences are simple statements.

> Soap melts in the bathtub.
>
> Every year Americans buy more bicycles than cars.
>
> The building burned down last night.

Making Mild Commands

Nonemphatic requests that do not ask a question also end in a period.

> Please go with me to the lecture.

Consider your opponent's views carefully when you are making an argument.

Lend me the car, and I'll do the shopping.

Using Indirect Questions

Statements about questions end in a period. In the following examples, the words *why, where, who,* and *how* ask questions indirectly.

People wonder why they have to pay such high taxes.

She asked me where I had gone to college.

They demanded to know who was responsible for the killings.

He wanted to know how I had come to that conclusion.

21b
Using the Question Mark

Use a question mark after a direct question, but not after an indirect question.

Who wrote *One of Ours?*

She wanted to know who wrote *One of Ours.*

If a question ends with a quoted question, one question mark serves for both the question in the main clause and the question that is quoted.

What did Juliet mean when she cried, "O Romeo, Romeo! Wherefore art thou Romeo?"

If a question is quoted before the end of a sentence that makes a statement, place a question mark before the last quotation mark and put a period at the end of the sentence.

21b

?

"What was Henry Ford's greatest contribution to the industrial revolution in America?" he asked.

"What did the president know and when did he know it?" became the great question of the Watergate hearings.

Occasionally a question mark changes a statement into a question.

You expect me to believe a story like that?

He drove my car into your living room?

To emphasize parts of a series of questions, you can use question marks to separate them into fragments.

> And what will we leave behind us when we are long dead? Temples? Amphora? Sunken treasure?
>
> —MARYA MANNES

To express uncertainty about a word or a date, you may use a question mark. In such usage the question mark means that no one can be sure if the date or word is correct. You should never use such question marks merely to show that you have not bothered to look up the information.

> Napoleon Bonaparte's brother-in-law, Joachim Murat (1767?–1815), was king of Naples for seven years.

21c
Using the Exclamation Point

Use exclamation points (!) sparingly to convey surprise, shock, or some other strong emotion.

> The land of the free! This is the land of the free! Why, if I say anything that displeases them, the free mob will lynch me, and that's my freedom.
>
> —D. H. LAWRENCE

> Moon, rise! Wind, hit the trees, blow up the leaves! Up, now, run! Tricks! Treats! Gangway!
>
> —RAY BRADBURY

21c

!

Commands showing strong emotion also use exclamation points.

Stay away from the stove!

Help!

Avoid using too many exclamation marks because readers will not respond with the excitement that an exclamation mark is supposed to call up. For a mild statement, use a comma or a period.

"Ah, what a beautiful morning," she said, throwing the windows open onto the new day.

Socrates said, "Know thyself."

■ **Exercise 21.1** Use periods, question marks, and exclamation points where they are required in the sentences below.

1. He asked if Mr. Kuhns worked for UNESCO or for the FBI
2. "Was it you," she asked, "who painted that wall purple"
3. What did he mean when he asked me, "Is your car an antique"
4. Stolen The money was stolen Right before our eyes, somebody snatched my purse and ran off with it
5. "Help me" he said "I want to learn how to dance"
6. "Isn't the true folk instrument the dulcimer" she asked
7. You expect me to wear a clown costume and ride that unicycle to the mall
8. Pick up the papers Don't you think it's fair for each of us to try to keep this room clean
9. She asked if Sara changed the tire herself or waited for the tow truck to arrive
10. "Where will it end" he asked

■ **Exercise 21.2** Compare the effects of different punctuation marks on the sentences in each pair below. Imagine situations in which you might have used each version of each sentence.

1. **a.** You don't have to tell me.
   b. You don't have to tell me!
   c. You don't have to tell me?
2. **a.** You called the police.
   b. You called the police?
   c. You called the police!
3. **a.** What will you contribute—your time, your talent, or your money?
   b. What will you contribute? Your time? Your talent? Your money?

21c

!

22

USING COMMAS

When you speak, you pause to emphasize elements of a sentence and to catch your breath. Commas show these pauses within written sentences. Commas also set off sentence elements, clarify the relations of some sentence elements to others, and serve in standard ways in dates, addresses, and other conventional forms.

22a
Setting Off Independent Clauses

Use commas to set off independent clauses joined by the common coordinating conjunctions *and, but, or, nor, so, yet, for.*

> Her computer broke down, and she had to write with a pencil.
>
> He won the Heisman Trophy, but no pro team drafted him.
>
> The art majors could paint portraits, or they could paint houses.
>
> Many Americans did not at first understand jazz, nor did they enjoy listening to it.
>
> He strained to hear her, for she spoke barely above a whisper.
>
> Many people don't understand punctuation, yet they use it correctly anyway.
>
> Printing has made language much less flexible than it once was, so the rules of English grammar will probably not change much from now on.

Some writers do not separate short independent clauses with a comma.

> He stayed at home and she went to work.

22b
Setting Off Long Introductory Phrases and Clauses

Use commas after long introductory phrases and clauses. A long introductory phrase or clause is easier to read and understand when a comma separates it from the rest of the sentence.

> After he had sat in the hot tub for three hours, the fire department had to revive him.

> If you plan to lose fifty or more pounds, you should take the advice of a doctor.

> After standing as a symbol of oppression and fear for twenty-six years, the Berlin Wall at last was broken down.

> Hounded by the media after charges and countercharges in their child custody suit, Woody Allen and Mia Farrow have lost the cherished privacy of their personal lives.

Short opening phrases do not have to be set off by commas.

> After the game I drifted along with the happy crowd.

> Before the wedding they discussed household duties.

> In their coffeehouses eighteenth-century Englishmen conducted many of their business affairs.

Always put a comma after an introductory subordinate clause (as explained on p. 136).

> When we came out, we were not on the busiest Chinatown street but on a side street across from the park.
> —MAXINE HONG KINGSTON

22b

,

> Although the struggle and competition for national or international power may not be explained wholly and simply as analogous to the power drive in personal relations, the personal may provide significant insight into the political.
> —KENNETH B. CLARK

Commas also set off introductory interjections, transitional expressions, and names in direct address.

Yes, a fight broke out after the game.

Nevertheless, we should look on the bright side.

To be sure, no one was killed.

Consequently, we will play again next year.

I'll say this, Soon Lee. You understood him first.

Golda, come here right away.

Pablo, why are you doing this?

22c
Setting Off Clauses and Phrases That Modify

Setting Off Absolutes

Any absolute—a phrase that combines a noun with a present or past participle and that serves to modify the entire sentence (as discussed on p. 115)—must be set off from the rest of the sentence by a comma.

> **The bridge now built,** the British set out to destroy it.

> The snake slithered through the tall grass, **the sunlight shining now and then on its green skin.**

Setting Off Participial Modifiers

Use commas to set off participial modifiers at the beginning or end of a sentence.

> Having learned that she failed the test, Marie had a sleepless night.

> Resolving to study harder, the next morning she went directly to the library.

> They toiled all night on the engine, grinding and adjusting the valves, polishing the cylinders, cleaning the pistons, replacing the rings, installing a new fuel pump, and putting in new spark plugs and points.

> She rushed down the corridor, holding the report in her hand.

> We climbed the mountain, feeling the spring sunshine and intoxicated by the view.

22c

,

■ **Exercise 22.1** Put commas where they are needed in the following sentences.

1. Many graduates seek jobs in media and entertainment fields but opportunities for beginners are limited.

2. Having missed the plane we had to take the bus to New York.
3. Although you need to know grammar exercises in grammar cannot help you write well unless you read a lot.
4. Adrienne was to be sure a steady performer.
5. Nevertheless Greek wine has become popular in America and is often sold in restaurants that he said do not specialize in Greek food.
6. He fired to second his throw beating Henderson to the bag by a step.
7. Pay something if you can but if you cannot go in and enjoy the exhibit anyway.
8. After he had watched television all night long his eyes turned to egg white and his brain became glue.
9. With student populations increasing people with the Ph.D. degree can get jobs again.
10. Acknowledging dramatic increases in world temperature scholars are growing more and more alarmed about global warming.

Setting Off Nonrestrictive Clauses and Phrases

Use commas to set off nonrestrictive clauses and phrases. **Nonrestrictive clauses and phrases** can be lifted out of sentences without any resultant change in the primary meaning of the sentences. The paired commas that set off a nonrestrictive clause or phrase announce that these words provide additional information.

> My dog Lady, who treed a cat last week, treed the mailman this morning.

> In the middle of the forest, hidden from the rest of the world, stood a small cabin.

22c

,

Setting off a phrase or a clause with commas can often change the meaning of a sentence. In the first sentence below, the commas make the clauses nonrestrictive. There was only one commencement speaker, and that speaker happened to be a sleep therapist. In the second sentence, the absence of commas makes us suppose there must have been several speakers. The clause is **restrictive:** it defines the noun and is essential to its meaning. The writer must single out the one who spoke for three hours. By calling the speaker a sleep therapist, the writer says that although there were several speakers, there was only one who was a sleep therapist, and that person was the one who spoke for three hours.

The commencement speaker, who was a sleep therapist, spoke for three hours.

The commencement speaker who was a sleep therapist spoke for three hours.

■ **Exercise 22.2**   Use commas to set off clauses and phrases in the following sentences. In some you have a choice. You can make the clause or phrase restrictive by not setting it off with commas, or you can make it nonrestrictive by using commas. In such cases, explain the changes in meaning so that you may be clear as to what they are and why they occur. At times simple common sense will tell you whether to make the clause restrictive or nonrestrictive.

1. The chain saw which had a two-cycle engine gave him a sense of immense power as he took it in his hand and walked into the woods filled with oaks and maples.
2. Fly fishing a difficult and sometimes dangerous sport requires much more skill than fishing with worms from a boat on a still lake.
3. The McCormick reaper which was invented by Cyrus Hall McCormick vastly increased wheat production in the nineteenth century.
4. Farmers who are by profession often isolated and independent have never been drawn in large groups to communism, but they have been attracted by fraternal organizations which have helped them meet together to satisfy social and economic needs.
5. Bats flying mammals found all over the world probably seem odious to many people because they look like rats that fly.

22d
Separating Elements of a Sentence

22d

,

Use commas to separate elements of a sentence to avoid confusion.

Confusing

Every time John raced small boys could leave him behind.

No matter how fast he ran the course was too hard for him.

To John Smith seemed odd.

Revised

Every time John raced, small boys could leave him behind.

No matter how fast he ran, the course was too hard for him.

To John, Smith seemed odd.

22e
Separating Items in a Series

Use commas to separate items in a series. A **series** is a set of nouns, pronouns, adjectives, adverbs, phrases, or clauses joined by commas and—usually—a final coordinating conjunction. Note that American writers put a comma before the coordinating conjunction at the end of a series.

Nouns

Winston Churchill told the English people that he had nothing to offer them but blood, toil, sweat, and tears.

Carrots, sweet potatoes, and other yellow vegetables help prevent cancer.

Pronouns

You, we, and they all have some things in common.

We saw you, him, and her walking on the beach.

Adjectives

My teacher's notes were old, yellow, and worn.

She was a helpful, surprising, and amusing person.

Adverbs

The three outlaws walked slowly, silently, and cautiously into the Sunday school.

She played steadily, intently, and cautiously.

Phrases

The college raised fees, reduced maintenance, fired assistant professors, turned down the heat, but went bankrupt anyway.

Lincoln's great address commended government of the people, by the people, and for the people.

22e

,

Clauses

> The traffic was heavy, the parking lot was full, rain drenched the city, and I was late.

> She combed the dog's hair, he started the car, Jack brought down the ribbon, and we were all ready for the show.

22f
Separating Two or More Adjectives

Use commas to separate two or more adjectives before a noun or a pronoun if you can use the conjunction *and* in place of the commas.

> Lyndon Johnson flew a short, dangerous combat mission in the Pacific during World War II.
> (Lyndon Johnson flew a short **and** dangerous combat mission in the Pacific during World War II.)
> Computers are expensive, necessary, and complicated.
> (Computers are expensive **and** necessary and complicated.)

If you cannot make an *and* fit easily between the adjectives, omit the comma.

> A devastating civil war erupted following the government's collapse.

> Six thin green pines stood against the evening sky.

> Four old red coats lay piled in a corner.

Adjectives preceding the noun they modify do not require a dividing comma when they mention color, size, age, location, or number. But if you mention several colors or sizes or numbers before nouns, separate the adjectives with commas:

> The auto industry first painted its cars a universal black, but now assembly lines turn out thousands of green, silver, gold, blue, crimson, tan, gray, and brown cars.

22f/g

,

22g
Setting Off Direct Quotations

Use a comma with quotation marks to set off a direct quotation from the clause that names the source of the quotation.

When the source comes first, the comma goes before the quotation marks. When the quotation comes first, the comma goes before the last quotation mark.

She said, "I'm sorry, but all sections are full."

"But I have to have the course to graduate," he said.

"A rule is a rule," she said sweetly, "and you will just have to postpone your graduation."

No comma is used if the quotation ends in a question mark or an exclamation point.

"Do you believe in grades?" he asked.

"Believe in them!" she cried. "I've had them."

In some cases, a colon can be used before a quotation (26a).

■ **Exercise 22.3** Place commas where they belong in the following sentences.

1. The old gray mare is not the superb creature she used to be says the old song.
2. Three happy little children came to the door shouting "Trick or treat!"
3. The hospital smelled of floor wax linen and iodine.
4. She righted the boat ran up the sail grabbed the rudder and flew before the wind.
5. The storm broke suddenly and furiously the lightning crashed from a black sky and the cattle ran off into the dark.
6. "North Dakota is sky prairie wheat and hospitality" she said. "You must go there Charles. You will never see colors so pure land so vast or cities so clean."
7. The poor the speaker said commit far more violent crimes than do members of the middle class and the saddest thing he thought is that poor people are most likely to kill or maim members of their own families.
8. To be sure the recession is not limited to America.
9. Nevertheless Elton John's music still thrills audiences of preteen-age adolescents young working professionals and the mothers and fathers of people in both those groups.
10. Consuelo you must speak energetically sadly and eloquently.

22g

,

22h
Using Commas for Special Effect

Sometimes commas help achieve special effects, and sometimes their use is optional.

Substituting for Words

Use a comma to take the place of a word omitted from a sentence. A comma frequently takes the place of the conjunction *and,* and in some constructions it can take the place of other words as well.

> Power staggers forward, then falls facedown in the dust.
>
> —PHILIP CAPUTO

The comma can also take the place of *and* in a series.

> The joke was stale, flat, vulgar.

In sentences that express a contrast, the comma can stand for several words.

> Lombard the actress was funny, not sophisticated.
> She said her cat was big, bright, and fast, not economical.

Providing Emphasis

Use commas to give special emphasis to words and phrases, even when commas are not grammatically necessary. Here commas create the pauses that would occur if you were speaking the sentences aloud.

22h

,

> It seems impossible to get a saint, or a philosopher, or a scientist, to stick to this simple truth.
>
> —D. H. LAWRENCE

> He found hamlets of three decaying houses with the corrugated iron of their roofs grinding and clanking in a hot wind, and not a tree for miles.
>
> —WILLIAM GOLDING

Setting Off Parenthetical Elements

Use paired commas to set off parenthetical elements. **Parenthetical elements** are words, phrases, or clauses set within sentences which add further description to the main statement the sentence makes. Always set such elements off by paired commas—a comma at the beginning of the element and another at the end.

> Brian Wilson, however, was unable to cope with the pressures of touring with the Beach Boys.
>
> Senator Cadwallader, responding to his campaign contributions from the coal industry, introduced a bill to begin strip mining operations in Yellowstone Park.
>
> Our Latin teacher, Mr. Harrison, was devoted to making us love the language.
>
> Jeannine is, we agree, a great editor.

22i
Using Commas with Numbers, Names, and Dates

Commas play a special role in clarifying numbers, place names, and dates.

Separating Parts of Place Names and Addresses

Use a pair of commas to separate parts of place names and addresses.

> At Cleveland, Ohio, the river sometimes catches fire.

The comma separates the city, Cleveland, from its state, Ohio. Another comma comes after Ohio to set off the state from the rest of the sentence.

Commas set off pairs of an address in sentences and in addresses on letters and envelopes.

22i

,

> He lived at 1400 Crabgrass Lane, Suburbia, New York.

> My address is:
> 63 Oceanside Drive, Apartment 3
> Knoxville, TN 37916

Separating Parts of Dates

Use paired commas in dates when the month, day, and year are included.

On June 6, 1993, my parents reaffirmed their marriage vows in St. Patrick's cathedral.

On October 17, 1989, the largest earthquake in America since 1906 shook San Francisco.

No comma is necessary when the day of the month is omitted.

Germany invaded Poland in September 1939.

British and European writers use a form of the complete date that requires no comma at all.

She graduated from college on 5 June 1980.

Separating Digits in Numbers

Commas separate digits by hundreds except for years and references to page numbers.

Jackson received 647,276 votes in the 1828 presidential election.

The entry for Tennessee is on page 2304.

✔ CHECKLIST 22.1: **AVOIDING UNNECESSARY COMMAS**

- **Do not separate subject, verb, object.** A comma should not separate a subject from its verb or a verb from its object or complement unless a nonrestrictive clause or phrase intervenes.

  Faulty

  With trembing hand, the child grasped the spoon.
  The tulips that I planted last year, suddenly died.

  Correct

  With trembling hand the child grasped the spoon.
  The tulips that I planted last year, which seemed to be doing well, suddenly died.

- **Do not separate prepositional phrases from what they modify.** A prepositional phrase that serves as an adjective is not set off by commas from the noun or pronoun that it modifies.

  Faulty: The best part, of the meal, is coffee.

  A prepositional phrase that serves as an adverb is not set off from the rest of the sentence by commas.

  Faulty: He swam, with the current, rather than against it.

22i

,

■ Do not divide a compound verb with a comma.

Faulty: He ran, and walked twenty miles.

But if the parts of a compound verb form a series, set off the parts of the verb with commas.

He ran, walked, and crawled twenty miles.

■ Do not use a comma after the last item in a series unless the series concludes a cause or phrase set off by commas.

He loved books, flowers, and people and spent much of his time with all of them.

Three "scourges of modern life," as Roberts calls the automobile, the telephone, and the polyester shirt, were unknown little more than a century ago.

■ Avoid commas that create false parentheses.

Faulty: A song called, "Faded Love," made Bob Wills famous.

■ Do not use a comma to set off a dependent adverbial clause at the end of a sentence. In practice this rule means that you should not use a comma before words such as *because, when, since, while, as, neither,* and *either.*

Faulty: He looked forward every year to June, because he always made a long bike trip as soon as school was out.

But if the clause beginning with *because* begins the sentence, follow the rule on p. 313.

Because he always made a long bike trip as soon as school was out, he looked forward every year to June.

■ **Exercise 22.4** Use commas correctly in the sentences below.

1. The speaker was rude pompous tiresome.
2. She purchased eggs rolls and butter from a small corner store in Cincinnati Ohio on June 7 1993 just before her son's birthday.
3. I shall be thirty on April 7 1994 when I shall be in London England
4. Dugan takes the Ford Martha the Toyota.
5. Water flows over the rocks for a mile then plunges fifty feet into a lake.

22i

,

■ **Exercise 22.5** Eliminate the unnecessary commas in the following sentences. Be careful! Some of the commas belong where they are. If a sentence is correct as it is written, put a check by it.

1. According to Hedrick Smith of the *New York Times,* life for the average Russian, has been one long round, of corruption, lines, and alcoholism.

2. Events, in Yugoslavia, in the winter and spring, of 1992, made many people wonder if the cold war, was over.

3. A controversial issue, in 1992, was the recession, and whether the country was recovering or falling deeper into a very, unpleasant, economic situation.

4. A story in the Sunday, *New York Times,* of November 26, 1989, held that crack dealers on the street, did not make much money, and were terrorized, by their overlords, in the illegal, drug trade.

5. The Oakland, Athletics, swept the San Francisco, Giants, in the 1989, World Series, despite the disruption, of the earthquake.

6. John Grisham's, *The Firm,* and *A Time to Kill,* were two of the big, paperback best-sellers, of 1992.

7. It is sometimes not easy to tell, when you have drunk, too much beer to drive safely.

8. Since divorce has become common, in America, many children are growing up in homes with only, one parent.

9. With the lessening of restrictions, on travel between East, and West in the 1990s, many people hoped that the East, German athletes would compete, in more athletic contests, in the West.

10. Laptop computers became, much, much smaller than ever, some of them weighing less than three, or four, pounds.

22i

,

USING SEMICOLONS

The semicolon is a stronger mark of punctuation than the comma, and it can be used to join sentence elements that cannot be joined by a comma alone. Semicolons can join certain independent clauses and set off elements within a series when commas are used within the elements.

23a
Joining Independent Clauses

Use a semicolon to join independent clauses, either with or without the help of a coordinating conjunction or a conjunctive adverb.

> Silence is deep as eternity; speech is shallow as time.
>
> —THOMAS CARLYLE

> Before 8000 B.C. wheat was not the luxuriant plant it is today; it was merely one of many wild grasses that spread throughout the Middle East.
>
> —JACOB BRONOWSKI

In each example, two clauses are closely related—one of the reasons for using the semicolon. The writers could have separated the clauses with a period, but they chose semicolons to stress the relation of ideas in the clauses.

In the example below, the semicolon is not necessary, as the independent clauses are joined by the coordinating conjunction *but;* but by reinforcing the pause between clauses, the semicolon adds emphasis to the second one.

> In the first draft I had Bigger going smack to the electric chair; but I felt that two murders were enough for one novel.
>
> —RICHARD WRIGHT

In this example, a semicolon used by itself between two clauses implies a contrast between them.

> Lucy had completed the assignment; Philip had not.

Often we express such contrasts in **elliptical constructions,** in which commas substitute for words left out that are clearly understood.

> In America, traffic problems are caused by cars; in China, by bicycles.
>
> In the Middle Ages, many children were abandoned by their parents; by the nineteenth century, comparatively few.

Use a semicolon to join independent clauses separated by a conjunctive adverb. Conjunctive adverbs such as *however, nevertheless, moreover, then,* and *consequently* connect ideas between clauses, but they cannot work without the right punctuation. For these sentences, place a semicolon before the conjunctive adverb, and a comma after it.

> He had biked a hundred miles in ten hours; nevertheless, he now had to do a marathon.
>
> Sheila had to wait at home until the plumber arrived to fix the water heater; consequently, she was late for the exam.

■ **Exercise 23.1**   Review the following sentences for the proper use of semicolons. Supply semicolons where they are needed. Eliminate semicolons that are incorrectly used. If a sentence is correct as it stands, place a check beside it.

1. She was unable to keep the appointment; since she was delayed in traffic; because of the wreck.
2. The sun is our most potent source of energy, nevertheless, research in harnessing solar power has gone slowly.
3. The United States and Canada have relatively few varieties of poisonous snakes; but the climate is warm enough to allow many such snakes to flourish should they be accidentally introduced.
4. Western movies once showed hostile Indians attacking covered wagons drawn up in circles on the plains; although no such attack ever occurred in fact.
5. Videocassette recorders allow many people to rent movies on tape and to play them at home through their television sets moreover, the rental fee for the tape is much less than it woud cost a family to see a movie in a theater.

23a

;

6. Nuclear war is a horror that no one wants to imagine; yet imagining it may help us prevent it.
7. November is a month that is much abused and often unfairly so; true, the leaves fall, and cold weather begins; but November gives us three holidays—Election Day, Veterans Day, and Thanksgiving.
8. I like Brian De Palma's films, however, they sometimes scare me.

■ **Exercise 23.2** Punctuate the following sentences correctly.

1. Some were satisfied others disgruntled.
2. He needed seven hours of sleep a night she only five.
3. Cancer is more feared heart disease more fatal.
4. In her room there were three pictures in mine one in his none.

23b
Separating Elements in a Series

Use a semicolon to separate elements in a series when some of those elements contain commas. These elements can be a set of nouns, pronouns, adjectives, adverbs, phrases, or clauses.

> They are aware of sunrise, noon and sunset; of the full moon and the new; of equinox and solstice; of spring and summer, autumn and winter.
>
> —ALDOUS HUXLEY

23b
;

> The committee included Dr. Curtis Youngblood, the county medical examiner; Roberta Collingwood, the director of the bureau's criminal division; and Darcy Coolidge, the chief of police.

Use semicolons to separate elements that contain other marks of punctuation.

> The assignment will be to read Leviticus 21:1–20; Joshua 5:3–6; and Isaiah 55:1–10.

■ **Exercise 23.3** For each set below, write a single sentence using semicolons correctly. Make reference to all the people and identify them by their jobs.

1. Dr. Mary A. Carter is a professor of history. Mr. Glenn G. Swenson is a football coach. Dean Sylvia Paoli was the moderator of the discussion. Dr. Carter and Mr. Swenson debated the place of intercollegiate athletics in education.

2. Ronald Martin designs computers. Elizabeth Ingersoll is an architect. Joseph Greenberg is a science teacher in Bradford High School in Fulton, Maine. The three of them led a discussion on the future of home computers in business and education.

■ **Exercise 23.4** Explain the use of the semicolon in each sentence below.

1. George Bush was elected president in 1988; Bill Clinton, in 1992.

2. The company had branches in Cleveland, Ohio; Paris, Tennessee; Del Rio, Texas; and Reno, Nevada.

3. Our guests included John Fox, the administrative dean of the Graduate School; Bill Dean, a good friend; and Tom Fox, John's son.

4. She had appeared in summer stock in *Mary, Mary; The Prisoner of Second Avenue;* and *Come Back, Little Sheba.*

5. He visited us at Thanksgiving 1992 with his sister; afterward we never saw him again.

6. We cooked a large meal together; then we sat down together and ate.

7. Elizabeth claimed to despise Darcy; nevertheless, in the end she married him.

8. Alcohol is the most dangerous drug; nicotine kills almost as many.

9. A little exercise each day can lengthen your life; it can be as little as a walk around the block.

10. He asked me what I wanted; I could not tell him.

23b

;

USING APOSTROPHES

Apostrophes show possession and indicate omitted letters in words written as contractions. They are used in such a wide variety of ways that they can be confusing. Contractions offer little difficulty, but be sure to learn the difference between the possessive case and the plural form of nouns. The apostrophe is used to form the possessive case of all nouns and of many pronouns. It is not used to form a plural.

24a
Showing Possession

Writers can choose among several forms to indicate ownership or posses-sion. In special cases, these forms can also show that an entity has a particular attribute, quality, value, or feature.

Children's toys could mean: **Everybody's** dreams could mean:

toys *of children*   dreams *of everybody*

toys *for children*   dreams *for everybody*

toys *belonging to children*   dreams *everybody has*

toys *owned by children*   dreams *belonging to everybody*

toys *that children own*

   Most writers would use the first form above without spelling out one of the full phrases. Without such words as *of, for, belonging to,* and *owned by,* only the apostrophe plus *s* (*-'s*) conveys the intended sense of possession. Writers often use possessive forms even when the concept of possession seems uncertain. In the examples above, *everybody* does not possess *dreams* in the same way that *children* possess *toys.* Accepted usage also requires apostrophes with concepts of duration and of monetary value.

an **hour's** wait   two **minutes'** work

a **dime's** worth   five **dollars'** worth

Two elements are usually required to show possession correctly with an apostrophe. Someone or something is the possessor, and someone or something is possessed. The word for the possessor takes an apostrophe, either along with an -s or alone if the word already ends in -s. The word for person or entity being possessed usually appears just after the word with the apostrophe, as in *Jane's tools.*

THE POSSESSOR AND THE POSSESSED

	Possessor	Thing, attribute, quality, value, or feature possessed
the woman's shovel	woman's	shovel
a child's bright smile	child's	bright smile
Juanita's son	Juanita's	son
the robbers' clever plan	robbers'	clever plan
five dollars' worth	dollars'	worth
everyone's plans	everyone's	plans
babies' books	babies'	books

Sometimes the thing possessed precedes the possessor. Sometimes the sentence may not name the thing possessed, but its identity is clearly understood by the reader. Sometimes we indicate possession by using both the *of* form and an apostrophe plus *s* or a personal possessive pronoun.

The motorcycle is the student**'s.**

Is the tractor Jan Stewart**'s?**

I saw your cousin at Nicki**'s.**

He was a friend of Rocco**'s.**

This dress of Mother**'s** is out of style.

That child of **his** rakes our leaves every fall.

24b

24b
Distinguishing Between Plurals and Possessives

Most nouns require -s endings to show the plural form: boy/boys; girl/girls; teacher/teachers; song/songs. Possessive forms require the apostrophe plus *s* ('s) ending: boy/boy*'s*; girl/girl*'s*; teacher/teacher*'s*. The possessive form and the plural form are not interchangeable.

Incorrect: The teacher's asked the girl's and boy's for attention.

Correct: The teachers asked the girls and boys for attention.

An apostrophe plus *s* at the end of a word makes that word the possessor of something.

■ **Exercise 24.1**   Identify each word in the following list as plural or possessive; then use each word correctly in a sentence.

1. a. women	**b.** women's	**c.** woman's
2. a. man's	**b.** men's	**c.** men
3. a. child's	**b.** children	**c.** children's
4. a. cats	**b.** cat's	**c.** cats'
5. a. professor's	**b.** professors	**c.** professors'

■ **Exercise 24.2**   In each of the following sentences, underline the word that shows possession and put a check above the word that names the entity possessed. (The entity possessed may be understood but not named.)

1. Plucking feathers on turkeys is not everyone's idea of a good job.
2. If the responsibility is the mayor's, then our citizens' group should push her to act.
3. At Mario's, the waiters serve with elegance; the diner's pleasure is the staff's only concern.
4. She brought me six dollars' worth of flour.
5. They went on a week's vacation together.
6. Gloria's smile welcomes students to the Writing Center.

24c
Forming Possessives

24c
'
V

To form a possessive, add an apostrophe plus *s* to a noun or pronoun, whether it is singular or plural, unless the plural already ends in *s*; then add an apostrophe only.

Noun/pronoun		**As a possessive**
baby	singular	a baby's smile
men	plural	the men's club

Noun/pronoun		As a possessive
Wanda	singular	Wanda's sundae
hour	singular	an hour's time
anyone	singular	anyone's idea
children	plural	the children's papers
Keats	singular	Keats's books
babies	plural	the babies' smiles
companies	plural	the companies' employees

Most writers add both an apostrophe and a final *s* to one-syllable singular nouns already ending in -*s* and to nouns of any number of syllables if the final -*s* is hard (as in *hiss*).

James**'s** adventure, Ross**'s** flag, Elvis**'s** songs

Proper names of geographical locations and some organizations do not take apostrophes.

Kings Point, St. Marks Place, Harpers Ferry, Department of Veterans Affairs

For hyphenated words and compound words and word groups, add an apostrophe plus *s* to the last word only.

my father-in-law**'s** job

the editor-in-chief**'s** responsibilities

the union leader**'s** supporters

To express joint ownership by two or more people, use the possessive form for the last name only; to express individual ownership, use the possessive form for each name.

Felicia and Elias**'s** house

McGraw-Hill**'s** catalog

Felicia**'s** and Elias**'s** houses

the city**'s** and the state**'s** finances

24c

'
∨

■ **Exercise 24.3** Change each word in parentheses into the correct possessive form by adding an apostrophe alone or an apostrophe plus *s*. A word may require a plural form before you change it to a possessive.

Example:
The two (woman) **women's** cars blocked the driveway.

1. (Mr. Cass) _____ contribution to the primaries brought praise from the (governor) _____ reelection committee.
2. The (assistant editor) _____ idea was to run three (student) _____ biographies in each issue.
3. The (Lady) _____ Auxiliary League drew hundreds to its Fourth of July picnic; (everyone) _____ praise meant that the tradition would continue next year.
4. In (Dickens) _____ novel *Great Expectations,* (Pip) _____ adventures hold every (reader) _____ attention.

■ **Exercise 24.4**   Change the structures that show ownership to possessive forms that use apostrophes.

Example:
The announcement of the secretary of state
The secretary of state's announcement

1. the cars of Kim and Thai
2. a patent belonging to my sister-in-law
3. the book written by Julio Garcia and John Youngblood
4. the smile of Doris
5. the value of fifty cents

24d
Showing Omission

Use an apostrophe to indicate letters or numbers left out of contractions or letters omitted from words to show regional pronunciation. In a **contraction**—a shortened word or group of words formed when some letters or sounds are omitted—the apostrophe serves as a substitute for omitted letters.

24d
'
∨

it's	(for *it is* or *it has*)
weren't	(for *were not*)
here's	(for *here is*)
comin'	(for *coming*)

Apostrophes can also substitute for omitted numbers. "The '50s were a decade of relative calm; the '60s were much more turbulent." But it is usually better to spell out the decades. "Many people claim that the fifties were much more turbulent than we remember and that the sixties only continued trends begun a decade earlier.''

✔ CHECKLIST 24.1: AVOIDING INCORRECT APOSTROPHES

A common error is placing apostrophes where they don't belong. As you revise, check your apostrophes.

- Don't use an apostrophe plus *s* ('s) to show the plural of a letter, number, or word used as a word rather than as a symbol of the meaning it conveys. Underline such elements (to indicate that they would be set in italics if your story or essay were set in type) and add -s, without an underline.

  Committee has two *m*s, two *t*s, and two *e*s.

  There are twelve *no*s in the first paragraph.
  He makes his *2*s look like *5*s.

- To show possession with personal and relative pronouns and the pronoun *it,* use the special possessive forms, which never require apostrophes (my/mine, your/yours, his, her/hers, our/ours, their/theirs; whose, and its).

  His cooking won a prize.

  Its fur was shedding.

  They knew **our** secret.

  Is he a friend of **yours?**

  The rake is **hers.**

- When an apostrophe appears with an *s* in a pronoun, the apostrophe probably marks omissions in a contraction.

  It's too hot. (It + is)

  Who's there? (Who + is)

  If **you're** awake, please call. (you + are)

24d

∨

■ **Exercise 24.5** Correct any words in boldface either by removing incorrectly used apostrophes or by adding apostrophes where they belong. Some words are correct and require no change. Place a check above them.

1. **Iris** cat lost **its** way, but one **neighbors** boy helped her find it.
2. There **wasnt** enough attention placed on writing **skills'** in college English curricula in the **60s.**
3. In the word **occurrence,** the two *c*s and two *r*s confuse even college **students'.**
4. If the **ideas'** are **hers', it's** wise to give her credit for them.
5. Many **childrens parents'** bought these **dolls** before the **companies** recalled them at the **governments** request.

CHAPTER 25

USING
QUOTATION
MARKS

Quotation marks ("...") always work in pairs. They are used to enclose words, phrases, and sentences that are quoted directly. Titles of short works such as poems, articles, songs, and short stories also require quotation marks, as do some words and phrases that you wish to use in a special sense.

25a
Enclosing Direct Quotations

A **direct quotation** repeats the exact words of a speaker or of a text. Direct quotations from written material may include whole sentences or only a few words or phrases.

> James Baldwin wrote of his experience during his childhood, "The only white people who came to our house were welfare workers and bill collectors."

> James Baldwin wrote that the only white visitors he saw in his home as a child were "welfare workers and bill collectors."

The examples in the table on page 336 will help you see how direct quotations are used and punctuated in sentences.

In writing dialogue, use quotation marks to enclose everything a speaker says. When one person continues speaking, use quotation marks again if the quoted sentence is interrupted.

> "I don't know what you're talking about," he said. "I did listen to everything you told me."

Sentence: Quoted words first

Opening quotation mark   Capital letter

"The first thing that strikes one about Plath's journals is what

Closing quotation mark   End mark

they leave out," writes Katha Pollitt in *The Atlantic.*

Comma inside quotation mark   Lowercase letter

Sentence: Quoted words last

Comma   Opening quotation mark
                                Capital letter

In *The Atlantic,* Katha Pollitt writes, "The first thing that

Closing quotation mark

strikes one about Plath's journals is what they leave out."

End mark inside quotation mark

Sentence: Quoted words interrupted

Opening quotation mark   Closing quotation mark   Lowercase letter
    Capital letter   Comma inside quotation mark

"The first thing that strikes one about Plath's journals," writes

25a
" / "

Opening quotation mark   Closing quotation mark

Katha Pollitt in **The Atlantic,** "is what they leave out."

Comma   Lowercase letter   End mark inside quotation mark

Note that no comma precedes the quotation when it completes the meaning of the sentence and that the existing initial capital letter in the quotation is made into a lowercase letter:

James Baldwin wrote of his childhood experiences that "the only white people who came to our house were welfare workers and bill collectors."

An **indirect quotation** is a **paraphrase.** That is, you express in your own words the meaning of someone else's words. Quotation marks are not used with an indirect quotation.

Casey confessed that he enjoyed blowing the whistle more than anything else he did as a locomotive engineer.

Odette asked if she could borrow my chain saw.

When you quote more than four typed lines, set them off from the text. Start a new line for the quotation, type it double-spaced, and set every line off by a ten-space indentation from the left margin. Double-space above and below the quotation. *Be sure that you indent every line in a block quotation.*

Usually introduced by a colon, a block quotation is *not* set off by quotation marks. If the block includes a direct quotation, however, use quotation marks as they are found in the text. The example that follows shows you how to do this.

Some of the most interesting pages in Schorske's book describe how Sigmund Freud arrived at psychoanalysis and the interpretation of dreams and so made a revolution in our understanding of how the mind works. But as Schorske points out, the young Freud's first passion was not the working of the mind but classical archeology:

> He consumed with avidity Jakob Burckhardt's newly published *History of Greek Culture,* so rich in materials on primitive myth and religion. He read with envy the biography of Heinrich Schliemann, who fulfilled a childhood wish by his discovery of Troy. Freud began the famous collection of ancient artifacts which were soon to grace his office in the Berggasse. And he cultivated a new friendship in the Viennese professional elite—especially rare in those days of withdrawal—with Emanuel Loewy, a professor of archeology. "He keeps me up till three o'clock in the morning," Freud wrote appreciatively to Fliess. "He tells me about Rome."
>
> —CARL SCHORSKE

25a
"/"

Use block quotations sparingly because they cut down on readability. Try instead to paraphrase the material and include it in the text, giving proper credit to your sources (see 33b, c, and d).

Two or three lines of poetry may be run into your text, much like any other short quotation. Line breaks are shown with a slash.

> In the nineteenth century Wordsworth wrote of the weary acquisitiveness of our modern age: "The world is too much with us; late and soon, / Getting and spending, we lay waste our powers: / Little we see in Nature that is ours."

Longer verse quotations are indented block-style, like long prose quotations. If you cannot get an entire line of poetry on a single line of your typescript, you may indent the turned line four spaces to the right of the line above it.

> Ah, what can ever be more stately and admirable to me
>   than mast-hemm'd Manhattan?
> River and sunset and scallop-edg'd waves of flood-tide?
> The sea-gulls oscillating their bodies, the hay-boat in the twilight,
>   and the belated lighter?
> What gods can exceed these that clasp me by the hand, and with
>   voices
> I love call me promptly and loudly by my nighest name as I
>   approach?
>
> —WALT WHITMAN

A pair of single quotation marks (made with the apostrophe on the typewriter) is used to set off quotations within quotations.

> What happened when the faculty demanded an investigation of dishonest recruiting practices in the athletic department? The president of the university said, "I know you're saying to me, 'We want an honest football team.' But I'm telling you this: 'I want a winning football team.' "

25b
Using Other Punctuation with Quotation Marks

A comma or period at the end of a quotation is always set before the last quotation mark. A question mark is set before the last quotation mark if the quotation itself asks a question. Punctuation marks that come before the quoted material are not included within quotation marks.

"The worst movie I've ever seen is *Jaws*," he said.

"How can you say that?" she asked. "I loved *Jaws*.

"How can I say that?" he said. "I'll tell you how I can say that; I can say that because I saw it eight times!"

She said, "I think *Jaws II* is even better." Then she asked, "Have you seen it?"

"Yes," he replied. "I have. I saw it four times."

"Then," she countered, "do you still say, 'The worst movie I've ever seen is *Jaws*'?"

Standard practice is to place the period before the final quotation mark even when the quotation is only one or two words long. A question mark or an exclamation point is placed after the last quotation mark if the quoted material is not itself a question or an exclamation.

He had what he called his "special reasons."

Why did he name his car "Buck"?

"Because," she said, "people pass it all the time."

Standard practice is to put colons and semicolons after the final quotation mark.

"I think the jokes in this book are terrible"; she made the remark at the top of her voice, and since I wrote the book, I was hurt.

Dean Wilcox cited the items he called his "daily delights": a free parking place for his scooter at the faculty club, a special table in the club itself, and friends to laugh with after a day's work.

25b

" / "

■ **Exercise 25.1**   Punctuate correctly the following sentences. Some sentences require no additional punctuation.

1. I want you to write a book Ted told me one night.
2. He said Give me a manuscript, and I'll get it published.
3. She told me that she would rather play tennis than eat.
4. He said to his friend I bought the car on credit.
5. The wind is rising she shouted Make the boats secure The hurricane is coming.

25c
Enclosing Titles

Use quotation marks to set off a variety of titles, such as essays, book chapters or sections, short poems, short stories, songs, articles in periodicals, radio or television program episodes, and for all unpublished works. Use italics, or underlining, for all other titles (see p. 396).

> "How to Die: The Example of Samuel Johnson" is the title of a recent article in the *Sewanee Review.*
>
> The chapter was called "Another Question of Location."

Note that the titles of songs and short poems are usually put in quotation marks. Often the distinction is based on whether the work was published separately or included in a larger work. Works published separately appear in italics. Titles of long poems are put in italics. In manuscripts and typescripts prepared with printers that do not have an italic font, underline to show what would be italicized in print (see 30a).

> Robert Herrick wrote the poem "Upon Julia's Clothes."
>
> George Noel Gordon, Lord Byron, wrote *Childe Harold's Pilgrimage.*
>
> John Milton wrote "On Shakespeare" in 1630, thirty-seven years before *Paradise Lost,* his major poetic work.

QUOTATION MARKS TO ENCLOSE TITLES

Essays

"A Hanging"
"Once More to the Lake"

25c
" / "

Book chapters or sections

"The Girl in Conflict" (Chapter 11 of *Coming of Age in Samoa*)
"Science and Technology" (Part IV of *The Universal Almanac*)

Short poems

"Daffodils"
"Love Song"

Short stories

"A Wagner Matinee"
"The Tell Tale Heart"

Songs

"My Way"
"Friends in Low Places"

Articles in periodicals

"Post-Soviet Baltic Republic: Still Stunted and Struggling" (in the *New York Times*)
"Scotland Yard of the Wild" (in *American Way*)

Radio and television program episodes

"I Can't Remember" (on *48 Hours*)
"Voyage of the Hokule' a" (on *Best of National Geographic*)
"The Final Problem" (on *Sherlock Holmes Mysteries*)

25d
Indicating Special Use

Use quotation marks to show that someone else has used a word or phrase in a special way that you or the general public may not use or agree with completely.

> The "worker's paradise" of Stalinist Russia turned out to be a combination of slums, shortages, secret police, and slave-labor camps.
>
> George had the "privilege" of working his way through school by cleaning bathrooms.
>
> For them, getting "saved" is clearly only the first step.
>
> —FRANCES FITZGERALD

Sometimes inexperienced writers use quotation marks to apologize for the informality of certain expressions. They want to indicate their awareness that such expressions are not usually found in serious writing. They think the quotation marks show readers that they know better.

25d
" "

Apologetic

People in California are "laid back."

You can accomplish great things only if you "keep your nose to the grindstone."

I thought he was "cute."

In fact, quotation marks used in this way only mark the writer as inexperienced. Experienced writers simply avoid using slang, clichés, and expressions that call for an apology. When you are tempted to use apologetic quotation marks, take time to think of a better way of expressing yourself.

Revised

People in California pride themselves on living for pleasure without taking anything too seriously.

You can accomplish great things only if you pay attention to what you are doing.

I thought he was attractive.

But if you have a good reason for using a cliché or a slang expression and are sure you can justify its use, use it—without quotation marks.

■ **Exercise 25.2** In some of the following sentences, quotation marks are incorrectly used. Correct any incorrect usages, and put a check by those instances in which quotation marks are used in the right way.

1. "Traditional Principles of Rhetoric" is the title of a chapter in Kenneth Burke's book "A Rhetoric of Motives."
2. "Gee whiz," he said, "I could rap with you all night long."
3. When I waited to do my term paper until the night before it was due, I was really "up the creek without a paddle."
4. "And the Thunder Rolls" is a song Garth Brooks sings.
5. I wanted to know if I could bring my "kids" to the party.
6. She was "put off" by my reaction to her paper.
7. "To His Coy Mistress" is a celebrated poem by Andrew Marvell.
8. Most "utopian" communities emphasize rigid conformity, hard work, and puritanical ethics.
9. "Lochinvar" is a rousing poem by Sir Walter Scott.
10. Hitler's "triumph" was Germany's "tragedy."

25d
" / "

✔ CHECKLIST 25.1: **PLACING PUNCTUATION WITH QUOTATION MARKS**

Convention calls for the placement of other marks of punctuation inside closing quotation marks. Some cases do require other punctuation outside quotation marks. And you often have to take into account the meaning of the sentence in relation to the material in quotation marks. As you revise, look for closing quotation marks and these marks of punctuation. Make sure that you place them in the right order.

- Periods always belong inside quotation marks.
- Commas always belong inside quotation marks.
- Semicolons always belong outside quotation marks.
- Colons always belong outside quotation marks.
- Exclamation points belong inside quotation marks if they are part of the statement or title quoted but outside quotation marks if they are end marks for the entire sentence.
- Question marks belong inside quotation marks if they are part of the question or title quoted but outside quotation marks if they are end marks for the entire sentence.

25d

" **/** "

OTHER MARKS OF
PUNCTUATION

End marks, commas, semicolons, apostrophes, and quotation marks are the most common marks of punctuation in English. Additional marks give more subtle meaning to your written expression. These include dashes, colons, parentheses, brackets, slashes, ellipses, and hyphens.

26a
Using Dashes

The dash (—) sets off words, phrases, and sometimes whole sentences so that they receive special emphasis. Think of the dash as a very strong pause intended to give special emphasis to what follows—and sometimes to what comes immediately before. Sometimes dashes are paired—as in the first example below—and sometimes they are not.

> A Wisconsin man traveling on horseback had the lower parts of his boots—brand-new ones, be it noted—eaten by wolves, but managed to save his toes.
>
> —RICHARD ERDOES

> I think this is the most extraordinary collection of human talent, of human knowledge, that has ever been gathered at the White House—with the possible exception of when Thomas Jefferson dined alone.
>
> —JOHN F. KENNEDY

On the typewriter the dash is made with two hyphens in a row. There is no space between the hyphens and no space between the dash and the word on either side of it, nor is there any other mark of punctuation on either side of the dash. Handwritten and typeset dashes are single, unbroken lines about as wide as a capital *M*.

```
Coca-Cola, potato chips, and brevity--these are the marks of
a good study session in the dorm.
```

Often the dash sets off nouns placed for special emphasis at the beginning of a sentence and then summarized by a pronoun after the dash, as you see in the sentence above. The dash sometimes can set off an independent clause within a sentence. In such sentences, the content of the set-off independent clause is not essential to the main assertion of the sentence. It is added information.

> Love, with Chaucer, is something tender and vulnerable—it must be protected from the sniggers of a callous world, from the cynicism bred by casual conquest, from the damage done by blurted-out ugly words.
>
> —HANS P. GUTH

When used in pairs, dashes serve to separate parenthetical statements more closely related to the sentence than parentheses would allow but less closely related than a pair of commas would imply (see 22c).

> What she gets—and enjoys—from me is a youthful perspective.
>
> —JUDITH VIORST

> Age groups and the part they have played in American culture—or indeed in any culture—are a subject that has seldom been thoroughly discussed.
>
> —MALCOLM COWLEY

Overuse of the dash can distract readers. You should use the dash only for special emphasis.

26b
Using Colons

26a/b
— :

Use the colon (:) to link independent clauses, to introduce direct quotations and lists, and to set off words and phrases at the end of a sentence. The colon also separates titles and subtitles and the numbers of chapters and verses of the Bible, and it is used in other specialized situations.

The colon links independent clauses when the second clause restates or elaborates on the first. Use it when you want to emphasize the second clause.

Mau Mau emerged as a secret society as a result of a prolonged breakdown of Kikuyu tribal life under European influence: the name is a corruption of '*Uma Uma*' (Out! Out!)—given as a warning when police were approaching.

—PENELOPE MAUNSELL

Until recently, women in Switzerland had an overwhelming political disadvantage: they could not vote.

Of this I am sure: Martin will arrive late, talk loudly, and eat too much.

Instead of a comma, you can use a colon as a more formal way of introducing a direct quotation. The use of the colon before a direct quotation adds additional separation between your statement and the quotation.

"Don't speak of it," she said in a reciting voice and choosing her words sadly and carefully: "It was a stroke."

—V. S. PRITCHETT

Later she recalled the hours Faulkner spent helping her to recover hope: "He kept me alive," she said.

—DAVID MINTER

Colons are often used to introduce **block quotations,** which are set off from regular text by spaces and indents, especially if the introduction previews the quotation.

Dickens had contempt for lazy people. Some of his worst characters are those who lie about, waiting for others to wait on them. Here is the way he introduces Mrs. Witterly in *Nicholas Nickleby:*

> The lady had an air of sweet insipidity, and a face of engaging paleness; there was a faded look about her, and about the furniture, and about the house altogether. She was reclining on the sofa in such a very unstudied attitude that she might have been taken for an actress all ready for the first scene in a ballet, and only waiting for the drop curtain to go up.

26b

:

Colons also introduce itemized lists.

During its first four years the Virginia venture had failed to meet three basic needs: political stability, economic prosperity, and peaceful Indian relations.

—ALDEN T. VAUGHAN

The colon *cannot* be used to introduce a simple series. To correct the sentence below, remove the colon altogether:

> During its first four years the Virginia venture had failed to meet: political stability, economic prosperity, and peaceful Indian relations.

Some writers capitalize the first letter of the first word after a colon if a complete sentence follows the colon.

> He is kind: Innumerable unknowns in dire need have received financial help from Sinatra.
>
> —ISOBEL SILDEN

By convention, colons separate a main title from the subtitle. The first word of the subtitle is always capitalized.

> *Doing Without: Meeting the Energy Crisis in the 1980s*

Colons intervene between Bible chapters and verses.

> Young writers should take Proverbs 12:1 as a motto.

To indicate the time of day, use a colon between the hour and the minutes.

> He woke up at 6:30 in the morning.

Colons follow salutations in business letters.

> Dear Mr. Clinton:

26c
Using Parentheses

26b/c

: ()

Parentheses ((. . .)) always work in pairs. Use them to set off information that breaks the flow of thought within a sentence or a paragraph. Parentheses enclose material that is not as important as material set off by commas or dashes (see 22c, 26a).

> The first money you get for a book will probably be your advance; as a rule, half of that is paid when you sign your contract (or as soon thereafter as the legal department and the accounting department

fill out the appropriate forms), and the other half comes due when you deliver a satisfactory manuscript.

—JUDITH APPLEBAUM and NANCY EVANS

At another barrier a seaman held back Kathy Gilnagh, Kate Mullins, and Kate Murphy. (On the *Titanic* everyone seemed to be named Katherine.)

—WALTER LORD

When parentheses enclose a whole sentence, a period comes after the sentence but before the final parenthesis, as in the second example above. A sentence that appears inside parentheses *within a sentence* is neither capitalized nor closed with a period.

John Henry (he was the man with the forty-pound hammer) was a hero to miners fearing the loss of their jobs to machines.

But a question mark or an exclamation point may follow a parenthetical sentence within a sentence.

John Henry (did he really swing a forty-pound hammer?) was a hero to miners fearing the loss of their jobs to machines.

John Henry (he swung a forty-pound hammer!) was a hero to miners fearing the loss of their jobs to machines.

Parentheses are used to enclose many kinds of numbers within a text. In some forms of annotation (see 33g), parentheses enclose page numbers of a book referred to throughout a paper. Parentheses also enclose cross-references to other parts of a book.

26c

()

Stevens writes that the demands of their offices turn the best university presidents into machines (43).

Carmichael says that the argument Stevens makes is nonsense because (1) university presidents don't work as well as machines, (2) university presidents don't do any real work at all, and (3) universities would be better off if they were run by faculty committees.

Readers tend to find many parenthetical numbers distracting because the numbers interrupt the flow of thought. If the numbers within parentheses were left out of the example above and the statements set off by commas alone, the passage would be more readable.

Using Brackets

Use brackets to set off material within quoted matter that is not part of the quotation.

> Samuel Eliot Morison has written, "This passage has attracted a good deal of scorn to the Florentine mariner [Verrazzano], but without justice."

In this sentence, a writer is quoting Morison. But Morison's sentence does not include the name of the "Florentine mariner." The writer adds the name—Verrazzano—but places it in brackets so that readers will know the identity of the mariner Morison is talking about.

Sometimes material in brackets explains or corrects something that is quoted.

> Vasco da Gama's man wrote in 1487, "The body of the church [it was not a church but a Hindu shrine] is as large as a monastery."

Brackets are also used around words that you insert within a quotation to make it fit the style or grammar of your sentence.

Full quotation

I went back to the country and farmed a crop of tobacco with my dad that next year. For all the work I put in I didn't make half as much as I'd been making at the factory, so, after the market closed, I wandered back to town and started looking for another job.

—ANN BANKS

Edited quotation

Jim Wells came off the farm to work in a cigarette factory in North Carolina during the depression. He was fired because he hit a foreman who mistreated him, and, he said, "I went back to the country and farmed a crop of tobacco with my dad that next year [but] I didn't make half as much as I'd been making at the factory." The only thing he could do was to go back to the city and look for another job.

The bracketed word *but* makes the sentence read smoothly. It eliminates the need for an ellipsis (see 26f).

Brackets may enclose the word *sic* (Latin for "thus") after quoted matter that looks like a mistake. *Sic* lets the reader know that the quotation is presented exactly as it appears in its source and that you, the writer, are aware of the error it contains.

The dean said, "Those kids is [*sic*] going to get kicked out of school for saying I don't know no [*sic*] grammar."

Brackets are sometimes used to enclose editorial notes, page numbers, or other documentation inserted in a text.

26e
Using Slashes

The slash has very limited uses. As a rule, use the slash only to show divisions between lines of poetry when you quote more than one line of a poem as part of a sentence. Poetry shown as a block quotation replicates the original lines, and does not require slashes.

Sophocles wrote of the uncertainty of human knowledge: "No man can judge that rough unknown or trust in second sight/For wisdom changes hands among the wise."

Occasionally the slash is used to show that something happened over a couple of calendar years.

The book sold well in 1988/89.

But it is usually better to use *and* or show inclusive dates with a hyphen.

26d/e

[ ] /

The book sold well in 1976 and 1977.

The book sold well in 1988–89.

Some writers use the slash to substitute for the conjunction *or* or as a marker between the words *and* and *or* when the words suggest options.

The course was offered credit/noncredit.

The winner will be chosen by lot, and he/she will drive a new car home.

You can buy the toaster oven and/or the microwave.

Most writers, however, consider such usage awkward. It is usually better to rephrase the sentence.

Students who took the course received no grades. If they satisfied the requirements, they got credit; if they did not, they received no penalty.

The winner, to be chosen by lot, will drive a new car home.

You can buy the toaster oven or the microwave, or both.

Do not use a slash to show alternate pronouns. See Chapter 11 for less awkward ways of avoiding bias in writing.

26f
Using Ellipses

If you wish to shorten a passage you are quoting, you may omit some words. To show readers that you have done so, use three spaced periods, called an **ellipsis.**

Full quotation

In the nineteenth century, railroads, lacing their way across continents, reaching into the heart of every major city in Europe and America, and bringing a new romance to travel, added to the unity of nations and fueled the nationalist fires already set burning by the French Revolution and the wars of Napoleon.

Edited quotation

In his account of nineteenth-century society, Wilkins argued that "railroads . . . added to the unity of nations and fueled the nationalist fires already set burning by the French Revolution and the wars of Napoleon."

26e/f

/ ...

Most writers do not use ellipses to indicate that words have been left out at the beginning or the end of a quotation. Academic writers occasionally use ellipses to show omissions at the beginning or at the end of a quotation. The primary function of the ellipsis is to show that something has been left out of the middle of a quotation.

Ellipsis marks may be used at the end of a sentence if you mean to leave a thought hanging, either in your own prose or in something you are quoting. You do this to suggest that you are not sure how the thought might be ended. If you use an ellipsis at the end of a sentence, add a fourth spaced period.

> Oh God, I'm scared. I wish I could die right now with the feeling I have because I know Momma's going to make me mad and I'm going to make her mad, and me and Presley's gonna fight.... "Richard, you get in here and put your coat on. Get in here or I'll whip you."
>
> —DICK GREGORY

The ellipsis should serve only as a means of shortening a quotation, never as a device for changing its fundamental meaning or for creating emphasis where none exists in the original.

■ **Exercise 26.1**

1. Write three sentences using dashes and three using parentheses. What difference, if any, do you find in the effects of using the two punctuation marks?
2. Go to the periodical reading room of your library and look at *Time, Newsweek, Ebony, Sports Illustrated, Popular Mechanics,* or the *New York Times Magazine.* Find sentences that use parentheses and sentences that use the dash. Copy as many of them as you can find. What can you say about the ways these punctuation marks are used?
3. Write a paragraph in which you quote something and insert material within brackets in the quotation. Also delete material and replace it with an ellipsis correctly. Explain what you have done.

■ **Exercise 26.2**   Explain the use of dashes and parentheses in the following sentences. Is the punctuation appropriate to the meaning? What other punctuation might serve as an alternative?

26f

...

1. An air-cooled engine requires no antifreeze in winter (an advantage), but it must be fairly small for the cooling to work (a disadvantage).
2. Diesel engines are fuel efficient and durable—but they are expensive to manufacture.
3. The Ford Motor Company paid workers five dollars a day (people said Henry Ford was undermining capitalism by paying so much) to build the Model T on assembly lines before World War I.
4. The rotary gasoline engine (the first popular model sold in the United States was the Japanese Mazda) was smooth, quiet, and durable, but it burned 15 percent more fuel than conventional engines—a reason for its swift demise.

5. Mechanical automobile brakes operated with springs, levers, and the physical strength of the driver—a strength that might not be sufficient to stop a car hurtling down the highway at forty miles per hour.

26g
Using Hyphens

Hyphens are bridges between words. The use of hyphens to form compound words is discussed in 27e.

Hyphens are also used to divide words at the end of lines when the entire word will not fit on a line. Generally, you should avoid breaking words this way because such divisions slow your readers down. Never divide the last word on a page. Leave yourself wide margins, and you will rarely have to divide a word.

When you must break a word, put a hyphen at the end of the first line only, not at the start of the next line. The general rule is to divide words only between syllables. If you are unsure about how to break a word into syllables, consult your dictionary (see p. 200). The following pointers will help you to divide words correctly.

Never divide one-syllable words.

Incorrect

None of us at the dean's luncheon thought that the dean **wo- uld** arrive in tattered jeans and a torn undershirt.

His weird and uncontrollable **la- ugh** echoed down the corridor.

Never divide a word if the division leaves only one letter at the end of a line or only one or two letters at the beginning of a line. Avoid breaking such words as *hap·py, could·n't, read·er, o·pen, light·ly,* and *hat·ed.*

26g

-

Incorrect

Lamont Harris wore his new tuxedo to the **o- pening** of the exhibition.

Naomi Lee Fong, who graduates today, never felt so **hap- py** in her life before.

Divide compound words into the words that make them up or at the hyphen if the word contains a hyphen. Compound words such as *hard-*

working, rattlesnake, bookcases, and *paperwork* should be broken only between the words that form them: *hard-working, rattle-snake, book-cases, paper-work.* Compound words that already have hyphens, such as *brother-in-law, self-denial, ex-convict,* and *anti-Semitic,* are broken after the hyphens only.

Incorrect

She loves being a detective, but she hates the paperwork.

I gave my old fishing rod to my brother-in-law, and he will sell it at his yard sale.

When two consonants come between vowels in a word you are divid-ing, make the split between the two consonants. Do not split the two consonants if the division does not reflect pronunciation. In the following words, for example, make the split where the dot appears.

ter·ror   run·ning
shel·ter   bril·liant

In a word like *respire,* however, you would have to divide the word after the prefix *re* and not between the *s* and the *p,* because the word is pro-nounced *re·spire* and not *res·pire.*

Avoid confusing word divisions. Sometimes part of a divided word forms a shorter word that can mislead your readers. In such cases, write the complete word or break the word where it will not cause confusion. The table shows some misleading divisions and some possible alternatives.

CONFUSING WORD DIVISIONS

Divisions to avoid	Possible alternatives
a-toll	atoll
at-tire	attire
bar-row	barrow
fat-uous	fatuous
his-torian	histor-ian
im-pugn	impugn
mud-dled	muddled
pig-mentation	pigmen-tation, pigmenta-tion

26g

-

Be especially careful if you allow a word-processing program to hyphenate for you. Most computer-controlled hyphenation cannot follow the many subtleties of proper English hyphenation. If you cannot turn the hyphenation function off, go through your essay and check every computer-made end-line hyphenation against your dictionary and the guidelines given here. No doubt you'll find many mistakes.

■ **Exercise 26.3**   Show where the following words can be divided if you must hyphenate them at the end of a line. Some words can be divided in more than one place. If a word cannot be divided, put a check alongside it.

1. typewriter
2. grasses
3. record (noun)
4. record (verb)
5. indignation

6. taxed
7. loved
8. pruning
9. roughly
10. England

26g

-

UNDERSTANDING MECHANICS

IMPROVING SPELLING

Correct spelling is a sign of literacy. If you misspell words, your readers may understand you, but they will be less likely to respect you. Frequent or even occasional misspellings in your writing can make people believe that you are careless or ignorant, and if that happens, you will have to work twice as hard to make them take you and your thoughts seriously.

This chapter provides some suggestions to help you toward better spelling.

27a
Reading and Pronouncing Carefully

Some common words are frequently misspelled because people misread them or mispronounce them. Of course, pronunciations vary from region to region, and no list can include all mispronunciations that lead to spelling trouble. But if you study the following list, you can train your eye and your ear to spot the parts of common words that often cause spelling errors.

COMMONLY MISPRONOUNCED WORDS

accident**ally**	NOT	accident**ly**
arith**m**etic	NOT	arith**e**metic
ath**l**etics	NOT	ath**e**letics
can**di**date	NOT	can**ni**date

COMMONLY MISPRONOUNCED WORDS   (continued)

chi**mn**ey	NOT	chi**ml**ey
cor**por**ation	NOT	co**per**ation
disas**tr**ous	NOT	disas**ter**ous
drow**ned**	NOT	drown**ed**ed
envi**ron**ment	NOT	envi**rer**ment
every**b**ody	NOT	**ever**body
every**th**ing	NOT	**ever**thing
Fe**bru**ary	NOT	Fe**bu**ary
gen**eral**ly	NOT	gen**r**ally *or* gen**er**ly
gover**nm**ent	NOT	gover**m**ent
heigh**t**	NOT	heigh**th**
hund**reds**	NOT	hund**ereds** *or* hu**nerds**
irre**le**vant	NOT	irre**ve**lant
la**bora**tory	NOT	la**bra**tory *or* la**ber**tory
li**brar**y	NOT	li**berr**y
lit**era**ture	NOT	lit**ra**ture *or* lit**er**ture
mathe**ma**tics	NOT	math**ma**tics
mischiev**ous**	NOT	mischiev**ious**
op**tim**ist	NOT	op**tom**ist
peremptory	NOT	**pre**emptory
performance	NOT	**pre**formance
perspiration	NOT	**pre**speration
prescription	NOT	**per**scription
privi**le**ge	NOT	priv**le**ge
production	NOT	**per**duction
pro**gram**	NOT	prog**rum**
pub**licly**	NOT	pub**lically**
repre**se**nt	NOT	re**per**sent
sopho**mo**re	NOT	soph**mo**re
stren**gth**	NOT	stren**th**
stud**ious**	NOT	stud**jous**
tempera**ment**	NOT	temper**ment**
temper**a**ture	NOT	tem**per**ture, tem**pra**ture, *or* tem**perchoor**
wond**rous**	NOT	wond**erous**

Some common plurals my be misspelled because they are mispronounced. Misspelling is especially common in the plurals of words ending in *-ist* or *-est*. The plural of *scientist* is *scientists*. The final combination *ts* sounds like the *tz* in *Ritz* or the *ts* in *fights*. Because this *ts* is difficult for some people to pronounce, they often leave it off, thinking almost unconsciously that the *s* sound in *ist* or *est* is sufficient to make the plural. But the plurals of such words always require a final *-s*. Other words with a difficult *s* sound in the final syllable sometimes trouble writers in forming the plural. Here are some plurals to remember.

COMMONLY PRONOUNCED PLURALS

biologist**s**	disc**s**	nest**s**	rasp**s**
desk**s**	humanist**s**	racist**s**	socialist**s**

27b
Distinguishing Homophones

Be especially careful of words that sound alike or nearly alike but have different meanings and different spellings. These are **homophones.** English has lots of homophones; some of the most frequently used ones are included in the table. Study these words. If you don't immediately recognize the distinctions in meanings, look up pairs (or, in a few cases, triplets and quadruplets) in a dictionary. Also look carefully at these words each time you use one in your writing to make sure you have selected the right one. Keep a list of the homophones that have given you trouble in the past.

COMMON HOMOPHONES

affect, effect	foreword, forward
all, awl	hear, here
complement, compliment	its, it's
council, counsel	lead, led
discreet, discrete	lightening, lightning

COMMON HOMOPHONES   (continued)

made, maid	sea, see
pail, pale	stationary, stationery
pair, pare	straight, strait
peace, piece	than, then
pedal, petal	their, there, they're
peer, pier	to, too, two
plain, plane	vain, vane, vein
principal, principle	way, weigh
rain, reign, rein	who's, whose
right, rite, write, wright	your, you're
role, roll	

**27c
Learning the Principles of Spelling**

Some principles of English spelling are so generally true that learning them will help you be a better speller.

Distinguishing Between *ei* and *ie*

When you are deciding between the combinations *ei* and *ie*, consider the previous letter and the sound of the word. When these letters sound like the *ee* in *see*, usually place the *i* before *e*.

   believe, relieve, grief, chief, yield, wield

But there are exceptions. When preceded by *c*, the spelling is nearly always *ei*.

   receive, deceive, ceiling, conceit

When the sound is like *ay* in *bay* or *May*, the spelling is nearly always *ei*.

   neigh, feign, neighbor, weigh

Then there are some renegades.

seize, caffeine, codeine

The familiar jingle is worth recalling: Write *i* before *e* except after *c*, or when sounded like *a* as in *neighbor* and *weigh*. But as for most other words with different sounds, it's best to memorize the spellings.

stein, weird, foreign, height, forfeit, pietism, sierra, pierce, pier, pie, pied, fiery, sieve

■ **Exercise 27.1**   Some of the following words are misspelled. Spell them correctly. Put a check by each word in the list that is spelled correctly.

1. friendly	**6.** believing
2. weight	**7.** conceive
3. grievous	**8.** liesure
4. beleif	**9.** frieghten
5. freight	**10.** heir

■ **Exercise 27.2**   Fill in the blanks in the following words with *ei* or *ie* to make the words correct. Explain the reasons for your choices.

1. s ___ zure	**6.** v ___ n	**11.** l ___ n
2. rec ___ pt	**7.** d ___ gn	**12.** n ___ ther
3. perc ___ vable	**8.** hyg ___ ne	**13.** n ___ ce
4. b ___ ge	**9.** th ___ f	**14.** conc ___ t
5. r ___ n	**10.** fr ___ ze	**15.** dec ___ t

Adding Suffixes

English builds words and changes the meanings of words by adding **suffixes,** or endings. Here are some general patterns in changes in the spelling of the root word when suffixes are added.

Words ending in a silent -*e*

Before adding the suffix -*ing*, drop a final silent -*e* from the root word.

force/forcing,   surprise/surprising,   manage/managing,   hope/hoping,   scare/scaring,   come/coming,   pave/paving,   become/becoming,   fume/fuming

There are a few exceptions to this rule.

dye/dyeing (to avoid confusion with *dying*)

hoe/hoeing (to avoid mispronunciation)
shoe/shoeing (to avoid mispronunciation and confusion with *show-ing*)

A final, silent -*e* on a root word is always dropped before the suffix -*ible.*

force/forcible

Though the silent -*e* of the root is usually dropped before the ending -*able,* the *e* is retained often enough to make this principle uncertain. It is best to memorize the words.

observe/observable, advise/advisable, move/movable (*sometimes* moveable), argue/arguable, debate/debatable

knowledge/knowledgeable, manage/manageable, peace/peaceable, notice/noticeable, change/changeable, embrace/embraceable

A final silent -*e* that is preceded by another vowel is always dropped before a suffix.

argue/argument, true/truly

Words ending in -*y*

When adding the suffix -*ing* to a word ending in -*y,* retain the -*y.*

study/studying, rally/rallying, enjoy/enjoying, cry/crying, ready/readying, steady/steadying, lay/laying

When a final -*y* follows a consonant in the root word, change the *y* to *i* before adding an ending other than -*ing.*

merry/merriment, merriest, merrier
happy/happier, happiness, happiest
rally/rallies, rallied, rallier
supply/supplier, supplies, supplied
pity/pitiless, pitiable, pitiful
mercy/merciful, merciless
kingly/kingliness
ugly/uglier, ugliest, ugliness

When a final -*y* follows a vowel in the root word, keep the *y* when adding an *s* to make the plural of a noun or the third-person singular of a verb.

valley/valleys, defray/defrays, delay/delays, dismay/dismays, enjoy/enjoys, toy/toys, ploy/ploys

Always keep the final *-y* when forming the plural of a person's name.

Joe and Mary Kirby/the Kirbys

To form the past tense of verbs ending in a final *-y* preceded by a vowel, generally keep the final *y* and add the suffix *-ed*.

play/played, dismay/dismayed, enjoy/enjoyed

But there are important exceptions.

pay/paid, say/said, lay/laid

■ **Exercise 27.3**   Add the suffix indicated for each of the following words. Be sure to change the spelling of the root word when such a change is appropriate.

1. advance + ing	**6.** sally + s
2. highboy + s	**7.** sense + ible
3. learn + able	**8.** pray + ed
4. horrify + ing	**9.** quality + s
5. quote + able	**10.** solicit + ing

Words ending in a consonant

Pay attention to words formed when a suffix that begins with a vowel is added to a root that ends in a consonant. These suffixes are *-ing, -er, -est, -ed, -ence, -ance, -ible, -able,* and *-ened*.

With most words of one syllable ending in a consonant immediately preceded by a vowel, double the final consonant.

grip/gripping, quip/quipped, stun/stunning, quit/quitting, plan/planned, sad/saddest, scar/scarring

If the root word ends with two consecutive consonants or with a consonant preceded by two consecutive vowels, do not double the final consonant before suffixes that begin with vowels.

tight/tighter, stoop/stooping, straight/straightest, sing/singer, deep/deepened, creep/creeping, crawl/crawler

If the root word has more than one syllable, and if the accent of the root falls on the last syllable, usually double the final consonant.

occur/occurrence, refer/referred, rebut/rebutting, concur/concurring

But if the final consonant of the root is preceded by a consonant or by two consecutive vowels, or if the accent shifts from the final syllable of the root when the suffix is added, don't double the final consonant.

depart/departing, ferment/fermenting, repair/repairing, refer/reference

If the final consonant is *-l*, check your dictionary. The increasing preference for the words listed below and others is not to double the final *-l*.

cancel/canceling, pencil/penciling, travel/traveled, unravel/unraveled

And there are, as always, exceptions that have to be memorized.

fit/fitted BUT benefit/benefited
ship/shipping BUT worship/worshiped

This rule sounds so complicated that you may think it better to memorize the spellings of all these words rather than to memorize the rule. But give the rule a try: it does work!

Adding Prefixes

Most standard **prefixes**—letters attached to the beginnings of words that change their meanings—do not require changing the spelling of the prefix or the root word. Before root words beginning with vowels, prefixes ending in vowels sometimes require a hyphen (see 27e).

appear/disappear	create/procreate
eminent/preeminent	satisfy/dissatisfy
operate/cooperate	spell/misspell
usual/unusual	

27c

spell

■ **Exercise 27.4**   Use the rules you have learned to add the indicated suffixes to the root words below. Explain why you change some roots to add the suffix and why you leave other roots unchanged. The exercise will help you most if you discuss your choices with other members of the class.

1. attend + ance	**10.** map + ing	**19.** spot + y
2. din + ed	**11.** submit + ing	**20.** star + ing
3. strip + ing	**12.** reckon + ed	**21.** confer + ence
4. dine + ing	**13.** detest + able	**22.** pin + ed
5. mar + ed	**14.** soon + est	**23.** disdain + ed
6. despair + ed	**15.** omit + ed	**24.** drown + ing
7. bob + ing	**16.** silly + est	**25.** pretend + ed
8. accept + ance	**17.** depend + ence	
9. dip + er	**18.** prefer + ing	

Forming Plurals

Plurals of nouns are formed according to some general rules. Most nouns simply add a final *-s.*

> grove/groves, boat/boats, cobra/cobras, bank/banks, scientist/scientists, moralist/moralists, gripe/gripes, gasp/gasps, disc/discs

Even acronyms and decades are made plural by the addition of *-s.*

> Some critics say that there have been two **FBIs**—the one before the death of J. Edgar Hoover and the one that came later on.
> The **1890s** are popularly called the Gay Nineties because of the extravagant pleasures of the rich during that decade.

Exceptions based on endings

Nouns ending in certain letters are exceptions to this rule.

When the singular of a noun ends in *-s, -x, -ch,* or *-sh,* add *-es* to form the plural.

> kiss/kisses, Marx/the Marxes, Mr. Jones/the Joneses, church/churches, dish/dishes

If a noun ends in *-y* preceded by a consonant, change the *y* to *i* and add *-es* to form the plural; if the final *y* is preceded by a vowel, keep the *y* and add *-s* to make the plural.

> beauty/beauties, sally/sallies, glory/glories, city/cities, country/coun-

tries, destiny/destinies, crudity/crudities, ray/rays, boy/boys, joy/joys, valley/valleys

When a noun ends in *-o* in the singular, form the plural by adding *-s* or *-es*. The best practice here is to look these plurals up in a dictionary.

hero/heroes, solo/solos, tomato/tomatoes, folio/folios, potato/potatoes, flamingo/flamingos *or* flamingoes, piano/pianos, manifesto/manifestos *or* manifestoes, veto/vetoes

To form the plurals of some nouns ending in *-f,* change the final *f* to *v* and add *-es.* If a silent *e* follows the *f,* also change the *f* to *v.*

leaf/leaves, hoof/hooves, knife/knives, life/lives, wife/wives, self/selves

But many nouns ending in *f* form their plurals by the standard addition of *-s,* and modern practice favors standardizing plurals this way.

chief/chiefs, roof/roofs

Irregular plurals

Some nouns have irregular plurals formed by changes in internal vowels or the addition of endings that don't include *-s.* These are some of the oldest and most familiar words in the English language.

child/children, goose/geese, man/men, woman/women, ox/oxen, tooth/teeth, mouse/mice

Some nouns are the same in the singular and plural.

deer/deer, fish/fish *or* fishes, fowl/fowl *or* fowls, moose/moose

Compound nouns

Compound nouns generally form plurals by the addition of *-s* or *-es.*

babysitter/babysitters, millrace/millraces

But when the first element of the compound is the most important word, the *-s* or *-es* is added to it.

attorney general/attorneys general, mother-in-law/mothers-in-law, father-in-law/fathers-in-law, court-martial/courts-martial, passerby/passersby

Latin and Greek words

Many Latin and Greek words have become part of the English language. To form the plurals of such words with the singular ending *-um* or *-on,* drop these endings and add *-a.*

> addendum/addenda, criterion/criteria, datum/data, medium/ media, phenomenon/phenomena

Some writers now treat *data* as though it were singular, but the preferred practice is still to recognize that *data* is plural and takes a plural verb.

> The data *are* clear on this point: the pass/fail course has become outdated by events.

Like *data,* the word *media* requires a plural verb. *Agenda,* by contrast, is now fully accepted as a singular form.

The plurals of a few nouns ending in *-is* are formed by changing this ending to *-es.*

> analysis/analyses, basis/bases, crisis/crises, thesis/theses

A few words with Latin roots ending in a vowel and an *x* may change to *-ices* when the plural is formed.

> appendix/appendices, index/indices (math), vortex/vortices

But today *-es* is the preferred form for the plurals of these words.

> appendixes, indexes (book), vortexes

A few English words with Latin roots ending in *-us* form their plurals by changing the *-us* to *-i.*

> alumnus/alumni, tumulus/tumuli, cumulus/cumuli, hippopotamus/ hippopotami *or* hippopotamuses, calculus/calculi, cactus/cacti

Even fewer words with Latin roots ending in *-a* form their plurals by changing the *-a* to *-ae.*

> alumna/alumnae

■ **Exercise 27.5** Form the plural of each of the following words. Check your plurals against those given in a dictionary when you have finished. (Chapter 12 discusses how to use a dictionary.)

1. mess	**13.** phlox	**25.** prophecy
2. harp	**14.** rest	**26.** symposium
3. disco	**15.** antenna	**27.** fungus
4. arch	**16.** handful	**28.** fascist
5. banjo	**17.** day	**29.** scientist
6. hello	**18.** money	**30.** neurosis
7. dodo	**19.** son-in-law	**31.** rest
8. grief	**20.** sheep	**32.** risk
9. radius	**21.** cow	**33.** critic
10. buffalo	**22.** garnish	**34.** soprano
11. elegy	**23.** vertebra	**35.** locus
12. harpy	**24.** rabbi	

27d

Using Lists of Words to Improve Spelling

The following lists of words misspelled in student papers were compiled a few years ago by New York State. Of the more than 31,000 misspelled words gathered by English teachers throughout the country, 407 were misspelled more frequently than others. These words are arranged in categories in descending order of difficulty. Study the list carefully. It will help if you have someone read the words aloud to you so that you can try to spell them without looking at them.

WORDS MOST FREQUENTLY MISSPELLED

Words misspelled 100 times or more

believe	description	occasion
belief	describe	occur
		occurred
benefit	environment	occurring
benefited		occurrence
beneficial	exist	
	existence	perform
choose	existent	performance
chose		
choice	its	personal
	it's	personnel
definite		
definitely	lose	precede
definition	losing	
define		principle
	necessary	principal
	unnecessary	

**27d
spell**

Words misspelled 100 times or more   (continued)

privilege	similar	too
professor	success	two
profession	succeed	to
receive	succession	write
receiving	than	writing
referring	then	writer
separate	their	
separation	they're	
	there	

Words misspelled 50 to 99 times

accommodate	control	intelligence
achieve	controlled	intelligent
achievement	controlling	interest
acquire	controversy	interpretation
affect	controversial	interpret
affective	criticism	led
all right*	criticize	loneliness
among	decision	lonely
analyze	decided	marriage
analysis	disastrous	Negro
apparent	embarrass	Negroes
argument	equipped	noticeable
aguing	equipment	noticing
began	excellent	origin
begin	excellence	original
beginner	experience	passed
beginning	explanation	past
busy	fascinate	possess
business	forty	possession
category	fourth	prefer
comparative	grammar	preferred
conscience	grammatically	prejudice
conscientious	height	prevalent
conscious	imagine	probably
consistent	imaginary	proceed
consistency	imagination	procedure
	immediate	prominent
	immediately	

* Although some dictionaries accept the spelling *alright,* most list it as non-standard usage. Most college instructors regard *alright* as a misspelling.

Words Misspelled 50 to 99 times   (continued)

psychology
psychoanalysis
psychopathic
psychosomatic

pursue

realize
really

repetition

rhythm

sense

shining

studying

surprise

thorough

tries
tried

useful
useless
using

varies
various

weather
whether

Words Misspelled 40 to 49 times

accept
acceptance
acceptable
accepting

accident
accidentally

acquaint
acquaintance

across

aggressive

appear
appearance

article

athlete
athletic

attended
attendant
attendance

challenge

character
characteristic
characterized

coming

convenience
convenient

difference
different

disappoint

discipline
disciple

dominant
predominant

effect

exaggerate

foreign
foreigners

fundamental
fundamentally

government
governor

hero
heroine
heroic
heroes

humor
humorist
humorous

hypocrisy
hypocrite

incident
incidentally

independent
independence

liveliest
livelihood
liveliness
lives

mere

operate

opinion

opportunity

paid

particular

philosophy

planned

pleasant

possible

practical

prepare

quantity

quiet

recommend

ridicule
ridiculous

speech

sponsor

summary
summed

suppose

technique

transferred

unusual
usually

villain

woman

27d
spell

Words misspelled 30 to 39 times

advice
advise

approach
approaches

author
authority
authoritative

basis
basically

before

careless
careful

carrying
carried
carries
carrier

conceive
conceivable

codemn

consider
considerably

continuous

curiosity
curious

dependent

desirability
desire

efficient
efficiency

entertain

extremely

familiar

finally

friendliness
friend

fulfill

further

happiness

hindrance

influential
influence

knowledge

laboratory

maintenance

ninety

oppose
opponent

optimism

parallel

permanent

permit

physical

piece

propaganda
propagate

relieve

religion

response

satire

significance

suppress

temperament

therefore

together

undoubtedly

weird

where

whose

you're

Words misspelled 20 to 29 times

accompanying
accompanies
accompanied
accompaniment

accomplish

accustom

actually
actuality
actual

adolescence
adolescent

against

amateur

amount

appreciate
appreciation

approximate

arouse
arousing

attack

attitude

boundary

Britain
Britannica

capital
capitalism

certain
certainly

chief

clothes

completely

counselor
counsel
council

curriculum

dealt

Words misspelled 20 to 29 times   (continued)

despair
disease
divide
divine
especially
excitable
exercise
expense
experiment
fallacy
fantasy
fantasies
favorite
fictitious
field
financier
financially
forward
guarantee
guaranteed
guidance
guiding
hear
here
huge
hungry
hungrily
hunger
ignorance
ignorant
indispensable
intellect
interfere
interference
interrupt
involve
irrelevant

laborer
laboriously
labor
laid
later
leisure
leisurely
length
lengthening
license
likeness
likely
likelihood
luxury
magazine
magnificent
magnificence
maneuver
mathematics
meant
mechanics
medicine
medical
medieval
miniature
mischief
moral
morale
morally
narrative
naturally
noble
obstacle
omit
peace
perceive
persistent
persuade

pertain
phase
playwright
politician
political
primitive
regard
relative
remember
reminisce
represent
roommate
sacrifice
safety
satisfy
satisfied
scene
schedule
seize
sentence
sergeant
several
shepherd
simply
simple
sophomore
source
story
stories
straight
strength
strict
substantial
subtle
suspense
symbol
synonymous

Words misspelled 20 to 29 times   (continued)

tendency	those	vacuum
themselves	thought	view
them	tragedy	whole
theory	tremendous	yield
theories		

27e
Using Hyphens

Hyphens are used to form compound words and to avoid confusion. Hyphens relate both to spelling and to style, and in using hyphens writers often have several options. For example, you could write *life-style* or *life style* or *lifestyle* and be correct in each case. A dictionary is the best help when you are unsure about using a hyphen.

The points below explain the most regular uses of hyphens.

Joining Noun Forms

Often in modern American English, a hyphen joins two nouns to make one compound word. Scientists speak of a *kilogram-meter* as a measure of force, and personnel managers speak of a *clerk-typist*, an employee who does general office work plus typing. The hyphen lets us know that the two nouns work together as one. Here are some other examples.

city-state	scholar-poet
composer-conductor	writer-editor

As compound nouns that once were new constructions come into general use, their hyphens tend to disappear. The nouns come to be written as one word, such as *housefly*, *firelight*, *firefight*, and *thundershower*.

A noun can also be linked with an adjective, an adverb, or another part of speech to form a compound noun.

accident-prone	cat-hater
break-in	dog-lover
by-product	first-rate

Hyphens also join nouns designating family relationships and compounds of more than two words.

brother-in-law	mother-in-law	stay-at-home
sister-in-law	father-in-law	stick-in-the-mud

Linking Modifiers to Avoid Confusion

Hyphens often help us sort out modifiers that come before the word they modify. If we say "He was a hard running back," we might mean that he was hard and that he was also a running back. If we say "He was a hard-running back," we mean that he ran hard. If we say "She was a quick thinking person," we might mean that she was quick and that she was also thinking. If we say "She was a quick-thinking person," we mean that she thought rapidly.

Notice that the hyphenated words in these examples employ adverbs (*hard, quick*) that do not end in *-ly*. When adverbs end in *-ly*, they do not require a hyphen if they modify an adjective that in turn modifies a noun.

They explored the **newly discovered** territories.

They endured his **clumsily arrogant** bragging.

Modifiers that are hyphenated when they are placed *before* the word they modify are usually not hyphenated when they are placed *after* the word they modify.

He was a **crisis-and-confrontation** politician.

His politics were a mix of **crisis and confrontation.**

It was a **bad-mannered** reply.

The reply was **bad mannered.**

Attaching Prefixes

Hyphens are used to attach prefixes to some words. Often, for example, a hyphen joins a prefix and a capitalized word.

anti-Semitic, un-American, pre-Columbian

Some prefixes are attached to a few words with hyphens even though the main word is not capitalized.

all-conference, ex-husband, self-interest, vice-president

Most prefixes, however, are not attached by hyphens. The prefix is simply joined to the stem with no punctuation.

antisocial	nonjudgmental	superpower
atypical	postwar	undersea
extracurricular	preliterate	

In some cases hyphens are retained to distinguish meanings or aid pronunciation.

co-op, co-worker, re-cover, re-create

Some proper nouns that are joined to make an adjective are hyphenated.

the Franco-Prussian war, a Mexican-American heritage, the Sino-Japanese agreement

Some numbers are hyphenated.

three-fourths of a gallon, thirty-odd, twenty-five

Often you will encounter variant spellings of the same word. Usually these variants are caused by differences in British and American practice.

plow/pough   theater/theatre
center/centre   humor/humour

In your own writing you should follow American practice. See Chapter 12, Using the Dictionary.

✔ **CHECKLIST 27.1: IMPROVING YOUR SPELLING**

- Make yourself realize the importance of good spelling, and resolve to spell correctly.
- Write down every word you misspell. Keep a spelling log or journal. Practice frequently misspelled words over and over again to help fix the correct spelling in your mind and in your fingers. Good spelling is a habit of both mind and hand.
- Pronounce words carefully. Many people misspell words because they pronounce them incorrectly.
- Learn to distinguish homophones—words pronounced alike but with different meanings and spellings. Study these words each time you encounter them to make sure you've used the right one.
- Learn the rules that generally hold for spelling, and learn the exceptions to those rules. Most rules have only a few exceptions. When

you have learned the exceptions, you will find that the rules themselves tend to stay in your mind.

- Try to group your errors. Misspellings often fall into patterns—errors with suffixes or plurals, for example.
- Proofread your writing carefully. Misspellings creep into the prose of the best of writers when they are in a hurry, when they are thinking ahead to their next thought as they write, or when they do not wish to break their train of thought to look up a troublesome word.
- Use your dictionary frequently when you proofread your work. Whenever you wonder about the correctness of your spelling of a word, look it up. Writing continually and using a dictionary continually are two excellent ways to become a good speller.
- Learn to write with a computer, and use the spell checker on your word-processing program. But always remember that your spell checker cannot tell the difference between the meanings of words. If you write "their" when you should write "there," the spell checker cannot help you. Your best habit is always to have a dictionary nearby when you write.

■ **Exercise 27.6**   Rewrite the following sentences to correct misspellings. Hyphenate words when necessary.

1. He beleived that the badly damaged plane could land safly.
2. The love them today leave them tomorrow philosophy is probly on the decline becaus people now unnerstan it's hypocricy.
3. His nervous laff was a hinderence to his carreer.
4. She remained an optomist though her experence told her that optomists often have trouble accomodating themselves to a pityless city.
5. He had a tendancy to miss classes as a sophmore, and his teachers were ill mannered enough to take attendence.

■ **Exercise 27.7**   Add hyphens only where they are needed in the following words and phrases. Defend your choices.

1. an off color remark
2. narrow minded
3. preChristian
4. self motivated
5. her daughter in law
6. a fast sailing ship
7. blue green algae
8. a well meaning act
9. faintly heard whisper
10. king of Austria Hungary

CHAPTER 28

CAPITALIZING CORRECTLY

Capital letters give readers signals about sentence patterns, names, titles, and pronouns. Many rules for use of capitals have been fixed by custom, but the rules change all the time. A standard dictionary is a good guide to capitalization. In most college dictionaries names that should always be capitalized are entered with capitals; all others are entered in lowercase (or small) letters. (Remember that capitalizing a word means that only the first letter in the word is capitalized; all other letters in the word appear in lowercase.)

28a
Capitalizing the First Word of a Sentence

The capital letter at the beginning of a sentence signals the reader that a new unit of thought is about to begin. Together with the punctuation mark at the end of the previous sentence, it makes reading easier.

Because robots greatly reduce human error, the products they manufacture are of a much more uniform quality. But because they reduce human employment, robots risk eliminating part of the market for which their products are destined.

In sentence fragments used for special effects, capitalize the first word.

But aside from good hair grooming, they are oblivious to everything but each other. Everybody gives them a once-over. Disgusting! Amusing! How touching!

—Tom Wolfe

Why did she lie under oath on the witness stand to defend her husband? Because she knew he was innocent? No, because she knew he was guilty.

Some writers who ask a series of questions by using fragments do not capitalize the first word of each fragment.

How many individuals can we count in society? how many actions? how many opinions?

—RALPH WALDO EMERSON

The more common practice is to capitalize the first word in each fragment that answers a question.

And what are the fundamentals? Reading? Writing? Of course not!

—SLOAN WILSON

Most writers do not capitalize the first word of an independent clause immediately following a colon.

If a person suffer much from sea-sickness, let him weigh it heavily in the balance. I speak from experience: it is no trifling evil, cured in a week.

—CHARLES DARWIN

But some writers do capitalize the first word after a colon.

The answer is another question: How many days must go by before millions of people notice they are not eating?

—*The New York Times*

The first word in an independent clause following a semicolon is never capitalized unless it is a proper noun (see 28c).

All in all, however, outside support counted for little; the men of the village did the work themselves.

—OSCAR HANDLIN

28b
Capitalizing Proper Nouns and Their Abbreviations

Proper nouns are the names of specific people, places, or things, names that set off the individual from the species. Proper nouns include names like *Jane* (instead of the common noun *person*), *France* (instead of the common noun *country*), and *Empire State Building* (instead of the common noun *building*).

The table shows examples of proper nouns.

TYPES AND EXAMPLES OF PROPER NOUNS

Names and nicknames of people

Wolfgang Amadeus Mozart, Ernest Hemingway, Cecil Fielder, Ella Fitzgerald, John F. Kennedy, Sandra Day O'Connor, Ulysses S. Grant, Gore Vidal, Joan Didion, the North Carolina Tarheels

Names of places

France, the United States of America, Tennessee, the Panama Canal, Back Bay, the Mississippi Delta, the North Shore, the Irunia Restaurant, the Sierra Nevada, the Great Lakes

Official names of organizations, organized events, courses

Phi Beta Kappa, the U.S. Department of Defense, the Authors' Guild of America, the University of Notre Dame, Cumberland College, Ford Motor Company, the Roman Catholic Church, the American Red Cross, the Boy Scouts of America, the NCAA, the NAACP, Renaissance Weekend, Rosebowl, Triple Crown, History 351: Old South and Civil War

Days of the week, months, special days

Monday, July, Veterans Day, Christmas, Labor Day, Halloween, Yom Kippur, Earth Day, Pearl Harbor Day, Fourth of July

Ethnic groups, nationalities, and their languages

Greeks, Chinese, Americans, Arabs, Turks; Greek, Chinese, English, Arabic, Turkish

Members of religious bodies and their sacred books and names

Jews, Christians, Baptists, Holy Bible, God, Allah, Hindus, Jesus Christ, Holy Spirit, the Koran, the Torah, Pentecostals, Christian Scientists

Historical events, names of movements, and titles of works
World War II, the Louisiana Purchase, Impressionism, the Bill of Rights, *Moby Dick,* "To Autumn"

Place names of regions are generally capitalized if they are well established, like *the Midwest* and *Central Europe,* but do not capitalize directions, as in *turn south.*

While holidays and names of months and days of the week are capitalized, seasons, such as *summer,* are not.

The words *blacks* and *whites* generally are not capitalized when they are used to refer to ethnic groups, but many writers follow individual choice in this matter. The older and now less favored word *Negro* is capitalized.

Many religious terms such as *sacrament, altar, priests, rabbi, preacher,* and *holy water* are not capitalized. The word *Bible* is capitalized (though *biblical* is not), but it is never capitalized when it is used as a metaphor for an essential book, as in this sentence: "His book *Winning at Stud Poker* was for many years the *bible* of gamblers."

Pronoun references to a deity worshiped by people in the present are sometimes capitalized, although some writers use capitals only to prevent confusion.

> Allah, so Muslims believe, sent Mohammed to deliver **His** word to the world.

> God helped Abraham carry out **His** law.

In each of the sentences above, the capitalization of the pronoun *His* helps avoid confusion. If the pronoun were not capitalized, readers might not be able to tell if it referred to Allah or Mohammed in the first sentence, or if the law mentioned in the second sentence was God's or Abraham's.

> God acts for his own purposes and according to his own wisdom.

In this sentence the pronoun *his* is not capitalized, since no confusion would result. You may choose to capitalize the pronoun if you wish.

Pronoun references to deities no longer worshiped are not capitalized.

> Jupiter, the Roman god of thunder and lightning, led a tempestuous love life that often got **him** into deep trouble with **his** wife, Juno.

Sometimes words not ordinarily capitalized take capitals when they are used as parts of proper names.

My **aunt** is arriving this afternoon.
My **Aunt Lou** tells fantastic stories that I think she makes up.

I have to go to the **bank** before we leave.
The **Cambridge Bank** is on the corner.

I graduated from **high school** in 1989.
I went to **Lenoir City High School.**

Such appellations as *Mother, Father, Cousin, Brother,* and *Sister* may replace proper names in speech and writing. If you intend to refer to a specific individual, capitalize the word.

I still miss **Mother,** although she has been dead for over a decade.

He supposed that **Grandfather** would come to his aid again, as he had so many times in the past.

But most of the time even these words are not capitalized, since they do not replace a proper name. Whether you capitalize such words depends on your intention.

I asked my **mother** to wake me at 5:00 a.m.

Some titles that may be capitalized before a proper name are often not capitalized when they are used after the name.

Everyone knew that **Governor** Grover Cleveland of New York was the most likely candidate for the Democratic nomination.

The most likely candidate for the Democratic nomination was Grover Cleveland, **governor** of New York.

Writers and editors do not agree on the capitalization of titles. *President of the United States,* or the *President* (meaning the chief executive of the United States), is frequently but not always capitalized. Practice varies with other titles also. Some writers say, "I will speak to the *Governor* about your wish to give him a new Cadillac for his personal use." Others say, "The *governor* of this state received a Cadillac last week from an old political friend and business associate." Most writers say, "The *president* of this university has seventeen honorary degrees." Others will say, "The *President* of this university would rather have a winning football team than seventeen honorary degrees." An internal memorandum circulated among university faculty would probably capitalize references to the president.

In general, editors and writers are tending to capitalize less, but it is still important to be consistent. If you write "the **P**resident of the Univer-sity," you should also write "the **C**hair of the **H**istory **D**epartment." If you write "The **p**resident of the **u**niversity," you should also write "the **c**hair of the **h**istory **d**epartment." And, of course, if you say "the **P**resident of the **U**niversity" in one place, you must capitalize in the same way whenever you write "the **P**resident of the **U**niversity."

Words derived from proper nouns generally keep the capitals of the original words.

> Miltonic, Reaganomics, Hodgkin's disease, Hollywoodiana, Siamese cat

When proper names describe or identify common nouns, the nouns that follow are generally not capitalized.

> Sanka brand, Russian history, French fries, Pennsylvania-Dutch shoo-fly pie, English literature

Brand names and trademarks are capitalized (Apple computer, Mac II, Big Mac), but some former proper nouns and brand names have be-come common nouns and no longer require capitalization.

> diesel, levis, pasteurization

Use capitals for abbreviations made from capitalized words or for words formed from the initial letters of words in a proper name. These words, called **acronyms,** are discussed in 29b. Acronyms of three or more letters do not generally use periods between the letters.

> WAC, FBI, NOW, UNESCO, ANZAC, NCAA, SWAT

Abbreviations used as parts of proper names usually take capitals.

> T. S. Eliot; Sammy Davis, Jr.; Maria Lopez, M.D.

28c
Capitalizing Titles of Literary and Art Works

Capitalize the major words of the title of any piece of writing, the title of a work of art or architecture, or the name of a ship. Do not capitalize the articles (*a, an,* and *the*) or prepositions and conjunctions of fewer than five letters unless they begin the title. Capitalize the first word after a colon or semicolon in a title.

Book: *Two Years Before the Mast*

Play: *The Taming of the Shrew*

Architecture: the *Eiffel Tower*

Ship: the *Titanic*

Painting: *Mona Lisa*

Magazine article: "Beating the Market: How to Get Rich on Stocks"

Magazine or journal: *Time*

Essay: "On Old Age"

Poem: "Ode on a Grecian Urn"

Music: "The Star-Spangled Banner"

Note that the preposition *Before* in the first title is capitalized. The general rule is that a preposition or conjunction of five letters or more is capitalized.

✔ CHECKLIST 28.1: USING CAPITALS APPROPRIATELY

As you revise your drafts, check to make sure you are using capital letters appropriately. Look for these instances.

- Sentence conventions
  after periods
  the pronoun *I*
  at the beginning of dialogue and quotations
  sometimes after colons
- Names of people
- Place names and names of areas and regions
- Historical events and movements
- Titles of works of literature, art, music, and architecture
- Names of institutions, groups, and organizations
- Titles of classes
- Names of religions, races, nationalities, and sacred things
- Days, months, holidays
- Names derived from proper nouns

28d
Capitalizing Dialogue and Quotations

When you include spoken dialogue in quotation marks, capitalize the first word.

> "You're going to kill us both!" she shouted.
>
> "Calm down," he shouted back. "I spent just thirty minutes learning to drive this motorcycle, and we're already doing a hundred miles an hour."
>
> She cried, "Help!"

Indirect quotations and questions require no capitals for words attributed to a speaker or writer.

> She said that jazz was one of the many contributions of blacks to world culture.
>
> He asked me which I liked better, bluegrass music without drums and electrically amplified instruments, or the more modern country music that is akin to soft rock.

The first word of quotations from printed sources is capitalized if the quotation is introduced as dialogue.

> Jim, the narrator of *My Antonia,* concludes: "Whatever we had missed, we possessed together the precious, the incommunicable past."

But when a quotation from a printed source is only an element in your sentence, not a sentence on its own, the first word is not capitalized.

> Jim took comfort in sharing with Antonia "the precious, the incommunicable past."

Many authors in earlier centuries and some writers today—especially poets—have used capitals in eccentric ways. If you are quoting a text directly, reproduce the capitalization used in the source, whether or not it is correct by today's standards.

> Sun and moon run together in one of Pyramus's speeches, "Sweet Moon, I thank thee for thy sunny Beams."
>
> —ELIZABETH SEWELL

28e
cap

Capitalizing Consistently and Carefully

Use capitals consistently when you have a reason for doing so, but avoid them when they are not necessary. When capital letters are optional, select one system and stick to it. Consistency is important.

Some inexperienced writers are tempted to use capitals for emphasis, and they capitalize too much. Unnecessary capitals may confuse readers or irritate them. In modern prose, the tendency is to use lowercase whenever possible.

■ **Exercise 28.1**   Follow the directions in each item below, and write full-sentence responses. Observe the conventions of proper capitalization.

1. Name the professor in your school whose lectures you find most interesting.
2. Name the city and state (or city and country) where you were born.
3. Name a supermarket at which you or your family members buy groceries.
4. What is your favorite season of the year?
5. In what direction must you walk or ride to get to campus?
6. In what region of the country did you grow up?
7. What two academic subjects do you enjoy most?
8. Name a book you enjoyed reading recently.
9. What is your favorite TV show?
10. Name your favorite holiday.
11. What is your favorite flower?
12. What was the name of your high school? (Use the words *high school* immediately after the name of the institution.)

■ **Exercise 28.2**   Fill in the correct capital or lowercase letters in the blanks below. Explain your choices.

1. __hen __overnor Blankenship stood on the steps of the state __apitol __uilding and said to the __resident of the __nited __tates, "__he states in the __outh need more of the __overnment's support," my neighbors on Main __treet applauded wildly.
2. __t the __an __iego __oo last summer, I disliked the __onkeys and the __pes because they looked so much like little men and women in a cage, but I was fascinated by the __eptile __ouse, where I saw the __frican __ock __ython as well as the __ndian __obras and the __oa __onstrictor.

3. __f you take __ociology 320, a __ourse in the __ociology of __eligion, you will learn to understand some of the strengths of __rotestantism, __udaism, and __oman __atholicism.

■ **Exercise 28.3**   Rewrite the following sentences, using capital and lowercase letters correctly.

1. during Summer i like to visit the Ski Resorts in vermont, where few visitors disturb my meditations among the Fir Trees and the Maples that dot the Landscape.

2. when I was a child, thanksgiving day was one of my favorite holidays, not only because my aunts and uncles always came over for a huge dinner but also because my mother and father took the friday after thanksgiving off and the whole family went shopping at lakeland mall.

3. in your sophomore course in english literature next fall, you may read at least one novel by daniel defoe, whose book *robinson crusoe* is sometimes called the first novel in the english language.

4. when we had our accident, we were taken to memorial hospital on greeley parkway, where a man in a white coat named thomas babington examined us and told us there was nothing wrong with us.

5. later, when i discovered that i had a fractured skull and that my brother had a broken leg, we sued the hospital, but the hospital claimed that mr. babington was only visiting the emergency room that day and was not an employee of memorial hospital at all. he was a chef in a local restaurant.

USING NUMBERS AND ABBREVIATIONS

Variations in the styles of authors, the demands of editors, and the requirements of various kinds of writing make it difficult to fix rules for using numbers and abbreviations. In some newspapers and some magazines, the use of figures to express numbers may be common. In books, figures and abbreviations are less common, at least in the body of a text. In footnotes, bibliographies, scientific or technical reports, letters, charts, tables, and graphs, figures and abbreviations must be used no matter what the publication.

You should use figures sparingly for numbers in standard essays, and you should use abbreviations for words only when convention allows. Spell out most abbreviations when you use them the first time in an essay.

29a
Spelling Out Numbers

Spell out numbers up to one hundred and round numbers over one hundred. But when there are a great many numbers and spelled-out numbers would take a great deal of space, use figures, even in the body of an essay.

> six cartons   BUT   181 cartons
>
> twenty-four dollars   BUT $23.88
>
> forty thousand children   BUT   39,658 children
>
> three million chickens   BUT   4,623 chickens

Try to avoid starting a sentence with a number, but if you must, spell the number out.

29b
Using Figures

Use figures for statistical comparisons, for quantitative information, and for dates, times of day, and addresses.

In writing about some subjects, especially technical subjects, numbers are so frequent that you should write them as figures.

> The original plan for the house called for a dining room that would be 18 × 25 feet and a living room that would be 30 × 34 feet with plate-glass windows at each end.

Note that in this example the word *by* in the measurements is also abbreviated as ×.

In nontechnical writing, figures are used to express percentages, but spell out *percent*.

> Nearly 60 percent of those who went to the polls voted to reject the referendum.

Dates that include the year usually appear as figures, but some writers prefer to spell them out.

October 9, 1893	the ninth of October 1893
9 October 1893	October ninth (NOT October 9th)
the 1960s	the nineteen-sixties
1929–1930	from 1929 to 1930

The time of day followed by the abbreviation A.M. or P.M. is always expressed in figures. If you use the less technical forms *in the morning* or *in the evening*, spell out the numbers.

> 6:00 A.M., 6 A.M., 8:15 P.M.
> six o'clock in the morning
> a quarter past eight in the evening

Street and highway numbers almost always appear as figures. When a house number and the number of a street come together in an address, then one of the numbers is written out.

1 Park Avenue	850 Fifteenth Street
Apartment 6J	State Highway 2
Interstate 80	

✔ **CHECKLIST 29.1: HANDLING NUMBERS**

Your use of spelled-out numbers or figures should be consistent and make the text flow. Ask yourself these questions.

- Are numbers spelled out up to 100?
- Are round or approximate numbers spelled out?
- Do sentences begin with numbers or years?
- Are figures used appropriately in dates, years, times, and addresses?
- If a discussion involves many numbers, statistical comparisons, or quantitative information, are figures used?

29c
Spelling Out Words

In formal essay writing, spell out most words rather than abbreviate them.

Spell out unfamiliar abbreviations

Abbreviations may cut down readability, since a general audience may be unfamiliar with them or may not recognize them at all. But in some technical writing such as memos or reports intended for a limited audience, you may use abbreviations that are standard to that audience.

Not: Dr. Ruth and SOL Dean Th. Luciano discussed the std. rules about hab. corp. proceedings in the pol. cts. as they might apply to studs. arrested on DWI charges in the commercial dist. alg. Mass. Ave.

But: Dr. Ruth Smith and School of Law Dean Thomas Luciano discussed the standard rules about habeas corpus proceedings in the police courts as they might apply to students arrested on charges of driving while intoxicated in the commercial district along Massachusetts Avenue.

Spell out the names of countries, cities, boroughs, and states and the words *Avenue, Boulevard, Highway, Street, River,* and *Mountains* and words like them used as parts of proper names when they appear in the body of your prose.

The Catskill Mountains of New York flank the Hudson River to the west.

Veterans Highway crosses Deer Park Avenue.

Cherokee Boulevard in Knoxville, Tennessee, runs by the Tennessee River.

See Chapter 38 for how to treat street and state abbreviations in addresses.

Spell out the names of months and days of the week, and spell out people's names.

In September and October, Charles visits the botanical gardens every Sunday.

Avoid the ampersand

Use an ampersand only if it is part of an official name.

Loneliness and poverty often accompany old age.

The stock index published by Standard & Poors is one of the most important economic documents in America.

The pistol was a Smith & Wesson.

Spell out parts of publications, company names

Spell out the words *pages, chapter, volume,* and *edition* and the names of courses of study, and words such as *company, brothers,* and *incorporated* unless they are abbreviated in official titles.

Chapter 16 presents new developments in open-heart surgery.

The eleventh edition of the Encyclopedia Britannica has thousands of pages without one typographical error.

Freshman Composition 102 is a prerequisite for Communications 201.

You may use abbreviations for *page, chapter,* and *edition* in footnotes, endnotes, and bibliographical references (see Chapter 33).

Use the abbreviation *Inc., Corp., Co.,* or *Bros.* only when it is part of the official title of a company.

His brothers formed a toy company called Kidstuff, Inc., and later changed the name to Goldstein Bros.

Avoid the use of *etc.*

It is almost always better to name the items you intend to blanket under the abbreviation *etc.* than to use the abbreviation as a catchall. If you don't want to make a long list, use *and so on, and so forth, for example,* or *such as.*

This garden is good for planting lettuce, broccoli, spinach, radishes, onions, and other cool-weather vegetables.
or
This garden is good for planting cool-weather vegetables—broccoli and spinach, for example.
or
This garden is good for planting vegetables such as lettuce and broccoli.

When you do use *etc.,* do not put the conjunction *and* before it. The abbreviation *etc.* stands for the Latin *et cetera* or *et caetera,* which means ''and the rest,'' so the *and* is included in the abbreviation itself.

29d
Abbreviating Familiar Titles

The general guideline about avoiding abbreviations does not apply to commonly abbreviated titles that always precede the person's name. These include *Mr., Mrs., Ms., Dr., St., the Rev., the Hon., Sen., Rep.,* and *Fr.*

Fr. Louis joined our monastery twenty years ago.

Mrs. Jean Bascom designed the brick walkway in front of our building.

Dr. Epstein and Dr. Kwang consulted on the operation.

The Rev. Dr. Karl Barth visited Gettysburg, Pennsylvania, shortly before he died.

Mr. Roger Jackson will marry Ms. Joan Wilkerson.

Many women prefer the title *Ms.* instead of *Miss* or *Mrs.* (see Chapter 11). Strictly speaking, *Ms.* is not an abbreviation, since it does not stand for a word. But it is used in the same way *Mr.* and *Mrs.* are used—before a name. The title *Miss* is not an abbreviation, so it is not followed by a period. It always precedes the name.

Some abbreviations are always used after a proper name. Usually they indicate academic or professional degrees or honors. Note that a comma is placed between the name and the abbreviation and that a space follows the comma.

Robert Robinson, Jr.   Elaine Leff, C.P.A., LL.D.
Kai-y Hsu, Ph.D.   Michael Bartlett, Esq.
Maria Tiante, M.D.

But spell out titles used without proper names.

> Mr. Carew asked if she had seen the doctor.

Notice that when an abbreviation ends a sentence, the period at the end of the abbreviation itself will serve as the period of the sentence. If a question mark or an exclamation point ends the sentence, you must place such a punctuation mark *after* the period in the abbreviation.

> When he was in the seventh grade, we called him "Stinky," but now he is William Percival Abernathy, Ph.D.!
>
> Is it true that he now wants to be called Stanley Martin, Esq.?

29e
Using Acronyms

If you use the name of an agency or an organization frequently in an essay or a report, you may abbreviate it to make the repetition less tedious. Write out the name of the agency or the organization the first time you use it, and give the abbreviation in parentheses.

> The Student Nonviolent Coordinating Committee (SNCC) was far to the left of other civil rights organizations, and its leaders often mocked the "conservatism" of Dr. Martin Luther King, Jr. SNCC quickly burned itself out and disappeared, but some scholars now give the organization much credit for some of the progress made in civil rights during those hard years.

Abbreviations of agency names that can be used as nouns or adjectives are called **acronyms.** Some, such as SNCC, are pronounced as words ("snick"). Acronyms of three or more letters generally do not use periods, but if you elect to use them, do so consistently.

> CIA, EPA, JFK, NAACP, NASA

Many government agencies are regularly referred to by their acronyms or abbreviations, especially in publications that mention them frequently. Often these abbreviations are so well known that they do not require any explanation.

> The FBI entered the case immediately, since under the Lindbergh Act kidnapping is a federal crime.

29f
Using Other Common Abbreviations

Abbreviate words typically used with times, dates, and figures.

6 P.M. OR 6:00 P.M.	A.D. 1066	
9:45 AM OR 9:45 A.M.	6000 rpm	
498 B.C.		

Note that instead of B.C., many writers now use B.C.E., "Before the Common Era." If a year stands alone, without B.C. or B.C.E., it is assumed to be A.D.

29g
Avoiding Latin Abbreviations

In text, use English translations rather than Latin abbreviations.

compare	cf.
for example	e.g.
and others	et al.
and so on, and so forth, and the rest	etc.
in the same place	ibid.
that is	i.e.

Although new documentation systems for research papers use a minimum of abbreviations, you may come across the Latin abbreviations in your own reading and research. A list of the most familiar abbreviations appears in 33h.

■ **Exercise 29.1**   Rewrite the following sentences, using numbers and abbreviations appropriately.

1. Dr. Muscatel's house was on 2d. Ave. near the warehouse of the Ledbetter bros.
2. The dr. got up early every a.m. and stayed in her office in the p.m. until the last patient had left.
3. You could call him in the middle of the night, & the rev. would come to your house in 20 minutes.
4. When you saw him on the st., he always seemed deep in thought.
5. 1936 was the year he moved here, & FDR was Pres. of the USA.

CHAPTER 30

USING ITALICS

Some words and phrases need to be set off as distinctive. The titles of novels you refer to in an essay for an American literature class, for example, need to look different from regular text.

Confusing: Hawthorne's Scarlet Letter set him apart from the New England writers of his day.

The reader who did not know that *The Scarlet Letter* is the title of a novel might think that Hawthorne wrote with red ink or had a correspondent named Scarlet!

To set off certain words and phrases, printers use *italics,* a typeface in which the characters slant to the right. Since most typewriters and many computer printers lack an italic face, and since it is impossible to make italics in handwriting, writers preparing manuscripts underline the words a printer would set in italics. An underline is, in fact, a typesetter's mark indicating that a word or words is to be set in italics.

Handwritten

Katharine Hepburn gives one of her best performances in The African Queen.

Typed

```
Katharine Hepburn gives one of her best performances in The
African Queen.
```

Printed

Katharine Hepburn gives one of her best performances in *The African Queen.*

30a
Treating Titles of Works of Art

Underline titles of books, magazines, journals, newspapers, plays, films, artworks, long poems, pamphlets and other short works published separately, and musical works.

> Joan Didion, a former editor of *Vogue* and the *National Review,* received glowing reviews in the *New York Times* for her novel *A Book of Common Prayer.*

> Picasso's *Guernica* captures the anguish and despair of violence.

> Plays by Shakespeare provide details and story lines for Verdi's opera *Falstaff,* the musical comedy *Kiss Me, Kate* by Cole Porter, and Franco Zeffirelli's film *Romeo and Juliet.*

In book titles, *a, an,* or *the* as a first word is capitalized and underlined, but *the* is not generally treated as part of the title in names of newspapers and periodicals.

Quotation marks distinguish the titles of short works—essays, newspaper and magazine articles and columns, short stories, television and radio programs, short poems, songs, chapters or other book subdivisions. Quotation marks are also used for titles of unpublished works, including student papers, theses, and dissertations (see p. 340).

> Elizabeth Cullinan's ''Only Human'' appears in a collection of her stories called *Yellow Roses.*

The Bible and other sacred books such as the Koran are exceptions.

> The Book of Ecclesiastes provides some of the most haunting phrases in the Bible.

Do not underline the title of your paper on the title page or place it in quotation marks. These conventions are used to refer to titles in writings about them, not in the writings themselves.

30b
Italicizing Foreign Terms

Underline most foreign words and phrases to indicate italics.

They are wise to remember, however, one thing. He is Sinatra. The boss. *Il Padrone.*

—GAY TALESE

Chota hasari—the little breakfast—consists of a cup of tea at five-thirty or six in the morning, with possibly some fruit or toast served with it. At eleven or at midday a heavier meal is eaten, *chapatis*—thin unleavened wheat cakes—and curry, with *dal*—a kind of lentil soup—and curds and sweets of some sort.

—SANTHA RAMA RAU

Memphis, in fact, was definitely the mecca, yardstick and *summum bonum.*

—TERRY SOUTHERN

Many foreign words have become so common in English that everyone accepts them as part of the language, and they require no underlining or italics. Some examples are rigor mortis (Latin), pasta (Italian), sombrero (Spanish), bête noire (French), and festschrift (German). Notice that in the quotation from Terry Southern above, the proper noun Mecca is used as a common noun meaning any place where large numbers of people go to have some uplifting experience (see 28c).

Some foreign words are still borderline, and some writers underline them while others do not. Examples are *ex nihilo* (Latin for "from nothing"), *imprimatur* (Latin for "Let it be printed"), and *Weltanschauung* (German for "world view"). Often the preference of the writer or the need for a special effect dictates the decision to underline or not.

Dictionaries offer some help. By labeling as *French* a phrase like *mise-en-scène,* for example, a dictionary guides your decision to underline. Some dictionaries have special sections headed "Foreign Words." Others italicize foreign words when they appear. But writers must use their own judgment about the borderline words. Here it is good to consider your audience and to try to imagine the expectations that readers may bring to your work. Within an essay, be consistent in italicizing foreign words and phrases that appear more than once.

30c
Italicizing Words Used as Words

Underline (to indicate italics) words or phrases you use as words rather than for the meaning they convey.

The use of the word *glide* at the end of the last stanza is effective and gives just the amount of emphasis required at the end of the poem.

—CLEANTH BROOKS AND ROBERT PENN WARREN

And if the word *integration* means anything, this is what it means: that we, with love, shall force our brothers to see themselves as they are, to cease fleeing from reality and begin changing it.

—JAMES BALDWIN

Letters used alone also require underlining to show italics.

The word *bookkeeper* has three sets of double letters: double *o,* double *k,* and double *e.*

Some writers use quotation marks to show that words are being used as words.

When I was in graduate school in the late fifties, ''criticism'' was still a fighting word.

—GERALD GRAFF

30d
Using Italics for Emphasis

Sometimes writers are tempted to italicize words to show the kind of emphasis they'd make in speaking. Use italics for this purpose only occasionally. Too many italicized words will tire readers; their eyes may leap over the underlined or italicized words—the very opposite effect from what you intended. Too much emphasis may mean no emphasis at all.

Weak: You don't *mean* that your *teacher* told the whole *class* that *he* did not know the answer *himself?*

Revised: Your teacher admitted that he did not know the answer? That is amazing.

An occasional word in italics helps you emphasize a point.

That advertisers exploit women's subordination rather than cause it can be clearly seen now that *male* fashions and toiletries have become big business.

—ELLEN WILLIS

It now seems clear that we are not going to improve instruction by finding *the* method or methods that are good for all peoples.

—K. PATRICIA CROSS

In written dialogue, writers may use italics to emphasize words to show the rhythms of speech used by characters.

The lady, however, regarded it very placidly. "I shouldn't have gone if she *had* asked me."

—HENRY JAMES

As they turned to him, Blackburn said: "Can *you* give *me* a few minutes, Dr. Howe?" His eyes sparkled at the little audacity he had committed, the slightly impudent play with hierarchy.

—LIONEL TRILLING

30e
Other Uses of Italics

By convention, the names of ships appear in italics, as do the names of air and space vehicles. The names of trains do not.

I packed my valise, and took passage on an ancient tub called the *Paul Jones* for New Orleans.

—MARK TWAIN

Many style manuals also recommend the use of italics for court cases.

In *Brown* v. *Board of Education of Topeka* (1954), the U.S. Supreme Court ruled that segregation in public schools was unconstitutional.

■ **Exercise 30.1**   Underline any words or phrases that require italics in the following sentences.

1. An advertisement in the San Diego Evening Tribune announced a cruise on the Queen Elizabeth II, but after I read Katherine Anne Porter's novel Ship of Fools, a vacation on the sea per se did not interest me.
2. Time reported that Da Vinci's painting The Last Supper had deteriorated seriously from pollution and neglect.
3. The word hopefully is common nowadays, but many people who take writing seriously object to it because they think the words I

hope or we hope or it is hoped usually express the meaning more clearly.

4. By the time the police discovered the body, rigor mortis had set in, and Inspector Michaelson told reporters from the Times and the Globe that death had taken place circa twelve hours before.

5. Russell Baker's column Observer appears in the New York Times several days a week.

■ **Exercise 30.2** Rewrite the following sentences to eliminate excessive emphasis. You may change the wording. You may also change the order of the sentences.

1. Mr. Watt promised that this was *absolutely* the last time that he or *any other* member of his department would even *mention* digging a coal mine in Yellowstone National Park.

2. Who could *possibly* have known that the landing gear *was* defective and that the pilot was *drunk?*

3. The crew of the space shuttle *firmly* believed that the *engineering problems* of the flight were less serious than the *psychological problems* of living so close together under such a demanding routine.

4. *Anyone* desiring to change sections *must* file a form with the registrar *before* Friday afternoon.

5. Do you *really* like *country* music?

✔ **CHECKLIST 30.1: SETTING OFF WORDS AND PHRASES**

As you revise, look for words and phrases that should be distinguished by italics (underlines) or quotation marks. Be sure they are correctly set off from the rest of your text. Pay attention to the following types of words and phrases.

Titles of published works

■ Are the titles of works published separately (including books, magazines, journals, newspapers, plays, films, art works, long poems, pamphlets, and musical works) set off in italics?

■ Are the titles of short works, including essays, newspaper and magazine articles and columns, short poems, television programs, songs, chapters and other book subdivisions, set off in quotation marks?

■ Are titles of unpublished works set off in quotation marks?

Foreign terms

■ Are unusual foreign terms set off in italics?

■ Are italics used consistently for these terms?

Words as words

■ Are words and letters discussed as such italicized to clarify your meaning?

Emphasis

■ Is italic used for emphasis only when absolutely necessary?

PART SEVEN
WRITING A RESEARCH PAPER

PART EIGHT
OTHER WRITING TASKS

SPECIAL
WRITING
TASKS

PART
SEVEN

WRITING
A RESEARCH
PAPER

CHAPTER
31

STARTING
A RESEARCH
PROJECT

Research projects rely on careful investigation of varied sources in the library and elsewhere. These sources include not just the obvious books, periodicals, and reference items but also films, plays, concerts, television programs, videotapes, audiotapes, records, computer programs, microfilms, and microfiches. Anything that can provide accurate information efficiently is a tool in the researcher's hands. Thus, research might include interviews; a reporter digging into corruption among city officials, for example, needs firsthand contact with municipal leaders and their aides. Often research begins with telephone calls and casual conversations with your friends, instructors, or other experts who can help set you on the path to information quickly.

The chapters in this part of the handbook use two student papers as models, tracing their development from selecting a topic, through researching and writing, to preparing the final copy. The final copies of both papers are presented in Chapter 34. One paper is an analysis of short stories by Willa Cather. This paper draws on the documentation methods established by the Modern Language Association of America (MLA) and recommended for research in literature and the humanities. Because the conventions of writing about research vary from discipline to discipline, we also include a paper on a scientific topic, the phenomenon of black holes. This paper draws on the documentation methods established by the American Psychological Association (APA) and recommended for research in the social sciences. The more you know about the conventions of the various disciplines, the easier it will be for you to investigate sources and to present your findings for different courses of study.

Thinking through a research paper is much like thinking through any other written composition, even though research papers differ in content and format from other kinds of papers. The planning guidelines set forth in these chapters should help you produce a successful paper.

Choose a subject that interests you, and develop a limited topic by doing prewriting exercises and using the library. Discuss the topic with friends or your instructor.

Start with a general subject that fits both your own interests and your assignment. Think about various topics within that general area; then discuss them with people you know. Try brainstorming, jotting down ideas in an informal list, asking yourself questions about your subject, writing nonstop, or developing a subject tree (illustrated in 1a).

Prewriting exercises will help you explore what you already know about the subject and identify areas you would like to know more about. See, for example, how developing an informal list helped the writer of the paper on Cather to narrow diffuse ideas to a topic of more manageable proportions.

Informal list

Willa Cather

novel <u>My Antonia</u> my favorite in high school English

realistic picture of life on the frontier

hard existence for women

good descriptive detail

simple writing style, deep feelings though

hard to leave behind your family and move West

read one of Cather's short stories, "Sculptor's Funeral"

good short story writer: picture of the hard life for the
    artist on the western plains

maybe read some other stories by Cather?

women as central characters? difference of effects of hard
    life on men and women?

making a new life in a new territory you're not prepared for

dangers of famine, weather, Indians

Where and how was Cather educated?

What was her life like as a writer?

What did other writers think of her work? book reviews?

Cather's view of her art? What was she trying to achieve in her stories and novels?

31a

topic

Once you have a preliminary idea for your paper, browse through the library. Check the library catalog, general reference books, and periodical indexes to see what others have written on your topic. Preliminary reading in books and magazines helps you decide on the suitability of your topic and limits and sharpens its focus. This early exploring of books and magazines will also help you develop your topic and organize your later research.

How narrow a topic must you choose? The answer to that question depends on your interests, the nature of the assignment, the required length of the paper, the number and quality of available library materials, and the time you have to do your assignment. But try to narrow your topic as much as possible, because narrow topics allow you to use enough specific examples and details to keep readers interested. In the following examples, note how students narrowed their topics until they reached promising starting points for their papers.

Literature	Astronomy
Short stories	Current questions about the universe
↓	↓
Willa Cather's short stories	Black holes
↓	↓
The theme of isolation in Cather's short stories	How black holes might be located in space
↓	↓
The theme of isolation in two stories by Cather	Various techniques used in the search for black holes

As you do preliminary research, you may discover that you need to limit your topic further. Carefully limiting your topic will help you exclude many fruitless areas before you investigate them. For instance, if the writer of the paper on Cather's stories had not narrowed her topic from the informal list above, she would have wasted time researching Cather's later novels, Cather's views on naturalism in fiction, or the ups and downs of her reputation among critics.

When you think that you have a workable topic, talk further about it with your instructor or with friends before you begin serious research. At this point, discussions with people whose judgment you trust can help you test your ideas and can lead to reshaping that may save time and work later on.

■ **Exercise 31.1***   Choose one of the general subjects below, and refine it until you identify at least one topic suitable for a research paper. Then repeat the process for two additional general subjects. You may wish to choose one of these narrowed-down topics for your own research paper. (Exercises marked with an asterisk [*] in this chapter and in Chapters 32 through 34—that is, Exercises 31.1, 31.2, 31.3, 31.4, 32.1, 32.2, 32.3, 34.2, 34.5, 34.6—are designed to help you with your research project.)

1. black politicians
2. mental illness
3. Vincent van Gogh
4. drug use in the United States
5. preschool education
6. the new Europe
7. women corporate leaders
8. the history of the theater
9. cowboys
10. political cartoons
11. exercise
12. Carl Sandburg's poetry
13. country music
14. existentialism
15. computers
16. mass transportation
17. rain forests
18. surrogate mothers
19. illegal aliens
20. one-act plays

31b
Learning About Libraries

Learn about the various libraries available to you. As you narrow your topic, check the library facilities on your campus and in the surrounding community.

If your college has only one library, that may simplify your life, but it may also limit your resources. Most large universities have several specialized libraries. Your school may have both an undergraduate library and a graduate or a main library; it may have a science library and various other special collections. Many cities have large public libraries, and in cities that have several colleges, students in one school often can use the libraries of all the others.

The concept of the library is changing rapidly because new technologies to preserve information are competing with books and periodicals for shelf space. Many libraries collect phonograph records, films, audio- and videotapes, photographs, and microfilm or microfiche. **Microfilm** is a film on which printed materials are photographed, greatly reduced in size. **Microfiche** is a sheet of microfilm that can accommodate and preserve many pages of printed text in reduced form. Many libraries are now beginning to store information on compact disks that can be retrieved by computer.

31c

sources

Once you have chosen your topic and put an initial limit on it, talk with a reference librarian who can tell you what resources are available for your research. Librarians enjoy helping people, and you can save time if you let them help you. Most librarians know not only the resources available in their own libraries, but also those you can consult elsewhere in the region. Ask for help at the very beginning. And as you write, ask for help whenever you need it.

31c
Locating Sources

Find out what has been written about your subject, and record preliminary sources by using the library catalog, indexes to periodicals, reference books, and other sources.

Using the Library Catalog

A library **catalog** lists all the books owned by your library. Most libraries use card catalogs. Some libraries use bound volumes. Modern automation makes catalogs available on microfilm, microfiche, computer files, compact disks, or a combination of these forms. Learn your library's catalog system as soon as you can; your librarian will help you use it efficiently.

If your library provides a card catalog, these cards are arranged alphabetically in drawers, usually located near the circulation desk. At large schools with several libraries, each library has a card catalog. You may also find a union catalog in the main library listing all the holdings of the school's libraries, including the names of the libraries where the books can be found.

In the card catalog of your library, you will find that every book is listed on at least three cards: an *author card*, a *title card*, and a *subject card*. If it covers several subjects, the same book may be listed on several subject cards. If your library's catalog is computerized, every book will have an entry in the same three areas: an *author entry*, a *title entry*, and a *subject entry*. You can find these entries by following the instructions at user computer terminals.

Library Catalog Entries: Automated System

Author entry

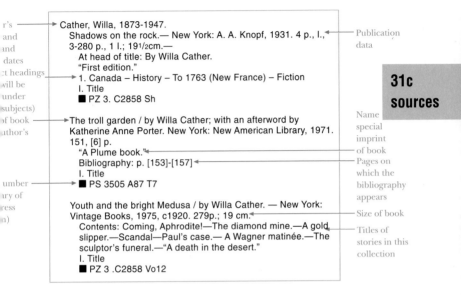

r's
and
and
dates
ct headings
vill be
under
subjects)
of book
uthor's

umber
ary of
ress
n)

Cather, Willa, 1873-1947.
    Shadows on the rock.— New York: A. A. Knopf, 1931. 4 p., l.,
    3-280 p., 1 l.; 19¹/₂cm.—
       At head of title: By Willa Cather.
       "First edition."
     1. Canada – History – To 1763 (New France) – Fiction
    I. Title
    ■ PZ 3. C2858 Sh

The troll garden / by Willa Cather; with an afterword by
Katherine Anne Porter. New York: New American Library, 1971.
151, [6] p.
    "A Plume book."
    Bibliography: p. [153]-[157]
    I. Title
    ■ PS 3505 A87 T7

Youth and the bright Medusa / by Willa Cather. — New York:
Vintage Books, 1975, c1920. 279p.; 19 cm.
    Contents: Coming, Aphrodite!—The diamond mine.—A gold
    slipper.—Scandal—Paul's case.— A Wagner matinée.—The
    sculptor's funeral.—"A death in the desert."
    I. Title
    ■ PZ 3 .C2858 Vo12

Publication
data

**31c
sources**

Name
special
imprint
of book
Pages on
which the
bibliography
appears

Size of book
Titles of
stories in this
collection

Title entry

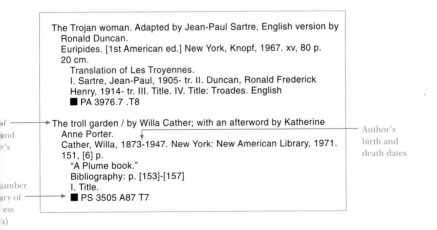

of
and
r's

umber
ary of
ess
n)

The Trojan woman. Adapted by Jean-Paul Sartre, English version by
Ronald Duncan.
    Euripides. [1st American ed.] New York, Knopf, 1967. xv, 80 p.
    20 cm.
      Translation of Les Troyennes.
     I. Sartre, Jean-Paul, 1905- tr. II. Duncan, Ronald Frederick
     Henry, 1914- tr. III. Title. IV. Title: Troades. English
    ■ PA 3976.7 .T8

The troll garden / by Willa Cather; with an afterword by Katherine
    Anne Porter.
    Cather, Willa, 1873-1947. New York: New American Library, 1971.
    151, [6] p.
      "A Plume book."
      Bibliography: p. [153]-[157]
     I. Title.
    ■ PS 3505 A87 T7

Author's
birth and
death dates

Card Catalog Entries

Title entry

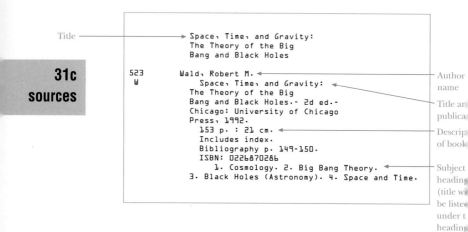

Title ──────→
523
W

**31c
sources**

```
                    Space, Time, and Gravity:
                    The Theory of the Big
                    Bang and Black Holes

        523     Wald, Robert M. ◄──────            Author
        W            Space, Time, and Gravity: ◄   name
                  The Theory of the Big
                  Bang and Black Holes.- 2d ed.-   Title an
                  Chicago: University of Chicago    publica
                  Press, 1992.
                     153 p. : 21 cm. ◄──────        Descrip
                     Includes index.                of book
                     Bibliography p. 149-150.
                     ISBN: 0226870286
                        1. Cosmology. 2. Big Bang Theory. ◄  Subject
                  3. Black Holes (Astronomy). 4. Space and Time.  headin
                                                     (title wi
                                                     be liste
                                                     under t
                                                     heading
```

Libraries use a number system to organize books according to type and topic. To find a book, you need the **call number,** which appears in the catalog entry and on the spine of the book. Many libraries use the

Author entry

```
Call number ──►523      Wald, Robert M.
(Dewey         W            Space, Time, and Gravity:
Decimal                  The Theory of the Big
System)                  Bang and Black Holes.- 2d ed.-
                         Chicago: University of Chicago
                         Press, 1992.
                            153 p. : 21 cm.
                            Includes index.
                            Bibliography p. 149-150. ◄──────   Pages o
                            ISBN: 0226870286                    which
                               1. Cosmology. 2. Big Bang Theory.  bibliogr
                         3. Black Holes (Astronomy). 4. Space and Time.  appears
```

Subject entry

```
┌─────────────────────────────────────────────────────────────┐
│                                                               │
│  ►Black Holes (Astronomy)                                     │
│                                                               │
│   523      Wald, Robert M.  ◄                                 │
│     W          Space, Time, and Gravity:  ◄                   │
│                The Theory of the Big                          │
│                Bang and Black Holes.- 2d ed.-                 │
│                Chicago: University of Chicago                  │
│                Press, 1992.                                   │
│              ►153 p. : 21 cm.                                 │
│                Includes index.                               │
│                Bibliography p. 149-150.  ◄                    │
│                ISBN: 0226870286                              │
│              ►1. Cosmology. 2. Big Bang Theory.               │
│                3. Black Holes (Astronomy). 4. Space and Time. │
│                                                               │
└─────────────────────────────────────────────────────────────┘
```

Author's
name
Title
Publica-
tion
data

Pages on
which
bibliography
appears

31c

sources

Library of Congress classification system. Others use the older Dewey Dec-imal System or a combination of the two. Whatever catalog system a library uses will be displayed on charts near the catalog and the circulation desk.

As soon as you pick a topic, find the subject section of the catalog and list the books related to that topic. This list is the beginning of your preliminary list of sources. Then go to the author section of the catalog to see if authors listed under the subject heading have written other books on your topic.

Even at this early stage, list each promising source on a separate 3 × 5 inch bibliography card. Record full publishing data for all your books and articles. The data you will need include the author's full name, full title and subtitle of the book, its date and city of publication, and the publisher's name. (See the sample card, below.) Copy the names of editors and translators as well as volume numbers, names and numbers of series, and names of special imprints if any of this information appears in the catalog entry. When you actually have the book in hand, check the data on your bibliography card carefully against the information on the title page. Copying down full publishing data at this stage accomplishes two valuable tasks. First, it assures you that your notes are accurately and fully documented. Second, it saves you the trouble of going back to reference materials to copy data for your reference list after you have finished your research (see 33d and 33e).

Always include the call number at the bottom of your card. You must have this number to get the book. If your library's stacks are *open,* you will need the number to locate the general section in which the book is shelved and the book itself. If your library's stacks are *closed,* you will need the number to fill out the request slip for the book. Remember that the call number not only identifies the book but also classifies it by subject area. If you can go into the stacks in your library, check the shelves near the books you have found in the catalog. Scan books that look useful, and, if they are, jot down the titles and call numbers on bibliography cards so that you can go back to them later.

Sample bibliography card, book

> Wald, Robert M.
> *Space, Time, and Gravity: The Theory of the Big Bang and Black Holes.* 2nd ed. Chicago:
> University of Chicago Press, 1992
>
>   523
>   W

Sample bibliography card, periodical

> Saposnik-Noire, Shelley
> "The Silent Protagonist: The Unifying Presence of Landscape in Willa Cather's *My Antonia*"
> *Midwest Quarterly*
> 1990 Winter
> Vol. 31
> pages 171-79

✔ CHECKLIST 31.1: RECORDING PRELIMINARY DATA FOR SOURCES

As you start your research project, make a list of the sources you want to consult. Be sure to include all the information you'll need for your reference list. Recording complete data from the beginning will save you time and headaches later on. For convenience, place each source on a separate bibliography card so that you can arrange your cards by subtopic and alphabetize them. Here is the information you need to record for books and articles.

**31c
sources**

Books

- author's last name and full first name or two initials
- title of book, including subtitle
- edition of book, if any
- translator's or editor's name, if any
- series title and number, if any
- total number of volumes and volume number
- special imprints, if any
- place of publication
- publisher's name
- date (year) of publication

Articles

- author's last name and full first name or two initials
- title of article, including subtitle
- title of periodical
- volume number of periodical
- issue number of periodical, if any
- month or season of periodical, or exact date of publication if a daily or weekly
- inclusive pages on which article appears

Using Indexes to Periodicals

Your library will have a variety of indexes to **periodicals**—journals, magazines, newspapers. General indexes to periodical literature list journal articles. A good index usually lists articles by year of publication, under various subject headings; some indexes list works by authors' names as well. Some indexes also provide abstracts. An **abstract** summarizes the article, usually in a short paragraph, without evaluating it. Because this summary tells you much more than the title, it may save you considerable time.

31c
sources

Make bibliography cards for any articles that you think might relate to your subject. The data you record for periodicals include the name of the author, the title of the article, the title of the journal, the volume number of the journal, the year of publication, and the page numbers on which the article appears. Look at the formats for periodical entries on pages 455–457 and pages 564–566 before you prepare bibliography cards for periodicals; these formats show some of the other data you may need when you set up your reference list.

The periodical indexes have their own notation systems, and most of these formats do not match those required for documentation in your research papers. Unless you copy down data in the correct format on your bibliography cards, you may have trouble with citations in your paper. You may need to check the article itself for information missing from the index entry—the author's first name, for example. Index entries also include information not required in a listing of works cited, so you should not use an index entry as a model for your source card.

The Readers' Guide to Periodical Literature (1900–)

The Readers' Guide is the best-known general guide to many popular periodicals. It is issued regularly (about every month) in paper covers throughout the year, and annual volumes appear in hard covers, fully indexed. Entries in *The Readers' Guide* are arranged by subject and by author. There is a helpful page of suggestions about how to use each volume, as well as a key to abbreviations used in the index. Read this page first to save time and effort.

Sample subject and author entries appear below. Marginal notations explain the parts of the entries.

Readers' Guide, subject entry

Readers' Guide, author entry

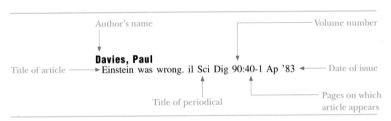

**31c
sources**

Other indexes

- *Access* (1975–) bills itself as "the supplementary index to periodicals," meaning that it indexes periodicals not included in *The Readers' Guide* and other general indexes. Even so, *Access* limits itself to the kind of periodical that you might find in a large magazine store.

- *America: History and Life* (1964–), an especially useful index for the research writer investigating any topic dealing with American (including Canadian) history and culture, includes not only citations to articles but also abstracts.

- *The British Humanities Index* (1962–), a British version of *The Readers' Guide,* indexes periodicals published in Great Britain and has a much broader range than its American counterpart because it includes scholarly and professional journals. It succeeds the *Subject Index to Periodicals,* published by the Library Association.

■ *Essay and General Literature Index* (1900–) lists essays and articles in essay collections in the humanities and social sciences.

■ *Humanities Index* (1974–) includes entries from more than 250 periodicals in archeology, classics, language, literature, history, philosophy, religion, the performing arts, and folklore, arranged by author and subject. Book reviews appear in a separate section at the end.

■ *MLA International Bibliography of Books and Articles on the Modern Languages and Literatures,* an annual five-volume bibliography issued by the Modern Language Association, offers a classified list and index by subject of selections on modern languages, literatures, folklore, and linguistics. It draws on hundreds of books and periodicals as well as films, sound recordings, microfilms, and other machine-readable materials.

MLA International Bibliography, entry

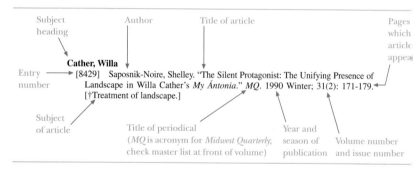

■ *The New York Times Index* (1913–), an indispensable resource, includes all stories that have appeared in the *New York Times,* giving the date of each story, the page and column number of the paper, and an abstract of the entry. Cross-references are numerous.

■ *Psychological Abstracts* (1927–) abstracts thousands of articles in psychology published every year, making it an excellent tool for any topic with a psychological dimension.

■ *Public Affairs Information Service Bulletin* (PAIS) (1915–), listing articles by subject, is a rich resource for almost any topic dealing with politics, economics, international relations, city planning, or other aspects of social or political life.

■ *Social Sciences Index* (1974–) covers periodicals in the fields of anthropology, criminology, economics, law, political science, psychology, and sociology, among other areas of interest to social scientists. Here, too, a separate section of book reviews appears in each issue. From 1965 to 1974, the *Humanities Index* and the *Social Sciences Index* were published as the *Social Sciences and Humanities Index*. From 1907 to 1965 the name of the combined index was the *International Index*.

31c
sources

Other indexes to periodical literature deal with specialized fields and include citations to specialized journals. Some articles they list may help you in the later stages of your research, after you have summarized the information about your topic and have developed a general idea of what you want to say about it. Here are a few specialized indexes.

Applied Science and Technology Index (1913–)
Art Index (1929–)
Arts and Humanities Citation Index (1978–)
Biography Index (1947–)
Biological and Agricultural Index (1964–)
Business Periodicals Index (1953–)
Current Index to Journals in Education (1969–)
Education Index (1929–)
Film Literature Index (1973–)
Index to U.S. Government Periodicals (1974–)
Music Index (1949–)
Social Sciences Citation Index (1973–)

Be sure to ask for help from your reference librarian, who will guide you to other indexes for topics dealing with other special fields.

Most periodicals publish their own annual indexes. When you work in a special field, consult the indexes of journals published in the field for articles useful for your research.

Using Standard Reference Books

When you write a research paper, you must do much more than merely repeat information you find in encyclopedias and dictionaries. But it is always a good idea to use such reference works for background information and perhaps for inspiration to guide you to other ways to explore your topic.

General encyclopedias

The reference section of your library will have several encyclopedias. Here are a few standard works you may wish to consult.

Collier's Encyclopedia
Dictionary of American Biography, 20 vols., plus supplements
Dictionary of National Biography, 21 vols., plus supplements (Britain)
Dictionary of American History, 8 vols.
Encyclopaedia Britannica
Encyclopaedia Judaica, 16 vols.
Encyclopaedia of Religion and Ethics, 13 vols.
Encyclopedia Americana
Encyclopedia Canadiana, 10 vols.
Encyclopedia of World Art, 15 vols.
The Golden Bough: A Study in Magic and Religion, edited by Sir James G. Frazer, 13 vols.
Harvard Dictionary of Music
The International Encyclopedia of Film
International Encyclopedia of the Social Sciences, 19 vols.
The McGraw-Hill Dictionary of Art
The McGraw-Hill Encyclopedia of Science and Technology, 15 vols.
New Catholic Encyclopedia, 15 vols.
The New Columbia Desk Encyclopedia
The New Grove Dictionary of Music and Musicians, 20 vols.
The New York Times Film Reviews
The Oxford Classical Dictionary, 2d ed.
The Oxford Dictionary of the Christian Church

Literary research materials

When you write research papers for literature courses, you have a large body of research materials to draw from, including several outstanding works.

■ *The Oxford Companion to American Literature*, 4th edition, edited by James D. Hart, offers biographies of American writers and summaries of literary works written in English by Americans. This volume pays little attention to literature not written by U.S. authors, and it ignores Latin American writers.

- *The Oxford Companion to English Literature,* 4th edition, edited by Sir Paul Harvey, presents biographies of British writers and summaries of their important works; it also gives writers' biographies and summarizes plots of European literary works considered influential in Britain and the United States.

- *The Oxford History of English Literature* comes in twelve volumes, each covering a period of literature and written by a distinguished specialist in that field.

- *The Year's Work in English Studies,* published in London annually since 1920, contains graceful, well-written summaries of books and articles published each year in the entire field of English literature.

- *Contemporary Authors* (1962–) is a multivolume series giving short biographies and publication information for twentieth-century writers.

- *Contemporary Literary Criticism* (1976–), another multivolume series, presents excerpts from reviews written by prominent critics of contemporary literature. The series has recently expanded to include film criticism.

- *The Harvard Guide to Contemporary American Writing,* edited by Daniel Hoffmann, 1979, surveys the works of the most prominent recent American writers.

31c
sources

Doing a Computer Search

Automated libraries now can store extensive information on sources and make the information quickly available to researchers. Using electronic reference lists, or **databases,** you can examine bibliographical information as well as abstracts, cross-references, or summaries from hundreds of different sources. Good databases currently are available on the natural, applied, and social sciences, and you can save time by consulting one suited to your topic.

A successful electronic search starts with key words, or **descriptors,** which signal an area of interest and allow the computer to call up the articles. Some databases ask you to specify descriptors by *author, title,* or *subject.* Others allow you to search the entire database for a key word. You should choose the most precise and specific descriptors that you can. A descriptor that is too general will yield hundreds or even thousands of entries. You could spend days going through them all, only to find the vast majority are of no use to you. One way to narrow a search while still using a broad descriptor is to limit it in time. You can start by looking only at the articles published this year, or in the 1990s.

Remember, the computer will look for exactly what you *write,* not necessarily what you mean. For instance, if you are doing a research paper on F. Scott Fitzgerald and your descriptor is *author: Fitzgerald, F. Scott,* you are unlikely to find any references, because Fitzgerald, who died in 1940, hasn't written any articles in a long time. However, you will find many entries under *subject: Fitzgerald, F. Scott* because there are many books and articles about him.

If you have questions about narrowing your field of search, most databases have on-line help. If the computer itself is unable to help you narrow your focus, your librarian can help you select more useful terms. Another approach is to look at a general index, like the *Readers' Guide to Periodical Literature,* under the general heading of your topic to see the various descriptors used there. For instance, the student interested in the general subject of *astronomy* would find seventeen subheadings as useful descriptors.

31c
sources

Database, subject entry

Subject heading ——————➤ **ASTRONOMY**
                         See also
                         Asteroids
                         Black holes (Astronomy)
Subheadings ——————➤ Comets
                         Constellations
                         Galaxies
                         Image processing—Astronomical use
                         Infrared astronomy
                         Meteors
                         Milky Way
                         Nebulae
                         Planets
                         Solar system
                         Stars
                         Sun
                         Telescopes
                         Ultraviolet astronomy
                         Universe

The student researching black holes used the *Wilson Indexes,* a magazine guide of 800 journals and periodicals. Most automated libraries have some computerized periodical index, such as the *Magazine Index, Infotract,* or *Nexis.* Using *astronomy* as a descriptor, the student learned that more than 2,500 entries were available, far too many to be useful. The descriptor *black holes* yielded 303, still too many. The student then chose to look only at articles published in the 1990s. Narrowing the search in this way produced 19 articles.

With most databases, you will be able to print out the titles the computer produces. Before you do, examine the number of citations and the format in which they will appear. You may want to narrow your descriptors further or develop new combinations. You can command the computer to provide simple bibliographical data, or you can request abstracts of articles as well as other relevant material. Ask only for what you need.

Database, sample printout

```
DWIL
SEARCH REQUEST: S=BLACK HOLES
WILSON RECORD-- 17 OF 303 ENTRIES FOUND
          SCREEN 17 OF 303

AUTHORS: CROSSWELL, KEN

ARTICLE TITLE:      THE BEST BLACK HOLE IN THE GALAXY.

SOURCE/DATE:        ASTRONOMY 20:30-7 MAR '92

SPECIAL FEATURES:   IL

SUBJECT DESCRIPTORS: BLACK HOLES(ASTRONOMY)
                     MILKY WAY
```

```
                GENERAL SCIENCE INDEX
COMMANDS
HO Holding          I  Index
N  Next record      G  Guide
P  Previous record  H  Help
```

```
DWIL
SEARCH REQUEST: K=BLACK HOLES
WILSON RECORD-- 19 OF 303 ENTRIES FOUND
          SCREEN 19 OF 303
AUTHORS: JOHN GRIBBINS

ARTICLE TITLE:      IS NAKEDNESS PERMITTED OUTSIDE
                    THE COSMIC EDEN?

SOURCE/DATE:        NEW SCIENTIST 134:15 APR '92

SPECIAL FEATURES:

SUBJECT DESCRIPTORS: SINGULARITIES (MATHEMATICS)
                     BLACK HOLES (ASTRONOMY)
```

31c
sources

Using Bibliographies and Notes

Look carefully at the scholarly books and articles you consult to find useful bibliographies and notes. References to other books and articles often lead to new and useful sources of information.

In a 1984 collection, *Critical Essays on Willa Cather* by John J. Murphy, the student writing on Cather discovered a three-page list of sources after one of the essays. There she found a reference to an article by Dayton Kohler in a 1947 issue of *College English.* Kohler's point about the effects of the barren landscape of the West on the human spirit helped the writer shape some of her ideas on Cather's stories.

31c

sources

■ **Exercise 31.2*** For any topic you narrowed down in Exercise 31.1, make a list of five indexes that you might use to help you locate articles in periodicals. Use the reference section of your library.

■ **Exercise 31.3*** If your library can do a computer search, make a list of key words relevant to your topic and check the list against the database descriptions. Print out a limited, focused list of sources.

■ **Exercise 31.4*** For any topic you narrowed down in Exercise 31.1, develop at least ten bibliography cards for books, periodicals, and other sources. Be sure to follow either the format suggested by your instructor or the format described in 31c as you copy the required data.

✔ **CHECKLIST 31.2:** LOCATING SOURCES

After you have decided on your topic, begin the serious search for sources. Here are some places to look.

- the subject catalog of your library catalog
- author entries for authors in the subject catalog, to see if these authors have published related works
- computer databases
- the library stacks where books related to your topic are shelved
- bibliographies and notes in books on your subject
- periodical indexes
- general encyclopedias
- other reference books
- conversations with specialists

CHAPTER

32

PLANNING A
RESEARCH PAPER

By this point in your research project, you've concentrated on selecting and narrowing a topic suitable for research and on identifying appropriate libraries, reference tools, and other materials for investigation. Your main tasks now are to shape your thoughts about your topic by exploring some sources and taking notes. You should also develop a flexible plan for your paper. As you read and evaluate what you have read, your topic may change focus or emphasis, and your plan, too, will change. Reading, note taking, and planning will help you produce a well-written paper.

32a
Developing a Thesis and a Rough Plan

After prewriting and after limiting your topic, explore some of your resources for information about it. Your purpose at this stage is to develop your ideas about the topic.

Doing research is more than simply gathering information; it is developing something of your own to say about what you have read. Don't worry about the number of people who have already written about your topic. Some careful thought about your resources at this stage will stimulate your own original ideas. As your thoughts take shape, put together a hypothesis and a rough plan. Both will help you concentrate on the topic you expect to develop in your paper.

A **hypothesis** is a debatable assumption that you have to prove. It can be thought of as an educated guess. After some early exploration of your topic, state tentatively what conclusion you expect your research to support. All researchers start with a hypothesis; it guides their investigations, helping them find appropriate sources and rule out others.

	Literature	**Astronomy**
Topic	The theme of isolation in two stories by Cather	Various techniques used in the search for black holes
	↓	↓
Hypothesis	In Cather's stories, characters isolated from familiar surroundings are severely affected physically and spiritually.	Black holes are almost impossible to find, despite astronomers' predictions.

32a

plan

The student writing on Cather noted a remark one critic made about how the American West affected the lives of characters in Cather's novels, especially characters moving to the West from more "civilized" Eastern societies. Was this true about characters in the short stories as well? As the student read Cather's stories and comments about them in secondary sources, she could identify details that seemed to show the effects of separation upon the body and spirit of central characters. Her hypothesis reflects the connection she sees between isolation from familiar worlds and its effects on people.

The student who chose the topic on black holes was struck by researchers' faith in the phenomenon of black holes despite the absence of real physical evidence. Physicists had defined black holes, predicted their presence, and suggested their origins, but no one had reported having found black holes. Could they be found? The student formulated a hypothesis: that black holes were almost impossible to locate.

As you continue reading and exploring, your hypothesis—even your topic itself—may change markedly. Other investigators may have disproved your idea. You may find that what seemed like promising sources offer little or no help. You may discover a new area of thought that reshapes your thinking and pushes you into new territory. At this stage, your hypothesis is tentative, as is your plan for the research paper itself. As your reading continues and your hypothesis becomes more precise, you will refine your thoughts and language and develop a carefully worded thesis for your paper. In the papers on Cather and on black holes (Chapter 34), you can see how the hypotheses changed as the writers thought about their topics during the course of their research.

After you state your hypothesis, sketch a rough plan, a brief list of the headings you intend to cover. The tentative thesis statement and the rough plans that follow guided the writers of the papers on Willa Cather and on black holes.

Literature

Plan: Write about the effects of isolation in Willa Cather's short stories
Tentative thesis: Cather's stories " 'A Death in the Desert' " and "A Wagner Matinee" deal with the theme of isolation.

1. Effects on characters' spirits
2. Effects on their appearance
3. How music is important

32b
plan

Astronomy

Plan: Write about the search for black holes
Tentative thesis: The search for black holes presents complex problems for astronomers today.

1. Definition
2. History of the idea
3. Early search
4. Pulsars
5. Binary stars
6. Current search

These preparatory steps bring your topic into focus for note taking and outlining. Of course, as you continue to read, you will make many changes, both in the thesis and in the rough plan.

■ **Exercise 32.1***   Do some preliminary reading to shape your ideas about the topic that you chose in Exercise 31.1. Then develop a tentative thesis and rough plan to guide your research.

32b
Using Primary and Secondary Sources

Read your sources with care, and take careful notes. Most of the sources you will use for a brief research paper will be *secondary*, although you should try to use *primary* sources whenever possible. **Primary sources** include works of literature, such as novels and poems; historical documents, such as diaries, letters, journals, speeches, and autobiographies; and interviews, private conversations, observations, and experiments. **Secondary sources** analyze and comment on other source material. The student writing about Willa Cather could use as a primary source one of Cather's short stories or novels or any of her other published works; as secondary sources, the student could use books or articles written about Cather or her fiction. Among the sources used for this paper, " 'A Death in the Desert' " and "A Wagner Matinee" are primary sources. Secondary sources include an article by Joseph X. Brennan, "Willa Cather and Music," and a book by David Dalches, *Willa Cather: A Critical Introduction.*

32b plan

Write your notes on 3 × 5 inch cards. Put only one idea on each card. Limiting your notes in this way will make it easier for you to organize your materials later (see 32c). Some students prefer larger index cards, but big cards make it tempting to copy down more information and more quotations than you need. Quote directly on your note cards only if you think you may use the quotation in your paper. Summarize or paraphrase many of your sources. Summarizing and paraphrasing force you to absorb the thoughts of your source and to express them in your own words rather than merely repeat them.

A **summary** is a sharply condensed version of an original source in your own words. A summary usually states the thesis briefly and gives the main idea of the original. Your purpose in a summary is to condense important information and to eliminate unessential points. A **paraphrase** is a much fuller summary; it may cite some of the evidence and use some of the words in the original source. A good paraphrase follows the line of reasoning in the original source and the sequence of ideas as well. In both paraphrases and summaries, you must acknowledge your sources.

Do not waste time copying down a long quotation or writing a paraphrase or a summary on a note card. Instead, make a signal card. On a **signal card,** note the page numbers where the information appears and record your thoughts about how a quotation might be used in your paper. Of course, you can't keep library books forever; so when you write signal cards, you should be ready to write your paper. If you think you may not have the book handy when you do write, copy down the material you need, either as a direct quotation or as a paraphrase. Because copying long direct quotations by hand leads to errors, you must proofread such passages with great care.

Copying machines are available in most libraries, and you can copy a page or two from a book or a periodical. (Such copying is strictly regulated by federal copyright laws, and your library may have regulations about the use of copying machines.) Remember that copying the source on a machine is no substitute for reading it. If you are going to use the source in your paper, you must read it carefully and make it part of your own thinking.

Often when you are taking notes, ideas about what you are summarizing, paraphrasing, or copying will occur to you. Be sure your notes distinguish your words and ideas from those of your source. In your paper you will have to identify the sources of all the ideas you have borrowed. If you do not make clear in your notes just whose ideas are whose, you may find yourself committing plagiarism (see 33b). Use parentheses, asterisks, arrows, or some other means to identify your own thoughts in your notes. Also, be careful to note page breaks when a quotation continues to another page. Only a small part of what you record on a note card may appear in the final draft of your paper, and you must be able to report the exact page reference for the quotation you use.

32b
plan

Below is an excerpt from pages 280–81 of Sharon O'Brien's *Willa Cather: The Emerging Voice* (New York: Oxford University Press, 1987) on Cather's "A Wagner Matinee." Various types of note cards prepared from the excerpt follow it. Note that the writer has identified the source at the top of each card in an abbreviated form. (Full bibliographical data will appear on the writer's bibliography cards; see 31c.)

Source

In "A Wagner Matinee," for example, Cather integrates a family story into her fiction: Georgianna and her husband measure off their quarter section of land by tying a cotton handkerchief to a wagon wheel and counting off the revolutions, as had Cather's Aunt Franc and her husband George Cather when they first arrived in Nebraska in the 1880s.[8] In the grim portrayal of Georgianna's Nebraska farm, Cather also drew on her own memories of the difficult transition from Virginia to Nebraska, using her memories of her grandparents' farmhouse in describing Georgianna's bleak environment. Her portrayal of the gifted woman starving for music amid the "silence of the plains" also owes something to her own experience of aesthetic deprivation in Nebraska, a feeling intensified retrospectively when she discovered what her prairie education lacked. As she told Will Owen Jones, the distaste she had felt for Nebraska was because she had been only half nourished there.[9] "The Sculptor's Funeral" also had real-life sources: Cather's witnessing an artist's funeral in Pittsburgh and, on another occasion, seeing the return of a Nebraska boy—in his coffin—to Red Cloud.

But there were dangers in turning from admiration to memory: the risk of punishment and retribution Cather had associated with self-exposure in her first college stories. After "A Wagner Matinee" appeared in *Everybody's Magazine* in 1904, a year before *The Troll Garden,* Cather faced a Nebraska uprising. The resulting controversy over the story was the "nearest she had come to personal disgrace," she told Viola Roseboro later.[10] Like "The Sculptor's Funeral" and Hamlin Garland's *Main-Travelled Roads*, "A Wagner Matinee" portrays the Midwest as a harsh, oppressive, and repressive environment. Family members were particularly insulted by the supposed portrait of Aunt Franc in Georgianna and informed Cather that it wasn't "nice" to say such things in print. Friends and neighbors found the grim depiction of Nebraska unfair, and Cather was even attacked in her hometown paper by her old friend and colleague Will Owen Jones. "If the writers of fiction who use western Nebraska as material would look up now and then and not keep their eyes and noses in the cattle yards," he complained in the *Journal*, "they might be more agreeable company" (*WWC*, p. 254).

In the quotation card below, the exact words of the source are in quotation marks. An arrow distinguishes the writer's thought from that of the source. The summary card highlights the points in the passage that concern the writer of the research paper. Note the many details omitted from the source. On the paraphrase card the notes closely follow the line of reasoning of the original, although the writer has used her own words to restate O'Brien's point. The few words in quotation marks are exact

O'Brien, *Cather*, p. 281
"Her portrayal of the gifted woman, starving for music amid the 'silence of the plains' also owes something to her own experience of aesthetic deprivation in Nebraska, a feeling intensified retrospectively when she discovered what her prairie education lacked.
→ Compare with Gerber and Stouck. This seems to be a major concern of Cather's - artist's survival on the frontier.

Summary card

O'Brien, _Cather_, p. 281
Cather's own experiences contribute to the grim
picture of Aunt Georgianna's Nebraska farm.
Cather's own sense of artistic loss and weakness
in education influences portrait of talented
woman hungering for music on the plains.

32b
plan

Paraphrase card

O'Brien, _Cather_, p. 281
In "A Wagner Matinee" Cather drew on personal experiences such
as measuring off land in Nebraska in the 1880s. Remembering her
move from Virginia and the farmhouse of her grandparents in
Nebraska, Cather portrayed "Georgianna's bleak environment."
The picture of Georgianna and her lack of music on the silent
plains relies on Cather's "own experience of aesthetic
deprivation in Nebraska" and her sense of what she missed in
her prairie education.
→ Where does phrase "silence of the plains" come from? Check
stories, also sources at notes 8 and 9.

■ **Exercise 32.2*** Take notes as you read and consult the various sources you have selected for your research. Use the note cards on pages 430 to 431 as models.

32c
Organizing Notes

Read and organize your notes carefully and use them to help you focus your ideas and develop your plan. Your tentative thesis and rough plan will guide your reading and note taking and will shape your thoughts about the topic. Your thoughts, in turn, will suggest changes in your thesis and plan. Don't worry if your thesis and plan change many times as you develop your outline, rough drafts, and final draft. Following a preliminary plan too rigidly keeps you from making the major changes in emphasis and organization that later reading and thinking often suggest.

If you have done your research carefully, you will have many note cards on which you have collected quotations, summaries, paraphrases, statistical information, and other data from your sources. Only one idea should appear on each card. Now read your notes over carefully and organize them so that you can develop your paper (see the Topic Summary Guide on the facing page).

In reading through your note cards, you should find that your material falls naturally into subject groups. The headings in your rough plan were your guide for taking and organizing notes from the beginning. By now you have probably clustered related data from various sources around the general headings. Yet as you reread your note cards, you will think of new major headings that bear on your topic and discover some old main headings that do not. You will also think of subheadings that flesh out the main headings.

At this point, you are ready to prepare a formal outline or to write a first draft. First, collect all your note cards, put them in order, and number them consecutively. Now you can prepare a summary guide that tells you, by number, where each note card fits into your plan. See the excerpts from the summary guides developed for the papers we have been tracking.

This kind of guide helps you arrange the note cards according to tentative headings. And because the cards are numbered and each card includes the author's name and the title of the book or the article, you can keep track of your sources as you go along.

This system allows you to experiment. You can group and regroup related data and ideas and shift the order of subject groups around before you make any final decisions. This experimentation also can help you develop your plan by suggesting more effective headings and subheadings.

■ **Exercise 32.3***   Continue reading about your topic and taking notes. Using the rough plan you formulated in Exercise 32.1, develop a more detailed plan.

**32c
plan**

Literature

TOPIC SUMMARY GUIDE

Headings	Note cards
Music connections	3, 4, 6, 9, 22, 26, 30, 31
Artistic deprivation	1, 7, 12, 13, 14, 28
Physical strain of prairie life	2, 18, 32, 36, 37
Imagery of West	5, 24, 25, 46, 53
Imagery of "civilized" life	19, 59, 63, 64, 65, 68

Astronomy

TOPIC SUMMARY GUIDE

Headings	Note cards
European investigation of black holes	3, 4, 6, 9, 22, 26
Definitions of black holes	1, 7, 12, 13, 14, 28
Finding black holes	2, 18, 32, 36, 37
Interpreting data	30, 31
Key researchers	5, 24, 25, 46, 53
Research methodology	5, 8, 17, 18, 55, 56, 57

✔ CHECKLIST 32.1: PLANNING A RESEARCH PAPER

Planning is crucial to the success of a research paper. Before you begin to write, be sure that you have completed all the planning steps.

32c
plan

- Prepare a preliminary list of sources.
- Develop a hypothesis and tentative thesis.
- Sketch out a rough plan.
- Read your sources.
- Take notes:
  - summarize
  - paraphrase
  - quote (use signal cards).
- Keep track of your sources; make sure that your notes distinguish your ideas from those of your sources.
- Read and organize your notes.

CITING AND DOCUMENTING SOURCES

A research paper requires a thoughtful balance between your own language and the words and sentences you borrow from other sources. Intelligent use of source material is the heart of research writing. As a general rule of thumb, use quotations only when you feel that the original wording will add significantly to your point. Students are often tempted to quote lengthy passages, but this is not a good practice unless you have a clear, specific purpose for doing so. A lengthy passage can be tedious if the reader does not see why you didn't summarize it. Select quotations carefully, and always keep them as short as possible.

To write a paper that does more than simply restate the ideas of others, you must interpret and evaluate source materials, provide commentary to clarify points, and assert your own conclusions. And you must acknowledge every source you use. You need to choose an appropriate and accepted method for citing and documenting materials you use in your paper.

33a
Integrating Sources into Your Writing

Integrating source material smoothly into your writing takes thought and care. The thesis of your paper will determine the points you make, but you will be supporting those points with ideas drawn from sources and written in a language and style that may be quite different from your own.

Quoting, Summarizing, and Paraphrasing

Following the methods you used to record your data (see 32b), you could quote the source directly, or you could summarize or paraphrase it. Suppose you wanted to use part of this passage, which appears at the end of the short story "A Wagner Matinee" by Willa Cather. The passage is about Aunt Georgiana, the main character.

**33a
cite**

Source

The concert was over; the people filed out of the hall chattering and laughing, glad to relax and find the living level again, but my kinswoman made no effort to rise. The harpist slipped its green felt cover over his instrument; the flute players shook the water from their mouthpieces; the men of the orchestra were out one by one, leaving the stage to the chairs and music stands, empty as a winter cornfield.

I spoke to my aunt. She burst into tears and sobbed pleadingly. "I don't want to go, Clark, I don't want to go!"

I understood. For her, just outside the door of the concert hall, lay the black pond with the cattle-tracked bluffs; the tall, unpainted house, with weather-curled boards; naked as a tower, the crook-backed ash seedlings where the dishcloths hung to dry; the gaunt, molting turkeys picking up refuse about the kitchen door.

—WILLA CATHER

One option is to quote the source exactly. You could quote a sentence or two to make your point, or you could present a longer quotation in block form, perhaps an entire paragraph. Either way, you must separate your ideas from those of your source. At the same time, you should blend your own words with the words of the writer you are quoting to produce a smooth and pleasing sentence. Later in this chapter you will learn the mechanics of documenting sources in a variety of citation systems (33d, 33e, 33f, 33g). Here we concentrate on how to make smoother connections between your prose and the prose of your source.

Quotation from source

In the last lines of "A Wagner Matinee" we can see the horrible tragedy of the transplanted artist, as Clark's aunt faces her life back home. Clark explains that "just outside the door of the concert hall, lay . . . the tall, unpainted house, with weather-curled boards" and "the gaunt, molting turkeys picking up refuse about the kitchen door" (115). It is the refuse of Aunt Georgiana's existence.

In this example, the writer uses her source to support the point she's making, the tragedy of the transplanted artist. Quotation marks are placed around each phrase copied from the source. The sentence that includes the quotation starting with "just outside the door of the concert hall" follows smoothly from the sentence before it. The tag "Clark explains that" helps the writer integrate the quoted material with her own writing. The writer uses the conjunction *and* to connect two parts of Cather's sentence that are separated in the original. The spaced periods, called **ellipses** (26f), shorten the quotation. Note how the writer comments on the quotation with her own thoughtful observation: the turkey's refuse is the refuse of Aunt Georgiana's existence. The parenthetical reference "(115)" is to the page number on which the quotation appears in Cather's story. Full documentation appears in the list of works cited (see 33d).

33a cite

Here is another way the writer could have quoted from her source.

Quotation from source

The final overwhelming images of the story show the utter
horror of the transplanted artist:

> For her, just outside the door of the concert hall, lay
> the black pond with the cattle-tracked bluffs; the
> tall, unpainted house, with weather-curled boards;
> naked as a tower, the crook-backed ash seedlings where
> the dishcloths hung to dry; the gaunt, molting turkeys
> picking up refuse about the kitchen door.

Here the long quotation supports the point the writer makes in the introductory sentence. Readers will read and see why the writer finds the images overwhelming. This type of long quotation, set apart from the writer's prose by indenting from the left, is called a **block quotation** (see 25a). Use the block form for a quotation of four or more typed lines. Note that quotation marks are not needed.

In the next examples, the author summarizes and paraphrases the source.

Summary

Cather leaves us with a grim picture of the life awaiting Aunt
Georgiana when she leaves the concert hall and returns to her
bleak homestead on the Nebraska frontier.

Paraphrase

We see a stark, ugly world awaiting Aunt Georgiana. When she
returns to her Nebraska homestead from the concert hall, she
must face "the black pond" surrounded by bluffs, a weather-

> beaten farmhouse, small ash trees "where the dishcloths hung
> to dry," and thin, bony turkeys pecking at garbage outside the
> kitchen (115).

In the **paraphrase,** which follows the original line of reasoning more
closely than the summary (see 32b), the writer uses quotation marks
around the phrases from the original.

You must use your judgment about when to use quotation marks for
individual words or for brief phrases borrowed from another source. Notice that the words *concert hall* appear in the original story, but in the
summary and the paraphrase these words are not enclosed within quotation marks. A good general rule is that when you use three or more
consecutive words from another source, you need quotation marks. Keeping this rule in mind will make you think about what you are doing and
will help you avoid the unconscious plagiarism that can get you into just
as much trouble as the deliberate act (see 33b).

■ **Exercise 33.1**   Select a passage from a magazine article or a book,
and write a paragraph in which you incorporate elements from the passage
into your own writing by following the directions below. Use appropriate
citations. Make a copy of the passage to show your instructor.

1. Write a brief summary of the passage as part of a paragraph that
   might appear in a draft of your paper.
2. Write a short paragraph in which you quote a few lines exactly
   from the passage.
3. Write a short paragraph in which you paraphrase the passage.

Commenting on Source Material

Although summaries of sources are important elements in most research
papers, you should provide more than summaries alone. Readers expect
you to guide them by explaining, interpreting, and evaluating source materials. You build paragraphs from quotations, summaries, or paraphrases
by giving your own thoughts on your topic.

Extensive research will shape your thoughts and opinions, and as you
continue examining different sources, you will formulate new ideas or
modify existing ones. Some of your sources may provide conflicting data.
Others may simply disagree in their interpretation of facts or even in their
definitions of key terms. Still others may offer opinions that challenge
what you have read elsewhere. Readers of your paper need your help in
sorting out the contradictions and in separating the important ideas from
the routine and the facts from the speculations.

Commenting on source material is not easy, but it is important. There are no exact rules to follow. A sensitive researcher learns from experience just when to shed light on a complex point or when to interpret or challenge an important idea. You should respect your sources, of course, but should not be intimidated by them. In citing authorities it is right to question their conclusions, to lay them alongside conclusions drawn by others, or to use them as springboards for your own conclusions. The following examples demonstrate how skilled writers can integrate source material while providing useful commentary on it.

33a
cite

> Cather's debut into fame was noted in volumes concerning American fiction, the first being Grant Overton's *The Women Who Make Our Novels*, issued late in 1918. A literary reporter rather than critic, Overton compiled information about all American female novelists of importance or popularity; but he did not prognosticate which of them, if any, might continue to be read fifty years hence. The order of his chapters was accidental and therefore meaningless; Willa Cather is sandwiched between one Grace S. Richmond, whose books were said to sell "faster than the books of any other American writer," and Clara Louise Burnham, author of "twenty-six books which have sold a half million copies." The thirteen pages Overton granted Cather are devoted largely to a biographical sketch (not always noted for accuracy) and to a summary of her achievement, drawn from reviews; these cover her work from *Alexander's Bridge,* which might have been written by Mrs. Wharton, through the indisputably personal triumph of *My Antonia.* Overton's judgments, reflecting a cross section of others' evalutions, emphasize the significance of Cather's early western experience, her controlled accessibility to it, her fidelity to character, and the esthetic delight furnished by her method.
>
> —PHILIP GERBER

Much more than a summary appears here. Certainly we learn the essence of Overton's entry on Cather and two of her contemporaries. But Gerber's comments and evaluations guide our perceptions. Note how he judges Overton's credentials as a writer about Cather, how he calls the order of chapters in *The Women Who Make Our Novels* meaningless, and how he questions the biographical accuracy in Overton's sketch of Cather. A reader unfamiliar with Overton has not only a summary of his work, but also an assessment of it from Gerber's perspective.

> Two of the shorter pieces in *The Troll Garden,* "A Wagner Matinee" and "The Sculptor's Funeral," take firm grip on the fatality of deprivation which was an inherent part of Miss Cather's native Ne-

braska material. "A Wagner Matinee" is a bleakly effective *récit,* holding in concentration the terrible spiritual toll taken by frontier life, especially upon women. An old aunt of the narrator, grizzled and deformed, comes to visit her nephew in New York; she had been a music teacher at the Boston Conservatory, and marriage had taken her to a Nebraska homestead fifty miles from a railroad, to live at first in a dugout in a hillside. He takes her to a concert. At the *Tannhäuser* overture, she clutches his coat sleeve. "Then it was I first realized that for her this broke a silence of thirty years; the inconceivable silence of the plains. . . ."

—Dorothy Van Ghent

Van Ghent's purpose is to summarize the main action of "A Wagner Matinee," but she provides her own interpretation as well. She classifies the story as a *récit*—a term usually reserved for short novels with simple narrative lines.

In the student's paper on Willa Cather note how the writer comments on source material in this instance, among many others:

> With a brilliant image Cather shows the conflicting forces of past and present in Katharine's life. In the Wyoming house, the music room makes Everett feel that he has stepped into a familiar New York studio almost exactly like his brother's, "so individual and poignantly reminiscent here in Wyoming" (71). As he sits chatting with Katharine, a window blind swinging in the wind reveals "the glaring panorama of the desert--a blinding stretch of yellow, flat as the sea in dead calm" (75). Blinding, yellow, flat, dead: so is Katharine's life away from the East, even in the studio room she has tried so hard to make like Adriance's.

The last sentence interprets for the reader the quotation from Cather's story "A Death in the Desert."

■ **Exercise 33.2**   Read the following passage from the book *Sociology* by Paul Horton and Chester Hunt. Write a paragraph or two in which you integrate this source into your prose by quoting and paraphrasing. Provide commentary on the quotations and paraphrases by offering your own clarifications, interpretations, or judgments.

Stereotypes.   A *stereotype* is *a group-shared image of another group or category of people.* Stereotypes can be positive (the kindly, dedicated family doctor), negative (the unprincipled, opportunistic politician), or mixed (the dedicated, fussy, sexless old-maid teacher). Stereotypes are applied indiscriminately to all members of the stereotyped group, without allowance for individual differences. Stereotypes are never entirely untrue, for they must bear *some* resemblance to the characteristics of the persons stereotyped or they would not be recognized. But stereotypes are always distorted, in that they exaggerate and universalize *some* of the characteristics of *some* of the members of the stereotyped group.

Just how stereotypes begin is not known. Once the stereotype has become a part of the culture, it is maintained by *selective perception* (noting only the confirming incidents or cases and failing to note or remember the exceptions), *selective interpretation* (interpreting observations in terms of the stereotype: e.g., Jews are "pushy" while gentiles are "ambitious"), *selective identification* ("they look like school teachers . . ."), and *selective exception* ("he really doesn't act at all Jewish"). All these processes involve a reminder of the stereotype, so that even exceptions and incorrect identifications serve to feed and sustain the stereotype.

—PAUL B. HORTON AND CHESTER L. HUNT

**33b
cite**

33b
Crediting Sources

You commit **plagiarism** whenever you present words or ideas taken from another person as if they were your own. The easiest way to avoid plagiarism is always to use quotation marks when you quote directly from a source and always to acknowledge a source when you borrow or even allude to someone else's ideas and language, even though you may not have used that person's exact words. Sections 33d, 33e, 33f, and 33g explain accepted methods of documentation and citation.

If you fail to follow these rules for borrowing from other writers, you may be guilty of plagiarism. The most obvious plagiarism is simply **copying,** either word for word or with a few words added or shifted around. Anyone who compares the source and the copy can recognize plagiarism instantly.

Mosaic plagiarism is using words or ideas of others indirectly and failing to credit the source. It may result when a well-meaning, uninformed writer takes bad notes or when a dishonest one deliberately attempts to deceive. Here is an example. The writer has added words and sentences, but anyone who reads the source and the plagiarism can tell that the latter depends entirely on the former.

Source

A territory is an area of space, whether of water or earth or air, which an animal or group of animals defends as an exclusive preserve. The word is also used to describe the inward compulsion in animate beings to possess and defend such a space. A territorial species of animals, therefore, is one in which all males, and sometimes females too, bear an inherent drive to gain and defend an exclusive property.

In most but not all territorial species, defense is directed only against fellow members of the kind. A squirrel does not regard a mouse as a trespasser. In most but not all territorial species—not in chameleons, for example—the female is sexually unresponsive to an unpropertied male. As a general pattern of behavior, in territorial species the competition between males which we formerly believed was one for the possession of females is in truth for possession of property.

—ROBERT ARDREY

Mosaic plagiarism

Territory may be defined as an area of space, water, earth, or air, which animals defend as an exclusive preserve. The word *territory* also describes the inner compulsion in living beings to own and defend such a space. In a territorial species, males and some females are driven to gain and defend their exclusive property against fellow members of the species. The female of most territorial animals is not responsive sexually to a male without property, and the competition between males that we once believed was for the possession of females is really for possession of property.

Plagiarism is a very serious offense. The prose we write ourselves is so individual that when we write something in a striking way or express a new idea, we have produced something that always belongs to us. To call someone else's writing your own is wrong and foolish. The student who plagiarizes can expect a failing grade on the paper and, in many schools, for the whole course. Plagiarism is an honors-code violation and is often grounds for expulsion.

Here is how the writer of the mosaic plagiarism could have avoided it by acknowledging the source of those thoughts, Robert Ardrey.

Revision

Ardrey defines territory as an area "whether of water or earth or air" which animals see as theirs exclusively and which they are driven by an "inward compulsion" to defend against members of their own species. A female in a territorial species is "sexually unresponsive to an unpropertied male." Ardrey believes that males do not compete for females. Instead, "the competition . . . is in truth for possession of property" (3).

You need not attribute information that is common knowledge. If you say that World War II ended in 1945, do not cite the source of your statement, since it is common knowledge. But if you do not know whether information is common knowledge or not, consult your instructor or an expert in the field.

**33c
cite**

✔ **CHECKLIST 33.1: AVOIDING PLAGIARISM**

- Always acknowledge your sources.
- Always keep your own notes and comments about a subject separate from the words you copy from other sources. Students sometimes commit plagiarism accidentally because their notes fail to distinguish between what is their own and what they have copied.
- Always use quotation marks when you are quoting directly, even if you choose to quote only a short phrase or clause.
- Even when you are not quoting directly from a source, always be sure to attribute striking ideas to the person who first thought of them.
- Always cite your sources for interpretations, statistical data, and facts that are not common knowledge.

33c
Using Various Formats for Documenting Sources

You must acknowledge information, ideas, and words borrowed from others. The format you use for acknowledging your sources may vary, depending on the discipline in which you are doing research. Most up-to-date documentation systems require internal (or parenthetical) citation. With **internal citation,** sources are enclosed in parentheses and are named in brief form directly in the text of the paper instead of in footnotes or in endnotes. This system also requires a list of references or works cited at the end of the paper, where sources are given in full. With **footnotes,** citations, keyed by numbers, appear at the bottom of the page. With **endnotes,** these notes appear at the end of the paper.

Because academic disciplines vary in the precise forms they require for documentation, you must follow the specific format that your instructor requests. Two of the most popular formats are those recommended by the

Modern Language Association of America (MLA) in its *MLA Handbook for Writers of Research Papers* and in its counterpart for scholars, *The MLA Style Manual*, and by the *Publication Manual of the American Psychological Association* (APA). This chapter focuses on these formats. In addition, you will see how to use other parenthetical documentation systems as well as footnotes or endnotes. Your instructor may require the documentation format recommended in the University of Chicago Press's *Chicago Manual of Style* or in Kate L. Turabian's *Manual for Writers of Term Papers, Theses, and Dissertations*. Many other manuals for researchers are also available.

33d
cite

33d
Using the MLA Format

Most research papers in the humanities use the MLA format. The main features of this format include parenthetical citations directly in the text, a list of works cited, and, when necessary, explanatory endnotes.

Using Parenthetical References

The MLA system uses an abbreviated format for documentation within the text. (A list of works cited, to be discussed shortly, supplies full publishing data.) A citation in the text typically includes:

- Author's last name
- Location of the material. Usually page numbers alone are enough; in a multivolume source, give the volume number as well. For literary works, you may want to give the act, scene, line, chapter, book, or stanza.

Remember, complete bibliographical information must appear in your list of works cited at the end of the paper. The following model will help you write your own sentences to indicate your sources. The complete entry for Van Ghent's book appears in the list of works cited on p. 509. (The full text from which the quotation in this model internal documentation is taken appears on pages 439–440.)

The key to successful parenthetical documentation is the complete list of works cited at the end of the paper. Every reference you make in your text must correspond to an entry on that list. Information you provide in the parenthetical documentation must match the information on your list of works cited.

Try to be concise and unobtrusive with your parenthetical references. Place them where pauses occur naturally in your sentences and as close as possible to the information you are identifying.

Model internal documentation; MLA format

```
Cather's "A Wagner matinee" shows "the terrible
spiritual toll taken by frontier life, especially
upon women" (Van Ghent 11).
```

Period at end of sentence

close parenthesis

Author's last name only

No comma or period here

Quotation ends here

Space only; no punctuation

Open parenthesis

Page number from work by author

33d cite

What you include in parentheses and what you include in the accompanying text will reflect your individual style as a writer. Feel free to experiment with different formats for references, remembering that what you include in your text determines what you include in the parenthetical documentation. If you use the author's name in a sentence, do not put that name in parentheses. If you do not name the author in your sentence, name him or her in parentheses.

We cannot show all the stylistic possibilities for internal documentation, but the following examples illustrate the simplest options. Wherever possible, these examples correspond to examples presented in later sections (Preparing a List of Works Cited, p. 450, and Using Footnotes or Endnotes, p. 472).

Parts of single-volume books or articles

Van Ghent believes that "A Wagner Matinee" is a story about "the terrible spiritual toll taken by frontier life, especially upon women" (11).

"A Wagner Matinee," as Van Ghent points out, "is a bleakly effective <u>récit,</u> holding in concentration the terrible spiritual toll taken by frontier life, especially upon women" (11).

In Cather's short story we see how life on the frontier imposes itself on a woman's spirit (Van Ghent 11).

It may be true that some of Cather's writing shows "the fatality of deprivation" (Van Ghent 11), but certainly a story like "A Wagner Matinee" also is a tribute to the power of art in human life.

> Van Ghent highlights the bleak, deprived life of Aunt
> Georgiana (11).

To cite an entire work rather than a part of it, name the author in the text and avoid a parenthetical reference.

> Dorothy Van Ghent comments on all of Cather's novels.

> An interesting collection of Greek and Roman myths appears in
> the volume by Mark Morford and Robert Lenardon.

> Clifford Morgan, Richard King, and Nancy Robinson have
> provided a basic text for beginning students of psychology.

> Albert Baugh and his colleagues trace the growth and
> development of English literature from the Middle Ages to the
> twentieth century.

Multivolume works

In the example below, the number before the colon in parentheses refers to the volume; the number after the colon refers to the page number. The "vii" tells you that the quotation comes from the preface; pagination in the preface or other front matter in a book is generally in lowercase roman numbers.

> Sir Thomas Browne's <u>Pseudodoxia Epidemica</u> was "no hasty
> compilation, but was the product of many years of patient
> thought, reading, observation, and experiment" (2: vii).

The following parenthetical reference is to an entire volume of a multivolume work and not to any particular part of that volume. Here you use a comma to separate the author's name from the volume number, and you use the abbreviation for *volume.*

> Modern readers may be mystified by the range of classical
> allusions in the <u>Pseudodoxia Epidemica</u> (Browne, vol. 2).

Works cited by title only

For parenthetical references to a work that appears in the list of works cited by title only, use a shortened version of the title. Omit the page number if the article is brief; otherwise include the page number after the title.

> Cather had already published <u>The Troll Garden</u> and <u>Song of the
> Lark</u>, but it was <u>My Antonia</u> that widened her reputation in
> 1918 ("Cather").

Works by a corporate author

This reference is to *The Humanities in American Life,* prepared by a committee. The committee is listed in the publication as the author.

> In 1980 the Commission on the Humanities recommended that
> "the humanities, sciences, and technology need to be
> substantially connected" (21), but we have made little
> progress toward that goal.

33d cite

Two or more works by the same author

If you use two or more books by the same author, you'll need to include the title, or a shortened form of it, in parenthetical references to works by this author; otherwise the reader will have no way of knowing which work by that author you are citing. A comma follows the author's name if you use it in the parenthetical reference. If you put the author's name in the text, give only the title and the page reference, as in the second example below. For this example, two of Farrington's books, *The Philosophy of Francis Bacon* and *Aristotle: Founder of Scientific Philosophy,* would appear in the list of works cited.

> Bacon condemned Plato as "an obstacle to science"
> (Farrington, <u>Philosophy</u> 35).

> Benjamin Farrington points out that Aristotle's father,
> Nicomachus, a physician, probably trained his son in
> medicine (<u>Aristotle</u> 15).

Literary works

For classical literary works in several editions, readers find it useful to have more than just page numbers in a reference. Chapter, book, act, scene, line, and stanza numbers make it easier to find materials in any copy of a novel or play. In the parenthetical reference, cite the page number first, then use a semicolon, and then give this information, using accepted abbreviations.

> In the opening sentence of <u>Lord Jim</u>, Conrad shows us the
> physical power of his hero (3; ch. 1).

> Marlowe says that what set Brown apart from other scoundrels
> "was the arrogant temper of his misdeeds and a vehement scorn
> for mankind at large and for his victims in particular"
> (Conrad 352-53; ch. 38).

More than one work in a single reference

When you cite more than one work in a single parenthetical reference, use semicolons to separate the works. The first two entries in the parenthesis below are to complete articles; the last entry ("Van Ghent 20–21") is to specific pages in Van Ghent's article. Because a parenthetical reference that is too long will distract readers, you may want to use a footnote or endnote to cite multiple sources.

> Several critics refer to the place of music in Cather's art (Giannone; Brennan; Van Ghent 20—21).

Indirect sources

You should take material from original sources whenever you can. But when the original is unavailable and you have only an indirect source (for example, a published account of someone's spoken comments), use the abbreviation "qtd. in" in your parenthetical reference, right before your citation. For this example, the list of works cited would include a reference to Turnball, not to Baker.

> Wolfe was upset at an anonymous criticism of his play The Mountains. He told his teacher at Harvard, George Pierce Baker, that "if I knew who wrote that, I would no longer be responsible for my actions" (qtd. in Turnball 54).

Plays, concerts, films, and television programs

> Linda Lavin's performance in Broadway Bound by Neil Simon pleased most of the New York drama critics.

> In The Unforgiven Clint Eastwood continues to impress audiences with his skills as an actor and a director.

■ **Exercise 33.3**   Write a sentence that quotes, summarizes, or paraphrases a portion of each selection below. Within your sentence, provide documentation for the source according to the MLA guidelines. Publishing data appear in parentheses following the quotation; you will not have to use all the information, however.

1. "When Shakespeare came to London from Stratford-on-Avon, the new poetry, which was to crown the last decades of the sixteenth century and the beginning of the seventeenth, was already established. Its arrival had been announced in 1579 by the publication of Spenser's *The Shepherd's Calendar*." (The selection is from *Shakespeare's Songs and Poems,* edited by Edward Hubler. The quotation is from pages xii–xiii. The book was published in 1959 by McGraw-Hill in New York.)

2. "Every summer, one of the nation's longest-running and most hotly contested photo competitions takes place at the offices of Sierra Club Books in San Francisco. Between 50,000 and 100,000 color transparencies are submitted for publication in the four Wilderness calendars, and the flood of entries keeps a small army of freelance photo editors and clerks busy from July to November." (The selection is from an article called "Wilderness Pin-Ups by Sierra Club" by Catherine Kouts in *Publishers Weekly,* vol. 225, no. 17, April 27, 1984, p. 41.)

33d cite

3. "The Greeks' most important legacy is not, as we would like to think, democracy; it is their mythology. Even though in the second century A.D. a mysterious voice was heard exclaiming 'great Pan is dead,' the Greek gods and many obscure and irrational stories about them lived on in the imaginations of artists and writers, no matter how often or in how many different ways Christians and philosophers tried to dismiss the myths as frivolous or harmful. And even in the twentieth century, when man has acquired greater power than ever before to alter the natural world, the old myths continue to haunt us, not just in the form of nymphs and shepherds on vases or garden statuary, but in many common assumptions about the shape of human experience. The notions—now presumably obsolete—that a man should be active and aggressive, a woman passive and subject to control by the men in her family, are expressed in virtually every Greek myth, even the ones in which the women seek to gain control of their own lives. That the most important phase of a woman's life is the period immediately preceding her marriage (or remarriage) is preserved in the plot of many novels, as is the notion that virginity, or at least celibacy, offers a woman a kind of freedom that she is no longer entitled to when she becomes involved with a man." (The selection is from p. 207 of an article called "Women in Greek Myths" by Mary R. Lefkowitz. The article appears on pp. 207–19 of the Spring 1985 *American Scholar,* vol. 54, no. 2. *The American Scholar* is a journal that numbers pages continuously throughout the annual volume and is published in Washington, D.C., by Phi Beta Kappa.)

Using Explanatory Notes

When you use parenthetical references in your research paper, you can also use footnotes or endnotes to provide additional information that you do not want to include in the text of your paper. In notes, you can provide evaluative comments on your sources or other relevant information that does not fit neatly in your text. Or to avoid the distraction of a long parenthesis including several citations, you can use a note to list multiple citations.

Indicate notes by a raised number in the text. Put your explanatory notes before your list of works cited, on a separate page under the heading "Notes."

Notes to explain

Notes can offer explanations that would be out of place in the text. In the following example, the writer uses a parenthetical reference to cite the page, "(107)," from which she quotes the words "at once pathetic and grotesque." She uses the note to explain information that does not belong in the text itself. In addition, she cites a reference to a critical piece about Cather.

> Earlier, when Clark received the letter from Howard announcing Aunt Georgiana's arrival, Clark says that her name called up her figure, "at once pathetic and grotesque" (107).[1]

> [1]Cather's family and friends objected to her portrait of Nebraska life when this story first appeared in Everybody's Magazine. A good friend, Will Jones, complained that strangers would always associate Nebraska with Aunt Georgiana's terrible shape, her false teeth, and her yellow skin. Cather denied that she wanted to disparage her homeland but admitted that her family felt insulted: "They had already told her that it was not nice to tell such things" (Woodress 117).

Notes to cite multiple sources

In the example below, the inclusion of seven references in a parenthetical citation in the text would distract readers. The note permits the writer to cite multiple sources without intruding in the text.

> Music is a very important element in much of Cather's fiction.[2]

> [2]Giannone; Brennan, "Willa Cather"; Brennan, "Music"; Gerber 71-73; Bloom and Bloom 123; Daiches 8; Van Ghent 20-21.

Preparing a List of Works Cited

You must provide a list of works cited for readers of your research paper. A **list of works cited** is an alphabetical list of books, articles, and other sources (such as films, interviews, or dramatic productions) that you consulted in doing your research. All the citations in your paper will be keyed to this list of research materials. (If you use print materials only, your list will be called a **bibliography**.)

If you make bibliography cards carefully (as discussed in 31c), you can produce a list of works cited without much trouble. Each card will have all the data you need to prepare your list for the final draft of your paper.

The following models show you how to document the usual kinds of sources for your research. If you cite some special sources (cartoons, computer programs, musical compositions, works of art), you should consult the *MLA Handbook* itself.

33d cite

Books and reference works

Model entry (MLA) in a list of works cited; book with one author

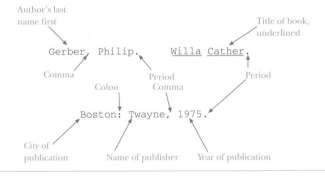

The periods set off three major elements in the entry: the author's name, the title, and the publication data. Note that the MLA style does not include the abbreviation for the state after the city. If the entry requires more than one line, indent the second line and all other lines in the entry five spaces.

Sometimes other facts are required, as in the following example. Note that for ranges of numbers, the MLA system does not repeat the digit for hundreds.

> McCray, Curtis L. "Kaptain Kronkite: The Myth of the Eternal Frame." <u>Television: The Critical View</u>. Ed. Horace Newcomb. 2nd ed. New York: Oxford UP, 1979. 319–33.

McCray is the author of an essay in the second edition of a book edited by Newcomb. Newcomb collected a number of essays and prepared them for publication, hence his designation as editor (Ed.) of the book. The book is in its second edition (2nd ed.), which means that one earlier version exists but that the researcher used the more recent book. Note the short form *Oxford UP* for *Oxford University Press.* Short forms for publisher's names are acceptable.

An anthology The abbreviation *ed.* says that Wolfe is the editor of this collection. If the author is a compiler (of a bibliography, for example) or a translator, use *comp.* or *trans.* after the name.

Wolfe, Don M., ed. <u>American Scene: New Voices</u>. New York: Stuart, 1963.

A book by two or more authors The abbreviation *ed.* here stands for *edition.* An arabic number (with an appropriate suffix to show that the number is ordinal) indicates the edition number. The abbreviation *et al.* is short for the Latin *et alii,* meaning "and others"; when a work has more than three authors, *et al.* replaces the names of all authors but the first. Notice that the name of the first author is the only one that appears last name first.

Morgan, Clifford T., Richard A. King, and Nancy M. Robinson. <u>Introduction to Psychology</u>. 6th ed. New York: McGraw, 1979.

Baugh, Albert C., et al. <u>A Literary History of England</u>. New York: Appleton, 1948.

Van Der Post, Laurens, and Jane Taylor. <u>Testament to the Bushmen</u>. London: Rainbird, 1984.

Two or more books by the same author When you list more than one book by the same author, give the author's name in the first entry only. For each succeeding entry, instead of the author's name type three hyphens and a period, then skip a space and type the title. The hyphens always stand for the author's name exactly as it appears in the entry that comes directly before. (Brooks's name is repeated in the third entry because hyphens would have referred to his name only; he is one of two authors of *Understanding Poetry.*) If the author is an editor, a compiler, or a translator, use a comma after the hyphens and put the correct abbreviation—*ed., comp.,* or *trans.*—before the title. All works listed for the same author appear alphabetically by title.

Brooks, Cleanth. <u>Fundamentals of Good Writing: A Handbook of Modern Rhetoric</u>. New York: Harcourt, 1950.

33d cite

---. <u>The Hidden God: Studies in Hemingway, Faulkner, Yeats,
Eliot, and Warren</u>. New Haven: Yale UP, 1963.
Brooks, Cleanth, and Robert Penn Warren, eds. <u>Understanding
Poetry</u>. 3rd ed. New York: Holt, 1960.
Farrington, Benjamin. <u>Aristotle: Founder of Scientific
Philosophy</u>. New York: Praeger, 1969.
---. <u>The Philosophy of Francis Bacon</u>. Chicago: U of Chicago
P, 1964.

**33d
cite**

A book with corporate authorship A corporate author might be
a commission, committee, or other work by a group whose members aren't
identified on the title page as authors.

Commission on the Humanities. <u>The Humanities in American
Life: Report of the Commission on the Humanities</u>.
Berkeley: U of California P, 1980.

A book with no author's name The citation begins with the title.
In the list of works cited, alphabetize the citation by the first word other
than an article.

<u>Greece: 1974</u>. Athens: National Tourist Organization of
Greece, 1973.

A selection from an anthology Page numbers indicate where the
essay being cited appears in the longer work.

Sewell, Elizabeth. "Bacon, Vico, Coleridge, and the Poetic
Method." <u>Giambattista Vico: An International
Symposium</u>. Ed. Giorgio Tagliacozzo and Hayden V.
White. Baltimore: Johns Hopkins P, 1969. 125-36.

A preface, an introduction, a foreword, or an afterword If you
are citing one of these elements and not the main work, the name of the
writer of the element begins the entry, followed by the name of the element you are citing. Quotation marks or underlining is unnecessary. When
the writer of the element is different from the author of the book, use the
word *By* after the title and cite the author's full name, first name first. If
the writer of the element is the same person who wrote the book, use only
the last name after the word *By*. In the first entry, Gardner wrote the
foreword; Penrose wrote the book. In the second entry, the writer of the
preface is also the author of the book.

Gardner, Martin. Foreword. <u>The Emperor's New Mind</u>. By
    Roger Penrose. New York: Oxford UP, 1989. v-vii.
Fowles, John. Preface. <u>Islands</u>. By Fowles. Boston:
    Little, 1978. 1-2.

A work in more than one volume The first entry says that the work is in four volumes and that the researcher used them all. The second entry says that only the second volume was used.

Browne, Thomas. <u>The Works of Sir Thomas Browne</u>. Ed.
    Geoffrey Keynes. 4 vols. London: Faber, 1928.
Browne, Thomas. <u>The Works of Sir Thomas Browne</u>. Ed.
    Geoffrey Keynes. Vol. 2. London: Faber, 1928. 4 vols.

An edited book Harris prepared this work of Buck's for publication. The entry indicates that citations in the text of the paper are to Buck's writing. If the citations are to the editor (his introductory comments, for example), his name would begin the entry. See the entry for Gardner, above.

Buck, Pearl. <u>China as I See It</u>. Ed. Theodore F. Harris. New
    York: Day, 1970.

A translation If your citations are to the translator's comments, and not to the translation itself, use the translator's name to begin the entry. See the entry for Gardner, above.

Maffei, Paolo. <u>Beyond the Moon</u>. Trans. D. J. K. O'Connell.
    Cambridge: MIT P, 1978.

A publisher's imprint An imprint is the name a publisher sometimes gives to a special group of books to be published under that name. Doubleday, for example, uses the imprint Anchor; Avon uses Camelot; New American Library uses Mentor. When a publisher's imprint appears on the title page, give the imprint name before the publisher's name. Use a hyphen between them.

Lévi-Strauss, Claude. <u>Tristes Tropiques</u>. New York:
    Pocket-Simon, 1977.

A republished book The original edition appeared in 1959; the writer of the paper used the edition republished by Bantam in 1966.

Knowles, John. <u>A Separate Peace</u>. 1959. New York: Bantam,
    1966.

A reference book   Material from a well-known reference work such as the *Encyclopedia Britannica* does not require full publication data, but you should note the year of publication. The title in quotation marks is the entry name.

> "Black Holes." The New Encyclopedia Britannica: Ready
>   Reference. 1992 ed.

For a signed article in an encyclopedia, include the author's name. Sometimes only initials appear after the article; in that case check the list of initials in the index or in some other volume of the encyclopedia to find out the author's full name.

**33d
cite**

> Moore, Norman. "Hodgkin, Thomas, M.D." Dictionary of
>   National Biography. 1908.
> Naylor, John Henry. "Peninsular War." Encyclopedia
>   Britannica: Macropaedia. 1974.

Pamphlets, bulletins, and public documents   For a work issued by a government, the name of the government comes first, then the name of the agency. *GPO* is the Government Printing Office.

> United States. Congressional Budget Office. Proposition
>   13: Its Impact on the Nation's Economy, Federal Reve-
>   nues, and Federal Expenditures. Washington: GPO, 1978.
> National Academy of Sciences. Committee on Water, Division
>   of Earth Sciences. Alternatives in Water Management.
>   National Research Council Publication No. 1408.
>   Washington: National Academy of Sciences, 1969.

A work in a series   Neither underlined nor in quotation marks, the name of the series appears after the title of the book.

> Swimming Medicine IV. International Series on Sports
>   Sciences 6. Baltimore: University Park P, 1978.

Journals, magazines and newspapers

The author's name, the article title, and the publication data are also the main elements in the entry for a journal article. Note that citations include both the title of the article and the title of the journal in which the work appears.

An article in a journal that numbers pages separately in each issue of an annual volume   If each issue in a volume is numbered, include the issue number in the citation. Write the volume number, then

33d cite

Model entry (MLA) in a list of works cited; article in a journal with pages numbered continuously throughout the annual volume

Author's last name first — Comma — Open quotation mark for title of article

Saposnik-Noire, Shelley. "The Silent
— Period

Protagonist: The Unifying Presence of

Landscape in Willa Cather's My
— Close quotation mark

Ántonia." Midwest Quarterly
— Period — Colon — Title of journal, underlined

Volume number —→ 31 (1990): 71-179.
— Year of publication (in parentheses) — Pages on which article appears — Period

a period, then the issue number. If the journal uses only issue numbers, treat them like volume numbers.

> Jewell, Walter. "The Contribution of Administrative
> Leadership to Academic Excellence." WPA: Writing
> Program Administration 3.3 (1980): 9-13.

An article in a monthly or bimonthly magazine   Neither volume number nor issue number is needed. Abbreviate the names of months.

> Rees, Martin J. "Black Holes in Galactic Centers."
> Scientific American Nov. 1990: 56-66.

An article in a weekly or biweekly magazine   Include the full date of publication.

```
Weiss, Rick.  "Snakebite Succor: Researchers Foresee
        Antivenom Improvements."  Science News  8 Dec. 1990:
        360-63.
```

An unsigned article in a magazine   The citation begins with the title and is alphabetized by the first word other than an article.

```
"And Now, Robodoc!"  Time  23 Nov. 1992: 23.
```

33d
cite

An article in a daily newspaper   For the readers' convenience in locating the article, the section designation *a* appears along with the page number. If an edition is named on the masthead, specify the edition (*natl. ed.* or *late ed.*, for example) after the date. Use a comma between the date and the edition. The plus sign (+) indicates that the article continues, but not on consecutive pages.

```
Angier, Natalie.  "Cheetahs Appear Vigorous Despite
        Inbreeding."  New York Times  10 Nov. 1992: C1+.
```

Special works

Unpublished dissertations and theses   These works are not published, so their titles appear in quotation marks.

```
Eisenberg, Nora.  "The Far Side of Language: The Search for
        Expression in the Novels of Virginia Woolf."  Diss.
        Columbia U, 1977.
```

Book reviews   Citations to reviews include the name of the reviewer and the name of the author of the work reviewed, as well as the title of the review and the title of the work reviewed.

```
Kaminer, Wendy.  "The Wrong Men."  Rev. of In Spite of
        Innocence: Erroneous Convictions in Capital Cases, by
        Michael L. Radelet, Hugh Adam Bedau, and Constance E.
        Putnam.  Atlantic  Dec. 1992: 147-50.
```

Material from computer services   The following article, originally published in the *Atlantic,* was retrieved from Dialog, one of the computer services available in some libraries.

05049972 DIALOG File 647: MAGAZINE ASAP *This is the FULL TEXT*

A.E. Housman and Willa Cather. (the authors' meeting in 1902)

Sorel, Nancy Caldwell

Atlantic v259 p83(1) July, 1987

SOURCE FILE: MI File 47

CODEN: ATMOA

ARTICLE TYPE: biography

AVAILABILITY: FULL TEXT Online LINE COUNT: 00031

BIOGRAPHEE: Cather, Willa--biography; Houseman, A.E.--biography

DESCRIPTORS: poets--biography; Novelists--biography

    A. E. HOUSMAN AND WILLA CATHER

    "MANY YEARS AGO when I was very young and foolish" was how Willa
Cather would later begin the story. In fact she was nearing thirty
that summer of 1902, when, in Europe for the first time, she
resolved to call on A. E. Housman. She had been captivated by the
bittersweet ballads of A Shropshire Lad; her own first book of
poems, April Twilights, would come out the following year. In
Housman she saw a kindred spirit. Nature was a malevolent force:
certainly in Nebraska that was so. She made the pilgrimage to
Shrewsbury and Ludlow and gazed with reverence on Housman's hills.
Then, one afternoon in London, her friends Isabelle McClung and
Dorothy Canfield in tow, she boarded a bus to Highgate in the firm
belief that "if one admired a writer very much one had a perfect
right to ring his doorbell."

    What she did not anticipate was that the door at 17 North Road
would be opened by so cordial a landlady, that they would be so
graciously asked inside, and that the poet himself (although
shabbily dressed) would descend the stairs open-armed to greet them.
But, of course, it was all a mistake. Housman was expecting three
Canadian cousins whom he had never met, and he thought--but never
mind. Perhaps they would like to come upstairs?

    Housman's bachelor rooms were as dog-eared as their inhabitant,
who was clearly distressed at facing three strange young ladies (and
three yet to come). Willa and Isabelle opened the conversation with
the trip to Ludlow. No response. Willa moved on to his poetry and
what it meant to her, but from that he visibly retreated. In the

```
    uneasy pause that followed, Housman turned to the silent Dorothy

    (she had neither gone to Ludlow nor read his poetry) and ascertained

    that she was a scholar of pre-classic Latin--his own field! His

    reticence vanished. He became absolutely expansive--but neatly

    deflected every effort to shift the conversation back to poetry.


    On the return bus her friends saw that Willa was crying, a fact she

    never mentioned in later years. By then, she, too, did not suffer

    fans gladly.


              COPYRIGHT The Atlantic Monthly Co. 1987
```

Cite computer service material as you would cite other print materials, but include a reference to the service at the end of your entry. Provide the publication information given by the service as well as the name of the service and the accession (or identifying) numbers within the service.

> Sorel, Nancy Caldwell. "A. E. Housman and Willa Cather."
>   <u>Atlantic</u> July 1987: 83. Dialog file 647, item 05049972.

Recordings   The entry starts with the composer, followed by the title of the work. The major performers appear after the word *with*. *Cond.* is an abbreviation for *Conductor* and *Orch.* is an abbreviation for *Orchestra*. LDR-73002 is the catalog number.

> Verdi, Giuseppe. <u>La Traviata</u>. With Joan Sutherland,
>   Luciano Pavarotti, and Matteo Manuguerra. Cond.
>   Richard Bonynge. National Philharmonic Orch. and
>   London Opera Chorus. London, LDR-73002, 1981.

Performances: plays, concerts, films, television or radio programs, interviews   In the first entry the abbreviation *dir.* is for *director*. The date given is that of the performance cited.

> Saks, Gene, dir. <u>Lost in Yonkers</u>. By Neil Simon. With Lucie
>   Arnaz. Richard Rogers Theater. New York. 27 Nov.
>   1992.
> <u>The Mother</u>. By Paddy Chayevsky. Dir. Delbert Mann. Philco
>   Television Playhouse. NBC, 4 Apr. 1954.
> Coppola, Francis Ford, dir. <u>Bram Stoker's Dracula</u>. With
>   Gary Oldman, Winona Ryder, Anthony Hopkins, and Keanu
>   Reeves. Columbia, 1992.

Rutter, John, cond. New England Symphonic Ensemble.
　　Concert. Carnegie Hall, New York. 29 Nov. 1992.
Sills, Beverly. Telephone interview. 6 Dec. 1981.

Final list of works cited

Your list of works cited, placed at the end of your paper, must include data for all the materials you used. A list that also includes data for materials consulted but not cited is headed "Works Consulted." For a sample of a full "Works Cited" list, see pp. 507–509.

**33d
cite**

✔ **CHECKLIST 33.2: PREPARING A LIST OF WORKS CITED, MLA STYLE**

- Set up your list on a separate page at the end of your paper.
- Type the title ("Works Cited," "Works Consulted," or "Bibliography") about one inch from the top of the page, and double-space before you type the first entry.
- Arrange all your entries alphabetically according to the author's last name, but do not number them. The author's last name goes first, then the first and middle names.
- If several entries are by the same author, give the author's name in the first entry only. For succeeding entries, replace the author's name with three hyphens, followed by a period.
- List all entries without authors alphabetically according to the first word in the title other than an article.
- Do not separate books from periodicals. Strict alphabetical order guides the arrangement of entries. (For advanced research projects, writers sometimes separate primary from secondary sources.)
- Start the first line of each entry at the left margin. Indent succeeding lines five spaces. Double-space within entries and between them.

Model list of works cited, MLA style (excerpt)

Works Cited

Bloom, Edward A., and Lillian D. Bloom. Willa Cather's Gift
　　of Sympathy. Carbondale: Southern Illinois UP, 1962.
Brennan, Joseph X. "Music and Willa Cather." University
　　Review 31 (1965): 257-64.
---. "Willa Cather and Music." University Review 31 (1965):
　　175-83.
"Cather." World Scope Encyclopedia. 1955 ed.
Cather, Willa. On Writing. New York: Knopf, 1949.

■ **Exercise 33.4**   Using the models in 33d, write correct entries for the following sources to be included in a list of works cited. (You may not need all the data that appear in each group.)

1. *Writing in the Arts and Sciences,* a 1981 textbook published by Winthrop Publishers, Inc., in Cambridge, Massachusetts. The authors, in the order in which they appear on the title page, are Elaine Maimon, Gerald L. Belcher, Gail W. Hearn, Barbara F. Nodine, and Finbarr W. O'Connor.

2. An article by Paul Moses called "Debate Over, Bishops Reach Out," in *Newsday,* a Long Island, New York newspaper. The article appeared on Friday, November 20, 1992, on page 5 and continued on page 41.

33e
cite

3. A book by Stewart C. Easton called *Roger Bacon and His Search for a Universal Science,* published by Greenwood Press of Westport, Connecticut, in 1970.

4. In the quarterly journal *American Scholar,* an essay called "A Culture of One's Own" by Quentin Anderson. The article appeared in Autumn 1992, volume 61, on pages 533–551. *American Scholar* is published by Phi Beta Kappa in Washington, D.C. It is paginated continuously throughout an annual volume.

5. Volume 1 of the two-volume edition of *Joseph Conrad: Life and Letters,* edited by G. Jean-Aubry and published in 1927 by Doubleday in Garden City, New York.

■ **Exercise 33.5**   Return to Exercise 31.4 and write a list of works cited, including any five sources.

33e
Using the APA Format

The *Publication Manual of the American Psychological Association* (APA) provides guidelines for writers of research papers in the social sciences and other academic areas. APA addresses its manual to writers aiming at publication in one of the many APA journals. It recommends that students writing papers in APA style follow supplementary guidelines established by their colleges. If you are told to use the APA *Publication Manual,* check with your instructor for further directions. For example, APA manuscripts submitted for publication require an **abstract,** which is a short, comprehensive summary of the paper. Yet at the instructor's request, many undergraduate papers written in the APA format use an outline instead of an abstract.

Like the MLA, the APA recommends short references documented within the text and a complete list of sources, called **references,** at the end of the paper. The APA parenthetical citation includes the author's last name and the year of publication. In general, page numbers are included only for direct quotations, not paraphrases or summaries.

Using Parenthetical References in the Text

33e
cite

Model internal documentation; APA format

Periodic emission of radiation from black holes suggests gravitational collapse is not as final as once believed (Hawking, 1988).

Author's name — Comma — Date of publication — Period

Here are some other examples.

Hawking (1988) interprets periodic emission of radiation from black holes as an indication that gravitational collapse is not as final as once believed.

In 1988 Hawking wrote that gravitational collapse may not be as final as previously believed.

Multiple publications in one year

If an author has published more than one work in a single year, these works will appear alphabetically by title in the reference list. For the first work, place an *a* after the year; for the second, place a *b*, and so on. T. G. R. Bower, for example, published two books in 1977, *The Perceptual World of the Child* and *A Primer of Infant Development.* In alphabetical order by title, they are labeled 1977a and 1977b. In the reference below, the writer of the paper calls attention only to *A Primer of Infant Development.*

Bower (1977b) discusses the stages of a child's development.

Multiple authors

The following examples show how to cite references with multiple authors. In the APA system, if a source has five authors or fewer, cite them all in the first reference. Use an ampersand for *and.* For two authors only, name them both each time you cite their material. For more than two but fewer than six, subsequent references use *et al.* after the first author's name. (As explained earlier, the abbreviation *et al.* is for the Latin phrase *et alii*, meaning "and others." Do not underline the abbreviation. Do not use a period after *et*; do use a period after *al.*) If your source has six authors or more, use *et al.* after the first name each time you cite the work. Use the date in each case.

> Some psychologists see suicide attempts as a gamble (Lester & Lester, 1971).
>
> An important study connects birth order and a child's need to conform (Becker, Lerner, & Carroll, 1966).
>
> Conformity also relates to group pressure (Becker et al., 1966).

33e cite

Works with no author listed

When the author is unnamed, cite in the text the first few words of the entry that appears in the reference list. Use quotation marks around the title of a chapter or article, and underline the title of a book or periodical. Include the year. Note that the title of an article in the list of references will not appear in quotation marks.

> Women over fifty who are widowed about twelve years report satisfaction and optimism in their lives ("Time Improves," 1992).
>
> In preparing text for publication writers should sketch technical drawings with precision and with symbols clear and consistent with the text (McGraw-Hill Author's Book, 1984).

Page citations

If you want to cite a specific part of your source, put the page number(s) you've taken your information from after the date. Use *p.* and *pp.* as the abbreviations. For ranges of numbers, repeat all digits.

> A six-year-old child who could not speak, Isabelle was "apparently unaware of relationships of any kind" (Mason, 1942, p. 299).

Preparing a List of References

At the end of your paper, beginning on a separate page headed "References," list the sources you cited. Arrange entries alphabetically by author's last name. If two or more works are by the same author, arrange them chronologically by year of publication. If an author has published two or more works in the same year, arrange them alphabetically by title, disregarding articles, and label them *a*, *b*, and so on, following the year.

Books and reference works

Model entry (APA) in a reference list, book with one author

33e
cite

The periods set off four major elements in the entry: the author's name, the year of publication, the title, and other publication data. Notice that only the first word of the title is capitalized. Proper nouns and the first word of the subtitle, if any, are capitalized too. If the city of publication is not well known or could be confused with another location, give the state or country. For states, use postal abbreviations, not traditional abbreviations. Do not abbreviate *University* in a publisher's name, but give as brief a form of a publisher's name as is intelligible.

A book by two or more authors or editors   All authors' or editors' names appear last name first, with commas separating them. Notice that an ampersand is used instead of the word *and*. The abbreviation *Eds.*, in parentheses, says that Lewis and Rosenblum are the editors of this collection.

> Lester, G., & Lester, D. (1971). Suicide: The gamble with death. Englewood Cliffs, NJ: Prentice-Hall.
> Lewis, M., & Rosenblum, L. A. (Eds.). (1974). The effect of the infant on its caregiver. New York: Wiley.

Journals, magazines, newspapers

The author's name, the year of publication, the article title, and other publication date are also the main elements in the entry for a journal

Model entry (APA) in a reference list, article in a journal with pages numbered continuously throughout an annual volume

Author's last name and initial or initials

Year of publication in parentheses

Title of article

Dervin, D. (1992). Feminizing Freud: A psychohistorical

Periods

perspective on four pioneering women analysts. Journal

Commas

of Psychohistory, 19, 479-491. ← Period

Title of journal, underlined   Volume number, underlined   Pages on which article appears

33e cite

article. Note that citations include both the title of the article and the title of the journal in which the work appears. For the title of the article, only the first word, proper nouns, and the first word of the subtitle, if any, are capitalized. For journal titles, all words except articles, conjunctions, and prepositions of less than four letters are capitalized. Article titles appear without quotation marks. Journal titles are underlined. For page numbers, all digits are repeated.

An article in a journal that numbers pages separately in each issue of an annual volume   If each issue in a volume is numbered, include the issue number in the citation. The number 23 after the title is the volume number. The number 3 in parentheses after the volume indicates the issue number.

> Labouvie-Vief, G. (1980). Beyond formal operations: Uses and limits of pure logic in life-span development. Human Development, 23(3), 141-161.

An article in a monthly or bimonthly magazine or daily newspaper   A comma separates the year of publication from the month. Use *pp.* to abbreviate *pages* only for magazine and newspaper entries, not for journals. Do not abbreviate months.

> Shepard, Nathaniel, Jr. (1981, October 11). Strong gun law sought in Chicago. New York Times, p. 38.
>
> Wang, P. (1992, December). Put your money worries behind you. Money, pp. 76-87.

An article with no author's name   The citation begins with the title. In the reference list, alphabetize the citation by the first important word in the title. The reference in the text will be a short version of the title and will appear in quotation marks.

> Time improves lives of older widows.   (1992–1993, December–
>   January).   <u>Modern Maturity</u>, p. 8.

Final reference list

The reference list names all sources cited in the text. The list is alphabetical by author, with the exceptions noted above. It begins on a separate page headed "References."

✔ CHECKLIST 33.3: PREPARING A REFERENCE LIST, APA STYLE

- Set up your list on a separate page at the end of your paper.
- Type the title "References" about one inch from the top of the page, and double space before you type the first entry.
- Arrange all entries in alphabetical order according to author's last name. Do not number entries. Do not separate books from periodicals.
- If any authors appear more than once, arrange their entries chronologically, from earliest to latest.
- If any authors have published more than one work in a year, place them alphabetically by title and label them *a, b, c,* and so forth, after the year.
- List entries without authors alphabetically according to the first important word in the title.
- Type the first line of each entry flush with the left margin. Indent three spaces all other lines within each entry. Double-space within entries and between them.

Model APA reference list, APA style (excerpt)

References

Hawking, S. W.   (1988).   <u>A brief history of time</u>.   New York:
      Bantam.

Lane, E. (1992, November 20). Black hole snapshot:
   Scientists think that's what Hubble photo may be.
   <u>Newsday</u>, p. 7.
Wald, R. M. (1992). <u>Space, time, and gravity: The theory of
   the big bang and black holes</u>. (2nd ed.). Chicago:
   University of Chicago Press.

■ **Exercise 33.6**   Return to Exercise 33.3. Revise your parenthetical documentation according to the APA format, and prepare a reference list for the three sources.

**33f
cite**

■ **Exercise 33.7**   Return to Exercise 31.4. Select any five entries and prepare a reference list according to the APA format.

33f
Comparing the MLA and APA Citation Systems

The MLA and APA systems are the most frequently used research documentation systems in the college curriculum. You should be able to shift from one to the other with a minimum of difficulty as your instructors explain their research paper requirements. You will use the MLA system for courses in humanities, literature, history, religion, communications, and education, among others. Courses in the social sciences—psychology, sociology, political science, economics, statistics, for example—may require the APA system, as may research projects in sciences like biology, chemistry, physics, and geology.

To help you use both systems more easily, we provide on facing pages two text excerpts that are exactly the same. The text and references come from the student paper on black holes. One uses the MLA citation system, and the other uses the APA citation system. Marginal comments indicate important features of each system. In addition, you will find two excerpts from the listed references used in the black holes paper; one excerpt is in MLA style and the other, using the same books and periodicals, is in the APA style. A complete version of the black holes paper in APA style appears in Chapter 34.

MLA Style

If a star's mass is low enough, the star can support itself against gravitational collapse. If not, the gravity continues to shrink the area, which makes the nuclear fuel burn faster and faster. As the fuel becomes exhausted, the star grows colder while the density increases. Jastrow explains what happens next:

> At that point, the mass is so compact that the force of gravity at the surface is billions of times stronger than the force of the sun. The tug of that enormous force prevents the rays of light from leaving the surface of the star. (65)

Without the fuel to maintain equilibrium, the star eventually becomes infinitely dense: a black hole!

While gravitational collapse takes place, other strange things happen. As the gravity becomes proportionally more massive, information from the star takes longer and longer to emerge. In a normal star like the sun, light waves are bent by the strong gravitational field. But in a black hole, the gravity is extremely strong; "light cones are bent inward so much that light can no longer escape" (Hawking 87).

This means that as a star collapses it eventually becomes invisible. Worse yet, the dimensions of the star shrink until it becomes a hole not only in space . . . .

Margin notes:

Source named in text; no date required

Quotation of four lines or more set up as block quotation and indented ten spaces

Specific page citation in parentheses; no abbreviation for *page*

Parenthetical citation: author's name and page number without punctuation

---

Works Cited

Dupree, Andrea K., and Lee Hartman. "Hunting for Black Holes."
    Natural History Oct. 1979: 30-37.
Hawking, Stephen W. A Brief History of Time. New York: Bantam
    Books, 1988.

APA Style

If a star's mass is low enough, the star can support itself against gravitational collapse. If not, the gravity continues to shrink the area, which makes the nuclear fuel burn faster and faster. As the fuel becomes exhausted, the star grows colder while the density increases. Jastrow (1979) explains what happens next:

> At that point, the mass is so compact that the force of gravity at the surface is billions of times stronger than the force of the sun. The tug of that enormous force prevents the rays of light from leaving the surface of the star. (p. 65)

Without the fuel to maintain equilibrium, the star eventually becomes infinitely dense: a black hole!

While gravitational collapse takes place, other strange things happen. As the gravity becomes proportionally more massive, information from the star takes longer and longer to emerge. In a normal star like the sun, light waves are bent by the strong gravitational field. But in a black hole, the gravity is extremely strong; "light cones are bent inward so much that light can no longer escape" (Hawking, 1988, p. 87).

This means that as a star collapses it eventually becomes invisible. Worse yet, the dimensions of the star shrink until it becomes a hole not only in space . . . .

Margin notes (left):
Source named in text; date of publication in parentheses

Quotation of forty words or more indented five spaces

Parenthetical citation: author's name, date, and page number separated by commas

Margin notes (right):
Specific page citation—with abbreviation *p.* for "page"—in parentheses

References

Dupree, A. K., & Hartman, L. (1979, October). Hunting for black
     holes. Natural History, pp. 30-37.
Hawking, S. W. (1988). A brief history of time. New York: Bantam.
Jastrow, R. (1979). Red giants and white dwarfs. New York: Warner.

MLA STYLE HIGHLIGHTS

Form

- Title (Works Cited) centered; no quotation marks, no underlining
- Double space throughout
- Second line of continuing entry indented five spaces
- Periods separate three main elements: author's name, title, publication data. Period completes entire entry.

**33f
cite**

Elements of Entries

Author. Last name and full first name for authors up to three; for more than three authors, name the first, followed by *et al.* First author listed with last name first, second and third authors listed first name, then last; *and* connects names of final two authors.

Title. Title follows author's name. Titles of articles and chapters are in quotation marks; first letter of all major words is capitalized. Book and periodical titles are underlined; first letter of all major words is capitalized. Book titles are followed by a period, but no mark of punctuation follows a journal title.

Publication data. For books, city of publication, colon, publisher's name (shortened or with appropriate abbreviations), comma, year of publication. For journals with continuous pagination, volume number, year in parentheses, colon, inclusive page numbers. For monthly periodicals, month (abbreviated except May, June, July) and year, colon, inclusive page numbers. For weeklies and dailies, day, month, year, colon, inclusive page numbers. Do not use *p.* or *pp.* Do not repeat digits for hundreds.

APA STYLE HIGHLIGHTS

Form

- Title (References) centered; no quotation marks, no underlining
- Double space throughout
- Second line of continuing entry indented three spaces
- Periods separate four main elements: author's name, year of publication, title, other publication data. Period completes entire entry.

Elements of Entries

Author. Last name first and initials for all authors up through five; for six or more authors, name the first, followed by *et al.* An ampersand (&) connects names of final two authors.

Date. Date, in parentheses, follows author's name. Books require year of copyright. For monthly magazines, year, comma, month. For daily newspapers and weekly and biweekly magazines, year, comma, month, day. Do not abbreviate month.

Title. Title follows date. Book titles are underlined and in lowercase letters, except for first word of title, first word of subtitle (generally after a colon in the title), and proper nouns. Titles of articles and chapters are not underlined or enclosed in quotation marks and follow same guidelines as books for uppercase and lowercase letters. Titles of periodicals are underlined; first letter of all major words is capitalized.

Publication data. For books, city of publication, colon, brief form of publisher's name (but do not abbreviate *university*). For journals with continuous pagination, comma follows journal title, then volume number underlined, comma, inclusive page numbers (no *p.* or *pp.*). For monthly, weekly, daily periodicals, comma follows periodical title, then *p.* (page) or *pp.* (pages), inclusive page numbers. Repeat all digits in ranges.

**33g
cite**

33g
Using Other Systems of Parenthetical References

Your instructor may recommend the number reference system or a full publication data system for citing sources in your paper.

Using the Number System

The number system requires an arabic number for each entry in the list of works cited; these numbers appear in the parenthetical citation, too. A comma separates the number of the entry from the relevant page number, and the entry number is often underlined, as you see below. With such a system, references included in the list of works cited may be arranged in any useful order, such as the order in which the writer cites the references in the text.

> Hawking is essentially the creator of this definition of
> black holes (2, 112).

Giving Full Publication Data in Parenthetical References

If you are required to give full parenthetical citation, use square brackets to replace the parentheses you would ordinarily use around city, publisher, and date. Full publication information in parenthetical references is rare; it distracts readers from the text and does not provide for a list of works cited, which readers always find useful. Occasionally, however, you will see this system in a bibliographic study or in a work that cites only a few references.

> Hawking interprets periodic emission of radiation from black holes as an indication that gravitational collapse is not as final as once believed (<u>A Brief History of Time</u> [New York: Bantam, 1988] 112).

33h
Using Footnotes or Endnotes

Although internal citation is now much preferred as a system of documentation, many researchers in the past used a system of numbered notes to document their sources accurately. In such a system, notes provide full publishing information.

Footnotes appear at page bottoms, numbered consecutively throughout the paper. **Endnotes** are numbered consecutively at the end of a work. As you do research in older texts, you no doubt will come across footnotes and endnotes.

Below you will find a model footnote entry for a book and a journal article. The entries correspond to the models provided in 33d and are based on the MLA system. In footnotes and endnotes, a comma separates the author's name from the title. Parentheses set off the publication data from the rest of the reference, and, as in bibliographic entries, you can always use the short form of the publisher's name. A period completes the entry. Raised a half space above the line, the number of each note comes after a five-space indentation. Continuing lines of each note are flush with the left margin.

Model footnote or endnote, book with one author

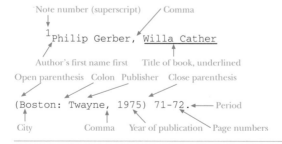

Model footnote or endnote entry, article in a journal with pages numbered continuously throughout an annual volume

33h cite

Later References to the Same Source

With full publication data in a previous note, writers use a shortened form of citation in each later reference to the source. Generally, these references include only the author's last name and the page number. Although the *MLA Handbook* discourages the use of the Latin abbreviation *ibid.* (for *ibidem,* meaning "in the same place"), the form persists in academic writing. *Ibid.* indicates that the citation appears in exactly the same source as in the preceding note. Capitalize *ibid.* as the first word of the sentence in the note, but do not underline it, and always use a period after the abbreviation. The samples below of first and later citations show both styles.

¹Bernard Baum, "Willa Cather's Waste Land," <u>South Atlantic Quarterly</u> 48 (1949): 590.

²Philip Gerber, <u>Willa Cather</u> (Boston: Twayne, 1975) 71-72.

³Baum 593.

⁴Baum.

⁵Gerber 72.

~~~~~~

¹Bernard Baum, "Willa Cather's Waste Land," <u>South Atlantic Quarterly</u> 48 (1949): 590.

²Ibid. 592.

³Philip Gerber, <u>Willa Cather</u> (Boston: Twayne, 1975) 72.

⁴Ibid.

⁵Baum 592.

Abbreviations

The Modern Language Association recommends that writers avoid using some Latin abbreviations that at one time were standard in research papers. You will encounter these abbreviations in your reading, however, and you should know what they mean. The following list includes familiar abbreviations for bibliographical citations, along with some of the short forms of Latin terms you may encounter.

33h
cite

anon.	anonymous	n., nn.	note(s), as in *p. 24, n. 2* or *p. 24n*
bk., bks.	book(s)		
c., ca.	circa (about), used with approximate dates	n.d.	no date (of publication)
		no., nos.	number(s)
		n.p.	no place (of publication) or no publisher
cf.	*confere* (compare)		
ch., chs., chaps.	chapter(s)		
col., cols.	column(s)	n. pag.	no pagination
comp.	compiler, compiled by	op. cit.	*opere citato* (in the work cited)
cond.	conductor	orch.	orchestra
dir.	director	p., pp.	page(s)
diss.	dissertation	passim	throughout
ed., eds.	edition(s) or editor(s)	pt., pts.	part(s)
		qtd.	quoted
et al.	*et alii* (and others)	q.v.	*quod vide* (which see)
ff.	and the following pages, as in *pp. 85ff.*	rev.	revision, revised, revised by; or review, reviewed by
ibid.	*ibidem* (in the same place)	rpt.	reprint, reprinted
illus.	illustrated by, illustrator, illustration(s)	sc.	scene
		sec., secs.	section(s)
		st.	stanza
l., ll.	line(s)	trans.	translator, translated by, translation
loc. cit.	*loco citato* (in the place cited)	univ.	university
ms, mss	manuscript(s)	vol., vols.	volume(s)

CHAPTER

34

DEVELOPING, WRITING, AND REVISING A RESEARCH PAPER

By this time you are almost ready to begin writing. You have investigated sources and taken careful notes. You can see relations between ideas. You note contradictions and differences of opinion. Your ideas form and re-form; your tentative thesis develops; you read further to explore a point you missed or to check on a point you're not sure of.

You need to think carefully about your thesis now. Your reading and other research should focus your thoughts and allow you to state your point clearly and accurately. You may find that a formal outline helps you organize your paper. A formal outline provides an orderly visual scheme of the paragraphs with main and subordinated points clearly related. From your outline you can write first and subsequent drafts. You will need to revise your research paper several times, paying attention to all the special details of documentation as well as to the general concerns of manuscript preparation. The research papers included in this chapter are models.

34a
Revising the Thesis

After studying your rough plan, your tentative thesis, and your notes (which you now have in order), reevaluate your thesis. Here are the tentative theses for the papers on Cather and on black holes. Notice how the writers of these papers continue to refine their theses.

	Literature	**Astronomy**
Tentative thesis	In Cather's stories, characters isolated from familiar surroundings are severely affected physically and spiritually.	Black holes are almost impossible to find, despite astronomers' predictions.
	↓	↓

**34a
rev**

	Literature	**Astronomy**
Revised thesis	Cather's " 'A Death in the Desert' " and "A Wagner Matinee" show people who are isolated from familiar environments.	Astronomers are finding it very difficult to discover and investigate black holes.
	↓	↓
A second revised thesis	The central characters in Cather's " 'A Death in the Desert' " and "A Wagner Matinee" show the effects of an untamed country on people from a stable, civilized world.	As new ideas evolved about the universe, scientists tried to confirm the existence of black holes, which in the past were only theoretical possibilities.
	↓	↓
Final copy	In two particular stories, " 'A Death in the Desert' " and "A Wagner Matinee," the central characters bear the burden of escape and isolation from familiar, stable traditions in a "new country."	But because black holes are impossible by definition to detect directly, the search to confirm their existence is an outstanding instance of theoretical and practical science working together.

■ **Exercise 34.1** Examine the development of topics to thesis statements for the papers on Cather and on black holes (pp. 425–427, 475–476). Comment on the evolution of the theses. What was each writer's original idea? How did it change? How does the final copy reflect the concerns of the writer's early thinking?

34a
rev

■ **Exercise 34.2*** Study your notes, and revise your thesis.

34b
Writing a Formal Outline

Your instructor may require a formal outline, or you may find an outline useful in your efforts to refine your plan. A formal outline gives you an orderly visual scheme of your ideas. As you set down these ideas, use roman numerals for the most important points, capital letters for the next most important points, arabic numbers for supporting points under lettered points, and lowercase letters for the smallest items you include in the outline. Further subordination is possible, but you will rarely need to use as many as four levels. For most papers, two or three levels of subordination will do. The scheme is shown on page 478.

Once you have grouped large, related ideas in your notes, label them with accurate, mutually exclusive, logically arranged headings. Follow your rough plan, but concentrate on making headings sufficient in number and breadth to cover the topic properly.

As you look over these headings, you may see a need for some changes in organization. Make whatever changes you need to shape your ideas, and then fill in supporting information under each major heading. Watch for and delete any overlap or repetition of ideas. Watch for proper sequence of ideas.

All outlines follow the same format, but you can write them as topic outlines or sentence outlines. In a **topic outline,** you write out points as brief capsules of meaning. Each item must communicate an idea, of course, but the items need not be full sentences. In a **sentence outline,**

34b

rev

Roman numerals for major headings.

I. Period _____

Uppercase letters for first-degree subheadings.

A. Period _____
B. _____

Arabic numbers for second-degree subheadings.

1. Period _____
2. _____
3. _____

Lowercase letters for third-degree subheadings.

a. Period _____
b. _____

Uppercase letter for next first-degree subheading.

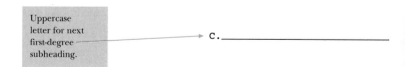

C. _____

Roman numerals again.

II. _____

each point appears as a complete grammatical statement, with a subject and a predicate. The sentence outline requires more effort: it asks you to name what you are going to talk about and also to indicate what you are going to say about it. For this reason, a sentence outline may be more productive, but a topic outline can be just as helpful if you think it through just as carefully.

Two rules govern the construction of every formal outline:

34b

rev

1. Every entry requiring division must be divided into at least two parts. When you divide a topic, you must have two or more subheadings under it. If you can come up with only one subpart, incorporate it into the main heading; it belongs there. In short, a *I* requires a *II*; an *A* requires a *B*; a *1* requires a *2*; an *a* requires a *b*.
2. Main headings must be parallel in form, and subheadings under each main heading must be parallel in form.

For the paper on black holes, the student prepared the topic outline on pages 511–512. The sentence outline on pages 486–487 shows you the skeleton of the Cather paper on pages 489–503. Study the outlines carefully and use them as models for form and style.

The rules will help you to construct a clear and useful outline. But remember that you should never be bound to your outline as you write. Feel free to use the ideas that come to all writers, ideas they did not have when they planned their work. In fact, you may prepare the formal outline *after* you write the paper. Every essay that has a logic and structure can be outlined; so you should be able to outline your essay once you have completed it. Then the outline will help you check that you have constructed a logical and clear piece of prose, that you have put everything in its proper place, and that you have developed a thesis in a thoughtful and well-written series of paragraphs leading to a conclusion.

■ **Exercise 34.3**   Discuss the strengths and weaknesses in the following outline. Look especially at the relation of the thesis to the points in the outline; look at the main headings and subordinate points; look at the form of the outline, including divisions and the use of numbers and letters. Which points are clear? Which points are not?

Outline

Thesis: A study of liberal arts and sciences is valuable for
students seeking careers in business.

  I. Exclusion of liberal arts and science courses from
business curricula

    A. Need for specialized business courses for job
training

  II. An understanding of people

    A. Value of psychology and sociology

      1. In a study of personality and group dynamics

    B. Value of natural sciences in seeing problems and in
stating and in finding solutions to them

    C. Insights into human character from literature

      1. Complete personality studies from fiction

      2. Opportunities to share thoughts of pressured
characters

  III. Recognition by businesses today of capabilities
developing from employees' varied educational
backgrounds

    A. Strong qualities of character

    B. Ability to deal with future technologies

  IV. Transmission of humanity's cherished values

■ **Exercise 34.4** Examine the outline of the papers on Cather
(pages 486–487) and on black holes (pages 511–512). How do the outlines
reflect the correct format for formal outlining?

■ **Exercise 34.5*** As your instructor directs, prepare a formal outline for your research paper. Use a *topic* or a *sentence* outline according to
your instructor's wishes.

34c
Writing the First Draft

Using your rough plan, your formal outline, and your note cards, write a rough draft of your research paper. This is not final copy, and the point is not to say everything perfectly but simply to flesh out what you have to say. Once you have paragraphs drafted, use them to adjust and refine the rough plan or your formal outline.

At this stage you will have a rough draft but a nearly final outline. Your outline should now be a guide to the next draft, although as new ideas come to you in the process of creating that draft, you may need to refine the outline further. Throughout the writing process, the outline enables you to check the logic of your progress from one point to the next. The outline also helps you check the accuracy and the consistency of your argument and the balance among sections.

As you write your draft, you will be drawing on your note cards. Review 33a, on integrating source material into your own writing. Be sure to acknowledge all sources, using the citation and documentation system your instructor requires. Use the checklist below as a guide.

34c
rev

✔ CHECKLIST 34.1: REVISING A RESEARCH PAPER

Revising is quality control. It may be the most important step you take in turning a good paper into a great one. For a full array of issues to consider as you revise, see Checklist 2.2. Here are some questions to ask yourself about a research paper.

- Is my thesis clear? Does it state accurately the intent of the paper?
- Have I done more than simply summarize other sources? Have I made appropriate commentary on source materials?
- Do my source materials—quotations, summaries, paraphrases—support my points throughout?
- Do my ideas follow logically? Are transitions clear?
- Are all sources clear? Have I always indicated my source of ideas even when paraphrasing or summarizing? Are citations unobtrusive and correctly written?
- Are sources listed with full publication data on a separate page at the end of my paper?

34d
Editing the First Draft and Preparing the Final Version

Take the time to polish your prose, also checking carefully for clarity of language and ideas and for conciseness; also check paragraph and sentence structure, grammar, spelling, and mechanics. (Use relevant checklists in Chapters 4–30.) Check the accuracy of quotations, summaries, and paraphrases. Avoid plagiarism by citing sources clearly and consistently (see 33d, 33e, 33f, and 33g). Most instructors ask that you type long papers, and you should follow the guidelines for manuscript preparation carefully (see Checklist 2.3). Handwritten research papers are hard to produce neatly because of their length, and they are difficult to read. If, with your instructor's permission, you choose to write your final copy in longhand, take special pains to produce a neat, clear manuscript.

Number all pages consecutively in the upper right corner, starting with page 1 of the text. Some writers type their last name before the page number in case pages are misplaced. APA style recommends a short form of the title instead of the author's last name. Do not use a period, hyphen, or the word *page* (or the abbreviation *p.*) with the page number. Remember that endnotes and the list of works cited count in the total pagination of your paper. Do not paginate the title page or cover sheet. The outline is paginated with lowercase roman numerals (i, ii, iii).

✔ **CHECKLIST 34.2:** ASSEMBLING THE FINAL COPY OF A RESEARCH PAPER

As you get ready to submit your research paper, make one final check that all the elements are in order. Final copy for a research paper or a term paper usually includes, in this order:

■ Title page. The *MLA Handbook* suggests that the author's name, the class, the date, and so on appear on the first page of the paper, an inch down from the top and an inch from the right. The title is centered, four spaces above the text of the paper. But when formal outlines are required, many instructors prefer a title page. (Sample title pages appear on pp. 485 and 510.) APA recommends a title page.

- Formal outline or abstract.
- The body of the essay.
- Endnotes. If you use parenthetical documentation, endnotes or foot-notes will be minimal. If your instructor requires footnotes, place them at the bottom of pages. In APA style endnotes follow the list of references.
- List of works cited (MLA) or references (APA).

**34e
rev**

34e
Examining Sample Research Papers

The research papers that follow illustrate many of the suggestions made in this chapter. The paper on Willa Cather uses the MLA system of citing sources in the text. Facing page annotations explain essential features of this paper in the MLA format. The paper on black holes uses the APA citation format. Here we provide annotations in the margin in order to point out key elements of an APA style paper. Examine the papers and the explanatory comments, and use them as models whenever you en-counter problems in setting up research papers of your own.

■ **Exercise 34.6***   After reading the sample papers and following the guidelines in 34c, prepare the final copy of your research paper. Observe your instructor's specific requirements.

34e
rev

(t-a) Title: one-third down, centered and double-spaced

(t-b) Cather used double quotation marks around the title of the story to show her debt to Robert Browning's poem "A Death in the Desert," which gave Cather her title. The title of the story, then, is written as a quote within a quote.

(t-c) Leave two inches before typing the next line.

(t-d) The writer's name, the instructor's name, the course and section number, and the date the paper is submitted, all centered and double-spaced.

(t-a)

Isolation and Escape

in

(t-b)

Cather's " 'A Death in the Desert' "

and

"A Wagner Matinee"

(t-c)

by

(t-d)

Shirley Hawkins

Mr. C. Prager

English 101, Section 4

April 7, 1990

i

Thesis: The central characters in Willa Cather's stories " 'A Death
in the Desert' " and "A Wagner Matinee" show the effects of an
untamed country on people from a stable, civilized world.

I. The main characters show the physical burden of living in the
barren West.

   A. In " 'A Death in the Desert' " Katharine Gaylord, self-
isolated in the Cheyenne of her youth, is dying of
tuberculosis.

   B. In "A Wagner Matinee" Aunt Georgiana is a wreck after thirty
years on the Nebraska frontier.

II. The characters are also burdened by the toll on their spirits.

   A. Wyoming is for Katharine a spiritual desert.

      1. She misses her former life as a famous singer.

      2. The emptiness of the desert intrudes on the room she
modeled after music studios in the East.

      3. She will never return to art.

      4. Her death separates her from art no more surely than did
her life.

   B. Georgiana's spirit also suffers the deprivations of frontier
life.

      1. In a world of worries about survival she had little
opportunity to enjoy the music she has loved so much.

      2. When she returns to Boston, the prairie world is always
painfully close.

III. Cather uses music to identify the pain of separation from
civilization and life in a primitive setting.

ii

A. For Katharine Gaylord music symbolizes the swift passage of her own life.

    1. Both life and artistic achievement are too brief.

    2. In a new sonata she recognizes her own personal tragedy of isolation from music.

B. The music Aunt Georgiana hears echoes her particular condition.

    1. The overture to <u>Tannhäuser</u> reflects her own struggle between art and the frontier.

    2. Other selections echo the opposing forces in her life.

IV. Cather acknowledged that the theme of escape ran through her work.

(1-a) The writer's last name and the page number appear near the top of all pages; outline is paginated in roman numerals, and text is page 1; margins are 1 to $1^1/_2$ inches.

(1-b) Title is centered two inches from the top of the page.

34e
rev

(1-c) *qtd. in Woodress:* the source of the quotation from Fisher is *Willa Cather* by James Woodress (listed among works cited, p. 10 of the essay). As Fisher's original article was not available, the writer used a secondary source.

(1-d) *Gerber, preface:* the quotation appears in the preface, which is unpaginated in Gerber's book (listed among works cited, on p. 10 of the essay).

(1-e) The thesis clearly states the topic. The introduction builds to the thesis. Here is an earlier draft of the student's introduction:

Dorothy Canfield Fisher was a friend of Willa Cather's from college days at the University of Nebraska. She wrote an essay on Cather's works for the New York *Herald Tribune* in 1933. She said: "The one real subject of all her books is the effect a new country—our new country—has on the people transplanted to it from the traditions of a stable, complex civilization" (qtd. in Woodress 247). Fisher was answering complaints by critics about disconnectedness in Cather's novels. But even in Cather's short stories, you can see that Fisher is right. The central characters in the stories generally are hurt by their escape from familiar places to a new one.

(1-f) The words *character* and *story* and the repeated reference to separation connect the paragraphs. The first sentence of this paragraph corresponds to the major heading I in the outline. The rest of this paragraph and the next develop subhead I.A in the outline.

(1-g) The summary gives only essential details to help readers who may not know the story.

(1-a)

Hawkins 1

(1-b)

Isolation and Escape in

Cather's " 'A Death in the Desert' "

and "A Wagner Matinee"

In a 1933 essay for the New York <u>Herald Tribune</u> Dorothy
Canfield Fisher wrote about her friend from college days at the
University of Nebraska. "I offer you a hypothesis about Willa
Cather's work: the one real subject of all her books is the effect a
new country--our new country--has on the people transplanted to it
from the traditions of a stable, complex civilization" (qtd. in

(1-c) Woodress 247). Fisher was addressing complaints by contemporary
critics who saw disconnectedness in Cather's writing, and Fisher
wanted to show that novels like <u>A Lost Lady</u> and <u>Shadows on the Rock</u>

(1-d) had a common bond (Gerber, preface). But even in Cather's first
collection of short stories, <u>The Troll Garden</u>, published in 1905,

(1-e) readers can see that Fisher's comment is valid. In two particular
stories, " 'A Death in the Desert' " and "A Wagner Matinee," the
central characters bear the burden of escape and isolation from
familiar, stable traditions in a "new country."

(1-f)   The physical appearance of the main character in each story
shows the strain of the separation she lived through. When we first
see her in " 'A Death in the Desert,' " Katharine Gaylord, a former

(1-g) singer, is dying of lung disease in Cheyenne, Wyoming, the home of
her youth. In the past she had lived in New York and Chicago and had

34e

rev

(2-a) The quotation blends with the writer's own prose. The parenthetical citation indicates that the quoted words appear on page 72 of the collection *The Troll Garden,* abbreviated here as *TG.* The title is required along with Cather's name because the list of works cited contains other works by Cather.

(2-b) The writer has paraphrased from the words Katharine Gaylord speaks in the story. Here is the original source:

Formerly, when it was not *if* I should ever sing Brunnhilde, but quite simply when I *should* sing Brunnhilde, I was always starving myself and thinking what I might drink and what I might not. But broken music boxes may drink whatsoever they list, and no one cares whether they lose their figure.

(2-c) The writer interprets the quotations she has presented.

(2-d) Corresponding to subhead I.B of the outline, this paragraph briefly summarizes important plot elements in "A Wagner Matinee." Note the smooth integration of a quotation from the story in the opening sentence.

(2-e) The page number alone is enough in parentheses here. Readers know that the discussion is still about "A Wagner Matinee."

(2-f) The superscript 1 corresponds to endnote 1 on page 9 of the essay.

traveled throughout Europe with the brilliant yet selfish composer
Adriance Hilgarde, a man she loved deeply without his knowing it.

Now Everett Hilgarde, Adriance's brother and an almost exact
look-alike for the famous musician, observes Katharine, who is being
destroyed by her long illness. Her loose-fitting gown could not

(2-a)

hide "the sharp outlines of her emaciated body, but the stamp of her
disease was there; simple and ugly and obtrusive, a pitiless fact
that could not be disguised or evaded" (Cather, TG 72). She has
stooped shoulders; she sways unevenly when she walks; and her face
is "older, sadder, softer" (72) than when Everett saw her a long time

(2-b)

ago. Self-exiled in the Gaylords' house, Katharine refers to

(2-c)

herself as a broken music box (81). Her physical decay reflects her
separation from the lively world of art she once knew.

(2-d)

In "A Wagner Matinee" Aunt Georgiana, a former music teacher at
The Boston Conservatory, returns to Boston--"the place longed for
hungrily half a lifetime" (Cather, TG 110). For thirty years she
had tended a ranch on the desolate Nebraska frontier. Her nephew
Clark, who spent some of his boyhood years on the farm with her and

(2-e)

his uncle Howard, notes her "misshapen figure" (108), her "soiled
linen duster," and her stooped shoulders "now almost bent together
over her sunken chest. . . . She wore ill-fitting false teeth, and
her skin was as yellow as a Mongolian's from constant exposure to a
pitiless wind and to the alkaline water which hardens the most

(2-f)

transparent cuticle into a sort of flexible leather" (109).[1]
Earlier, when Clark received the letter from Howard announcing Aunt
Georgiana's arrival, Clark said that her name called up her figure,
"at once pathetic and grotesque" (107). Clark himself knows about

(3-a) The opening sentence corresponds to the major heading II in the outline. The subhead A identifies the character to be discussed here. Second-level subheads 1, 2, 3, and 4 correspond to details introduced and expanded upon in succeeding paragraphs.

(3-b) The quotation card for this source appears below. Note that the writer quotes only the most relevant point and changes the tense of the verb *imposed* so that it fits into her sentence. The brackets show that she supplied the *s*.

34e
rev

> Kohler, "WC," 9.
> "To a generation coming to maturity between wars, Miss Cather already seemed a little old-fashioned. It was true that she did not always flatter the West, and her stories were filled with images of the waste that its barren loneliness imposed upon the human spirit."
> ✱ Good statement to support Fisher's point -- tough new world's effect on the spirit.

(3-c) Since the sentence identifies Porter as the source, only the page number is required as documentation. For full publishing data, readers can check the list of works cited, where Porter's afterword has a separate entry.

(3-d) This paragraph develops the second-level subhead II.A.1 and II.A.2.

(3-e) The writer interprets and evaluates Cather's image.

(3-f) Here is the signal card that the writer made out and in 4-a below, the quotation from " 'A Death in the Desert' "

> Cather, "Death in the Desert," 74-75.
> Quote about Everett talking with Katharine - as desert suddenly glares through window -- good to show contrast between two worlds tugging at Katharine.

the pains of that frontier life; when he thinks of corn-husking days on the ranch, he says, "I felt the knuckles of my thumb . . . as though they were raw again" (107).

(3-a)   But Cather's stories show more than just the effects of the untamed West on a person's body. They also show "the waste that its **(3-b)** barren loneliness impose[s] upon the human spirit" (Kohler 9). It is true that for Katharine Gaylord, life in the West has not caused her bodily pain. Still, her physical condition is a symbol of the barren life the former artist must live now as she is dying of tuberculosis. As Katherine Anne Porter says in her 1952 afterword to The Troll Garden, "Wyoming is for her not only an earthly desert **(3-c)** but one of the heart, the mind, the spirit" (151). Forced to leave the life of musical fame that she once had, she is very unhappy, her brother says, dying "like a rat in a hole, out of her own world, and she can't fall back into ours" (Cather, TG 69).

(3-d)   We can see how much that former life meant to Katharine and how deeply she misses it. It is easier to die in the West, she maintains: "to go East would be dying twice" (70). It is not that Wyoming is a new land for her--she grew up there as a child--but it **(3-e)** is a land now alien to her spiritual needs. With a brilliant image Cather shows the conflicting forces of past and present in Katharine's life. In the Wyoming house, the music room makes Everett feel that he has stepped into a familiar New York studio **(3-f)** almost exactly like his brother's, "so individual and poignantly

**34e
rev**

(4-a) Note the writer's interpretation. Here is the paragraph from the short story:

"I remember," Everett said seriously, twirling the pencil between his fingers and looking, as he sat with his head thrown back, out under the red window blind which was raised just a little, and as it swung back and forth in the wind revealed the glaring panorama of the desert—a blinding stretch of yellow, flat as the sea in dead calm, splotched here and there with deep purple shadows; and, beyond, the ragged-blue outline of the mountains and the peaks of snow, white as the white clouds.

(4-b) This paragraph develops points II.A.3 and II.A.4 in the outline.

(4-c) The writer has paraphrased Bloom and Bloom:

This avowed hostility between the artist and society gave her the subject for an undergraduate theme, which was published in the *State Journal,* on Thomas Carlyle's fierce withdrawal from social concerns. Later, in " 'A Death in the Desert,' " she further alluded to the alienation as a "long warfare" so futile and enervating that it can only distract the artist's attention from his singular purpose.

(4-d) The opening sentence places the issues of frontier life and artistic fulfillment in a larger critical context and provides a thoughtful bridge to the discussion of "A Wagner Matinee." The parenthetical documentation identifies three critics who have called attention to the issue emphasized here. Full documentation is given in the list of works cited.

(4-e) The point here matches the first-level subhead II.B in the outline.

(4-f) Brief details of the plot explain Aunt Georgiana's reactions in Boston.

reminiscent here in Wyoming" (71). As he sits chatting with
Katharine, a window blind swinging in the wind reveals "the glaring
panorama of the desert--a blinding stretch of yellow, flat as the

(4-a) sea in dead calm" (75). Blinding, yellow, flat, dead: so is
Katharine's life away from the East, even in the studio room she has
tried so hard to make like Adriance's.

(4-b) Only Everett with his tales of city life and, finally (at
Everett's prompting), a letter from Adriance with a copy of a new
sonata he has just written cheer Katharine up somewhat. But it is
very clear from her regular conversations with Everett that her
desperate longing for the art she once knew and her own fate not to
achieve it are the great ironies of the story. When the singer
dies, Cather writes, "the madness of art was over for Katharine"

(4-c) (86). As Bloom and Bloom have noted (151), Cather was fascinated by
the artist isolated from society. In the portrait of Katharine
Gaylord, we see that the singer's death separated her from art no
more surely than the final years of her life.

(4-d) Many critics note Cather's concern with the difficulties an
artist has in leading a satisfying life on the harsh frontier
(Gerber 44; Bloom and Bloom 8; Stouck 299). As with Katharine

(4-e) Gaylord, "the fatality of deprivation" (Van Ghent 11) has a serious
effect on Clark's Aunt Georgiana in "A Wagner Matinee." Yet
Georgiana's circumstances are somewhat different from Katharine's.
Passionate love, not illness, has removed her from the civilized

(4-f) world of Boston. Against her family's wishes, she eloped with a
shiftless village boy who was nine years younger than she
was. Howard led her to the Nebraska homestead, which she did not

(5-a) **This paragraph develops the second-level subhead II.B.2 in the outline.**

(5-b) **Compare the quotation with the paragraph from which it comes. The ellipsis indicates the omission of words that the writer believed were unnecessary for her point.**

The concert was over; the people filed out of the hall chattering and laughing, glad to relax and find the living level again, but my kinswoman made no effort to rise. The harpist slipped its green felt cover over his instrument; the flute players shook the water from their mouthpieces; the men of the orchestra went out one by one, leaving the stage to the chairs and music stands, empty as a winter cornfield.

(5-c) **The writer's evaluation here emphasizes the importance of the image and justifies the use of the long quotation that follows.**

(5-d) **This quotation occupies more than four typed lines and therefore is set off from the text as a block quotation. Introduced by a colon, the quotation starts on a new line indented ten spaces from the left margin. Quotation marks are not used, and all lines are double-spaced. As the quotation is part of a single paragraph, no further paragraph indentation is necessary. When a quotation is set off, the parenthetical reference comes after the end mark. (The options of quoting, summarizing, or paraphrasing the original source are discussed in 33a.)**

leave for many years. Their lives were always threatened by roving
bands of Indians and insufficient supplies. A little parlor organ
and church singing provided the only music she heard during all that
time. Clark recalls that once, as he practiced at the organ, she
told him in a quivering voice, "Don't love it so well, Clark, or it
may be taken from you" (Cather, TG 110).

(5-a)   Unlike Katharine in her permanent exile, Aunt Georgiana returns
to her former world of art. Clark takes her to a performance of the
symphony orchestra. Here, too, Cather's images weave together the
civilized world and the grim prairie. Clark wonders how much of her
ability to understand music "had been dissolved in soapsuds or
worked into bread or milked in the bottom of the pail" (114). At the
end of the concert, Aunt Georgiana sits weeping as the musicians
(5-b)   file out, "leaving the stage . . . empty as a winter cornfield"
(5-c)   (115). The final overwhelming image of the story shows the utter
horror of the transplanted artist:

(5-d)   For her, just outside the door of the concert hall, lay
                the black pond with the cattle-tracked bluffs; the tall
                unpainted house, with weather-curled boards; naked as a
                tower, the crook-backed ash seedlings where the
                dishcloths hung to dry; the gaunt, molting turkeys picking
                up refuse about the kitchen door. (115)

It is the refuse of Aunt Georgiana's existence. Clark realizes that
no matter how painful a human life, the soul always can be revived.
Yet we must wonder if, in fact, he did a service for his aunt by
reawakening her to the joys she had missed for so long. We

(6-a) Note the pair of single quotation marks within the pair of double quotation marks to indicate a quotation within a quotation.

(6-b) The opening sentence corresponds to major heading III in the outline.

(6-c) The superscript 2 corresponds to endnote 2 on page 9 of the essay. It cites seven sources, and, as a parenthetical documentation in the text, would have been too long.

(6-d) The citation indicates a paraphrase. Although the writer's language is original, she nonetheless acknowledges the source of her ideas. Merely changing Brennan's words does not change the fact that the ideas are his. This is what he wrote:

It seems likely, too, that she subscribed to a prevalent nineteenth-century view (one prevalent even yet, for that matter) that music is the supreme art, that the musical experience—in its sensuous immediacy, its emotional intensity and profound spiritual appeal—is the most rapturous, most transcendent, the most certainly ineffable of all aesthetic experiences. In Willa Cather's fiction, at any rate, it is the musical moment which is generally employed to characterize a transcendent rhapsodic emotion that drenches the soul in its intensity but eludes all precise definition.

(6-e) The opening sentence corresponds to outline point III.A. The rest of the paragraph develops outline points III.A.1 and III.A.2.

(6-f) The writer interprets the meaning of the image and relates it to the thesis of the paper.

(6-a)   understand, as Clark does at the end, when she "burst into tears and
sobbed pleadingly. 'I don't want to go, Clark, I don't want to
go!' " (115). Yet, of course, go she must.

(6-b)   It is obvious that Katharine and Georgiana are both very much
involved in music, and in the two stories, music helps Cather show
how dramatic the separation from civilized society can be for a
person isolated in a primitive setting. Music is a very important

(6-c)   element in much of Cather's fiction.[2] Of all the arts, Cather saw
music as the most dynamic form in our culture--even more dynamic
than literature. Through the power of music Cather characterizes an
emotion so powerful that it goes beyond ordinary limits to saturate

(6-d)   the human soul (Brennan, "Music" 175).

(6-e)   Richard Giannone sees music for Katharine Gaylord in " 'A Death
in the Desert' " as a symbol of how swiftly her life is passing.
Though art is humanity's supreme effort, it is futile, finally,
because life and artistic achievement are so brief (41).
Transplanted now from the life of art, she realizes her dilemma as
she listens to Adriance's composition. As Everett plays the piece,
Katharine recognizes its great tragic themes. Adriance's
achievement prods her own suffering. "This is my tragedy, as I lie
here spent by the racecourse," she proclaims, "listening to the feet
of the runners as they pass me. Ah, God! The swift feet of the

(6-f)   runners!" (81). The feet of the runners are elements of that
stable, complex world, to use Fisher's terms again, from which
Katharine was transplanted. Adriance's music tells her of the
"tragedy of the soul" and "the tragedy of effort and failure, the

(7-a) The opening sentence corresponds to III.B in the outline. The rest of the paragraph expands on III.B.1.

(7-b) This paragraph develops point III.B.2 in the outline.

thing Keats called hell" (Cather, TG 81). It is, of course,
Katharine's own failure that she recognizes in the sonata.

(7-a)   In "A Wagner Matinee" the musical selections at the concert echo
the themes of the story. The first piece Aunt Georgiana hears is
the overture to Tannhäuser, one of Wagner's early operas. The
overture starts with the Pilgrim's Chorus, the solemn chanting of
travelers on their way to Rome (Ewen 673). Giannone says that the
motif in this chorus "represents the ecstasy of sacred yearnings"
(43). Then the Venusberg motif begins, the music of the sensual,
tempting, yet disturbing world of Venus and her followers. Giannone
sees this as a contrasting world of profane longings. He points out
that in the overture to Tannhäuser, Wagner presents the "struggle
between the sacred and profane in man" (43). For Aunt Georgiana,
the sacred is her higher yearning for art and music; the profane is
the dry prairie in an unfriendly world. The terrible tragedy here,
Giannone suggests, is that "in the tug between 'the inconceivable
silence of the plains' and 'the little parlor organ,' silence won"
(43).

(7-b)   Other selections that Aunt Georgiana hears at the matinee,
including excerpts from The Flying Dutchman and Tristan and Isolde,
similarly reflect the battle between the opposing forces that she so
fully embodies. The last piece, Siegfried's funeral march from the
Ring cycle, signals the defeat of Wagner's hero, just as it predicts
Aunt Georgiana's defeat--her return to Nebraska after the concert
ends. Unlike many of Wagner's operas, "A Wagner Matinee" does not
end in glory or victory, with good overpowering evil. Art does not

34e

rev

(8-a) The conclusion reminds readers of the introduction and the important point made by Fisher. This paragraph is not simply a restatement of the introductory paragraph. The writer provides interesting background information as she explains Cather's own reaction to her friend's criticism. The conclusion builds further credibility for the thesis of the paper. The writer is implying that even Cather might acknowledge that the two stories treated the lives of women transplanted to a new country from stable societies.

(8-b) The citation "Cather" refers to an encyclopedia entry in the list of works cited.

(8-c) Here the writer draws upon another primary source to make an important point. Note again the smooth integration of source material.

(8-d) The conclusion highlights major points made throughout the research paper.

win (here, nor do sacred yearnings. Nothing redeems Aunt

Georgiana's fate (Giannone 45).

(8-a)   By 1933, when Dorothy Canfield Fisher was writing her essay for

the Tribune, Cather was highly sensitive to comments by critics.

Honored for literary accomplishments with the Prix Femina Americain

(8-b)   ("Cather"), she nonetheless was attacked by many of her

contemporaries (Murphy and Synnott 12-14). After she read a

prepublication copy of Fisher's essay, Cather sent her friend a

telegram asking her to give up the project. As for Fisher's idea

that Cather's fiction deals with the effects of a new country on

people removed to it from a civilized world, Cather unhappily

"summarized this thesis in one word, 'escape' " (Woodress 247). Yet

she recognized that this theme ran through her work. Just a few

(8-c)   years later she would write in a letter to The Commonweal, "What has

art ever been but escape?" (On Writing 18). In " 'A Death in the

Desert' " and "A Wagner Matinee" Cather explores the complex theme of

(8-d)   escape by showing artistic women transplanted from civilized

societies into hostile worlds.

34e

rev

(9-a) These notes correspond to the superscripts that appear on pages 2 and 6 of the research paper. Notes generally go on a separate page at the end of the text with the word *Notes* centered one inch from the top. Notes are double-spaced and indented five spaces from the left margin. If more than one line is required, subsequent lines are flush with the left margin. Some instructors require the notes to be placed at the bottom of the page on which the matching numeral appears in the text. See 33g.

(9-b) Note the format of the multiple references. The writer separates the references with semicolons. No page numbers follow the first three references because in each case the writer is referring to the whole book or article.

(9-a)

Notes

[1]Cather's family and friends objected to her portrait of Nebraska life when this story first appeared in Everybody's Magazine. A good friend, Will Jones, complained that strangers would always associate Nebraska with Aunt Georgiana's terrible shape, her false teeth, and her yellow skin. Cather denied that she wanted to disparage her homeland but admitted that her family felt insulted: "They had already told her that it was not nice to tell such things" (Woodress 117).

(9-b)

[2]Giannone; Brennan, "Willa Cather"; Brennan, "Music"; Gerber 71-73; Bloom and Bloom 123; Daiches 8; Van Ghent 20-21.

In this list of works cited, entries are listed alphabetically by author's last name or, as with unsigned works, by the first main word of the title. Books and articles are not separated.

(10-a) A book with two authors. *UP* stands for *University Press.*

(10-b) Three hyphens followed by a period indicate a work by the author of the previous entry. Both citations here are journal articles with pages numbered consecutively throughout an annual volume. The articles are listed alphabetically by the first word of the title.

(10-c) An article in an encyclopedia.

(10-d) A republished book. The date of the original edition is 1905; the date of the current edition is 1971. Also, this NAL book has a special imprint, Plume, which precedes the publisher's name.

(10-e) Standard reference to a book with one author.

(10-f) An entry for an encyclopedia in only one edition. Ewen wrote the particular entry and the rest of the book as well. He is author of the article and author of the encyclopedia. Hence, his name appears in two places.

(10-g) Murphy's complete book is *not* cited in the text of the paper and hence might seem out of place here. However, since the writer of the paper used *two* articles from this anthology, she lists the collection itself and then cites the articles with *cross-references* to this main entry. See 10-i below.

(10-h) Murphy's name is spelled out here as well as in the previous entry. The first entry is a book published under his name alone. If the list included other books by Murphy alone, three hyphens and a period would appear in place of his name in the second and subsequent entries (as in 10-b). The three hyphens, however, stand for only the name or names of authors in the preceding entry. Since the authors of "The Recognition of Willa Cather's Art" are Murphy *and* Synnott, both names are listed.

(10-i) A cross-reference. "Murphy 1–28" refers readers to *Critical Essays on Willa Cather,* the main entry for Murphy. The numbers 1–28 identify the pages on which this essay is found.

(10-a)   Works Cited

Bloom, Edward A., and Lillian D. Bloom. <u>Willa Cather's Gift of</u>

   <u>Sympathy</u>. Carbondale: Southern Illinois UP, 1962.

Brennan, Joseph X. "Music and Willa Cather." <u>University Review</u> 31

   (1965): 257-64.

(10-b) ---. "Willa Cather and Music." <u>University Review</u> 31 (1965): 175-83.

(10-c) "Cather." <u>World Scope Encyclopedia</u>. 1955 ed.

Cather, Willa. <u>On Writing</u>. New York: Knopf, 1949.

(10-d) ---. <u>The Troll Garden</u>. 1905. New York. Plume-NAL, 1971.

(10-e) Daiches, David. <u>Willa Cather: A Critical Introduction</u>. Ithaca:

   Cornell UP, 1959.

(10-f) Ewen, David. "Tannhäuser." <u>The New Encyclopedia of the Opera</u>. By

   Ewen. New York: Hill, 1971.

Gerber, Philip L. <u>Willa Cather</u>. Boston: Twayne, 1975.

Giannone, Richard. <u>Music in Willa Cather's Fiction</u>. Lincoln: U of

   Nebraska P, 1968.

Kohler, Dayton. "Willa Cather: 1876-1947." <u>College English</u> 9

   (1947): 8-18.

(10-g) Murphy, John J., ed. <u>Critical Essays on Willa Cather</u>. Boston:

   Hall, 1984.

(10-h) Murphy, John J., and Kevin A. Synnott. "The Recognition of Willa

(10-i)   Cather's Art." Murphy 1-28.

(11-a) Porter's afterword, published in 1952, appears in the volume of *The Troll Garden* already cited under Cather's name. The cross-reference "Cather, *Troll Garden*" is used instead of "Cather" because another book by Cather appears in the list.

34e

rev

(11-b) Another cross-reference to Murphy.

(11-c) A book in a series. When the title page indicates that the book is part of a series, put the series name (without quotation marks or underlining) and number before the publishing data.

(11-a) Porter, Katherine Anne. Afterword. 1952. Cather, <u>Troll Garden</u>
          134-51.

(11-b) Stouck, David. 1905. "Willa Cather's Last Four Books." Murphy
          290-304.

(11-c) Van Ghent, Dorothy. <u>Willa Cather</u>. U of Minnesota Pamphlets on
             American Writers 36. Minneapolis: U of Minnesota P, 1964.

          Woodress, James. <u>Willa Cather</u>. 1970. Lincoln: Bison-U of Nebraska
             P, 1975.

1

Title

The Continuing Search for Black Holes

Name and
other
information
required by
instructor

Richard Lanier

Ms. J. Clay

English 101.6

November 15, 1993

Continuing Search, 2

Thesis: As new ideas evolved about the universe, scientists tried to confirm the existence of black holes, which in the past were only theoretical possibilities.

Topic outline (see 34b)

I. Black holes vs. ordinary stars

    A. Definition of black holes

    B. Contrary forces on ordinary stars

       1. Expansion from nuclear burning

       2. Compression from gravity

    C. Theory of formation of black holes

       1. Shrinking gravity's effect on burning fuel

       2. Lack of light

II. History of the search for black holes

Letters and arabic numbers for subordinate points

    A. Problems in finding them

       1. Their invisibility

       2. Their infinitesimal size

       3. Their place in theories of the universe

    B. Developing ideas through the early 1960s

       1. Einstein's predictions

       2. Later confirmations

III. Modern investigations in physics and astronomy

    A. Discovery of pulsars

    B. Quantum mathematics and black hole possibilities

    C. Idea of binary relationships

IV. Continuing search through X-rays

    A. Uhuru satellite and X-ray detection

    B. X-ray star called V861 Sco

    C. Intensive X-ray searches

        1. Imaging from Einstein Observatory

        2. New information from ROSAT satellite

        3. Hubble telescope picture of NGC 4261

V. Hawking's theory and future possibilities for black holes

The Continuing Search for Black Holes

One of the most dramatic and exciting scientific concepts to emerge during the last twenty-five years is the black hole. Scientists suspected the possible existence of black holes in the late 1800s, but it was only in the twentieth century that changes in theoretical physics forced astronomers to start looking for them. So much about black holes runs contrary to our ordinary experience of life that they are difficult to imagine. But because black holes are impossible by definition to detect directly, the search to confirm their existence is an outstanding instance of theoretical and practical science working together.

Stars, like people, have a life span between birth and death. Unlike people, dying stars can end up in a variety of ways--as supernovas, neutron stars, or pulsars. In all of these cases, they are still objects in the universe and still contribute to the cosmic balance. But some dead stars may become black holes, in which case they are no longer part of the universe at all.

What exactly is a black hole? Black holes are collapsed stars, which "contain the strongest gravitational forces in the known universe" (Shipman, 1980, p. 15). Not all stars are massive enough to collapse. Our own sun, for instance would have to have a mass at least one and one-half times greater with the same volume before a gravitational collapse could begin to take place. In a healthy

Marginal notes (left margin):

ort title and
ge number
pear at the
 of all
ges;
argins are 1
1 1/2 inches

le repeated

troduction
ilds to
esis

esis:
mpare with
evious
rsions (see
a)

finition and
planation of
ack hole

arenthetical
ation:
thor, date,
ge number.
e reference
t on p. 15.

star, like our sun, the force of gravity is balanced by internal

Reference to diagram

forces, like the gas pressure from nuclear reactions taking place,

as shown in Figure 1. As Stephen W. Hawking (1988) points out, this

state is similar to a balloon, where the gas inside exerts enough

pressure to keep the rubber from collapsing. In a star, super-hot

matter is like the gas in a balloon and gravity acts like the rubber

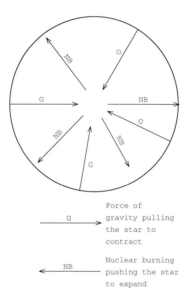

Figure 1. Forces acting on stars.

Continuing Search, 6

itations
nnecessary,
riter's own
ords and
eas

coating. When stars get old, their nuclear fuel runs low, and gravity overwhelms the other forces. The star begins to shrink, reducing the volume and forcing the remaining fuel to burn faster. The smaller area makes the remaining matter interact much more intensely than before.

If a star's mass is low enough, the star can support itself against gravitational collapse. If not, the gravity continues to shrink the area, which makes the nuclear fuel burn faster and faster. As the fuel becomes exhausted, the star grows colder while the density increases. Jastrow (1979) explains what happens next:

uotation of
ore than
orty words
ouble-
paced and
et off without
uotation
arks

> At that point, the mass is so compact that the force of gravity
> at the surface is billions of times stronger than the force of
> the sun. The tug of that enormous force prevents the rays of
> light from leaving the surface of the star. (p. 65)

Without the fuel to maintain equilibrium, the star eventually becomes infinitely dense: a black hole!

utline point
C.1

While the gravitational collapse takes place, other strange things happen. As the gravity becomes proportionally more massive, information from the star takes longer and longer to emerge. Eventually the laws governing the normal universe break down in the vicinity of the dying star. In a normal star like the sun, light waves are "bent" by the strong gravitational field. But in a black hole, the gravity is extremely strong; "light cones are bent inward so much that light can no longer escape" (Hawking, 1988, p. 87).

This means that as a star collapses it eventually becomes invisible. Worse yet, the dimensions of the star shrink until it

becomes a hole not only in space, but in time as well. Jastrow
(1979) describes the process of collapse:

> The star's volume becomes smaller and smaller; from a globe
> with a two-mile radius it shrinks to the size of a pinhead,
> then to the size of a microbe, and still shrinking, passes into
> the realm of distances smaller than any ever probed by man. At
> all times the star's mass of a thousand trillion trillion tons
> remains packed into the shrinking volume. But intuition tells
> us that such an object cannot exist. At some point the
> collapse must be halted. Yet according to all the laws of
> twentieth century physics, no force, no matter how powerful,
> can stop the collapse. (p. 65)

In the late eighteenth century, scientists like Mitchell and
Laplace had suggested that a star with sufficiently massive gravity
would not allow light to escape and would seem like a dark hole in
space (Hawking, 1988). But for nearly one hundred and fifty years,
practical scientists refused to accept this conclusion because they
knew too little about the nature of light and gravity.

Outline point II.B.1

In the first part of this century, Einstein's Theory of
Relativity changed the way people thought about light, gravity, and
time. One aspect of his theory was that gravity caused a
deformation even of empty space and that this deformation would
curve the universe until it folded over on itself. During World War
I, a German astronomer named Karl Schwarzschild first formulated the
idea of a black hole. He believed that such an object could exist

Citation to encyclopedia article

Superscript 1
corresponds
to footnote 1
on page 16 of
the essay

if we assume that light is affected by the force of gravity
("Schwarzschild," 1990).[1]

In 1919 Sir Arthur Eddington confirmed Einstein's prediction.
During a solar eclipse, Eddington's tests on whether rays of light
actually were "twisted" by the gravitational field of the sun offered
experimental proof that Einstein's theory was correct (Davies, 1980,
p. 135). In the 1920s, one of Eddington's students, Subrahmanyan
Chandrasekhar, rediscovered the idea that a star's gravity might be
so massive that not even light could escape. The work of
Chandrasekhar was very controversial. Eddington and even Einstein
could not accept the possibility of such an object.

In 1939 J. Robert Oppenheimer--later to become famous for his
role in creating the atom bomb--and his student Hartland Snyder
suggested that a black hole might result from the collapse of
enormous, massive stars several times larger than our sun (Dupree &
Hartman, 1979). But since no telescope could see these objects if
they existed, astronomers pursued other areas of exploration and the
whole subject was largely forgotten.

By the 1960s, Schwarzschild, Chandrasekhar, and Oppenheimer
had contributed theoretical work that was sound in terms of
Einstein's theory, but their notions were contrary to everyday
experience and suggested disturbing consequences. No one could
resolve the matter, because there are no black holes in our
immediate galactic neighborhood. This is a good thing, because, as
Wald (1992) points out, "if a black hole were close enough to be
'seen' directly, its gravitational field would be greater than that
of the sun" (p. 108).

**Article, two
authors**

**Quotation
within a
quotation in
single quotes**

Outline point III

Only in the last twenty-five years have we developed the practical tools to explore more deeply into the universe and, ultimately perhaps, to confirm black hole theories. In 1967, Jocelyn Bell, an astronomy student at Cambridge, discovered pulsars, objects in the sky that emit regular pulses of energy. At first, Bell believed that she had found alien transmissions, but eventually she realized that pulsars were, in fact, neutron stars. These were stars that had collapsed until the protons, the positively charged particles in atoms, and electrons, which are negatively charged particles, had been forced together to form neutrons, or electrically neutral particles (Thorne, 1977).

The inner space of the atoms in these neutron stars had been so reduced that the stars were only ten miles in diameter, far too small for optical telescopes to reveal. But the neutron stars gave off powerful radio waves, intense radiation created as the compressed atoms collided with each other. Radio telescopes can pick up this radiation, which "sweeps through space like the light

Integrated quotation (see 33a)

from a revolving lighthouse beacon. If the earth happens to lie in the path of the rotating beam, it will receive a sharp burst of radiation once every turn of the pulsar" (Jastrow, 1979, p. 63). This discovery of neutron stars revived interest in the concept of black holes.

At the same time, two other Cambridge scientists, Roger Penrose and Stephen Hawking, began contributing new theoretical work to the subject of black holes. Although they did not know it at the time, their work was similar to the predictions of Michell and Laplace. But unlike their predecessors, Penrose and Hawking were armed with quantum mathematics. When they suggested "an event horizon," drawn over the singularity point of a black hole and the normal universe, they had enough calculations to support the idea. Many other scientists began to take the possibility of black holes seriously.

That meant that direct astronomical confirmation might never reveal the existence of a black hole. But because of its massive gravitational field, scientists could detect the effects of black holes without direct evidence by observing the strong gravitational force of a black hole on luminous objects in its immediate vicinity.

Outline point III.C

Astronomers have known for a long time about binary stars (double stars that revolve around each other), and two Russians, Y. B. Zel'dovich and O. K. Guseynov, began compiling a list of stars that were orbiting in pairs with a dark companion. It does not necessarily follow, of course, that a dark companion is a black hole. Zel'dovich and Guseynov's work could also suggest planets. However, astronomers assumed that if the dark companion were a black hole, the star should be losing stellar material into the massive gravitational field. This action is illustrated in Figure 2 with the black hole enlarged in scale compared to the visible star.

In theory, as the stellar gas gets closer to the black hole, it will accelerate until it is traveling at a speed approaching the speed of light (Dupree & Hartman, 1979). When the molecules of gas moving at such a terrific speed collide with each other and with the surface of the black hole itself, the collision should give off

Article, three authors

enormous quantities of X-rays (Jones, Forman, & Liller, 1974). So a

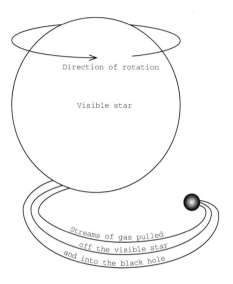

Direction of rotation

Visible star

Streams of gas pulled
off the visible star
and into the black hole

Figure 2. The Pull of stellar gas.

star with an apparent wobble in space, with no detectable partner and giving off huge quantities of X-rays, might be paired with a black hole.

As a result of this theory, the search to confirm the possible existence of black holes shifted to equipment that detected strong sources of X-ray and radio emissions. Unfortunately, the earth's atmosphere absorbs X-rays. So the search for black holes could not continue until satellites with X-ray telescopes were launched into space.

Outline point IV

Continuing Search, 12

One of the early probes was the <u>Uhuru</u>, a joint Italian and American satellite launched in 1970. It probed an X-ray source called Cygnus X-1. (Stars are named for the constellations where they are found and according to a system of grid marks set on standard photographs of each segment of the sky.) Initially, the mass of the unseen companion pulling on Cygnus X-1 was estimated to be eight times that of the sun (Thorne, 1977). More recent estimates lower that figure to six (Hawking, 1988), but whichever figure is correct, this mass is too great to be a neutron star. Scientists conclude that the companion in all probability is a black hole.

Outline point IV.B — Another possible location of a black hole is in V861 Sco. The object apears to be connected to a dark companion, and it is curious because it generates a large, luminous ultraviolet flare. William Oegerle and Ronald S. Polidan of Princeton University were intrigued by this flare. Thomson (1979) reported on their findings:

> From the optical properties of V861 Sco, they could determine an orbital period of seven days. They figure that the mass of the primary star is between 20 and 50 times that of the sun. The unseen companion is between 7.5 and 13 solar masses. This **Ellipsis shows omission** — rules out a neutron star or a white dwarf. . . . Either ought to have much less mass. It is possible in theory to link the ultraviolet flare with an X-ray flare. X-ray flares are seen in these X-ray binaries and they are explained by changes in the gas flow between the two objects. So it all looks good provided V861 Sco really is the X-ray source. (p. 25)

In 1979, the orbiting Einstein Observatory was launched. It

Outline point IV.C.2

conducted an X-ray imaging survey of the sky and identified nearly 60,000 sources of X-ray radiation.

In 1990, the United States, Britain, and Germany launched the ROSAT satellite, the most powerful X-ray telescope yet devised. ROSAT, short for Roentgen Satellite, is named after the discoverer of X-rays. Its mission is to scan the X-ray sources that the Einstein Observatory identified, but with three times the resolution power of that earlier probe. ROSAT has already provided glimpses of another potential black hole, LMC X-1 (Cowen, 1991).

But ROSAT and the Hubble telescope, launched in 1991, have shown the clearest picture to date of what a black hole might look like. Evidence for black holes can be found in many parts of the universe, even in other galaxies like the M51 galaxy which, like our own galaxy, appears to have a massive black hole at its center. According to Rees (1990), black holes may be an integral part of the formation of galaxies themselves. And recently Hubble sent back a picture of what may be a massive black hole in the core of galaxy NGC 4261. Astronomers apparently no longer doubt that there are objects of massive gravitation at work in the universe (Lane, 1992, p. 7).

Commentary on source (see 33a)

Although black holes seem like depressing ends for stars, Stephen Hawking's recent work suggests that they may not be so final after all. As black holes accumulate matter, they may reach a point at which the process of contraction reverses, and a massive disgorging of material may result in quasars, quasi-stellar objects, that appear to be rotating faster than the speed of light. ROSAT reveals dozens of previously unknown quasars, and perhaps as the scientific community digests this information, we may come to

understand the relation between quasars and black holes. We may
also find that both new theories in physics and new explorations in
space once again will lead us to reevaluate our concepts of the way
the universe works.

References
page for cited
works (see
33e)

References

Cowen, R. (1991, June 29). ROSAT revelations. <u>Science News</u>, pp.
    408-410.

Davies, P. (1980). <u>The runaway universe</u>. New York: Penguin.

Dupree, A. K., & Hartman, L. (1979, October). Hunting for black
    holes. <u>Natural History</u>, pp. 30-37.

Hawking, S. J. (1988). <u>A brief history of time</u>. New York: Bantam.

Jastrow, R. (1979). <u>Red giants and white dwarfs</u>. New York:
    Warner.

Jones, C., Forman, W., & Liller, W. (1974). X-ray sources and
    their optical counterparts. <u>Sky and Telescope</u>, <u>48</u>, 289-291.

Lane, E. (1992, November 20). Black hole snapshot: Scientists
    think that's what Hubble photo may be. <u>Newsday</u>, p. 7.

Rees, M. J. (1990, November). Black holes in galactic centers.
    <u>Scientific American</u>, pp. 56-66.

Schwarzschild, Karl. (1990). In <u>Encyclopaedia Britannica</u>
    <u>Micropaedia</u> (Vol. 10, p. 548). New York: Encyclopaedia
    Britannica.

Shipman, H. L. (1980). <u>Black holes, quasars and the universe</u> (2nd
    ed). Boston: Houghton Mifflin.

Thomson, D. (1979, July 14). V861 Sco's UV flare. <u>Science News</u>,
    p. 25.

Thorne, K. S. (1977). The search for black holes. In <u>Cosmology</u>
    <u>+1</u> (pp. 66-70). San Francisco: Freeman.

Wald, R. M. (1992). <u>Space, time, and gravity: The theory of the</u>
    <u>big bang and black holes</u>. (2nd ed). Chicago: University of
    Chicago Press.

Footnotes

Content footnotes at foot of page where referenced or following list of references.

[1] In 1798 the French mathematician and astronomer Pierre Simon de Laplace hinted at the possibility of phenomena like black holes, but he never used the term.

EIGHT

OTHER WRITING TASKS

WRITING LOGICAL ARGUMENTS

We argue to persuade others to accept a point of view. In ordinary speech, the word *argument* is often associated with anger and conflict. But in writing, and especially in research papers, *argument* means a conflict of opinions, not of people. The writer of an argumentative paper strives by reason and logic to persuade readers to accept his or her point of view or conclusion. A good argument is carefully stated and well supported by evidence; it makes friends, not enemies.

35a
Differentiating Between Argument and Persuasion

Persuasion includes any means by which we get people to do what we want them to do. You can persuade some people to buy a certain brand of beer by showing them funny commercials featuring the beer. You can persuade others to give money to help the homeless by showing them photographs of homeless people living in the streets. You might be able to persuade your parents to lend you the family car for the weekend because you want to go to a party.

Persuasion includes argument. An **argument** is a carefully reasoned conclusion derived from evidence. We make arguments to prove that our point of view is more logical than others. We argue that our interpretation of *Hamlet* or of a short story or novel is the correct one, and we quote from the text to support our conclusion. You want your readers to think through your argument and agree with you. The primary appeal of argument is to reason, to judgment. You evaluate evidence and draw conclusions that seem to be inescapable or at least extremely probable.

The parts of an argument are tightly connected. These logical connections can be built on two kinds of reasoning: inductive and deductive. **Inductive reasoning** moves from particular examples to general truths.

Statistics show that cigarette smokers are ten times more likely than non-smokers to get lung cancer. The examination of thousands of specific events leads to a general truth: cigarette smoking is dangerous to health. **Deductive reasoning** moves from a general truth we know to a conclusion about a specific instance. Deductive reasoning may start with a general truth that has been proved by induction. Cigarette smoking is dangerous to health; therefore, if you smoke cigarettes, you will probably not live as long as a nonsmoker.

35b
Using Inductive Reasoning

The most common way to reason is by induction: we have specific experiences and move from them to general conclusions about what they prove or mean.

Some inductions require rigorous study. Arguments about medical research, for example, often stand on years of experiments. We conclude that cigarette smoking causes lung cancer because the disease is common among heavy cigarette smokers and relatively uncommon among non-smokers. But we do not know what agent in cigarette smoke causes the cancer, and we cannot observe the smoke acting to make a cancer. Our conclusion is based on *statistics,* a number of instances that seem to have meaning when we construct a generalization that explains them. Some conclusions can be drawn from only one instance. If you accidentally burn yourself with a lighted match, you conclude that matches should be handled with care. You do not have to burn yourself over and over again. The same is true if you slip on an icy sidewalk. You do not have to fall again and again to prove to yourself that ice can be dangerous.

**35b
argue**

Here an argument based on induction is presented by Jane Brody, nutrition expert for the *New York Times,* writing about cholesterol.

> In a famous study of 12,000 middle-aged men in seven developed countries, Dr. Ancel Keys and his coworkers from the University of Minnesota found that the people of east Finland had the highest death rate from diseases of the coronary arteries—220 per 10,000 men in a five-year period—the highest percentage of saturated animal fats in their diet (22 percent of total calories were saturated fats, mostly from cheese, butter, and milk), and the highest blood cholesterol levels. The United States was not far behind in coronary deaths (185 per 10,000) and blood cholesterol levels.
>
> But in Mediterranean countries like Greece and Italy, where the fat is mostly of vegetable origin and therefore unsaturated and lacking cholesterol, early death from coronary heart disease was far less com-

mon. And in Japan, where only 10 percent of the diet is fat and most of that is polyunsaturated fat from vegetable sources (only 3 percent of total calories is saturated fat), the cholesterol levels were very low and the death rate from coronary artery disease was only 20 per 10,000.

—JANE BRODY

The conclusion to which this assembled evidence points is that a diet high in cholesterol leads to heart attacks. Here is induction in action.

Inductive arguments begin as people study issues and raise questions that are not easily answered. Often people develop hypotheses or theories to explain the facts and then study the evidence inductively to see if they are true. That is what nutrition experts did in the studies Jane Brody cites.

Gathering Facts

35b argue

Inductive argument always involves a gathering of facts and the drawing of a conclusion from those facts. Here are some simple examples.

Fact	Conclusion
More than one thousand people were vaccinated against small-pox during a great epidemic that swept our state early in the century. Not one of those people got the disease. Not one of the people who did get the disease had been vaccinated.	Vaccinations against smallpox prevented the disease.
My next-door neighbor got into a fight last week with the mail carrier because he said the mail carrier made too much noise walking up on the porch to deliver the mail. The same neighbor was arrested at a high school basketball game Tuesday night because he started a fight with an official over a foul call. He threatened to fight the trash haulers because they made so much noise with his garbage cans, and the paper boy refused to deliver papers anymore after my neighbor yelled at him for being late.	My neighbor has a bad temper.

Making Inferences

An **inference** is a conclusion arrived at through reasoning or implication. When we infer, we use some previous experience or knowledge to make sense of something we observe. If someone smiles at us, we infer friendly feelings because when people have smiled at us in the past, they have been showing friendly feelings. If we wake up in the night and hear a drumming of water on the roof, we infer that it is raining, though we cannot see the rain fall. We have heard rain fall on our roof before, and we recognize the sound when we hear it. If we see fire trucks roaring down the street, their sirens wailing and all the fire fighters looking grim, we assume there is a fire somewhere. Inference is not certainty. A smile may mask evil intent; some practical joker may have turned a hose on our roof; the fire fighters may be going out for coffee. But none of these possibilities is as likely as the expectation we have as a result of our experience. A smile is probably a sign of friendship; water drumming on the roof is probably rain; and the fire trucks screaming down the street are probably going to a fire.

Charles Darwin, the nineteenth-century naturalist, always asked questions as he studied facts. He wondered, for example, how certain plants that grew in ponds and marshes came to be spread across the oceans so that the same varieties grew thousands of miles apart. In his travels he noticed that the types of marsh grass that grew along the shores of North America also grew along the coasts of Europe, yet the animals in these widely separated regions differed considerably. Darwin could understand why aquatic plants (seaweed and so on) might have a wide range. But how did plants with roots in the soil spread around the earth? To solve the problem he made an inference.

**35b
argue**

With respect to plants, it has long been known what enormous ranges many fresh-water and even marsh species have, both over continents and to the most remote oceanic islands. This is strikingly illustrated, according to Alph. de Candolle [A French botanist], in those large groups of terrestrial plants, which have very few aquatic members; for the latter seem immediately to acquire, as if in consequence, a wide range. I think favourable means of dispersal explain this fact. I have before mentioned that earth occasionally adheres in some quantity to the feet and beaks of birds. Wading birds, which frequent the muddy edges of ponds, if suddenly flushed, would be the most likely to have muddy feet. Birds of this order wander more than those of any other; and they are occasionally found on the most remote and barren islands of the open ocean; they would not be likely to alight on the surface of the sea, so that any dirt on their feet would not be washed off; and when gaining the land, they would be sure to fly to their natural fresh-water haunts. I do not believe that botanists are aware how charged the mud of ponds is with seeds; I have tried several little experiments, but will here give only the most striking case: I took in February three tablespoonfuls of mud from three different points, beneath water, on the edge of a little pond: this mud when dried weighed only $6\frac{3}{4}$ ounces; I kept it covered up in my study for six months, pulling up and counting each plant as it grew; the plants were of many different kinds, and were altogether 537 in number; and yet the viscid mud was all contained in a breakfast cup! Considering these facts, I think it would be an inexplicable circumstance if water-birds did not transport the seeds of fresh-water plants to unstocked ponds and streams, situated at very distant points. The same agency may have come into play with the eggs of some of the smaller fresh-water animals.

—CHARLES DARWIN

Forming Plausible Conclusions

35b

argue

Darwin's conclusion is plausible. To say that a conclusion is *plausible* is to say that we can believe it even if we cannot prove it by observation. Most argumentation is based on plausible reasoning rather than on direct observation. When we can observe something directly, we do not have to argue about it.

Induction builds on facts and arrives at an explanation that tries to account for everything we know. But we may lack the key observation that will prove our conclusion beyond all doubt. We can only infer a conclusion. Scientists often make observations of several facts (they usually call these facts *phenomena*) and try to explain them in a logical way. They arrive at a *theory* that explains the facts—an inference, a conclusion that seems to arise naturally from what they know.

An inductive argument proceeds from the gathering of facts and the explanation of how these facts are related. That is, an inductive argument involves analyzing facts and deciding which of them are causes and which of them are effects. Sometimes that analysis leads to an obvious conclusion: cigarette smoking causes lung cancer. But sometimes the conclusions are not so obvious. When a fifty-five-mile-an-hour speed limit was imposed on American highways after the fuel crisis of 1973, traffic fatalities dropped dramatically. Did the lowered speed limit cause this drop? Or did the completion of the American interstate highway system, which occurred about the same time, cause the drop? You must study the issue and gather many data before you can make a compelling argument on either side.

Weighing Possible Conclusions

Inductive arguments may lead to a clearly plausible point of view. For many centuries, no one knew what caused typhoid fever. Once scientists observed under the microscope that the blood of everyone who had typhoid fever contained certain bacteria that were not seen in the blood of people free of the disease, the most plausible inference was that those bacteria caused the disease.

But often in the arguments you make in college papers, in position papers in business or professional life, and in writing about public issues, you discover many plausible sides to an argument. Arguments that have only one side are rarely interesting. So you must assemble the facts and decide what you want to argue. Your decision may depend on how you interpret those facts, or it may depend on what you value in those facts. In either case, you must gather as many factors as you can to be certain that you are being fair to the evidence and let readers know that you know what you are talking about.

✔ CHECKLIST 35.1: **APPLYING INDUCTIVE REASONING**

■ What question do I want to ask of the data?
■ Do I have enough specific facts to suggest an answer to the question?
■ How are these facts related to one another?
■ What answer takes into account the most evidence?
■ Can I suggest other plausible answers to the question?
■ Have I been fair to the evidence that opposes my answer?

**35b
argue**

■ **Exercise 35.1** Construct a brief argument from the following group of statements to answer the question, Should the library of Sourmash State University be kept open on Friday nights? Assume that each statement is true; consequently you can use each statement in your argument.

The administration of Sourmash State University wants to close the school library at 6:00 p.m. on Fridays. Accounts figure that it costs an average of $984.62 for heat, lights, and personnel to keep the library open from 6:00 p.m. until 11:00 p.m. Closing the library will mean a saving of about $10,000 every ten weeks, or about $30,000 during the academic year. An average of five student readers and one professor use the library on Friday night. On the average, ten books were checked out of the library on each of the last ten Fridays that the library was open. "We are trying to save money so student tuitions will not rise," President Vessie Reins told the faculty in explaining the decision to shut the library. One of the students who uses the library every Friday night is senior Helen Walden. Her novel *Late Hours* won the Pulitzer Prize last year and has been translated into seventeen languages. The one professor who uses the library on Friday nights is Judith Franklin, of the Women's Studies Program. She has completed three volumes of a projected six-volume history of American women writers. Critic and activist Helen Garfield Black says that Franklin's literary history of women writers will change the way literature is taught in American universities for the next century. Should the administration close the library on Friday nights?

35c
Using Deductive Arguments

When we reason deductively, we begin with a general truth and use it to give meaning to a fact. A deductive argument is an application of the general to the specific so that a conclusion may be drawn. The general truth is supposedly accepted by everyone likely to be interested in the argument.

35c
argue

Constructing a Syllogism

Deductive reasoning proceeds through a syllogism. In a **syllogism,** the general truth includes the specific case and is the cause of the conclusion. The general truth is called the *major premise,* the specific case is called the *minor premise,* and the conclusion shows what the major premise proves about the minor premise. Here is a standard syllogism.

> **Major premise:**   All men are mortal.
> **Minor premise:**   Socrates is a man.
> **Conclusion:**   Socrates will die.

The general truth accepted by everyone is that all men are mortal. That is, all men will eventually die. No one who reads the argument can deny that assumption. The specific case here is a statement joining Socrates to the general truth by remarking that he is an individual member of the class of beings called men. The conclusion then follows. You can always rephrase a syllogism to use the word *because* or *since* in the statements you make in conclusions derived from the general truth.

All men are mortal; since Socrates is a man, he is mortal.

The major premise in a syllogism is always a broad generalization; the minor premise is always a statement somehow included within the major premise. The conclusion follows necessarily because of the relation of the major premise and the minor premise. Here are more syllogisms based on deductive reasoning:

Major premise: This textbook is revised every three years.

Minor premise: Three years have passed since the last edition of this textbook appeared.

Conclusion: A new edition of this textbook will appear this year.

Major premise: Rain nearly always falls soon after the barometer falls rapidly when the air is warm and moist.

Minor premise: The barometer is falling fast, and the air is muggy and hot.

Conclusion: It is going to rain.

Major premise: Medical research has proved that excessive drinking of alcohol damages the heart, the digestive tract, and other organs of the body, and that heavy drinking is often associated with cancer, insomnia, psychological depression, high blood pressure, and the breakdown of the immune system.

**35c
argue**

Minor premise: My Aunt Mabel drinks a quart of whiskey a night.

Conclusion: Aunt Mabel will probably not live to a healthy old age.

Major premise: The ability to write well is a great advantage to business and professional people.

Minor premise: I write well.

Conclusion: I have an advantage if I go into business or professional life.

These syllogisms are not quite so solid as the one about Socrates. Socrates has to be mortal because all men eventually die. But Aunt Mabel may live to be ninety-five, and the ability to write well does not guarantee success in business or professional life. When we reason about most subjects to make an argument, the syllogisms we use may not fall together with the certainty of a good key turning a lock. If the major premise is not true, the syllogism will not be true. If the major premise is flawed or not accepted by others, the syllogism built on it will not be convincing.

Major premise: Nonsmokers will never die.

Minor premise: My cousin Horace is a nonsmoker.

Conclusion: Horace will never die.

All people eventually die, whether they smoke cigarettes or not. Although Cousin Horace may live longer than a chain smoker, he will eventually die.

> **Major premise:** First-rate rock composers are much more creative than composers of classical music.
>
> **Minor premise:** John Lennon was a first-rate rock composer.
>
> **Conclusion:** John Lennon was more creative than Beethoven.

The syllogism might stand among people who accept the major premise. But lovers of classical music, especially lovers of Beethoven, would reject the conclusion because they reject the supposed general truth from which the conclusion is drawn. Lovers of the Beatles might accept the syllogism, but it would not convince those on the other side.

35c

argue

Constructing an Argument with Syllogisms

You may find several syllogisms in the same argument. The following paragraph contains two syllogisms.

> In the Declaration of Independence, Thomas Jefferson wrote that people established government and entrusted it with power to preserve their rights to life, liberty, and the pursuit of happiness. A government can legitimately exercise those powers that the people consent to yield to it. The government of King George III of England had not protected those rights; it had, instead, violated them by taking the lives of Americans, by attempting to destroy their liberty, and by making it impossible for them to pursue happiness. Americans did not consent to those actions. Therefore, Jefferson argued, the English government was not a legitimate government; and since it was not a legitimate government, Americans owed it no allegiance. Since they did not owe allegiance to the English government, Americans had a right to abolish it and establish another government in its place.

Here are the syllogisms:

> **Major premise:** Governments, which were established by the people to preserve their rights to life, liberty, and the pursuit of happiness, may legitimately exercise those powers to which the people have consented.
>
> **Minor premise:** The government of King George III had taken actions to which the American people had not consented.
>
> **Conclusion:** King George's government was not legitimate.

Major premise: People have a right to abolish a government that is not legitimate.

Minor premise: King George's government was not legitimate.

Conclusion: Americans had a right to abolish King George's government.

■ **Exercise 35.2**   Construct syllogisms from the arguments in the following paragraphs:

1. Universities exist to further the intellectual life of their students and faculty and society at large. The intellectual life is not cheap. It costs money for faculty, money for the buildings where classes are conducted, money for libraries, and money to keep those libraries open at night. Judith Franklin furthers the intellectual life of society every Friday night when she works in the library. The university should support her by keeping the library open so she can work. She is doing what Sourmash University exists to do.

2. Lightning can kill. Bike riders sometimes believe that they are protected from lightning because they are on rubber tires. They think that the rubber protects them by preventing the lightning from running through them into the ground. But that belief is a superstition. Lightning can strike bikers. It kills some cyclists every year. So when a thunderstorm blows up and you are on your bike, seek shelter at once.

3. You can do thousands of things with computers—word processing, complicated math, architectural modeling, graphic design, and more. The more elaborate your computer, the more you can do with it. But the more elaborate your computer, the more it will cost. Most students use their computers only for word processing. Therefore, if you are going to use your computer only to write papers, avoid buying an expensive and elaborate computer.

35c

argue

■ **Exercise 35.3**   Study the following syllogisms. Which of them are good syllogisms, and which are bad? What is wrong with the bad ones?

1. **Major premise:** Good teachers always give students good grades.
   Minor premise: I got a bad grade in my writing class.
   Conclusion: I had a bad teacher.
2. **Major premise:** Professional athletes make a lot of money.
   Minor premise: I love basketball.
   Conclusion: I should spend all my time practicing so I can become a professional basketball player.
3. **Major premise:** Taxes are necessary to support state and federal governments.

Minor premise: Taxes on cigarettes provide a substantial proportion of government revenue.
Conclusion: We should encourage people to smoke cigarettes.
4. **Major premise:** Sunburns cause skin cancer.
  Minor premise: My skin is very sensitive.
  Conclusion: I should avoid sunburn.

Making Assumptions

In making a deductive argument, we often do not spell out the entire syllogism. We assume that the major premise is clear to readers even if we do not state it. We assume that they accept it. Sometimes we call an unexpressed major premise an **assumption.** Here are some examples.

**35c
argue**

Professor Churl promised us that half our grade would depend on our research paper. We all worked night and day on those papers. I spent every night for three weeks in the library working on mine. But then he said that the term papers were all so good that he would have to give everyone in the class an A if he kept his word. So he counted the term papers as only one-tenth of the grade and said the other nine-tenths would come from the midterm and the final.

Here is the syllogism with the major premise stated.

Major premise: Professors who break their promises to students are unfair.

Minor premise: Professor Churl broke his promise.

Conclusion: Professor Churl was unfair.

Here is another example.

Many American students make a spelling mistake when they form the plurals of words ending in *-est* and *-ist*—words such as *guest, nest, humanist, scientist,* and *colonist.* They do not add a final *s.* The plurals of these words are *guests, nests, humanists, scientists,* and *colonists.* The error seems to come about because these students fail to form the plurals of these words correctly when they speak. It is difficult to make the *s* sound after *-ist,* so many Americans pronounce the singular and the plural the same way. Therefore they spell them the same way. The rule is simple: To make the plural of all words ending in *-est* or *-ist,* add the letter *s.*

Major premise: Mispronunciations may cause misspellings.

Minor premise: Students often mispronounce words such as *guests, nests, humanists, scientists,* and *colonists.*

Conclusion: The mispronunciation causes these plurals to be spelled without the final *s,* as if they were singular nouns.

✔ **CHECKLIST 35.2: CONSTRUCTING DEDUCTIVE ARGUMENTS**

Constructing a deductive argument requires logic. To be certain your argument is logical, ask yourself these questions.

- Can readers locate the syllogisms in my argument?
- Can readers locate incomplete syllogisms, or assumptions, in my argument?
- Will my major premises be accepted by my readers?
- Will my assumptions in my incomplete syllogisms, or assumptions be accepted by my readers?
- Does each minor premise truly fit its major premise or assumption?
- Do my conclusions follow logically from my major premise and my minor premise?

35c

argue

■ **Exercise 35.4** Find the implied major premise in each syllogism embedded in the following paragraphs.

1. Sylvester Pecks has been campaigning to be elected governor of the state, telling us that he won the Congressional Medal of Honor in Vietnam. He has limped to the platform again and again to tell us how he was wounded in the leg holding his position against overwhelming enemy attack. But now it turns out that he spent the entire Vietnam war in Switzerland acting as a security guard for a girls' school. The headmaster of that school has come forward to tell us that Mr. Pecks broke his leg when he fell through a kitchen window one night as he was making off with steaks from the school's refrigerator. The headmaster has produced medical records from a Swiss hospital to support his claim. Do not vote for Sylvester Pecks.
2. Rattlesnakes abound in the Wyoming countryside around Independence Rock, one of the great landmarks along the old overland trail followed by the pioneers on their way to California and Oregon. Climbing up Independence Rock is a great adventure, and from the top you can see for miles across the rolling prairie.

But be sure you wear tall boots as you walk through the high grass around the rock, and be careful where you put your hands.

3. A recent survey revealed that the average American watches seven hours of television a day. If the average American spent half that much time reading, we would have one of the most knowledgeable citizen bodies in the world. As it is, Americans, entertained by television and neglecting their books, are woefully ignorant of simple facts necessary to understand the world. Another recent survey disclosed that one-third of the students in a large American university could not locate the continent of Europe on a map of the world. Almost half of all Americans claim that they have never read a book through in their lives. Because they watch television and do not read, Americans run the risk of being unable to make policy decisions that may help them survive as a nation.

35d

argue

■ **Exercise 35.5**   Write a paragraph in which you imply a major premise to support an argument.

35d
Arguing from Authority, Testimony, and Personal Experience

In addition to arguments constructed inductively and deductively you can also build your case on authority, testimony, and personal experience.

Arguing from Authority

If you should write a paper arguing that the characters in Shakespeare's *A Midsummer Night's Dream* are not profound, you may quote the Shakespearean scholar David Young, who has written on that subject and reached a similar conclusion. Young is an authority who strengthens your case because he is known to have studied Shakespeare and to have written a great deal about the plays, especially about the comedies.

Never be afraid to ask for help on a paper. People who have become authorities in their fields usually enjoy talking with students. Are you writing a paper about changes in the countries of Eastern Europe where communist regimes held power for so long? There is probably a professor on your campus who teaches Russian history and who can talk to you about events in Russia and other countries in Eastern Europe. Go talk to that person. He or she can become an authority for your paper.

Any time you quote facts from a book or cite an author's opinion to support your own in an argument paper, you are arguing from authority. (The use of quotations and citations of sources is discussed in 33a.) When you do research, you know enough to be on the lookout for evidence that can give authority to the assertions you make in a paper. But even when you do random reading or when you listen to lectures in other disciplines or watch television or go to the movies, keep your eyes open for materials you can use in your paper.

The following paragraphs present an argument from authority. The historian David McCullough has investigated the recurring attacks of asthma that afflicted young Theodore Roosevelt, later president of the United States. What causes asthma? McCullough believes the disease is at least partly *psychosomatic*, that is, caused by the mental state of the victim rather than by germs, viruses, or some other physical entity. (The nickname *Teedie* in the selection was given young Theodore Roosevelt by his family, and McCullough uses it to indicate the child.)

35d

argue

In 1864, or two years after the infant Teedie's asthma had begun, a highly important work was published in Philadelphia, a book of 256 pages titled *On Asthma*. The author was an English physician, Henry Hyde Salter, a very keen observer who as the father of an asthmatic child had "experienced the horrors" of the disease. . . . Salter had found no abnormalities in the lungs of his asthmatic patients, no trace of the disease in either the respiratory or circulatory system, and hence concluded that the trouble lay in the nervous system. Asthma, a disease of "the direst suffering," a disease "about whose pathology more various and discrepant ideas prevail than any other," was "essentially a *nervous* disease."

Sudden "mental emotion," Salter said, could bring on an attack and abruptly end one. He did not know why, only what he had observed. He reported on a patient whose attack ceased the moment he saw a fire outside the window and another who had his asthma stop when put on a fast horse. Still other patients found that as soon as they neared the doctor's office, their asthma vanished, "suddenly and without any apparent cause except the mental perturbation at being within the precincts of the physician." The onset of an attack, he noted, was frequently preceded by a spell of depression or "heaviness" (what Teedie called feeling "doleful"), and twenty years in advance of what might be regarded as the first studies in the psychosomatic side of asthma he reported on a small boy who "found his disease a convenient immunity from correction."

"Don't scold me," he would say, if he had incurred his father's displeasure, "or I shall have the asthma." And so he would; his fears were as correct as they were convenient.

—DAVID MCCULLOUGH

Arguing from Testimony and Personal Experience

When we argue from testimony, we say that something happened to us and that this happening proves a point that we wish to make or that it proves our entire argument. Your personal experience may support an argument only if the experience has given you enough information to support generalizations that will help the case you are trying to make. If you have not learned from your experience, your argument may be weakened by inadequate support. Here is an argument from personal experience.

> Disneyland has been criticized for giving a sanitized version of American history, for trivializing international relations and national differences, and for taking all the frightening moments out of fairy tales. But I visited Disneyland with my two children last summer, and we loved it. Yes, it is a form of escapism. But why else do we go to an amusement park? Only a new form of puritanism requires us to be serious every moment about everything. Sometimes we have to relax. And I can't think of a time when I have been happier than I was sitting with my seven-year-old and my five-year-old in Dumbo, the Flying Elephant, circling round and round, suspended over the crowds by the strong steel arms of a friendly Disneyland machine that rotated us in the friendly sunshine.

**35e
argue**

35e
Building a Good Argument

Not every statement can be argued or is worth arguing. Not every statement can stand up in the face of contrary evidence. As you select an argument, be sure you can defend it. As you shape your argument, be sure you present your ideas courteously and without committing common fallacies.

Selecting a Topic

Begin by selecting a topic that is manageable and debatable.

A limited topic

Avoid arguments that are so broad that you can write only a series of assertions. You must gather enough information to know what you are talking about. Topics too broad require more knowledge than you can gather during the term.

You cannot argue in only a few pages that the American government is spending too much money for defense unless you are an expert on the federal budget, particularly on military spending. Even then, you can make that argument work in so short a paper *only* because you are a recognized authority. But you can argue in a brief paper that military spending involves a lot of waste—*if* you can gather evidence of that waste. You can get this information from magazine articles and newspaper stories and from budget hearings recorded in the *Congressional Record*. Many of these sources will be in your school library.

Your argument must be limited enough to state clearly. Your readers must know what you want to prove. Otherwise your argument will be useless.

A topic that lends itself to debate

A strong argument starts with a limited topic that lends itself to debate. If people can take sides on the issue, it's probably a good topic—provided it is limited enough to allow you to know it thoroughly and argue it convincingly. To test a topic for argument, you might ask if anyone cares to debate it.

35e
argue

Statement	Debatable?
Shakespeare wrote some interesting plays.	No. Few people would disagree with this topic.
Radio stations should not be allowed by the federal government to play rock music with lyrics that glorify drugs or casual sex.	Yes. Many people think that something should be done to protect young children from such music; others think that a prohibition against such music would violate the First Amendment to the Constitution, with its guarantee of free speech.
Private persons should not be allowed to own pistols.	Yes. Many people, citing the number of murders committed with pistols, think that private ownership of handguns should be banned. Many others believe that such a ban would restrict the freedom of law-abiding gun owners.
We should find a cure for AIDS.	No. AIDS is one of the epidemic diseases of our age, and all serious people believe we should find a cure for it.

Statement	Debatable? *(Con't)*
AIDS victims should be quarantined.	Yes. Many people believe AIDS victims should be kept away from society to protect those who do not have the disease. Others argue that the disease cannot be transferred by casual social contact and that quarantine of its victims would be cruel and inhuman.

35e

argue

Controversy is not essential for good argument. People do not have to be passionate about the subject. But the topic must be debatable. Often controversial topics (such as abortion, welfare, and legalizing drugs) have been argued so much that fresh insights are hard to come by. Do not argue an issue unless you have something new to say about it. It is almost never good to write an argument without reading what other people have written on the subject.

Matters of taste are seldom debatable. It is difficult to argue that a movie or a novel or a short story or a play is good or bad. People often disagree; what seems to be trash to one critic may seem like a masterpiece to another. Many people love the novel *Moby Dick;* others find it boring. Horror movies scare some people; they strike others as silly.

You can argue, however, that a movie or something you read contradicts itself or that it presents stereotypes or that it glorifies violence; you can argue that a movie is complicated, that it addresses this or that issue in society, that it strives for this or that effect. But the simple argument that the movie—or whatever—is "good" or "bad" will carry little weight.

■ **Exercise 35.6**   Which of the following statements would make good arguments? Which cannot be argued in a college paper seven or eight pages long? Write a short paragraph explaining your response to each suggested argument.

1. William Faulkner used descriptions of light in his novels to help emphasize the moods of his characters.
2. Mark Twain's novel *Huckleberry Finn* contains much that can injure the feelings of modern African Americans.
3. The movie *Star Wars* was the most brilliant film ever produced by Hollywood.
4. The movie *Star Wars* uses clichés developed in Hollywood westerns, but reinvents them by transposing them to outer space.
5. Everyone who drives to school would be happier if there were more free parking spaces.

■ **Exercise 35.7** Here are suggested topics for argument papers. Which are debatable, and which are not?

1. The law should ban smoking in all public places.
2. War is one of the great sources of misery in our time.
3. Women in the army should take part in combat.
4. The president of the United States holds great responsibility.
5. A constitutional amendment should outlaw any desecration of the American flag.

Considering Contrary Evidence

The facts rarely line up neatly on one side of any debatable issue. Debatable topics are debatable *because* they have at least two sides. Evidence can be interpreted in different ways. If you are to be fair-minded and reasonable, you must consider the opposing arguments. It is unfair to misquote or misrepresent the opposition. You must think out the opposing point of view as carefully as you can and be sure you represent it correctly.

In dealing with contrary evidence, you have three options: you can point out that it is invalid; you can admit its validity but point out its inferiority; or you can change your mind.

35e
argue

Invalidating contrary evidence

You can argue that the contrary evidence is invalid because it has been misinterpreted by your opponents and that it therefore does not damage your position.

> It is true that keeping the library open on Friday nights costs the university nearly a thousand dollars a week. People who want to close the library argue that all that money will be saved if we take this step. But they have forgotten that when the building is closed, we must pay the salary of a security guard. They have forgotten that even when the building is closed, the lights must be kept on for security, and the heat remains on to protect the books from dampness. They have forgotten that library personnel on duty at night are students working their way through college and that to cut off their pay might be to exclude them from higher education.

Discrediting contrary evidence

You can concede the contrary evidence but argue that your point of view is still superior.

> I do concede that only a handful of people use the library on Friday nights. Although those who want to close the library overestimate the money they would save, I concede that they would indeed save some

money. But why does a university exist? It exists to promote the life of the mind, to expand the intellect and the imagination, to produce knowledge. By keeping the library open on Friday nights, the university confirms these purposes to the handful of people who work there. The books two of these people have written confirm the purposes of the university to the thousands of people who read those books. Through these writers, the university reaches out to readers who can never enter the campus.

The student union is also open on Friday nights. I have checked into the costs of operating the union on those nights. They amount to some six thousand dollars an evening. I am not opposed to keeping the union open on Friday nights. But I do say that a university that saves a little money by closing its library while it keeps open its pool-rooms, its bowling alleys, its subsidized soda fountains, and its movie auditorium is selling its soul to the accountants and losing its fundamental purpose.

<table>
<tr><td>**35e**</td></tr>
<tr><td>**argue**</td></tr>
</table>

Acknowledging contrary evidence

Sometimes you may find it effective to develop your argument by the means by which you come to the position. Or, in the course of thinking about your topic, you may change your mind. Chronicling that process is itself a strong argument.

I once believed in legalizing marijuana. Smoking the weed made people feel good. It seemed to have no harmful effects, and it was not addictive, like alcohol or nicotine. Users said that marijuana did not impair vision or judgment, so drivers high on marijuana could operate cars and trucks in perfect safety. But now a considerable body of research has been built up to prove that marijuana *does* have harmful effects. Smoking marijuana is just as hard on the lungs as smoking tobacco. It does appear to be addictive. And marijuana has been implicated in several private-plane crashes, automobile wrecks, and, recently, train wrecks. It is not the harmless pleasure it once appeared to be, and I now think there are powerful reasons *not* to legalize the drug.

Using a Courteous Tone

Too often, writers of argument papers believe that they can win their argument only by assaulting and insulting everyone who disagrees with them. Fair-minded readers quickly reject writers who argue as though they were at a shouting match. You should learn to argue by friendly persuasion.

It is the fashion today to argue that Machiavelli's *The Prince* is a work of genius and to condemn the critics who have condemned Machiavelli through the centuries. No doubt Machiavelli was a brilliant observer of the sixteenth century and understood the tactics of the petty princes who ruled the Italian city-states. They were immoral men, and Machiavelli described their immorality in elaborate detail. Much of the criticism that has been leveled against Machiavelli through the years should be directed against those princes. He considered himself to be a sort of reporter, describing in great detail how they grasped power and held on to it. One can even argue that like the Christian thinkers of the Middle Ages, Machiavelli believed that human beings were selfish and ignorant, slaves of a flawed human nature.

But despite the brilliance of his observations and the blame that can be placed on the rulers he observed, Machiavelli himself can still be chilling. No particle of sympathy for the victims of those princes penetrates his stately prose. He seems to be above concern for the suffering of the innocent. He was passionately dedicated to building an Italian state strong enough to repel the French, German, and Spanish invaders. But nothing in his writings indicates dedication to human rights or even awareness that human beings have rights. No matter how highly we praise his genius, we must recognize that something is lacking in his spirit.

35e argue

The tone of the preceding paragraphs does not insult those who have said that Machiavelli was a genius and that he has been judged too harshly by later writers. It makes an argument based on evidence and treats those who have expressed different views gently.

Avoiding Fallacious Reasoning

Some reasoning may appear at first to be logical, but on examination the fallacies or errors in reasoning appear. Certain common fallacies appear again and again in arguments we see in political debate, in advertising, in editorial writing, and indeed in almost every public forum. Learn to recognize the common fallacies and to avoid them in your own writing.

Improper cause and effect

The mere fact that happening B occurred after happening A is not proof that A caused B. You must make a stronger connection than mere sequence to establish cause and effect. Many superstitions arise because people make connections between events that have no real relation except that one happened after the other.

> A black cat walked across my path last night, and when I got home, discovered that my house had been robbed. The black cat brought me bad luck.

> Since radio, television, and the movies began emphasizing stories about crime, crime has steadily increased; therefore, radio, television, and the movies have been responsible for the increase in the crime rate.

Crime increases for many reasons. We might make the argument if we interviewed several convicted criminals who said they had been motivated by the broadcast media and the movies to commit crime. Or if we could discover a rash of crimes identical to some crime that had been shown in a television story or a movie, we might have some indication that that medium increased the crime rate. But the mere fact that the crime rate rose after such stories became popular in the media is not evidence that the media caused the crimes. We might also discover that the crime rate had increased since television started broadcasting more basketball games. Would you argue that basketball broadcasts had increased crime?

35e

argue

Too little information for generalization

When you engage in inductive reasoning, you gather facts and arrive at generalizations. If you don't gather enough facts, you may make a faulty generalization.

> In many of his novels, William Faulkner wrote about terrible happenings in the American South. Therefore Faulkner must have hated the South.

> In his novel *The Turn of the Screw,* Henry James wrote about two ghosts who attempted to corrupt two little children. Therefore James believed in ghosts.

> I was in Paris last summer, and a French police officer was very rude to me when I asked him how to find the Louvre Museum. "You are standing next to it," he said. All the French are rude.

> My Uncle Herbert smokes two packs of cigarettes a day and is eighty-five years old. Therefore all the talk about the dangers of cigarette smoking is a lie.

Either/or reasoning

Pushing an argument to the extremes weakens it. Don't demand that your readers accept one of two extreme positions.

Either we must stop our children from listening to rock music or civilization will crumble.

Either you buy the new supercharged TurboLemon convertible when our sale ends or you will never have such an opportunity again in your life.

Either people must understand Shakespeare or they cannot consider themselves educated.

The straw man

A *straw man* is a weak or imaginary argument that you attribute to your opponent for the sole purpose of refuting it and seeming to advance your point. This strategy is designed to make readers (or hearers) think the opponent's position is so indefensible that no sensible person could possibly hold back. Often the attack on the straw man is a variation of the either/or fallacy.

35e
argue

Statement: In the United States, prayer in public schools offers many difficulties. It is difficult for sincerely religious people to keep from trying to influence others to accept their point of view. Prayers may easily become sermons. Different people use different forms of prayer. Christians customarily pray with their eyes closed; Jews pray with their eyes open; Americans of some other faiths pray by chanting. Children of various religious backgrounds are forced by law to go to school. But they should not be forced to worship God in a way that contradicts their own beliefs or the beliefs of their parents. The United States is the most religious of all the industrial countries, and we may suggest that religion has flourished here because it has not been forced on anyone. We would do well to ponder this question: Is religion helped by being prescribed by law, no matter how inoffensive the form may seem to those who prescribe it?

Reply: My opponent has questioned the value of prayer in the public schools. Only an atheist would do such a thing. He does not believe in God. He denies that we owe reverence to our Creator. He has blasphemed the Almighty by saying that little children should not pray to Him. It is his kind that will destroy our country, for if we forsake God, God will forsake us. I do not say that he is a Communist, but I say that he is playing into the hands of the Communists by denying God just as they deny God. If you vote for my opponent, my beloved friends, you are voting against religion.

The *ad hominem* argument

An *argumentum ad hominem* is an "attack on the person." The writer (or speaker) avoids the central issue of the opponent's argument and instead attacks the opponent's character.

> My opponent spent an hour last night explaining his economic policies to the nation on television. He advanced columns of figures about jobs and about workers and employment and inflation. He gave us a six-point program that he said would reduce inflation, increase employment, strengthen the dollar, and control the federal deficit. These items were very interesting, but I could not think about them very much because as the cameras zoomed in on him, I realized that he dyes his hair. Now I ask you, what kind of man dyes his hair? Can you believe in such a man? Would any of you women out there marry a man who dyes his hair? People who dye their hair are lying about themselves. And my friends, a man who lies about himself will lie about the budget of the United States. Look at me! I am totally bald. I have an honest, pure-bald head. Look at me, and see a man who believes in the truth. Look at my opponent and see a man who lies about his hair and his age and about anything else that will help him get elected president of the United States.

Begging the question

Begging the question is a fallacy in deductive reasoning that occurs when the person presenting the argument evades or sidesteps the real question by assuming it is established or proved. The person who begs the question states the major premise in such a way that it is a conclusion, without allowing an argument to decide the merits of the case.

> He could not be lying because he is president of the Campus Society for Moral Uplift.

Here is how this statement would be set up in a syllogism.

Major premise: The president of the Campus Society for Moral Uplift cannot tell a lie.

Minor premise: He is president of the Campus Society for Moral Uplift.

Conclusion: Therefore he cannot tell a lie.

If we accept the major premise, we have no argument. But the major premise begs the question by assuming a perfect correlation between top status in the Campus Society for Moral Uplift and honesty. That correlation cannot be assumed, and the premise is false. Moreover, if the president of the Campus Society for Moral Uplift was charged with lying, the argument should turn on the evidence, not on his position in a campus club.

The red herring

A **red herring** is any issue introduced into an argument that distracts attention from the main issue. People often introduce a red herring when they think they are about to lose an argument. The original red herring was a smoked salt fish with a strong taste and smell. Farmers who wanted to keep fox hunters from galloping across their crops and ruining them would drag a red herring along the edge of their fields to throw the dogs off track.

> That rugged-looking cowboy smokes a famous cigarette in beautiful magazine ads that show stunning color photographs of the American West. You can almost smell the fresh air and feel the glory of space in those ads. You can look at that beautiful scene and that handsome face and know that cigarettes are not nearly as bad for your health as the surgeon general claims they are.

**35e
argue**

The advertisers of cigarettes know that medical evidence is solidly against smoking. So they present red herrings, beautiful ads that feature beautiful people doing athletic or robust things while they smoke. The ads distract attention from the central issue—whether people should smoke or not.

■ **Exercise 35.8**   Read the following sentences, and identify the logical fallacies.

1. Anyone who claims that Americans have the right to burn the flag hates the United States.
2. Forty years ago, when my opponent was a freshman in college, he plagiarized a term paper and had to withdraw from school for a year. That proves he is a dishonest person and does not deserve your vote.
3. If you do not read Plato and Aristotle, you are contributing to the moral laxity of our times.
4. Anyone who thinks Stephen King writes serious novels is a fool.
5. I cannot write about this book because I dislike it so much.
6. I would not want my daughter to be a soldier because it is not ladylike to carry a gun.
7. Religious people are ignorant.
8. Morals have fallen in America because of television.

9. Athletes in television commercials drink beer; so I will drink beer, too.

10. Writing cannot be taught; so I will not take a writing course.

✔ **CHECKLIST 35.3: MAKING SOLID ARGUMENTS**

As you select your topic for an argument and frame your position, ask yourself these questions to be sure you are on track. Ask yourself these questions again as you revise your first draft, to be sure you are staying on track.

- Is my argument worth making?
- Does anyone dispute my argument?
- Can I make my argument in the space and time I have available?
- Can I develop my argument by reasoning, or can I only assert my opinions?
- Are my inductions logical?
- Are my syllogisms logical?
- Have I considered contrary arguments?
- Have I been courteous to my opponents?
- Are there any logical fallacies in my argument?
- Is my conclusion supported by my evidence?

35e argue

WRITING ABOUT LITERATURE

Many of your English courses will require you to write about novels, short stories, poems, or plays that you read on your own or that you study and discuss in class. An essay on a literary subject shows your understanding of the work you have read. Such an essay is always critical in the sense that it states your position on, attitude toward, or opinion of the work and provides details to support your point.

36a
Analyzing the Assignment

Your instructor may have a specific goal in asking you to write about a piece of literature. For example, your assignment may be to write about sound images in *The Tempest,* to analyze the theme of Melville's story "Bartleby the Scrivener," to compare two love sonnets by Keats, or to trace the development of a character in a novel. Or your instructor may give a general assignment—to write about a specific literary work or to choose a work on your own and write about it. In these last two cases you have to define the terms of the assignment yourself.

The student whose paper appears at the end of this chapter received this assignment. Read "in Just-" by E. E. Cummings and write an essay of about two or three typed pages that explains the meaning of the poem. The class was studying poetry and had read and discussed some of Cummings's other poems. The text of "in Just-" appears on pages 564–565.

Both specific and open-ended writing assignments about literature almost always require **analysis.** When you analyze something, you scrutinize its parts in order to understand the whole. You look closely at the words and sentences, the motivations and the actions of the characters, the events of the narrative, and the writer's techniques, among other elements. Analysis often involves **interpretation,** an explanation of what you think the work means, and **evaluation,** your opinion and judgment of the literary work. Analysis and interpretation lead to evaluation. You should base your judgments on thorough analysis and careful interpretation.

36b
Reading Actively

Don't write until you've read the work carefully several times. You cannot write a good paper about a work that you have read only once. When you read a text several times, you will begin to notice things that deepen your appreciation and enlarge your understanding of it. That detailed knowledge is a resource that will enable you to write a good paper.

Read actively. If you own the book, underline words and phrases and make notes to yourself in the margin. Some students of literature make their own indexes on the blank pages at the back of a book, especially in longer works. They copy a key phrase and the number of the page on which the phrase appears. They write down the names of characters and the first page on which each character appears. Sometimes they write a short summary of the character's qualities. Summarizing the main events in the plot is a good idea, too. Always record the page numbers in your notes and summaries. Later, when you begin to write about the work, you can find important passages easily.

To read literature actively is to ask questions. Stimulate your mind by posing questions about literary selections and seeking answers to them as you read. When you examine some of the approaches to writing about literature in 36e, you will find questions that will help you understand a novel, short story, poem, or play. Not all the questions will apply to every work. But if you keep them in mind as you read, you will become a more attentive reader, and you will see things in the literature that will help you write about it. Chapters 37 and 39 suggest other ways to read actively.

36c
Developing a Thesis

Follow the guidelines for prewriting presented in Chapter 1 as you prepare to write an essay about a piece of literature. Do brainstorming, make an informal list, or use a rough outline. Keep returning to the literary text as you shape your ideas.

Develop a tentative thesis for your paper. Before you begin writing your thesis statement, look at your assignment again. You may be able to use some of its language in your thesis. For example, if your assignment is to explain how Iago convinces Othello of Desdemona's guilt, your tentative thesis might be, "Iago convinces Othello of Desdemona's guilt by means of carefully developed circumstantial evidence."

See the research paper on Willa Cather in Chapter 34. Willa Cather wrote about harsh and grim life on the Great Plains and how that life deprived people of certain kinds of culture and beauty. You can see how the writer of this paper developed that theme in two of Cather's short stories. This research paper goes beyond a mere summary of the plot.

To develop such themes, you must study a text, think about it, read it again and again, and write down various ideas to try out as paper topics. These ideas may become an informal outline built around a central thesis. You may have to write a draft before your most important idea becomes clear; then you will have to write at least one more draft to develop it.

Use the guidelines in 1f as you formulate your thesis. Remember that your thesis should be flexible and probably will change as you write successive drafts. As with other kinds of writing, the thesis should state a concrete position that you can argue about. Both your topic and your opinion about it should be stated clearly.

**36c
lit**

The student who wrote about Cummings's poem developed his thesis in three stages.

Tentative thesis	Cummings's "in Just-" is about a group of children who respond to the whistle of the balloonman on a spring afternoon.
Revised 1	In the poem "in Just-" Cummings paints a child's world in the child's own terms.
Revised 2	In the poem "in Just-" E. E. Cummings presents a child's world filled with childhood's delights and dangers.
Final copy	The poem "in Just-" presents an entirely familiar world of children at play in the spring. Yet the poet's unusual use of language shows us the subtle dangers lurking about the delights and pleasures we all associate with childhood.

The tentative thesis is not a thesis at all. It is a summary of the action. It makes no arguable point. The first revised thesis does make an assertion, but it is too broad and not well focused. The second revised thesis makes an arguable assertion that is sufficiently limited for a brief literary paper. For the final copy (pp. 566–71), the student revised the thesis again.

When you write and revise, you must be sure to keep your paper focused on one leading idea. The writer of the paper about Willa Cather in Chapter 34, is not concerned about how Cather got from her birthplace in Virginia to Nebraska. Nor is the writer concerned about the many nineteenth-century stories about artistic young women dying of tuberculosis. These are interesting subjects. They might make interesting topics for other papers. But this paper is about the effect of the vast spaces of the Great Plains and the hardships of life there on two people with a great love of music and the culture that music reflects. The writer would have spoiled the effect if she had been distracted by these other ideas and had neglected her central theme.

36d
lit

36d
Considering Audience and Purpose

Your audience for a paper on a literary subject is usually your instructor. In most cases your instructor is familiar with the work he or she has asked you to write about and does not need a detailed plot summary.

Unless your assignment explicitly requires you to do so, avoid writing an extensive plot summary. Of course, you may have to refer to elements in the plot to make your point. But your instructor does not want to read a paper that tells her something she already knows quite well. She wants to see your mind at work. She wants you to think about the piece and to develop ideas that your reading has stimulated in your mind. Write your essay as if both of you know the work and you want to tell her some things you have learned about it.

Your purpose in writing will influence the outcome of your paper. If you are writing an essay with limits defined by your instructor—about two pages (500–750 words), for example—make your point quickly and offer supporting detail and no more. If the assignment is due within a few sessions, you should avoid an overly ambitious plan that draws upon extensive use of secondary sources and other library materials. For brief interpretive essays, most instructors expect you to develop ideas from the primary text itself. If you have been given a substantial amount of time to carry out the assignment, library research is probably a requirement. Chapters 31 through 34 present a research paper on a literary topic and show you how the paper was developed.

36e
Considering Approaches to Literary Analysis

You may take any of a variety of approaches when you write about literature and you may ask several kinds of questions as you think about your assignment.

Writing About the Characters

If you decide to focus your essay on character in a work of literature, think about the way the author develops the characters and the relation of character to other aspects of the work, such as plot, structure, and meaning.

Begin by identifying the most important characters in the work. How are they related to each other? How do they relate to each other? Does one character dominate the work, or do several characters share the action equally? What exactly do the characters do? Do they talk more than they act? Do the characters' actions match their talk, or do they talk one way and act another? What do the actions and the talk reveal about the characters? What makes you sympathize with or like one or more of the characters? What makes you unsympathetic toward or dislike one or more of the characters? What moral values do the characters have? How do the characters judge their own situation? What do characters learn in the course of the action? How do characters change? How do what characters learn relate to the work's theme or meaning? If there is a narrator, what additional perspective does this character introduce? For more questions regarding narrators, see below.

36e
lit

Writing About the Plot and Setting

The **plot** is the action of a work; the **setting** is the place and time of the action. Writing about the plot means analyzing the relation of one event to another or the effects of the action on the characters or the effects of the characters on the action. Writing about the setting means trying to present your sense of why the author chose to create the scene as he or she did. The setting involves not only a specific location but also a broader environment of history and geography.

You can raise many questions about plot and setting. How has the author arranged and connected the events? Are the events told in the order in which they occur or in some other order? How does a single important event relate to other events? Where does the action of the work take place? Is there any significance to the setting where the action takes place? What period or periods of time does the work embrace? Why do you suppose the writer set the work in that time? What surprises you in the work? Why are you surprised?

Writing About the Structure of the Work

Literature falls into **genres,** or types. Short stories are one genre. Other genres are plays, poetry, novels, and essays. Screenplays represent a new literary genre. Each genre has a different formal structure. If you decide to focus your essay on the structure of a work of literature, you will need to analyze its elements in light of the expectations of its genre.

Here are some questions to consider. How has the author put the pieces together? How do the various chapters or stanzas or acts relate to each other? What particular chapter or stanza or act stands out for any reason? Why does it stand out? How is the work similar to or different from work in the same literary category, or genre? All poems belong to the genre of poetry, but the structure of a poem by E. E. Cummings is very different from the structure of a poem by John Keats or Thomas Hardy. And, despite similarities, one poem by Cummings is very different from other poems by Cummings. How does the author meet or challenge your expectations for the genre?

Writing About the Tone of the Work

The **tone** is the author's attitude toward the subject. How does the author feel about the characters and their actions, and how does the author make you feel about them? Is the tone impartial, serious, mocking, condemning, playful? What accounts for the author's attitude toward the subject? Why do you think the author wrote the work?

Considering tone usually means considering the speaker, or **narrator,** the person through whose eyes and lips we learn about the events. All narrators have a **point of view,** or perspective. What is the narrator's point of view? Is the story told by a third-person narrator, someone who is not a character in the piece? Or is it told by a first-person narrator? Does the third-person narrator follow one character exclusively, or does the point of view shift from character to character? How much does the narrator know about the characters he or she describes? Are his or her perceptions reliable? How does the narrator's knowledge affect what we as readers know about the action of the work? You never should assume that the narrator in any work is the same as the author of the work. What is the relation between the narrator and the author?

Writing About Language and Style

The **language** comprises the words the writer uses. **Style** includes language as well as sentence structure, usage, and diction. Imagery, figurative language, and symbolism (see Chapter 9 and 36f) contribute to style. Some questions to ask about language and style are:

- Are the words informal, colloquial, formal?
- What kinds of words does the author seem to like?
- Which words does the author repeat frequently?
- Which words seem to have special meaning for the author?
- Where and how has the author used sensory language?
- Are the images original?
- Can you identify a pattern in the uses of imagery?
- How do figurative expressions contribute to the style and meaning of the work?
- Does something in the work appear to stand for something else? That is, does some word, some action, some description or character make you think of something beyond it?
- How are the sentences structured—are they simple or complex, long or short?
- Which sentences do you like and why?
- What special qualities of style do you notice?

**36e
lit**

✓ CHECKLIST 36.1: **CONSIDERING APPROACHES TO LITERARY ANALYSIS**

In analyzing a work of literature, consider the following elements. You may decide to concentrate on any one of them, but in doing so, consider their interrelationships.

- the characters
- the plot and/or the setting
- the structure of the work
- the tone of the work
- the language and style of the work

■ **Exercise 36.1**   Read "A Rose for Emily," by William Faulkner. Answer in brief paragraphs the following questions about the story.

1. Who is the narrator in the story?
2. Where and when does the story take place?
3. How long a time does the story cover?
4. How old is the narrator?

5. How does Faulkner prepare us for the surprise ending?
6. How is Miss Emily Grierson related to her town?
7. What does Miss Emily say in the story?
8. What do you notice about the style of the work?

36f
Using the Language of Literary Analysis

Literary analysis often involves interpretation and evaluation. As you write about literature, use the language writers and critics use in the study of this art form.

Understanding Key Literary Devices and Terms

Literary critics identify literary devices that have helped writers achieve certain effects. Often these devices help integrate the whole piece for the reader and perhaps reveal an unexpected meaning that makes the text more vivid and more memorable. When you recognize such devices and know their names, you can write about them more effectively and make your papers about literature more interesting. Here are some common literary devices.

Climax

The **climax** of a literary work is that point toward which the entire piece seems to be directed. Usually literary works end shortly after the climax. The problems are resolved or made clear; some point of understanding is reached; the major action of the story takes place.

The climax of Faulkner's "A Rose for Emily" is the point at which the astonished citizens of Miss Emily's little town break into a room of her house after her funeral and discover the corpse of Homer Baron lying in the bed and a strand of Miss Emily's "iron-gray" hair lying on the pillow beside the corpse.

Being able to identify the climax will help you see more clearly all the devices the author is using to keep you reading to see how everything turns out and to see the relation of the various parts of the work to the whole.

Irony

A writer or speaker who uses **irony** means something different from the literal meaning of the words. Sometimes the writer means something entirely opposite from the words in the text. The most famous irony in

English is Jonathan Swift's "A Modest Proposal." Swift, enraged by England's exploitation of Ireland in the eighteenth century, was especially concerned about the neglect of poor Irish children while members of the English upper classes lived in luxury. He wrote:

> I have been assured by a very knowing American of my acquaintance in London, that a young healthy child well nursed is at a year old a most delicious, nourishing and wholesome food, whether stewed, roasted, baked, or boiled, and I make no doubt that it will equally serve in a fricassee, or a ragout.

Swift was not serious about serving little Irish children up for food. But he was serious in his belief that the rich, especially the rich English lords of Ireland, were treating the poor like animals.

Dramatic irony comes from characters in plays, poems, or stories who present or encounter a reality that is the opposite of appearances.

Shakespeare often uses dramatic irony in his plays. Macbeth is told that he will not die until Birnam Wood comes to Dunsinane Castle. He thinks he is secure because he does not believe a forest like Birnam Wood can move; but then Macduff's soldiers cut branches from the trees of Birnam Wood and use them as camouflage to disguise their movements, and so Birnam Wood comes to Dunsinane—and Macbeth is defeated and killed. Dramatic irony is common in all forms of literature.

In all irony, the audience must know that it is irony. In well-done ironic pieces, we know throughout that we are reading something not meant to be taken literally. Inexperienced writers may fail because they know they are writing with irony but do not give their readers any clues. Therefore the readers take their words literally.

36f

lit

Hyperbole

Hyperbole is exaggeration so extravagant that no reasonable person would take it for literal truth.

> The father of this pleasant grandfather, of the neighbourhood of Mount Pleasant, was a horny-skinned, two-legged, money-getting species of spider, who spun webs to catch unwary flies, and retired into holes until they were entrapped. The name of this old pagan's God was Compound Interest. He lived for it, married it, died of it. Meeting with a heavy loss in an honest little enterprise in which all the loss was intended to have been on the other side, he broke something— something necessary to his existence; therefore it couldn't have been his heart—and made an end of his career.

> —CHARLES DICKENS, *Bleak House*

Dickens here amuses himself by going back into the genealogy of the Smallweed family, characters in *Bleak House* that Dickens holds up to ridicule. He wants to show us that the entire family of Smallweeds was greedy, heartless, and cruel.

Understatement

Like exaggeration, **understatement** often pops up in ordinary speech, especially in humorous statements intended to defuse a tense situation. Your roommate comes in and starts throwing books against the wall one by one and screaming at the top of his voice because he received a grade of C− on a paper that he was certain would get an A. You say, "I believe you're upset."

Here is Mark Twain describing a celebration of the Fourth of July on an American ship in the Mediterranean during one of his trips to Europe.

> The speeches were bad—execrable, almost without exception. In fact, without *any* exception, but one. Capt. Duncan made a good speech; he made the only good speech of the evening. He said:
>
> "LADIES AND GENTLEMEN:—May we all live to a green old age, and be prosperous and happy. Steward, bring up another basket of champagne."
>
> It was regarded as a very able effort.
>
> —MARK TWAIN, *The Innocents Abroad*

"It was regarded as a very able effort" expresses the enormous relief of the passengers that they were about to be treated to champagne rather than a long speech.

Allusion

When writers make **allusions,** they refer to something indirectly without precisely identifying it. It may be a literary work, a historical event, a work of art, a person, or something else. In writing papers about literature, you should be especially interested in allusions to other written works.

> Methought I saw my late espousèd saint
>   Brought to me like Alcestis from the grave
> Whom Jove's great son to her glad husband gave,
> Rescued from death by force, though pale and faint.
>
> —JOHN MILTON, "On His Dead Wife"

At the beginning of this famous sonnet, Milton alludes to the classical myth of Alcestis, the wife of King Admetus of Thessaly. She sacrificed her life to save her husband, and later Zeus (or Jove, as the Romans called him) permitted Hercules to go down into the realm of the dead and bring her back to her husband. Milton also alluded frequently to the Bible.

An allusion can often be used as the topic of a paper about literature because the allusion may provide a key to understanding the work. In poetry particularly, an allusion may give the key to the entire work.

Recognizing Symbols and Images

Fiction writers, dramatists, and poets sometimes use language that makes us think both of the literal truth they are describing and of something beyond that truth. The reverberations that symbols set up broaden and intensify the meaning of the literary work.

To find images and symbols in literature, you must read the text carefully and look closely at individual words to see what special meanings the writer may have poured into them. Look especially at words that are frequently repeated. You must also be well read and familiar with the cultural context of the work.

> Still falls the Rain—
> Dark as the world of man, black as our loss—
> Blind as the nineteen hundred and forty nails
> Upon the Cross.
>
> —Edith Sitwell, "Still Falls the Rain"

36f
lit

The English poet Edith Sitwell wrote these lines about the German air raids over London in 1940, early in World War II. We may see in the image of the cross the suffering of innocent humankind from war throughout the 1,940 years since Christ.

COMMON LITERARY DEVICES

Climax	The point toward which the entire piece is directed.
Irony	The use of words to express a meaning opposed to the literal meaning.
Dramatic irony	The use of characters who present or encounter a reality that is the opposite of appearances.
Hyperbole	Exaggeration so extravagant that no one would mistake it for the literal truth.
Understatement	A moderate statement in ironic contrast to what the situation warrants.
Allusion	An incidental, indirect reference to someone or something.
Symbols and images	Language that suggests or stands for something beyond its literal meaning.

■ **Exercise 36.2** Read the poems "Richard Cory," by Edwin Arlington Robinson; "Ozymandias," by Percy Bysshe Shelley; and "Death and Co.," by Sylvia Plath. See how many literary devices you can find in each poem.

36g
Writing About Literature: A Sample Paper

Use your prewriting to guide you as you develop the first and later drafts of your essay on a literary topic. Be prepared to revise your thesis as your ideas take shape. Return often to the work you are writing about.

Write your essay as you would an essay on any topic. Write an introduction followed by paragraphs that support your points with specific details. Make your conclusion a natural ending.

One further point: Write about your literary topic in the present tense. The convention in discussing literature and other works of art is to assume that the work "happens" each time it is read, viewed, heard, or studied. Notice in the student paper that follows how the writer uses the present tense to describe what Cummings achieves in his poem: "Cummings *uses* words and images that reflect a child's perception of the world"; "But beneath this simple word *is* a much more complex one"; "the poet *raises* the questions but *provides* no definite answers."

The following essay about a literary subject was written in response to the assignment asking for an analysis of E. E. Cummings's poem "in Just-." The full text of the poem appears below.

in Just-
spring   when the world is mud-
luscious the little
lame balloonman

whistles   far   and wee

and eddieandbill come
running from marbles and
piracies and it's
spring

when the world is puddle-wonderful

36g
lit

the queer
old balloonman whistles
far   and   wee
and bettyandisbel come dancing

from hop-scotch and jump-rope and

it's
spring
and
   the

      goat-footed

balloonMan   whistles
far
and
wee

**36g
lit**

✔ **CHECKLIST 36.2: REVISING AN ESSAY ABOUT LITERATURE**

As you revise your essay about literature, attend to all the concerns that have been emphasized in this handbook. Review Checklist 2.2 and 34.1 in particular. Then ask yourself these questions.

- Did I examine the assignment carefully?
- Did I read and reread the literary work actively so that I understand it well?
- Did I do prewriting to develop my ideas on the work?
- Did I state my thesis as a hypothesis that I can argue intelligently?
- Did I offer specific details to support my thesis?
- Did I quote accurately? Did I enclose in quotation marks any exact words that I used from the literary work?
- Did I avoid extensive plot summaries?
- Did I demonstrate my understanding of the work by analyzing it carefully? Did I address literary terms and devices, where appropriate?
- Did I consider my audience and purpose?

(1-a) The short introduction states the thesis succinctly. Compare this final thesis with the tentative and revised theses on page 555.

36g
lit

(1-b) The writer analyzes the language and draws details from the poem. Note the quotation marks enclosing words quoted from the poem and the slash indicating the end of one line and the beginning of the next. See 26e.

(1-c) Note that the writer offers no summary of the poem, as none is needed to understand this essay, but does express his own thinking about the poem.

(1-d) "But" and "this simple world" connect this paragraph with the preceding one.

Delights and Dangers of Childhood

(1-a)   E. E. Cummings's poems show an inventive, playful use of words
and sentence structure to force readers to consider common ideas and
feelings in a new context. The poem "in Just-" presents an entirely
familiar world of children at play in the spring. Yet the poet's
unusual use of language shows us the subtle dangers lurking about
the delights and pleasures we all associate with childhood.

Cummings uses words and images that reflect a child's
perception of the world. He calls the world "mud-luscious" and
"puddle-wonderful." With those phrases we can feel a child's delight
at springtime. The games abandoned at the balloonman's call--
(1-b)   "marbles and / piracies" and "hop-scotch and jump-rope"--accurately
show us children at play. Cummings runs the names of the children
together on the page so that we hear them just as children would say
(1-c)   them, "eddieandbill" and "bettyandisbel." In addition, the
balloonman "whistles far and wee," a child's excited expression
certainly. The words "it's spring" are repeated twice, again to show
the innocent excitement of youngsters outdoors after the spring
rain.

(1-d)   But beneath this simple world is a much more complex one. The
balloonman has a peculiar, ominous power over the children. They
stop everything, running and dancing to see him. On one level, of
course, it is not surprising for children to greet a neighborhood
visitor who sells balloons. Yet Cummings calls him "lame," "queer,"

(2-a) By explaining the allusion to the satyrs, the writer enriches our understanding of the poem.

(2-b) The writer comments on structure. Any phrase repeated in a short poem demands consideration. The writer makes an interesting point about the phrase "far and wee."

(2-c) Again, an explanation of an allusion puts the poem in a broader context.

(2-d) The writer offers his view of the theme of the poem. Clearly he reached this conclusion after considering many elements of the poem, such as language, style, character, and setting.

(2-e) Analyzing a key phrase, and relating it to the structure of the poem, is a good strategy here.

(2-a) and "goat-footed." In Greek mythology, the satyrs, creatures who enjoyed wild merrymaking, were humanlike gods with goats' features. By alluding to the satyrs, the poet implies something sinister.

(2-b)   The phrase for the sound of the balloonman's whistle, "far and wee," which is used three times in this poem of twenty-four very short lines, also suggests something unusual, even dangerous. Why "far"? Will the sound transport the children far away? Can children far away hear it? Although Cummings's piper is more contemporary--he uses a whistle instead of a flute--the poet certainly is alluding

(2-c) here to the Pied Piper of Hamelin, who enchanted all the children with his magic flute and lured them away from their town.

(2-d)   In a sense, then, the poem may be viewed as a story of the loss of innocence awaiting children as they grow up. In a secure world of play there are no troubles. But evil and danger are imminent, maybe even necessary for passage into adulthood. These ideas help call

(2-e) attention to the phrase "in Just-" / "spring." (Cummings probably used an uppercase letter for the j in Just for emphasis. The only other capital letter in the poem is for the word Man in balloonMan, when the word appears for the third time. Even the children's names are set in lowercase letters.)

    Does the word Just mean "only," suggesting that spring alone, the season of growth and renewal, is the time of joy in a child's life? Or is the message darker, perhaps even ironic? If spring is "just," meaning fair or honorable, where is the justice in children (or their childhoods) being stolen away? Perhaps Cummings is saying

(3-a) The questions are interesting, especially in light of the writer's conclusion: "the poet raises the questions but provides no definite answers."

**36g
lit**

that spring is not just at all, that its delights are merely

seductions. What makes the poem so compelling and provocative is

(3-a)   that the poet raises the questions but provides no definite answers.

37

WRITING ACROSS THE CURRICULUM

Most college courses require writing—short papers, research papers, reports, perhaps even journals that may give an account of your reading and your thoughts about it. The advice we give in this handbook will help you in all these writing assignments.

But different courses have different requirements for writing. A physics professor may ask you to write a lab report describing an experiment demonstrating the forces that operate on a moving body, such as a ball rolling down an inclined plane. A biology course may require you to write a lab report on cell division in a Petri dish. A business course might concentrate on case studies and reports. A history professor may ask you to relate the events that led to the outbreak of the first World War or to explain the thought of an important woman in history or to discuss a controversy among historians. A philosophy course may require a number of short papers developing abstract concepts or steps in logic. An economics professor may ask you to write a paper explaining the ripple effects that sweep through an economy from a change in the minimum wage law or the tax structure. In all these disciplines you may be asked to write reports that show that you have read and understood assigned books and articles.

These different kinds of papers require the same prewriting techniques, the drafting, the revising, and the proofreading that are the subject of this handbook. This chapter suggests ways you can apply these techniques in writing across the curriculum.

✔ **CHECKLIST 37.1: UNDERSTANDING THE WRITING ASSIGNMENT**

Your instructors are the authorities for what you write in college courses. Listen carefully to what they tell you, and follow their instructions. If they give you written handouts to guide your work, read them carefully. If they do not provide handouts, perhaps you should request them.

For each writing assignment, be sure you understand its purpose and elements as well as the mechanics of length and date due. Consider these questions.

- Does the assignment call for a report or an essay? That is, does the assignment require you primarily to assemble information, or does it require you to collect information and interpret it?
- What are the key words in the assignment? *discuss,* explain, *compare,* evaluate; *why, when, who, where, what.* How do these key words define what you must write?
- How long will the paper be?
- What is the deadline for the assignment?
- Where will you find the evidence to help you write the assigned paper? The library? By observation or field trip? By experiment in the laboratory?
- Will your paper have parenthetical references and a list of works cited or references, or will it be sufficient to mention your few sources in the text?
- Will your instructor look at a draft of the paper before you hand in the final copy?
- Will your instructor let you work on the paper with another student in the class?
- What information from other courses or disciplines will help you write this paper?
- Have you had any personal experiences that may help make the points you want to make in the paper?

37a
curric

Reading Actively

Good writing begins with active reading. Study every subject and course you take in college with an active and critical mind. Don't be passive. Don't accept everything you read merely because it is on the page. Don't accept everything you hear merely because a college professor said it. Ask yourself why people write things, say things, demonstrate things. Ask what your own observations mean.

Read, observe, think, and write with questions in mind. Compare data. Be skeptical. Don't be content with reading one source. Read several sources for the same subject and compare them. How different are histories about Martin Luther written by Catholics, Protestants, Jews, and those with no religion at all? How do astronomers and other scientists differ in their thinking about black holes? How different are the views of women about the works of Ernest Hemingway from the views of men? How does gender shape literature and affect literary criticism?

Try to read as though you were a detective in a mystery novel trying to make all the evidence add up to something. Ask if there is any reason you should *not* believe something you see in a film or hear on tape or read in a book or article. Ask yourself about the motives of writers. What biases do they have? What are they trying to prove? Can you tell if they are not giving you all the information you need? Have they not thought to ask questions that you can ask of their material?

37a
curric

Thinking Critically

To write a good paper, you must engage your mind with your subject. That is thinking critically. To think critically is to ask questions about everything you read and to look for meanings that aren't immediately obvious. The critical thinker reads between the lines of texts, considers motives, ponders biases, asks what else needs to be known before a judgment can be made. Such thinkers never take anything for granted. They never read passively. They read and listen and observe skeptically—not out of an angry spirit of contrariness but out of curiosity and a desire to get to the bottom of things.

Drawing Inferences

When you read actively and think critically, you make connections. You connect elements of the work you are reading. You connect ideas from the work with facts you already know and ideas that grow out of them. You put facts and ideas together to draw inferences (see 35b).

An **inference** is not a bare opinion. It is a plausible judgment arrived at by comparing something we are studying with something else we know. An inference is believable on the basis of the evidence, but it often cannot be proved beyond the shadow of a doubt. When you draw inferences in a paper, you put texts and observations in a larger context. You provide meaning. You explain things.

According to an old legend, Sir Isaac Newton observed an apple fall while he sat in a garden in England. He asked himself what force made the apple fall. In pondering this question—or one like it—he inferred that bodies attracted each other by a force called *gravity,* which meant only "the quality of being heavy." No one has ever been able to explain this force. But Newton was able to describe it mathematically and to demonstrate that it was constant throughout the universe, at least as far as it was possible to observe it in his day.

Newton's original inference was very simple—a force exists in bodies that causes them to attract each other. Your inferences may also be simple, but they can lead to interesting arguments that suggest relationships among different pieces of evidence.

Relationships and motives can be very complex. In an American history course you might want to write a paper on the concept of states rights held by political figures in the southern United States long before the Civil War. They seem to have been sincere in their belief that the federal government had no right to coerce the people of Georgia or Mississippi to do anything they did not want to do. But did states rights have any content other than the right to deprive black citizens of civil rights given all Americans by the U.S. Constitution? Could any issue besides race have caused the Civil War? Did southern politicians ever make another important case that might have defined states rights? These are complicated questions that can be approached by trying to infer the real meaning of texts behind the words.

Like Newton, you begin with a fundamental question and expand it into a wide investigation of related questions. You cannot answer these questions off the top of your head. You must read carefully and widely. You must move back and forth between evidence and inference to establish the basis for your conclusions.

■ **Exercise 37.1**   Study the following text, and show where the writer is reporting information. Where is this writer drawing an inference and expressing an opinion?

> Arthur M. Schlesinger was for many years regarded as one of the great liberal historians of our times. He wrote three admiring books on Franklin D. Roosevelt's New Deal and another book about the administration of John F. Kennedy in whose administration he served. Both these men were heroic figures to him, as was Woodrow Wilson, the president of the United States during World War I.
>
> Yet it is curious to see how little discussion Schlesinger gives to racism in the United States in the first volume of his three books on the New Deal, *The Crisis of the Old Order,* published in 1957. That was three years after the Supreme Court outlawed racial segregation in the public schools, two years after the Reverend Martin Luther King, Jr., had led blacks in Montgomery, Alabama, to victory over segregation in the city's bus system. It was at a time when racial discrimination was being talked about all over the country.

37a
curric

Yet except for a brief discussion of the revival of the Ku Klux Klan during and after World War I, Schlesinger hardly speaks of racism at all. The word "Negro"—the word commonly used to describe black Americans in 1957—does not appear in his index. He expresses his approval of Woodrow Wilson for Wilson's plan for a League of Nations. But as president of the United States, Woodrow Wilson introduced racial segregation into the Federal Civil Service, including the United States Post Office. Schlesinger passes that fact over in silence. It is as if Schlesinger simply did not think matters of race were important enough to mention. Or it may be that he did not want to say anything bad about politicians he regarded as liberal and heroic—including Woodrow Wilson. Therefore, it seems, Schlesinger praises them and remains silent about their vices.

—DICK CURRY

■ **Exercise 37.2**   Now that you have had some practice in looking at a text where inferences are made, read carefully the following excerpt from a book by William J. Bennett, who was secretary of education under President Ronald Reagan. Read the text, and write down all the questions you can think of about it. Then look at the questions that we have provided. How do your questions compare with ours?

A third key education reform is parental choice—full, unfettered choice over which schools their children will attend. In a free market economy, those who produce goods and services are ultimately answerable to the consumer; if quality is shoddy, the consumer will buy someone else's product. It doesn't work that way in public education, though. Even when armed with adequate information about school quality (which they rarely have), parents in most places around the country are not permitted to transfer their children from a bad school to a good one.

In a sharp break with my predecessor, Terrel H. Bell, I immediately voiced strong support for vouchers and tuition tax credits when I became Secretary of Education. "The idea of choice is an idea whose time has come," I said at a news conference announcing our proposal. The proposal urged that the federal Chapter I program (compensatory education for the disadvantaged) be administered through vouchers (averaging $600 each) in order to give students from less fortunate environments the chance to choose private schools, too. As I told the National Catholic Educational Association in 1985: "All parents, regardless of income, should be able to choose places where they know their children will learn. And they should be able to choose environments where their own values will be extended instead of lost. It's possible that there are some public schools nobody would choose. They are so bad that they might suddenly find themselves without any students. But I have no idea why we should be interested in protecting schools like that from competition—or any schools from competition. Our worst schools are non-competitive schools, and that's no coincidence."

—WILLIAM J. BENNETT, *The Devaluing of America*

If you are writing about Bennett's remarks for a course in sociology or political science or education, here are some questions you might ask as a prewriting exercise to help you write a paper about his views.

1. Does Bennett approve of our present public school system?
2. What does he think will happen if competition is introduced into the public school system?
3. How many poor children might choose a private school if they received vouchers worth $600 each from the federal government?
4. Will $600 pay the tuition at a private school?
5. How does Bennett's proposal relate to the idea of separation of church and state?
6. Who are the people most likely to oppose or support Bennett's proposals?

37b
curric

All these questions require further research. But by asking them and others, you are reading actively, thinking critically, drawing inferences, and on your way to writing a paper about Bennett's proposals.

37b
Approaching Texts Critically

All disciplines require you to write about **texts,** either written texts or the "texts" that you observe in the area you are studying. A motion picture can be a "text"; so can a balance sheet or a dissected frog. A painting, a sculpture, a building, a billboard, a television commercial, an athletic uniform, or even a whole city can also be a text in this definition. All these objects present us with different meanings, some obvious, some obscure. As you write about texts, you discover relationships and learn to ask questions that help you understand not only the subject you are investigating but the nature of truth itself.

When you prepare to write in any college class, first consider your texts. Approach your writing assignment by focusing first on these texts. You may wish to do as many writers do and use a notebook to collect your thoughts.

Summarizing and Interpreting

Begin by writing a one-page interpretive summary of the text. Write on one page a brief statement of what is in the book, the article, the short story, the poem, the letter, or whatever written text you have before you. If the text is a painting, a building, a tool, a specimen, or some other meaningful object, describe it briefly. You will find that the effort to describe physical objects helps you see them better. Then try to say what you think the text means. How does it fit with the other information you have about your subject? How do you think you can use the text as you write about it?

If you are writing about a written text, choose a passage that has a special resonance to you, something that you notice, that seems to speak out. We all read things now and then that make us say suddenly, "That's great!" Or we read sentences that convey some thought that we have been groping for ourselves. These meaningful passages can be the basis of interesting structural and thematic discussions. It is always good to look for sentences that hold the key to the meaning of the entire text.

If your text is an object such as a work of art, describe the part of it that stands out to you. If you are looking at a painting of a human figure in an art history course, you may decide whether the face is individual, realistic, abstract, or idealized. Does the face look serene, troubled, loving, angry, determined? Try to decide why the face makes such an impression on you. Speculate on the painter's intention in portraying the face in that way.

In a geology course, you may be on a field trip to study the effects of glaciation, and your "text" may be a landscape with rounded valleys and rocky mountainsides that show the effects of glaciers scraping along the ridges.

Examining Premises and Contradictions

Every text makes some assumptions and contains some inherent contradictions. Pick out the contradictions you see or infer, and try to decide how important they are. For example, isn't it odd that in Shakespeare's *Henry V* the English victory at Agincourt causes the slaughter of several thousand Frenchmen and yet immediately after it King Henry marries the princess of France, Katherine, who seems to love him? What does that seeming contradiction mean?

Perhaps your text is a document. In a political science class, you might be asked to write about the Constitution. What are its assumptions? What are its contradictions? The Declaration of Independence, for example, had stated that "all men are created equal." How did it happen, then, that the Constitution acknowledged slavery? The Fourteenth Amendment, passed in 1868, affirmed that all persons born or naturalized in the United States are citizens. How did it happen, then, that women were not allowed to vote in federal elections until 1920? Examining assumptions and contradictions can often point you straight at the heart of crucial social problems.

For a visual text, ask similar questions. What purpose is served in nature by having a frog's front legs so small compared to the back legs? Why did Picasso paint figures with the faces flattened out and the eyes in the wrong places? Why do medieval paintings show the birth of the Virgin Mary taking place in great castles when according to the New Testament she and her husband Joseph were poor people? Why do advertisers make beer commercials so funny? Why do advertisements for cigarettes show young, healthy people smoking in scenic outdoor settings?

**37b
curric**

Uncovering Sources

Where did the writer get his or her information? How does the writer use these sources? In formal academic essays, the sources are clearly stated. It's often fascinating to see how a writer uses primary sources to produce a secondary source.

But how do poets get their information? Where does Toni Morrison get the material for her fiction? Where did the ideas for the Constitution come from? What are the sources a historian uses to write about the assassination of John F. Kennedy?

The same questions can be asked of visual objects. How did a photographer take pictures of starving people in Somalia? Did she stand close up to these dying people, or did she stand off at a distance and shoot with a telephoto lens?

What are the impressions of nature we get from the wildlife photography we see so frequently on television? What is the significance of some of the images of science writing—the web of life, the chain reaction in atomic explosions?

How may a photograph of political figures have been cut to eliminate some of them and emphasize others? Why do photographs of Franklin Roosevelt show him sitting down or focus only on his face above a podium?

What subjects did a nineteenth-century French painter choose? Did he paint inside or outside? Why did he paint the same subjects again and again?

What are the sources for a work of music? Has the composer used folk songs, national anthems, or works of other composers?

Analyzing Images and Implications

Images are easy to identify in literary works. The sun and the moon recur in images throughout Shakespeare's plays. But images recur in all kinds of prose. Why do pronouncements from presidents and other government officials so often use images taken from war? Why do some public figures use images from sports? Why, in traditional English, were ships and countries described as *she*? Why do the British have a *mother country* and the Germans a *fatherland*? Think about images in the texts you study and the language you use and try to understand what they seem to imply.

Visual objects also convey images. Why do churches have steeples? Why are women in sculptures of the nineteenth and twentieth centuries so often presented bare-breasted or even nude, while male statues usually have their private parts covered up? Why do women's fashions often emphasize their bodies, while men's fashions obscure their bodies? But in Henry VIII's day male fashions highlighted male bodies—why? Why are American and British graveyards so often laid out like parks with grassy lawns and great trees, while southern European graveyards are often cramped and treeless, the tombs pushed up against one another, and scarcely ever shaded by trees? Why do presidential candidates now present themselves to be photographed in running shorts or in otherwise informal dress, while presidential candidates of an earlier time were nearly always photographed in suits and ties? Why are Coke bottles subtly shaped like the female body? What does the female body have to do with advertising and sales? What does that say about American culture? A photograph of a Yoruba dancer in Africa shows him wearing a painted mask. What possible meaning can the mask have? Why have Chinese artists been so fascinated with dragons? What can the smears of color in a Mark Rothko painting signify?

Images convey meaning. Notice them and write about them. Sometimes meaning is conveyed not so much by imagery as by implication. Write about meanings that may not be obvious but seem to be implied. What does it mean when so many people who commit crimes now claim that they are the real victims: "I sexually harassed various female employees in my office because I was a victim of alcoholism, and I could not help myself?" What does it mean when a government official uses the passive voice, saying something like this: "Mistakes have been made. Money has been lost. Perhaps crimes have been committed. The matter is under investigation."

Why did athletic teams once commonly name themselves "Redskins," "Indians," "Braves," and "Seminoles"? Why is so much glass used in modern high-rise architecture?

Texts have their mysteries, their secrets, their conundrums that no interpreter can ever quite tease out. The silences of a text are often as provocative as its words. When you write about the things you do not

37b

curric

understand, you often discover that others find those passages mysterious. And you may discover their meaning, too.

Making Comparisons

Compare one text to other texts by the same writer, artist, scientist, architect, or thinker. Compare one situation to another. Compare one time period to another. Compare one person to one or more other persons. Compare the work of one scientist to that of another. Compare different paintings by the same artist. Compare the same subject as it was painted by several artists.

Always be sure your comparisons are instructive, that they genuinely add to knowledge about an important subject. A recent article in the *New Yorker* compared Margaret Mitchell's *Gone With the Wind* with the "plantation novels" that came before it and with the racism of movies such as *Birth of a Nation*. The comparison was illuminating.

Don't fall into the error of the writer who once compared the sea and the desert: They are both big, they are inhospitable to human beings, but there is a lot more going on under the surface than you may think. Anyone must ask in reading such a comparison, "So what?" When you do any kind of writing—but especially when you compare one thing with another—ask yourself, "So what?" What does it matter? What value is there to the comparison?

37b curric

■ **Exercise 37.3** Read ten pages in one of the books or articles you are studying in a course you are taking. Subject those ten pages to the approaches described in this section. Summarize them briefly, pick out a sentence or two that seems especially important, look for assumptions and contradictions, find the sources. Are there any images in the text? If so, what impression do they convey? What is implied in the text? What don't you understand about it? Is it useful to compare this text with another? Now consider how these approaches would help you write about the text for a class writing assignment. Sketch a brief outline for a paper.

✔ **CHECKLIST 37.2: WHAT IS A TEXT?**

Expand your notion of *text*. Think of texts as literary works but also as documents, films, works of art, musical scores, artifacts, objects, substances, specimens. By expanding your notion of text, you can approach writing assignments in any discipline as you would approach a writing assignment about a work of literature. Follow these steps.

- Write a one-page interpretive summary or description.
- Select passages or elements that attract your attention.
- Examine premises and contradictions.
- Look for sources.
- Analyze images.
- Explore implications.
- Identify what you don't understand and ask why.
- Compare the text with others.

37c
Using Evidence

All writing assignments, in every discipline, depend on evidence. Unless you are a well-known expert in the field you are writing about, your bare opinion will not count for anything with your readers. You must provide reasons for them to accept your point of view. Instructors in all your college courses want you to support your opinions with evidence that places you solidly within the **discourse community** of the discipline they teach. You must be able to support your writing with evidence that those who know the discipline will find plausible.

Like texts, evidence need not be limited to literary works or documents. Evidence can be letters you find in a library, observations you make on field trips, experiments, interviews, statistical tables, and public opinion polls. If you dissect a frog in a biology laboratory, you observe the evidence of the frog's body.

Distinguishing Primary and Secondary Sources

Most sources of evidence are classified as *primary* or *secondary*. Be sure you understand the difference.

Primary sources

Primary sources are the fundamental building blocks of research. They provide the most direct information because they are the sources nearest to your subject. Primary sources may come from the era you are writing about. Often they come from the person you write about or the people who knew the person.

For example, if you write about how President Woodrow Wilson installed racial segregation in the U.S. Civil Service, your primary sources would include the Wilson Papers edited in many volumes by Arthur Link and others at Princeton University Press. These papers include almost everything Wilson wrote that has survived, including speeches, letters, memos, articles, lecture notes, and others. Books Wilson published are not included in the Wilson Papers because they are available in libraries. But these books would also be primary sources for Wilson's thought. Primary sources might also include the correspondence and diaries of people who had had conversations with him or who had observed him during his lifetime. Primary sources for this writing assignment would also include government documents.

Primary sources for a study of crime in your town would include police reports, court reports, and statistics compiled by various law-enforcement agencies. They might also include records of conversations with or writing by convicted criminals, by those who have been accused of crime, or by victims of crime, by police officers, and by others somehow directly connected with crime and its causes and effects.

The primary sources for a topic in astronomy would include data gathered by astronomers from their observations of stars and planets or other phenomena of the universe. The primary sources of a topic in medical science might be statistics on the spread of a disease such as AIDS or cancer or the common cold. They might also include direct microscopic examination of agents that cause these diseases or of the bodily tissue that they affect.

**37c
curric**

Secondary sources

Secondary sources are reports and essays written about primary sources. Many people have written about Woodrow Wilson, segregation, crime, astronomy, and disease. A biography of Wilson is a secondary source. So is an article about Wilson in a historical journal. A history of segregation such as C. Vann Woodward's *The Strange Career of Jim Crow* is a secondary source. An essay on Shakespeare's play *Romeo and Juliet* by G. Blakemore Evans is a secondary source for the play.

Secondary sources in the sciences are somewhat more difficult to define. An essay written by a scientist presenting research methods and results is a primary source. But an essay written by a scientist such as Stephen J. Gould about the research of others is a secondary source—a very fine one. Secondary sources convey important information, and they may include arguments or opinions by scholars and others. An essay you write about a scientific subject is a secondary source.

When you use secondary sources, try to discover how reliable they are. A documentary or film that interprets a historical event is a secondary source, as it compiles primary sources—photographs, original footage—to present a point of view. The celebrated documentary by Ken Burns on the Civil War presents many extraordinary images and texts from that tragic conflict. Millions of Americans saw it. But it contains many errors—

such as Abraham Lincoln's age when he died. Do not assume that facts presented in secondary sources are true. Before you use facts, try to verify them in primary or other secondary sources.

A much different example is the 1991 motion picture *JFK* directed by Oliver Stone. It claims that President John F. Kennedy's assassination in 1963 was the work of a conspiracy of government officials who wanted Kennedy out of the way so they could send more American troops to Vietnam. Stone's film suppresses a great deal of evidence that runs counter to his point of view, and it uses evidence in an imbalanced way to make it support his conspiracy theory. No reputable historian of the assassination has taken the movie seriously. You should not use such questionable sources as authority in your writing.

All secondary sources are to some degree unreliable. All are subject not only to human error but to the frames of mind of those who created them. Read secondary sources actively and critically, and try to find out something about the writers, their use of evidence, their points of view, and their reputation among experts in the field.

37c
curric

Secondary sources that become primary sources

Whether a source is primary or secondary may depend on your topic. For example, if you write an essay on changing ways that American movies have portrayed the family, the primary source for your paper will be the movies themselves. You may use a videocassette recorder to look at dozens of movies and to make your judgments. Your secondary sources will be essays by critics who have written about those movies and by scholars who have studied the family in the United States.

But if your topic is film criticism, what people have written about movies becomes your primary source. Perhaps you are writing about *Casablanca*. Because your topic is not the movie but what writers have said about it, your primary sources are the reviews that were published in 1942, when the movie came out, as well as what later scholars and other writers have said about the film.

Why Primary Sources Are Best

Always use primary sources when you can. They grant your writing an authority that secondary sources alone can seldom bring to your work. Use your library; look at videos and documentaries; listen to oral history tapes; interview people; conduct polls or experiments. Use as many different kinds of primary sources as possible.

By using primary sources, your facts are likely to be accurate and convincing. Your study of primary sources may actually reveal something new or show that a secondary source is wrong. For example, Longfellow's poem on the midnight ride of Paul Revere is a secondary source for the first battle of the American Revolution, but it is so familiar to every American that its recounting of events is often taken as fact. According to the poem Paul Revere was in Boston, knowing that the British were about to send troops to destroy the weapons and supplies the citizens of Massachusetts had been collecting to oppose British rule. Longfellow has Revere telling a friend to post lanterns in the steeple of Old North Church to signal whether the British were going to march out of Boston by land or be transported by boats over the Back Bay. If they were going by land, they would have been taking the road to Worcester. If they were ferried across the Back Bay, they would have been going to Concord. Then Revere has a friend row him across the Charles River where he waits for the lanterns to be hung. So Longfellow has Revere say:

> He said to his friend, "If the British march
> By land or sea from the town tonight,
> Hang a lantern aloft in the belfry arch
> Of the North Church tower as a signal light,—
> One if by land and two, if by sea;
> And I on the opposite shore will be,
> Ready to ride and spread the alarm
> Through every Middlesex village and farm."

But when we look at Revere's own story of what happened that night, we discover that there were other riders across the Charles River and the Back Bay and that Revere had the lanterns posted before he was himself rowed across to ride out through the countryside. Revere also explains that he was captured near Lexington and that, although he got away from the British, he was not able to ride on into Concord to spread the alarm.

You may not be tempted to use poetry as a source for historical fact, but keep in mind that although historians claim no "poetic license," they are neither infallible nor free of bias. Using primary sources allows you to bypass one layer of potential error.

**37d
curric**

37d
Writing for Academic Disciplines

Like reading actively and thinking critically, writing makes connections. Each sentence, each paragraph, each section draws on what you know, what you can prove, what you infer. Each builds on what you have written and looks to what you will write next. As you write, you put facts and thoughts together and establish relations between them. The very act of writing helps you organize knowledge and present it in a form that not only communicates with other readers but also helps you see connections and meaning in what you know.

College writing across the curriculum demands similar techniques and approaches. But the form that writing takes can differ significantly from one discipline to another. This chapter concludes with explanations and examples of some types of writing you may be asked to do in college classes. In other chapters we have already covered formal arguments, interpretive essays, and research papers (see Chapters 1 and 31–34), so here we will look only at reports, summaries or abstracts, lab reports, case studies, and position papers.

37d
curric

Writing a Report

The **report** provides information in a readable form and does not emphasize original thinking by the author. A report may be a summary of reading or a description of an experiment done in the laboratory. It may be a description of a painting or of a field trip.

An instructor may assign a report to be sure that you have done the required reading and that you know how to draw the information in these texts together into a coherent whole. If you are on a field trip in an archeology or geology or anthropology course, you may collect information and write it up as a report.

Reports thus use both primary and secondary sources. They may include interpretation, but usually do so by quoting recognized authorities in a particular field. The writer does not express an opinion in his or her own voice; rather, the writer will say something like this:

> The historian David Sacks says that Bristol was the most important English port for commerce with the New World during the seventeenth and eighteenth centuries.

The student writer of the report would not give his or her own answer to the question, "What makes Ross run?" Instead, the student quotes an authority:

> When Ross Perot re-entered the 1992 presidential campaign, the *New York Times* writer Michael Kelly asked, "What makes Ross run?" The answer, Kelly said, was simple. "The point is to gain attention."

A report may examine two sides of a question. In 1992, for example, some nutritionists published their opinion that cow's milk is bad for people because it has many risky side effects for some human beings. Other medical authorities said nonsense, that milk is an excellent food and that the nutritionists opposed to milk were in reality trying to get Americans to become vegetarians. The controversy went on for several weeks in the media, both in magazines and newspapers and on television.

A person writing a report on the argument would try to tell both sides of the story as fairly as possible and would not overtly favor one side or another. Objectivity is one of the primary qualities of the report. When you write a report, you do not express your own opinion. You let readers make up their own minds.

Preparing Summaries or Abstracts

Summaries or **abstracts,** as they are called in some disciplines, are valuable ways of extracting important information. The writer must choose the most important information and ideas and present them in a summary form, often in a single paragraph. As summaries and abstracts are usually based on a single text, they use a primary source or a secondary source, but not both. Some research papers, especially in the sciences, require that an abstract be submitted with the paper.

An abstract of an article is a summary that allows a researcher to decide quickly whether or not to read the whole work. Published abstracts usually appear at the beginning or the end of the articles they summarize. You can use abstracts to file information you collect during your research. Here is a sample abstract.

37d
curric

Abstract

As an unmarried daughter of the provincial upper bourgeoisie, Catherine des Roches (1542–1587) would have encountered pressure to conform to the expectation that she marry. Instead, she chose a studious life of learning and the companionship of her scholarly mother. Included among her extensive published writings is her paraphrase of the Song of the Valiant Woman from Prov. 31:10–31 in which she justifies her unusual career. This study analyzes how des Roches adapted a popular religious text to validate her choice of life-style, and to critique the humanistic/Reformed imperative that women of her class seek an authoritative identity solely within the home.

Writing Lab Reports

A **lab report** is a report of an experiment you do in a laboratory as part of a science course. The lab report describes the materials you use in the experiment, narrates the process of the experiment from start to finish, and gives its results.

The lab report allows your instructor to see if you have done the experiment correctly. The structure required by the report helps train your mind in the orderly methods and precise observations on which good science depends.

Lab reports are based on observation; the experiment is the primary "text." No secondary sources are consulted. Lab reports differ from one discipline to another. In a chemistry or a biology or a physics course, you may be asked to make an experiment in the laboratory and to report the steps you take and the results you get. You will take careful note of the quantities you use, the times involved in the various steps, and the precise results of the experiment.

Here is an example of a lab report in an introductory physics class.

Lab Report

Physics 221

Object of the Experiment: To demonstrate the transfer of energy in moving bodies that collide with one another.

Materials for the Experiment: A baseball, a basketball, and a flat floor.

The Experiment: I held a basketball four feet from the floor in one hand and with the other hand I held a baseball on top of the basketball so that the baseball rested on the basketball. Quickly removing the hand supporting the basketball, I let the two balls fall together on the floor, the baseball atop the basketball. When the basketball struck the floor, it did not bounce. But the baseball on top of it rebounded about sixteen feet in the air. I repeated this experiment several times, and the results were the same each time.

The principles of physics illustrated by the experiment are the conservation of energy and the conservation of momentum. The law of the conservation of energy holds that although energy can be transferred, it cannot be created or destroyed; the law of the conservation of momentum holds that for every action there is an equal reaction. Energy is defined as the ability of a body to do work; momentum is defined as velocity times mass.

The basketball is approximately three times as heavy as the baseball. Their mass thus adds up to a factor of four. When the basketball and the baseball are held four feet above the floor, they represent potential energy--a potential to do work. When they are dropped together, they fall at the same velocity towards the floor. When the basketball strikes the floor, it rebounds according to the law of the conservation of momentum that for every action there is an equal reaction. In the instant of impact, it is traveling upward while the baseball is traveling downward, and they are traveling at the same rate of speed. The basketball rebounds from the baseball, but since it cannot move through the floor, and since it is the heavier object, all the energy of its fall is transferred back to the baseball by the law of the conservation of momentum. When a heavy object collides with an object one-third its weight, all the energy is transferred to the lighter object. Since the balls were held four feet above the ground, and since the mass of the basketball represents three and the mass of the baseball represents one, there is a total mass of four. Since the basketball cannot move, the total energy of the falling mass, four, is transferred to the baseball, which bounces four times as high as the distance the baseball and the basketball were held off the floor. By the law of the conservation of energy, the potential energy of the baseball at the height of its trajectory thus is the total of the potential energy of baseball and basketball together at the start of the experiment.

In geology or botany courses, a lab report may involve identifying specimens of rocks or plants. In such a report, you will note the various qualities of the specimens and key them to a handbook. Your report will describe the step-by-step progress of your identification.

Writing Case Studies

Case studies are narratives that describe situations or problems that require a decision. Case studies are presented as instructional devices in education and psychology classes, in law schools and business schools, and in workshops for management training.

Case studies used for instruction are usually based on real situations and presented objectively so that students can analyze the case and select a solution they can describe and justify. Students generally write up their solutions in the form of an argument (see 37d).

Here is a sample case study that might be used in an education course.

A Case Study

Disruption in the Classroom

The Complaint

Jack B. is a fifth-grade student in the Sunnybrook School. He is white, middle-class, somewhat small for his age and according to his test scores, of high intelligence, though his grades have always been low. He has been a terror to his teachers since he was in first grade. He often disrupts class by throwing books, picking fights with other children both male and female, and by shouting out "Hail Columbia!" while the teacher is going over lessons with the class.

One day when the teacher had a small bouquet of flowers in a vase on her desk, Jack walked up to sharpen a pencil and snatched up the flowers and poured them on the head of a larger boy who was reading a book on the front row. The boy so abused stood up and struck Jack in the face, bloodying his mouth. The teacher separated them with difficulty, and Jack's mother was called to the school and asked to take him home for the day.

The next day instead of shouting "Hail Columbia" during lessons, Jack shouted, "I'm flower champion of the world." He began tearing pages out of one of his textbooks. Again his mother was called to school and asked to take him home for the day.

These disruptions have gone on for five years.

A Case Study, 2

Personal History

Jack's father and mother were divorced when he was two years
old, and his father left the state. Jack has not seen him since, and
the father provides no support for him. Jack is an only child. His
mother is a successful lawyer, expert in contracts and bankruptcy,
with an income that allows her to own a large house with a swimming
pool and a live-in maid who takes care of Jack through the day. The
mother works long hours and often comes home late at night while
Jack is in bed. His mother's parents live on a farm in another
state. Jack visits them in the summertime, rides horses, watches his
grandfather milk cows, and goes out into the fields when hay is cut.
He is happy on the farm and never wants to return to the city at the
end of the summer.

Jack has few friends because he is so quarrelsome. He spends a
great deal of time alone in his room when he is at home. On weekends
he sometimes goes with his mother to movies and likes violent films.
He likes to sing, and he collects compact disks and sings along with
the vocalists. Sometimes his mother takes him to concerts. He likes
all kinds of music but especially loves blues and rock. Even in a
classical music concert he sits very still and listens with close
attention.

Conceptionalization and Treatment

Jack's problems seem to be related to loneliness. He has never
known his father, and he scarcely knows his mother. They spend very
little time together. His love for music seems to be an example of

music having power to tame the most savage soul. His outbursts in school seem to get attention--any attention by any way, even if the attention he gets is negative. He has not been around other children very much and has very little sense of how to relate to them.

The counselor requested a series of interviews with Jack's mother and discussed several possibilities for treatment. One was that the mother make an adjustment in her own life to give more time to Jack. She has promised that she will try, but she worries that as a single parent, she has financial responsibilities that must be met, and she is afraid that if she gives up income today, she may not have anything to live on at some later time when some accident might deprive her of a job.

The counselor has made an effort to persuade her to discuss these fears with a skilled therapist; it seems that these fears are unwarranted. Perhaps treatment of the mother's anxiety over money will lead to her willingness to work less and to spend more time with Jack.

The counselor has also persuaded Jack to enroll in a children's chorus after school. He is one of the youngest members, but the chance to sing every day has made him much happier. He has met other children who love to sing, and he has made some friends among them.

Jack has also been enrolled in a Saturday swimming group that helps drain off some of his excess energy. The counselor has found a college student on a nearby campus to be Jack's "big brother." The two of them go to the movies and to other functions together, and Jack seems to have developed a real trust in him.

Prognosis

At this moment the prognosis seems borderline hopeful. Jack's mother has promised she will spend more time with her son, although as yet she has continued to postpone reducing her time at the office. Jack has several friends in the chorus and at the swimming pool where he goes on Saturday, and his "big brother" notes an improvement in Jack's social skills. Jack's teachers report that he seems quieter, happier, less intent on disruption. But he still sometimes breaks out into song or irrelevant talk in class.

Discussion

This seems to be a straightforward case, but one with no easy solution. Jack's loneliness would be solved if he had a brother or sister or if his mother could stay home with him more. His new friends at the pool and in the chorus are not sure about him. One of them says Jack is too "clingy." That is, he wants to be with the friend all the time. The main task is to give Jack a feeling of companionship and belonging, to provide a sense of worth that will allow him to be quiet in the proper places for silence. The counselor at the school is looking carefully at the situation.

Writing Short Position Papers

Short papers that respond to reading assignments or to problems posed in a class are sometimes called **position papers.** This type of writing is often required in college ethics courses. The instructor poses an ethical problem: Suppose a bank robber has taken a hostage during a failed robbery and threatens to shoot the hostage if he is not allowed to go free. Would it be ethical for authorities to lie to the terrorist to rescue the hostage?

Because position papers ask for a response to a situation, they have no primary sources. But the student may elect to buttress his or her response by reference to or quotation from authorities. These would serve as secondary sources.

Position papers are usually no more than two pages long. You must get right to the point, explain the problem, give your solution to it, and stop.

**37d
curric**

Whenever you send out a business letter, a job application, a memo, or a résumé, you can expect to be judged on the form of what you have written as well as on the content. If you misspell words, type over errors without first removing them, or leave smudges and stains on what you send out, you can expect readers to conclude that you are sloppy and careless in your work. If you do not use the standard business forms, readers will assume you do not know how to use them. If you do not communicate information in a clear and structured way, readers will think you are disorganized. But if your business correspondence is written clearly, directly, and neatly, your business audience will be inclined to take you seriously.

This chapter examines some of the kinds of writing common in the workplace. In addition to business letters and memos, we present some advice for preparing a résumé and applying for a job.

38a
Following Accepted Standards for a Business Letter

In the block style, the major parts of the letter are set flush with the left margin. Do not indent for paragraphs. Indicate paragraphs by leaving a line of space between the last line of one paragraph and the first line of the next.

Letterhead stationery

If you are writing for a business firm or a professional organization, you will probably use stationery with a printed letterhead at the top. The letterhead will give the name of the firm, its address, and often some sort of advertising slogan. You begin such letters with the date, written a couple of spaces under the letterhead. You may center the date, or you may move it to the right or left side of the page.

Space down three or four lines, and type the name and address of the person to whom you are sending the letter. The address of the recipient of your letter is called the **inside address.** Space down three or four lines and type the salutation. Double space, and begin your first paragraph. Do not indent the paragraph. Unlike student papers submitted to college instructors, business letters are single spaced. At the end of the paragraph, double space and begin the next paragraph.

When you have finished the letter, double space and type the complimentary close, again starting flush with the left margin. Space down four lines and type your name. If you have a title, write it just under your typed name. Sign your name with a pen in the space between the complimentary close and your typed name.

If you enclose anything with the letter, space down another two lines and write "Enclosure" or "Enclosures" flush with the left margin.

A sample business letter on letterhead stationery, typed in the block format form, is shown on page 597.

**38a
business**

Stationery without a letterhead

If you write to a business or to an institution as an individual, not as a representative of an organization, type your letter on unlined, sturdy bond paper, $8\frac{1}{2} \times 11$ inches. Type your own address at the top of the page, starting in the center. Put the date under your address. Then follow the instructions given above for using letterhead stationery.

Modified Block Style

In the block format, every line of the letter except the heading begins flush with the left margin. This format is common in business writing because it is efficient. Word processing programs on computers can be set up to produce the block format automatically, and the writer can move swiftly through the letter.

Some businesses prefer the modified block format. The only difference here is that the complimentary close is centered and the first letter of the typed name of the letter writer is placed four lines directly under the first letter of the typed complimentary close.

Address and Salutation

For the inside address, include the title of the addressee—the person to whom you are writing. The title may appear immediately after the name, or it can be put beneath the name.

International Automobile

3821 Oceanside Drive • Bancroft, Idaho 83217 • Telephone: 208-489-0199

Dealers in Antique Car Replacement Parts

July 29, 1994

Ms. Lenore P. Raven, President
Nevermore Antique Car Restorations, Inc.
35 Oak Street
Belmont, Massachusetts 02178

Dear Ms. Raven:

Thank you for your letter of July 14 inquiring about parts for the
standard six-cylinder 1948 Chevrolet Fleetmaster engine. I am happy
to tell you that we do carry pistons, rods, and crankshafts for that
engine. I am enclosing a price list for the various parts. Shipping
charges are included in the prices. We ship by United Parcel Service
on the day orders are received. We can arrange overnight delivery at
an additional charge.

We accept payment by Visa, MasterCard, or American Express, or money
order or certified check.

Thank you for thinking of International Automobile.

Yours sincerely,

Roderick Usher

Roderick Usher
President and General Manager

Enclosure

28 Horseshoe Lane
Fair Hills, New York 10020
March 15, 1994

Mr. Basil Carmine
Ajax Industrial Chemicals
3939 Gentilly Boulevard
New Orleans, Louisiana 70126

Dear Mr. Carmine:

Last week I bought a fifty gallon drum of your industrial strength
floor cleanser for my automotive repair business. According to your
advertisement in the February Mechanic's Companion, your cleanser,
Wipe Out, is guaranteed to remove all oil and grease from garage
floors.

I carefully followed your directions in applying the cleanser. I
spread the powder over the grease and oil stains on the floor of my
establishment and hosed down the powder with water. You can imagine
my astonishment when your cleanser began to boil violently and to
give off thick red fumes that forced us to evacuate the building.

When we were finally able to reenter the building the next day, we
discovered that Wipe Out had eaten large holes in the concrete floor
underneath the stains.

I have discussed the situation with my lawyer, Rosalyn East, of
East, Burns, and Tavern, and she has advised me to ask you to pay for
repairs. Several reputable contractors are preparing estimates,
which I shall forward to you.

If you are unwilling to pay for the repairs, we shall have no
recourse but to sue you and your firm under state and federal laws
regulating interstate commerce and false and misleading
advertising. I hope that a lawsuit will not be necessary. And I look
forward to your reply.

Yours sincerely,

Glenda Ruby

Glenda Ruby
President, Southside Garage, Inc.

Ms. Glenda Ruby
President, Southside Garage, Inc.
28 Horseshoe Lane
Fair Hills, New York 10020
or
Ms. Glenda Ruby, President
Southside Garage, Inc.

Never abbreviate titles. Do not write:

Ms. Glenda Ruby, Pres.

Mr. Sylvan Glade, Asst. Mgr.

Instead, write:

Ms. Glenda Ruby, President

Mr. Sylvan Glade, Assistant Manager

Some titles ordinarily are placed before the name in the inside address, and some of these titles can be abbreviated:

Dr. Ishmael Romer
Dean Ivy Wallace
Bishop Bernard Law
The Rev. Hiram Welch
Captain Jennifer Jones
Sister Mary Annunciata

38a
business

The salutation, always followed by a colon in a business letter, greets the person who receives the letter. It is placed flush with the left margin, below the inside address and separated from the inside address by a double space.

Use the addressee's last name in the salutation. Do not address the person by his or her first name unless you are very good friends. Never address by first name a person you have not met or one you know only slightly.

Always say "Dear _____." Do not say "Hi," "Hi there," "Greetings," or anything else that attempts to be cute. The conventions of business writing require the traditional salutation.

Use *Messrs.* (the abbreviated plural of the French *Monsieur*) when you address more than one man. When the addressees are two or more women, use *Mmes.* (the abbreviation of *Mesdames*).

Here are some sample salutations acceptable to most people.

Dear Ms. Ruby:
Dear Dr. Farnsworth:
Dear Messrs. Doolittle and Kreisburg:
Dear Mmes. Cohen and Grey:
Dear Miss Williams:

To avoid unnecessary reference to marital status, many writers favor *Ms.* as a title for women (see 29d). This usage has won wide acceptance, and many women prefer it. However, *Miss* and *Mrs.* are still acceptable, and you should use one of these forms of address if you know that the person you are addressing prefers it. Note whether she has indicated any preference by the way she has typed her name on any letter she has written to you or on the envelope. If she has supplied no clue, use *Ms.*

In writing to business organizations or to someone whose name you do not know, use one of the following kinds of salutation.

Dear Registrar:
Dear American Express:
Dear Sir or Madam:
Dear Sir:
Dear Madam:
Gentlemen:
Mesdames:
Dear Colleagues:
To whom it may concern:

A good dictionary will provide correct forms of addresses and salutations in the special cases of elected government officials, judges and justices, religious leaders, military personnel, and others.

The Body of the Letter

Get to the point quickly, and let your reader know what you want. Business letters are like college papers: they should have a thesis. You write a letter to get the recipient to do something or to believe something. You do not write a business letter to ramble on about all sorts of things that may be on your mind. You may write a business letter to apply for a job, to report on something you have done, to request information, to complain, to apologize, to ask advice, to give information, to develop a plan, or for many other reasons. You should make your purpose clear within the first two sentences of your letter.

Dear Mr. Armstrong:

As president of the Environmental Coalition, I am sending you this letter by certified mail to inform you that we are suing you in federal court to shut down your factory on the Hiwassee River. I have written you several times on this matter, but you have not responded. In the meantime, the pollutants from your factory continue to kill fish by the thousands. So we have no recourse but to sue, and we have taken the first steps to get our suit before the court. You will be hearing from the court and from our lawyers shortly.

Dear Dr. Farnsworth:

I would like to apply for the job of dental hygienist that you have advertised in today's *Morning Bugle*. I worked as a hygienist for ten years in Dallas, Texas, before my wife was transferred here by her business. I am enclosing my résumé, and I would welcome an opportunity to talk with you about the position.

Business people do not have time to study a letter in search of the writer's meaning. They want to know right away what the writer wants of them. You should express that purpose as quickly and as directly as possible. Practice getting to the point as quickly as you can.

38a business

Style and tone

Many people think that a good business letter must be bland and impersonal or that the writer must use complicated language to impress the recipient. Less frequently, they think they must use slang or other informal language to attract attention. In fact, a business letter should be simple and direct. It should be natural and courteous, neither too formal nor too informal. It should not contain slang or jargon. Study these examples.

Unnatural: I want to take this opportunity to inform you of the important fact that I am most seriously interested in the announcement of the accounting job that you advertised last week.

Too informal: The accounting job you guys are offering in the latest *Daily Snort* sounds like a real grabber. Count me in. I look forward to pressing the flesh and to throwing all the facts on the table.

Natural: I want to apply for the accounting job you announced in today's *Times-Standard*.

Unnecessarily complex: In your recent communication dated March 16, you asked us to enumerate, categorize, and prioritize the need-based scholarship applicants eligible for financial aid under Title 6 of the Federal Grants Act of 1987. We are able to report that we have now enumerated, categorized, and prioritized the need-based scholarship applicants eligible for financial aid.

Simple and direct: In your letter of March 16, you asked us to count the students who need financial aid, to classify them according to the sort of help they need, and to decide which of them should have preference. Here are our findings.

Length

Whenever possible, keep a business letter to one page. Longer letters burden the people who must read them. They often obscure your meaning. Since business letters almost always ask for some action on the part of the recipient, you may feel that you have to argue your case at length. Sometimes you do indeed have to write a longer letter. But it is usually much better to make your request clearly, briefly give reasons for your request, and close as quickly as possible. Readers of business letters appreciate brevity and clarity.

**38a
business**

Final paragraphs

Having stated or explained your business, say clearly what you want the recipient to do next. You may be ordering merchandise; you may be asking for information; you may be requesting agreement; you may be asking for a proposal; you may be asking how a complaint will be met; you may be asking for a response to a report. Most business letters expect a response, and you should spell out clearly what sort of response you expect. Do you want the person to telephone you? Do you want to meet with the person? Do you want a report? Do you want a replacement for faulty merchandise?

Now and then you may not need a response to the letter. You may, for example, acknowledge receipt of a report and thank the writer for her hard work in putting together information you have requested. You do not expect the recipient to respond to a thank-you note.

You should always maintain a courteous and businesslike tone in your letters, but avoid clichés. Don't end your letters with a worn-out expression of gratitude such as "Thank you for your time," "Thank you for your consideration of this request," or "I await the courtesy of a reply." If you write in a friendly tone, you can close the letter immediately after you have stated your business and no one will accuse you of discourtesy. If you want to thank your recipient for something specific, you can do that. The writer of the preceding letter closed with a friendly expression of expectation. You can often close with a pleasant word about future relations. But avoid formula closings.

DUNHAM ENGINEERING

31 Pine Crest Industrial Park
Atlanta, Georgia 30375

November 21, 1994

Mr. Michael Elia, President
Rocky Mountain Scenic Railroad, Inc.
1313 Grand View Street
Boulder, Colorado 80832

Dear Mr. Elia:

I want to arrange a day-long scenic excursion on your railroad for
approximately a thousand people on Saturday, May 6, 1995. At that
time, the National Association of Subdivision Engineers will be
having its annual convention in Denver. We are sure to have at least
a thousand people who would enjoy such a trip. We would like to
leave around 9:00 A.M. and to return to Boulder around 2:30 or 3:00
P.M. We would like to charter our own train, and we would like to
stop for a picnic lunch in the middle of the day.

Please let me know if your line is available for such a trip, and, if
it is, quote me your group rates. Please tell me also if you are able
to provide the lunch or if we should arrange to have it catered by
another firm.

Many people have spoken to me of the beauty of your rail route and
the courtesy of your service. I look forward to an enjoyable day on
your line.

Yours sincerely,

David Dunham

David Dunham
President

✔ **CHECKLIST 38.1: WRITING A BUSINESS LETTER**

Business correspondence is to the point. Be sure business letters include the following:

- Return address
- Date
- Recipient's address
- Salutation
- Body
  - In the first sentence, give the purpose of the letter.
  - Tell the recipient what you want.
  - Give brief reasons for what you want.
  - Tell what the recipient can do next.
  - Close the letter.
- Complimentary close
- Signature and typed name

Closing and Signing the Letter

Letters usually close with one of the endings below. A capital letter always starts the first word of the complimentary close; a comma always follows the complimentary close.

Yours truly,	Sincerely,
Very truly yours,	Sincerely yours,
Yours very truly,	Yours sincerely,
Cordially,	Cordially yours,
Respectfully,	Respectfully yours,
Regards,	Best regards,

The signature appears in a four-line space between the complimentary close and the typed name of the writer. Most writers avoid adding a professional title (such as attorney-at-law) or a degree (such as Ph.D.) after their typed name. However, to indicate their official capacity, writers who have a business title often use it.

Sincerely yours,   Very truly yours,

Carolyn Garfield   W. Prescott Blast
Marketing Manager   Dean of the Faculty

Addressing the Envelope

Address the envelope to include all essential information required for postal delivery. The address centered on the envelope is the same as the inside address; the return address in the upper left of the envelope includes the sender's name and address. Write out all words according to standard practice (see 29c), although you may elect to use either conventional or postal abbreviations for the names of states.

```
Julie Holden
3200 Lake View Drive
State College, PA 16801



                        Ms. Delores Smith
                        Personnel Manager
                        Farm Journal, Inc.
                        230 West Washington Square
                        Philadelphia, PA 19105
```

Fold $8\frac{1}{2} \times 11$ stationery in thirds so that it fits a standard $4 \times 9\frac{1}{2}$ envelope. Fold the bottom third up, then the top third down, leaving about a quarter inch between the top edge of the paper and the bottom fold so that your recipient can open the letter easily. For smaller business envelopes, fold standard paper in half from the bottom up; then fold the paper in thirds, left side first, right side over left.

■ **Exercise 38.1**   Write a letter to a local business requesting a catalog or other information you'd like to have. Use the Yellow Pages of your phone book or your school newspaper as a source of names and addresses. Pay close attention to correct format of the letter and the envelope.

Writing a Memo

Modern business runs on **memos**—memorandums or short communications exchanged within an office or between offices in the same firm. As the name indicates, *memo* usually refers to something that should be remembered by people on the staff. Most conferences in a well-run business result in a memo that records what was decided. Supervisors in such businesses use memos to make announcements. Memos are usually kept on file. They are often used to trace the development of policy.

A good memo has many of the qualities of the business letter. But since the memo usually goes out to several people—perhaps hundreds of people—at once, it usually lacks some of the personal conventions of letters.

Formatting a Memo

Memos are intended for quick reading. The first four lines show the date and a summary of essential information introduced by key words:

To:

From:

Subject:

A memo begins with a date in the upper right corner of the page. But instead of the salutation "Dear Ms. Adams," the memo begins with a general address, usually preceded by *To* followed by a colon. The recipients are assumed to be within the organization, so the memo does not include an inside address other than the classification of the people who are to receive the memo.

The memo does not have a complimentary close, and it usually does not have a signature. Instead, the name of the writer of the memo appears after *From* followed by a colon. The writer's initials are then written by hand next to the name. The writer's title may or may not appear on the memo.

A good memo announces the subject on a third line after the word *Subject* followed by a colon. See sample standard headings (page 607).

March 21, 1993

To: All the staff
From: RCM **RCM**
Subject: Midterm grades

November 28, 1992

To: All coaches
From: Jack Booster, president of the
university **JB**
Subject: The upcoming NCAA investigation
of our athletic program

January 7, 1993

To: Department supervisors
From: Michele Johnson, Affirmative Action
Officer **MJ**
Subject: Affirmative Action guidelines

July 29, 1994

To: All members of the staff
From: LB **LB**
Subject: Dental care

We have made arrangements with the North Slope Community Health
Group for complete dental care for employees of the company and
their families. Your cost will be a $5.00 monthly fee that will be
added to the medical insurance deduction in your paycheck. The
company will defray all other costs for each employee enrolled in
the dental plan.

The enclosed brochure from the North Slope Community Health Group
will answer many of your questions about the plan. If you have
further questions, please call Dr. Jerry Pullem at North Slope at
524-7529.

You must enroll in the plan by September 30. If you wish to enroll,
please sign the enclosed form and return it to me. Your payroll
deduction will begin with your October paycheck.

Composing the Body of a Memo

Like a good business letter, a good memo should be brief and to the point. It should treat only one subject. It should be clear. If some response is required, the expected response should be spelled out. The memo does not have a complimentary close or a signature at the bottom. Study the sample memo on page 607.

38c
Applying for a Job

Some of the most important writing you may ever do is applying for a job. Be sure your résumé and cover letter reflect you, and all you have learned in your writing course, at your best.

Preparing a Résumé

A standard **résumé** presents an overview of your education, your work experience, your interests, and other pertinent personal data. Formats for résumés vary. Some are in the form of paragraphs, giving full information about past experience relevant to the job for which the writer is applying. Others are brief summaries. All good résumés include the information potential employers need to know about their workers.

As the sample shows, you should type your résumé and lay it out attractively. Be sure entries are parallel and that all spacing and capitalization are consistent. Be sure to proofread your résumé carefully, and have someone else proofread it for you, too. A mistake in a résumé can cost you an interview—or a job. Because a brief résumé helps a prospective employer evaluate your record quickly, you should try to keep your presentation to a single page. Do not inflate your résumé with unnecessary details in an effort to make it seem more impressive than it really is. If you are just starting a career, no one will expect you to be rich in experience and skills.

- **Personal data.** Give your name, current address, home address (if it is different from your current address), zip code, and telephone number with the area code. Mention any special abilities, such as fluency with languages other than English or experience in using business machines or computers. Mention any travels that might be relevant to the job.

- **Career objective.** Express your interest in a specific kind of position by stating your immediate and perhaps also your long-range objectives realistically.
- **Education.** List the schools you attended, beginning with high school. Start with your most recent school and work backward. Give your dates of attendance and the degrees you received. Include any honors or awards you won, your major, and any courses you think qualify you especially for the job you are seeking.
- **Work experience.** List the jobs you have held, the dates of your employment, the names of your supervisors, and a brief description of your duties. Again, start with the most recent job and work backward.
- **Special interests.** To reveal details about yourself as an individual, you may wish to include information about hobbies, membership in clubs and organizations, volunteer work, or any special talents you have. Be sure to mention interests that might be useful in the job you are applying for. If you have won any awards, you might want to mention them, too.
- **References.** Give the names, addresses, and telephone numbers of people who will attest to your character and skill as a student and a worker. Be sure to ask permission from anyone you list as a reference, and be sure to select people who know you well and will write or speak strongly in your behalf. People you use as references should write directly to the prospective employer, or they may expect to receive a phone call from the prospective employer. You may send copies of letters that you have received in the past, commending you for your work, and sometimes you may send letters of recommendation that you have solicited from various people. But some employers tend to disregard such letters, preferring instead those written directly to the employer in your behalf.

**38c
business**

Preparing a Cover Letter

When you send your résumé to a prospective employer, enclose a letter that catches attention by its careful statement of your qualifications. Among the scores of responses a personnel director receives after a job is advertised, your letter must stand out if you are to receive the consideration you want. Yet your letter must not violate the conventions of courtesy and restraint that have developed in business correspondence over the centuries. You are best served if you present your strongest qualifications clearly, briefly, and carefully.

Julie Holden

Current address	**Home address**
8200 Beaver Avenue	R.D. 2, Box 9
State College, PA 16801	Manheim, PA 17545
Tel.: (814) 998-0004	Tel.: (717) 777-7888

Career objective
A position of responsibility on the editorial staff of a magazine or publishing firm.

Education
1989-1993
The Pennsylvania State University, B.A. in English (June 1993).
Grade point average: 3.25 of 4.0. **Honors**: Dean's List.
Major courses: Article Writing, News Reporting, Magazine Journalism, Style Problems, Sociology, Rural Community Services.

1986-1989
Central High School, Manheim, Pennsylvania

Experience
Summers of 1991 and 1992
Clerical assistant at Central High School under the supervision of Mr. Horace K. Williams, Manheim, Pennsylvania. Duties included microfilming, typing, and filing.

Summers of 1989 and 1990
Farmhand on the Schwarzmuller Dairy Farm under the supervision of Mr. Robert Wilkes, Manheim, Pennsylvania. Duties included field work (operating tractors and implements) and barn work (feeding and cleaning).

Special interests
Painting, photography, gardening, macramé.

References

Professor Carolyn Eckhardt	Mr. Horace K. Williams
Department of English	Guidance Counselor
The Pennsylvania State University	Central High School
University Park, PA 16802	Manheim, PA 17545
Phone: (814) 987-2268	Phone: (717) 998-8768

Route 2, Box 9
Manheim, Pennsylvania 17545
February 22, 1994

Ms. Delores Smith
Personnel Manager
Farm Journal, Inc.
230 West Washington Square
Philadelphia, Pennsylvania 19105

Dear Ms. Smith:

I would like very much to become an editorial assistant at <u>Farm Journal</u>. My four
years of education at the Pennsylvania State University and my twenty years'
experience as the daughter of a farming couple have given me the knowledge and
background necessary to do this job.

Like many of your readers, I was born and raised on a farm. I have planted corn,
mowed hay, and delivered calves. I share with your readers an appreciation of farm
life and an understanding of the independent farmer's problems.

As you will see from my résumé, I am graduating from the university in June with a
bachelor of arts degree and a double major in English and sociology. In my classes I
have practiced and refined my knowledge of writing and editing and have studied the
problems of producing magazines. Now I would like to apply what I have learned.

I will be in Philadelphia the week of March 21. If we could arrange for an interview
on the morning of March 23, I would be most grateful. I will call you before that day
to see if it is convenient or to see if we can make an appointment at another time.

I look forward very much to meeting you.

Sincerely,

Julie Holden

Julie Holden

Encl.

Because a job-application letter is usually accompanied by a full résumé, you do not need to list educational background, work experience, and other interests. Instead, use the letter to highlight the special talents you bring to the position. Make your letter specific. Don't be satisfied with saying, "I have had much valuable experience that will help me do this job."

The letter reproduced on page 611 is forceful and concise. Note that each paragraph serves a specific function. The first states the writer's purpose in sending the letter. The second describes how the writer's background would help her do the job well. The third paragraph explains how the writer's education has prepared her for this job. The last paragraph asks for an interview. Everything is to the point.

■ **Exercise 38.2**   Prepare a résumé that highlights your education and job experience as well as other key information shown in the sample on page 610 and the Checklist below.

✔ **CHECKLIST 38.2: PREPARING A RÉSUMÉ**

Your résumé is an important document you will have throughout your working life. You will need a résumé for applying for student work-study programs, part-time jobs, summer jobs, and your first job upon graduation. Here are some things to include and attend to.

A résumé should include:

■ personal data
■ career objective
■ education
■ work experience
■ special interests
■ references

Be sure your résumé is:

■ attractively laid out
■ consistent in format and wording
■ error free

CHAPTER 39

IMPROVING STUDY TECHNIQUES

Develop your study skills by applying techniques for improving your comprehension and retention of what you read. Learn to take useful notes when you read and when you listen to lectures. Studying is an active, continual process that requires planning, repetition, and *writing* to help you remember and use information.

39a
Planning

Develop a realistic weekly plan for studying. Consider all the demands on your time—eating, sleeping, attending classes, doing homework, exercising, socializing, commuting, watching television—and set aside time for studying. Some students make a weekly chart of their activities. If you do block in regular activities and study time on a calendar, leave a number of free periods so that you have time for relaxing and for making adjustments. When exams or special projects come up, for example, you'll need blocks of time over several days, even weeks, to complete work on time. Try to avoid cramming for tests, because the stress it produces prevents deep learning and memory. If you must cram, try to outline the major points you need to cover and concentrate on learning the central ideas and facts.

39b
Reading Actively

You can improve your ability to learn and retain material by approaching your reading with a clear plan and by taking various kinds of notes.

Surveying

Scanning the text for information without reading every word gives you an outline of the material so that you can focus on what you are about to read. When you survey a book, look for chapter titles and subtitles, headings and subheadings, charts, graphs, illustrations, and words in boldface or italics. Skim the opening and closing paragraphs of a chapter or of chapter sections. Surveying of this kind can give you the sense of a book very quickly.

Questioning

Once you have looked through the material, jot down some questions about it. Writing will help make things stick in your mind, and your written questions will provide a good short review. It is always better to write your own questions, but if there are questions at the end of a chapter, let them guide your reading.

Keeping questions in mind as you read will get you actively involved in the material at hand. Your reading now has a purpose: you are trying to find answers to your questions.

39b
study

Summarizing

Learn how to make summaries. When you read, try to summarize every paragraph by composing a simple, short sentence. Put the author's thoughts into your own words. Don't try to duplicate the style of the book or article you are reading. Putting somebody else's ideas into your own words is a good way of making sure you truly know those ideas.

Underlining has several disadvantages. Obviously, you cannot underline in a library book. If you underline material, you will have to own the book. Underlining is also a passive approach. When students come back to passages they have underlined, they often cannot remember why they underlined them in the first place. Most people underline too much, and the result is boring and confusing. Underlining is never as effective as writing a short summary sentence for each paragraph or each page. A summary sentence ensures that you will reconsider the thoughts in the book, translate them into your own words, and put them on paper.

Comparing

You can also help retain information by looking for the same topic or closely related information in another source. Your instructor may require you to buy one or more books for the course, and you should read these books and make notes about them. But it is also an excellent idea to look up the topics in some of the many reference books available in the library. Try an encyclopedia, various dictionaries, and other reference books your librarian can help you find. (Many of these reference books are listed in 31c of this handbook.)

When you read the same information presented in slightly different ways, you will find that each source has some detail the others do not have. Variety in your learning can be a wonderful help in remembering. If you have taken careful notes on the various things you have read, you should remember more easily.

Analyzing

Another required skill is the ability to analyze, to tell what things mean, to discover how they fit with other things you know. Here again, writing will help you to study. Many instructors advise students to keep a notebook in which they jot down their notes from sources on one page and their thoughts about those notes on a facing page. If you ask yourself questions about the things you put down, you will develop your analytical powers. Pay attention to your own feelings. Do you like a book? Make yourself set down reasons why you like it. Do you dislike a book? Again, write down the reasons for your preference. Whether you feel interested, bored, repelled, or excited, ask yourself what there is in the book (or movie or whatever else you may be studying) that arouses such feelings. Then write your reasons down. You do not have to like a work of literature or art or history merely because someone else does. But you should be able to justify your opinions to others and to yourself. As you get into the habit of writing down these justifications, you will find your analytical ability steadily improving.

39b study

Expanding Your Vocabulary

With the aid of a dictionary, keep a written record of new words; write them on index cards or in a notebook. Include correct spelling, pronunciation clues, clear definitions that you write yourself, and a phrase or a sentence using the word properly. Arrange the words in related groups to help yourself study (business words, economics words, psychology words, literature words, and so on). Incorporate any new words into your speaking and writing vocabulary. Here is an example:

> puerile (PYOO ar il)
> juvenile in a bad sense. People who are puerile are not just children; they are <u>childish</u>. He was <u>puerile</u> when he refused to let her name appear before his on the program for the play.

Reviewing

Immediately after you finish reading, and at convenient intervals thereafter, look over the questions, notes, summaries, or outlines you have created from your reading. Don't try to read every word of the original material in the book or article every time you review. Skim over it. You will learn better from many rapid readings than from one or two slow readings. Skimming will help you get the shape of the material in your mind. As you study your own notes, you will recall many of the supporting details.

Use your written work to help you complete your assignments. It often helps if you close the book, put away your notes, and try to jot down from memory a rough outline of what you are studying. The more ways you can write about material you are learning, the more effectively you will learn it.

39c
study

39c
Taking Notes

Taking good notes requires practice. Some students tape-record lectures so they can listen again to what the instructor has said. But even if you have a tape recorder and the instructor is willing to be recorded, good notes can still help you understand and remember the lecture.

Never try to write down everything you hear in the lecture as it is going on. Unless you know shorthand, you cannot write as fast as a person speaks, and while you are struggling to get a sentence down, the lecturer will have gone on to another point. In your haste, you may garble both what has been said and what is being said.

Your best bet is to write down words, phrases, and short sentences. Use these jottings to stimulate your memory later on. As soon as possible after the lecture is over, take your notes to a quiet place and try to write down as much of the lecture as you can remember. If you do this regularly, you probably will find yourself remembering more and more of each lecture.

Once you have written up your notes, compare what you have with the notes taken by another member of the class. If four or five of you get together to share your notes, you will each acquire an amazingly complete set, and in your discussions of gaps and confusions, you will further your learning.

Don't try to sit for hours without a break. Get up every forty-five minutes or so and walk around the room and stretch. Then sit back down quickly and go to work again. Taking a break will relax your body and perhaps stimulate your mind to some new thought that you can use when you start studying again.

For the sake of good order, don't keep your notes for all of your courses in one notebook. You can keep track of your notes much more easily by using a separate notebook for each course. At graduation, you will have an orderly record of your college education.

✔ CHECKLIST 39.1: IMPROVING STUDY TECHNIQUES

Consider these techniques to help you learn and retain what you have learned.

- Plan a reasonable study schedule; don't get caught having to cram.
- Survey each text chapter before you read it.
- Take advantage of chapter outlines and summaries, time lines, key words, discussion questions, and other study devices your textbooks may provide.
- Make up questions so that you can read with a purpose.
- Summarize rather than underline.
- Consult a variety of sources.
- Analyze what you read.
- Look up and learn unfamiliar words.
- Use a separate notebook for each course.
- Take notes in class quickly; then rewrite and summarize your notes as soon after class as possible.
- Review your notes and reading assignments.
- Compare your notes with classmates; set up a study group for sharing notes and discussing issues as well as anticipating assignments and test questions.

39c
study

40

WRITING AN ESSAY EXAM

Most college courses require students to write a midterm and a final examination and perhaps other exams as well. The pressure of time during an examination makes this kind of writing especially challenging, but essay examinations call for the same skills demanded by other kinds of writing. Here are some points to note.

40a
Preparing for the Exam

In some ways, preparing for an essay exam is like preparing for any writing assignment. Use the prewriting techniques described in Chapter 1 as you think about the material you will be tested on. Jot down ideas, ask the journalist's questions, draw a subject tree to tie facts and ideas together.

Reviewing Notes

If you have taken adequate notes on lectures and assigned readings (Chapter 39), preparing for the exam should not be overwhelming. Read your text summaries, the notes you have written in the margins of your text, and in your course notes. Underline key words and phrases. Develop outlines. Your goal should be to highlight the major concepts and details the exam is likely to cover.

Anticipating Questions

Imagine that you are the instructor, and write out the questions that you would give. Merely writing questions down helps you organize your mind to answer them. You will often be surprised at how close you can come to the questions that appear on the examination.

40b
Taking the Exam

Be sure to give yourself every advantage in taking an essay exam—or any exam for that matter. Arrive early; don't put yourself under extra pressure by being late. Bring all the supplies you will need—pens, pencils, erasers, paper, bluebooks.

Reading the Questions

When the examination is before you, read it through carefully and spend a minute or two thinking about it. You may find that a later question reminds you of information that is useful for an earlier question. Be sure you understand exactly what each question is asking you to do. Most essay questions contain a cue word that indicates exactly what you are supposed to do: *describe, identify, compare, contrast, explain, analyze,* and so on. A great many students go wrong on exams because they read the questions hastily and misunderstand them, not responding to the cues in the question.

40b
essay

Outlining Responses

Next, jot down a few words to help guide your answer. They will provide a brief outline for you to use in developing your answer, and they will nearly always stimulate your mind to think more clearly about the question. The two or three minutes you spend reading the question and writing down words to help you answer it will save you much time in the actual writing. Suppose you have a question such as this.

> What were the major causes of World War I? Which of these causes do you think was most important in the conflict that broke out in the summer of 1914? Justify your opinion.

Look at the question carefully: it is really *two* questions. The first one requires you to name several causes of World War I. The second requires you to make a choice among the causes you have named, and then to give reasons for your answer.

Once you understand the question, you are ready to start jotting down words and phrases to help form your answer. You begin by asking yourself who took part in the war as it developed in the summer of 1914—information you should remember readily if you have taken careful notes from your lectures and your reading. You remember that Germany and Austria-Hungary stood on one side and that against those two powers stood Serbia, Russia, Belgium, France, and Great Britain. Then you write phrases like these:

Russia vs. Austria-Hungary in the Balkans/Sarajevo
Germany vs. France and England; Alsace-Lorraine/naval race
Germany vs. Russia; Germans fear Russians; Schlieffer Plan
Neutral Belgium in the way of German army
Most important cause: German fear of Russia

40b essay

Beginning to Write

With these notes before you, you can begin to write. Although you should not waste time restating the essay question in a formulaic manner, often you can use part of the language provided in the question to begin your answer. A well-constructed essay question is often packed with information, and you can borrow from the question as you frame your response. Look at some typical essay questions and the opening sentences students wrote on their examinations.

Course	Question	Response
Marketing	Explain the general selling process that many salespeople use as they sell a product.	Although the selling process varies from person to person, most salespeople follow a general and definable process as they sell products.
Biology	Give a biological definition of aging, and show how the rates of aging vary among animal species.	Any biological definition of aging must begin with a consideration of genetics, which provides the basis of maximum life expectancies among animal species.

Economics	Explain how Keynesian economists attempt to achieve a stable economy through monetary policy.	The goal of monetary policy is economic stability, and Keynesians see monetary policy as moving through a complicated system of causes and effects.
Psychology	Identify the hierarchy (ladder) of needs that, according to Maslow, lead to self-actualization, and explain the elements in the hierarchy.	Abraham Maslow identified a hierarchy of five general needs leading to self-actualization.
Philosophy	Define metaphysics, and explain how Bergson took a new look at the concept handed down from Aristotle.	From classical Greece onward, human beings have sought knowledge for its own sake: "All men by nature desire to know," writes Aristotle in his *Metaphysics*. But Henri Bergson, a twentieth-century philosopher, looked at the concept anew and pointed out that we are using the wrong methods to discover answers to a key metaphysical question: What is there? or What is real?

**40b
essay**

Justifying Opinions with Concrete Details

Many responses to essay questions are so vague and general that instructors wonder whether the students who wrote them ever came to class. A good answer mentions names, dates, facts, and specific details. A good answer also carries an argument and makes a point—just as any other good piece of writing does. Your first paragraph, even your first sentence, should provide a clear statement of your thesis. Lay out the structure of your essay in the introduction. The reader of an essay exam wants to know immediately what you intend to prove and how you intend to prove it.

A good answer to the question about World War I might read something like this.

> In the summer of 1914, Europe was an arena of peoples who hated each other. The Germans hated the English because the English had a great empire and they themselves had little. The English hated the Germans because, since 1896, the Germans had been building a huge navy under the goading of the German Kaiser, Wilhelm II. The British believed that this German navy was to be used against them, and when the Kaiser sided with Britain's enemies in the Boer War, the British people saw their darkest suspicions confirmed.
>
> The French hated the Germans because the Germans had annexed the French territories of Alsace and Lorraine after the Franco-Prussian War of 1870-1871; the French wanted their land back and spoke continually of "revenge." The Germans heard that talk about revenge and hated the French for not adjusting to the new reality of Europe, which in the German view meant German domination of the continent.

40b essay

The writer establishes her thesis in the first sentence. She proposes the theory that national hatreds were a major cause of World War I by giving specific reasons for each country's hatred of another country, including appropriate names and dates.

Reviewing and Improving Your Answer

Once you have written your response, read it over. Though you cannot rewrite it, you can often improve it by making minor corrections and additions. You were probably writing fast. If you left words out or misspelled them, make corrections now.

As you review, look especially for ways to strengthen general statements by making them more specific. Simply adding a name, a date, or a factual detail may transform a vague claim into a specific reference that will demonstrate knowledge of the subject.

Vague: Though others flew before them, the Wright brothers are credited as the first to fly.

Specific: Because their powered flights of December 17, 1903, were recorded by witnesses and photographs, the Wright Brothers are credited as the first to fly.

Vague: Time is an interesting concept in Faulkner's "A Rose for Emily."

Specific: In Faulkner's "A Rose for Emily" we have a narrator who seems to be older than Miss Emily Grierson and lives longer than she does. Who is this narrator? How is the narrator related to time?

Vague: John Donne's poem "Death Be Not Proud" ends up being hopeful.

Specific: John Donne's poem "Death Be Not Proud" addresses Death as a person and exalts human nature by condemning the traditional claim that Death finally triumphs over humankind.

■ **Exercise 40.1**   Compare the list of questions on pages 620–621 with the opening sentence responses by student writers. What elements have the writers repeated from the question? What elements of their own have they introduced to establish a thesis?

40b essay

✔ CHECKLIST 40.1: **TAKING AN ESSAY EXAM**

Doing well on an essay exam requires more than knowing the material. You also must organize it and write about it within a strict time limit. Here are some tips.

- ■ Read the entire exam.
- ■ Be certain you understand every question and are aware of all their parts.
- ■ Make brief notes outlining your response to each question.
- ■ Begin writing, working your thesis sentence into the first paragraph of your answer.
- ■ Back up your generalizations with concrete details.
- ■ When you have finished writing, read the question again to be sure that you have answered all its parts.
- ■ Review, correct, and strengthen your answer.

40c
Writing an Essay Exam: A Sample Answer

The following essay was written in response to an examination question in an introduction to psychology course. The question was "Identify the hierarchy (ladder) of needs that, according to Maslow, lead to self-actualization, and explain the elements in the hierarchy."

■ **Exercise 40.2** Evaluate the student essay on the hierarchy of needs. What are its strengths? Weaknesses? Has the writer answered the question?

■ **Exercise 40.3** Select an essay-type question from the exercises in the textbook of any course you are currently taking. Following the recommendations in this chapter, write a draft response to the question. Share your essay with others in your writing class or with your writing instructor.

Opening
paragraph
1. States
   thesis
2. Repeats
   key words
   from
   question

Abraham Maslow identified a hierarchy of five general needs leading to self-actualization. Arranged from lowest to highest, these needs, Maslow says, must be satisfied in order, with self-actualization the last (and most difficult) to achieve.

Specific
details that
identify the
elements of
the hierarchy

The first need on the ladder of needs is physiological. This need includes hunger, thirst, sex--survival, in general. Second is the safety need, such as stability, security, and order. Third is love needs and belongingness; this includes needs for identification, affiliation, and the all-important affection. The fourth needs to be met before the final need of self-actualization are esteem needs, including the needs for success, self-respect, and prestige.

Examples
continue
identification
and provide
analysis

To explain the needs hierarchy, psychologists often provide the example of a starving man. That person is concerned only with obtaining food for today. He doesn't think about tomorrow (the safety need) until he is assured that his most basic physiological need (hunger) is met. When today's meal is certain, he can plan for meeting his physiological needs regularly and can concern himself with safety needs, next in the hierarchy. Those needs met, he can address belonging and love needs. At each rung on the ladder of motives we see the same set of priorities. When all other needs are met, people can strive to do what they enjoy and succeed at and thus become self-actualizing, that is, satisfying the need to realize potential and latent abilities.

New
paragraph:
new point in
explanation

Unfortunately, most people do not become self-actualizing. They get stuck on one of the steps of the ladder and do not move ahead. Despite noticeable examples of hunger throughout the world, most societies do provide an environment in which basic physiological needs can be met, and so most of us move up the ladder to <u>safety</u> needs. These hold most of our attention throughout life. We become intensely focused for example, on job security or the need for protection against crime. Only when we can assure the continued atmosphere of safety do we strive for love and then esteem.

Further points in analysis

Of course, any discussion of the needs hierarchy is of necessity oversimplified. In truth people easily fall back to lower rungs on the ladder when conditions in their lives or environment change. War, for example, with its threats to life and its deprivations can thrust a person already meeting belonging needs into a preoccupation with physiological needs (finding food), which have a much lower order in the hierarchy. Additionally, we often try to meet two different needs at the same time--for instance physiological and safety or belongingness and esteem. Because, according to Maslow, higher level needs can be fulfilled only when lower needs are met, the higher order motives (including self-actualization) often go unrealized. When people cannot achieve the higher rungs on Maslow's ladder, they can grow frustrated and conflicted.

Short summary paragraphs

The needs hierarchy and the various elements in each category provide a helpful method for understanding human motivation and conflict.

USING A WORD PROCESSOR

By all means learn to use computers and word-processing programs before you leave college. The computer has become a standard medium of communication. Word-processing programs enable you to make sweeping revisions or small changes with relative ease. They are fun to use, and they often give writers a sense of control over their work which they lacked when they were doing everything with a pencil or even with a typewriter.

Choose a word-processing program that you can learn easily and that someone you know is using successfully. Manuals are notorious for poor writing. If you cannot understand the manual, you can always consult a friend who knows the program.

Learn to compose at a keyboard. It is a much faster and more convenient way of writing than longhand. To use a computer, you must be able to use a keyboard, so if you don't know how to type, take the time to learn.

Computers eliminate much of the physical labor of writing, but you still have to work hard. No computer can think for you or tell you what you ought to say. But the computer, a good word-processing program, and a printer will make some of your choices easier. Revision becomes much easier, and as we have said so frequently, revision is the heart of writing. A computer is useful to a writer in a variety of ways: you can use it to take notes, to store data, and to create outlines as well as to write and revise your papers and prepare the final copy.

41a
Taking Notes and Storing Data

You can make many of your notes with a computer and a word processor. Book stands that hold books open and upright beside the keyboard are available in office supply shops and many campus bookstores.

Taking notes on a computer gives you several advantages. You can find them quickly by using the *search* command on your word-processing program. For example, suppose you are reading stories by the writer Peter Taylor for a literature paper on his work and you notice how often he mentions mirrors. You think you might mention that detail, perhaps even make a paper out of it. But you don't yet know. So you make this note.

The person in the mirror now eyed him curiously, even incredulously, and momentarily he resented the intrusion of this third, unfamiliar person on the scene, a person who, so to speak, ought still to have been asleep beside his wife back there in the family's guest room.

—"At the Drug Store," *The Collected Stories of Peter Taylor*

(New York: Penguin Books, 1986), p. 117

41a

wp

You might want to add a thought of your own about the use of the mirror in this passage. When you have made several dozen notes, you may want to recover all those places where Taylor mentions a mirror. All you have to do is command your word processor to search for the word *mirror*. It is a much faster process than keeping notes on 3 × 5 cards and having to shuffle through them when you sit down to work on your paper.

In making notes, you may make a file in which you put the full bibliographical information for every source you consult. If in that file you have the full information for *The Collected Stories of Peter Taylor,* you need type only *Taylor* and a page number with your note on mirrors. All good word-processing programs have another feature you can use in your writing. By using only a few keystrokes, you can copy quotations from your note file into the body of the paper you are writing. Not only is the process much easier than typing the quotation over again; it also cuts down your chances of making a copying error.

In taking notes with a computer, you should avoid the temptation to take too many notes or to copy too much *verbatim* (word for word) from the source. You should summarize most information, perhaps using only sentence fragments or abbreviated sentences. So, for the quotation above, you might write:

Taylor, mirrors, p. 117, *Collected Stories*

Then your computer file serves as an annotated index of your sources. Seeing the word *mirrors* on your computer, you can pick up the book of short stories and turn quickly to the passage. It is always a good idea to make comments on the notes you take. Your thoughts as you write the note should also go into your computer file, marked in some clear way that allows you to distinguish between what you are thinking and what you are seeing in the source.

Avoid taking so many notes that doing the research becomes a substitute for writing the paper. Many writers, both experienced and inexperienced, take so many notes and do so much research that they never get around to writing.

You can set up a separate computer file for each set of notes—a file for English literature, another for history, another for chemistry, and so on. You can set up a bibliography file, listing the various books and articles you use in a research project. You can make a directory that might, for example, combine all the files of notes made in various English courses you have taken in college. You can add files and notes throughout your formal education and afterward.

41b
Creating Outlines

41b
wp

The same features that make a word-processing program a good note file can also help you in outlining a paper. You can construct an outline on your word processor and then move the various parts around easily to achieve a more effective organization. As you work, you can gradually fill in your outline, using sample sentences and paragraphs that you can later fit into your paper. You can try out introductions and conclusions to see which of them best express your purposes.

If you have consulted several sources, you can often put your paper together by transferring notes from your note file to the place where you think they ought to fit in your outline. You can try different arrangements and experiment with different organizations. You can save the various versions of your expanded outlines, print them out, and compare them to see which seems to suit your purposes best.

Some word-processing programs now have built-in outlining functions, and some outlining programs with special functions are on the market. These outliners allow you to put your final paper together easily from an extended outline merely by pressing a few function keys. But by using the *search* and *copy* functions of any program, you can use it as an outliner.

If you use the computer to outline and to arrange your notes in organized blocks, you will see more clearly that writing is seldom a linear process in which one sits down and starts writing a paper from the beginning and goes straight through to the end. Writing is nearly always a process by which the writer brings chunks of material together and then blends them into a whole.

41c
Writing and Revising the Paper

Computers permit you to write more quickly than by hand or typewriter. But be careful. Sometimes your fingers can fly faster than your brain can think. Unless you write carefully, you may spend all the time you thought you saved in revising.

Revising

When you have used a computer for a while, you will learn to revise on the screen, inserting here, deleting there. But you should always print your work out and read it on paper, at least for the final run-through. Read with a pencil in hand to mark those places where you want to revise.

Be sure to give special attention to two errors common in word processing. One is deleting too much; the other is not deleting enough.

Often a writer will produce a sentence like this:

41c

wp

> Mr. Harrington, who has been convicted of car theft, said that his criminal record had nothing to do with his present effort to become city fire inspector, since cars had nothing to do with city buildings.

The writer, looking at this long sentence, naturally thought of ways of shortening it. And so he deleted some words. But as people often do in using computers, he deleted too much.

> Mr. Harrington, of car theft, said that his criminal record had nothing to do with his present effort to become city fire inspector, since cars had nothing to do with city buildings.

He had to insert a word he had accidentally deleted:

> Mr. Harrington, convicted of car theft, said that his criminal record had nothing to do with his present effort to become city fire inspector, since cars had nothing to do with city buildings.

Another error is failure to delete enough. A writer wrote this:

> Custer seemed to think that a dramatic victory over the Sioux Indians in 1876 would make him a national hero and might make him president in the election later that year.

In looking at her sentence, the writer decided to revise and came up with this:

> Custer seemed to think that a slaughtering the Sioux Indians would make him a national hero and might make him president in the election later that year.

The writer decided to make Custer's intentions more vivid by changing "a dramatic victory over" to "slaughtering." So she deleted and inserted. But she has not deleted the article *a,* thus leaving the sentence confused. It should be this:

> Custer seemed to think that slaughtering the Sioux Indians would make him a national hero and might make him president in the election later that year.

Computers allow you to move groups of words or, indeed, whole pages from one part of your essay to another by using a few function keys. You can try out a great many forms for the information you present. But you need to make the parts you move fit into their new spot. Read your work over again to be sure that you have not moved something without proper regard for the new context or that you have not left a noticeable hole in the place where the moved text was originally located. Working on a computer grants marvelous efficiency to the writing process. But it does not take away the requirement of any writer to read the text again and again and again to see that everything hangs together as it should.

41c

wp

Keep your successive drafts, on either backup disks or printouts or both. You may decide that you want to return to an earlier version of a sentence or a paragraph.

Checking for Repetitions

All writers have certain words or expressions they like and therefore tend to use too often. If you think you have used some stylistic mannerism too frequently, use the *search* function on the word-processing program to see how many times you have used it in your paper. For example, you may like the word *doggedly.* Search your paper to see how many times you have used it. If you have used it more than once, you should probably find a synonym.

Sometimes, especially in a long paper, you may repeat information unnecessarily. If you write a paper about southern literature, you might mention Peter Taylor as someone whose writing has little to do with the agrarian tradition of much southern writing. Suppose you are writing and think you may have said that earlier. It's easy to search for *Taylor* in your preceding text to see if you have given the information before.

You can apply the recommendations of this handbook by searching in your writing for words and usages we have warned you against. Are you afraid that you have used needless intensifiers such as *absolutely, definitely,* and *incredibly?* Search for them on the computer and decide if you want to eliminate them. Do you think you may have overused modifiers such as *very, rather,* and *really?* Search for them on the computer, and see if you can eliminate them where they turn up.

Checking Spelling

Many word-processing programs come with dictionaries that allow you to check the spellings of words in your text. These dictionaries are usually smaller than standard desk dictionaries. Most collegiate desk dictionaries list about 150,000 words; a dictionary on a word-processing program usually has around 50,000 words. Geographical, biographical, and specialized names and terms are not usually included in a computer dictionary, but you can add them to the dictionary.

The computer dictionary, often called a *spell checker,* is usually activated when one or more function keys are pressed while the cursor is on the word whose spelling you wish to examine. The computer will usually give you a message telling you whether the word is in the computer's dictionary. If it *is* in the dictionary, you may assume only that the word exists in English. You may need to check the entry in your desk dictionary to be sure you have got the word you want. **Homophones**—words pronounced alike but with different meanings—can trip you up (see 27b). Your computer spell checker may tell you *there* is spelled correctly, but if you meant *they're* or *their,* you've still spelled the word wrong. If the word is *not* in the dictionary as you have spelled it, either you have misspelled it or the computer dictionary does not include it. You might get a message, for example, that the word *dilettante* is not in your computer's dictionary. But on consulting your desk dictionary, you discover that you have spelled the word correctly! So you should never depend on the computer dictionary alone; use it in conjunction with a good desk dictionary.

Some dictionary programs can be set to work as you are typing. A quiet buzzer sounds each time you type a word not in the computer's dictionary. Such a function not only helps you with your spelling but also warns you against typographical errors. The computer will buzz if you misspell the word *believe* by writing "beleive." It will also buzz if you reverse letters in the word *the* so that you get "teh." The computer dictionary can be a valuable aid in proofreading.

41d
Preparing the Final Copy

Computers make life easier for writers but sometimes harder for readers. Be sure you do not let technology burden your readers. You can be courteous in the kind of printer you use for your final drafts and in the way you manage computer paper.

Selecting a Printer and Paper

Computer printers are of three main types. Laser printers are fast, and they have the clearest typeface. Letter-quality printers are heavy and slow, but they also have an excellent typeface, comparable to that of a good electric typewriter. Dot-matrix printers are perhaps the most common and reliable printers generally available. They make characters out of combinations of little dots; the dots are pressed onto the paper by tiny wires pushed through an inked ribbon, and the effect is like the appearance of the lights that form letters and numbers within a square on a scoreboard.

Dot-matrix type has improved dramatically over the years, but some models still make characters that are difficult to read. If you use a dot-matrix printer, be sure that it makes letters with true descenders. That is, the *g, j, p, q,* and *y* should have tails that come below the baseline of the rest of the type. The dots should also be close enough together to make legible letters. Before you use or buy a dot-matrix printer, look at a document that printer has produced. Can you read the document without being distracted by the type? If you have any doubts, find another printer.

Beware of printers that work with thermal-sensitive paper. These printers are often advertised as needing no ribbon; they make an impression by applying heat to treated paper. Such printers are fast and quiet. But often the type fades quickly as chemical changes take place in the paper. You can write something on thermal-sensitive paper and discover in a few months that you have nothing but blank sheets in your file! (Always be careful around any kind of dot-matrix printer; in operation, the printing head is extremely hot and can cause severe burns.)

Be sure the ribbon on your printer is dark enough to provide legible copy. The ribbons on dot-matrix printers wear out rapidly. A faint, scarcely legible type in dot matrix can make life even more difficult for a hard-pressed instructor.

Computer paper may be fed into the printer on a continuous roll. A perforated strip on each side allows a tractor feed to roll the paper line by line into the printer so that the paper does not wrinkle or twist on the roller. When you hand in your paper, be sure to tear off the perforated strip that has been used by the tractor feed. Be sure, too, to separate the pages. Don't hand in a continuous roll of printed pages! Instructors become justifiably annoyed if they have to separate individual sheets and put a student's work together before they can read and grade it.

Computer paper is notoriously poor in quality. Nearly all computer printers, however, will accept ordinary white bond paper. Although you must feed bond paper into some printers one sheet at a time, the greatly improved appearance justifies the extra effort.

Formatting the Document

Formatting a computer document involves laying out pages by adjusting the margins and line spacing, placing material (including page numbers) at the head and the foot of each page, setting the number of lines of type that will appear on a page, and determining the positions of the subheads.

41d

wp

In word processing, as in typing, take care to provide good margins—usually an inch and a half on the left side and at least an inch at the top, the right side, and the bottom. A little practice with your computer and your word-processing program should make it easy for you to set these margins. With most word-processing programs, you can justify the right margin. However, unless your word-processing program and your printer will do proportional spacing, it's always better to leave your right margin unjustified.

Always number your pages. Word-processing programs can set numbers at the top or the bottom of each page, and they can enter the number or set it on the right or left side. It's usually a good idea to number pages at the top. Page numbers are usually set as headers or footers. A *header* is a line of type that goes across the top of every page; a *footer* is a line of type that goes across the bottom of every page. You can add other information as well—the title of your paper, your last name, the date. It's generally good to keep headers and footers simple so they will not distract from the body of the text. Headers and footers should be separated from the body of the text by one line of space if the text is single-spaced and by two lines of space if the text is double-spaced.

All student papers should be double-spaced. When you prepare the computer to paginate, you must tell it how many lines to put on a page. If you double-space on $8\frac{1}{2} \times 11$ paper, you will usually have a header with a page number and about 27 lines of text. A page that ends with a subhead, with the material that the subhead introduces on the next page, looks imbalanced. Consult your program manual to find out how to make the computer move your heading to the top of the next page, where it belongs. Every time you repaginate your text after inserting or deleting material, check through your work to be sure you have not pulled or pushed a subhead to the bottom of a page.

Don't overuse the variety of typefaces your computer or printer may offer you. Boldface and italic are the only special typefaces you need for most work. Avoid eccentric typefaces. Never turn in papers written in a script or gothic typeface.

41e
Housekeeping

Computer data are stored by means of electric impulses that are translated onto disks by much the same sort of process that makes tape recordings. Small disks, measuring either $3\frac{1}{2}$ inches or $5\frac{1}{4}$ inches across, are called *floppies* and can be carried around and used in various compatible computers. Hard disks with vast storage capacities are sealed and fixed in the computer and are not intended to be moved from computer to computer.

All these disks are extremely fragile. Floppies can be ruined if they are placed too close to the speakers of a stereo set or even too close to the video monitor of the computer itself. Floppies are also sensitive to dust, to cracker crumbs, to fingerprints, to spilled coffee, and to anything else that touches the magnetic surface. Hard disks are sealed against dust and may give good service for several thousand hours. But all hard disks fail eventually. The failure comes suddenly, without warning. The hard disk simply fails to record data or to give data back to the computer screen.

Once a disk is ruined, the data you have put on it—a copy of your research paper, for example—may be gone forever. And even if you can retrieve the data by some of the technology now available, the process is time consuming and sometimes expensive.

So you should always make backup copies of your work. That means that you should copy the work on one disk to another amd keep the two disks in separate places so that if something happens to one, you will not lose your data. If you are using a hard disk, back your work up on floppies. If your computer fails, you can take your floppies to another compatible computer and go back to work with a minimum of lost time and with no lost data. Whenever you can do so, it's a good idea to print your work out at the end of a session with the computer. Printing the work out takes more time than making a backup disk. If you have a printed copy of your work, you may suffer the inconvenience of having to type it over again to store it on a disk. But at least you have your work.

✔ **CHECKLIST 41.1:** WRITING WITH A WORD PROCESSOR

Using a word processor may make writing easier, but it sometimes makes revising harder. Word processors can lull you into thinking your paper is better than it is. Always print out a draft, and revise it in the old-fashioned way—in pencil. When you return to the keyboard, keep these cautions and functions in mind.

- Revise carefully to be sure you delete neither too little nor too much and that you insert or move text to the right place.
- Use the *search* function to prevent repetitions.
- Use the spell checker to check your spelling; then confirm any word you're still uncertain of in your desk dictionary.
- Select a printer and typeface that are easy to read.
- Format your document with your readers in mind.
- Back up everything.

41e
wp

ESL
APPENDIX

ESL 1

Subjects: Subject Pronouns

In some languages the subject pronoun can be omitted if the reference to a preceding noun is clear. In English, such pronouns must always be included:

> *No:* My sister lives in Woodland. Is a small city.
> *Yes:* My sister lives in Woodland. *It* is a small city.
>
> *No:* My brother has a large practice. It is a dentist.
> *Yes:* My brother has a large practice. *He* is a dentist.
>
> *No:* The peony bloomed. Is a beautiful flower.
> *Yes:* The peony bloomed. *It* is a beautiful flower.

ESL 2

Subjects: Prepositional Phrases

A prepositional phrase cannot be used as the subject of a sentence. Use a noun or add a subject pronoun after the prepositional phrase:

> *No:* In my town is very safe.
> *Yes:* My town is very safe.
>   In my town it is very safe.
>
> *No:* With my sister go to school.
> *Yes:* I go to school with my sister.
>   With my sister, I go to school.
>
> *No:* In the house is warm.
> *Yes:* It is warm in the house.
>   In the house it is warm.

ESL 3

Subjects: *It* and *There* in Deferred Subjects

In some languages, you can omit *it* or *there* as a subject and still have a complete sentence. In English, these words must always be included.

> *No:* Is not good to miss class.
> Are many reasons to get to class on time, too.

> *Yes:* It is not good to miss class.
> There are many reasons to get to class on time, too.

ESL 4

Verbs: Phrasal Verbs

Some English verbs combine with adverbs or prepositions (called particles) to form two- and three-word *phrasal verbs* with new and different meanings. The words that make up phrasal verbs often have different meanings in combination than they do separately. The meaning of *put up with* (to tolerate or endure), for example, is different from the individual meanings of *put* or *up* alone.

Phrasal verbs are used more in conversation and informal writing than in academic writing. They are common in idiomatic expressions, often follow no general rules, and must usually be learned or looked up in a dictionary. They are also easy tests of fluency in speaking and writing.

Mistakes in choice of particle and placement of parts of the phrasal verb can destroy or change meaning. To avoid such mistakes, keep these points in mind:

Phrasal verb particles, unlike prepositions that follow verbs, cannot be separated and moved to other parts of the sentence. The entire phrasal verb may come at the end of the sentence, as in "What time did you *get in?*" (What time did you arrive?)

(continues on next page)

ESL 4 (continued)

Phrasal verbs can be transitive or intransitive, and some have both transitive and intransitive forms. For instance, *wake up* can be used in the following ways:

It's time to *wake up*.
Please *wake* me *up* at 6:00.

Some verbs and prepositional phrases cannot be separated by other words; some can be. There is no general rule.

"*Look* the word *up*" is correct.
"*Look* the child *after*" is wrong. It must be "*Look after* the child."

Objects of transitive phrasal verbs that cannot be separated should follow the complete verb, as in "*Look over* the assignment."

Noun objects of phrasal verbs that can be separated can be placed after the verb, or between verb and particle(s), as in "*Hand in* the test" or "*Hand* the test *in*."

Pronoun objects always come between verb and particle(s), as in "*Look* him *over*."

Common Phrasal Verbs

ask out	drop in	go out (with)
break down	drop off	go over
break up (with)	drop out (of)	grow up
bring up	figure out	hand in
burn down	fill in	hand out
burn out	fill up	hang out
burn up	find out	hang up
call back	get along (with)	have on
call in	get away (from)	help out
call off	get away (with)	keep on
call up	get back	keep out
catch up (with)	get in	keep out (of)
check in	get on (with)	keep up (with)
check out	get out	leave out
check up (on)	get over	look after
come out	get up	look into
cross out	give back	look out (for)
cut out	give in	look over
cut up	give up	look up

ESL 4 (continued)

make up (with)	shut off	try on
pass out	shut up	try out (for)
pick out	speak out	tune in (to)
pick up	speak up	tune up
put away	stand up (for)	turn down
put back	stay up	turn in
put off	take after	turn off
put on	take care (of)	turn on
put out	take in	turn out
put up (with)	take off	turn up
quiet down	take out	wake up
run across	take over	watch out (for)
run into	tear down	wear out
run out (of)	tear up	wrap up
show off	think over	use up
show up	throw up	

ESL 5

Verbs: Nonprogressive Verbs

Stative verbs are verbs that do not denote action. Instead they express a mental or emotional state or describe some property of their subject. These verbs do not take the progressive form:

No: I am preferring Beethoven's piano sonatas to any of his other works.
Yes: I prefer Beethoven's piano sonatas to any of his other works.

Certain verbs are always stative:

know, realize, understand, recognize, suppose, imagine, doubt, remember, forget, want, need, prefer, mean, love, like, hate, fear, envy, mind, care, possess, own, belong, seem

Other verbs are sometimes active, depending on the intended meaning:

be, have, taste, smell, hear, sound, feel, see, look, appear, weigh, cost

Juan's drawings *looked* very professional.
While the committee *was looking* at Juan's drawings, the room became silent.

Verbs: Errors in the Use of Verbs

With do in negatives and questions: Using third-person singular and past tense endings is incorrect.

> *No:* I didn't understood the assignment.
> *Yes:* I didn't understand the assignment.

With auxiliaries: Using third-person singular and past tense endings with verbs following *can* and *may* is incorrect.

> *No:* Mai can helps you with your homework.
> *Yes:* Mai can help you with your homework.

With verb endings for infinitives: Using third-person singular and past tense endings with infinitives used as objects is incorrect.

> *No:* Karl liked to studied in the library.
> *Yes:* Karl likes to study in the library.
> Karl liked to study in the library.

Verbs: Gerunds and Infinitives

Gerunds and infinitives can be objects or complements of verbs. Some verbs must be followed by infinitives; some verbs must be followed by gerunds; some verbs can be followed by either form.

Infinitives as objects of verbs often give a sense of purpose or signify that something is expected or anticipated. Gerunds as objects of verbs indicate that something is known or real. So all of these are correct:

> I like to swim. I like swimming. I enjoy swimming.

And these are not correct:

> I enjoy to swim. I wanted going to the movies.

Deciding which form to use can be a problem in English, since the choice depends on both the meaning and the particular verb. Here are some techniques to help avoid mistakes:

- An infinitive shows action after the time of the main verb: "I forgot to hand in that paper."
- A gerund indicates action before the time of the verb: "I forget handing in that paper."

An infinitive indicates an effort: "Try to make an outline before you write your essay."

A gerund indicates an experiment: "Try making an outline before you write your essay."

An infinitive indicates a purpose: "I stopped to talk to the teacher after class." "I stopped talking to the teacher after he insulted me."

Here are some common verbs and their complements:

These common verbs are followed by infinitives:

advise	encourage	make	refuse
agree	expect	mean	remind
allow	fail	need	request
appear	forbid	offer	require
ask	go (purpose)	order	see (purpose)
cause	hear	permit	seem
command	hesitate	persuade	teach
compel	hope	plan	tell
consent	instruct	prepare	trust
dare	intend	pretend	wait
decide	invite	promise	want
deserve	learn	propose	warn

These common verbs are followed by gerunds:

admit	discuss	imagine	quit
advise	dislike	keep (on)	recall
appreciate	encourage	mention	require
avoid	enjoy	mind	resent
can(not) help	excuse	miss	resist
consider	feel like	object to	risk
delay	finish	postpone	suggest
deny	forbid		

These verbs can be followed by an infinitive or a gerund with little or no difference in meaning. Generally, an infinitive expresses an action, a gerund expresses a process.

attempt	can(not) stand	like	see
begins	continue	love	stand
can(not) bear	hate	prefer	start

A few verbs can take either an infinitive or a gerund depending on the meaning.

remember, forget, regret

Verbs: Sequence of Tenses in Conditional Sentences

Verb forms in conditional sentences with *if* or *unless* present special problems. There are three basic kinds of conditional sentences: factual, predictive, and imaginative. Each has different rules.

Purpose of Sentence	Time of Occurrence
To state a general truth (factual)	present
To describe habitual action (factual)	present
	past
To express an inference (predictive)	present
	past
Make a promise or prediction (predictive)	future
To describe an event that is possible but not likely, or one that is not possible (imaginative)	present
	past

ESL 8 (continued)

Verb Form in If Clause	Verb Form in Independent Clause
If people lack social ties,	they become depressed.
If Rosa is lonely,	she goes to the Student Union.
If Rosa was lonely,	she called her mother.
If Milna is in bed early,	*present or must* + *verb stem* she must be sick.
If her light was on,	*past or must* + *present perfect* she must have been awake.
If my symptoms get worse,	I'll call the doctor.
Unless you study,	you'll get poor grades.
past (plural form of be) If I studied harder,	*would* + *stem* I would get all A's.
If I were a genius,	I wouldn't have to study.
past perfect If I had studied harder,	*would* + *present perfect* I would have aced that test.
If I had been a genius,	life would have been easier.

ESL 9

Objects: Position of Indirect Object

An indirect object can also be placed after a direct object. When this happens, it becomes part of a prepositional phrase. The preposition *for* is used after verbs such as *make* and *sing,* which suggest an action on someone or something else's behalf; *to* is used following verbs such as *give* and *tell,* which may imply a transaction between two individuals. A very few verbs, such as *ask* and *demand,* take the preposition *of.*

Usually, either position is acceptable:

Rogelio made *me* a copy of his notes.
Rogelio made a copy of his notes *for me.*

Here are some exceptions:

If the direct object is a pronoun, the indirect object must be placed in a prepositional phrase.

I gave them back *to him* the following day.

The same rule holds if either the direct or the indirect object has lengthy modifiers:

The instructor provided extra time *for all the students who needed help.*

The indirect object must not be expressed in a prepositional phrase following verbs like *cost* and *charge:*

The company charged *us* extra for the duplicates.

The trip cost *the family* a great deal of money.

ESL 10

Nouns: Types of Nouns

Nouns are names of persons, places, things, ideas, actions, and states of existence. Any word can be a noun if in a given context it can be given a name. There are several types of nouns in English, and some of the types overlap. Here is a brief list of the types, with definitions and some examples.

From the point of view of grammar and correct usage, collective nouns and the count/noncount (mass) categories are the most complicated and need special attention [see ESL 11, Count and Noncount (Mass) Nouns].

Type	Function	Examples
common nouns	name things according to a general class	desk, street, tractor, teacher
proper nouns	name specific people, places, things; capitalized	George Washington, Italy, the White House
concrete nouns	name entities we know from our own experience	tree, house, computer, highway, dog, cat
abstract nouns	name entities that we do not know except mentally, like ideas and states of existence	friendship, ambition, haste, serenity, happiness, life, death
collective nouns	name groups; can be singular or plural	team, crew, audience, class, government
count nouns	name entities that can be counted as individual units	friend, apple, lake, room, desk, shoe
noncount (mass) nouns	name entities that cannot be counted as individual units	sugar, rice, water, life, peace

Nouns: Count and Noncount (Mass) Nouns

Two types of nouns can cause difficulty because of a feature called *countability:*

Count nouns name items that can be counted as individual units.

Noncount or mass nouns name items that cannot be counted.

Here are some familiar categories of mass or noncount nouns:

Groups/substances consisting of similar items: furniture, machinery, rice, flour, sugar

Fluids and gases: water, milk, air, hydrogen, ozone

Games: chess, tag, hide-and-seek, mah-jongg

Substances: wood, metal, cotton, wool, velvet, leather

Abstractions: life, death, beauty, peace, cooperation, ignorance, serenity

Nouns formed from verbs: swimming, skiing, eating, seeing, walking, running

To use these nouns correctly, several points of grammar are important:

Noncount or mass nouns cannot be made plural; count nouns can be:

I drink water every day.
I broke two glasses today.

ESL 11 (continued)

Noncount or mass nouns take the third-person singular verb:

Water is good for you.
The machinery needs repair.
The sand is soft.

A few nouns can be either count or noncount depending on emphasis. If the focus is on a concrete example, they are count; if the focus is on a class, they are noncount.

Dieters should avoid recipes that contain egg. [noncount; mass]

That recipe calls for three eggs. [count; concrete]

Count and noncount nouns use different articles or determiners:

With count nouns: a/an, many/few/a, few/each/every/several

With noncount nouns: much/little/a little

With both types: all, some, any, a lot of/ lots of, plenty, none of

Here are some examples:

I have many friends in New York. [count]

We wished them much happiness in the future. [noncount]

They have some apples and some sugar. [both]

Determiners: Using Articles Correctly

One of the easiest tests of a fluent, idiomatic speaker or writer of English is correct use of articles—*an/an* and *the.* In English, deciding whether to use an article and which article to use is sometimes difficult.

Articles (or determiners) are usually divided into two categories: definite or specific (*the*), and indefinite or nonspecific (*an/an, some,* no article). To avoid errors, think in terms of four choices: *a/ an, the, some,* or no article.

Here are some guidelines and examples to help in making the choice.

DEFINITE   Use *the* with:

1. Common nouns, singular or plural, and noncount nouns that are specific because:

The noun has been mentioned previously:
The college is building *the library.*

The noun is identified by a modifier:
The new library will be much better.

The item is known to your reader/listener:
Your school has *the best library.*

The item is unique:
The computer index is extremely helpful.

2. Singular common count nouns that are used to represent a class of things or people:

Our library has a good book on *the* panda.

3. Plural proper nouns or proper nouns that name oceans or rivers, a geographical region, an organization or federation, or a newspaper:

The Smiths are both librarians.
They sailed *the Atlantic.*
Cartier explored *the Northeast.*
New atlases do not list *the Soviet Union.*
The President's commission will present its report.
The Atlanta Constitution is a good paper.

INDEFINITE   Use *a/an* with:

1. Singular countable common nouns that are nonspecific because:

There has been no previous mention:
I have *a study carrel* in the library.

There is no restricting modifier:
There is *a copy machine* on the first floor.

Identity is not important to the context:
The change machine can change *a dollar.*

2. Singular countable nouns that are generic:

A computer is *an electronic tool.*

INDEFINITE   Use *some* with:

Plural or noncount nouns that refer to a specifiable quantity.

I have *some change* for the copy machine.
Bring *some money.*

INDEFINITE   Use no article with:

1. Plural or noncount common nouns that are nonspecific because:

There is no previous mention:
There are *pens* for sale.

There is no restricting modifier:
There are *computer terminals* on every floor.

Quantity and identity are not important:
The reference librarian has *scratch paper.*

2. Plural nouns used in an abstract or generic sense:

Carrels are enclosed study cubicles.

3. Singular proper nouns that name a person, a single country/city/continent/a mountain/lake/bay or a disease:

Newsweek is a popular weekly.
Lake Baikal in *Siberia* is very polluted.
Some of the patients have *diabetes.*

ESL 13

Adjectives: Adjective Placement

Where to place adjectives can sometimes be a source of confusion. In general, single-word adjectives should precede the noun they modify, and phrases or clauses that function as adjectives should follow the noun.

> *No:* She had brown hair and curly.
> *Yes:* She had brown, curly hair.
>   She had hair that was brown and curly.

When several single-word adjectives precede the noun, follow this order:

DETERMINER	QUALITY	SIZE	AGE	SHAPE
two	priceless	little	old	round

PARTICIPLE	COLOR	ORIGIN	NOUN	NOUN
handmade	blue	Swedish	wine	glasses

ESL 14

Adverbs: Placement of Adverbs and Adverbials

The placement of adverbs and adverbials (phrases that can function as adverbs) can present problems in speaking or writing English. These two general rules are reliable guides to correct, idiomatic expression:

1. Never put an adverb or adverbial between the verb and its object:

> *No:* Dr. Sanders gave *this morning* a memorable lecture.
> *Yes:* Dr. Sanders gave a memorable lecture *this morning.*

ESL 14 (continued)

2. When a sentence contains a series of adverbs or adverbials following the verb, the usual order is manner, place, time:

The students sat <u>attentively</u> <u>at their desks</u> <u>until class was</u>
               [manner]   [place]   [time]
<u>over</u>.

Other placement rules:

1. Indefinite adverbs and adverbials of frequency (*sometimes, occasionally, seldom*) appear in the middle (before the verb, or between the auxiliary and main verb):

We *seldom* go to the movies.
We have *seldom* seen them on campus.

2. Definite adverbs and adverbials of frequency (*every, once*) appear in initial or first position:

Every Thursday we have a seminar.
Once a year, I go home for a visit.

3. Adverbs and adverbials of place (*at school, on the corner*) and manner (*slowly, anxiously, confidently, with a smile*) go in initial or final position.

Let's meet *at school.*
They walked *slowly.*

4. Adverbs and adverbials of time (*lately, early, recently*) go in initial or final position:

Lately it's been raining a lot.
It's been raining a lot *lately.*
Can you come *early* ?

5. Adverbs and adverbials of direction (*to the market, in the east*) go only in final position:

The sun rises *in the east.*
The vendors are on their way *to the market.*

ESL 15

Prepositions: Choosing the Correct Preposition

English has more prepositions than many other languages, and there is much overlap in their use and meaning.

Prepositions of space and time, like *at, on, in, into, onto,* and *to,* are the most easily confused. This is because they are used not according to the noun that is the object, but according to the aspect of space and time that is emphasized, and/or the degree of precision needed:

at 8 P.M. (exact)
in the evening (indefinite)

Many other common prepositions, like *above* and *under,* have stable meanings that can be checked in a dictionary. Choosing the correct preposition in these cases is usually not a problem. But for the difficult ones, those that can shift the meaning of a phrase, the dictionary is not always enough. Here are some additional hints to help you avoid errors:

If the preposition is part of a verb phrase, check the phrasal verbs list in ESL 4. It lists the common verb-preposition combinations and their meanings. Such combinations are frequent in English, particularly in everyday conversation and writing.

The table below presents rules governing the use of prepositions of space and time, along with examples that show which preposition to use in which situation.

SPACE

A Point	A Surface	Enclosed
LOCATIONAL		
at at the car	*on* on the car	*in* in the car
at the library	on the floor	in the lobby
at 20 Oak Street	on Oak Street	in the gray house
DIRECTIONAL		
to to the car	*onto* onto the floor	*into* into the house

ESL 15 (continued)

TIME

Point	Day	Period or Unspecified
at at 10:00	*on* on Monday	*in* in May
at Christmas	on May 1	in spring
(season)	on Christmas	in 1992
at New Year	(day)	in the morning/ evening

ESL 16

Participles: Confusion of Past and Present Participles

Differences in meaning between the present participle and the past participle forms of verbs that describe states of mind such as *bore, excite, interest, annoy, challenge,* and *fascinate* can sometimes cause problems. Remember that a present participle describes an experience or a person causing that experience. A past participle describes a person's response to an experience. Here are some examples of correct and incorrect expressions:

No: The lecture was very bored because I am not interesting in biochemistry.

Yes: The lecture was very boring because I am not interested in biochemistry.

No: Jack was annoying when Mary was not exciting at his award.

Yes: Jack was annoyed when Mary was not excited at his award.

ESL 17

Clauses: Mixed Subordination and Coordination

Two clauses can be connected by either a subordinating clause or a coordinating conjunction, but not by both:

> *No: Although* Hang felt sick, *but* he still went to his math class.
> *Yes: Although* Hang felt sick, he still went to his math class.
>   Hang felt sick, *but* he still went to his math class.

> *No: Even though* he said we would go, *but* it rained.
> *Yes: Even though* he said we would go, it rained.
>   He said we would go, *but* it rained.

> *No: If* you would like to attend the concert, *and so* would I.
> *Yes:* You would like to attend the concert, *and so* would I.
>   *If* you would like to attend the concert, *so* would I.

ESL 18

Clauses: Relative Pronouns and Adjective Clauses

Adjective clauses modify a noun or a pronoun. A relative pronoun (*who, whom, which, that*) is used to connect the clause to the word it modifies. When and how to use these pronouns is often a source of difficulty. Here are some general guidelines.

- When the relative pronoun is the subject of the clause, it must always be included.

  My cousin *who* lives in St. Louis is very rich.

- When the relative pronoun is the object of the clause, it can be omitted. Both of these examples are correct:

  The house my cousin lives in is very big.
  The house *that* my cousin lives in is very big.

Clauses: Special Problems in Forming Adjective Clauses

The relative pronouns *who/whom, that,* and *which* function not only as subordinators but as the subject or object in the adjective clauses they introduce.

These adjective clauses should not include additional subject or object pronouns.

OBJECT
No: Tina saw two dresses at the mall *that she liked them.*
Yes: Tina saw two dresses at the mall *that she liked.*

SUBJECT
No: She bought the dress *that it was more expensive.*
Yes: She bought the dress *that was more expensive.*

The relative pronouns that introduce adjective clauses must always refer to a noun in the main clause.

No: Carlos threw the ball to *who* was at first base.
Yes: Carlos threw the ball to *the player who* was at first base.

Adjective clauses always immediately follow the noun they modify in the main clause.

No: Mai's cousin plays the piano very well *who lives in Pittsburgh.*
Yes: Mai's cousin *who lives in Pittsburgh* plays the piano very well.

ESL 20

Dictionaries: Choosing Word Reference Books

A good dictionary designed specifically for second-language students is the best source of information about word meanings. Such dictionaries will help you avoid several common problems.

Ordinary dictionaries frequently define difficult words with other difficult words. In the American Heritage Dictionary, for example, the word *haze* is defined as "Atmospheric moisture, dust, smoke, and vapor suspended to form a partially opaque condition." An ESL dictionary defines it more simply as "A light mist or smoke."

Bilingual or "translation" dictionaries frequently oversimplify word meanings. They give synonyms that do not reflect multiple meanings of words. As a result, a writer seeking to use *fresh* in an abstract sense might choose *green,* which in this meaning is not a synonym. For example,

> TV reporters are always in search of *green* news to attract viewers.

Thesauruses and abridged dictionaries also do not show shades of meaning. For example, if you were looking for a synonym for the word *way,* you might find *direction* and use it in this non-idiomatic fashion:

> Because of my limited English, math class is hard. I often solve problems in the wrong *direction.*

GLOSSARY
OF USAGE

Although the meanings of words often change through the years, clear communication is enhanced when these changes take place slowly and meanings are kept as constant as possible. The following words and expressions are often misused or used in nontraditional ways. Studying this list will help you improve your vocabulary and your precision in the use of words.

Accept/Except   *Accept* is a verb meaning "to receive willingly"; *except* is a preposition meaning "but."

Please *accept* my apologies.

Everyone *except* Carlos saw the film.

Advice/Advise   *Advice* is a noun; *advise* is a verb. The *c* in *advice* is pronounced like the *c* in *certain;* the *s* in *advise* is pronounced like the last *s* in *surprise.*

I took his *advice* about buying stock, and I lost a fortune.

I *advise* you to disregard his *advice.*

Affect/Effect   The verb *affect* means "to impress, to move, to change"; the noun *effect* means "result"; the verb *effect* means "to make, to accomplish"; the noun *affect,* meaning "a feeling or an emotion," is used in psychology.

Inflation *affects* our sense of security.

Inflation is one of the many *effects* of war.

Inflation has *effected* many changes in the way we spend money.

To study *affect,* psychologists probe the unconscious.

Ain't *Ain't* is an eighteenth-century contraction that has become a sign of illiteracy and ignorance; it should not be used in formal writing or speech.

All/All of; More/More of; Some/Some of Except before some pronouns, the *of* in these constructions can usually be eliminated.

> *All* France rejoiced.
>
> *Some* students cut class.
>
> *All of* us wish you well. [The pronoun *us* requires the *of* before it here.]

All right/Alright The spelling *alright* is an alternate, but many educated readers still think it is incorrect in standard written English.

> I told him it was *all right* to miss class tomorrow.

All together/Altogether *All together* expresses unity or common location; *altogether* means "completely," often in a tone of ironic understatement.

> At the Imitators-of-Elvis national competition, it was *altogether* startling to see a swarm of untalented, loud young men with their rhinestones, their dyed and greased hair, and their pretensions, gathered *all together* on a single stage.

Allusion/Illusion An *allusion* is an indirect reference to something; an *illusion* is a fantasy that may be confused with reality.

> He wrote to her of an "empty house," an *allusion* to their abandoned love affair.
>
> They nourished the *illusion* that they could learn to write well without working hard.

Almost/Most *Almost,* an adverb, means "nearly"; *most,* an adjective, means "the greater part of." Do not use *most* when you mean *almost.*

> He wrote her about *almost* [NOT *most*] everything he did.
>
> He told her about *most* things he did.

A lot *A lot* used as a synonym for *many* is always two words.

> She had *a lot* of reasons for disliking Carmichael.

Among/Between *Between* expresses a relation of two nouns; *among* expresses a relation involving more than two.

> The distance *between* Boston and Knoxville is a thousand miles.
>
> The desire to quit smoking is common *among* people who have smoked for a long time.

But throughout the history of English, *between* has sometimes been used with more than two nouns. It often has the sense of "within."

> He covered the space *between* the four corners of his yard with concrete.

Between is sometimes used for more than two when each noun is considered individually.

The treaty that was signed was *between* the United States, Israel, and Egypt. [Each country signed the treaty individually.]

Between usually expresses a more precise relation, and *among* is more general.

Amount/Number Things measured in *amounts* usually cannot be thought of as having any individual identity; things measured in *numbers* can be sorted out and counted separately.

The *amount* of oil left underground in the United States is a matter of dispute.

But the *number* of oil companies losing money is tiny.

Anxious/Eager Careful writers distinguish between these two words when they are used to describe feelings about something that is going to happen. *Anxious* means "fearful"; *eager* signals strong interest or desire.

I am *anxious* when I visit the doctor.

I am *eager* to get out of the hospital.

Anymore/Any more *Anymore* is an adverb always used after a negation; *any more* can be an adjective and a pronoun or noun, or it can be an adverb and an adjective.

I don't enjoy dancing *anymore*.

I can't stand *any more*.

I don't want *any more* peanut butter.

Anyone/Any one; Anybody/Any body; Everyone/Every one; Everybody/Every body *Anyone, anybody, everyone,* and *everybody* are indefinite pronouns; when the pronoun *one* or the noun *body* is modified by the adjectives *any* and *every,* the words remain distinct in space and spelling.

Anybody can make a mistake.

A good murder mystery accounts for *every body* that turns up in the story.

The Scots always thought that *any one* of them was worth three of the enemy.

Anyone can see that this book is complicated.

Apt/Liable/Likely *Apt* means that someone has a special talent for doing something; *liable* means having legal responsibility; *likely* conveys a general expectation or consequence.

The president is an *apt* negotiator.

If my singing breaks your chandelier, I am *liable* for damages.

People who picnic in the woods are *likely* to get poison ivy.

As Do not use *as* as a synonym for *since, when,* or *because.*

UNCLEAR: I told him that he should visit Alcatraz *as* he was going to San Francisco.

BETTER: I told him that he should visit Alcatraz *since* he was going to San Francisco.

UNCLEAR: *As* I complained about the meal, the cook said he didn't like to eat there himself.

BETTER: *When* I complained about the meal, the cook said he didn't like to eat there himself.

UNCLEAR: *As* American Indians fought as individuals and not in organized groups, no wagon train in the history of the West ever had to circle up and fight off a mass attack by an Indian tribe.

BETTER: *Because* American Indians fought as individuals and not in organized groups, no wagon train in the history of the West ever had to circle up and fight off a mass attack by an Indian tribe.

As/Like   In formal writing, avoid the use of *like* as a conjunction. Although this usage is becoming more common even among the educated, it still irritates so many people that you would be wise to avoid it.

NOT: He sneezed *like* he had a cold.

BUT: He sneezed *as if* he had a cold.

Like is perfectly acceptable as a preposition that introduces a comparison.

He rode his horse *like* a cavalry soldier.

The peas were *like* bullets.

At the closing bell, the children scattered from the school *like* leaves before the wind.

It is not necessary to substitute *as* for *like* any time *like* is followed by a noun unless the noun is the subject of a dependent clause.

She enjoyed tropical fruits *like* pineapples, bananas, oranges, and mangoes.

They did the assignments uncomplainingly, *as* they would have done nothing, uncomplainingly, if I had assigned them nothing.

It is now acceptable to use *like* before a noun when a verb is implied afterward.

She wants to sing *like* a bird.

He ran across the stage *like* a horse.

At   Avoid the use of *at* as a false particle to complete the notion of *where*.

NOT: Where is Carmichael *at?*

BUT: Where is Carmichael?

Awful/Awfully   Use *awful* and *awfully* only to convey the emotion of terror or wonder (awe-full).

The vampire flew out the window with an *awful* shriek.

Careful writers avoid the use of *awful* and *awfully* when they mean *very* or *extremely*.

Awhile/A while   *Awhile* is an adverb; *a while* is an article and a noun.

Many authors are unable to write anything else for *a while* after they publish their first novel.

Stay *awhile* with me.

Being as/Being that   These terms should not be used as synonyms for *since* or *because*.

> NOT: *Being as* the mountain was there, we had to climb it.
> BUT: *Because* the mountain was there, we had to climb it.

Beside/Besides   *Beside* is a preposition meaning "next to" or "apart from"; *besides* is both a preposition and an adverb meaning "in addition to" or "except for."

> The ski slope was *beside* the lodge.
> She was *beside* herself with joy.
> *Besides* a bicycle, he needed a tent and a pack.

Better   Avoid using *better* in expressions of quantity.

> Crossing the continent by train took more than [NOT *better than*] four days.

But that/But what   Avoid writing these phrases when you mean *that* in expressions of doubt.

> NOT: I have no doubt *but that* you can learn to write well.
> BUT: I have no doubt *that* you can learn to write well.

> NOT: I doubt *but what* any country music singer and writer has ever had the genius of Hank Williams.
> BUT: I doubt *that* any country music singer and writer has ever had the genius of Hank Williams.

Can't hardly   This is a double negative that is ungrammatical and self-contradictory.

> NOT: I can't hardly understand algebra.
> BUT: I can hardly understand algebra.
>   I can't understand algebra.

Case/Instance/Line   These words are often used in expressions that can be revised, made more clear, or shortened.

> NOT: In Murdock's case, I had to decide if he was telling the truth.
> BUT: I had to decide if Murdock was telling the truth.

> NOT: In that instance, Murdock lied.
> BUT: Murdock lied.
>   Murdock lied then, but he told the truth the rest of the time.

> NOT: Along that line, Murdock lied.
> BUT: Murdock lied when he said he was allergic to cats.

In many sentences, the use of *in that instance* or *along that line* or some other similar phrase keeps writers from being specific and their prose from being lively.

Censor/Censure   To *censor* is to keep a part or all of a piece of writing, a film, or some other form of communication from reaching its intended audience; to *censure* is to scold or condemn someone. Sometimes the censure is a formal act; sometimes it is a personal expression.

The Chinese government *censors* newspapers.

The House of Representatives *censured* Representative Larsonee for stealing from the Post Office.

Compare with/Compare to   When you wish to stress either the similarities or the dissimilarities between two things, use *compare to;* when you wish to stress both similarities and differences, use *compare with.*

She compared his singing to the croaking of a wounded frog.

Compared to driving a motorcycle, driving a sportscar is safer.

He compared Omaha with San Francisco.

The use of *compared with* means that he found some things alike in Omaha and San Francisco and some things that were not alike, and that he mentioned both the similarities and dissimilarities.

Complement/Compliment   A *complement* is something added to something else to complete it. A *compliment* is an approving remark. *Complimentary* is an adjective referring to something freely given, as approval or a favor.

He considers sauerkraut a perfect *complement* to hot dogs.

She received many *compliments* on her bulldozer.

All veterans received *complimentary* tickets.

His remarks were *complimentary.*

Convince/Persuade   *Convince* usually means to win someone over by means of argument; *persuade* means to move so some form of action or change by argument or by some other means. *Convince* should always take *that* with a clause; *persuade* is followed by *to.*

The experiment *convinced* him *that* light was subject to gravity.

The television images of people dying in Bosnia *persuaded* the president *to* send help from the United States.

Could of/Should of/Would of   These are ungrammatical forms of *could have, should have,* and *would have.* Avoid them and use the proper forms.

Differ from/Differ with   *Differ from* expresses a lack of similarity; *differ with* expresses disagreement.

The ancient Greeks *differed* less *from* the Persians than we often think.

Aristotle *differed with* Plato on some important issues in philosophy.

Different from/Different than   The idiom is *different from.* Careful writers avoid *different than.*

The east coast of Florida is *different from* the west coast.

Disinterested/Uninterested   To be *disinterested* is to be impartial; to be *uninterested* is to have no concern about something, to pay no attention, to be bored.

We expect members of a jury to be *disinterested.*
Most people nowadays are *uninterested* in philosophy.

Don't/Doesn't *Don't* is the contraction for *do not; doesn't* is the contraction for *does not.*
You *don't* know what you're talking about.
He *doesn't* either.
Some American speakers say *he don't* and *she don't,* but such usage is nonstandard and should be avoided.

Due to/Because *Due to* is an overworked, wordy, and often confusing expression when it is used to show cause.
WORDY: Due to the fact that I was hungry, I ate too much.
BETTER: Because I was hungry, I ate too much.
Most writers accept the causative use of *due to* in short phrases, such as "His failure was *due to* laziness." But such constructions can be vague and confusing. Whose laziness? His or someone else's? The sentence does not tell us. What about a sentence like this one: "Their divorce was due to infidelity." Whose infidelity? Were both partners unfaithful? Sentences that include an agent are almost always clearer and more vigorous.
He failed because he was lazy.
His unfaithfulness to her caused their divorce.
A good rule of thumb is to use *due to* only in expressions of time in infinitive constructions or in other contexts where the meaning is scheduled.
The plane is *due to* arrive at five o'clock.
He is *due to* receive a promotion this year.

Each and every Use one or the other but not both.
Every cow came in at feeding time.
Each bale has to be put in the barn loft.

Eager/Anxious *See* Anxious/Eager.

Either . . . or/Neither . . . nor Always singular when followed by a singular noun or pronoun.
Neither Kant *nor* Hegel enjoys much popularity today.
When things get calm, *either* he *or* she starts a fight.
Either has an intensive use that *neither* does not, and when it is used as an intensive, *either* is always negative.
She told him she wouldn't go *either.*

Eminent/Imminent/Immanent *Eminent* means "exalted," "celebrated," "well known"; *imminent* means "about to happen" or "about to come"; *immanent* refers to something invisible spread everywhere through the visible world.
Many *eminent* Victorians were melancholy and disturbed.
In August 1939 Europeans sensed that war was *imminent.*

Medieval Christians believed that God's power was *immanent* through the universe.

Enthused/Enthusiastic   Most writers and editors prefer the word *enthusiastic*.

The secretary of the interior was *enthusiastic* about the plans to build a high-rise condominium in Yosemite National Park.

Etc.   This is a Latin abbreviation for *et cetera*, meaning "and others" or "and other things." Since the *and* is included in the abbreviation, you should not write *and etc.* In a series, a comma comes before *etc.* just as it would come before the coordinating conjunction that closes the series.

Everyone/Every one   *See* Anyone/Any one.

Except/Accept   *See* Accept/Except.

Expect/Suppose   *Expect* means "hope" or "anticipate"; *suppose* means "presume."

I *expect* a good grade on my essay.

I *suppose* that he lost money on the horses.

Farther/Further   *Farther* is used for geographical distances. *Further* means "in addition" when geography is not involved.

Ten miles *farther* on is a hotel.

He said *further* that he was annoyed with the play, the actors, and the dog that bit him on stage.

The Department of State hired a new public relations expert so that *further* disasters could be more carefully explained to the press.

Fewer/Less   *Fewer* is the adjective for groups or collections whose parts can be counted individually; *less* as an adjective is used for things in bulk not commonly considered collections of individual entities.

Fewer people were at commencement this year.

Your argument has *less* substance than you think.

Flaunt/Flout   *Flaunt* means "to wave, to show publicly" with a delight tinged with pride and even arrogance; *flout* means "to scorn" or "to defy," especially in a public way, seemingly without care for the consequences.

He *flaunted* his wealth by wearing overalls lined with mink.

He *flouted* the traffic laws by speeding, driving on the wrong side of the road, and running through a red light.

Former/Latter   These words can refer only to one of two persons or things—in sequence, named first, named last.

John saw *Star Wars* and *The Empire Strikes Back*. He liked the former better than the latter.

If you are speaking of three or more things, use *first* and *last*.

Guy's closest friends were Paul, Curtis, and Ricco. The first was Greek, the second was English, and the last was Italian.

Get   *Get* is one of the most flexible verbs in English. But in formal writing, you should avoid some of its more colloquial uses, as in *get with it, get it all together, get-up-and-go, get it, get me,* and *that gets me.*

Good/Well   *Good* is an adjective; *well* is an adverb except when it refers to good health, in which case it is an adjective. Avoid confusing them.

I felt *good* after the doctor told me that I looked *well.*
She did *well* on the exam.

Half/Half a/A half of   Write *half, a half,* or *half a,* but not *a half a, a half of,* or *half of.*

Half the baseball players went out on strike.
Half a loaf is better than none unless you are on a diet.
I want *a half*-dozen eggs to throw at the candidate.

Hanged/Hung   People are *hanged* by the neck until dead; pictures and all other things that can be suspended are *hung.*

Hopefully   Since the 1960s, *hopefully* has come into common use as an adverb modifying an entire sentence. Many careful writers and speakers object to *hopefully* as a modifier of an entire sentence because it does not specify who has the hope.

Hopefully Franklin will play poker tonight.

Who has the hope, Franklin or the other players who hope to win his money? Or perhaps the hope is held by someone who yearns for Franklin to be out of the house this evening.

Franklin *hopes* to play poker tonight.
All his gambling friends *hope* that Franklin will play poker with them tonight.
I *hope* Franklin is going to play poker tonight.

If . . . then   Avoid the common redundancy that results when you use these words in tandem.

REDUNDANT: *If* I get my license, *then* I can drive a cab.
BETTER: If I get my license, I can drive a cab.
        Once I get my license, I can drive a cab.

Imply/Infer   To *imply* means to suggest something without stating it directly; to *infer* means to draw a conclusion from evidence.

By pouring hot coffee on his head, she *implied* that he should stop singing.
When she dozed off in the middle of his declaration of love for her, he *inferred* that she was not going to marry him.

In/In to/Into   *In* refers to a location inside something; *in to* refers to motion with a purpose; *into* refers to movement from outside to inside or from separation to contact.

Charles kept a snake *in* his room.
The dorm supervisor came *in to* kill it.

The snake escaped by crawling *into* the drain.

The supervisor ran *into* the wall, and Charles got *into* trouble.

Incredible/Incredulous   The *incredible* cannot be believed; the *incredulous* do not believe. Stories and events may be *incredible;* people are *incredulous.* Avoid using *incredible* and *incredibly* so loosely that your reader can tell that you were too lazy to think of a more precise and more vivid word.

Our *incredible* journey began with a bomb threat and ended with a robbery.

The audience was *incredulous* at his bizarre tale of why his shirt and trousers were torn.

Individual/Person   Avoid the use of *individual* as a pompous synonym for *person,* and avoid using *individuals* when *people* will do. *Individual* as either a noun or an adjective should be used only to show a contrast between a person or a single entity and the group. Even then, *person* or one of its cognates may often be used.

The Bill of Rights guarantees *individual* liberties.

OR: The Bill of Rights guarantees *personal* liberties.

The speech was directed to every *person* in the square.

BUT: One of the oldest political questions is the relation between the *individual* and society.

Inside of/Outside of   The *of* is unnecessary.

He was *inside* the house watching the pro football game on television.

She was *outside* the house mowing the lawn.

Irregardless   This is a nonstandard form of *regardless.* The construction *irregardless* is a double negative, since both the prefix *ir-* and the suffix *-less* are negatives.

It's/Its   *It's* is usually the contraction for *it is* but sometimes for *it has; its* is a possessive pronoun.

It's clear that *its* paint is peeling.

It's often been said that spelling is difficult.

Kind/Kinds   *Kind* is a singular form and must take singular verbs and modifiers.

This kind of house *is* easy to build.

These kinds are better than those kinds.

Kind, sort, and *type* are often overused in writing. Try to do without them unless the classification they imply is necessary.

AWKWARD: She was a happy kind of person.

BETTER: She was a happy person.

Lie/Lay   *Lie* means "to recline"; *lay* means "to place." Part of the confusion in the way we use *lie* and *lay* comes because the principal parts of the verbs are confusing. Study the following sentences.

INTRANSITIVE: I am going to *lie* down to sleep.
TRANSITIVE: He said he would *lay* the clothes carefully on the bed.
PRESENT: I often *lie* awake at night.
PAST: He *lay* on his stomach for a long time and listened intently.
PAST PARTICIPLE: He had *lain* there for an hour before he heard the horses.
PRESENT: He will *lay* the bricks in a straight line.
PAST: She *laid* her book on the steps and left it there.
PAST PARTICIPLE: He had *laid* away money for years to prepare for his retirement.

Literally   *Literally* indicates that an expression often used in a figurative way is to be taken as true in this case.
Literally thousands of people gathered for the funeral.
The writer knows that *thousands* is sometimes used to mean merely "a great crowd." He wants people to know that if they counted the crowd at the funeral, they would number thousands. *Literally* is often incorrectly used as an intensive adverb. Avoid this usage, which can sound misleading or even ridiculous.
He *literally* scared Grandpa to death.
His blood *literally* boiled.
Her eyes *literally* flashed fire.

Maybe/May be   *Maybe* is an adverb meaning "perhaps"; *may be* is a verb meaning "is possible."
Maybe he can get a summer job selling dictionaries.
That *may be* a problem because he doesn't know how to use one.

Moral/Morale   The noun *moral* means "lesson," especially a lesson about standards of behavior or the nature of life; the noun *morale* means "attitude" or "mental condition."
The *moral* of the story is that to have a friend you must be a friend.
Morale dropped sharply among the students when they discovered that they would be penalized for misspelling words.

More important/More importantly   The correct idiom is *more important,* not *more importantly.*
More important, if Jackson had not won the Battle of New Orleans, the city might have remained in British hands.

Myself (Himself, Herself, etc.)   Pronouns ending with *-self* are reflexive, referring to the noun or pronoun that is the subject of a sentence, or intensive, stressing the noun or pronoun that serves as the antecedent.
Hercules hurt *himself* when he cleaned the stables.
Standing in the doorway was Count Dracula *himself* with a silver goblet in his hand.
When you are unsure whether to use *I, me, she, her, he,* or *him* in a com-

pound subject or object, you may be tempted to substitute one of these pronouns. Don't do it.

NOT: The quarrel was between him and *myself.*

BUT: The quarrel was between him and me.

Nohow/Nowheres   These words are nonstandard for *anyway, in no way, in any way, in any place,* and *in no place.* Don't use these words in writing.

Of/Have   *See* Could of/Should of/Would of.

Off of   Omit the *of.*

He knocked the hide *off* the ball.

She took the painting *off* the wall.

Parameter/Perimeter   *Parameter* is a mathematical term referring to an arbitrary constant or an independent variable; *perimeter* means "limit."

The *parameters* were set to give the standard deviation from many distributions.

The *perimeters* of his biography of Theodore Roosevelt were set by Roosevelt's birth and death.

Parameter can sometimes be used correctly outside mathematics or computer science to mean some constant whose value varies, allowing us to measure other variables by it.

Because religion is a *parameter* of human life in all times and places, its effects on the relation between family and society may readily be observed.

Plus   Avoid using *plus* as a substitute for *and.*

SUBSTANDARD: He had to walk the dog, wash the dishes, and take out the garbage, *plus* he had to write a book.

STANDARD: He had to walk the dog, wash the dishes, take out the garbage, and write his book.

Practicable/Practical   *Practicable* is an adjective applied to things that can be done; practical means "sensible."

A space program that would land human beings on Mars is now *practicable,* but the journey would take a long time.

Many people don't think such a journey is *practical.*

Previous to/Prior to   Avoid these wordy and somewhat pompous substitutes for *before.*

Principal/Principle   *Principal* is an adjective meaning "first in importance" or a noun referring to the highest office in an organization or a capital sum that collects interest; *principle* is a noun referring to a standard for life, thought, or morals or the underlying unity that joins distinct phenomena.

The *principal* objection to our school's *principal* is that he had no *principles* in handling the endowment, investing it in the company owned by his wife.

Real/Really   Avoid the use of *real* when you mean *very.*

The cake was *very* good.

It is grammatically correct to use *really* for the adverb *very*, but *really* is overworked nowadays and should be given a rest, especially because it rarely adds anything worthwhile to a sentence. The overuse of *really* makes you sound insincere, as if you were trying to convince somebody of something without having any evidence at your command.

Reason is because   This is a redundant expression.

The reason he fell on the ice is *that* he cannot skate.

Relation/Relationship   A short while ago *relationship* was most commonly used for "blood kin." Now it has almost replaced *relation. Relationship* is called a "long variant" of *relation* by H. W. Fowler, a great authority on the English language. It says nothing that *relation* does not say, but often writers use it because it lets them imagine that they are saying much more than they are.

Respective   The word is almost always unnecessary in constructions like the following, and you can usually leave it out.

Charles and Robert brought in their *respective* assignments.

Set/Sit   *Set* is usually a transitive verb, taking a direct object, meaning "to establish" or "to place"; *sit* is usually intransitive, meaning "to place oneself in a sitting position." The principal parts of *set* are *set, set,* and *set.* The principal parts of *sit* are *sit, sat,* and *sat.*

DiMaggio *set* the standard of excellence in fielding.

The dog *sat* on command.

Occasionally *set* can be intransitive and *sit* transitive.

The concrete took a while to *set.*

He *sits* his horse like a champion.

Shall/Will   Not long ago, *shall* was the standard first-person future of the verb *to be* when a simple statement of fact was intended; *will* was the future for the second and third persons. But to say *I will, you shall, she shall,* or *they shall* implied a special determination to accomplish something.

I *shall* be forty-eight on my next birthday.

I *will* eat these cursed beets because they are good for me.

Now the distinction is blurred in the United States, although it is still observed in Britain. Most writers use *will* as the ordinary future tense for the first person.

We *will* come to New York next week.

Shall is still used in a few emphatic constructions in the second and third person.

They *shall* not pass.

You may take my life, but you *shall* not rob me of my dignity.

Some   Avoid the use of the adjective *some* in place of the adverb *somewhat.*

He felt *somewhat* better after a good night's sleep.

Somewheres   Don't use this nonstandard form for *somewhere*.

Sure   Avoid confusing the adjective *sure* with the adverb *surely*.

The hat she wore on the streetcar was *surely* bizarre.

Sure and/Sure to   *Sure and* is often used colloquially.

NONSTANDARD: Be *sure and* get to the wedding on time.

In formal writing, *sure to* is preferred.

Be *sure to* get to the wedding on time.

That/Which   A few writers use *that* as a restrictive pronoun to introduce restrictive clauses and *which* to introduce nonrestrictive clauses.

The bull *that* escaped ran through my china shop, *which* was located on the square.

This distinction has never been so widely observed or respected that it can be considered a rule of grammar. The distinction offers no help for restrictive and nonrestrictive phrases or for *who* and *whom* clauses, which can be restrictive or nonrestrictive. The best rule is to set off the nonrestrictive elements with commas and to avoid using commas with restrictive elements.

Their/There/They're   *Their* is a possessive pronoun; *there* is an adverb of place; *they're* is a contraction of *they are*.

They gave *their* lives.

She was standing *there*.

They're reading more poetry than they once did.

This here/These here/That there/Them there   Avoid these nonstandard forms.

Try and/Try to   *Try to* is the preferred form.

Try to understand.

Use/Utilize   *Utilize* seldom says more than *use*, and simpler is almost always better.

We must learn how to *use* computers.

Verbally/Orally   To say something *orally* is to say it aloud; to say something *verbally* is to use words. Many people confuse the two terms today, using *verbally* when they should use *orally*.

We agreed *orally* to get married, but when I asked her to confirm our engagement in writing, she refused.

His eyes displayed anger, but *verbally* he said only that he was disappointed.

Wait for/Wait on   People *wait for* those who are late; they *wait on* tables.

Wait for me.

Steve *waited on* four tables at the diner.

Which/Who/Whose   *Which* is used for things, *who* and *whose* for people.

The plane, *which* was late, brought the team home from California.

My lost fountain pen was found by a man *who* had never seen one before, *whose* whole life had been spent with ballpoints.

But *whose* is increasingly being used for things in constructions where *of which* would be awkward.

The cathedral, *whose* towers could be seen from miles away, seemed to shelter its city.

GLOSSARY OF
GRAMMATICAL TERMS

Grammar is the science of the English language; studying grammar helps us analyze and talk about everyday spoken and written communication. This handbook does not provide a comprehensive course in grammar but instead offers a general introduction to the scientific study of our language (see Chapters 13–20). The terms and definitions below expand some of the concepts introduced earlier.

Absolute phrase　A phrase made up of a noun or pronoun and a participle, extending the statement made by the sentence and modifying the sentence as a whole, not a particular element in it.

> The sun rose at six o'clock, *its red light throwing long shadows in the forest.*

When the participle is some form of the verb *to be,* it is often omitted.

> He flung the ball from center field, *his throw* [being] *like a bullet.*

Absolutes are common in modern English style; they allow compression of action and provide variety in sentences.

Abstract noun　A noun that does not call up a concrete memory involving sensual experience. Examples: *relation, idea, thought, strength, matter, friendship, experience, enmity.* An abstract noun refers to some quality *abstracted,* or drawn, from many different experiences, and it may be used to name many different kinds of experiences. Abstract nouns require the help of concrete nouns if they are to make sense.

Acronym　A noun made of the initials of an organization and sometimes pronounceable as if it were a word. Familiar acronyms include FBI (Federal Bureau of Investigation), CREEP (Committee to Re-elect the President), SNCC (Students Nonviolent Co-ordinating Committee), and HEW (Department of Health, Education, and Welfare). The forms of acronyms usually do not change, but the possessive case and the plural are formed in the same way as those of other nouns.

SNCC's first leader was Bob Moses.

Active voice   The voice of a verb used to report that the subject does something.

The guitar player *sang* tenor.

The active voice always makes a stronger sentence than the passive voice.

Adjectival   Any word or group of words (a phrase or a clause) that can be used as an adjective to modify a noun or pronoun. In the following examples, the adjectival words are in italics:

my book, *your* picture, *his* anger, *her* success

She painted the house *next door.*

The table *in the corner* belonged to me.

Writers *who write truly* always have readers.

Adjective   Word that modifies a noun or pronoun by describing some quality.

The *red* coat; the *blue* book

Adjectives can come before or after a noun:

The roof of the *old red* barn collapsed.

The barn—*old, weather-beaten,* and *abandoned*—finally collapsed in the last snow.

Adjectives can also come after a verb when they modify the subject. In this position they are *predicate adjectives.*

The barn was *red.*

Adjectives often change form to show comparison.

Her car is *big.*

Jack's car is *bigger.*

My car is *biggest* of all, and I can't afford to drive it.

She bought an *expensive* meal at the Ritz.

She bought a *more expensive* meal at the Algonquin.

But she bought her *most expensive* meal at Tommy's Lunch, since it gave her food poisoning and put her in the hospital for a week.

Adjective clause   Clause used to modify a noun or pronoun.

The car *that I drove then* appears in these old snapshots.

Adjective phrase   A phrase such as a prepositional phrase that modifies a noun or pronoun.

He came to the end *of the road.*

Adverb   Word commonly used to modify a verb, an adjective, or another adverb. Increasingly in modern English, adverbs are being used to modify whole sentences, though here the effect may be confusing. Adverbs tell us *when, where, why, how, how often, to what degree.*

They left *yesterday.*
The sun was *insufferably* hot.
The *more frequently* used room deteriorated *more seriously.*
Happily, the car hit the wall before it could hit me.

Adverbial, adverbial clause, adverbial phrase   A clause or phrase that acts as an adverb, usually modifying a verb in another clause but sometimes modifying an adjective or another adverb.

Adverbial clauses often begin with words like *when, because, although, since, if, whether, after,* and *before.*

> *After he lost at Gettysburg,* Lee knew he could not invade the North again.

> We often think that women's fashions in the nineteenth century were dull *because we see them only in black-and-white photographs.*

Any phrase used as an adverb is an adverbial phrase. The most common adverbial phrase is the prepositional phrase.

> You may find me *at home* this evening.

> We groped around *in the dark.*

Adverbial is a word sometimes used to describe a phrase or a clause that acts as an adverb. Sometimes nouns are pressed into service as adverbials.

> Many Americans go to church *Sundays.*

> We plan to go *home* for Thanksgiving.

Agreement between pronouns and antecedents   A matching in number and gender between pronouns and the nouns to which they refer.

> Most *Americans* pay too little attention to *their* bodies.

> *Emma Bovary* hated *her* dull life in *her* little town.

> *Flaubert* created in her *his* greatest character.

> *Anyone* dropping a course needs the signature of *his* or *her* faculty advisor.

Agreement between subjects and verbs   A matching in number between subjects and verbs. A singular subject must take a singular verb; a plural subject must take a plural verb.

> The *general* over all the armies *was* Eisenhower.

> The *horses run* nearly every day at Suffolk Downs.

> *Lee Ann* and *Tommy are playing* in the snow.

The greatest trouble in agreement between subjects and verbs usually comes in the third person singular, where *s* or *es* is added to the dictionary form of the verb.

> *She dances* with grace and strength.

> *He yearns* to return to the South.

The common contractions *don't* and *doesn't* give particular difficulty. Remember that *doesn't* is used in the third person singular in the present tense; *don't* is used in all other forms of the present tense:

> It *doesn't* matter now.

> They *don't* believe us.

She *doesn't* live here any more.

Appositive   A noun or noun phrase that identifies another noun or pronoun, usually by naming it again in different words. Appositives usually come after the nouns they identify.

This is my brother *John.*

They loved Chinese food—*tofu, rice, and sweet-and-sour sauces.*

Clarence Penn, *the children's leader at the YMCA,* loved to lead hikes.

Notice that the appositives have the same relation to the rest of the sentence as the nouns they identify. You can leave out either the appositive or the noun identified by the appositive and have a grammatically complete sentence.

The children's leader at the YMCA loved to lead hikes.

Article   The *indefinite articles* are *a* and *an;* the *definite* article is *the.* An article (sometimes called a *determiner*) sets off a noun or noun substitute in a sentence or phrase.

a broken toy

an unsettling thought

the treehouse

Auxiliary (helping) verb   A verb used to help form the proper tense of another verb in a clause. Common helping verbs are *am, is, are, was, be, been, being, were, do, did, does, have, has, had, shall, will, may, might, can, could, would, should, must,* and *ought. (See also* Verb.)

He *had been* sleeping before the earthquake hit.

Rock music *must* have some strange power over children.

They *have* invited Norman to the party, but he *has* not yet accepted.

She *should have been* studying but instead she *was* watching television.

Biased writing   Writing that fosters stereotypes or that demeans, ignores, or patronizes people on the basis of gender, age, religion, country of origin, physical abilities, sexual preference, or any other human attribute.

Case   Form of a noun or pronoun that shows a grammatical relation to some other part of the sentence. English has only three cases: the *subjective* (or *nominative*), the *possessive* (or *genitive*), and the *objective* (or *accusative*). Only pronouns change form from the nominative in both the possessive and the objective case. Nouns commonly change form only in the possessive.

To form the possessive of a singular noun, add *'s.* For nouns ending in *s,* some writers add only an apostrophe, others add *'s.*

Erasmus/Erasmus', Dick/Dick's, Germany/Germany's

Some pronouns have different forms of all three cases.

Nominative	Possessive	Objective
I	my/mine	me
who	whose	whom
we	our/ours	them
they	their/theirs	them
he	his	him

Some pronouns have only two forms.

Nominative	Possessive	Objective
you	your/yours	you
it	its	it
she	her/hers	her

Clause A group of grammatically related words that includes a subject and a predicate. An *independent* (or *main*) clause may stand alone as a sentence; a *dependent* (or *subordinate*) clause acts as a noun, an adjective, or an adverb for some element of another clause. Independent clauses are sometimes called *main clauses;* dependent clauses are sometimes called *subordinate clauses.*

He thought his book was a failure *because it lost money.*

The independent clause (beginning with ''He thought'') can stand alone as a sentence, the dependent clause (in italics) acts as an adverb modifying the verb *was* in the independent clause.

Clustering Tying together various related ideas; can be done by drawing a subject tree.

Collective noun A noun naming a group of people or things. In American English it is usually considered a grammatical singular. (*See also* Noun.)

The *team* was upset because of the penalty.

The *government* is the plaintiff in the case.

The *majority* is opposed to the measure.

Comma splice The misuse of a comma to join two independent clauses without the help of a coordinating conjunction. You can mend a comma splice by using a coordinating conjunction or by replacing the comma with a semicolon.

COMMA SPLICE: They gathered the wood, she built the fire.

REVISED: They gathered the wood; she built the fire.

They gathered the wood, and she built the fire.

Common noun   A noun that is not specific enough to be capitalized within a sentence. Common nouns are words like *desk, typewriter, chair, aircraft, automobile, glue, cow,* and *football.* (*See also* Noun.)

Comparative degree   *See* Comparison.

Comparison   Adjectives and adverbs can make comparisons. They indicate degrees by changing form or adding words.
The *positive degree* is the form that makes no comparison: *swift, quickly.*
The comparative degree compares no more than two things: a *swifter* boat, runs *more quickly.* Form the comparative degree by adding *-er* to the modifier or by using the word *more* or *less* before the modifier.
The *superlative degree* compares three or more things: the *swiftest* boat, runs *most quickly.* Form the superlative degree by adding *-est* to the modifier or by using the word *most* or *least* before the modifier. Exceptions exist, of course:

Positive	Comparative	Superlative
good	better	best
bad	worse	worst

Complement   A word or group of words that extends or completes the meaning of some other elements in a clause.
A *subject complement* usually follows the verb but adds something to the meaning of the subject. Subject complements can be nouns or adjectives:
> Her work was her *life.* [The noun *life* defines the subject, *work.*]
> Her work was *difficult.* [The adjective *difficult* modifies the subject, *work.*]

An *object complement* follows immediately after the direct object of a verb or another object in the sentence and extends or completes the meaning of the object.
> I wrote a letter to my sister *Nancy.* [*Nancy* is the complement of the object of the preposition, *sister.*]
> The university named her *president* last week. [*President* is the complement of the direct object, *her.*]

A *verb complement* can be the direct or indirect object of the verb: it can receive the action of the verb or show for whom or to whom the action is conveyed.
> He raised *money* for the campaign. [Direct object, *money.*]
> He gave *me* the money. [Indirect object, *me.*]

Complete predicate   The predicate, together with all the words that help make it a statement about the subject. (*See also* Predicate.)

Complete subject   The subject and the words that describe it. (*See also* Subject.)

Complex sentence   A sentence with an independent clause and at least one dependent clause. (*See also* Sentence.)

> If you want to write well, you must work hard.
> Because she worked hard, she received a promotion.
> Although he hates exercise, he ran six miles every morning.

Compound sentence   A sentence with at least two independent clauses joined by a comma and a coordinating conjunction or by a semicolon or a colon. (*See also* Sentence.)

> We faced strong opposition, but we won.
> She washed the clothes; he did the dishes.
> Their point was this: men and women should receive equal pay for equal work.

Compound subject   Two or more subjects connected by a conjunction. (*See also* Subject.)

Compound-complex sentence   A sentence that has at least two independent clauses and at least one dependent clause. (*See also* Sentence.)

> The Russians declared war on Germany, and the Germans invaded Belgium because a Serbian killed an Austrian prince.

Conditional mood   *See* Mood.

Conjugation   A listing of the various forms of a verb to show tense, person, number, voice, and mood.

Conjunction   Word that joins elements of sentences to one another. *Coordinating conjunctions* (*and, but, or, nor, for,* and sometimes *so* and *yet*) can join independent clauses. *And,* the most frequently used coordinating conjunction, can be used to join many different elements in a sentence, but all the elements joined by *and* must be grammatically equal. That is, you should not write a sentence like this one: "The house was large, old, and it had not been painted in years." Revise it: "The house was large, old, and weather-beaten."

Subordinating conjunctions (or *subordinators*) mark a dependent clause to come. Example: *although, after, because, when, before.*

Conjunctive adverbs connect ideas between clauses. Examples are *however, nevertheless, moreover, indeed, in fact,* and *as a result.* Conjunctive adverbs are not strong enough to join two clauses without the help of a strong punctuation mark such as the semicolon, as in this sentence: "The sea voyage was long and difficult; however, Darwin seemed to enjoy it." Conjunctive adverbs may be used to begin a sentence to indicate a strong relation between that sentence and the one immediately before it.

> Another way is not inevitable. Indeed, nothing in human life is inevitable except death.

Connotation The traditional collection of associations that surround the use of a word. If I say, "I *demand* an answer," the connotation is much less friendly than if I say, "I *request* an answer." If I say, "The orchestra *slogged through* Beethoven's Third Symphony," the impression is much less flattering to the orchestra than if I say, "The orchestra *marched* through Beethoven's Third."

Contraction A shortened word or group of words formed when some letters or sounds are omitted and replaced by an apostrophe. Contractions include forms such as *doesn't* for *does not, can't* for *cannot*, and *won't* for *will not*. Contractions are common in informal speech and writing; they are generally not used in formal writing. You may find contractions in a magazine article; you will probably not find them in a textbook.

Coordinating conjunction *See* Conjunction.

Coordination A grammatical structure that joins sentence elements so that they are of equal importance.
> They flew, but we drove.
> The bird tumbled from its perch and did a flip.

Correlative conjunctions Conjunctions, used in pairs, that connect sentence elements of equal value. Examples: *both . . . and, either . . . or, neither . . . nor, not only . . . but also.* (*See also* Conjunction.)

Count noun *See* Noun.

Dangling modifier An adjectival element, often at the beginning of a sentence, which does not correctly modify the grammatical subject.
> DANGLING MODIFIER: *Crushed by the debt on her credit cards*, it was difficult for her to understand that she was making $40,000 a year and was still broke.
> REVISED: Crushed by the debt on her credit cards, she could hardly understand that she was making $40,000 a year and that she was still broke.

Declarative sentence A sentence that makes a statement. Some writers define a *declarative sentence* as a sentence that begins with the subject followed by a verb without any intervening phrases or clauses.

Declension A table of all the forms of a noun or pronoun, showing the various cases. In English, a declension includes the forms of the nominative, the possessive, and the objective in the singular and the plural.

Degree *See* Comparison.

Demonstrative pronoun *See* Pronoun.

Denotation Primary meaning(s) of a word; the strict dictionary definition.

Dependent clause   *See* Clause.

Determiner   *See* Article.

Diagramming   A pictorial method of showing relationships among various grammatical parts of a sentence.

Direct and indirect quotation   In a *direct quotation,* the exact words of a source are given within quotation marks.

> The chair of the board said today, "I will not permit that no-good turkey of a president to dictate to this corporation."

In an *indirect quotation,* the sense of what has been said is given in a paraphrase; the exact words of the source are not used.

> The chair of the board declared that he would not allow the president to tell the corporation what to do.

Direct object   *See* Object.

Discourse community   A group with certain interests, knowledge, and expectations and with certain conventional ways of communicating with one another, such as baseball fans or biologists.

Double negative   A substandard construction that makes a negative statement by using two negative forms. A double negative can be a single word such as the nonstandard *irregardless* (which has a negative form, *ir-,* at the beginning and another negative form, *-less,* at the end). A double negative is more commonly two negative words, as in this sentence: "I *don't* have *no* reason to go there." To correct the sentence, remove one of the negatives: "I *don't* have a reason to go there," or "I have *no* reason to go there." A common double negative is the phrase *can't hardly,* as in the sentence "I *can't hardly* do that assignment." The sentence should read, "I *can hardly* do that assignment."

Ellipsis   An omission from within a direct quotation, marked by three spaced dots made with the period on the typewriter. You should mark an ellipsis by making a space after the last word you quote; setting a period after the space; making another space, another period, another space, a third period, and another space; and then typing the first word of the quotation beyond the omitted material.
A sentence from David McCullough's *Mornings on Horseback:*

> He must bide his time, maintain perfect decorum and silence, and so passive a role did not sit at all well with him.

The sentence quoted with an ellipsis:

> "He must bide his time, . . . and so passive a role did not sit at all well with him," McCullough said.

Notice that the comma after *time* is included before the ellipsis marks.

Elliptical construction   A sentence construction in which words have been left out but are clearly understood.

[what is] *More important,* we learned to write well.
They are older *than she* [is old].
We enjoyed France more than [we enjoyed] *Switzerland.*

Exclamatory sentence　A sentence that expresses strong emotion and ends with an exclamation point.

Expletive　The use of *there, here,* or *it* as the grammatical subject of a sentence, followed by a form of *to be.*

We saw that *there were* feathers beneath the fence.
"*Here are* footsteps in the mud!" she exclaimed.
It was only Lucinda the cat who had torn a pillow to shreds.

When *it* is used as an expletive, this pronoun is the grammatical subject of a clause.

It is said that his grandfather did time in prison.
It was all a mystery, and we were baffled.

Expository writing　Writing that presents, develops, and discusses ideas, rather than telling a story or describing how things look.

Fragment　*See* Sentence fragment.

Free modifier　A modifier, usually in the form of the present or past participle or participial phrase, that serves as an adjective modifying the subject but appearing after the verb. Free modifiers may be multiplied almost infinitely without confusing the sentence.

Hank Williams began his country music career as a young boy in Alabama, *playing* nightclubs called blood buckets, *writing* songs in cars between engagements, *drinking* too much whiskey, *making* his way painfully to the Grand Ole Opry and national fame.

Free writing　Writing nonstop for a stated time period, without any attention to coherence or organization to get ideas on paper and stimulate thinking.

Future perfect tense　*See* Tense.

Future tense　*See* Tense.

Gender　Sexual reference in grammar. Nouns and pronouns can have a masculine, feminine, or neuter *gender.* Many writers now make a special effort to use nouns that do not specify gender when both males and females may be included in the noun: *police officer* rather than *policeman, chair* or *chairperson* rather than *chairman, flight attendant* rather than *stewardess.*

Genitive case　*See* Case.

Gerund　The present participle of a verb (with the ending *-ing*) used as a noun.

Bicycling is my favorite exercise.

Helping verb   *See* Auxiliary verb.

Idiom   A word or expression that conveys a meaning established by custom and usage rather than by the literal definition. According to American English idiom, *making out* with someone is different from *making up* with that person. If you say you are *burned out* at your job, you are saying something different from what you mean if you say you are *burned up* at your boss.

Imperative mood   *See* Mood.

Imperative sentence   A sentence that gives a command or makes a request.

Indefinite pronoun   A pronoun (such as *anybody* or *everybody*) that does not require an antecedent noun or pronoun, although it may refer to a noun or pronoun that comes after it in a sentence or a paragraph. (*See also* Pronoun.)

Independent clause   *See* Clause.

Indicative mood   *See* Mood.

Indirect object   Noun or pronoun placed before a direct object and used to show for whom or to whom the action is conveyed by the verb. (*See also* Object.)

Indirect quotation   *See* Direct and indirect quotation.

Infinitive   A verbal in the form of the simple present and usually marked by the infinitive marker *to*. Infinitives can be used as nouns or adjectives or adverbs.

>   NOUN: *To die* may not be the worst thing one can do.
>   ADJECTIVE: She believed she had many books *to write*.
>   ADVERB: Most Americans are willing *to work*.

Inflection   Changes in nouns, pronouns, verbs, adjectives, and adverbs that make these words serve various functions in sentences. The inflections of nouns and pronouns are called *declensions,* the inflections of verbs are called *conjugations,* and the inflections of adverbs and adjectives are called *comparisons.*

Intensive pronoun   *See* Pronoun.

Interjection   A part of speech used to express sudden or strong feeling.
>   *Ouch!* That hurts!
>   *Hey!* You can't do that to me!

Interrogative pronoun   *See* Pronoun.

Interrogative sentence   A sentence that asks a question and that ends with a question mark.

Intransitive verb   Verb that reports an act or a state of being and does not take a direct object. Intransitive verbs that join a subject with a subject complement are called *linking verbs*. (*See also* Verb.)

> Jack *ran* all the way home.
> He *was* sick all that week.
> She *had been* an architect in Missouri.

Inverted object   A direct object that comes before the subject in a sentence, used only occasionally for sentence variety.

> Whiskey he drank by the barrel.

Inverted sentence   A sentence in which the subject comes after the verb. The most common inverted sentences begin with the adverb *there:*

> There is something in what you say.
> Ding, ding, ding went the bell.
> Far, far away sounded the trumpets against the hills.

Irregular verb   A verb whose simple past and past participle are not formed with the addition of the suffix *-ed*. These are verbs such as *come/came/come; think/thought/thought;* and *sit/sat/sat*.

Linking verb   A verb that joins a subject to its complement. The most common linking verbs are forms of the verb *to be,* but all the verbs of sense are also linking verbs, so you should follow them with an adjective form:

> I felt bad because he disliked my play.
> The spring rain smelled good.

Mass noun   *See* Noun.

Misplaced modifier   Phrase or clause misplaced in the sentence so that it modifies the wrong thing.

> Mrs. Hotchkiss, who loved Indian customs, served the Thanksgiving turkey in a sari and sandals.

Modifier   Any word or group of words used as an adjective or adverb to qualify another word or group of words. The *red* truck is set off from trucks that are not red, and the horse *in the field* is set off from horses not in the field. (*See also* Misplaced modifier, Nonrestrictive modifier, Restrictive modifier.)

Mood   The form of a verb that shows whether the writer or speaker thinks the action reported is true, false, or desirable.

The *indicative mood* reports actions that the writer assumes to be true:

> Cat books now *crowd* the best-seller list.

The *subjunctive mood* reports actions that the writer assumes are untrue or at least uncertain:

> If I *were* rich, I would do nothing but farm.

The subjunctive mood can report actions or states that may not be true but that the writer thinks are desirable:

Let justice roll down like waters and righteousness as a mighty stream.
The *imperative mood* expresses a command or a request for an action that
the writer or speaker thinks is desirable.

Get out of here!

Bring the books with you when you come.

The *conditional mood* expresses what might be true or false under certain
circumstances.

If Betty *is* right, Bob *is* in trouble.

If Betty *were* here, she *could explain* what happened.

Nonrestrictive modifier   A clause or phrase that adds to the description
of the word it modifies without being essential to the core assertion of the
sentence. Nonrestrictive modifiers are usually set off by commas from the
word they modify.

Faulkner, *who never finished college,* became one of America's greatest
writers.

He ran toward the sound of the train, *stumbling in the tall grass, laughing, longing to see the locomotive and the engineer.*

The DC-3, *one of the most durable aircraft ever built,* still flies the skies in
some parts of the world.

Noun   Nouns are names of persons, places, things, ideas, actions, and
states of existence. Any word can be a noun if in a given context it can be
a name. A sure test for a noun is whether it can have one of the articles—
a, an, or *the*—placed before it. The plurals of nouns are usually formed
with the additions of *-s* or *-es,* but there are exceptions: sheep/*sheep,* child/
children, and man/*men.*

Common nouns name things according to a general class: *desk, street,
tractor, welder. Proper nouns* name specific people, places, or things and are
spelled with initial capital letters: *Italy, the Department of Agriculture, Abraham
Lincoln. Abstract nouns* name entities that lack any specific associations with
sense experience: *friendship, ambition, relationship, haste, details. Concrete
nouns* name entities that we may recall from our own sense experience:
wood, house, computer, cigar, highway, truck stop, bulldozer. Collective nouns
name groups: *team, crew, church, synagogue, audience, department. Count nouns*
name entities that can be counted as individual units. *Mass nouns* name
entities that cannot be separated and counted as individual units.

The categories of nouns may overlap. The collective noun *community*
is also an abstract noun, since the idea of community is abstracted from
our observations of people acting together. *George Washington* is a proper
noun, since the name refers to a specific person and is capitalized; but it
is also a concrete noun, since the man George Washington was a person
whom we can identify by his picture and by works that have been written
about him.

Noun clause A dependent clause used as a noun.

They told me *where we would meet in Athens.*

Number The form of a noun, verb, or pronoun that indicates singular or plural.

Object A noun or pronoun that receives the action reported by a verb, a preposition, or a verbal. (Verbals are infinitives, participles, and gerunds.) Objects usually come after the element that conveys action to them. A *direct object* receives the action of a verb (or a verbal) and generally follows the verb in a sentence.

Politicians must raise *money* to be elected.

An *indirect object* is a noun or pronoun placed before a direct object and used to show for whom or to whom the action is conveyed by the verb.

He promised *me* a hot cup of coffee.

Infinitives and verbals may take objects too.

We hoped to give her the *victory.*

Pushing *the couch,* she injured her back.

Prepositions always take objects.

They swam across the *river* together.

Object complement A word or group of words appearing after an object in a sentence and further defining that object.

He named his son *Tsang-Jou.*

They called the storm a *hurricane.*

Objective case Any noun or noun substitute is in the objective case when it is a direct object, an indirect object, or the object of a preposition or verbal. (*See* Case.)

Parenthetical element An element not essential to the main assertion of the sentence. If a parenthetical element represents a large interruption of the flow of a sentence, it may be placed within parentheses or dashes. Nonrestrictive modifiers are sometimes called parenthetical, since their removal does not destroy or confuse the main assertion of the sentence. Some words and expressions such as *incidentally* and *to be sure* are also considered parenthetical.

Herbert Hoover detested Franklin Roosevelt (Hoover would scarcely speak to him during Roosevelt's inaugural in 1932) and went on denouncing the New Deal for years.

He disliked the country—its loneliness appalled him—and he refused to visit it, even to ski or picnic or hike.

Participial phrase *See* Phrase.

Participle *See* Past participle and Present participle.

Parts of speech The names given to words to describe the role they play in communication. The eight parts of speech are noun, pronoun, verb, adjective, adverb, preposition, conjunction, and interjection.

Passive voice Form of a verb phrase that causes the subject of a clause to be acted upon. The passive is always made with some form of the verb *to be* and a past participle. (*See* Active voice; Voice.)

Lincoln *was elected* President in 1860.

The houses on the hill *were* all *built* alike.

Past participle The third principal part of a verb, the form of a verb used with the helping verbs *have* and *had*. It usually ends in *-ed*, but irregular verbs have different endings. The past participle finds common use as an adjective.

The hymn, *sung* by the mighty choir, rolled out into the night.

Their *worn* faces showed the futility of their effort.

The past participle, used with some form of the verb *to be*, is necessary to the passive voice.

The azaleas *were dug up and taken* from the garden before dawn.

Person The form of a pronoun that tells whether someone or something speaks. (*I, me, we, our*), is spoken to (*you, your*), or is spoken about (*he, she, it, their, them*). Verbs also change to show person in some tenses, especially in the third person singular.

FIRST PERSON: *I cry* (or *we cry*) at sad movies.

SECOND PERSON: *You cry* at sad movies.

THIRD PERSON: *He cries* (or *they cry*) at sad movies.

Personal pronoun *See* Pronoun.

Phrasal verb Verb combined with an adverb or preposition to express a new or different meaning. *Put up with*, for example, has a different meaning from *put* or *up* alone.

Phrase A group of related words that has neither subject nor predicate, and that serves as a part of speech in a sentence.

VERB PHRASE: We *are toiling* in the vineyard.

PREPOSITIONAL PHRASE: We must work *until sunset*.

PARTICIPIAL PHRASE: *Leaping the fence*, the horse carried me swiftly to safety in the woods.

INFINITIVE PHRASE: Lyndon Johnson yearned *to be somebody important*.

GERUND PHRASE: *Walking the dog* was his only exercise. [noun]

ABSOLUTE PHRASE: The car crashed through the house, *the front wheels coming to rest on the living room sofa*.

Positive degree *See* Comparison.

Possessive case The form of a noun or pronoun that indicates possession or a special relation. Some pronouns can only indicate possession—*my, mine, our, ours, your, yours, their*. The possessive of nouns (singular or plural) and some pronouns is formed by an apostrophe and an *-s* added at the end—*anybody's, everyone's, Gertrude's, Hubert's, women's* bank, *children's* toys. The possessive of nouns ending in *-s* (singular or plural) is generally formed by the addition of an apostrophe alone—*James', Erasmus',* the class' responsibility, the *states'* governors. Some writers prefer to add *'s* even to those nouns that end in *-s* in the singular—*James's, Erasmus's.* (*See also* Case.)

Possessive pronoun   *See* Pronoun.

Predicate   Everything in a clause or sentence besides the subject and its immediate adjectives. The predicate declares something about the subject. The *complete predicate* includes everything in the sentence but the subject cluster; the *simple predicate* includes only the verb or verb phrase. In this example *the complete predicate, including the simple predicate, is in italics.*

> The art of the late twentieth century *has departed from all the rules that supposedly guided both painting and sculpture for centuries.*

Predicate adjective   An adjective that comes after a verb and modifies the subject. (*See* Complement.)

> She was *dignified.*

Predicate noun   A noun that comes after the verb and helps to identify the subject of the sentence. (*See* Complement.)

> Ms. Smythe was an *architect.*

Prefix   A letter or a group of letters, often derived from Latin or Greek, added to the beginning of a word to form another word. Common prefixes are *dis-, ir-, un-,* and *a-,* implying some kind of negation, as in *disbelief, irreplaceable, unreliable,* and *asymmetrical; ad-* means something added or joined to something else, as in *admixture.*

Preposition   A word that does not change its form and that, by joining with a noun object, brings the noun into the sentence to act as an adjective or adverb. Common prepositions are *about, above, across, after, against, outside, toward,* and *within.* A preposition and its object, the noun or pronoun, make a *prepositional phrase,* and the prepositional phrase almost always serves as an adjective or an adverb in the sentence where it is found.

Prepositional phrase   *See* Phrase.

Present participle   The form of a verb that ends with *-ing.* With the aid of auxiliary verbs, the present participle forms the progressive of the various verb tenses. Standing by itself, the present participle can be an adjective or an adverb.

> ADJECTIVES: *Staggering* and *shouting,* he protested his innocence.
> ADVERB: They went *singing* through the streets at Christmas.

Present perfect tense   *See* Tense.

Present stem   The present stem of every English verb except *to be* is the form used with the personal pronoun *I* in the present tense (I *go,* I *stop*). It is also the form of the infinitive (*to go, to stop*). The simple past of a

regular verb is formed by the addition of *-ed* or *-d* to the present stem, and the present participle is formed by *-ing* added to the present stem. If the present stem ends in *-e*, that letter is almost always dropped before *-ing* is added. Dictionaries list words in alphabetical order according to the spelling of the present stem; so the present stem is sometimes called the *dictionary form* of the verb.

Present tense   *See* Tense.

Prewriting   The first step in the writing process: preparation for writing. It can involve thinking and learning about your topic, jotting down ideas, asking the journalist's questions, free writing, clustering, and researching.

Principal parts of a verb   The present stem, the simple past, and the past participle of a verb. The various tenses of verbs are formed from their principal parts.

> PRESENT STEM: smile, do
> SIMPLE PAST: smiled, did
> PAST PARTICIPLE: smiled, done

Progressive tense   *See* Tense.

Pronoun   A word used in place of a noun. Many pronouns have an antecedent that comes before them either in the sentence where they are found or in an earlier sentence. But some pronouns such as *I, you, we, anybody,* and *everyone* may lack a formal antecedent, and sometimes the noun to which a pronoun refers may follow the pronoun in the text. Pronouns are generally classified in the following ways:

> PERSONAL: I, you, we, they, he, she, our
> RELATIVE: who, whom, which, that
> INTERROGATIVE: who? which? what?
> DEMONSTRATIVE: this, that, these, those
> INDEFINITE: anybody, anyone, everyone, everybody
> POSSESSIVE: my, mine, your, her, his, its, our, their
> REFLEXIVE: myself, yourself, oneself
> INTENSIVE: myself, yourself, oneself

The difference between reflexive and intensive pronouns depends on how they are used in a sentence. Their forms are the same. If the subject is in the same person as the pronoun and acts on it, the pronoun is reflexive, as in the sentence *I did all the damage to myself.* But if the pronoun serves to make a statement much more emphatic than it would be without the pronoun, we say that it is intensive, as in this sentence: *I said it myself.*

Proper noun   *See* Noun.

Quotation   *See* Direct and indirect quotation.

Reflexive pronoun   *See* Pronoun.

Regular verb   A verb whose simple past and past participle are both formed by the addition of *-ed* to the present stem: *play/played/played*. (*See also* Irregular verb.)

Relative pronoun   *See* Pronoun.

Restrictive modifier   A modifying element that defines or restricts the element it modifies, so that its removal from a sentence would confuse the sense of the main assertion.

> The bicycle *that I rode to the coast* had eighteen speeds.
> The man *in the gray suit and white hat* held the gun.
> The woman *who spoke* allayed the fears of the crowd.

Rhetorical question   A question asked so that the writer or speaker may provide an answer or may demonstrate to the audience that the answer is obvious. The rhetorical question is often a convenient device for getting into a subject or for shifting emphasis within an essay. It should not be overused.

> How long are we going to let a government of the people be the chief destroyer of the people's land?
> How can we explain the seeming shift between Thomas More's early humanism and his later fury toward the Protestants?

Run-on sentence   Two independent clauses run together with no punctuation to separate them. (*See also* Sentence.)

> Scientists, grammarians, and artists are all alike in one respect they depend on the work of others like themselves.
> I rose to applaud the mayor's speech then I tripped over the woman's handbag.

Sentence   A statement, question, or command made by a grammatical union between a subject and a predicate. The subject must be a noun or noun substitute, and the predicate must include a verb. The subject controls the verb, and the subject and the verb must agree in number. In a sentence that is not a command, the predicate makes a statement about the subject. In a question, the statement is made in the form of an inquiry that asks to know if the statement is true.

> The personal computer *will soon become as common in the American home as the sofa in the living room.*
> *Will* the personal computer *soon become as common in the American home as the sofa in the living room?*

Sentence fragment   A group of words that begins with a capital letter and ends with a closing mark of punctuation, but does not include a subject in grammatical union with a predicate. Correct a sentence fragment by giving it a subject or predicate (or both, when necessary) or by adding it to the sentence that comes directly before or after it.

FRAGMENT: The telephone dropped. *Onto the floor.*
Working at her desk. She suffered terribly.
Dr. Leyton introduced the visiting surgeon. *Who spoke formally without looking up from her notes.*

REVISED: The telephone dropped. It fell to the floor.
Working at her desk, she suffered terribly.
Dr. Leyton introduced the visiting surgeon, who spoke formally without looking up from her notes.

Simple predicate   The word (or words) that reports or states a condition, with all the describing words removed; the verb.

Simple sentence   A sentence with only one clause.
An orange sun dropped below the horizon.
Bob and Ray amused radio audiences for many years and helped define a new age of American comedy.
Some simple sentences are not very simple.
Catherine arrived in England in 1501 and immediately encountered the English hatred of foreigners, a hatred shown in the scorn heaped on her retainers; in the bitter stinginess of her royal father-in-law, Henry VII; and in the indifference of those around her to her comfort and even to her dignity.

Simple subject   The word(s) that serve as the focus of the sentence.

Subject   The noun or noun substitute about which the predicate of a clause or sentence makes its statement. The *simple subject* is the noun or noun substitute; the *complete subject,* or the *subject cluster,* includes all the immediate modifiers of the subject.
The absurd and angry group that assembled in a beer hall in Munich that night in 1923 was to create, a decade later, the most bloody revolution in German history.
A *compound subject* is two or more subjects connected by a conjunction.

Subject complement   *See* Complement.

Subjective case   *See* Case.

Subjunctive mood   *See* Mood.

Subordinate clause   *See* Clause.

Subordinating conjunction   *See* Conjunction.

Subordination   The act of placing some elements in sentences in a dependent relation with others so that readers will know what is important and what is not. So-called choppy sentences are usually sentences without adequate subordination.
The hunters walked for miles.
They did not know where they were going.

They had never been in the woods before.

Suffix An ending that changes the meaning of the word to which it is attached. The suffixes in the following words are in italics:

care/care*less,* delight/delight*ful,* boy/boy*ish,* visual/visual*ize*

Superlative degree *See* Comparison.

Syntax The part of grammar that defines the relations between sentences and between parts of sentences. In English syntax, the subject usually comes before the verb; prepositional phrases include a preposition and a noun or noun substitute that acts as the object of the preposition; and clauses serve as nouns, adjectives, or adverbs.

Tense The form of a verb that indicates time, whether present, past, or future. The *simple tenses* include the present, the past, and the future.

PRESENT: I *speak,* she *laughs*

PAST: I *spoke,* she *laughed*

FUTURE: I *shall* (or *will*) *speak,* she *will laugh*

The *perfect tenses* indicate time previous to the simple tenses. Perfect tenses are formed with the past participle and an auxiliary verb, *have* or *had.*

PRESENT PERFECT: I *have spoken,* she *has spoken*

PAST PERFECT: I *had spoken,* she *had spoken*

FUTURE PERFECT: I *shall have spoken,* she *will have spoken*

The *progressive tense* indicates continuing action. It is formed with the present participle and a form of the verb *to be* as auxiliary.

PRESENT PROGRESSIVE: I *am speaking.*

PAST PROGRESSIVE: She *was speaking.*

PAST PERFECT PROGRESSIVE: They *had been speaking.*

Tone The writer's attitude toward the subject—how the writer feels about characters and their actions, and how the writer makes the reader feel about them; the writer's perspective or point of view.

Transitive verb A verb that conveys action from a subject to a direct object. (*See* Verb.)

He *walked* his dog late last night.

She *bought* a new tennis racket.

Verb A word that reports an action or a condition; a word that makes an assertion. *Main verbs* combine with *helping verbs* to form the various tenses. *Intransitive verbs* report that the subject acts or exists in a certain condition; these verbs do not take a direct object. *Transitive verbs* carry action from the subject to an object. A verb can be transitive or intransitive, depending on its use in the sentence. *Linking verbs* join a subject with a complement, either a noun or an adjective. *Phrasal verbs* are combinations with an adverb or preposition that express a new or different meaning.

Jackson *smoked*. [intransitive]
Jackson *smoked* a pipe. [transitive; *pipe* is a direct object]

Verbal   Word formed from a verb that does not function as a verb. Verbals are gerunds, participles, and infinitives. A verbal cannot make an assertion about a subject by itself.

Verb complement   A direct or indirect object. (*See* Object.)

Verb phrase   A main verb and its helping or auxiliary verbs. A verb phrase gives a complete statement of tense.

I *am helping* with the project.
He *had been seen* in the vicinity.

Voice   The form of a verb used to indicate whether the subject does the acting (*active*) or is acted upon (*passive*).

ACTIVE VOICE: Ramon García *hit* the ball out of the park.
PASSIVE VOICE: A ball *was hit* out of the park by Ramon García.

Word order   Most English sentences begin with the subject, or with an adverb or adverbial. The subject usually comes before the verb. The direct object usually comes after the verb. An indirect object always comes between the verb and the direct object. Most adjectives come immediately before or after the noun or noun substitute they modify. Predicate adjectives or subject complements modify the subject of a clause but come after the verb. Adverbs may be separated from the word or phrase they modify.

ACKNOWLEDGMENTS

Carl Bereiter. Excerpt from "Genetics and Educability," from *Disadvantaged Child*, vol. 3, edited by Jerome Hellmuth. Reprinted with permission from Brunner/Mazel, Inc.

Jane Brody. Excerpt reprinted from *Jane Brody's Nutrition Book* by Jane Brody, by permission of W. W. Norton & Company. Copyright © 1981 by Jane E. Brody.

E. E. Cummings. "in Just-" is reprinted from *Tulips & Chimneys* by E. E. Cummings, edited by George James Firmage, by permission of Liveright Publishing Corporation. Copyright 1923, 1925 and renewed 1951, 1953 by E. E. Cummings. Copyright © 1973, 1976 by the Trustees for the E. E. Cummings Trust. Copyright © 1973, 1976 by George James Firmage.

Tom Cuthbertson. Excerpt from *Anybody's Bike Book* by Tom Cuthbertson. Copyright © 1979. Used with permission of Ten Speed Press, Box 7123, Berkeley, CA 94707.

Richard D. Daugherty. Excerpt from "People of the Salmon," from *America in 1942: The World of the Indian Peoples before the Arrival of Columbus*, edited by Alvin M. Josephy, Jr., Alfred A. Knopf, Inc., 1992. Reprinted by permission of the author.

Joan Didion. Excerpt from "Some Dreamers of the Golden Dream" from *Slouching Towards Bethlehem* by Joan Didion. Copyright © 1966, 1968 by Joan Didion. Reprinted by permission of Farrar, Straus & Giroux, Inc.

Rachel G. Fuchs and Leslie Page Moch. Excerpt from "Pregnant, Single and Far from Home: Migrant Women in Nineteenth-Century Paris," in *American Historical Review*, vol. 95, no. 4, October 1990. Reprinted by permission.

Philip Gerber. Excerpt from *Willa Cather* by Philip Gerber. Copyright 1975 and reprinted with the permission of Twayne Publishers, a division of G. K. Hall & Co., Boston.

Paul B. Horton and Chester L. Hunt. Excerpt from *Sociology,* 6th ed., by Paul B. Horton and Chester L. Hunt. Copyright © 1984. Reprinted by permission of Mc-Graw-Hill, Inc.

Nathan Irvin Huggins. Excerpt from *Black Odyssey* by Nathan Irvin Huggins. Copyright © 1977 by Nathan Irvin Huggins. Reprinted by permission of Pantheon Books, a Division of Random House, Inc.

Roy S. Johnson. Excerpt from the following article is reprinted courtesy of *Sports Illustrated* from the April 30, 1992 issue. Copyright © 1992, Time Inc. "None of Our Business: Arthur Ashe Is a Public Figure, but the Media Had No Right to Make His Illness a Public Matter" by Roy S. Johnson. All Rights Reserved.

Martin Luther King, Jr. Excerpt from "Letter from Birmingham Jail" from *Why We Can't Wait* by Martin Luther King, Jr. Reprinted by arrangement with the Heirs of the Estate of Martin Luther King, Jr., c/o Joan Daves Agency as agent for the Proprietor. Copyright 1963 by Dr. Martin Luther King, Jr. Copyright renewed 1991 by Coretta Scott King.

Maxine Hong Kingston. Excerpt from *The Woman Warrior: Memoirs of a Girlhood among Ghosts.* Reprinted by permission of Alfred A. Knopf, Inc.

David McCullough. Excerpt from *Mornings on Horseback* by David McCullough. Copyright © 1981 by David McCullough. Reprinted by permission of Simon & Schuster, Inc.

N. Scott Momaday. Excerpt from "The Becoming of the Native: Man in America before Columbus," from *America in 1492: The World of the Indian Peoples before the Arrival of Columbus,* edited by Alvin M. Josephy, Jr., Alfred A. Knopf, Inc., 1992. Reprinted by permission of the author.

The New Yorker. Two excerpts from "Talk of the Town" March 30, 1992 and April 6, 1992. Copyright © 1992; The New Yorker Magazine. Reprinted by permission; © The New Yorker Magazine, Inc.

Sharon O'Brien. Excerpts from *Willa Cather: The Emerging Voice* by Sharon O'Brien. Copyright © 1986 by Oxford University Press, Inc. Reprinted by permission.

Nell Irvin Painter. Excerpt from *Standing at Armageddon: The United States 1877-1919* by Nell Irvin Painter, W. W. Norton & Company, Inc., 1987.

Random House Webster's College Dictionary. Definition of the word "compare" and note on the word "lady" from *Random House Webster's College Dictionary* by Random House, Inc. Reprinted by permission of Random House, Inc. and McGraw-Hill, Inc.

Chet Raymo. Excerpt from "Science Musings," in *The Boston Globe,* January 19, 1987. Reprinted by permission of the author.

Reader's Guide to Periodical Literature. Entry for "Black Holes." Copyright © 1982 by the H. W. Wilson Company. Material reproduced by permission of the publisher.

Bernard Reich. Excerpt from "Themes in the History of the State of Israel," in *American Historical Review,* vol. 96, no. 5, December 1991. Reprinted by permission.

Jim Robbins. Excerpt from "Care for a Little Hellish Relish? Or Try a Hotsicle," in *Smithsonian,* January 1992. Reprinted by permission.

David Roberts. Excerpt from "Together, Scientists and Indians Explore the Conundrums of Casa Malpais," in *Smithsonian,* March 1992. Reprinted by permission.

Peter Mark Roget. "Humorist" from *Roget's International Thesaurus,* Fourth Edition, by Peter Mark Roget. Copyright © 1977 by Harper & Row Publishers, Inc. Reprinted by permission of HarperCollins Publishers.

Robert A. Rosenstone. Excerpt from "JFK: Historical Fact/Historical Film," in *American Historical Review,* vol. 97, no. 2, April 1992. Reprinted by permission.

Berton Roueche. Excerpt from "A Walk Along the Towpath" from *What's Left* by Berton Roueche. Reprinted by permission of Harold Ober Associates Incorporated. First published in *The New Yorker.* Copyright © 1962 by Berton Roueche. Copyright renewed 1990 by Berton Roueche.

Youngju Ryu. Excerpt from "Five Heroines for a Hard City," in *The New York Times,* April 4, 1992. Copyright © 1992 by the New York Times Company. Reprinted by permission.

Nancy Caldwell Sorel. Excerpt from "A. E. Housman and Willa Cather." Originally published in the July 1987 issue of *The Atlantic Monthly.*

E. M. Swift. Excerpt from the following article is reprinted courtesy of *Sports Illustrated* from the March 2, 1992 issue. Copyright © 1992, Time Inc. "Women of Mettle" by E. M. Swift. All Rights Reserved.

Lewis Thomas. Excerpt from "On Meddling," from *The Medusa and the Snail* by Lewis Thomas. Copyright © 1974, 1975, 1976, 1977, 1978, 1979 by Lewis Thomas. Used by permission of Viking Penguin, a division of Penguin Books USA Inc.

Wilcomb E. Washburn. Excerpt reprinted with the permission of Charles Scribner's Sons, an imprint of Macmillan Publishing Company from *Red Man's Law/White Man's Law* by Wilcomb E. Washburn. Copyright © 1971 Wilcomb E. Washburn.

Time. Excerpt from "Will Japan's Slump Stifle a U.S. Recovery?" in *Time,* March 23, 1992. Copyright 1992 Time Inc. Reprinted by permission.

INDEX

Each page number consists of two elements: the first element is either a chapter number and section letter (e.g., 17a) or an appendix abbreviation (e.g., ESL refers to the ESL Appendix, GU refers to the Glossary of Usage, and GT refers to the Glossary of Grammatical Terms); the second element after the colon refers to the page number(s) of the citation. Separate citations are indicated by semicolons. For example, 31c: 419–420 means that the entry is in chapter 31, section c, pages 419–420.

ESL APPENDIX